The Princeton Review®

6 Practice Tests for the

SAT®

The Staff of The Princeton Review

PrincetonReview.com

Penguin
Random
House

The Princeton Review
24 Prime Parkway, Suite 201
Natick, MA 01760
E-mail: editorialsupport@review.com

Published in the United States by Penguin Random House LLC, New York, and in Canada by Random House of Canada, a division of Penguin Random House Ltd., Toronto.

Terms of Service: The Princeton Review Online Companion Tools ("Student Tools") for retail books are available for only the two most recent editions of that book. Student Tools may be activated only twice per eligible book purchased for two consecutive 12-month periods, for a total of 24 months of access. Activation of Student Tools more than twice per book is in direct violation of these Terms of Service and may result in discontinuation of access to Student Tools Services.

ISBN: 978-1-101-91979-8
ISSN: 2377-7273

SAT is a registered trademark of the College Board, which does not sponsor or endorse this product.

Art, Mind, and Brain: A Cognitive Approach to Creativity. Gardner, Howard. Copyright (C) 1982. Reprinted with permission of the author.

"At Pluto, the End of a Beginning." Billings, Lee. Excerpted with permission. Copyright (C) 2015 Scientific American, a Division of Nature America, Inc. All rights reserved.

"A New Billion-Mile Journey for New Horizons." Scharf, Caleb A. Excerpted with permission. Copyright (C) 2015 Scientific American, a Division of Nature America Inc. All rights reserved.

"Does media multitasking always hurt?" Kelvin F. H. Lui, Alan C.-N. Wong, *Psychonomic Bulletin & Review.* August 2012, Volume 19, Issue 4, pp. 647-653. http://www.psychonomic.org

From *The New England Journal of Medicine,* Arias, Cesar A. and Murray, Barbara E., "Antibiotic-Resistant Bugs in the 21st Century--A Clinical Super-Challenge," Vol. 360, Pages No. 439-443, Copyright © 2009 Massachusetts Medical Society. Reprinted with permission from Massachusetts Medical Society.

Excerpt from "Noblesse Oblige? Social Status and Economic Inequality Maintenance among Politicians." Kraus, MW, Callaghan B (2014). PLoS ONE 9(1): e85293. doi: 10.1371/journal.pone.0085293.

Excerpt from "No Rest for the Weary: Migrating Songbirds Keep Their Wits without Sleep." (2004) PLoS Biol 2(7): e221. doi:10.1371/journal.pbio.0020221.

"Report Cards Give Up A's and B's for 4s and 3s." From *The New York Times,* March 24 (C) 2009 The New York Times. All rights reserved. Used by permission and protected by the Copyright Laws of the United States. The printing, copying, redistribution, or retransmission of this Content without express written permission is prohibited.

Excerpt from "A Sensory-Motor Control Model of Animal Flight Explains Why Bats Fly Differently in Light Versus Dark." Bar NS, Skogestad S, Marçal JM, Ulanovsky N, Yovel Y (2015). PLoS Biol 13(1): e1002046. doi:10.1371/journal.pbio.1002046

Excerpt from "Bring on the Hipsters: Gentrification is good for the poor." (C) The Economist Newspaper Limited, London.

Excerpt from "Identifying the Volcanic Eruption Depicted in a Neolithic Painting at Çatalhöyük, Central Anatolia, Turkey. Schmitt AK, Danišík M, Aydar E, Şen E, Ulusoy I, Lovera OM (2014). PLoS ONE 9(1): e84711. doi:10.1371/journal.pone.0084711

Reprinted by permission from Macmillian Publishers Ltd: *Nature News,* "Where in the world could the first CRISPR baby be born?" Ledford, Heidi, Vol. 526, No. 7573, (C) 2015.

Excerpt from "It's the Thought That Counts," Belk, Russell W. (C) 1976. Reprinted with permission from the author.

"Fracking's Future" originally appeared in the January-February 2013 issue of Harvard Magazine (115:3; 24-27). Permission granted by the authors: McElroy, Michael B. and Lu, Xi.

"Unchecked Fracking Threatens Health, Water Supplies." (C) 2015. Reprinted with permission from the Natural Resources Defense Council.

"The Current Political World-View, Education and Alienation," Murphy, John W. and Pardeck, John T. *International Journal of Adolescence and Youth,* Vol. 3, No. 1-2, 1991. Excerpt reprinted by permission of the publisher (Taylor & Francis Ltd, http://www.tandfonline.com).

Excerpt from "Processed foods: contributions to nutritions." Republished with permission of American Society for Nutrition, from *The American Journal of Clinical Nutrition,* Weaver, Connie M.; Dwyer, Johanna, Fulgoni, Victor L.; King, Janet C.; Leveille, Gilbert A.; MacDonald, Ruth S.; Ordovas, Jose; Schnakenberg, David, Vol. 99, No. 6, 2014; permission conveyed through Copyright Clearance Center, Inc.

Excerpt from "Big Food, Food Systems, and Global Health." Stuckler D, Nestle M (2012). PLoS Med 9(6): e1001242. doi:10.1371/journal.pmed.1001242.

Excerpt from "Hey, What about the 24th?" From Slate, May 2 © 2008 The Slate Group. All rights reserved. Used by permission and protected by the Copyright Laws of the United States. The printing, copying, redistribution, or retransmission of this Content without express written permission is prohibited.

"Arctic Sea Ice: What, Why, and What Next" originally appeared as a guest blog on Scientific American's website, September 21, 2012. Permission granted by the author, Naam, Ramez.

The Princeton Review is not affiliated with Princeton University.

Printed in the United States of America on partially recycled paper.

10 9 8 7 6 5 4 3 2 1

1st Edition

Acknowledgments

This edition would not have been possible without the extraordinary talent of and tireless effort by Amy Minster, Brian Becker, and Elizabeth Owens.

Special thanks to:

Chris Chimera
Anne Goldberg
Bobby Hood
Tony Krupp
Spencer LeDoux
Leah Murnane
Kay Robinson
Steve Voigt

Thanks to:

Lori DesRochers
Jim Havens
Jay Hilsenbeck
Lindsay Maxwell
Michelle McCannon
Ian Persits
Nicole-Henriette Pirnie
Rebecca Scott
Susan Swinford

National ACT & SAT Content Director, The Princeton Review

Jonathan Chiu

Contents

Register Your

1 Go to **PrincetonReview.com/cracking**

2 You'll see a welcome page where you can register your book using the following ISBN: 9781101919798.

3 After placing this free order, you'll either be asked to log in or to answer a few simple questions in order to set up a new Princeton Review account.

4 Finally, click on the "Student Tools" tab located at the top of the screen. It may take an hour or two for your registration to go through, but after that, you're good to go.

If you are experiencing book problems (potential content errors), please contact EditorialSupport@review.com with the full title of the book, its ISBN number (located above), and the page number of the error. Experiencing technical issues? Please e-mail TPRStudentTech@review.com with the following information:

- your full name
- e-mail address used to register the book
- full book title and ISBN
- your computer OS (Mac or PC) and Internet browser (Firefox, Safari, Chrome, etc.)
- description of technical issue

Book Online!

Once you've registered, you can...

- Check to see if there have been any corrections or updates to this edition
- Download additional bubble sheets and score conversion tables
- Get valuable college-planning information

The **Princeton** Review®

Chapter 1
Your Guide to Getting the Most Out Of This Book

WHAT'S INSIDE

Welcome to *6 Practice Tests for the SAT*. As you've probably already guessed, this book contains six full-length practice tests for the SAT, which we at The Princeton Review have created based off the information released by the College Board. We've rigorously analyzed available tests, and our content development teams have tirelessly worked to ensure that our material accurately reflects what you will see in terms of design, structure, style, and most importantly, the content on test day. We continually evaluate the data on each question to ensure validity and to refine the level of difficulty within each test to match that of the SAT even more closely, and you shouldn't hesitate to reach out to us at EditorialSupport@review.com if you feel something's amiss.

Even though the SAT has been redesigned, we are confident that if you work through these tests and evaluate your performance with our comprehensive explanations, you'll improve the skills that you need to score higher on the SAT. Use the included score-conversion tables to help you to assess and track your overall performance so that you get the most out of your test-prep, as well as in-depth explanations that not only explain how to get the right answer but also why the other choices are incorrect. Through careful self-assessment, you can correct any recurring mistakes, as well as identify any weaknesses or gaps in knowledge that you can then focus your attention on studying.

What Is The Princeton Review?
The Princeton Review is the nation's most popular test-preparation company. After thirty years in the business, our goal is to help students everywhere crack the SAT and a bunch of other standardized tests, including the PSAT and ACT as well as graduate-level exams like the GRE and GMAT. We offer courses and private tutoring for all of the major standardized tests, and we publish a series of books to help in your search for the right school. If you would like more information about how The Princeton Review can help you, go to PrincetonReview.com or call 800-2-Review.

HOW TO USE THIS BOOK

Each test is laid out as you'll encounter it on the SAT. While we recommend that you take each test in full, in accordance with the allotted times, and under conditions similar to those that you'll face on the day of the examination, you're welcome to focus on specific sections on which you'd like more practice.

Don't forget to carefully review our detailed explanations! Whether you get the question right or not, these explanations are packed full of our powerful SAT strategies and techniques, and might help you to save time on future questions, or to clarify where you might have gotten a right answer for the wrong reason.

WHEN YOU TAKE A TEST

Here are some suggestions for working through this book:

1. Keep track of your performance. Whether you're working through individual sections or taking each test as a whole, be sure to score yourself with the tables provided at the start of the explanations to each test. Include the time and date with each entry so that you can track your progress.

2.	The SAT is a timed test. You may be a star test-taker when you have all the time in the world to mull over the questions, but can you perform as well when the clock is ticking? Timing yourself will ensure you are prepared for the constraints of the actual test, just as our strategy filled explanations can help you to discover faster methods for solving questions.

3.	Don't cram it all in at once. It's hard enough to concentrate throughout one SAT—don't burn yourself out by taking multiple tests in a row. You wouldn't run two marathons back-to-back, so why treat your brain (which is like a muscle) in that way? Give yourself at least a couple of months before your anticipated "real" test date so that you can learn from any mistakes that were made on these practice tests.

4.	Accordingly, take time to analyze your performance between tests. As you actively review your work, your mind will be subtly taking notes and tweaking the way it handles future questions of a similar nature, shaving seconds off its processing time as it grows more accustomed to particular wordings or presentations.

Filling In Answers

It's not enough to get the right answer on the SAT quickly—you also have to accurately bubble it into a separate scantron sheet, and a surprisingly large number of mistakes can be made at this point, especially if you're skipping over certain questions along the way. To that end, we've included sample scantrons at the end of each test, which you can rip out of the book so that you get into the habit of rapidly transferring answers from the test itself to the scantron. (We've also included this in your online student tools, in case you'd rather print out a fresh copy.)

The SAT also includes Student-Produced Responses (grid-ins) for the two math sections. We've replicated those on the scantrons, so that you can practice correctly filling them in now. A version of the following directions should appear on the test itself, but rather than waste valuable time reading it later, take a moment to familiarize yourself with it now.

Directions: A Student-Produced Response question requires you to solve the problem and enter your answer by marking the circles in the special grid, as shown in the examples below. You may use any available space for scratch work.

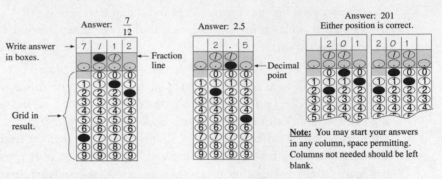

- Mark no more than one circle in any column.
- Because the answer document will be machine-scored, **you will receive credit only if the circles are filled in correctly.**
- Although not required, it is suggested that you write your answer in the boxes at the top of the columns to help you fill in the circles accurately.
- Some problems may have more than one correct answer. In such cases, grid only one answer.
- No question has a negative answer.
- **Mixed numbers** such as $3\frac{1}{2}$ must be gridded as 3.5 or 7/2. (If [3 1 / 2] is gridded, it will be interpreted as $\frac{31}{2}$, not $3\frac{1}{2}$.)

- **Decimal Answers:** If you obtain a decimal answer with more digits than the grid can accommodate, it may be either rounded or truncated, but it must fill the entire grid. For example, if you obtain an answer such as 0.6666..., you should record your result as .666 or .667. **A less accurate value such as .66 or .67 will be scored as incorrect.**

Acceptable ways to grid $\frac{2}{3}$ are:

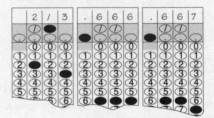

GOOD LUCK!

We know that the SAT may seem intimidating at first glance—but then again, after using this book, you'll be taking it on at seventh or eighth glance, so you're headed in the right direction. Also, as you prepare, whether you're stressed or relaxed, remember this key point:

The SAT doesn't measure the stuff that matters. It measures neither intelligence nor the depth and breadth of what you're learning in high school. It doesn't predict college grades as well as your high school grades do, and many colleges know there is more to you as a student—and a person—than how you fare on a single four-hour test administration on a random Saturday, Sunday, or Wednesday morning.

This is a high-stakes test, and you should absolutely work hard and prepare. But don't treat it like it's some mythical monster or world-ending catastrophe. It's just a test, and we at The Princeton Review know tests. We're here for you every step of the way.

Chapter 2
What You Need to Know for the SAT

GENERAL INFORMATION ABOUT THE SAT

Let's take a moment to discuss some SAT facts. Some of them may surprise you.

Wait, *Who* Writes This Test?

You may be surprised to learn that the people who write SAT tests questions are NOT necessarily teachers or college professors. The people who write the SAT are professional test writers, not superhuman geniuses, so you can beat them at their own game.

Who Writes the SAT?

Even though colleges and universities make wide use of the SAT, they're not the ones who write the test. That's the job of Educational Testing Service (ETS), a nonprofit company that writes tests for college and graduate school admissions, and the College Board, the organization that decides how the tests will be administered and used.

They've changed the SAT twice in the last ten years, and they've admitted that students can and should prepare for the test, which means that the test *can* be beaten, and as they say, practice helps to make perfect.

"Optional" Is as Optional Does

Though the SAT now refers to the essay as optional, there are some colleges that may require it. Before planning your test-day strategy, make sure you've researched each of the colleges you plan on applying to, and take the essay only if you have to.

What's on the SAT?

The redesigned SAT is 3 hours long, or 3 hours and 50 minutes long if you choose to take the "optional" essay. It includes four tests (and the essay).

- Reading Test: 65 minutes, 52 questions
- 10-minute break
- Writing and Language Test: 35 minutes, 44 questions
- Math Test (No Calculator): 25 minutes, 20 questions
- 5-minute break
- Math Test (Calculator): 55 minutes, 38 questions
- 2-minute break

- Essay; 50 minutes, 1 prompt

With the exception of the open-ended essay prompt and a few grid-in problems in the math section, everything else is multiple-choice, with four options for each question. Here's a brief rundown of what to expect.

Reading Test

Your score on the Evidence-Based Reading and Writing section of the SAT is comprised of your scores on the Reading Test and the Writing and Language Test. The Reading Test is 65 minutes long and consists of 52 questions, all of which are passage-based and multiple-choice. Passages may be paired with informational graphics, such as charts or graphs, and there will also be a series of questions based on a pair of passages. The selected passages will be from previously published works in the areas of world literature, history/social studies, and science. Questions based on science passages may ask you to analyze data or hypotheses, or to read graphs, while questions about literature passages will concentrate more on literary concepts like theme, mood, and characterization. The main goal is to measure your ability to both understand words in context and find and analyze evidence.

Writing and Language Test

The Writing and Language Test is 35 minutes long and consists of 44 questions, which are also multiple choice and based on several passages. However, instead of asking you to analyze a passage, questions will ask you to proofread and edit the passage. That means you'll have to correct grammar and word choice and make larger changes to the organization or content of the passage.

Math Test

You'll have a total of 80 minutes to complete the Math Test, which, as we mentioned earlier, is divided into two sections. The No-Calculator portion is 25 minutes, and has 20 questions, while the Calculator portion is 55 minutes, with 38 questions. Most questions are multiple-choice, but there are also handfuls of student-produced response questions, which are also known as grid-ins. (Instead of choosing from four answer choices, you'll have to work through a problem and then enter your answer on your answer sheet by bubbling in the appropriate numbers.) Exactly 13 of the 58 math questions will be grid-ins.

Optional Essay

Unlike other essays you may have seen on standardized tests, this one does not require you to write about a personal experience or to argue for or against a position. Instead, you'll have to read a short passage and explain how the author effectively builds his or her argument. The test writers want to see how you comprehend an idea and demonstrate that understanding in writing, using evidence from that author's text.

Table of Content
If you're super curious about the content that the Math Test covers, the test developers have cryptically designated the four main areas as (1) Heart of Algebra, (2) Problem Solving and Data Analysis, (3) Passport to Advanced Math, and (4) Additional Topics in Math.

Scoring on the SAT

The new SAT is scored on a scale of 400-1600, and also introduces a series of cross-test scores and subscores that analyze various proficiencies. Here's the breakdown:

- **Total score (1):** The sum of the two section scores (Evidence-Based Reading and Writing and Math), ranging from 400 to 1600
- **Section scores (2):** Evidence-Based Reading and Writing, ranging from 200-800; Math, also ranging from 200-800
- **Test scores (3):** Reading Test, Writing and Language Test, Math Test, each of which is scored on a scale from 10 to 40
- **Cross-test scores (2):** Each is scored on a scale from 10 to 40 and based on selected questions from the three tests (Reading, Writing and Language, Math):
  1) Analysis in History/Social Studies
  2) Analysis in Science
- **Subscores (7):** Each of the following receives a score from 1 to 15:

  1) Command of Evidence (Reading; Writing and Language)
  2) Words in Context (Reading; Writing and Language)
  3) Expression of Ideas (Writing and Language)
  4) Standard English Conventions (Writing and Language)
  5) Heart of Algebra (Math)
  6) Problem Solving and Data Analysis (Math)
  7) Passport to Advanced Math (Math)

A Note on Essay Scoring

If you choose to write the essay, you will be graded by two readers in three areas: Reading, Wring, and Analysis. You will be scored on a 2-to-8 point scale for each of the three areas.

Scoring Tricks

Unlike the old SAT, you will no longer be penalized for wrong answers on the SAT. This means that you should always guess, even in this means choosing an answer at random. Moreover, with the number of answer choices reduced from five to four, the odds of getting a right answer are better than ever, especially if you can use Process of Elimination (POE) to eliminate an answer choice or two.

Because time is at a premium on the test, don't be shy about bubbling in a guess on a question that you don't fully understand so that you can move on to questions that you feel more confident you can answer correctly (and quickly). That said, try to indicate which questions you've done this on so that if you have time left at the end of a test, you can return to those tricky questions and try to get a few extra points.

WHEN IS THE SAT GIVEN?

The SAT schedule for the school year is posted on the College Board website at www.collegeboard.org. There are two different ways to sign up for the test. You can either sign up online by going to www.collgeboard.org and clicking on the SAT hyperlink, or sign up through the mail with an SAT registration booklet, which may be available at your school guidance counselor's office.

Try to sign up for the SAT as soon as you know when you'll be taking the test. If you wait until the last minute to sign up, there may not be any open spots in the testing centers that are closest to you.

If you require any special accommodations while taking the test (including, but not limited to, extra time or assistance), www.collegeboard.org has information about applying for those. Make sure to apply early; we recommend doing so six months before you plan to take the test.

Stay on Schedule
Although you may take the SAT any time starting freshman year, most students take it for the first time in the spring of their junior year and possibly retake it in the fall of their senior year. In addition, you may also need to take SAT subject tests (many competitive colleges require them), so don't leave everything to the last minute. You can't take SAT and SAT Subject Tests on the same day. Sit down and plan a schedule.

Chapter 3
Practice Test 1

Reading Test

65 MINUTES, 52 QUESTIONS

Turn to Section 1 of your answer sheet to answer the questions in this section.

DIRECTIONS

Each passage or pair of passages below is followed by a number of questions. After reading each passage or pair, choose the best answer to each question based on what is stated or implied in the passage or passages and in any accompanying graphics (such as a table or graph).

Questions 1–10 are based on the following passage.

This passage is excerpted from Mary Shelley's Frankenstein, *originally published in 1818.*

My journey was very melancholy. At first I wished
to hurry on, for I longed to console and sympathize
with my loved and sorrowing friends; but when I drew
Line near my native town, I slackened my progress. I could
5 hardly sustain the multitude of feelings that crowded
into my mind. I passed through scenes familiar to my
youth, but which I had not seen for nearly six years.
How altered every thing might be during that time!
One sudden and desolating change had taken place;
10 but a thousand little circumstances might have by
degrees worked other alterations, which, although
they were done more tranquilly, might not be the
less decisive. Fear overcame me; I dared no advance,
dreading a thousand nameless evils that made me
15 tremble, although I was unable to define them. I
remained two days at Lausanne, in this painful state of
mind. I contemplated the lake: the waters were placid;
all around was calm; and the snowy mountains, 'the
palaces of nature,' were not changed. By degrees the
20 calm and heavenly scene restored me, and I continued
my journey towards Geneva. The road ran by the side
of the lake, which became narrower as I approached
my native town. I discovered more distinctly the
black sides of Jura, and the bright summit of Mont
25 Blanc. I wept like a child. "Dear mountains! My own
beautiful lake! How do you welcome your wanderer?
Your summits are clear; the sky and lake are blue and

placid. Is this to prognosticate peace, or to mock at my
unhappiness?"
30 I fear, my friend, that I shall render myself tedious
by dwelling on these preliminary circumstances;
but they were days of comparative happiness, and I
think of them with pleasure. My country, my beloved
country! Who but a native can tell the delight I took
35 in again beholding thy streams, thy mountains, and,
more than all, thy lovely lake! Yet, as I drew nearer
home, grief and fear again overcame me. Night also
closed around; and when I could hardly see the dark
mountains, I felt still more gloomily. The picture
40 appeared a vast and dim scene of evil, and I foresaw
obscurely that I was destined to become the most
wretched of human beings. Alas! I prophesied truly,
and failed only in one single circumstance, that in all
the misery I imagined and dreaded, I did not conceive
45 the hundredth part of the anguish I was destined to
endure. It was completely dark when I arrived in the
environs of Geneva; the gates of the town were already
shut; and I was obliged to pass the night at Secheron,
a village at the distance of half a league from the
50 city. The sky was serene; and, as I was unable to rest,
I resolved to visit the spot where my poor William
had been murdered. As I could not pass through the
town, I was obliged to cross the lake in a boat to arrive
at Plainpalais. During this short voyage I saw the
55 lightning playing on the summit of Mont Blanc in the
most beautiful figures. The storm appeared to approach
rapidly, and, on landing, I ascended a low hill, that I

CONTINUE ➡

might observe its progress. It advanced; the heavens were clouded, and I soon felt the rain coming slowly in
60 large drops, but its violence quickly increased.

While I watched the tempest, so beautiful yet terrific, I wandered on with a hasty step. This noble war in the sky elevated my spirits; I clasped my hands, and exclaimed aloud, "William, dear angel! This is
65 thy funeral, this thy dirge!" As I said these words, I perceived in the gloom a figure which stole from behind a clump of trees near me; I stood fixed, gazing intently: I could not be mistaken. A flash of lightning illuminated the object, and discovered its shape
70 plainly to me; its gigantic stature, and the deformity of its aspect more hideous than belongs to humanity, instantly informed me that it was the wretch, the filthy daemon, to whom I had given life. What did he there? Could he be (I shuddered at the conception) the
75 murderer of my brother? No sooner did that idea cross my imagination, than I became convinced of its truth; my teeth chattered, and I was forced to lean against a tree for support. The figure passed me quickly, and I lost it in the gloom.

1

Which choice best describes the developmental pattern of the passage?

A) A lighthearted description of an adventure

B) A dramatic response to a request for help

C) A profound analysis of an ancient curse

D) A melancholy recounting of a doomed homecoming

2

Which choice best describes what happens in the passage?

A) One character returns home to avenge the death of his brother.

B) One character fears his future in the hometown he left.

C) One character is afraid to return to a city haunted by an unknown monster.

D) One character worries that he won't be welcome at home.

3

Which emotion does the narrator most feel?

A) He feels joy at returning home.

B) He feels antagonism for the daemon.

C) He feels dread concerning his fate.

D) He feels sorrow over William's death.

4

Which choice provides the best evidence for the answer to the previous question?

A) Lines 34–36 ("Who but . . . lake")

B) Lines 42–46 ("I prophesied . . . endure")

C) Lines 58–60 ("It advanced . . . increased")

D) Lines 74–75 ("Could he . . . brother")

5

As used in line 28, "placid" most nearly means

A) palatial.

B) dull.

C) peaceful.

D) divine.

6

The main purpose of the first paragraph is to

A) represent a journey.

B) embellish an emotion.

C) provide a context.

D) establish a mood.

CONTINUE

7

Why does the narrator mention "a thousand little circumstances" (line 10)?

A) He fears a natural disaster and its aftermath.

B) He dreads the effects of a devastating incident.

C) He knows he could have stopped a tragedy.

D) He has incited a revolution to take down the government.

8

Which of the following provides the best evidence for the answer to the previous question?

A) Line 8 ("How altered . . . time")

B) Lines 9–13 ("One sudden . . . decisive")

C) Lines 50–52 ("The sky . . . murdered")

D) Lines 64–65 ("William, dear . . . dirge")

9

In the passage, the narrator addresses the tempest with

A) awe, but not fear.

B) ebullience, but not rage.

C) disconsolation, but not anger.

D) insanity, but not regret.

10

As used in line 66, "stole" most nearly means

A) loomed.

B) pinched.

C) wrapped.

D) displaced.

CONTINUE

Questions 11–20 are based on the following passage.

This passage is an excerpt from Howard Gardner, *Art, Mind and Brain*. © 1982 by Basic Books.

Twenty years ago psychology seemed a rather remote and sterile area to individuals interested in the full and creative use of the mind. The field harbored a
Line trio of uninviting specializations. There was academic
5 psychology, featuring the use of contrived laboratory apparatus to study the perception of visual illusions or the memorization of long lists of nonsense syllables. Such lines of study bore little evident relationship to human beings engaged in thought. There was
10 behaviorism, the approach that emerged from work with rats and pigeons. Behaviorists claimed that we act in the way we do because we are reinforced for doing so and, given their focus on overt activity, these scholars denied inner life—no thought, no fantasies,
15 no aspirations. Finally, there was psychoanalysis, which offered not only a controversial method of treatment but also an overarching theory of human nature. While psychoanalysis had a grandeur and depth that eluded both academic psychology and behaviorism, it strongly
20 accentuated human personality and unconscious problem-solving.

The cognitive revolution came in two parts. First, there was the frank recognition that one could—one must—take seriously human mental
25 processes, including thinking, problem-solving, and creating. Study of the mind once again became a proper scientific undertaking. Second, there was the demonstration by several researchers that human thought processes were characterized by considerable
30 regularity and structure. Not all of this cogitation took place in full view, nor could such cognitive processes always be either related to external stimuli or confirmed by introspection. But there was structure to thought processes, a structure the careful analyst could
35 help lay bare.

Many of us who were studying the behavioral sciences in the 1960s were swept up—and have remained inspired—by this revolution. For some, the appeal lay in computer programming and
40 artificial intelligence—the design of machines that display intelligence. For others, the thrill came in conducting careful laboratory experiments in which one could trace, on a millisecond-by-millisecond basis, an individual's mental process as he carried out

45 a multiplication problem, reasoned through a logical syllogism, or rotated an image of geometrical form in his head. Still others took roads that went through pedagogy, through anthropology, or through the neurosciences. In my own case, I found especially
50 appealing the approach to the mind put forth by structuralists working in the cognitive regions of several social sciences.

In the opening set of essays I lay out the principal assumption of this structuralist approach as it is
55 exemplified by the developmental psychologist Jean Piaget, the linguist Noam Chomsky, and the anthropologist Claude Levi-Strauss. These thinkers share a belief that the mind operates according to the specifiable rules—often unconscious ones—and that
60 these can be ferreted out and made explicit by the systematic examination of human language, action, and problem-solving. There are many intriguing differences among their approaches as well, and I review several of these: still, one finds throughout a
65 surprisingly (and reassuringly) common vision of what the human mind is like and how it can best be described for scientific purposes.

The structuralist approach to the mind has limitations. Those that are more germane, given my
70 own concern with artistic knowledge, derive from the essentially closed nature of structuralist systems. Though creative thought has not escaped their attention, each of the major cognitive structuralists views the options of human thought as in some way
75 preordained, limited in advance. This makes their work especially problematic for a study of mind where the major focus falls on innovation and creation, as in the fashioning of original works of art.

To my mind the limitation implicit in the standard
80 structuralist stance can be circumscribed by the recognition of one special feature of human thought —its ability to create and sponsor commerce through the use of various kinds of symbol systems. These symbol systems—these codes of meaning—are the
85 vehicles through which thought takes place: by their very nature they are creative, open systems. Through the use of symbols the human mind, operating according to the structuralist principles, can create, revise, transform, and re-create wholly fresh products,
90 systems and even worlds of meaning.

CONTINUE

11

The main purpose of the passage is to

A) review a set of essays on structuralism and creativity.

B) convince scientists to abandon behaviorist thought.

C) emphasize the limitations present in psychology.

D) present the author's view that structuralism allows for creativity.

12

The central claim of the passage is that

A) psychology has evolved since the 1960s before which it was too sedate and impractical for modern scientists.

B) traditional structuralist principles can allow for the possibility of human creativity.

C) behaviorists are limited in their scientific processes and have preordained views that humans act largely on their operant conditioning.

D) the author's opinions on creativity are revolutionary and supported by research in traditional psychology.

13

The author describes the different branches of psychology throughout the passage mainly to

A) guide the reader through a complete historic progression of a science.

B) establish his prominent and novel role within the psychological community.

C) highlight a difference that makes structuralism inferior to behaviorism.

D) show how the revolution of the 1960s affected psychology.

14

Gardner indicates that the cognitive revolution he describes in the passage was

A) a motivation for the author's exploration of creativity and structuralism.

B) a pertinent factor in revitalizing a dying field of science.

C) beneficial for interjecting thoughtful scientists back into the field of psychology.

D) more effective than previous changes to the perspective of psychologists.

15

Which choice provides the best evidence for the answer to the previous question?

A) Lines 8–9 ("Such lines . . . thought")

B) Lines 27–30 ("Second, there . . . structure")

C) Lines 36–38 ("Many of . . . revolution")

D) Lines 38–41 ("For some . . . intelligence")

16

The author characterizes the branch of psychology that became popular after the cognitive revolution mentioned in line 22 as using both

A) problem-solving and creating.

B) meticulousness and mathematics.

C) regularity and structure.

D) fantasy and aspiration.

17

Which lines best support the previous answer?

A) Lines 11–15 ("Behaviorists claimed . . . aspirations")

B) Lines 23–26 ("First, there . . . creating")

C) Lines 41–47 ("For others . . . head")

D) Lines 64–67 ("still, one . . . purposes")

CONTINUE

18

According to the passage, the author references Jean Piaget, Noam Chomsky, and Claude Levi-Strauss because they

A) represent different approaches to a unified belief about the mind.

B) present work that is inherently problematic when used in psychological discussions.

C) are psychologists who support his assumptions about structuralism.

D) published works that do not support the author's opinion on creativity.

19

The "original works of art" mentioned in line 78 mainly serve to emphasize how

A) admiring of artistic knowledge and endeavors the author is.

B) distorted the views of the structural psychologists are.

C) restricted the traditional structuralists' views on creativity are.

D) closed-minded and limited psychology is regarding artistic ability.

20

Which choice most closely captures the meaning of the "symbol systems" referred to in line 84?

A) Thought processes

B) Problematic methods

C) Structured principles

D) Representative expressions

CONTINUE ➤

Questions 21–31 are based on the following passages.

Passage 1 is adapted from Lee Billings, "At Pluto, the End of a Beginning." © July 2015 by *Scientific American*. Passage 2 is adapted from Caleb A. Scharf, "A New Billion-Mile Journey for New Horizons." © August 2015 by *Scientific American*. Lee Billings is a science journalist. Caleb Scharf is the Director of Astrobiology at Columbia University.

Passage 1

Early this morning, if all has gone well, the first golden age of interplanetary exploration will have come to a close. At 7:49 Eastern time, NASA's New
Line
5   Horizons spacecraft was slated to reach its primary target, Pluto and its moons, concluding what some call the preliminary reconnaissance of the known solar system.

Though it was conceived in the late 1980s, New Horizons wasn't launched until 2006, after long years
10 of delays, redesigns, and even near-death cancellations. Its unlikely five-billion-kilometer voyage to Pluto has been the work of decades. And yet today, at the climax of its mission, the spacecraft was expected to traverse the expanse of Pluto in less than three
15 minutes, whizzing 12,500 kilometers above the surface at nearly 50,000 kilometers per hour. From the start, the spacecraft was custom-built for speed. Carrying enough fuel to crash into orbit at Pluto would have made New Horizons too bulky, expensive, and slow to
20 even launch in the first place, so instead it will flyby and continue outward, on an endless journey into interstellar night.

During its brief close encounter, New Horizons will be too busy gathering data to immediately phone
25 home, instead using those precious moments to scrutinize the planet with a suite of seven instruments all running on a nightlight's share of electricity. Mission planners will only learn of the flyby's success later tonight, via a radio signal. Or, they could learn of
30 its failure by hearing nothing—the spacecraft has an estimated 1 in 10,000 chance of suffering a destructive high-speed collision with debris while passing through the Plutonian system.

Presuming New Horizons' flyby is successful, its
35 confirmatory signal traveling sunward at the speed of light will reach Earth some 4.5 hours after being transmitted, and is expected to arrive at 8:53 pm. Though the primary encounter is best measured in minutes and hours, the slow data-transmission rate

40 imposed by such vast distances ensures that New Horizons will be beaming its archived images home well into 2017.

Passage 2

What do you do when you've flown 3 billion miles through interplanetary space?
45   You keep going.

Although NASA's New Horizons mission has only just begun to transmit the bulk of the detailed scientific data from its history-making encounter with the Pluto-Charon system (at an excruciatingly slow 2 kilobits per
50 second) the spacecraft team has been hard at work on a critical, and time-sensitive, decision.

It had long been hoped that New Horizons would be able to deploy its instruments to study further objects in the Kuiper belt. But back in early 2014 it
55 wasn't clear that astronomers and planetary scientists were going to be able to find any suitable candidates within the range of trajectories that the mission—with its limited on-board fuel resources—could reasonably adjust to. Despite searching with Earth-bound
60 telescopes it was clear that our understanding of the number of objects smaller than Pluto (but still large enough to study) was incomplete, as candidates were in short supply.

Using the Hubble Space Telescope in the summer
65 of 2014, in what was a bit of a last-ditch attempt, there was huge relief as just five plausible targets finally revealed themselves, with two later confirmed to be good for an intercept.

The first of these, called PT1 (potential target one)
70 or more officially 2014 MU69, has now been chosen as the next goal for New Horizons.

This object is thought to be at most 30 miles across —akin to a cometary nucleus on steroids—and barely 1% the size of Pluto. In other words, it's an entirely
75 different beast than Pluto, but it may be the kind of body that helped form Pluto itself some 4.5 billion years ago, and it's within reach for New Horizons at a mere billion miles further along the interplanetary road.

CONTINUE ▶

21

In line 10, the author of Passage 1 mentions "delays, redesigns, and even near-death cancellations" primarily to

A) indicate why the ship was built for speed.

B) predict that not all may go well with the mission.

C) express concern that the ship may crash.

D) explain the period of time between the plan and its execution.

22

The author of Passage 1 indicates that the flyby over Pluto could have which outcome?

A) Scientists could receive data beginning at 7:49 Eastern time.

B) Scientists could receive no data from the ship.

C) Scientists could learn of the mission's failure through a radio signal.

D) Scientists could receive data after a delay of 3 minutes.

23

Which choice provides the best evidence for the answer to the previous question?

A) Lines 3–7 ("At 7:49 . . . system")

B) Lines 28–29 ("Mission planners . . . signal")

C) Lines 29–33 ("Or, they . . . system")

D) Lines 34–37 ("Presuming New . . . 8:53 pm")

24

As used in line 26, "suite" most nearly means

A) jacket.

B) room.

C) array.

D) candy.

25

What function does the discussion of the measurement of the primary encounter in lines 38-39 serve in Passage 1?

A) It supports a claim made earlier in the text.

B) It undermines an assumption made in the previous paragraph.

C) It emphasizes the relativity of time in measuring space.

D) It highlights the brevity of the encounter vs. the slow pace of the documentation.

26

The central claim of Passage 2 is that New Horizons has started to transmit information about Pluto but

A) it will then continue on an endless journey into night.

B) it is also on the way to its next observation.

C) plans for its next task need to be decided upon soon.

D) the preliminary reconnaissance of our solar system is complete.

27

As used in line 53, "deploy" most nearly means

A) mimic.

B) utilize.

C) release.

D) negate.

CONTINUE

28

Which statement best describes the relationship between the passages?

A) Passage 2 expresses concern about the dangers mentioned in Passage 1.

B) Passage 2 revises the interpretation of events described in Passage 1.

C) Passage 2 describes the next chapter in the story depicted in Passage 1.

D) Passage 2 provides qualified support for the successes celebrated in Passage 1.

29

The author of Passage 2 would most likely respond to the discussion of New Horizons' continued journey in lines 21-22, Passage 1, by claiming that the journey

A) will involve at least one further stop.

B) will not take place on a literal road.

C) will be endless.

D) will take a long time before return is possible.

30

Which choice provides the best evidence for the answer to the previous question?

A) Lines 46–51 ("Although NASA's . . . decision")

B) Lines 52–54 ("It had . . . belt")

C) Lines 69–71 ("The first . . . Horizons")

D) Lines 74–79 ("In other . . . road")

31

Which statement about New Horizons' journey is true about both passages?

A) Passage 1 contains an exaggeration, while Passage 2 contains an ironic understatement.

B) Passage 1 utilizes a metaphor, while Passage 2 relies on strict realism.

C) Passage 1 relies on allegory, while Passage 2 makes use of personification.

D) Passage 1 presents a history, while Passage 2 presents an anecdote.

CONTINUE

Questions 32–42 are based on the following passage and supplementary material.

This passage is adapted from Kelvin F. H. Lui and Alan C.N. Wong, "Does Media Multitasking Always Hurt? A Positive Correlation Between Multitasking and Multisensory Integration." © 2012 by Psychonomic Society, Inc.

Humans often engage in multitasking—that is, performing more than one task simultaneously or in rapid alternation. We can effortlessly talk to each other while walking and watch television while eating. Certain multitasking situations are more challenging because the tasks involved are more difficult or they concurrently engage overlapping processes and, thus, interfere with each other more. Talking on cell phones while driving is a good example. Sometimes, such difficulties can have serious consequences.

One way that modern technology has transformed human living styles is through the invention and popularization of various media of communication and interaction, including radio, television, telephone and text messaging, video games, computers, and the Internet. Media multitasking has thus grown into a popular phenomenon and even a way of life, especially among young people. The high accessibility of computers, in particular, has cultivated obsessive multitasking, due to the ease of switching between instant messaging, music, Web surfing, e-mail, online videos, computer-based games, computer-based applications, and so forth.

The immediate effects of media multitasking on one's memory, learning, and other cognitive functions have been a focus of recent research. It was found that watching TV while doing homework decreased participants' performance on the recognition of TV content. Besides, Furnham and Bradley found detrimental effects of background music on participants' performance in various cognitive tasks. Armstrong and Chung showed a negative effect of background television during science article reading on subsequent recall and recognition. Similarly, reading and watching video simultaneously impaired participants' performance on the reading task. Moreover, Hembrooke and Gay found that opening laptops and engaging in media multitasking behaviors during a lecture impaired students' memory for lecture contents.

Research also has examined the chronic effects of media multitasking. Kirschner and Karpinski found that heavy Facebook users reported having lower grade point averages (GPAs) and suggested the possible deleterious effect of simultaneously using Facebook with other activities. Besides, the amount of time spent on instant messaging was found to be negatively correlated both with cognitive performance in lab tasks and with GPA. While these two studies assumed that Facebook usage and instant messaging often co-occur with other activities and, thus, represent multimedia usage, they did not, however, exclude the simpler possibility that Facebook usage and instant messaging simply occupy the time that could be used for studying.

A recent large-scale study compared the way in which heavy media multitaskers process information differently from those who do not. Participants completed a self-report questionnaire in their study to indicate their level of media multitasking. It was found that heavy media multitaskers performed worse than light media multitaskers in several cognitive tasks that involved working memory, selective attention to task-relevant information in visual search, and surprisingly, task switching. It was suggested that heavy media multitaskers have developed the habit of simultaneously consuming information from multiple media and, thus, "breadth-biased cognitive control." As a result, heavy media multitaskers could not precisely differentiate between important information and distractors. They readily spread their attention to different sources of information regardless of whether they were relevant to the primary task at hand. This is why they were inferior to light media multitaskers in tasks that required one to disregard irrelevant information in the environment and in memory.

An intriguing possibility, however, is that their breadth biased cognitive control will lead to better performance if a task contains some unexpected information that is important to the task at hand. When a media multitasker reads, for example, he or she may more readily detect an SMS ringtone from a mobile phone, although the ringtone does not carry information useful for the primary task of reading. In fact, situations like that may actually be more representative of what happens in real life.

CONTINUE

In this study, our aim was to measure the potential difference between high and low media multitaskers in this tendency to capture information from seemingly
90 irrelevant sources. Specifically, we accessed how much one can integrate visual and auditory information automatically, using a visual search task in the pip-and-pop paradigm. In this paradigm, participants made speeded responses to indicate which of a horizontal
95 or vertical line segment was present among a number of oblique line segments of various orientations. Both target and distractor lines in the display changed color between red and green continuously. Participants performed the same search task on both tone-
100 absent (baseline) and tone-present trials, but only in tone-present trials was each target color change accompanied by a short auditory tone (the pip).

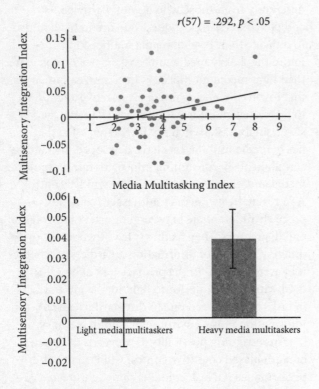

$r(57) = .292, p < .05$

a) Scatterplot between the multisensory integration index for accuracy and the media multitasking index.

b) Multisensory integration indices for light and heavy media multitaskers. Error bars indicate standard errors of the means.

32

The authors most likely use the examples in lines 3-9 of the passage to highlight that

A) multitasking is usually difficult and dangerous.

B) multitasking is a fairly common occurrence.

C) students who want to increase their grades should not multitask.

D) multitasking is an instinctual habit.

33

In line 7, the word "engage" most nearly means

A) marry.

B) capture.

C) employ.

D) absorb.

34

The study authors mentioned in paragraph 3 (lines 24–40) would likely describe "media multitasking" as

A) focused.

B) disadvantageous.

C) multifaceted.

D) chronic.

35

The authors indicate that Kirschner and Karpinski suggest grades decreased because students

A) used a social media platform while studying.

B) performed badly on tests due to fatigue.

C) spent too much time on Messenger.

D) spent too much time on Facebook in general.

CONTINUE ▶

36

Which choice provides the best evidence for the answer to the previous question?

A) Lines 26–29 ("It was . . . content")

B) Lines 42–46 ("Kirschner and . . . activities")

C) Lines 49–55 ("While these . . . studying")

D) Lines 56–58 ("A recent . . . not")

37

In the fifth paragraph (lines 56-76), the author indicates that, compared to heavy media multitaskers, light media multitaskers are more

A) distracted.

B) focused.

C) scholarly.

D) discriminating.

38

Which choice provides the best evidence for the answer to the previous question?

A) Lines 56–58 ("A recent . . . not")

B) Lines 65–68 ("It was . . . control")

C) Lines 73–76 ("This is . . . memory")

D) Lines 77–80 ("An intriguing . . . hand")

39

As used in line 57, "process" most nearly means

A) filter.

B) share.

C) digitize.

D) retain.

40

The authors refer to the pip-and-pop paradigm (lines 92-93) in order to

A) question a technique.

B) support a claim.

C) offer a clarification.

D) introduce a method.

41

In the graph following the passage, the line of best fit demonstrates that

A) light media multitaskers get good grades.

B) Kirschner and Karpinski's study was correct.

C) Facebook usage leads to lesser cognitive functions.

D) a weak data correlation exists in the study.

42

The authors of the study would likely attribute heavy media multitaskers' increased Multisensory Integration, as represented in the graph, to an ability to

A) discern important information in context.

B) spread their attention to multiple unrelated tasks.

C) display an increased level of sensitivity.

D) observe all details during a stressful event.

CONTINUE

Questions 43–52 are based on the following passage and supplementary material.

This passage is from Cesar A. Arias, M.D., Ph.D., and Barbara E. Murray, M.D., "Antibiotic-Resistant Bugs in the 21st Century—A Clinical Super-Challenge." © 2009 by *New England Journal of Medicine*.

In March 1942, a 33-year-old woman lay dying of streptococcal sepsis in a New Haven, Connecticut, hospital, and despite the best efforts of contemporary

Line

medical science, her doctors could not eradicate her

5 bloodstream infection. Then they managed to obtain a small amount of a newly discovered substance called penicillin, which they cautiously injected into her. After repeated doses, her bloodstream was cleared of streptococci, she made a full recovery, and she went

10 on to live to the age of 90. Sixty-six years after her startling recovery, a report described a 70 year-old-man in San Francisco with endocarditis caused by vancomycin-resistant *Enterococcus faecium* (VRE). Despite the administration, for many days, of the best

15 antibiotics available for combating VRE, physicians were unable to sterilize the patient's blood, and he died still bacteremic. We have almost come full circle and arrived at a point as frightening as the preantibiotic era: for patients infected with multi-drug

20 resistant bacteria, there is no magic bullet.

It is difficult to imagine under-taking today's surgical procedures, transplantations, cancer chemotherapy, or care of the critically ill or HIV-infected without effective antimicrobial agents.

25 Bacteria are champions of evolution, and a few microbes have adapted to a point where they pose serious clinical challenges for humans. Among the gram-positive organisms, methicillin-resistant *Staphylococcus aureus* (MRSA) and *E. faecium*

30 represent the biggest therapeutic hurdles. The evolution of MRSA exemplifies the genetic adaptation of an organism into a first-class multidrug-resistant pathogen. After the introduction of penicillin and, later, methicillin, *S. aureus* quickly developed

35 resistance to the β-lactam compounds, and by 2003 more than 50% of *S. aureus* isolates recovered in U.S. hospitals were MRSA.

Then MRSA began developing resistance to glycopeptides, first evolving, through largely undefined

40 mutations, low-level resistance to vancomycin, which was associated with a thickening of the pathogen's cell walls. Such isolates were designated VISA (or GISA), for vancomycin (or glycopeptide) intermediately resistant *S. aureus*. VISA is difficult for clinical

45 laboratories to detect, but its presence is associated with the therapeutic failure of glycopeptides. The break-points for susceptibility to vanomycin have therefore been changed, screening tests for VISA have been proposed, and much debate has ensued regarding

50 the usefulness of vancymycin in the treatment of serious MRSA infections.

Next, strains of MRSA with true, high-level resistance to vancomycin (vancomycin-resistant *S. aureus* or VRSA) emerged. Such resistance is due to

55 the acquisition of the *vanA* gene cluster, originally described in enterococci. Fortunately, fewer than a dozen such isolates have been reported (mostly in Michigan), and their dissemination appears to be limited, at least for now. VRSA, like other

60 strains of health-care associated MRSA, is often resistant to multiple drugs, including clindamycin, aminoglycosides, trimethoprim-sulfamethoxazole, rifampin, and fluoroquinolones.

CONTINUE ➤

	Antibiotic family				
Bacteria	**Penicillin**	**Aminoglycosides (including streptomycin)**	**Macrolides (including vancomycin)**	**Aminopenicillins (including methicillin)**	**Fluoroquinolones (including amikacin)**
	Resistance of bacteria to antibiotic family				
E. faecium			75%	19%	
M. tuberculosis			9%		47%
P. mirabilis	9%			22%	28%
CoNS			63%		50%
C. difficile			3%		
P. aeruginosa		15%			27%
E. coli	9%			22%	33%
Shigella		56%	14%	78%	0.2%
S. aureus				51%	0.8%
When Introduced	1940s		1950s	1960s	

43

Based on the passage, the authors' statement "We have almost come full circle … for patients infected with multi-drug resistant bacteria, there is no magic bullet" (lines 17–20) implies that

A) antibiotics are no longer used to treat bacterial infections.

B) the medical sciences have finally come around to antibiotic treatments and therapies.

C) there is currently no solution for how to treat multi-drug resistant bacteria.

D) vancomycin-resistant *Enterococcus faecium* is no longer treatable.

44

A student claims that antibiotic use has never been 100% effective in the treatment of a bacterial infection. Which of the following statements in the passage contradicts the student's claim?

A) Lines 8–10 ("After repeated . . . 90")

B) Lines 14–17 ("Despite the . . . bacteremic")

C) Lines 33–37 ("After the . . . MRSA")

D) Lines 56–59 ("Fortunately, fewer . . . now")

45

The authors use the word "evolution" in lines 25 and 31 to indicate that

A) only one type of bacteria, methicillin-resistant *Staphylococcus aureus*, has demonstrated significant resistance to antibiotics.

B) multi-drug resistant bacteria was an inevitable outcome of the evolution of medical science and prescription drug development.

C) antibiotics are not effective at treating specific strains of bacteria as those strains are significantly altered from their original presentation.

D) strains of bacteria previously known to scientists have entirely disappeared and been replaced by drug-resistant versions.

CONTINUE

46

In the second paragraph (lines 21–37), what do the authors claim to be a result of antibiotic resistance?

A) The disappearance of methicillin-resistant *S. aureus* (MRSA) and *E. faecium*.

B) The creation of a "magic bullet" antibiotic to treat patients infected with multi-drug resistant bacteria.

C) A significant increase in the numbers of deaths from bacterial infection in the United States.

D) The majority of clinically observed cases of *S. aureus* were resistant to at least one antibiotic treatment.

47

The authors' main purpose of including the information about MRSA's glycopeptide and vancomycin resistance is to

A) review the history of medical research, specifically antibiotic development and therapy.

B) present the progression a specific bacteria demonstrated to alternate treatment options.

C) provide a list of the most common antibiotics that are used to battle certain bacteria.

D) confirm the broad resistance of *S. aureus* to all known antibiotics

48

The authors' use of the words "appears" and "often" in lines 58–60 in the final paragraph functions mainly to

A) confirm that the levels and types of antibiotic-resistance of MRSA and VSRA are well known.

B) counter the claim that based on clinical results antibiotic resistance is slowing for MRSA and VSRA.

C) support the authors' call for greater attention and research funding for multi-drug resistant bacterial research.

D) emphasize the lack of certainty that surrounds our existing knowledge of multi-drug resistant bacteria.

49

Based on the table and passage, which choice gives the correct description of penicillin?

A) Penicillin was initially introduced for medical use in the first half of the twentieth century.

B) *Streptococcal sepsis* has not developed antibiotic resistance to penicillin.

C) Fewer bacteria have demonstrated resistance to penicillin than to fluoroquinolones.

D) More bacteria have demonstrated resistance to penicillin than to amikacin.

50

Do the data in the table support the authors' assertion that *S. aureus* and *E. faecium* represent the biggest therapeutic hurdles?

A) Yes, because collectively they show some level of resistance to three antibiotic families, which is more than any other single bacteria listed.

B) Yes, because the highest level of resistance either bacteria exhibits is 75%, the largest percent of resistance listed.

C) No, because the lowest level of resistance either bacteria exhibits is 0.8%, the smallest percent of resistance listed.

D) No, because collectively they show some level of resistance to three antibiotic families, which is fewer than any other single bacteria listed.

CONTINUE

51

According to the table, which of the following bacteria provides evidence in support of the answer to the previous question?

A) *M. tuberculosis*

B) *CoNS*

C) *Shigella*

D) *P. aeruginosa*

52

Based on the table, is Aminopenicillin-resistant *S. aureus* resistant to at least one member of the Fluoroquinolones family or none, and which statement made by the authors is most consistent with that data?

A) At least one; "Then MRSA . . . walls" (lines 38–42)

B) At least one; "VRSA, like . . . fluoroquinolones" (lines 59–63)

C) None; "Fortunately, fewer . . . now" (lines 56–59)

D) None; "VRSA, like . . . fluoroquinolones" (lines 59–63)

STOP
If you finish before time is called, you may check your work on this section only.
Do not turn to any other section in the test.

Writing and Language Test

35 MINUTES, 44 QUESTIONS

Turn to Section 2 of your answer sheet to answer the questions in this section.

DIRECTIONS

Each passage below is accompanied by a number of questions. For some questions, you will consider how the passage might be revised to improve the expression of ideas. For other questions, you will consider how the passage might be edited to correct errors in sentence structure, usage, or punctuation. A passage or a question may be accompanied by one or more graphics (such as a table or graph) that you will consider as you make revising and editing decisions.

Some questions will direct you to an underlined portion of a passage. Other questions will direct you to a location in a passage or ask you to think about the passage as a whole.

After reading each passage, choose the answer to each question that most effectively improves the quality of writing in the passage or that makes the passage conform to the conventions of standard written English. Many questions include a "NO CHANGE" option. Choose that option if you think the best choice is to leave the relevant portion of the passage as it is.

Questions 1–11 are based on the following passage.

"Made-Up" Science

When we hear about the opinions of "ten scientists" or "ten dentists," or we hear that things are "clinically proven" or "lab-tested," for [1] example, and we might expect to be reading scientific journals. However, these phrases and statistics are well-known outside of scientific circles because they are so commonly used in a less likely place: advertising. It's not enough for, say, a shampoo to promise clean hair: it seems the only way to sell shampoo is [2] by lowering the price and offering special deals and coupons.

1

A) NO CHANGE
B) example, consequently we
C) example: we
D) example, we

2

Which provides the most relevant detail?

A) NO CHANGE
B) to merge into larger corporations and reduce the number of shampoo brands.
C) by comparing the product to other products customers buy more regularly.
D) to promise 40% more volume and bounce or 60% fewer split ends than other brands.

CONTINUE

These claims are part of what has been called, since 1961, "cosmeutical" science. The word itself combines "cosmetics" and "pharmaceutical." Since the term was coined in 1961, cosmetics companies have been under more pressure to innovate, as competition grows and markets expand outside the United States. This pressure has led to an increased reliance on scientific data as a way to back up the advertisers' claims.

[1] But where exactly do these claims come from? [2] However, if these claims seem absurd at times, it's because they may come from nowhere at all. [3] A recent study of these scientific claims appears in the *Journal of Global Fashion Marketing*. [4] In this study, the researchers looked at over 300 advertisements from fashion magazines like *Elle*, **3** *Vogue*, and *Vanity Fair*. [5] The obvious answer would seem to be "the lab." **4**

To anyone who has ever **5** believed the truth-value of these advertisements (or of advertisements in general), the researchers' findings are probably not surprising. The researchers found that a mere 18% of the claims made in these advertisements were true. 23% of the claims were classified as "outright lies." **6** 42% were considered too vague to classify.

3

A) NO CHANGE
B) *Vogue* and,
C) *Vogue*; and
D) *Vogue*: and

4

To make this paragraph most logical, sentence 5 should be placed
A) where it is now.
B) before sentence 2.
C) before sentence 3.
D) before sentence 4.

5

A) NO CHANGE
B) pondered
C) questioned
D) skepticized

6

The writer is considering deleting the underlined portion. Should the writer do this?
A) No, because it demonstrates the most surprising of the researchers' findings.
B) No, because it completes the discussion of the data and is mentioned again in the passage.
C) Yes, because it is a reminder of how subjective the researchers' study truly was.
D) Yes, because the reader could deduce this information through simple mathematics.

CONTINUE

These findings are good for a laugh, but **7** they may have more serious implications as well. Although everyone knows that the Food and Drug Administration can **8** reign what goes *into* food and drugs, what is less known is that the FDA can also punish false advertising claims. That sizable 23% that is telling "outright lies" may have a federal agency investigating its claims, and these investigations **9** might have resulted in significant fines and lawsuits.

While this has obvious ramifications for the "outright lies," what can the FDA do **10** from that much larger share of "too vague" claims? These may be safe for the simple reason that they are too vague to be disproven. Whatever the FDA may decide to do, this research should still remind consumers about the potential perils of trusting the word of advertisers. **11** Thus, the claims are often harmless, but consumers want to believe that they are giving their hard-earned money to trustworthy organizations.

7
A) NO CHANGE
B) will have
C) may have
D) might be having

8
A) NO CHANGE
B) regulate
C) name
D) administrate

9
A) NO CHANGE
B) have resulted in significant fine's
C) may result in significant fines
D) may result in significant fine's

10
A) NO CHANGE
B) to
C) by
D) with

11
A) NO CHANGE
B) On the other hand,
C) True,
D) Nevertheless,

CONTINUE

Questions 12–22 are based on the following passage and supplementary material.

Gerry's Salamander

The United States is often lauded for its contributions to democracy in the world. When the process is allowed to work, democracy in the United States is truly admirable, and all of those who vote can feel that they are participating in the process in a significant way. **12** This being the case, there are some abnormalities in the history of U.S. elections that fall short of these expectations.

[1] One notable instance came in a state senate election in Massachusetts in 1812. [2] Unfortunately, it was not the last. [3] Shortly before this election, Elbridge **13** Gerry, then governor of the state, called for a redistricting that was supposed to reflect demographic shifts within the city. [4] To anyone paying attention, however, it **14** will become clear that this redistricting would benefit Gerry's own party, the Democratic-Republicans. [5] It was one of the first and most infamous works of political trickery in the history of the country. **15**

12
A) NO CHANGE
B) Happily,
C) Politically,
D) Unfortunately,

13
A) NO CHANGE
B) Gerry then governor of the state,
C) Gerry, then governor of the state
D) Gerry, then governor, of the state

14
A) NO CHANGE
B) would have become
C) became
D) becomes

15
To make this paragraph most logical, sentence 2 should be placed
A) where it is now.
B) after sentence 3.
C) after sentence 4.
D) after sentence 5.

CONTINUE

Gerry's tactics gave birth to a new term. The *Boston Gazette* poked fun at Gerry's redistricting **16** plan. This newspaper said that the newly created South Essex electoral district resembled a salamander on the map. This image, combined with the governor's name, came to be known by a very specific **17** name: gerrymandering. The practice unfortunately continues to be a tool of political manipulation to this day.

Particularly on the state and local levels, gerrymandering can have a tremendous influence on the outcome of an election. As the below graphic shows, gerrymandering can turn **18** voters against some of the legislative bodies in their state. In a population of 50 people, in which voting blocs lived in contained areas, different districting can result in vastly different outcomes, even where there is a clear advantage for one party. In the redistricting shown below, **19** 40% light gray voters can become 60% dark gray districts through the careful manipulation of the districts.

Gerrymandering, explained
Three different ways to divide 50 people into five districts

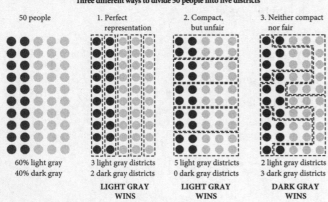

50 people	1. Perfect representation	2. Compact, but unfair	3. Neither compact nor fair
60% light gray 40% dark gray	3 light gray districts 2 dark gray districts	5 light gray districts 0 dark gray districts	2 light gray districts 3 dark gray districts
	LIGHT GRAY WINS	**LIGHT GRAY WINS**	**DARK GRAY WINS**

16

Which choice most effectively combines the two sentences at the underlined portion?

A) plan, when the paper said

B) plan, at which time the paper said

C) plan, saying

D) plan and they said

17

A) NO CHANGE

B) name: which was

C) name;

D) name. And it was

18

Which choice best completes the description of the purpose of gerrymandering?

A) NO CHANGE

B) a series of political factions against one another.

C) elections into long processes with delayed results.

D) electoral disadvantages into electoral advantages.

19

Which choice most accurately and effectively represents information in the figure?

A) NO CHANGE

B) 60% dark gray voters can become 60% light gray districts

C) 40% light gray voters can become 100% dark gray districts

D) 60% light gray voters can become 60% dark gray districts

CONTINUE ➤

Gerrymandering almost always benefits the parties in [20] power, not those out of power, because those are the parties that have the influence necessary to redistrict. Many perfectly viable candidates have been shut out by cruel and unfair districting practices. In this and in other political arenas, it is much easier to stay in power than to gain power.

The real victims of gerrymandering, however, are the voters. The process is used quite often to disenfranchise certain voters by making [21] they're votes less valuable. In "majority-minority" districts in particular, districts with large non-white populations, gerrymandering can discount the importance of particular races or classes of voters, many [22] of whose voting interests may go against those in power. The American voting system works, but only when all voters are given an equal say in the outcome of an election.

20

A) NO CHANGE
B) power usually,
C) power
D) power for the good

21

A) NO CHANGE
B) their
C) there
D) they are

22

A) NO CHANGE
B) voters'
C) of their
D) DELETE the underlined portion.

CONTINUE

Questions 23–33 are based on the following passage and supplementary material.

The Original Condition

If you've ever been to an art museum, you know the basic layout: long hallways and large rooms with paintings hung a few feet apart. You know how the paintings are **23** by certain means marked, and you know that the paintings have been arranged chronologically or thematically.

There's one thing, however, which you've definitely noticed even if you can't quite articulate it. Particularly when looking at old paintings, **24** paintings all have that vividly *new* look, whether they were painted in 1950 or 1450. Even where the subject matter is older, the colors are vibrant, and you're never forced to wonder exactly what the painting must have looked like in its original state. **25** The history of painting is nearly as long as the history of mankind.

23

A) NO CHANGE

B) marked,

C) being marked in a way,

D) by so means of marking,

24

A) NO CHANGE

B) you've surely noticed how *new* all the paintings look,

C) noticing the *new* look of all the paintings is something you can do,

D) the paintings always strike you as very *new* looking,

25

The writer is considering deleting the underlined sentence. Should the sentence be kept or deleted?

A) Deleted, because it strays from the paragraph's major focus by introducing an irrelevant fact.

B) Deleted, because it restates a historical detail that is provided in a later paragraph.

C) Kept, because it is a useful introduction to the topic of this paragraph.

D) Kept, because it provides a humorous anecdote regarding the work of art restorers.

CONTINUE

This incredible feat is the work of a highly specialized group: art restorers. Despite this specialization, the profession has exploded in recent years. **26** Art restoration has been growing steadily since 1930. While the job of an art restorer may seem fairly straightforward **27** when looking, the job is in fact quite complicated. Sometimes, as in the case of Michelangelo's famous sculpture David, the cleaning and restoration of artworks is a simple **28** matter, applying chemicals, washing away grime, and scrubbing off the dirt.

26

At this point the writer wants to add specific information that is consistent with the focus of the paragraph.

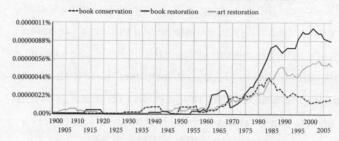

PERCENTAGE OF AMERICAN WORKFORCE IN 3 FIELDS

Which choice most effectively provides a sentence with relevant and accurate information from the graph above?

A) NO CHANGE

B) The number of book restorers who became art restorers tripled in 2000.

C) By the year 2020, it is predicted that art restoration will even eclipse art conservation.

D) From 1970 to 2005, the percentage of people working in art restoration has roughly tripled.

27

A) NO CHANGE

B) beholden,

C) at first glance,

D) under your gaze,

28

A) NO CHANGE

B) matter

C) matter:

D) matter;

CONTINUE ➤

29 With most paintings, however, the process is a good deal more involved because it is not necessarily just a matter of "cleaning" the older paintings. One cannot merely take a scrub brush to a centuries-old great work. Because of the wide range of restoration techniques, art restoration itself can be controversial business. For many years, before museums became the high-volume tourist attractions they are today, art "restorers" were typically artists themselves. They would project some image of what the painting must have looked like originally and apply a variety of techniques, up **30** to and including: repainting, to preserve this "original."

[1] Now, however, more attention is paid to the historical quality of the artworks. [2] Some art historians **31** who is writing today even go so far as to say that dirt and grime themselves are parts of the historical fabric of a painting and thus should be left in. [3] Others argue that the purity of the painting is all that matters. [4] They will restore the original look of a painting, even if that means "fixing" the painting by some non-paint means. **32**

Whatever methods they use, art restorers are more needed **33** for ever, but their work is also less permanent. In order to retain the integrity of the artwork in case the restorers make a mistake, all restoration must now be reversible, a reminder that art "history" is very much a thing of the present and the future.

29

A) NO CHANGE

B) Anyway,

C) In this sense,

D) Alongside cleaning,

30

A) NO CHANGE

B) to, and including,

C) to and including

D) to, and including:

31

A) NO CHANGE

B) who are

C) whom is

D) whom are

32

The writer wants to add the following sentence to the paragraph.

> For example, a recent restoration at Harvard's Art Museums involved precisely calibrated lights that would correct the color damage to a series of murals done by Mark Rothko in the 1960s.

The best placement for the sentence is immediately

A) after sentence 1.

B) after sentence 2.

C) after sentence 3.

D) after sentence 4.

33

A) NO CHANGE

B) by

C) what

D) than

CONTINUE ▶

Questions 34–44 are based on the following passage.

The Rise of *Hyperion*

Literary critics have always paid the most attention to "serious" authors. The great authors of recent memory, especially in American literature, have been distinctly "literary" authors: Toni Morrison, Philip Roth, Thomas Pynchon, and Jonathan Franzen. Often overlooked in this pantheon of great authors are the contributions of authors in non-traditional 34 modes. Specifically overlooked is the genre of science fiction. In some ways, the novel that has hearkened back to the great authors of the Victorian nineteenth century is not Morrison's *Beloved* or Roth's *American Pastoral* but *Hyperion* by Dan Simmons.

Simmons's novel was published in 1989, and it won the Hugo Award for best science-fiction novel that year. 35 All things considered, it is regularly listed among the greatest science-fiction novels of all time. The novel 36 that spawned a series of novels dealing with the same fantastic universe, the first of which was *The Fall of Hyperion*, published in 1990. *Hyperion* tells the story of seven pilgrims who travel to the distant world of Hyperion in an attempt to avert a galaxy-wide war between hostile factions. Because the pilgrims are 37 not sure in a complete way why they've been recruited for this "pilgrimage," they spend the long journey to Hyperion sharing 38 your stories, each of which illuminates the journey 39 while explaining this new fantasy world to the reader.

34

Which choice most effectively combines the sentences at the underlined portion?

A) modes, which notably include

B) modes, and overlooked in particular is

C) modes, specifically

D) modes, and one genre suffering neglect is

35

A) NO CHANGE

B) For all that,

C) To this day,

D) Check this out,

36

A) NO CHANGE

B) which,

C) is that which

D) DELETE the underlined portion.

37

A) NO CHANGE

B) not sure in their entirety

C) not entirely sure

D) lacking a complete sureness

38

A) NO CHANGE

B) their

C) our

D) everyone's

39

A) NO CHANGE

B) when

C) though

D) as if

CONTINUE

If this structure **40** of sound familiar, that's because it draws on some of the great classics of literature, most notably *The Canterbury Tales*, which itself is a kind of travel narrative, as it follows **41** pilgrims travel together to the Canterbury Cathedral. The name of the novel draws on a long literary history as well: poems by John Keats and novels by Friedrich Hölderlin and Henry Wadsworth Longfellow. **42** With all of these literary tributes, if great

A) NO CHANGE

B) and sounding

C) sounding

D) sounds

A) NO CHANGE

B) pilgrim's travels

C) pilgrim's traveling

D) pilgrims traveling

Which choice most effectively sets up the information that follows?

A) Dan Simmons must have studied the poems and essays of T.S. Eliot at some point in his life.

B) Even beyond these nominal debts, *Hyperion* pays homage to countless genres, including the war story and the detective novel.

C) But don't worry, there are still plenty of lasers and space ships in the book, too.

D) Although the critics of the early twentieth century probably would've loved it, many of them died before *Hyperion* was published.

CONTINUE ➡

works of literature are expressions of, as T.S. Eliot says, "tradition and the individual talent," then *Hyperion* is certainly a great work. [43]

In addition to its incredible achievements in terms of literary history, *Hyperion* is also a truly incredible work of science fiction. The future world it imagines is vivid, and its continuities with the contemporary world [44] is clearly defined. *Hyperion* is awash in literary laurels, but it is also an entertaining novel—quite a combination!

The fact that *Hyperion* is not as well known as some of the more accepted "classics" should make us wonder what we mean by this term "classics." We should also wonder what else we've been missing because it hasn't met our traditional criteria for greatness.

[43]

At this point, the writer is considering adding the following sentence.

> Some of T.S. Eliot's most famous poems are *The Waste Land* and "The Love Song of J. Alfred Prufrock."

Should the writer make this addition here?

A) Yes, because it helps to put the literary quality of *Hyperion* into its appropriate context.

B) Yes, because it names another series of works that are overlooked for being non-traditional.

C) No, because it introduces a new set of information that does not have a clear link to the rest of the passage.

D) No, because it disagrees with the passage's central claim that *Hyperion* is the greatest work of science fiction.

44

A) NO CHANGE

B) has been

C) being

D) are

STOP

If you finish before time is called, you may check your work on this section only.
Do not turn to any other section in the test.

Math Test – No Calculator

25 MINUTES, 20 QUESTIONS

Turn to Section 3 of your answer sheet to answer the questions in this section.

CONTINUE

1

During a certain week, Jan worked j hours each day for 3 days, and Noah worked n hours each day for 5 days. Which of the following represents the total combined number of hours worked that week by Jan and Noah?

A) $3j + 5n$

B) $5j + 3n$

C) $8jn$

D) $15jn$

2

If $\dfrac{y + 2}{5} = c$ and $c = 4$, what is the value of y ?

A) 16

B) 18

C) 20

D) 22

3

For $i = \sqrt{-1}$, what is the sum $(10 - 4i) + (3 + 6i)$?

A) $13 - 10i$

B) $13 + 2i$

C) $7 - 10i$

D) $7 + 2i$

4

$$(ab^2 + 4a^2 + 6a^2b^2) - (-ab^2 + 2a^2b^2 + 4a^2)$$

Which of the following is equivalent to the expression above?

A) $-2a^2b^2$

B) $-2a^2b^2 + 8a^2$

C) $2ab^2 - 2a^2b^2 + 8a^2$

D) $2ab^2 + 4a^2b^2$

CONTINUE

5

$$w = 3{,}150 + 450l$$

A marine biologist uses the equation above to estimate the weight, *w*, of a mature great white shark, in pounds, in terms of the shark's fork length, *l*, in feet. Based on the equation, what is the estimated weight increase, in pounds, for each foot of growth in fork length in a great white shark?

A) 3,150

B) 2,700

C) 1,350

D)   450

6

Juan is a book editor who is given a book to edit. The number of pages that he has left to edit at the end of each hour is estimated by the equation $P = 326 - 12h$, where *h* represents the number of hours spent editing the book. What is the meaning of the value 326 in this equation?

A) Juan edits pages at a rate of 326 per day.

B) Juan edits pages at a rate of 326 per hour.

C) Juan is given a total of 326 pages to edit.

D) Juan will finish editing the book in 326 hours.

7

If $\dfrac{x}{y} = 3$, what is the value of $\dfrac{12y}{x}$?

A)   4

B)   6

C)   8

D) 12

8

$$2y + x = -17$$
$$5x - 4y = -15$$

What is the solution (x, y) to the system of equations shown above?

A) (−7, −5)

B) (−4, −1)

C) (−3, 0)

D) (5, −11)

CONTINUE

9

$$c = \frac{\dfrac{r}{1,200}}{1 - \left(1 + \dfrac{r}{1,200}\right)^{-N}} M$$

In order to buy a house, a couple takes on a mortgage of M dollars at an annual rate of r percent to be paid off over N months. If the equation above is used to determine the monthly payment, c, that the couple needs to make to pay off the loan, which of the following expressions gives the value of M, in terms of c, r, and N?

A) $M = \left(\dfrac{r}{1,200}\right)c$

B) $M = \left(\dfrac{1,200}{r}\right)c$

C) $M = \dfrac{1 - \left(1 + \dfrac{r}{1,200}\right)^{-N}}{\dfrac{r}{1,200}} c$

D) $M = \dfrac{\dfrac{r}{1,200}}{1 - \left(1 + \dfrac{r}{1,200}\right)^{-N}} c$

10

A line in the xy-plane has a slope of $\dfrac{2}{3}$ and passes through the origin. Which of the following points lies on the line?

A) $\left(0, \dfrac{2}{3}\right)$

B) $(2, 3)$

C) $(6, 4)$

D) $(9, 4)$

11

$$f(x) = cx^2 + 30$$

For the function f defined above, c is a constant and $f(3) = 12$. What is the value of $f(-3)$?

A) -12

B) -2

C) 0

D) 12

CONTINUE

12

$$A = 240 - 20w$$

$$B = 320 - 30w$$

In the equations above, A and B represent the price per night for a room in Hotel A and Hotel B, respectively, w weeks after September 1 last autumn. What was the price per night in Hotel A when it was equal to the price per night in Hotel B?

A) $80

B) $160

C) $180

D) $220

13

If $a - 4b = 18$, what is the value of $\dfrac{3^a}{81^b}$?

A) 81^2

B) 9^6

C) 3^{18}

D) The value cannot be determined from the information given.

14

If $(ax + 3)(bx + 5) = 35x^2 + kx + 15$ for all values of x, and $a + b = 12$, what are the two possible values for k?

A) 46 and 50

B) 15 and 35

C) 21 and 25

D) 5 and 7

15

If $y > 5$, which of the following is equivalent to

$$\dfrac{1}{\dfrac{1}{y-4} + \dfrac{1}{y-3}}\ ?$$

A) $2y - 7$

B) $y^2 - 7y + 12$

C) $\dfrac{y^2 - 7y + 12}{2y - 7}$

D) $\dfrac{2y - 7}{y^2 - 7y + 12}$

CONTINUE ▶

DIRECTIONS

For questions 16-20, solve the problem and enter your answer in the grid, as described below, on the answer sheet.

1. Although not required, it is suggested that you write your answer in the boxes at the top of the columns to help you fill in the circles accurately. You will receive credit only if the circles are filled in correctly.

2. Mark no more than one circle in any column.

3. No question has a negative answer.

4. Some problems may have more than one correct answer. In such cases, grid only one answer.

5. **Mixed numbers** such as $3\frac{1}{2}$ must be gridded as 3.5 or 7/2. (If $\boxed{3\ 1\ /\ 2}$ is entered into the grid, it will be interpreted as $\frac{31}{2}$, not as $3\frac{1}{2}$.)

6. **Decimal Answers:** If you obtain a decimal answer with more digits than the grid can accommodate, it may be either rounded or truncated, but it must fill the entire grid.

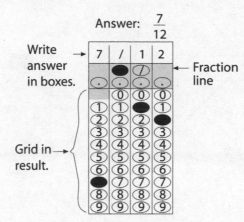

Answer: $\frac{7}{12}$

Write answer in boxes. — Fraction line

Grid in result.

Answer: 2.5 — Decimal point

Acceptable ways to grid $\frac{2}{3}$ are:

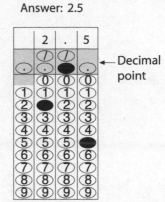

Answer: 201 – either position is correct

NOTE: You may start your answers in any column, space permitting. Columns you don't need to use should be left blank.

CONTINUE ➡

16

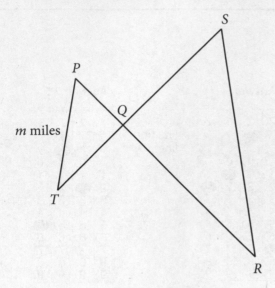

In a certain park, the layout of the six bicycle paths is shown in the figure above. The lengths of $\overline{PQ}$, $\overline{QT}$, $\overline{QS}$, and $\overline{SR}$ are 3 miles, 4 miles, 8 miles, and 10 miles, respectively. Paths $\overline{PR}$ and $\overline{ST}$ intersect at point Q, and $\angle TPQ$ is congruent to $\angle QRS$. What is the value of m?

17

If $y > 0$ and $y^2 - 36 = 0$, what is the value of y?

18

In a right triangle, one angle measures $d°$, where $\cos d° = \dfrac{5}{13}$. What is $\sin(90° - d°)$?

CONTINUE

19

If $c = 3\sqrt{5}$ and $5c = \sqrt{5z}$, what is the value of z ?

20

$$a + b = -10$$
$$2a + b = -33$$

What is the value of b in the system of equations shown above?

STOP

**If you finish before time is called, you may check your work on this section only.
Do not turn to any other section in the test.**

Math Test – Calculator

55 MINUTES, 38 QUESTIONS

Turn to Section 4 of your answer sheet to answer the questions in this section.

DIRECTIONS

For questions **1-30**, solve each problem, choose the best answer from the choices provided, and fill in the corresponding circle on your answer sheet. For questions **31-38**, solve the problem and enter your answer in the grid on the answer sheet. Please refer to the directions before question 31 on how to enter your answers in the grid. You may use any available space in your test booklet for scratch work.

NOTES

1. The use of a calculator **is permitted**.
2. All variables and expressions used represent real numbers unless otherwise indicated.
3. Figures provided in this test are drawn to scale unless otherwise indicated.
4. All figures lie in a plane unless otherwise indicated.
5. Unless otherwise indicated, the domain of a given function f is the set of all real numbers x for which $f(x)$ is a real number.

REFERENCE

$A = \pi r^2$
$C = 2\pi r$

$A = \ell w$

$A = \frac{1}{2} bh$

$c^2 = a^2 + b^2$

Special Right Triangles

$V = \ell wh$

$V = \pi r^2 h$

$V = \frac{4}{3}\pi r^3$

$V = \frac{1}{3}\pi r^2 h$

$V = \frac{1}{3}\ell wh$

The number of degrees of arc in a circle is 360.
The number of radians of arc in a circle is 2π.
The sum of the measures in degrees of the angles of a triangle is 180.

CONTINUE

1

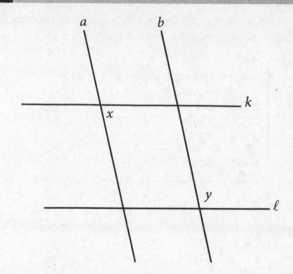

In the figure shown above, lines a and b are parallel and lines k and ℓ are parallel. If the measure of $\angle x$ is 75°, what is the measure of $\angle y$?

A)   15°

B)   75°

C) 105°

D) 165°

2

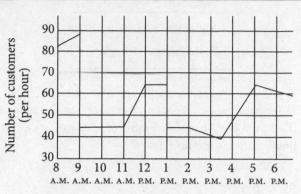

The graph above shows the number of customers per hour at a coffee shop. Over which of the following intervals is the number of customers strictly decreasing then strictly increasing?

A) From 9 A.M. to 12 P.M.

B) From 12 P.M. to 2 P.M.

C) From 2 P.M. to 5 P.M.

D) From 3:30 P.M. to 6:30 P.M.

3

If $y = \dfrac{x}{k}$, where k is a constant, and $y = 5$ when $x = 30$, what is the value of y when $x = 42$?

A)   6

B)   7

C) 10

D) 17

CONTINUE

1 kilogram = 1,000 grams

10 decigrams = 1 gram

A pharmacy sells a certain type of medication in 1-decigram doses. Based on the information shown in the box above, three kilograms of medication contain how many 1-decigram doses?

A)   300,000

B)   30,000

C)   3,000

D)   300

5

If $6x - 4$ is 11 less than 25, what is the value of $9x$?

A)   3

B)   8

C)   18

D)   27

6

Which of the graphs below best illustrates a strong positive correlation between h and p ?

A)

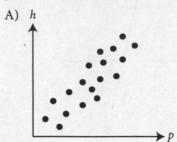

B)

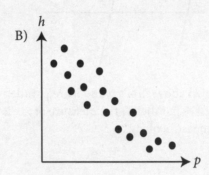

C)

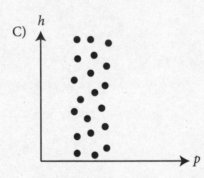

D)

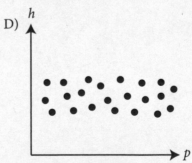

CONTINUE

Questions 7 and 8 refer to the following information.

$$p = 101 + 10.094d$$

The total pressure on an object submerged in the ocean depends on the depth of the object beneath the surface. The formula above shows the relationship between p, pressure, in kilopascals, and d, depth, in meters.

7

At which of the following depths will the total pressure be closest to 200 kilopascals?

A)   8 meters

B)   9 meters

C)   10 meters

D)   11 meters

8

Which of the following formulas expresses depth in terms of pressure?

A) $d = \dfrac{p}{10.094} - 101$

B) $d = \dfrac{10.094}{101 - p}$

C) $d = \dfrac{p + 101}{10.094}$

D) $d = \dfrac{p - 101}{10.094}$

9

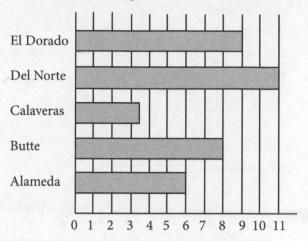

Wind Turbine Operation in Five Counties

The number of wind turbines in use in five counties is shown in the graph above. If there are a total of 3,750 wind turbines operating in these five counties, which of the following is an appropriate label for the horizontal axis of the graph?

A)   Number of wind turbines (in tens)

B)   Number of wind turbines (in hundreds)

C)   Number of wind turbines (in thousands)

D)   Number of wind turbines (in tens of thousands)

CONTINUE

10

For how many values of k is it true that $|k - 3| + 2$ is equal to one?

A) None

B) One

C) Two

D) More than two

11

Number of Residents in Each of 14 Apartments

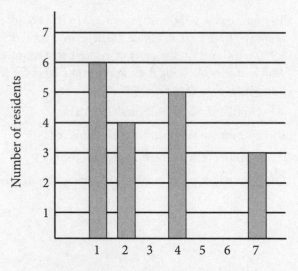

Number of apartments

According to the histogram shown above, which of the following is closest to the average (arithmetic mean) number of residents per apartment?

A) 3

B) 3.25

C) 3.5

D) 4

12

Which of the following integers CANNOT be a solution to the inequality $6x - 4 \leq 7x - 3$?

A) 1

B) 0

C) –1

D) –2

13

Weights of potatoes (in ounces)								
2	3	3	4	4	4	5	5	6
6	7	7	7	7	8	8	9	9

An agriculture class harvested 18 potatoes from the school garden and compiled the weights of the potatoes in the table above. If the 2-ounce measurement is removed from the data, which of the following statistical measures of the values listed will change the least?

A) The mean

B) The median

C) The range

D) The total

CONTINUE

14

$$p + x > y$$
$$r - x < -y$$

In the xy-plane, $(2, 2)$ is a solution to the system of inequalities shown above. Which of the following must be true about p and r?

A) $p < r$

B) $r < p$

C) $p + r = 0$

D) $|p| = |r|$

15

	Political Party			
	Liberal	Conservative	Independent	Total
Men	59	74	62	195
Women	82	63	55	200
Total	141	137	117	395

A group of voters in country X responded to a poll that asked which political party they planned to vote for. The table above shows the results of the polling data. Which of the categories below accounts for approximately 15 percent of all poll respondents?

A) Men voting Liberal

B) Men voting Independent

C) Women voting Conservative

D) Women voting Liberal

CONTINUE

Questions 16 and 17 refer to the following information.

Total Cost of Renting a Car by the Day

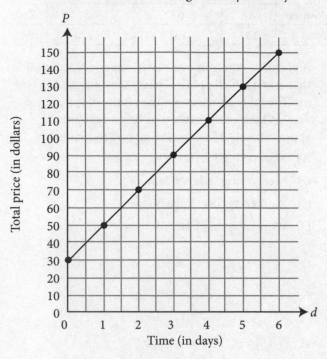

The graph above shows the total price *P*, in dollars, to rent a car for *d* days.

16

What does the slope of the graph represent?

A) The total number of cars rented

B) The initial cost of renting a car

C) The average increase in price to rent a car for each additional day

D) The total number of days for which a car is rented

17

Which of the equations below shows the relationship between *d* and *P* ?

A) $P = 25d$

B) $P = d + 30$

C) $P = 10d + 30$

D) $P = 20d + 30$

CONTINUE

18

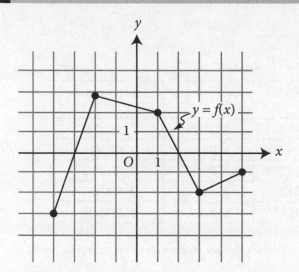

The figure above shows the complete graph of the function *f* in the *xy*-plane. For which of the following values of *x* is $f(x)$ at its maximum?

A) −4

B) −3

C) −2

D) 3

19

The price of a train ticket purchased in the train station or from a conductor is 15 percent less during off-peak hours than it is during peak hours. If a ticket is purchased from the conductor, an 11 percent surcharge is added to the price. Alec purchased a ticket from the conductor during off-peak hours and paid a total of *t* dollars. Which of the following, in terms of *t*, represents the price he would have paid if he had purchased the ticket in the train station during peak hours?

A) $\dfrac{t}{0.96}$

B) $0.96t$

C) $\dfrac{t}{(0.85)(1.11)}$

D) $(0.85)(1.11)t$

20

Number of Exercise Sessions per Week

	0–2	3–5	More than 5	Total
Group 1	13	22	15	50
Group 2	11	18	21	50
Total	24	40	36	100

The table above was compiled by a nutrition researcher studying how often people exercise when asked to keep a log of their exercise sessions. Group 1 was comprised of people who regularly eat snacks, and Group 2 was comprised of people who rarely eat snacks. If one person is randomly chosen from among those who exercise fewer than six times per week, what is the probability that this person belonged to Group 1 ?

A) $\dfrac{35}{64}$

B) $\dfrac{50}{64}$

C) $\dfrac{29}{100}$

D) $\dfrac{35}{100}$

21

A service station sells gasoline for $3.25 per gallon and diesel fuel for $3.00 per gallon. On Monday, the service station's revenue from selling a total of 131 gallons of gasoline and diesel fuel was $404.25. How many gallons of diesel fuel did the service station sell on Monday?

A) 35

B) 55

C) 76

D) 86

CONTINUE

Questions 22 and 23 refer to the following information.

Total Budget Spending in One U.S. State by Category, 2010–2014

Year	K-12 education	Higher education	Public assistance	Medicaid	Corrections	Transportation
2014	3,635,265	3,099,112	29,450	2,990,415	930,525	1, 556,244
2013	3,677,428	2,734,615	45,873	3,005,188	820,855	1,873,618
2012	3,715,853	2,550,665	55,645	3,020,012	773,420	1,721,682
2011	3,747,921	2,309,789	54,321	2,984,375	694,011	1,388,904
2010	3,785,200	2,104,214	55,787	3,001,650	632,350	1,434,006

The table above summarizes annual spending, in thousands of dollars, for six categories of spending in one U.S. state, 2010-2014.

22

Of the following, which category's ratio of its 2010 spending to its 2014 spending is nearest to the higher education category's ratio of its 2010 spending to its 2014 spending?

A) K-12 education

B) Medicaid

C) Corrections

D) Transportation

23

Which of the following is the best approximation of the average rate of change in spending on public assistance from 2012 to 2014 ?

A) $6,000,000

B) $10,000,000

C) $13,000,000

D) $26,000,000

CONTINUE

24

A fish leaps vertically upward from the surface of a lake at an initial speed of 9 meters per second. The height h, in meters, of the fish above the surface of the water s seconds after it leaps is given by the equation $h = 9s - 4.9s^2$. Approximately how many seconds after the fish leaps will it hit the surface of the lake?

A) 2.0

B) 2.5

C) 3.0

D) 3.5

25

A circle in the xy-plane is centered at $(3, 0)$ and has a radius with endpoint $\left(1, \dfrac{8}{3}\right)$. Which of the following is an equation of the circle?

A) $(x - 3)^2 + y^2 = \dfrac{10}{3}$

B) $(x + 3)^2 + y^2 = \dfrac{10}{3}$

C) $(x - 3)^2 + y^2 = \dfrac{100}{9}$

D) $(x + 3)^2 + y^2 = \dfrac{100}{9}$

26

A square lawn has a length of 8 feet and a width of 8 feet. Eight researchers each examine a randomly chosen region of the field; all regions are square with length and width of one foot. The researchers count the number of seedlings in each region that have reached a height of at least 2 inches. The table below shows the resulting data.

Region	1	2	3	4
Number of seedlings	82	87	95	99
Region	5	6	7	8
Number of seedlings	102	106	111	115

Which of the following best approximates the number of seedlings that are at least 2 inches high in the entire lawn?

A)   80

B)   640

C)   800

D) 6,400

27

A zoologist is studying the reproduction rates of two different breeds of chinchillas in country Y. He discovered that the Eastern chinchillas in his study produced 30 percent more offspring than the Western chinchillas did. Based on the zoologist's observation, if the Eastern chinchillas in his study produced 143 offspring, how many offspring did the Western chinchillas produce?

A) 100

B) 103

C) 110

D) 186

CONTINUE

28

When polynomial $g(x)$ is divided by $x - 4$, the remainder is 3. Which of the following statements about $g(x)$ must be true?

A) $g(-4) = 3$

B) $g(4) = 3$

C) $x - 4$ is a factor of $g(x)$.

D) $x + 3$ is a factor of $g(x)$.

29

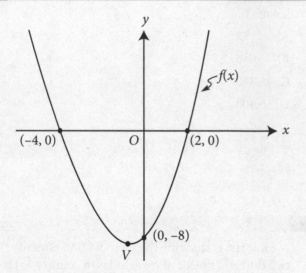

The figure above shows the graph in the xy-plane of the function $f(x) = x^2 + 2x - 8$. Which of the following is an equivalent form of the function f that includes the coordinates of vertex V as constants in the function?

A) $f(x) = (x + 1)^2 - 9$

B) $f(x) = x(x + 2) - 8$

C) $f(x) = (x - 2)(x + 4)$

D) $f(x) = (x + 2)(x - 4)$

30

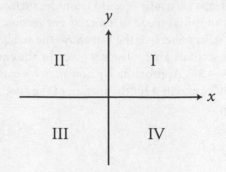

If the system of inequalities $y \geq x + 2$ and $y \geq \dfrac{1}{3}x - 1$ is graphed in the xy-plane shown above, how many quadrants will contain solutions to the system?

A) 4

B) 3

C) 2

D) 1

CONTINUE

DIRECTIONS

For questions 31-38, solve the problem and enter your answer in the grid, as described below, on the answer sheet.

1. Although not required, it is suggested that you write your answer in the boxes at the top of the columns to help you fill in the circles accurately. You will receive credit only if the circles are filled in correctly.

2. Mark no more than one circle in any column.

3. No question has a negative answer.

4. Some problems may have more than one correct answer. In such cases, grid only one answer.

5. **Mixed numbers** such as $3\frac{1}{2}$ must be gridded as 3.5 or 7/2. (If is entered into the grid, it will be interpreted as $\frac{31}{2}$, not as $3\frac{1}{2}$.)

6. **Decimal Answers:** If you obtain a decimal answer with more digits than the grid can accommodate, it may be either rounded or truncated, but it must fill the entire grid.

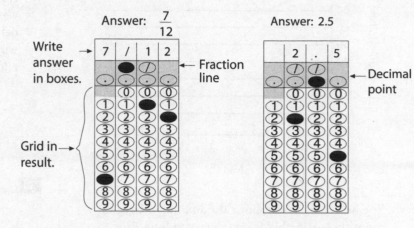

Answer: $\frac{7}{12}$ — Write answer in boxes. — Fraction line — Grid in result.

Answer: 2.5 — Decimal point

Acceptable ways to grid $\frac{2}{3}$ are:

Answer: 201 – either position is correct

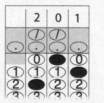

NOTE: You may start your answers in any column, space permitting. Columns you don't need to use should be left blank.

31

Amount of Greg's Heating Bill Each Month
from January to June

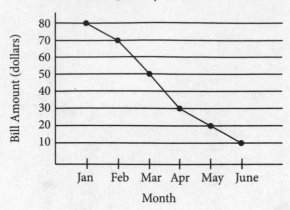

The line chart above shows the amount of Greg's monthly heating bill from January to June. The amount of his bill in April was what fraction of the amount of his bill in February?

32

A worker at a shoe factory is required to box at least 8 pairs of shoes per minute, but is not allowed to box more than 12 pairs of shoes per minute. According to this information, what is a possible amount of time, in minutes, that it could take the worker to box 168 pairs of shoes?

33

Safety regulations in a certain building require that the elevator not carry more than 1,600 pounds. A delivery driver will enter the elevator with a pallet containing a certain number of identical cartons that weigh 45 pounds each. If the combined weight of the delivery driver and the empty pallet is 250 pounds, what is the maximum number of cartons that will be allowed by the building's safety regulations?

34

├— 9 inches —┤

An aluminum can in the shape of a right circular cylinder has a <u>diameter</u> of 9 inches and a volume of 81π cubic inches. What is the height of the can, in inches?

CONTINUE

35

For what value of x is the expression

$$\frac{2}{(x-6)^2 + 4(x-7) + 8}$$ undefined?

36

A train passes through the Appleton train station every 20 minutes. The first train each day passes through at 6:00 A.M., and the last train passes through at 10:40 P.M. How many trains pass through the Appleton station in one day?

Questions 37 and 38 refer to the following information.

Helene purchased a $50 savings bond, issued by city A, which earns interest that is compounded annually. She uses the expression $50(1.03)^t$ to find the value of the savings bond after t years.

37

What is the annual interest rate, expressed as a percentage, earned by the savings bond? (Disregard the percent sign when gridding in your answer.)

38

Helene's sister Carolyn purchased a $50 savings bond issued by city B. Carolyn's bond has an interest rate, compounded annually, that is 1 percent greater than the interest rate earned by Helene's bond. After 12 years, the value of Carolyn's bond will be how much greater than the value of Helene's bond? (Round your answer to the nearest cent and disregard the dollar sign when gridding in your answer.)

STOP

If you finish before time is called, you may check your work on this section only.
Do not turn to any other section in the test.

SAT Essay

DIRECTIONS

The essay gives you an opportunity to show how effectively you can read and comprehend a passage and write an essay analyzing the passage. In your essay you should demonstrate that you have read the passage carefully, present a clear and logical analysis, and use language precisely.

Your essay must be written on the lines provided in your answer sheet booklet; except for the planning page of the answer booklet, you will receive no other paper on which to write. You will have enough space if you write on every line, avoid wide margins, and keep your handwriting to a reasonable size. Remember that people who are not familiar with your handwriting will read what you write. Try to write or print so that what you are writing is legible to those readers.

You have 50 minutes to read the passage and write an essay in response to the prompt provided inside this booklet.

REMINDER

— Do not write your essay in this booklet. Only what you write on the lined pages of your answer booklet will be evaluated.

— An off-topic essay will not be evaluated.

CONTINUE

As you read the passage below, consider how Eleanor Roosevelt uses

- evidence, such as facts or examples, to support claims.
- reasoning to develop ideas and to connect claims and evidence.
- stylistic or persuasive elements, such as word choice or appeals to emotion, to add power to the ideas expressed.

Adapted from Eleanor Roosevelt, "The Struggle for the Rights of Man." The speech was delivered to the United Nations in Paris, France on September 28, 1948.

1   I have come this evening to talk with you on one of the greatest issues of our time—that is the preservation of human freedom. I have chosen to discuss it here in France, at the Sorbonne, because here in this soil the roots of human freedom have long ago struck deep and here they have been richly nourished. It was here the Declaration of the Rights of Man was proclaimed, and the great slogans of the French Revolution—liberty, equality, fraternity—fired the imagination of men. I have chosen to discuss this issue in Europe because this has been the scene of the greatest historic battles between freedom and tyranny…

2   We must not be confused about what freedom is. Basic human rights are simple and easily understood: freedom of speech and a free press; freedom of religion and worship; freedom of assembly and the right of petition; the right of men to be secure in their homes and free from unreasonable search and seizure and from arbitrary arrest and punishment.

3   We must not be deluded by the efforts of the forces of reaction to prostitute the great words of our free tradition and thereby to confuse the struggle…

4   There are basic differences that show up even in the use of words between a democratic and a totalitarian country. For instance "democracy" means one thing to the U.S.S.R. and another the U.S.A. and, I know, in France. I have served since the first meeting of the nuclear commission on the Human Rights Commission, and I think this point stands out clearly.

5   The U.S.S.R. Representatives assert that they already have achieved many things which we, in what they call the "bourgeois democracies" cannot achieve because their government controls the accomplishment of these things. Our government seems powerless to them because, in the last analysis, it is controlled by the people. They would not put it that way —they would say that the people in the U.S.S.R. control their government by allowing their government to have certain absolute rights. We, on the other hand, feel that certain rights can never be granted to the government, but must be kept in the hands of the people…

CONTINUE

6   I think the best example one can give of this basic difference of the use of terms is "the right to work." The Soviet Union insists that this is a basic right which it alone can guarantee because it alone provides full employment by the government. But the right to work in the Soviet Union means the assignment of workers to do whatever task is given to them by the government without an opportunity for the people to participate in the decision that the government should do this. A society in which everyone works is not necessarily a free society and may indeed be a slave society; on the other hand, a society in which there is widespread economic insecurity can turn freedom into a barren and vapid right for millions of people.

7   We in the United States have come to realize it means freedom to choose one's job, to work or not to work as one desires. We, in the United States, have come to realize, however, that people have a right to demand that their government will not allow them to starve because, as individuals, they cannot find work of the kind they are accustomed to doing, and this is a decision brought about by public opinion which came as a result of the great depression in which many people were out of work, but we would not consider in the United States that we had gained any freedom if we were compelled to follow a dictatorial assignment to work where and when we were told. The right of choice would seem to us an important, fundamental freedom.

8   The place to discuss the issue of human rights is in the forum of the United Nations. The United Nations has been set up as the common meeting ground for nations, where we can consider together our mutual problems and take advantage of our differences in experience... It is now as always our hope that despite the wide differences in approach we face in the world today, we can with mutual good faith in the principles of the United Nations Charter, arrive at a common basis of understanding.

Write an essay in which you explain how Eleanor Roosevelt builds her argument that the United Nations should create a Universal Declaration of Human Rights. In your essay, analyze how Roosevelt uses one or more of the features listed in the box above (or features of your own choice) to strengthen the logic and persuasiveness of her argument. Be sure that your analysis focuses on the most relevant features of the passage.

Your essay should not explain whether you agree with Roosevelt's claims, but rather explain how Roosevelt builds an argument to persuade her audience.

END OF TEST

DO NOT RETURN TO A PREVIOUS SECTION.

1.

YOUR NAME: _____
(Print)
Last   First   M.I.

SIGNATURE: _____ DATE: __ / __ / __

HOME ADDRESS: _____
(Print)
Number and Street

_____
City   State   Zip Code

PHONE NO.: _____
(Print)

IMPORTANT: Please fill in these boxes exactly as shown on the back cover of your test book.

2. TEST FORM

6. DATE OF BIRTH

Month	Day		Year	
JAN				
FEB	0	0	0	0
MAR	1	1	1	1
APR	2	2	2	2
MAY	3	3	3	3
JUN		4	4	4
JUL		5	5	5
AUG		6	6	6
SEP		7	7	7
OCT		8	8	8
NOV		9	9	9
DEC				

3. TEST CODE **4. REGISTRATION NUMBER**

7. SEX
- MALE
- FEMALE

The **Princeton** Review®

5. YOUR NAME

First 4 letters of last name				FIRST INIT	MID INIT

(bubbles A–Z)

Test ➊

Start with number 1 for each new section.
If a section has fewer questions than answer spaces, leave the extra answer spaces blank.

Section 1—Reading

1. A B C D
2. A B C D
3. A B C D
4. A B C D
5. A B C D
6. A B C D
7. A B C D
8. A B C D
9. A B C D
10. A B C D
11. A B C D
12. A B C D
13. A B C D
14. A B C D
15. A B C D
16. A B C D
17. A B C D
18. A B C D
19. A B C D
20. A B C D
21. A B C D
22. A B C D
23. A B C D
24. A B C D
25. A B C D
26. A B C D
27. A B C D
28. A B C D
29. A B C D
30. A B C D
31. A B C D
32. A B C D
33. A B C D
34. A B C D
35. A B C D
36. A B C D
37. A B C D
38. A B C D
39. A B C D
40. A B C D
41. A B C D
42. A B C D
43. A B C D
44. A B C D
45. A B C D
46. A B C D
47. A B C D
48. A B C D
49. A B C D
50. A B C D
51. A B C D
52. A B C D

Section 2—Writing and Language Skills

1. A B C D
2. A B C D
3. A B C D
4. A B C D
5. A B C D
6. A B C D
7. A B C D
8. A B C D
9. A B C D
10. A B C D
11. A B C D
12. A B C D
13. A B C D
14. A B C D
15. A B C D
16. A B C D
17. A B C D
18. A B C D
19. A B C D
20. A B C D
21. A B C D
22. A B C D
23. A B C D
24. A B C D
25. A B C D
26. A B C D
27. A B C D
28. A B C D
29. A B C D
30. A B C D
31. A B C D
32. A B C D
33. A B C D
34. A B C D
35. A B C D
36. A B C D
37. A B C D
38. A B C D
39. A B C D
40. A B C D
41. A B C D
42. A B C D
43. A B C D
44. A B C D

The Princeton Review®

Test ❶ Start with number 1 for each new section.
If a section has fewer questions than answer spaces, leave the extra answer spaces blank.

Section 3—Mathematics: No Calculator

1. Ⓐ Ⓑ Ⓒ Ⓓ
2. Ⓐ Ⓑ Ⓒ Ⓓ
3. Ⓐ Ⓑ Ⓒ Ⓓ
4. Ⓐ Ⓑ Ⓒ Ⓓ
5. Ⓐ Ⓑ Ⓒ Ⓓ
6. Ⓐ Ⓑ Ⓒ Ⓓ
7. Ⓐ Ⓑ Ⓒ Ⓓ
8. Ⓐ Ⓑ Ⓒ Ⓓ
9. Ⓐ Ⓑ Ⓒ Ⓓ
10. Ⓐ Ⓑ Ⓒ Ⓓ
11. Ⓐ Ⓑ Ⓒ Ⓓ
12. Ⓐ Ⓑ Ⓒ Ⓓ
13. Ⓐ Ⓑ Ⓒ Ⓓ
14. Ⓐ Ⓑ Ⓒ Ⓓ
15. Ⓐ Ⓑ Ⓒ Ⓓ

16. 17. 18. 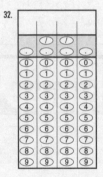 19. 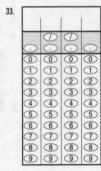 20.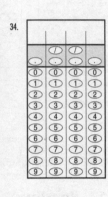

Section 4—Mathematics: Calculator

1. Ⓐ Ⓑ Ⓒ Ⓓ
2. Ⓐ Ⓑ Ⓒ Ⓓ
3. Ⓐ Ⓑ Ⓒ Ⓓ
4. Ⓐ Ⓑ Ⓒ Ⓓ
5. Ⓐ Ⓑ Ⓒ Ⓓ
6. Ⓐ Ⓑ Ⓒ Ⓓ
7. Ⓐ Ⓑ Ⓒ Ⓓ
8. Ⓐ Ⓑ Ⓒ Ⓓ
9. Ⓐ Ⓑ Ⓒ Ⓓ
10. Ⓐ Ⓑ Ⓒ Ⓓ
11. Ⓐ Ⓑ Ⓒ Ⓓ
12. Ⓐ Ⓑ Ⓒ Ⓓ
13. Ⓐ Ⓑ Ⓒ Ⓓ
14. Ⓐ Ⓑ Ⓒ Ⓓ
15. Ⓐ Ⓑ Ⓒ Ⓓ
16. Ⓐ Ⓑ Ⓒ Ⓓ
17. Ⓐ Ⓑ Ⓒ Ⓓ
18. Ⓐ Ⓑ Ⓒ Ⓓ
19. Ⓐ Ⓑ Ⓒ Ⓓ
20. Ⓐ Ⓑ Ⓒ Ⓓ
21. Ⓐ Ⓑ Ⓒ Ⓓ
22. Ⓐ Ⓑ Ⓒ Ⓓ
23. Ⓐ Ⓑ Ⓒ Ⓓ
24. Ⓐ Ⓑ Ⓒ Ⓓ
25. Ⓐ Ⓑ Ⓒ Ⓓ
26. Ⓐ Ⓑ Ⓒ Ⓓ
27. Ⓐ Ⓑ Ⓒ Ⓓ
28. Ⓐ Ⓑ Ⓒ Ⓓ
29. Ⓐ Ⓑ Ⓒ Ⓓ
30. Ⓐ Ⓑ Ⓒ Ⓓ

31. 32. 33. 34. 35.

36. 37. 38.

Chapter 4
Practice Test 1:
Answers and
Explanations

PRACTICE TEST 1 ANSWER KEY

Section 1: Reading				Section 2: Writing & Language				Section 3: Math (No Calculator)				Section 4 : Math (Calculator)		
1.	D	27.	B	1.	D	23.	B	1.	A	11.	D	1.	C	20.	A
2.	B	28.	C	2.	D	24.	B	2.	B	12.	A	2.	C	21.	D
3.	C	29.	A	3.	A	25.	A	3.	B	13.	C	3.	B	22.	C
4.	B	30.	C	4.	B	26.	D	4.	D	14.	A	4.	B	23.	C
5.	C	31.	A	5.	C	27.	C	5.	D	15.	C	5.	D	24.	A
6.	D	32.	B	6.	B	28.	C	6.	C	16.	5	6.	A	25.	C
7.	B	33.	C	7.	A	29.	A	7.	A	17.	6	7.	C	26.	D
8.	B	34.	B	8.	B	30.	C	8.	A			8.	D	27.	C
9.	A	35.	A	9.	C	31.	B	9.	C	18.	$\frac{5}{13}$	9.	B	28.	B
10.	A	36.	B	10.	D	32.	D	10.	C			10.	A	29.	A
11.	D	37.	D	11.	C	33.	D			19.	225	11.	D	30.	B
12.	B	38.	C	12.	D	34.	C			20.	13	12.	D	31.	$\frac{3}{7}, \frac{6}{14},$
13.	D	39.	A	13.	A	35.	C					13.	B		.428
14.	A	40.	D	14.	C	36.	D					14.	B		or
15.	C	41.	D	15.	D	37.	C					15.	A		.429
16.	B	42.	B	16.	C	38.	B					16.	C	32.	Any value
17.	C	43.	C	17.	A	39.	A					17.	D		from 14
18.	A	44.	A	18.	D	40.	D					18.	C		to 21,
19.	C	45.	C	19.	D	41.	D					19.	C		inclusive
20.	D	46.	D	20.	C	42.	B							33.	30
21.	D	47.	B	21.	B	43.	C							34.	4
22.	B	48.	D	22.	A	44.	D							35.	4
23.	C	49.	A											36.	51
24.	C	50.	D											37.	3
25.	D	51.	C											38.	8.76
26.	B	52.	B												

For self-scoring assessment tables, please turn to page 565.

PRACTICE TEST 1 EXPLANATIONS

Section 1: Reading

1. **D** This question asks about the developmental pattern of the passage, so it should be answered after the specific questions. Look for clues in the text that indicate the mood and story of the passage. This particular passage moves from glum to foreboding. The narrator is nervous on his journey, but he states that when he sees the city he foresees his bleak future. Since the narrator discusses the past, he goes further to confirm it: *I prophesied truly, and failed only in one single circumstance, that in all the misery I imagined and dreaded, I did not conceive the hundredth part of the anguish I was destined to endure.* Choice (A) refers to the joy he felt at seeing his native land, but that is only a half-right answer because it does not address the negative mood and events. The passage says nothing about the narrator responding to a request for help, so (B) is incorrect. The author describes the daemon, but the passage does not mention an ancient curse, so (C) is incorrect. Choice (D) accurately describes the narrator's mood and final despair. Choice (D) is the correct answer.

2. **B** This question asks about what happens in the passage, making it a straightforward question to answer after the specific questions have been answered. Choice (A) goes beyond the information in the passage, since there is no mention of any plans the narrator has to avenge his brother's death. Choice (B) accurately addresses the feeling of anxiety the narrator has throughout the passage, as seen in the fourth paragraph when he says, *The picture appeared a vast and dim scene of evil, and I foresaw obscurely that I was destined to become the most wretched of human beings.* Keep (B). Choice (C) describes the narrator's fear of returning home to the monster, but the passage discusses how the narrator seems to be more afraid of what has changed and how his future may be affected, so it can be eliminated. Choice (D) addresses how the narrator becomes anxious about returning home, but he says he *longed to console and sympathize with my loved and sorrowing friends*, so it seems that he isn't afraid he will not be welcome. Choice (B) is the correct answer.

3. **C** The question asks which emotion the narrator *most* feels. Because the question uses the word *most*, this indicates there may be more than one emotion the narrator feels. The answer to this question is the one that the narrator feels most strongly. Notice that the following question is a best evidence question, so this question and Q4 can be answered in tandem. Look at the answers for Q4 first. The lines in (4A) mention *the delight [the narrator] took*, so look to see if those lines support any answers in Q3. Choice (3A) mentions the *joy...at returning home.* Connect those two answers. Next, consider the lines for (4B). The narrator says that he *prophesied truly... all the misery I imagined...anguish I was destined to endure.* He's looking into the future and seeing terrible things. Consider the answers to Q3. Choice (3C) mentions *prescience concerning his fate*, which is a paraphrase of *looking into the future.* Connect (3C) and (4B). The

lines in (4C) mention the coming storm, which is not referenced in any of the answers to Q3. Eliminate (4C). Choice (4D) mentions the narrator's reaction to the daemon, but does not reference any emotion. Eliminate (4D). Without any support from Q4, (3B) and (3D) can be eliminated. Consider the remaining pairs of answer choices in the context of the passage. The emotion the narrator feels *most* is negative, so (3A) and (4A) can be eliminated. Choices (3C) and (4B) are the correct answers.

4.   **B**   (See explanation above.)

5.   **C**   This is a Vocab-in-Context question. Use the context to substitute another word based on the clues in the text. The passage says *all around was calm; and the snowy mountains, 'the palaces of nature,' were not changed. By degrees the calm and heavenly scene restored me, and I continued my journey towards Geneva.* Therefore, *placid* must mean something like *peaceful* or *calm.* Choices (A), (B), and (D) can all be eliminated. Choice (C) is the correct answer.

6.   **D**   The question asks about the *main purpose* of the first paragraph, so the correct answer will accurately summarize the paragraph. The author starts the passage by saying *My journey was very melancholy* and later describes his *painful state of mind* to set a tone for what will come. The author's choices create a negative mood for the reader. Choice (A) is incorrect, since the paragraph isn't written to represent anything. Choice (B) says that the author exaggerates the narrator's emotion, but the narrator is feeling a profound sort of dread, so there's no exaggeration. Choice (C) says that the paragraph is there to give context, but the narrator doesn't mention his brother's death explicitly or the daemon until later in the passage. Choice (D) best explains that the paragraph is there to establish the mood as the narrator returns home. Choice (D) is the correct answer.

7.   **B**   This question asks why the narrator uses a particular phrase. Carefully read the window to look for clues to indicate the narrator's meaning. His focus is on how things may have changed in the six years he's been gone (*How altered everything might be during that time*). Although *one sudden and desolating change had taken place*, the narrator goes on to say that *other alterations* had possibly been worked by those *thousand little circumstances*. Of these little circumstances, he says that *although they were done more tranquilly, [they] might not be the less decisive.* Therefore, although there was only one major change, significant changes could also have come from smaller events that were individually less traumatic but still added up to something big. Choice (A) can be eliminated because the change that happened (the loss of the narrator's brother) was not connected to a natural disaster. Choice (B) is a good paraphrase of the prediction, so don't eliminate it. The narrator never mentions his role in the murder or any way he could have affected the outcome, so eliminate (C). Choice (D) can be eliminated because there is never any mention of politics. Choice (B) is the correct answer.

8.   **B**   This is a best evidence question with a clear window. Simply consider the lines used to predict the answer to Question 7. The textual evidence used to answer Q7 was in the lines *One sudden and desolating change had taken place; but a thousand little circumstances might have by degrees*

worked other alterations, which, although they were done more tranquilly, might not be the less decisive. Choice (B) is the correct answer.

9. **A**   This question asks about how the narrator addresses the tempest. Find evidence in the text to support how the narrator feels about the storm. He states, *While I watched the tempest, so beautiful yet terrific, I wandered on with a hasty step. This noble war in the sky elevated my spirits; I clasped my hands, and exclaimed aloud, "William, dear angel! This is thy funeral, this thy dirge!* Although the rain is pelting him and lightening is flashing, his spirits are high. Thus, the *awe but no fear* in (A) looks good. Don't eliminate it. He describes the storm as *violent* and *terrific*, so a word that means overjoyed is too positive, making (B) incorrect. While he is sad about William's death, he is not sad about the storm, making (C) incorrect. It is possible that the narrator is a little dramatic, but there is no evidence to prove that he is crazy. Therefore, (D) is incorrect. Choice (A) is the correct answer.

10. **A**   This is a Vocab-in-Context question. Use the context to substitute another word based on the clues in the text. The passage says, *I perceived in the gloom a figure which stole from behind a clump of trees near me.* The figure is emerging from behind the tree, so *stole* must have something to do with how the figure is moving. Put in *emerged* or *stepped out from behind*. Eliminate any answers that have nothing to do with that prediction. That eliminates (B) and (C). To *loom* means to *come into view in indistinct and enlarged form*, and *displaced* means *to move out of the usual place*. Based on the context, it would make more sense for the monster to move out from its position behind the trees. Choice (A) is the correct answer.

11. **D**   This is a main purpose question, so even though it's the first question for the passage, it should be done at the end. It asks about the main purpose, so the correct answer should address why the passage was written. In the fourth paragraph, the author does mention *a set of essays*, but this passage is an introduction for those essays, not a review of them. Eliminate (A). Choice (B) is incorrect because the author does not use persuasive language, nor is there an argument for or against any field in this passage. Eliminate it. Choice (C) can be eliminated because, while the author does mention the limitations of Piaget and others, he goes on to reconcile those limitations with his own scientific views, so that's not the main purpose of the passage. Choice (D) sums up the information that the author provides in the passage. He introduces psychology and its fields of study to get to the point of how structuralism has influences on his own work. Choice (D) is the correct answer.

12. **B**   This question asks about the *central claim* of the passage. This is a general question, so it should be answered after all the specific questions have been answered. The central claim of the passage is related to the main purpose: what is the most important part of the author's argument? The author's main point is that structuralism provided a wider range of avenues for psychologists to explore the mind. Choice (A) does not match this prediction because, while it might make sense that the author thinks pre-1960s psychology was *sedate and impractical*, that isn't actually in the text. Eliminate (A). Choice (B) is supported by the final paragraph, so keep it.

Choice (C) is partially true in that behaviorists believe that humans *act in the way we do because we are reinforced for doing so,* but that is not the central claim in this passage. Also, there is no evidence their views are *preordained,* so this choice can be eliminated. Choice (D) can be eliminated because there is no evidence that the author's work is revolutionary. Although that word appears earlier in the passage, it does not refer to the author's work. Choice (B) is the correct answer.

13. **D** This question asks about the reason the author *describes different branches of psychology* throughout the passage. In the first paragraph he mentioned *academic psychology, behaviorism, and psychoanalysis.* He labels these three as *uninviting specializations.* Then he mentions the *cognitive revolution* in the 1960s in the second paragraph, and he goes on to further describe how the revolution *inspired* those in the field who became and remained interested in the *structuralist approach.* The correct answer should address this shift. Choice (A) does not match the prediction because the author's goal is to present the shift, not to simply lay out the history. Choice (B) does not match because there is no evidence that the author is in any way prominent in the scientific community. It can be eliminated. Choice (C) can be eliminated because the author never makes any reference to structuralism being *inferior to behaviorism.* In fact, the author seems to feel more positively about structuralism than behaviorism. Choice (D) is consistent with the prediction and is the correct answer.

14. **A** This question is in a paired set with Q15. This question asks what the author indicates about the *cognitive revolution* in the passage. The author is positive about the revolution, mentioning that the revolution made the study of the mind *a proper scientific undertaking.* He also says the revolution provided a *structure to thought processes.* In the third paragraph, he says many in the behavioral sciences in the 1960's were *swept up—and have remained inspired—by the revolution.* Choice (A) matches the idea that the author was *swept up* by the revolution, so keep that answer. Choice (B) can be eliminated because there is no evidence that psychology was ever a dying science. Choice (C) can be eliminated because while the author hints at a revitalization of psychology due to the revolution, the thoughtfulness of previous psychologists was not mentioned or questioned. Choice (D) does not match any of the predictions because there is no mention of changes prior to the 1960s. Choice (A) is the correct answer.

15. **C** This is a best evidence question, so consider the lines used to predict the answer to Q14. Choice (C) is the correct answer.

16. **B** This question and Q17 are a general paired set, so they can be answered in tandem. Consider the lines given in Q17 and see if those lines can be used to support any of the answers in Q16. Choice (17A) supports (16C), so draw a line to connect those answers. Choice (17B) might initially look good because the words *problem-solving* and *creating* also show up in (16A), but those words describe mental processes, not the psychology. Eliminate (17B). Choice (17C) supports (16B), so draw a line connecting those answers. Choice (17D) does not support any of

the answers for Q16, so that answer can be eliminated. Look back at the answers for Q16. Neither (16A) nor (16D) has support, so both of those can be eliminated. This leaves two pairs of answers: (16C)/(17A) and (16B)/(17C). Look back at the question. It asks about the branch of psychology that became popular *after the revolution*. The description of behaviorism in (17A) is from before the revolution. That pair can be eliminated, leaving (16B) and (17C) as the correct answers.

17. **C** (See explanation above.)

18. **A** This question asks about the author's reason for mentioning Piaget, Chomsky, and Levi-Strauss. In the fourth paragraph, the author says these scientists (*psychologist, linguist, and anthropologist*) *exemplify the principal assumption* of the structuralist approach. Choice (A) matches the prediction, so keep it. Choice (B) can be eliminated because their work is not *inherently problematic*; it is just not fully in line with the views of the author. Choice (C) can be eliminated because the author notes that these men are not all psychologists: Chomsky is a linguist and Levi-Strauss is an anthropologist. Choice (D) can be eliminated because there is no evidence that these men have published anything that would not agree with the author's conclusions about creativity and structuralism. Choice (A) is the correct answer.

19. **C** This question asks about the author's use of the phrase *original works of art*. In the fifth paragraph, the author discusses the *limitations* of the structural approach. He uses the *original works of art* as an example in which the structuralists' ideas about human thought were *problematic for a study of mind where the...focus falls on innovations and creativity*. Choice (A) does not work because it does not address the *limitations*. Eliminate it. Choice (B) can be eliminated because the author makes the point that the structuralists' view are *limited*, but he never argues that the views are *distorted*. Choice (C) is a good paraphrase of the text, so keep it. Choice (D) is too broad in its mention of *psychology* and incorrect in its assessment of psychology as *closed-minded*. Choice (C) is the correct answer.

20. **D** This question asks about the meaning of the *symbol systems*. The author states that those systems are *codes of meaning* and *vehicles through which thought takes place*. Choice (A) is incorrect because while the symbol systems are used in thought processes, they are not the thought processes themselves. Choice (B) is incorrect because symbol systems reconcile the issue with creativity and structuralism. Choice (C) is incorrect because the author does not refer to the systems as *principles,* but as a *feature of human thought*. Choice (D) is correct because the symbols are the way the human mind makes meaning. Choice (D) is the correct answer.

21. **D** This question asks about the author's purpose in mentioning *delays, redesigns, and even near-death cancellations*. Use the given line reference to find the window in the passage. The earlier part of the sentence makes a contrast between the conception of New Horizon *in the late 1980s* and its launch in *2006*, so look for an answer choice that deals with a time delay. Choice (A) deals with speed, not a span of time. Choices (B) and (C) deal with possible problems with the mission, and are thus irrelevant to time delay. Choice (D) deals with a time delay between

a plan and its execution. Plan matches *conception*, and execution matches *launch*. Choice (D) is the correct answer.

22. **B** This question asks what outcome the author says could result from the flyby over Pluto. Use the key word *flyby* to locate the window at the end of paragraph 2. The following paragraphs both describe possible results of the flyby, so look for an answer there. Choice (A) mentions 7:49 Eastern time, which is from paragraph 1. Choice (B) states that no data might come in, which matches *its failure by hearing nothing*. Choice (C) contains *mission's failure* and *radio signal*, which match phrases from paragraph 3, but (C) is deceptive—the text states that scientists will learn of the *success* through *a radio signal*. Choice (D) mentions receiving data after a delay, which matches paragraph 3, but (D) specifies the delay as 3 minutes, a number mentioned in paragraph 2. Choice (B) is the correct answer.

23. **C** This question asks for the best evidence for the answer to Q22. Since the sentence in paragraph 3 containing *its failure by hearing nothing* supported that answer, eliminate answer choices from other paragraphs, then compare the remaining answer choices to select the best match. Choice (C) contains the phrase *its failure by hearing nothing*, so that is the correct answer.

24. **C** This is a Vocab-in-Context question, so find the word *suite* in line 26 and cross it out. Replace it with another word that makes sense in the context of the text. A word like *group* or *collection* would make sense, so use such a word to compare to the answer choices. Choice (A) may recall suit, which looks like *suite*, but has a different meaning. Choice (B) is one meaning of *suite*, but not in this context. Choice (C) means arrangement. Keep any unknown words, just in case they are correct, and only eliminate ones that are definitely incorrect. Choice (D) may recall sweet, which has the same pronunciation as *suite*, but not the same meaning. Since (A), (B), and (D) are wrong, the correct answer must be (C), even if this was a previously unknown word. Choice (C) is the correct answer.

25. **D** This question asks why the author discusses the measurement of the primary encounter. Use the given line reference to find the window. The sentence containing *primary encounter* begins with *Though*, so the author is establishing a contrast. Although that encounter *is best measured in minutes and hours*, the sentence goes on to emphasize how long it will take for the data to all be sent to Earth. Look for an answer choice that makes a contrast between a short amount of time and a long amount of time. Choice (A) references an earlier claim that could be supported by this discussion, but no earlier claims are supported by this discussion. Choice (B) refers to an undermined assumption, but there is no assumption and nothing is undermined. Choice (C) is about time, but does not match the prediction. Choice (D) is about time, and it matches the prediction, since it indicates a contrast between something fast and something slow. Choice (D) is the correct answer.

26. **B** This question asks about the main idea of Passage 2. Because it is a general question, it should be done after all the specific questions. It begins with the first part of a contrast, that *New Horizons has started to transmit information about Pluto*, but then the question ends with a

but. Find something in the text that contrasts with the idea of New Horizons reaching Pluto. The end of the passage mentions another target for New Horizons *a mere billion miles further along the interplanetary road.* The correct answer will have something to do with further goals for New Horizon. Choice (A) might intially look attractive because New Horizons is going to *continue on...into the night,* but (A) has nothing about the next mission. Choice (B) is a solid paraphrase of the prediction, so don't eliminate it. Choice (C) might be true, but it isn't the contrast given in the passage. Eliminate it. Choice (D) is not mentioned in Passage 2. Choice (B) is the correct answer.

27.   **B**   This is a Vocab-in-Context question, so find the word *deploy* in line 53 and cross it out. Replace it with another word that makes sense in the context of the text. A word like *use* would make sense. Look for an answer choice that matches this prediction. Choice (A) might recall the word *decoy.* Choice (B) matches the prediction. Choice (C) does not match the prediction. Choice (D) might recall the word *destroy.* Choice (B) is the correct answer.

28.   **C**   This question asks how the passages relate to each other. Because it is about both passages, it should be done after all the specific and general questions about the individual passages. Both passages inform readers about the objects New Horizons will encounter and study (Pluto, and then something beyond), and both have a positive tone. Choice (A) mentions *concern* and *dangers,* which do not match the prediction. Choice (B) mentions a *revision,* but there is no revision. Choice (C) is a possible match to the prediction: The *story* could be *the first golden age of interplanetary exploration,* and the *next chapter* could be the search for new objects beyond the solar system. Choice (D) mentions support, but there is no *qualified* support of Passage 1 by Passage 2. Choice (C) is the correct answer.

29.   **A**   This question asks how the author of Passage 2 would most likely respond to something specific in Passage 1. Note the main idea of Passage 2, and use the given line reference to find the window in Passage 1. The continued journey is referred to in Passage 1 as an *endless journey into interstellar night.* Passage 2 describes the journey as having a target, rather than lacking an end or a goal, so look for an answer that fits this prediction. Choice (A) is possible, since New Horizons will now head toward *PT1 (potential target one) or more officially 2014 MU69.* Choice (B) is a true statement, but one that does not answer this question. Choice (C) fits Passage 1, not Passage 2, and (D) makes a statement not supported by either text. Choice (A) is the correct answer.

30.   **C**   This question asks for the best evidence for the answer to Q29. Since paragraph 6, which contains *PT1 (potential target one) or more officially 2014 MU69,* supported that answer, eliminate answer choices involving other paragraphs, then compare remaining answer choices to select the best match. Choice (A) is from paragraph 3. Choice (B) is from paragraph 4. Choice (C) is from paragraph 6, and contains the predicted phrase. Choice (D) is from paragraph 7. Choice (C) is the correct answer.

31. **A** This question asks which statement is true about New Horizons' journey in both passages. Passage 1 depicts an *endless journey into night*. Passage 2 names a stopping point located *a mere billion miles further*. Choice (A) could be true, since the journey could end and since a billion miles is described with the word *mere*. Choice (B) mentions metaphor and strict realism, neither of which have textual support. Choice (C) mentions allegory and personification. Although Passage 2 may personify the spacecraft as a person (*What do you do? … You keep going*), no allegory appears in the text. Choice (D) may be tempting, due to the mention in Passage 1 of *a golden age*, but Passage 2 does not present an anecdote. Choice (A) is the correct answer.

32. **B** This question asks what the authors intend to highlight with their examples. Use the given line references to find the window. Choice (A) contradicts that we can *effortlessly* talk and walk. Choice (B) fits the claim that *Humans often engage in multitasking*. Choice (C) does not match the first paragraph. It is deceptive, because later there is discussion about multitasking and lower grades, but this is a correlation. Choice (C) suggests that doing one thing can cause the other. Choice (D) does not match the first paragraph. Later, the authors suggest that multitasking could have some evolutionary benefits, but this is not the same as instinctual and is not why the examples of multitasking are mentioned. Choice (B) is the correct answer.

33. **C** This is a Vocab-in-Context question, so find the word *engage* in line 7 and cross it out. Replace it with another word that makes sense in the context of the text. A word like *use* or *require* would make sense, so use such a word to compare to the answer choices. Choice (A), *marry*, recalls a different meaning of *engage*. Choice (B), *capture*, does not fit the prediction. Choice (C), *employ*, matches the prediction *use*. Choice (D), *absorb*, does not fit the prediction. Choice (C) is the correct answer.

34. **B** This question asks what the authors would most likely say about media multitasking. Use the line reference provided to find the window, and locate something the authors actually did say. Paragraph 3 begins by mentioning that *recent research* has examined effects of *media multitasking*. The rest of the paragraph presents results that are described as *detrimental … negative …* and twice the word *impaired* is used. Thus, select an answer choice that summarizes these meanings. Choice (A), *focused*, is positive. Choice (B), *disadvantageous*, fits the prediction. Choice (C), *multifaceted*, is either neutral or positive. Choice (D), *chronic*, is negative, but fits the prediction less well than (B). Choice (B) is the correct answer.

35. **A** This question asks for something specific the author says about Kirschner and Karpinski, namely: what do they suggest is the reason that grades decrease? Use the names as lead words to locate the window. This is paragraph 4. The second sentence reads: *Kirschner and Karpinski found that heavy Facebook users reported having lower grade point averages (GPAs) and suggested the possible deleterious effect of simultaneously using Facebook with other activities.* Thus, look for an answer choice that closely matches this sentence. Choice (A) could fit, since Facebook is a social media platform. Keep it for now. Choice (B) could be true, but it does not fit the prediction because

there is no mention of social media. Choice (C) could be true, but does not fit the prediction because there is no mention of Messenger in the prediction. Choice (D) mentions Facebook, but the prediction was about using Facebook while doing other things, like homework, not about spending too much time on Facebook in general. Choice (A) is the correct answer.

36.   **B**   This is a specific best evidence question, so simply consider the lines used to predict the answer to Q35. Lines 43–46 were used to predict the answer to Q35, so (B) is the correct answer to this question.

37.   **D**   This question asks what the large-scale study authors assume to be true about light media multitaskers as compared to the heavy media multitaskers. Use the lines provided to find the window. Much of the paragraph is about heavy media multitaskers, but the final sentence says that heavy media multitaskers are *inferior to light media multitaskers in tasks that required one to disregard irrelevant information in the environment and in memory*. Thus, look for an answer choice showing that light media multitaskers are better at disregarding irrelevant information. Choice (A), *distracted*, suggests the opposite of this prediction. Choice (B), *focused*, fits this prediction. Keep it for now. Choice (C), *scholarly*, has nothing to do with this prediction. Choice (D), *discriminating*, fits this prediction. Compare the remaining answer choices. Choice (B) is further away from the text's focus on sorting through relevant information. This choice also doesn't work because the heavy media multitaskers are focused, just on broader information. Choice (D) is closest in meaning to the text. Choice (D) is the correct answer.

38.   **C**   This question asks for the best evidence for the answer to Q37. Since the prediction came from paragraph 5, eliminate answer choices from other paragraphs first. Choice (38A) is from paragraph 4; eliminate it. It supports (37C), but is not relevant here. Choices (38B) and (38C) are from paragraph 5; keep them for now. Choice (38D) is from paragraph 6; eliminate it. Also, it supports nothing from Q37. Choice (38B) is about heavy media multitaskers, but Q37 asked about light media multitaskers; eliminate it. Choice (38C) is about light media multitaskers, and contains the phrase used to predict the correct answer to Q37. Choice (38C) is the correct answer.

39.   **A**   This is a Vocab-in-Context question, so find the word *process* in line 57 and cross it out. Replace it with another word that makes sense in the context of the text. Given the focus of the rest of the paragraph on sorting, distinguishing or discriminating between relevant and irrelevant information, use one of these verbs as a prediction. Choice (A), *filter*, fits this prediction. Choice (B), *share*, does not fit because the passage discusses how multitaskers bring in information, not how they send it out. Choice (C), *digitize*, makes no sense. Choice (D), *retain*, does not fit the prediction. Choice (A) is the correct answer.

40.   **D**   This question asks why the authors refer to the *pip-and-pop paradigm*. Use the line reference provided to find the window. In paragraph 7 the authors state what they were trying to measure, then mention the pip-and-pop paradigm, then go on to describe how the paradigm works.

Choose an answer choice that fits this outline of paragraph 7. Choice (A) does not fit, since the authors are not questioning a technique. Choice (B) does not fit, since there is no claim that would be supported. Choice (C) can be eliminated because the authors are introducing the pip-and-pop paradigm, not clarifying it. Choice (D) could fit, since the paradigm is an experimental method, and since they are introducing it before explaining what it is. Choice (D) is the correct answer.

41. **D**   This question asks for the most accurate interpretation of the line of best fit on the graph following the passage. Notice that the line has a positive slope, and that $r = 0.292$. The term r represents the correlation between the two factors on the X and Y graphs. Also notice what the X and Y axes represent: media multitasking and multisensory integration. Choice (A) is incorrect, because neither the graph nor the text indicate what grades light media multitaskers get. Choice (B) is incorrect because the study in question deals with a different topic than Kirschner and Karpinski's study. Choice (C) is incorrect, because neither the graph nor the text discuss cognitive functions. Choice (D) is true: The data are not tightly grouped around the line of best fit, so although there is a correlation, it is weak. Choice (D) is the correct answer.

42. **B**   This question asks how the study's authors would interpret a specific finding presented in the graph. First look at the graphs themselves: both indicate that heavy media use is positively correlated to multisensory integration. To answer the question of how the authors would interpret this finding, look at the passage. Paragraphs 5 and 6 discuss heavy media multitaskers. Paragraph 5 focuses on their weaknesses in distinguishing between data, while paragraph 6 focuses on their strengths in being aware of multiple data. Heavy media multitaskers may have *better performance if a task contains some unexpected information that is important to the task at hand. When a media multitasker reads, for example, he or she may more readily detect an SMS ringtone from a mobile phone, although the ringtone does not carry information useful for the primary task of reading.* Choice (A) describes a strength of low media multitaskers, rather than heavy media multitaskers. Choice (B) fits the prediction, since reading and hearing a ringtone match *multiple unrelated tasks.* Choice (C) could be true, but it is too general to fit the prediction. Choice (D) is more specific, but claims too much. The passage mentioned reading and ring tones. Choice (D) claims that heavy media multitaskers observe *all* details, and during a *stressful* event. This does not fit the passage. Choice (B) is the correct answer.

43. **C**   The question asks what the authors' statement implies. Use the given line reference to find the window in order to answer this question. This sentence summarizes the paragraph, which begins by describing a woman who was surprisingly cured by the use of antibiotics early in the twentieth century and a man who wasn't cured six decades later. The authors' statement *we have come full circle* indicates that we are medically back to pre-antibiotic days, and the fact that there is *no magic bullet* indicates there is no solution to this problem. It does not indicate that antibiotics are no longer used to treat bacterial infections, only that antibiotics are increasingly ineffective; eliminate (A). Based on the paragraph it is clear that doctors were on board

with the use of antibiotics before this article was written, which eliminates (B). Choice (C) is supported as the author states there is *no magic bullet*, or solution, as to how to treat antibiotic-resistant bacteria as illustrated in the paragraph. Keep it. Choice (D) is deceptive; although this paragraph does mention *E. faecium*, it does not say that it is no longer treatable at all; it only states that one case was not treatable with antibiotics. Eliminate (D). Choice (C) is the correct answer.

44. **A**   This questions asks which statement would contradict the claim that *antibiotic use has never been 100% effective in the treatment of a bacterial infection*. Use the given line references provided in the answer choices to find a statement that contradicts this statement. Choice (A) describes a successful use of antibiotic treatment for a bacterial infection, which would contradict the idea that antibiotics have never been 100% effective. Choice (B) describes an unsuccessful application of antibiotics to treat a bacterial infection; this supports the claim in the question so (B) should be eliminated. Choice (C) discusses how bacteria developed resistance to certain antibiotics, but it does not indicate the success rate of those antibiotics prior to that resistance. As this choice neither supports nor contradicts the claim, eliminate (C). Choice (D) can be eliminated for the same reason; it does not contain any specific information about the success, or lack thereof, of antibiotic treatments against bacteria. Choice (A) is the correct answer.

45. **C**   This question asks what a word, *evolution*, indicates in the passage. Use the given line references to find the windows in order to answer this question. The sentences that contain *evolution* in them are discussing *adaptation*, with the first sentence focusing on bacteria as a group and the second focusing on MRSA specifically. As it is not only one bacteria discussed in both lines, (A) should be eliminated because it is too limited. Although the sentences do discuss evolution and drug-resistant bacteria, neither indicate that the evolution was *inevitable*, so (B) should be eliminated. These lines do indicate that it is the adaptability of bacteria that enables them to resist antibiotic treatment, which supports (C). Keep (C). While the passage does say that bacteria have adapted and evolved, there is no indication that any specific strains have disappeared, eliminating (D). Choice (C) is the correct answer.

46. **D**   This question asks about a specific claim. As the window given is very large (an entire paragraph) and antibiotic resistance is the main focus of the passage, it is likely that the authors say there are many things that could be a result of antibiotic resistance. In this case, it would be most effective to check each answer choice against what is stated in the passage and use POE. Choice (A) can be eliminated as the paragraph indicates that those strains have actually become more difficult to overcome, not that they have disappeared. Choice (B) can be deleted as it is a reference to an entirely different paragraph (paragraph 1), and it is incorrect—there is no *magic bullet* according to the passage. Choice (C) can be eliminated as deaths are not mentioned in this paragraph. Choice (D) is supported by the paragraph as it states that *S. aureus quickly developed resistance to the β-lactam compounds*, which fits that *S. aureus* is resistant to at least one antibiotic treatment. Choice (D) is the correct answer.

47. **B**   This question asks why the author included information about MRSA's glycopeptide and vancomycin resistance. As no reference is included, use chronological order and lead words to locate the window of the passage in which these terms appear, which is in the third paragraph. This paragraph reviews MRSA's history of resistance in relation to glycopeptides and vancomycin and medical changes that resulted from that resistance. Choice (A) can be eliminated as it is much too broad and the paragraph does not contain information about the medical research that went into developing antibiotics. Choice (B) correctly reflects the fact that a history of a bacteria's resistance to differing antibiotics is reviewed. Keep (B). Choice (C) is not supported by the paragraph; not only is there no reference to these being the most common antibiotics used, the information indicates that they are no longer effective at treating a specific bacteria. Eliminate (C). Choice (D) is another choice that is too broad because it refers to all antibiotics, but only certain ones are mentioned. Eliminate (D). Choice (B) is the correct answer.

48. **D**   This question asks about the function of the words *appears* and *often*. Use the reference window, the final paragraph, to read these words in context. The author uses *appears* when referring to the fact that the dissemination of certain *isolates appears to be limited, at least for now* and *often* when referring to the fact that VRSA is *often resistant*. These sentences indicate a lack of certainty and specificity: strains of a bacteria are referred to as having *true* resistance, rather than *100%* or some other resistant measurement, spread *appears* to be limited rather than is or isn't limited, a bacteria is *often* resistant rather than a specific percent resistant. All of these words indicate a lack of certainty. This best matches (D). Choice (A) is incorrect as no levels of anything are confirmed in this paragraph. Choice (B) is incorrect as clinical results are not discussed in this paragraph. Choice (C) is incorrect as there is no call for greater attention or funding for this area of science. Choice (D) is the correct answer.

49. **A**   This questions asks for an answer that is supported by both the table and the passage. Locate where penicillin is discussed in the passage. In the first paragraph penicillin is discussed in the context of curing a woman of streptococci in 1942. The only answer that is supported by this is (A), since the passage refers to penicillin as a newly discovered substance when it was administered in 1942. This is also supported by the chart as the "when introduced" row indicates it was introduced in the 1940s, or in the first half of the twentieth century. Choice (B) is supported by the passage, but is not supported by the graph. Eliminate it. Choice (C) is supported by the graph, but not the passage, so it can also be eliminated. Choice (D) can be eliminated, because there isn't any data about the bacteria's resistance to amikacin specifically. Choice (A) is the correct answer.

50. **D**   This question asks if the data in the table supports the authors' assertion that *S. aureus* and *E. faecium* represent the biggest therapeutic hurdles. In order to be the biggest therapeutic hurdles, this would mean that they have great resistance to many antibiotics. Check each answer choice against the information provided in the graph. Choice (A) can be eliminated as other bacteria demonstrate levels of resistance to more than three antibiotic families. Choice (B) can be eliminated as 75% is not the greatest percentage of antibiotic resistance listed on the graph;

Shigella has a 78% resistance to aminopenicillins. Choice (C) is incorrect as there is an even lower percentage of resistance, 0.2%, found on the table. Choice (D) stresses that *S. aureus* and *E. faecium* do not represent the biggest therapeutic hurdles because other bacteria demonstrate resistance to many more antibiotics than these do. The number of antibiotics other bacteria are resistant to create a greater challenge in treatment, based on the general information contained in the passage. Choice (D) is the correct answer.

51. **C** This questions asks for a bacteria on the table that supports the answer to the previous question. As the answer to the previous question was (D), *S. aureus* and *E. faecium* do not represent the biggest therapeutic hurdles because other bacteria demonstrate resistance to many more antibiotics than they do, the correct answer choice will be a bacteria with resistant to a greater number of antibiotics than *S. aureus* and *E. faecium*. These two have a combined resistance to three antibiotics families. Choice (C), *Shigella*, shows resistance to four families of antibiotics. Choice (C) is the correct answer.

52. **B** This question asks whether or not something is true based on the table, and then what line from the passage also supports that information. First determine if Aminopenicillin-resistant *S. aureus* is resistant to at least one member of the Fluoroquinolones family. Looking at *S. aureus* on the table, it is clear that it shows resistance to the Fluoroquinolones family, even though it's only a small percentage. Eliminate (C) and (D). Between (A) and (B), only (B) contains any information regarding the Fluoroquinolones family. Choice (B) is the correct answer.

Section 2: Writing and Language

1. **D** This question has answers with Stop punctuation, so use the vertical line test. In this sentence, the idea before the punctuation is *When we hear about the opinions of "ten scientists" or "ten dentists," or we hear that things are "clinically proven" or "lab-tested," for example* is incomplete. Therefore, it cannot precede a colon, eliminating (C), nor can it precede the combination of a comma and a coordinating conjunction, eliminating (A). Choice (B) adds an unnecessary word, thus making (D) the best answer.

2. **D** The following paragraph refers to *These claims*, suggesting that there must be some claim in the sentence in question, preferably one that refers back to some of the pseudoscientific claims at the beginning of the paragraph. Choices (A), (B), and (C) offer irrelevant pieces of information that do not support these claims, so they can be eliminated. The most *relevant* detail, therefore, comes from (D), which offers one of *these claims*.

3. **A** In this sentence, *Elle*, *Vogue*, and *Vanity Fair* comprise a list of three things. On the SAT, that list needs to be separated by commas, including one before the word *and*. Choice (A) is the only one of the answer choices that provides this comma in the appropriate spot.

4. **B** Sentence 5 refers to an *obvious answer*, suggesting that the sentence will come after a question. Look for question marks! Only sentence 1 contains a question (real or implied), so sentence

5's *obvious answer* must follow sentence 1's question. Choice (B) best captures this positioning within the paragraph.

5. **C** This sentence states that the researchers' findings are *not surprising*. The paragraph goes on to describe how deceptive many of these advertising claims are. Who, therefore, would not be surprised to find that a set of ads is deceptive? Not someone who believes the ads, eliminating (A), nor someone who has merely thought about those ads, eliminating (B). Choice (C) provides the hint of skepticism that the question needs. Choice (D) would seem to provide this skepticism as well—the only problem is that *skepticized* is not actually a word, thus eliminating (D).

6. **B** The previous sentences in this paragraph provide the first parts of the researchers' findings. With the categories of *true* and *"outright lies,"* it is not necessarily clear what the third category will be. Therefore, the sentence should be kept because it completes the researchers' findings, as (B) suggests.

7. **A** This sentence is separated into two parts by a comma and a coordinating conjunction. This combination requires two complete ideas on either side of it. The only answer choice that creates a complete idea after the conjunction is (A), which completes the sentence to say *they may have more serious implications as well*.

8. **B** Choose the word that has the most specific and consistent meaning within the context. In this sentence, that word is *regulate*, (B), because the word clearly describes what the FDA is capable of doing. Choices (A) and (C) don't make sense in the context. While it might seem logical that the Food and Drug Administration would *administrate*, as in (D), there is not proof from the passage that the FDA *administrates* what can go into makeup.

9. **C** The early part of this sentence contains the verb *may have*, which suggests a hypothetical situation happening in either the present or the future. Choices (A) and (B) place the verb in the past tense, which is not consistent with the rest of the sentence. Choice (D) can be eliminated because it introduces an unnecessary apostrophe. Choice (C) provides a consistent verb without excessive apostrophes.

10. **D** Choices (A) and (C) can be eliminated immediately because those prepositions do not pair idiomatically with the verb *to do*. Choice (B) can also be eliminated because the FDA is not doing anything *to* the claims. Instead, as (D) implies, the FDA may do something *with* the claims, such as punish or correct them.

11. **C** Choice (A), *Thus*, implies causation, but there is no causation between this sentence and the last. Choices (B) and (D) imply a contrast where there is no contrast. The best answer in this case comes from (C), *True*, which suggests a kind of concession on the part of the author.

12. **D** There is a contrast in this sentence between something *truly admirable* and something that *fall[s] short of these expectations*. The word that links the ideas, therefore, must imply some kind

of contrast. Of the answer choices, only (D) does so. While the essay is about politics, there is no need for the word *Politically* in this sentence.

13.   **A**   The phrase *then governor of the state* describes *Gerry*, but it does not restrict either the meaning or completeness of the sentence. In this sense, the remark is unnecessary in that it provides information parenthetically. As such, the remark should be offset with a pair of commas, as in (A).

14.   **C**   The action described in this sentence occurs in 1812, which is to say, the past. Therefore, the verb should reflect this past tense, thus eliminating (A) and (D). Of the remaining two verbs, (C) is more concise, and (B) rather wordily implies that the action described in the sentence may not have happened.

15.   **D**   The sentence *Unfortunately, it was not the last* should follow a sentence that mentions some *first*, which sentence 5 does. While sentence 2 may sound fine where it is now, there is no good reason to keep it there. It separates the *election* mentioned in sentence 1 from the *election* reference in sentence 3. Sentence 5's use of the word *first* provides a much better reason for the placement of sentence 2, which should therefore go after sentence 5, as (D) states.

16.   **C**   The question asks for a way to combine the two sentences. In questions like these, look to the shortest option first, particularly because the desire to combine sentences is fundamentally a desire for conciseness. In this case, (C) is the shortest, and it is not missing any information that the other answers possess. Therefore, (C) can be said to provide the most effective combination of the two sentences.

17.   **A**   Choices (B) and (D) should be eliminated right away because they provide a number of words that are unnecessary and make the wording of the sentence awkward. One of the remaining answers has Stop punctuation, so use the vertical line test. In order to choose between a colon and a semicolon remember this: A semicolon joins two complete ideas, whereas a colon only requires a complete idea before. In this case, the single word *gerrymandering* is not a complete idea, so the semicolon can't be used, thus eliminating (C) and leaving (A) as the correct answer.

18.   **D**   As described by the passage, the desired effect of gerrymandering is the acquisition of political advantage through demographic redistricting. While the events described in (A), (B), and (C) may be outcomes of gerrymandering, they do not describe its purpose. Only (D) describes the purpose, as it cites the desire to gain political advantage.

19.   **D**   Follow the percentages carefully. The un-districted figure on the far left shows 60% light gray voters and 40% dark gray voters. The distribution of these voters does not change, but the method of division on the far right of the figure shows how these voters can be rearranged in such a way as to create 3 dark gray districts and 2 light gray districts, or 60% dark gray districts from 60% light gray voters. Choice (D) best captures these percentages.

20. **C** Choices (A) and (D) give information that is implied by the words *benefits* and *in power*. Because those choices give redundant information, they can be eliminated. Then, (B) adds another unnecessary word, so it too can be eliminated. This leaves only (C), which is more concise than the other choices but accomplishes the same basic goal.

21. **B** This sentence describes the votes *belonging to* the voters. Therefore, the sentence requires the possessive form of the word *their*, as it is given in (B).

22. **A** While it may seem desirable to DELETE underlined portions whenever possible, doing so here would create a grammatical error, namely a comma splice between two complete ideas. Choices (B) and (C) would create the same problem. Only (A) correctly situates the idea within the sentence's given punctuation.

23. **B** All of the answer choices say essentially the same thing, so choose the answer that does so most concisely and clearly. Choice (B) provides this answer in that it says in a single word what the longer answers say with more words.

24. **B** This sentence begins with the modifier *Particularly when looking at old paintings*. The thing that this modifies should come directly after the modifier. The *paintings* cannot be *looking at old paintings*, thus eliminating (A) and (D). Choice (C) can be eliminated because *noticing* is not what is *looking at old paintings*. Only (B) provides a viable answer in suggesting that *you* are *looking at old paintings*.

25. **A** On the SAT, every sentence should have a clear, definable role within a paragraph, a role that is consistent with the theme of that paragraph. While the sentence in question is interesting, it does not have a clear role within the paragraph, so it should be deleted, thus eliminating (C) and (D). Then, the sentence should be deleted because it is irrelevant to the topic of the paragraph, as (A) states.

26. **D** Check the answer choices against the graph shown in the question, and use POE. The light gray line given in this figure represents the percentage of the workforce that works in art restoration. This line has a small bump from 1900 to 1910 and then disappears until approximately 1945, after which time it generally rises. Choice (A) is incorrect because the field did not begin growing in 1930, nor can it be said to rise steadily at any point after that. Choice (B) can be eliminated because it states that book restorers became art restorers, which is not supported in the graph, nor would the doings of book restorers be relevant to this passage. Choice (C) can be eliminated because the curves shown in the graph do not extend to 2020, nor is there any indication that the art-restoration line will overtake the art-conservation line at any point. Choice (D) is therefore the correct answer—it describes what is shown in the chart. In 1970, the percentage of people working in art restoration was just under 22 (leaving out all of the zeros) and by 2005, the number was just under 66, or roughly triple.

27. **C** Choice (A) can be eliminated because it is not clear whom or what the phrase *when looking* is meant to describe. Choice (B) does not make sense in the context. Choice (D) does not contain a meaning consistent with the sentence's intended meaning. Only (C) can work in the sentence, which indicates a contrast between the simplicity the viewer may see *at first glance* and the true *complicated* nature of what the viewer is seeing.

28. **C** The word *matter* is not part of the list at the end of this sentence, thus eliminating (A). The word *matter* is an introduction to the list. It should therefore be offset by some punctuation, eliminating (B). One of the remaining answers has Stop punctuation, so use the vertical line test. In order to choose between a colon and a semicolon, remember this: a semicolon requires complete ideas both before and after it whereas a colon only requires a complete idea before. In this case, the list after the punctuation is not a complete idea, so only a colon will work, making (C) the correct answer.

29. **A** The previous sentence refers to what happens *sometimes*. This sentence describes what happens more often. The transition between these two ideas must therefore include some transition from *some* to *most*, as only (A) does.

30. **C** A colon must be preceded by a complete idea. The idea *They would project some image of what the painting must have looked like originally and apply a variety of techniques, up to and including* is not complete and therefore cannot precede a colon, eliminating (A) and (D). Then, if there is no particular reason to use a comma (or any punctuation, for that matter), don't use that punctuation. Choice (C) contains no punctuation, and none is needed, thus making (C) the correct answer.

31. **B** The subject *some art historians* is plural, so it requires a plural verb, thus eliminating (A) and (C). Then, because the word *who* is the subject of the verb *are*, it should be kept in the subject form, as in (B). The object form *whom* would not apply in this case (because one would not say *them are writing today*), eliminating (D).

32. **D** The sentence in question provides an *example* of something that must be described in the preceding sentence. The best option for that preceding sentence must be sentence 4, which describes restoring paintings by *non-paint methods*. The sentence in question describes fixing a painting by relighting it, one example of these *non-paint methods*. The sentence should therefore be placed after sentence 4, as (D) indicates.

33. **D** The word *more* in this sentence implies a comparison. The word in the underlined portion must therefore indicate some comparison, as only (D) does.

34. **C** The question asks for a way to combine the two sentences. In questions like these, look to the shortest option first, particularly because the desire to combine sentences is fundamentally a desire for conciseness. In this case, (C) is the shortest, and it is not missing any information that the other answers possess, so (C) provides the most effective combination of the two sentences.

35. **C** The previous sentence describes an event in the past. This sentence describes an event in the present. Therefore, the transition should somehow address this shift in time, which only (C), *To this day*, does.

36. **D** When given the option to DELETE the underlined portion, it is usually best to choose that option unless there is a very good reason not to. In this case, the information in the underlined portion and its alternatives are not needed. In fact, deleting the underlined portion fixes what would otherwise have been a sentence fragment. As a result, (D), DELETE, is the best possible answer.

37. **C** All of the answer choices say essentially the same thing, so choose the answer that does so most concisely and clearly. Choice (C) provides this answer in that it says in fewer words what the other answers say with more words.

38. **B** When unsure which pronoun to use, find the original noun to which the pronoun is referring. In this case, that is actually another pronoun, *they*, which refers to the noun *pilgrims*. The only pronoun consistent with both words is therefore *their*, or (B).

39. **A** This sentence states that two things are happening simultaneously: the pilgrims figure out why they have been chosen for the pilgrimage as the reader learns more about the fantasy universe. Therefore, the underlined portion should contain some indication of this simultaneity. Of the available choices, only (A) does so. Choice (B) also provides some indication of time, but it implies a cause-and-effect that is not contained in the meaning of the sentence.

40. **D** The word *If* implies some complete action or thought. Of the available answer choices, only (D) completes that thought, creating the idea *If this structure sounds familiar*.

41. **D** There are only two reasons to use apostrophes: possession and contraction. Neither of those reasons apply here, thus eliminating the answers with apostrophes, (B) and (C). Then, within this sentence, the word *traveling* should describe the pilgrims. The word without the –*ing* ending is either a verb or a noun, so it cannot fulfill this function. Only (D) has the appropriate ending and the appropriate lack of apostrophes.

42. **B** The next sentence begins *With all these literary tributes*. Therefore, this sentence should contain more literary tributes, a continuation of the list begun earlier in this paragraph. The phrase *pays homage* in (B) best indicates these literary tributes, so (B) is the only one among the answer choices that has a discernible connection to the following sentence.

43. **C** While the information in the proposed sentence is true, this is not an essay about T.S. Eliot, so additional information about Eliot would not contribute in a substantial way to the essay as a whole. Therefore, the sentence should not be included, thus eliminating (A) and (B). Then, the sentence should be excluded because it is irrelevant, not because it contradicts any of the essay's claims, making (C) the best answer.

44. **D** When a question is testing verbs, check the subject. In this case, the subject is the word *continuities*, which is plural. Therefore, all singular verbs, as in (A) and (B), can be eliminated. Choice (C) creates a sentence fragment. Therefore, only (D) completes the sentence and is appropriately consistent with its subject.

Section 3: Math (No Calculator)

1. **A** Write an expression for the number of hours each of the two people has worked. Jan worked j hours a day for 3 days, so she worked a total of $3j$ hours. Noah worked n hours a day for 5 days, so he worked a total of $5n$ hours. Therefore, the total hours worked by Jan and Noah combined is the sum of these two, which is $3j + 5n$. These are not like terms, so they cannot be combined or simplified further. The correct answer is (A).

2. **B** Plug $c = 4$ into the right side of the equation to get $\dfrac{y + 2}{5} = 4$. Multiply both sides of the equation by 5 to get $y + 2 = 20$. Subtract 2 from both sides to get $y = 18$, which is (B).

3. **B** Even though this looks complicated, start by combining like terms. Add the real terms, 10 and 3, to get 13. Then, add the imaginary terms, $-4i$ and $6i$, to get $2i$. Add these two to get $13 + 2i$, which is (B).

4. **D** Simplify this expression by combining like terms in bite-sized pieces. Start with the ab^2 terms. The $-ab^2$ term from the second polynomial is subtracted from the ab^2 in the first. $ab^2 - (-ab^2)$ $= ab^2 + ab^2 = 2ab^2$. Eliminate any choice that does not include $2ab^2$: (A) and (B). Now look at the a^2 terms. The $4a^2$ term from the second polynomial is subtracted from the $4a^2$ term in the first. $4a^2 - 4a^2 = 0$. Therefore, the correct answer cannot have an a^2 term. Eliminate the remaining choice that does, which is (C). The correct answer is (D).

5. **D** The weight of a mature great white shark is estimated by $w = 3{,}150 + 450l$, where l is the fork length in feet. The question asks for the estimated weight increase in pounds for each foot of growth. To determine this, plug in values for l that show a one foot increase. First, plug in $l = 2$. If $l = 2$, then $w = 3{,}150 + 450(2) = 4{,}050$. Then plug in $l = 3$. If $l = 3$, then $w = 3{,}150 + 450(3) = 4{,}500$. The increase is $4{,}500 - 4{,}050 = 450$. Therefore, the correct answer is (D).

6. **C** The number of pages Juan has left to edit is represented by the equation $P = 326 - 12h$, where h represents the number of hours worked. The question asks for what 326 represents in this equation. Since P is a number of pages, 326 must also be a number of pages, so eliminate (D). Choices (A) and (B) each deal with a rate. In order to turn a rate into an amount, the rate must be multiplied by time. Since h represents time, the coefficient on time, 12, must represent the rate rather than 326. Therefore, eliminate (A) and (B). Only (C) remains, so it must be correct. To understand why it is correct, plug in $h = 0$. If $h = 0$, then $P = 326 - 12(0) = 326$.

Therefore, after working for 0 hours at the start of the project, he has 326 pages left to edit. Therefore, the correct answer is (C).

7. **A** The question says that $\dfrac{x}{y} = 3$. Plug in values of x and y that satisfy this equation. Let $x = 6$ and $y = 2$. Plug these values into the expression $\dfrac{12y}{x}$ to get $\dfrac{12(2)}{6} = \dfrac{24}{6} = 4$. Therefore, the correct answer is (A).

8. **A** To solve this problem, plug in the answers. Test the points in the answer choices by plugging them into the two equations. In order to be the solution of the system of equations, a point must satisfy both equations. Start with (A): $(-7, -5)$. Plug these values into the first equation to get $2(-5) + (-7) = -17$. This is true, so plug the values into the second equation to get $5(-7) - 4(-5) = -15$. Since this is also true, the correct answer is (A).

9. **C** The equation includes a very complicated fraction. However, the equation asks for the value of

M, which is not part of the fraction but rather the value that is being multiplied by the fraction.

In order to isolate a variable that is multiplied by a fraction, multiply both sides by the recipro-

cal. On the right side of the equation, the fractions cancel, isolating M. On the left side, the

reciprocal is multiplied by c to get $\dfrac{1 - \left(1 + \dfrac{r}{1,200}\right)^{-N}}{\dfrac{r}{1,200}}\,c$. Therefore, the correct answer is (C).

10. **C** The question asks about a line in the xy-plane. Any such line can be defined by the equation $y = mx + b$, in which m is the slope and b is the y-intercept. The question says that the slope is $\dfrac{2}{3}$, so $m = \dfrac{2}{3}$. The question also says that the line passes through the origin, which is the point $(0, 0)$. Since the y-intercept is the point at which the x-coordinate is 0, the origin must be the y-intercept, so $b = 0$. Thus the equation of the line is $y = \dfrac{2}{3}x + 0$, or $y = \dfrac{2}{3}x$. Plug the points in the answer choices into this equation. Start with (A). Plug in the values from (A) to get $\dfrac{2}{3} = \dfrac{2}{3}(0)$. Since this is false, eliminate (A). Try (B). Plug in the values from (B) to get $3 = \dfrac{2}{3}(2)$. Since this is false, eliminate (B). Try (C). Plug in the values from (C) to get $4 = \dfrac{2}{3}(6)$. Since this is true, select (C).

11. **D** Since $f(3) = 12$, plug this into the function equation to get $f(3) = c(3)^2 + 30 = 12$. Therefore, $9c + 30 = 12$. Subtract 30 from both sides to get $9c = -18$. Divide both sides by 9 to get $c = -2$.

Plug this into the original equation to get $f(x) = -2x^2 + 30$. The question asks for $f(-3)$, so plug in $x = -3$ to get $f(-3) = -2(-3)^2 + 30 = -2(9) + 30 = -18 + 30 = 12$. The correct answer is (D).

12. **A** The question asks for the price per night when it is the same for both hotels. Since the two equations given are for the price per night in the two hotels, set the two expressions for the prices equal: $240 - 20w = 320 - 30w$. Add $30w$ to both sides to get $240 + 10w = 320$. Subtract 240 from both sides to get $10w = 80$. Divide both sides by 10 to get $w = 8$. This represents the number of weeks, but the question asks for the price per night. Plug this value of w into the equation for A. $A = 240 - 20(8) = 240 - 160 = 80$, which is (A).

13. **C** The question asks for the value of $\dfrac{3^a}{81^b}$. To divide numbers with exponents, the bases must be the same. Convert the denominator to a base of 3: since $81 = 3^4$, $81^b = (3^4)^b$. When raising a number with an exponent to an exponent, multiply the exponents, so $81^b = (3^4)^b = 3^{4b}$. Therefore, $\dfrac{3^a}{81^b} = \dfrac{3^a}{3^{4b}}$. When dividing numbers with exponents and the same base, subtract the exponents, so $\dfrac{3^a}{81^b} = \dfrac{3^a}{3^{4b}} = 3^{a-4b}$. The question also says that $a - 4b = 18$, so $\dfrac{3^a}{81^b} = \dfrac{3^a}{3^{4b}} = 3^{a-4b} = 3^{18}$. Therefore, the correct answer is (C).

14. **A** The question gives a quadratic in both factored and expanded form. Get them in the same form by expanding the factored quadratic on the left side. Use FOIL on $(ax + 3)(bx + 5)$. Multiply first terms to get $(ax)(bx) = abx^2$. Compare this to the x^2 term on the right side, $35x^2$. Therefore, $ab = 35$. Since $ab = 35$, consider the factors of 35. There are two pairs of factors: 1, 35 and 5, 7. Since the question says that $a + b = 12$, a and b must be 5 and 7, but there is no way to determine the order. Therefore, consider both $a = 5$, $b = 7$ and $a = 7$, $b = 5$. If $a = 5$ and $b = 7$, the equation becomes $(5x + 3)(7x + 5) = 35x^2 + kx + 15$. To get the value of k, determine the coefficient on the x-term of the quadratic expression on the left. To do this, find the product of the outer terms and the product of the inner terms, which are $25x$ and $21x$, respectively. Add these products to get $25x + 21x = 46x$, so, in this case, $k = 46$. Eliminate any choice that does not include 46: (B), (C), and (D). Therefore, the correct answer is (A). (To determine the other possible value, plug in $a = 7$ and $b = 5$ to get $(7x + 3)(5x + 5)$. Multiply outer terms to get $35x$. Multiply inner terms to get $15x$. Add the products to get $50x$, so $k = 50$.)

15. **C** Rather than dealing with complicated fractions, simplify the fractions by plugging in. The question says that $y > 5$, so plug in $y = 6$ to get $\dfrac{1}{\dfrac{1}{6-4} + \dfrac{1}{6-3}}$. The fraction simplifies to $\dfrac{1}{\dfrac{1}{2} + \dfrac{1}{3}}$. Now, add the fractions in the denominator, using the bowtie method.

$$\overset{3 \quad + \quad 2}{\dfrac{1}{2} \underset{\times}{\overset{+}{\searrow\swarrow}} \dfrac{1}{3}} = \dfrac{5}{6}$$

Therefore, the original fraction is equivalent to $\dfrac{1}{\frac{5}{6}}$. When dividing by a fraction, flip the

bottom fraction and multiply. Therefore, $\dfrac{1}{\frac{5}{6}} = \dfrac{\frac{1}{1}}{\frac{5}{6}} = \dfrac{1}{1} \times \dfrac{6}{5} = \dfrac{6}{5}$, so $\dfrac{6}{5}$ is the target

number. Plug $y = 6$ into the answer choices and eliminate any choice that is not

equal to $\dfrac{6}{5}$. Since (A) and (B) are not fractions, eliminate them immediately. Try

(C). $\dfrac{y^2 - 7y + 12}{2y - 7} = \dfrac{6^2 - 7(6) + 12}{2(6) - 7} = \dfrac{36 - 42 + 12}{12 - 7} = \dfrac{6}{5}$, so keep (C). Try (D).

$\dfrac{2y - 7}{y^2 - 7y + 12} = \dfrac{2(6) - 7}{6^2 - 7(6) + 12} = \dfrac{5}{6} \neq \dfrac{6}{5}$, so eliminate (D). The correct answer is (C).

16. **5** First label the figure. Label $\overline{PQ}$ with length 3, $\overline{QT}$ with length 4, $\overline{QS}$ with length 8 and $\overline{SR}$ with

length 10. When a question involves two triangles, determine whether they are similar. Simi-

lar triangles, by definition, have three pairs of congruent corresponding angles. However, since

the measures of the angles in all triangles have a sum of 180°, it is only necessary to show that

two pairs of corresponding angles are congruent. The question says that $\angle TPQ$ is congruent to

$\angle QRS$. Also, $\angle PQT$ and $\angle SQR$ are vertical angles, so they are also congruent. Thus, the two tri-

angles are similar. Similar triangles have a consistent proportion between corresponding sides

(sides that are opposite congruent angles). The question asks for the value of m, or the length

of $\overline{PT}$, which corresponds with $\overline{SR}$. Use the lengths of another pair of corresponding sides, $\overline{QT}$

and $\overline{QS}$, to set up a proportion: $\dfrac{m}{10} = \dfrac{4}{8}$. Cross-multiply to get $8m = 40$. Divide by 8 to get

$m = 5$. Therefore, the correct response is 5.

17. **6** To solve the equation $y^2 - 36 = 0$, add 36 to both sides to get $y^2 = 36$. Take the square root of

both sides to get $y = \pm 6$. However, the question specifies that $y > 0$, so $y = 6$.

18. $\dfrac{5}{13}$ Draw the right triangle. Label one of the non-right angles with measure $d°$. Since $\cos = \dfrac{adj}{hyp}$

and $\cos d° = \dfrac{5}{13}$, label the side adjacent to d as 5 and the hypotenuse 13. Using the Pythago-

rean Theorem (or the 5-12-13 Pythagorean triple), the missing side has length 12. Since the angles in a triangle have a sum of 180, label the missing angle x and set up the equation $d + x + 90 = 180$. Subtract 90 from both sides to get $d + x = 90$, and subtract d from both sides to get $x = 90 - d$. The question asks for the sine of this angle. Since $\sin = \frac{opp}{hyp}$, find the side opposite this angle, which is 5, and the hypotenuse, which is 13, to get $\sin(90° - d°) = \frac{5}{13}$. Alternatively, note that the angle of measure $(90° - d°)$ is the complement of the angle of measure $d°$. The sine of an angle is equal to the cosine of its complement. Therefore, $\sin(90° - d°) = \cos d° = \frac{5}{13}$. Either way, the answer is $\frac{5}{13}$.

19. **225** The question asks for the value of z. The second equation, $5c = \sqrt{5z}$, is in terms of c and z, so plug in the value of c to get $5(3\sqrt{5}) = \sqrt{5z}$. Simplify the left side to get $15\sqrt{5} = \sqrt{5z}$. Since the equation involves square roots, square both sides to get $(15\sqrt{5})^2 = (\sqrt{5z})^2$. Square each factor to get $(15)^2(\sqrt{5})^2 = (\sqrt{5z})^2$ and $(225)(5) = 5z$. Divide both sides by 5 to get $225 = z$. The answer is 225.

20. **13** To determine the value of b, stack the equations and cancel the a terms. To do this, make sure that the a term coefficients are opposites. Multiply the first equation by -2 to get $-2a - 2b = 20$. Stack this below the second equation, $2a + b = -33$, and add the two equations.

$$
\begin{array}{r}
2a + b = -33 \\
-2a - 2b = 20 \\
\hline
0a - b = -13
\end{array}
$$

Therefore, the new equation is $0 - b = -13$ or $b = 13$. Thus, the correct response is 13.

Section 4: Math (Calculator)

1. **C** When two parallel lines are intersected by a third line, or by two or more parallel lines, remember this simple rule: All the small angles are the same; all the big angles are the same; and any small angle + any big angle = 180°. "Small" angles are less than 90°, and "big" angles are greater than 90°. In this question, x is a small angle, and y is a big angle, so $x + y = 180°$. Substitute the given value: $75° + y = 180°$. Subtract 75° from both sides to get $y = 105°$. The answer is (C).

2. **C** Work through the answer choices one at a time. For (A), the number of customers stays the same from 9:00 A.M.–11:00 A.M., then increases from 11:00 A.M.–12:00 P.M., so eliminate (A). For (B), the number of customers stays the same from 12:00 P.M.–1:00 P.M., drops suddenly, then stays the same from 1:00 P.M.–2:00 P.M., so eliminate (B). Choice (C) looks good; the

number of customers decreases from 2:00 P.M.–3:30 P.M., then increases from 3:30 P.M.–5:00 P.M. Finally, in (D), the number of customers increases from 3:30 P.M.–5:00 P.M., then decreases from 5:00 P.M.–6:30 P.M. This is a trap answer that does the opposite of what the question asks for, so eliminate (D). The correct answer is (C).

3. **B**   Start by plugging in the values given for x and y, then solve for k. If $5 = \dfrac{30}{k}$, then $5k = 30$ and $k = 6$. It is given that k is a constant, which means that its value doesn't change (whereas x and y are variables, so their values do change). Now plug in the values for the second scenario: $y = \dfrac{42}{6}$, so $y = 7$, which is (B).

4. **B**   Set up a proportion. First convert the 3 kilograms into grams: $\dfrac{1\,\text{kg}}{1{,}000\,\text{g}} = \dfrac{3\,\text{kg}}{x\,\text{g}}$, so $x = 3(1{,}000) = 3{,}000$ grams. Next, convert the 3,000 grams into decigrams: $\dfrac{1\,\text{g}}{10\,\text{dg}} = \dfrac{3{,}000\,\text{g}}{x\,\text{dg}}$, so $x = 10(3{,}000) = 30{,}000$ decigrams, which is (B).

5. **D**   The simplest way to solve this problem is to translate it into an equation and solve for x. The statement *6x – 4 is 11 less than 25* can be translated as $6x - 4 = 25 - 11$. Simplify the right side: $6x - 4 = 14$. Add 4 to both sides: $6x = 18$. Divide by 6: $x = 3$. Be careful not to fall for (A); read the full question! The question asks for the value of $9x$, and $(9)(3) = 27$, so the answer is (D).

6. **A**   When a question contains a scatterplot, draw a line of best fit through the dots, so that roughly half the dots are above the line, and half are below. If the line of best fit has a positive slope, it means that h and p have a *positive correlation* (the question might say "association" rather than "correlation"). If the line has a negative slope, it means that the two quantities have a *negative correlation*, as in (B). If there is no clear relationship between the variables, there is *no* correlation. If the dots in the scatterplot are packed relatively closely, the correlation is *strong*; if they are far apart, the correlation is *weak*. Fortunately, there's no need to choose between strong and weak here. The answer is (A).

7. **C**   Plug in 200 for p and solve for d: $200 = 101 + 10.094d$. Subtract 101 from both sides: $99 = 10.094d$. Divide both sides by 10.094 to get $d = 9.808$. The question asks for the closest answer, so round to the closest integer, which is 10. The correct answer is (C).

8. **D**   The fastest way to solve this question is to use algebra. Start by isolating the term that contains d by subtracting 101 from both sides: $p - 101 = 10.094d$. Divide by 10.094: $\dfrac{p - 101}{10.094} = d$. Now simply write the expression in reverse so that d is on the left side: $d = \dfrac{p - 101}{10.094}$. This matches (D), so that's the correct answer. As an alternative, plug in to solve the problem.

Plug in 2 for *d* and solve for *p*: 101 + (10.094)(2) = 121.188 = *p*. Now plug these values into the answers and pick the one that works. Only (D) matches.

9. **B** Add up the number of wind turbines shown on the graph: 9 + 11 + 3.5 + 8 + 6 = 37.5. Now try the answer choices. Start with (B) or (C), then move higher or lower if the first choice doesn't work. Try (C): 37.5 × 1,000 = 37,500, which is too big. Try (B): 37.5 × 100 = 3,750, which is correct.

10. **A** When the SAT mixes math symbols and words, try translating the words into a math equation. In this question, the phrase $|k - 3| + 2$ *is equal to one* translates to $|k - 3| + 2 = 1$. To isolate the absolute value expression, subtract 2 from both sides to get $|k + 3| = -1$. Here's the tricky part of the question: An absolute value expression can never be negative, so no values of *k* would make this expression true. Therefore, the answer is (A).

11. **D** Read carefully! There are 14 apartments: 1 apartment with 6 residents, 2 with 4 residents, 4 with 5 residents, and 7 with 3 residents. Add up all the residents: 6 + 4 + 4 + 5 + 5 + 5 + 5 + 3 + 3 + 3 + 3 + 3 + 3 + 3 = 55. Divide by the number of apartments: $\frac{55}{14} = 3.929$. This is closest to 4, so the answer is (D).

12. **D** There are two ways to tackle this problem: solve algebraically or plug in the answers. To solve algebraically, subtract 6*x* from both sides to get $-4 \leq x - 3$. Then add 3 to both sides to get $-1 \leq x$ or $x \geq -1$. Since *x* must be –1 or greater, –2 cannot be a solution, so the answer is (D). To plug in the answers, start with (B) or (C). Here, it makes more sense to start with (B), because 0 is a very easy number to plug in. Plugging in 0 gives $-4 \leq -3$, which is true, so eliminate (B). Now try (C): $-10 \leq -10$, which is true, so eliminate (C). Finally, try (D): $-16 \leq -17$, which is false, so the answer is (D).

13. **B** To calculate (or estimate) mean, median, or range, it's best to save mean for last, since it's usually the most time-consuming to calculate. Start with the easiest part: the total. If 2 is removed, the total will change by 2. The range is the difference between the largest and smallest term. The range now is 9 – 2 = 7, but if 2 is removed, the smallest term will be 3, so the range will be 9 – 3 = 6, and the range changes by 1. To find the median in a set with an even number of terms, take the average of the two middle terms. Here, the two middle terms are both 6, so 6 is the median. If 2 is removed, there will be 17 terms, so the 9th term will be the median. Since the new 9th term will be 6, the median will not change at all. This makes it unnecessary to calculate the average. The average is the total divided by the number of things, so if 2 is removed from the total and 1 from the number of things, the average will change. Therefore, the answer is (B).

14. **B** Plug (2, 2) in for *x* and *y*, and solve for *p* and *r*. In the first inequality, *p* + 2 > 2, so *p* > 0. In the second inequality, *r* – 2 < –2, so *r* < 0. Since *r* is negative and *p* is positive, *r* must be less than *p*, so the answer is (B).

15. **A** When a question says approximately, go ahead and approximate. The total, 395, is close to 400, so 15% of 400 = $\frac{15}{100} \times 400 = 60$. Often this would be enough to find the correct answer, but in this case there are two answers, 59 and 62, that are very close, so try them both. $\frac{59}{395} \times 100 = 14.94\%$. That looks good, but try (B), just to be safe: $\frac{62}{395} \times 100 = 15.7\%$, which rounds to 16%, which is not correct. The correct answer is (A).

16. **C** Slope is rise divided by run, or vertical change divided by horizontal change. For each additional day, the price increases by \$20, so the slope, $\frac{20}{1}$, is equivalent to the average daily price increase. The correct answer is (C).

17. **D** When the SAT asks for the relationship between two variables, they are asking for an equation. In this case, it's the equation of a line, and all the answer choices are in slope-intercept form. The slope is 20 (as calculated for the previous question). Notice on the graph that when $d = 0$, $P = 30$, so the y-intercept is 30. The equation of a line in slope-intercept form is $y = mx + b$, where m is the slope and b is the y-intercept. In this question, $m = 20$ and $b = 30$, so the equation is $y = 20d + 30$, and the answer is (D). Plugging in values from the graph can also determine the correct equation.

18. **C** Remember that $f(x) = y$. The maximum y-value on this line graph is 3, and when $y = 3$, $x = -2$, so the answer is (C). In this type of question, if they ask for an x-value, the corresponding y-value is likely to be a trap answer (in this case (D) is the trap).

19. **C** When there are variables in the answers, plug in. Start from the simplest price, which is a peak ticket bought in the station. Let's say that price is \$100. Then an off-peak ticket purchased in the station will be 15% off, or \$85. For an off-peak ticket purchased from the conductor, there is an 11% surcharge, so $\frac{11}{100} \times 85 = 9.35$, and \$85 + \$9.35 = \$94.35. This is the value of t, and the question is asking for the value of a peak ticket bought in the station, which is \$100. Now plug $t = \$94.35$ into the answer choices, and choose the one that equals \$100; the correct answer is (C).

20. **A** In most SAT questions, all the information matters. But, once in a while, there will be unnecessary information designed to create confusion. In this question, it is not necessary to know the total number of people, nor whether they eat snacks or not. A person is being randomly chosen from *among those who exercise fewer than six times per week*, so only the first two columns in the table matter. There are a total of 24 + 40 people who exercise fewer than 6 times per week and, of those people,

13 + 22 = 35 of them are in group 1. Use the probability formula: $probability = \dfrac{want}{total} = \dfrac{35}{64}$. The correct answer is (A).

21. **D** This question can be solved two ways: as a system of equations, or by plugging in the answers.

To solve with equations, start by assigning variables. Make g the number of gallons of gasoline and d the number of gallons of diesel. Now write two equations: $3.25g + 3d = 404.25$ and $g + d = 131$. To get the value for d, try to make the g values disappear. Multiply the 2nd equation by -3.25 to get $-3.25g - 3.25d = -425.75$. Stack and add the two equations to get

$$\begin{aligned} 3.25g + \quad 3d &= 404.25 \\ -3.25g - 3.25d &= -425.75 \\ \hline -0.25d &= -21.5 \end{aligned}$$

Divide by -0.25 to find that $d = 86$, so the correct answer is (D).

A safer method is to plug in the answers. Start with (C). If the station sold 76 gallons of diesel, then the station sold $131 - 76 = 55$ gallons of gasoline. The revenue from diesel would be $76 \times \$3 = \$228$, and the revenue from gasoline would be $55 \times \$3.25 = \$178.75$, for a total of $\$228 + \$178.75 = \$406.75$, which doesn't match the total sales of $\$404.25$ given by the problem. Since the total was too high, move to (D), where more of the cheaper diesel fuel was sold: If the station sold 86 gallons of diesel, then the station sold $131 - 86 = 45$ gallons of gasoline. The revenue from diesel would be $86 \times \$3 = \$258$, and the revenue from gasoline would be $45 \times \$3.25 = \$146.25$, for a total of $\$258 + \$146.25 = \$404.25$, which matches the total sales given by the problem. The correct answer is (D).

22. **C** With the ugly numbers in the chart, approximation is helpful here. The ratio of 2010 higher education spending to 2014 higher education spending can be estimated as 2.1 million to 3.1 million, or even more approximately as 2:3. The only other column that is close is corrections, which can be estimated as 630,000 to 930,000, also fairly close to 2:3. The correct answer is (C).

23. **C** When questions ask for an approximate value, round the numbers to avoid unnecessary math. Round public assistance spending in 2012 to $\$56,000$ and round 2014 spending to $\$30,000$. Subtract to get an approximate difference of $\$26,000$. Divide by two to get an average of $\$13,000$. Read carefully: The chart values are in *thousands of dollars*, so multiply by 1,000 to get the actual rate of change of $\$13,000,000$, which is (C).

24. **A** When the fish hits the surface of the lake, the height will be 0, so plug 0 into the equation: $0 = 9s - 4.9s^2$. From here, the easiest thing to do is plug in the answer choices. Start with (C): $(9)(3) - (4.9)(3^2) = 27 - 44.1 = -17.1$. This negative value means that the fish has gone 17 meters below the surface. Choice (C) is too big, so try (B). It's also too big, so the answer must be

(A). Double check to be sure: $9(2) - (4.9)(2^2) = 18 - 19.6 = -1.6$. The question is asking for an approximate answer, and (A) is closest, so that's the correct answer. The problem can also be solved by factoring $h = 9s - 4.9s^2$ into $h = s(9 - 4.9s)$. The solutions for s in this equation are $s = 0$ (the time when the fish began the leap) and $9 - 4.9s = 0$ (the time when the fish hit the water). Solve the latter for s: $9 = 4.9s$, so $s = \dfrac{9}{4.9} = 1.84$ seconds, which is closest to (A).

25. **C** The equation of a circle centered at (h, k) is $(x - h)^2 + (y - k)^2 = r^2$. Therefore, the left side of the equation must be $(x - 3)^2 + y^2$. Eliminate (B) and (D). To narrow it down further, find the radius by drawing a triangle and finding the legs to plug into the Pythagorean Theorem (this is safer than trying to remember the distance formula).

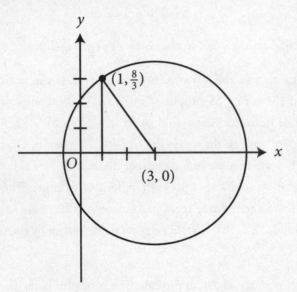

The base is 2 and the height is $\dfrac{8}{3}$, so use the Pythagorean Theorem to find the radius. $2^2 + \left(\dfrac{8}{3}\right)^2 = r^2$, so $4 + \dfrac{64}{9} = r^2$, or $\dfrac{36}{9} + \dfrac{64}{9} = \dfrac{100}{9} = r^2$. It's not necessary to take the square root, because the only piece missing from the circle formula is r^2. The correct equation is $(x - 3)^2 + y^2 = \dfrac{100}{9}$, which is (C).

26. **D** When dealing with area questions, always calculate the areas—don't make assumptions. The area of the lawn is $8 \times 8 = 64$ square feet. There are 8 samples, and each sample is $1 \times 1 = 1$ square foot, so the total area sampled is $\dfrac{8}{64} = \dfrac{1}{8}$ of the total area. Next, since the question asks for approximation, approximate the total number of seedlings. Notice that the middle values are very close to 100, and

the highest and lowest values are almost equidistant from 100, so the average number of seedlings in a sample is about 100. Therefore, the total number of seedlings in all the samples is approximately $100 \times 8 = 800$, and the total number of seedlings in the lawn is approximately $800 \times 8 = 6,400$. The correct answer is (D).

27. **C** The easiest way to solve this question is to plug in the answers. Start with (B). If there were 103 Western chinchilla offspring, then the Eastern chinchilla produced $103 \times \dfrac{30}{100} = 30.9$ more offspring than the Western chinchilla, totaling 133.9. Since 133.9 does not match the 143 offspring specified by the problem, eliminate (B) and move to a larger number. Try (C): If there were 110 Western chinchilla offspring, then the Eastern chinchilla produced $110 \times \dfrac{30}{100} = 33$ more offspring than the Western chinchilla, totaling 143, which matches the number specified in the problem. Therefore, the answer is (C).

28. **B** The opening sentence, *when polynomial g(x) is divided by x − 4, the remainder is 3,* means that if an x-value of 4 is plugged into the polynomial, the corresponding y-value will be 3. This fact can be represented with the equation $g(4) = 3$, so (B) is correct. Without knowing this, the question is pretty tough. However, it is possible to plug in, with a little knowledge about how remainders work. Consider an easier question: When a number is divided by 5, the remainder is 3. What is one value for the number? It's fairly easy to come up with an answer to this question, such as the number 13. A simple way to find a quotient with a certain remainder is to double (or triple, etc.) the number, and add the remainder. So, double 5 and add 3, and the result is 13. The same thing can be done in this more difficult question. The divisor is $x − 4$, so double it and add 3: $2(x − 4) + 3 = 2x − 5$. This polynomial meets the requirements of the question and can be used to test the answers. For (A), plug $x = −4$ into the polynomial: $2(−4) + 5 = −3$, so (A) is false. For (B), $2(4) − 5 = 3$, so (B) looks good, but be sure to check all four answers. For (C), remember that if $x − 4$ is a factor of $g(x)$, then 4 is a solution, and plugging 4 into the equation should yield zero. But working through (B) already demonstrated that $2(4) − 5 = 3$, so (C) is false. For (D), plug −3 into the equation: $2(−3) − 5 = −11$, so (D) is false, and the answer is (B).

29. **A** The question gives an equation in *standard* form, which is $y = ax^2 + bx + c$, and asks for the equation in *vertex* form. The vertex form of a parabola is $y = a(x − h)^2 + k$. It's called vertex form because the vertex of the parabola is at (h, k). The x-coordinate of the vertex will always be the average of the x-coordinates of any two points that have the same y-value. The graph gives two points on the y-axis (these are the *solutions* or *zeros* of the equation), so find the average of the x-coordinates:

$\dfrac{-4+2}{2} = -1$, so $h = -1$. From the graph, it also looks like the y-coordinate of the vertex is -9, so $k = -9$, making the vertex $(-1, -9)$. Now look at the answers. Choice (A) is in vertex form, and the vertex it shows is $(-1, -9)$, so the correct answer is (A).

30. **B** To answer this question, use the provided quadrant drawing to make a quick sketch with both equations drawn. It is not necessary to make a perfectly accurate graph; just get the general idea. For this system of inequalities, any solutions must be above *both* lines (because the solutions must be greater than both $y \geq x + 2$ and $y \geq \dfrac{1}{3}x - 1$), so shade in this area as shown below:

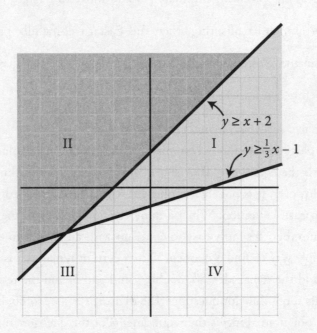

As the sketch shows, there are solutions in Quadrants I, II, and III, but not in IV. Therefore, the answer is (B).

31. $\dfrac{3}{7}, \dfrac{6}{14}, .428$ or $.429$

Locate the values for April and February, and write them as a fraction: $\dfrac{30}{70}$. This fraction won't fit into the grid-in box, so either reduce it or convert it into a decimal.

32. **Any value from 14 to 21, inclusive**

If the worker boxes 8 pairs of shoes per minute, it will take $\dfrac{168}{8} = 21$ minutes to box all the shoes. If the worker boxes 12 pairs per minute, the same task will take $\dfrac{168}{12} = 14$ minutes. Therefore, any answer from 14 to 21 is valid. An easy way to solve a question like this is to just plug in a value within the given range. Suppose the worker boxes 10 pairs per minute. Then it will take $\frac{168}{10} = 16.8$ minutes to complete the task. This is a valid answer, and it is faster than finding the boundaries of the range.

33. **30** Begin by subtracting the weight of the driver and the pallet: $1,600 - 250 = 1,350$. Now divide by the weight of the boxes: $\frac{1,350}{45} = 30$. Therefore, 30 is the maximum number of boxes that can be safely loaded into the elevator.

34. **4** The formula for the volume of a cylinder is $V = \pi r^2 h$, so plug the given information into the formula. The radius is $\frac{9}{2}$, so $81\pi = \pi\left(\frac{9}{2}\right)^2 h$. Divide both sides by π and square the fraction on the right: $81 = \frac{81}{4}h$. Divide both sides by $\frac{81}{4}$ to get the correct answer, which is 4.

35. **4** A fraction is undefined if the denominator is zero, so set the denominator equal to zero: $(x - 6)^2 + 4(x - 7) + 8 = 0$. Now solve for x by using FOIL and distributing where necessary: $x^2 - 12x + 36 + 4x - 28 + 8 = 0$. Combine like terms: $x^2 - 8x + 16 = 0$. Factor the equation: $(x - 4)^2 = 0$. Take the square root of both sides: $x - 4 = 0$. Add 4 to both sides: $x = 4$. The correct answer is 4.

36. **51** The trains arrive at 6, 6:20, 6:40, then 7, 7:20, 7:40, then 8, 8:20, 8:40, and so on. There are three trains per hour, so count the number of hours—using a pencil to keep track if necessary. There are 17 hours, and $17 \times 3 = 51$, so the correct answer is 51.

37. **3** For this question, it helps to know the compound interest formula, which is $A = P\left(1 + \frac{r}{n}\right)^{nt}$, where A is the total amount, P is the principal or initial amount, r is the interest rate (expressed as a decimal), n is how many times per year the rate is compounded, and t is the number of years. That may seem complicated, but usually the interest is compounded once a year, so $n = 1$, and the formula can be simplified to $A = P(1 + r)^t$. Therefore, the interest rate expressed as a decimal is 0.03. Multiply by 100 to express the interest rate as a percentage: $(0.03)(100) = 3$, which is the correct answer.

38. **8.76** It helps to solve question 37, the easier question of the pair, before solving this one. Helene's interest rate, from the answer to question 37, is 3%, so to find her total after 12 years, use the formula above: $A = 50(1.03)^{12} = 71.29$. Carolyn earns 1% more, so her total is $A = 50(1.04)^{12} = 80.05$. Subtract the first total from the second to get 8.76, which is the correct answer.

Chapter 5
Practice Test 2

Reading Test

65 MINUTES, 52 QUESTIONS

Turn to Section 1 of your answer sheet to answer the questions in this section.

DIRECTIONS

Each passage or pair of passages below is followed by a number of questions. After reading each passage or pair, choose the best answer to each question based on what is stated or implied in the passage or passages and in any accompanying graphics (such as a table or graph).

Questions 1–10 are based on the following passage.

This passage is excerpted from Miguel de Cervantes, *Don Quixote,* originally published in 1605 and translated by John Ormsby in 1885.

At this point they came in sight of thirty or forty windmills that are on that plain.

"Fortune," said Don Quixote to his squire, as soon
Line as he had seen them, "is arranging matters for us better
5 than we could have hoped. Look there, friend Sancho Panza, where thirty or more monstrous giants rise up, all of whom I mean to engage in battle and slay, and with whose spoils we shall begin to make our fortunes. For this is righteous warfare, and it is God's good
10 service to sweep so evil a breed from off the face of the earth."

"What giants?" said Sancho Panza.

"Those you see there," answered his master, "with the long arms, and some have them nearly two
15 leagues* long."

"Look, your worship," said Sancho. "What we see there are not giants but windmills, and what seem to be their arms are the vanes that turned by the wind make the millstone go."

20 "It is easy to see," replied Don Quixote, "that you are not used to this business of adventures. Those are giants, and if you are afraid, away with you out of here and betake yourself to prayer, while I engage them in fierce and unequal combat."

25 So saying, he gave the spur to his steed Rocinante, heedless of the cries his squire Sancho sent after him, warning him that most certainly they were windmills

and not giants he was going to attack. He, however, was so positive they were giants that he neither heard the
30 cries of Sancho, nor perceived, near as he was, what they were.

"Fly not, cowards and vile beings," he shouted, "for a single knight attacks you."

A slight breeze at this moment sprang up, and the
35 great vanes began to move.

"Though ye flourish more arms than the giant Briarus**, ye have to reckon with me!" exclaimed Don Quixote, when he saw this.

So saying, he commended himself with all his
40 heart to his lady Dulcinea, imploring her to support him in such a peril. With lance braced and covered by his shield, he charged at Rocinante's fullest gallop and attacked the first mill that stood in front of him. But as he drove his lance-point into the sail, the wind whirled
45 it around with such force that it shivered the lance to pieces. It swept away with it horse and rider, and they were sent rolling over the plain, in sad condition indeed. Sancho hastened to his assistance as fast as his ass could go, and when he came up found him unable
50 to move, with such a shock had Rocinante fallen with him.

"God bless me!" said Sancho, "did I not tell your worship to mind what you were about, for they were only windmills? And no one could have made any
55 mistake about it but one who had mills of the same kind in his head."

CONTINUE ►

"Hush, friend Sancho" replied Don Quixote, "the fortunes of war more than any other are liable to frequent fluctuations; and moreover I think, and it is
60 the truth, that the same sage Friston*** who carried off my study and books, has turned these giants into mills in order to rob me of the glory of vanquishing them, such is the enmity he bears me; but in the end his wicked arts will avail but little against my good sword."

*   seven miles
**   a hundred-armed giant from Greek mythology
***   the magician (El Sabio Frestón), an imaginary character who Quixote imagines as the thief of his books and the enchanter of the windmills

---

1

Which choice best summarizes the passage?

A) An adventure goes awry when two young men decide to pretend they are in a great battle due to their longing for adventure.

B) A great warrior and his faithful steed single-handedly vanquish an army of giants in a mystical tale.

C) Two knights find themselves in an argument over what is really happening in their immediate surroundings.

D) A knight with an altered perception of reality engages in what he believes to be a battle of good versus evil.

2

The main purpose of the opening sentence of the passage is to

A) inform the reader of the true setting of the story for later plot purposes.

B) elaborate on the importance of technological advances during the Middle Ages.

C) describe the field on which a great battle is about to take place.

D) provide detailed imagery to enhance the mood of the following story.

3

During the course of the first six paragraphs (lines 1–24), the main character's focus shifts from

A) recollection of past victories to the prospect of imminent defeat.

B) reflection on the role of money in warfare to the role of God in battle.

C) generalization of how to wage a successful battle to specific rules of combat.

D) evaluation of an enemy before him to an argument with his faithful companion.

4

The phrase "sweep so evil a breed from off the face of the earth" at the end of the second paragraph mainly has which of the following effects?

A) It establishes the story as a horror story that will primarily focus on the evil in the world.

B) It informs the reader that Don Quixote is in fact a prophet who receives orders from God to go into battle.

C) It indicates the grandiose view that Don Quixote has of the battle he is about to undertake.

D) It demonstrates to the reader the dangers of taking religious fanaticism to the point of violence.

5

The passage indicates that Don Quixote would characterize his charge into battle as

A) ridiculous.

B) insane.

C) unexceptional.

D) brave.

CONTINUE

6

The passage indicates that Sancho views Don Quixote as a

A) boss who endangers his employees.

B) superior who needs looking after.

C) skillful leader to follow into battle.

D) pious man who requires help.

7

Which choice provides the best evidence for the answer to the previous question?

A) Lines 20–21 ("It is . . . adventures")

B) Lines 21–24 ("Those are . . . combat")

C) Lines 25–28 ("So saying . . . attack")

D) Lines 41–43 ("With lance . . . him")

8

The passage indicates that Don Quixote does not believe Sancho's description of the "giants" (line 17) because

A) Sancho's eyesight is not as good as Don Quixote's.

B) Don Quixote claims Sancho is not as brave as he is when it comes to battle.

C) Don Quixote knows more about Friston's schemes than Sancho does.

D) Don Quixote believes Sancho is too busy praying to pay attention.

9

Which choice provides the best evidence for the answer to the previous question?

A) Lines 13–15 ("Those you . . . long")

B) Lines 16–19 ("Look, your . . . go")

C) Lines 21–24 ("Those are . . . combat")

D) Lines 32–33 ("Fly not . . . you")

10

At the end of the passage, the reference to Friston mainly has the effect of

A) giving the reader greater insight into how Don Quixote perceives reality.

B) revealing the evil in the world that Don Quixote is fighting his battle against.

C) explaining to the reader the detailed history of how Don Quixote came to see things.

D) illustrating for the reader the evil that can come from personal misunderstandings.

CONTINUE ➡

Questions 11–20 are based on the following passage.

This passage is adapted from Susan B. Anthony's 1873 address to Post Office Districts of Monroe on women's suffrage.

Friends and Fellow-citizens: I stand before you tonight, under indictment for the alleged crime of having voted at the last Presidential election, without
Line having a lawful right to vote. It shall be my work this
5 evening to prove to you that in thus voting, I not only committed no crime, but, instead, simply exercised my *citizen's right,* guaranteed to me and all United States citizens by the National Constitution, beyond the power of any State to deny.

10 Our democratic-republican government is based on the idea of the natural right of every individual member thereof to a voice and a vote in making and executing the laws. We assert the province of government to be to secure the people in the
15 enjoyment of their unalienable rights. We throw to the winds the old dogma that governments can give rights. Before governments were organized, no one denies that each individual possessed the right to protect his own life, liberty and property. And when 100 or
20 1,000,000 people enter into a free government, they do not barter away their natural rights; they simply pledge themselves to protect each other in the enjoyment of them, through prescribed judicial and legislative tribunals. They agree to abandon the methods of brute
25 force in the adjustment of their differences, and adopt those of civilization.

Nor can you find a word in any of the grand documents left us by the fathers that assumes for government the power to create or to confer rights.
30 The Declaration of Independence, the United States Constitution, the constitutions of the several states and the organic laws of the territories, all alike propose to protect the people in the exercise of their God-given rights. Not one of them pretends to bestow rights.

35 "All men are created equal, and endowed by their Creator with certain unalienable rights. Among these are life, liberty and the pursuit of happiness. That to secure these, governments are instituted among men, deriving their just powers from the consent of the
40 governed."

Here is no shadow of government authority over rights, nor exclusion of any from their full and equal enjoyment. Here is pronounced the right of all men, and "consequently," as the Quaker preacher said, "of
45 all women," to a voice in the government. And here,

in this very first paragraph of the declaration, is the assertion of the natural right of all to the ballot; for, how can "the consent of the governed" be given, if the right to vote be denied. Again:

50 "That whenever any form of government becomes destructive of these ends, it is the right of the people to alter or abolish it, and to institute a new government, laying its foundations on such principles, and organizing its powers in such forms as to them shall
55 seem most likely to effect their safety and happiness."

Surely, the right of the whole people to vote is here clearly implied. For however destructive in their happiness this government might become, a disfranchised class could neither alter nor abolish it,
60 nor institute a new one, except by the old brute force method of insurrection and rebellion. One-half of the people of this nation today are utterly powerless to blot from the statute books an unjust law, or to write there a new and a just one. The women, dissatisfied as
65 they are with this form of government, that enforces taxation without representation,—that compels them to obey laws to which they have never given their consent,—that imprisons and hangs them without a trial by a jury of their peers, that robs them, in
70 marriage, of the custody of their own persons, wages and children,—are this half of the people left wholly at the mercy of the other half, in direct violation of the spirit and letter of the declarations of the framers of this government, every one of which was based
75 on the immutable principle of equal rights to all. By those declarations, kings, priests, popes, aristocrats, were all alike dethroned, and placed on a common level politically, with the lowliest born subject or serf. By them, too, men, as such, were deprived of their
80 divine right to rule, and placed on a political level with women. By the practice of those declarations all class and caste distinction will be abolished; and slave, serf, plebeian, wife, woman, all alike, bound from their subject position to the proud platform of equality.

CONTINUE

11

The central problem that Anthony explains in the passage is that women have been

A) prevented from voting, which is a violation of their human rights.

B) prevented from participating in Congress, which has led to the creation of unjust laws.

C) too kind and just, while men are cruel and unfair.

D) denied equal access to schools, which has prevented them from attending college.

12

Anthony uses the phrase "grand documents" (lines 27–28) mainly to refer to the

A) paper the Declaration of Independence was written on.

B) letters from a grand jury.

C) President's personal notes.

D) important legislation the country was founded on.

13

Anthony claims that which of the following was a purpose of the Declaration of Independence?

A) The protection of human rights

B) The bestowal of human rights

C) The creation of human rights

D) The prevention of violence

14

Which choice provides the best evidence for the answer to the previous question?

A) Lines 4–9 ("It shall . . . deny")

B) Lines 27–29 ("Nor can . . . rights")

C) Lines 30–34 ("The Declaration . . . rights")

D) Lines 50–55 ("That whenever . . . happiness")

15

As used in line 33, "the exercise" most nearly refers to

A) an activity.

B) a workout.

C) a use or application.

D) a process.

16

It can be reasonably inferred that "natural right" (line 47) was a term generally intended to

A) describe the right of men and women to vote.

B) criticize the right of women to run for office.

C) advocate for the right to bear arms.

D) introduce the origin of the fifth amendment.

17

As used in line 59, "class" most nearly means

A) subject.

B) group.

C) genus.

D) stylish.

18

Anthony contends that the situation she describes in the passage shows that the U.S. Government has

A) established laws denying women's suffrage.

B) denied participating in an unjust system.

C) considered women superior to men.

D) dethroned kings for political equality.

CONTINUE

19

Which choice provides the best evidence for the answer to the previous question?

A) Lines 1–4 ("Friends and . . . vote")

B) Lines 35–40 ("All men . . . governed")

C) Lines 50–55 ("That whenever . . . happiness")

D) Lines 75–78 ("By those . . . serf")

20

Lines 61–75 of the seventh paragraph are primarily concerned with establishing a contrast between

A) those with power and those without.

B) poor men and rich men.

C) social customs and religious customs.

D) laws and guidelines.

CONTINUE

Questions 21–30 are based on the following passage and supplementary material.

This passage is adapted from the U.S. Geological Survey, "Ground Water." © 1999 by the U.S. Department of the Interior.

Although there are sizable areas where ground water is being withdrawn at rates that cause water levels to decline persistently, as in parts of the dry
Line Southwest, this is not true throughout the country. For
5 the Nation as a whole, there is neither a pronounced downward nor upward trend. Water levels rise in wet periods and decline in dry periods. In areas where water is not pumped from aquifers in excess of the amount of recharge to the aquifer—particularly in the
10 humid central and eastern parts of the country—water levels average about the same as they did in the early part of the twentieth century.

A major responsibility of the U.S. Geological Survey is to assess the quantity and quality of the
15 Nation's water supplies. The Geological Survey, in cooperation with other Federal, State, and local agencies, maintains a nationwide hydrologic-data network, carries out a wide variety of water-resources investigations, and develops new methodologies for
20 studying water. The results of these investigations are indispensable tools for those involved in water-resources planning and management. Numerous inquiries concerning water resources and hydrology are directed to the Survey and to State water-resources
25 and geological agencies.

To locate ground water accurately and to determine the depth, quantity, and quality of the water, several techniques must be used, and a target area must be thoroughly tested and studied to identify hydrologic
30 and geologic features important to the planning and management of the resource. The landscape may offer clues to the hydrologist about the occurrence of shallow ground water. Conditions for large quantities of shallow ground water are more favorable under
35 valleys than under hills.

Rocks are the most valuable clues of all. As a first step in locating favorable conditions for ground-water development, the hydrologist prepares geologic maps and cross sections showing the distribution and
40 positions of the different kinds of rocks, both on the surface and underground. Some sedimentary rocks may extend many miles as aquifers of fairly uniform permeability. Other types of rocks may be cracked and broken and contain openings large enough to carry

45 water. Types and orientation of joints or other fractures may be clues to obtaining useful amounts of ground water. Some rocks may be so folded and displaced that it is difficult to trace them underground.

Next, a hydrologist obtains information on
50 the wells in the target area. The locations, depth to water, amount of water pumped, and types of rocks penetrated by wells also provide information on ground water. Wells are tested to determine the amount of water moving through the aquifer, the
55 volume of water that can enter a well, and the effects of pumping on water levels in the area. Chemical analysis of water from wells provides information on quality of water in the aquifer.

Evaluating the ground-water resource in developed
60 areas, prudent management of the resource, and protection of its quality are current ground-water problems. Thus, prediction of the capacity of the ground-water resource for long-term pumpage, the effects of that pumpage, and evaluation of water-
65 quality conditions are among the principal aims of modern-day hydrologic practice in achieving proper management of ground water.

Ground water, presently a major source of water, is also the Nation's principal reserve of fresh water. The
70 public will have to make decisions regarding water supply and waste disposal-decisions that will either affect the ground-water resource or be affected by it. These decisions will be more judicious and reliable if they are based upon knowledge of the principles of
75 ground-water occurrence.

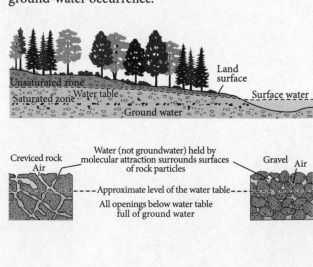

CONTINUE

21

According to the Geological Survey, the capability to assess the nation's water supplies is significant primarily because

A) the study of such water supplies will provide critical information to plan future infrastructure.

B) the study of water supplies will allow agencies to plan and manage all water resources.

C) it will enable researchers to assess the quantity and quality of nationwide hydrologic data.

D) it will enable scientists to verify the depth and location of ground water.

22

Which choice provides the best evidence for the answer to the previous question?

A) Lines 6–7 ("Water levels . . . periods")

B) Lines 20–22 ("The results . . . management")

C) Lines 47–48 ("Some rocks . . . underground")

D) Lines 56–58 ("Chemical analysis . . . aquifer")

23

The third paragraph serves mainly to

A) propose a new method and detail its efficacy.

B) explain different methods for finding a natural resource.

C) address a need for making a discovery.

D) describe how a hydrologic instrument is implemented.

24

As used in line 32, "occurrence" most nearly means

A) plan.

B) happening.

C) event.

D) presence.

25

As used in line 52, "penetrated" is closest in meaning to

A) drained.

B) inserted.

C) excavated.

D) breached.

26

Based on information in the passage, it can reasonably be inferred that ground water occurrence

A) is produced only by the flow of rain water through permeable rock in a valley.

B) could be located by proximity to landscape features such as hills and existing wells.

C) might be relatively constant across large landscapes but is affected by many seasonal variables.

D) achieves roughly the same depth regardless of the occurrence and persistence of surface water.

27

Which choice provides the best evidence for the answer to the previous question?

A) Lines 6–12 ("Water levels . . . century")

B) Lines 26–31 ("To locate . . . resource")

C) Lines 31–35 ("The landscape . . . hills")

D) Lines 36–41 ("As a . . . underground")

28

In the figure, which hydrologic or geologic layer holds only moisture with molecular attraction?

A) Unsaturated zone

B) Surface water

C) Creviced rock

D) Water table

CONTINUE

29

Which concept is supported by the passage and by the information in the figure?

A) Rock orientation can affect mapping the occurrence of ground water.

B) Rock orientation changes based on the type and orientation of the rock.

C) Rock orientation is determined by the folds and crevices in a rock.

D) Rock orientation is fairly uniform for some sedimentary rocks.

30

How does the figure support the author's point that rock orientation affects aquifer characteristics?

A) It presents numerous types of rocks folding and turning to block or allow ground water to pass through.

B) It depicts the variation in rock orientation on ground water supplies in a certain cross section.

C) It demonstrates how rock orientation is the best ground water indicator out of many other landscape features.

D) It shows that rock orientation allows ground water to extend as aquifers for miles.

CONTINUE

Questions 31–41 are based on the following passage and supplementary material.

This passage is adapted from Chester Lloyd Jones, "Bananas and Diplomacy." © 1913 by *The North American Review*.

To those in world-trade, names of countries and regions suggest their products. It has always been so. The East Indies four hundred years ago meant spice; two hundred years ago China meant silks and tea;
5　Canada meant fur. The Caribbean to Queen Elizabeth meant gold—it was the route of the treasure ships of Spain—to Washington it meant sugar and molasses, and to our children it will mean bananas.

The Panama Canal has so occupied our attention
10　for the last decade that we have overlooked a significant economic change taking place independently of the forces which promise so radically to change the transportation routes of world commerce. Economists tell us that the trend of Caribbean diplomacy will be
15　determined by the banana crop. At the beginning of the twentieth century, there are food products that will exercise an influence upon international politics unconnected with the Panama Canal and of an importance which can be measured only in prophesy.
20　The market for bananas in the United States was developed largely through the efforts of one man. Forty years ago, Captain L. D. Baker was engaged in trade between the Orinoco River and Boston. On one trip he called at Port Morant, Jamaica, for a cargo of
25　bamboo for paper-making and carried back a few bunches of bananas, then a curiosity in the New England markets. The venture proved profitable and the captain thereafter made several trips a year to Port Antonio, Jamaica, to take cargoes of bananas to
30　Boston.

How important the trade has become is illustrated by the figures of exports. In 1911 there were sent from Caribbean countries in the export trade 52,936,963 bunches, which, on the average of 140 bananas to
35　the bunch, represents a total of over 7,400,000,000 bananas. In 1912 the continental United States alone consumed 44,520,539 bunches, or over sixty bananas for each man, woman, and child. Two facts appear from the following figures: with the exception of the
40　Canary Islands, all the countries producing large quantities of bananas for export border the Caribbean, and the United States consumes 85 percent of all bananas exported—five times as much as all the rest of the world.

Banana Supply of the United States 1912

Jamaica	15,467,918
Honduras	7,151,178
Costa Rica	7,053,664
Panama	4,581,500
Cuba	2,478,581
Nicaragua	2,270,100
Guatemala	2,017,650
Colombia	1,542,988
Mexico	817,006
British Honduras	557,160
Dominican Republic	304,000
Dutch Guiana	261,548
Others	17,246
Total	44,520,539

The world supply in 1911 as shown by the same records was:

Country of Origin	Quantity (Bunches)
Dominican Republic	404,000
Mexico (Frontera Province)	750,000
Honduras	6,500,000
Costa Rica	9,309,586
Jamaica	16,497,385
Colombia	4,901,894
Panama	4,261,500
Canary Islands	2,648,378
Cuba	2,500,000
Nicaragua	2,225,000
Guatemala	1,755,704
British Honduras	525,000
Dutch Guiana	387,516
Others	250,000
Total	52,915,963

45　The business, especially when the fruit must be sent long distances, demands organization for collecting fruit from small planters and large capital for steamers with refrigerating appliances. In fact, reliance on private planters has proven unsatisfactory and the
50　big banana-marketing companies now own extensive plantations throughout the West Indies and on the mainland.

CONTINUE ▶

The increased production of the banana in its natural state and the diversification of its uses promise
55 to introduce a new and hitherto neglected factor in our food supply. If present development continues, it will raise the Caribbean region from its dependence on foreign markets for food to one of the regions from which an important part of the world's food-
60 supply will be drawn. The wheat fields of the Dakotas and Manitoba will meet as one of their competitors in feeding the world the banana plantations of the American Mediterranean.

These figures show that the world is just awakening
65 to the value of the banana as food. If the present development continues, the acreage devoted to banana-growing must rapidly increase. Improved refrigeration and quick steam service will continue to widen the area in which the product can be marketed.
70 The development of the banana-flour industry also promises to open a market for the product of areas too distant to profit by the demand of fresh fruit, just as the perfection of the manufacture of copra, the dried meat of the coconut, has opened up a new industry reaching
75 to the farthest islands of the Pacific.

Great as the blessings of the Panama Canal will be to the trade of the world and to that of the United States in particular, we must not let the new markets which it will develop beyond the Isthmus make us
80 forget that region so rich in possibilities which lies this side of the continental divide and so much nearer our own markets. Friendship with our near neighbors is no less important than the good will of people over wide seas. One of the most important, and from our past
85 experience let us remember, one of the most delicate problems with which our men of state have to deal is the diplomacy of the Caribbean.

31

The main purpose of the passage is to

A) examine the impact of an export on the global economy.

B) posit that bananas will become the new gold standard.

C) consider a dilemma brought about by global economics.

D) argue that international politics bars the Caribbean from gaining financial independence.

32

The main purpose of the second paragraph (lines 9-19) is to

A) illustrate how exports will skyrocket with the completion of the Panama Canal.

B) introduce an idea not widely associated with a familiar region.

C) prove that bananas will dominate the economy of the twentieth century.

D) provide support that economists correctly prophesy that the Panama Canal will radically change world commerce.

33

As used in line 17, "exercise" most nearly means

A) operate.

B) exert.

C) train.

D) maneuver.

34

Which choice best supports the author's claim that bananas are likely to play a significant role in the global economy?

A) Lines 1–5 ("To those . . . fur")

B) Lines 13–15 ("Economists tell . . . crop")

C) Lines 42–44 ("United States . . . world")

D) Lines 60–63 ("The wheat . . . Mediterranean")

35

As used in line 82, "friendship" most nearly means

A) affection.

B) fondness.

C) collusion.

D) cooperation.

CONTINUE

36

The main idea of the final paragraph (lines 76–87) is that

A) friendship is important and often overlooked in the global economy.

B) the Panama Canal has proven to be a great blessing in international trade.

C) new markets will emerge beyond the Isthmus, calling for change in the global economy.

D) the Caribbean may prove to be an important component of the global economy in coming decades.

37

In the passage, the author anticipates which of the following potential difficulties for the banana industry?

A) Transporting bananas large distances requires certain technology to be successful.

B) Steamers are the best way to transport large quantities of bananas.

C) The banana flour is produced in areas too distant to be reached.

D) The banana industry will be surpassed by copra exports.

38

Which choice provides the best evidence for the previous question?

A) Lines 15–19 ("At the . . . prophesy")

B) Lines 45–48 ("The business . . . appliances")

C) Lines 48-52 ("In fact . . . mainland")

D) Lines 70–75 ("The development . . . Pacific")

39

Data in the tables provide most direct support for which idea in the passage?

A) Countries other than the United States are beginning to learn about bananas as food.

B) The increased production of the banana is the beginning of an economic revolution in the Caribbean.

C) Acreage toward banana-growing must increase to accommodate increased production.

D) The export numbers in the tables show an upward trend in banana consumption.

40

Data in the tables indicate that the greatest difference between U. S. banana supply exports in 1912 and world banana supply in 1911 is from which country?

A) Honduras

B) Panama

C) Jamaica

D) Nicaragua

41

Data in the table of the world supply in 1911 most strongly support which of the following statements?

A) Panama and Columbia combined supplied more bananas than did Jamaica in 1911.

B) The profits earned from bananas did not fluctuate.

C) Dutch Guiana produced the fewest bananas in 1911.

D) Colombia exported more bananas in 1911 than did Cuba.

CONTINUE

Questions 42–52 are based on the following passages.

Passage 1 is adapted from Jonah Lehrer, "The Neuroscience of Music." © 2011 by *Wired*. Passage 2 is adapted from Jeanette Bicknell, "Musical Thrills and Chills." © 2011 by *Psychology Today*.

Passage 1

Why does music make us feel? On the one hand, music is a purely abstract art form, devoid of language or explicit ideas. And yet, even though music says

Line little, it still manages to tickle some universal nerves.
5 When listening to our favorite songs, our body betrays all the symptoms of emotional arousal. The pupils in our eyes dilate, our pulse and blood pressure rise, the electrical conductance of our skin is lowered, and the cerebellum, a brain region associated with bodily
10 movement, becomes strangely active. Blood is even re-directed to the muscles in our legs. (Some speculate that this is why we begin tapping our feet.) In other words, sound stirs us at our biological roots.

We can now begin to understand where these
15 feelings come from, why a mass of vibrating air hurtling through space can trigger such intense states of excitement. A new paper by a team of Montreal researchers marks an important step in revealing the precise underpinnings of "the potent pleasurable
20 stimulus" that is music. The scientists asked ten individuals who experience chills to instrumental music to bring in their playlist of favorite songs – virtually every genre was represented, from techno to tango – and played them the music while their brain
25 activity was monitored.

Because the scientists were combining methodologies (PET and fMRI) they were able to obtain an impressively precise portrait of music in the brain. The first thing they discovered is that music
30 triggers the release of dopamine in both the dorsal and ventral striatum. This isn't particularly surprising: these regions have long been associated with the response to pleasurable stimuli.

The more interesting finding emerged from a
35 close study of the timing of this response, as the scientists looked to see what was happening in the seconds *before* the subjects got the chills. In essence, the scientists found that our favorite moments in the music were preceded by a prolonged increase of
40 activity in the caudate. They call this the "anticipatory phase" and argue that the purpose of this activity is

to help us predict the arrival of our favorite part. This subregion of the striatum has been typically implicated in learning of stimulus-response associations and
45 in mediating the reinforcing qualities of rewarding stimuli such as food. In other words, the abstract pitches have become a primal reward cue, the cultural equivalent of a bell that makes us drool.

Passage 2

People who are strongly affected by music
50 sometimes claim that it gives them chills down their spine and makes their hair stand on end. (The technical term is "piloerection".) When we are affected in this way by music, art, or by the grandeur of nature, what exactly is going on? Can some kind of
55 evolutionary explanation help us make sense of the experience?

One of the most intriguing explanations for music's "chill" effect has been offered by neuroscientist Jaak Panksepp. Panksepp found that chills and piloerection
60 were most likely to be associated with sad music, and with the bleak simplicity of a solo soprano voice or instrument emerging from a relatively richer musical background. A great example occurs in Whitney Houston's version of Dolly Parton's song "I Will
65 Always Love You," when the words of the title are repeated at the beginning of the third rendition of the chorus. Panksepp offers an evolutionary explanation for the origin of the chill phenomenon, whether the music involved is a popular song, operatic aria, or
70 instrumental work. He argues that chills may emerge from brain dynamics associated with the perception of social loss, specifically with separation calls. Separation calls are cries by young animals that inform parents of the whereabouts of offspring that have become
75 lost. The "coldness" of chills may provide increased motivation for social reunion in the parents.

Recent experimental work by Mathias Benedek and Christian Kaernbach offers some support for Panksepp's hypothesis. Subjects listened, on
80 headphones, to four short musical selections and four short audio excerpts from film soundtracks. Researchers monitored their physical responses, including skin conductivity, and cardiovascular and respiratory measures, and set up a camera to record
85 piloerection. They found that some of the listeners'

CONTINUE

responses, specifically short-term increases in heart-rate and in respiration depth, were consistent with the physiological reactions usually associated with non-crying sadness. While the existence of a connection

90 between pilocrection and sadness lends some support to Panksepp's ideas, researchers did not find much evidence for any connection between piloerection and a sense of coldness.

42

The author of Passage 1 indicates which of the following about the caudate?

A) It emerges from a close study of response times.

B) It is involved in learning associations.

C) It causes the chill experience.

D) It helps reinforce qualities of food.

43

Which choice provides the best evidence for the answer to the previous question?

A) Lines 6–10 ("The pupils . . . active")

B) Lines 29–31 ("The first . . . striatum")

C) Lines 37–40 ("In essence . . . caudate")

D) Lines 42–46 ("This subregion . . . food")

44

The author of Passage 1 indicates that music

A) may preclude feeling states.

B) often derives from feeling states.

C) can evoke feeling states.

D) could contain ideas of feelings.

45

As used in line 5, "betrays" most nearly means

A) demonstrates.

B) turns against.

C) undermines.

D) misleads.

46

The author of Passage 2 refers to "coldness" (line 75) primarily to

A) outline the chill effect of music.

B) illustrate an evolutionary explanation.

C) associate it with sadness.

D) trace the origin of piloerection.

47

According to the author of Passage 2, what do Panksepp and Benedek and Kaernbach have in common?

A) They undertook experiments to study the chill effect.

B) They argue for an evolutionary explanation of the chill effect.

C) They draw a connection between piloerection and sadness.

D) They draw a connection between piloerection and happiness.

48

The reference to the song "I Will Always Love You" has primarily which effect?

A) It exemplifies when piloerection is likely to occur.

B) It serves to console young when they are separated from their parents.

C) It provides support for Benedek's hypothesis.

D) It shows an example of bleak repetition.

CONTINUE ▶

49

The main purpose of both passages is to

A) highlight recent methods of learning music through neuroscience.

B) show the superiority of neuroscience over merely psychological analysis of responses to music.

C) explain how music can evoke feelings in scientists.

D) show the relevance of neuroscience to understanding responses to music.

50

Which choice best describes the relationship between the two passages?

A) Passage 1 examines an evolutionary explanation of piloerection, while Passage 2 considers the findings of a study of the chill response.

B) Passage 1 considers positive emotional responses to music, while Passage 2 considers the relevance of negative emotions to musical responses.

C) Passage 1 reviews recent research, while Passage 2 reviews more established theories.

D) Passage 1 relies on the methods of neuroscience, while Passage 2 considers only theoretical work.

51

On which of the following points would the authors of both passages most likely agree?

A) Although music is generally abstract, it can affect us in quite concrete ways.

B) The use of tests such as PET and fMRI is a superior way of obtaining a precise understanding of the role of music in the brain.

C) The neuroscience of emotion and the study of musical response can both help illuminate phenomena such as the chill response.

D) The chill effect of music can be seen along with the expression of both positive and negative emotions.

52

Which choice provides the best evidence that the author of Passage 1 would agree to some extent with the argument attributed to Panksepp in lines 70-72, Passage 2?

A) Lines 1–3 ("On the . . . ideas")

B) Lines 12–13 ("In other . . . roots")

C) Lines 29–31 ("The first . . . striatum")

D) Lines 46–47 ("In other . . . cue")

STOP

If you finish before time is called, you may check your work on this section only.
Do not turn to any other section in the test.

No Test Material On This Page

Writing and Language Test

35 MINUTES, 44 QUESTIONS

Turn to Section 2 of your answer sheet to answer the questions in this section.

DIRECTIONS

Each passage below is accompanied by a number of questions. For some questions, you will consider how the passage might be revised to improve the expression of ideas. For other questions, you will consider how the passage might be edited to correct errors in sentence structure, usage, or punctuation. A passage or a question may be accompanied by one or more graphics (such as a table or graph) that you will consider as you make revising and editing decisions.

Some questions will direct you to an underlined portion of a passage. Other questions will direct you to a location in a passage or ask you to think about the passage as a whole.

After reading each passage, choose the answer to each question that most effectively improves the quality of writing in the passage or that makes the passage conform to the conventions of standard written English. Many questions include a "NO CHANGE" option. Choose that option if you think the best choice is to leave the relevant portion of the passage as it is.

Questions 1–11 are based on the following passage.

Streaming Something Beyond Hard Work

There is no question that the American workforce has changed, regardless of whether one believes it has changed for better or worse. In the 1940s, the United States led the world in most economic categories, and its businesses were some of the most praised in the world. By the 1980s, however, the dominance of the United States had been challenged by industries the world over, and the economy was measured in terms of global effects rather than national ones.

This **1** growing and enlarging competition has unfortunately led to a loosening of companies' responsibilities toward their employees. Retirement

1
A) NO CHANGE
B) increased competition
C) increased competing among countries
D) larger spirit of competitiveness for all

CONTINUE

pensions are largely a thing of the past. **2** Moreover, whereas someone born in the 1940s might have expected to spend his or her entire career with a single company. Many of whom now swap through four or five "careers" throughout a single working life.

This trend has intensified recently, particularly in **3** Silicon Valley startups. One of the major success

Which choice most effectively combines the underlined sentences?

A) Moreover, whereas someone born in the 1940s might have expected to spend his or her entire career with a single company; many workers now swap through four or five "careers" throughout a single working life over the course of it.

B) Swapping jobs is, moreover for instance, a thing that new workers do now, whereas those in the 1940s would have been more likely to work for a single company for their entire careers.

C) Moreover, whereas someone born in the 1940s might have expected to spend his or her entire career with a single company; many workers now swap through four or five "careers" throughout a single working life.

D) Moreover, whereas someone born in the 1940s might have expected to spend his or her entire career with a single company, now the norm has workers swapping through four or five "careers" throughout a single working life.

At this point, the author is considering adding the following information.

> the fast-paced, forward-thinking, occasionally ruthless world of

Should the writer make the addition here?

A) Yes, because it shows the author's ability in finding apt adjectives.

B) Yes, because it creates a richer description of the company discussed in the essay.

C) No, because it lengthens the sentence unnecessarily with information that is given elsewhere.

D) No, because it is not the kind of thing that would be acceptable to say in the workplace.

CONTINUE

stories from among these many-sided companies **4** that is Netflix, the streaming and DVD-mailing giant, who may have been singlehandedly responsible for ending the lifespans of both the video store and the DVD in only a few short years. Netflix's compulsively innovative methods have changed the way that those living in the United States and in many other parts of the globe interact with visual media, especially in movie theaters, on home entertainment systems, and on **5** computers.

6 For all this, Netflix has become famous (or infamous) for changing its employees' relationship to the workplace. Netflix's staff is relatively lean, and employees are incredibly well treated. Their salaries are higher than those of other Silicon Valley businesses, and the employees are given *unlimited* (yes, you read that correctly) vacation time. Furthermore, as Netflix continues to push beyond the traditional boundaries of film and TV, the company affords its employees the opportunity to be on the cutting edge of change.

4

A) NO CHANGE
B) that are
C) is
D) are

5

A) NO CHANGE
B) machines used for computing.
C) PCs and Macs with the capacity to stream.
D) intelligent machines.

6

A) NO CHANGE
B) Irregardless,
C) Thus,
D) Furthermore,

CONTINUE

All of Netflix's success comes at a price, however. **7** Just putting seriously all of it right out there, employees at Netflix are warned not to think of the job as one that they will keep "for life." Netflix is not concerned with traditional ideas of "hard work:" **8** to come to work on time, staying late, and showing loyalty to the company. Instead, Netflix is concerned only with *results*. Just ask the computer programmers who started Netflix's streaming service and then were let go when the service became so successful that Netflix had to use Amazon.com's servers instead. While these employees had done about as good a job as one could do, **9** yet they were fired the moment they were no longer needed.

Indeed, as companies continue to tighten their belts and their responsibility to be profitable remains, they will demand more of their employees and withdraw some of the comfortable **10** premising that the employees of earlier eras relied on. **11** This may be the workplace of the future, and we can only hope that employees will adapt as well as they have to past changes.

7

Which choice most effectively sets up the idea given in the second part of this sentence?

A) NO CHANGE

B) Turned off by the company's rudeness,

C) Having no idea what they're walking into,

D) From the first day on the job,

8

A) NO CHANGE

B) coming

C) come

D) workers coming

9

A) NO CHANGE

B) and

C) because

D) DELETE the underlined portion.

10

A) NO CHANGE

B) premise

C) promises

D) promising

11

Which statement most clearly ends the passage with a restatement of the writer's primary claim?

A) NO CHANGE

B) This is the end of employment as we know it, and we should all head for the hills.

C) You can try to get a job at Netflix, but they're not really hiring all that often.

D) If you've ever been fired or laid off from a job, you know how difficult it can be.

CONTINUE

Questions 12–22 are based on the following passage.

Television—Not So Bad After All?

— 1 —

A mere ten years ago, surveys recorded data that showed the average American viewer to watch four hours of television a day. Television was a central part of the American household. Now that the Internet has come to supplant television's central role in American culture (as people spend more time watching six-second videos on Vine, reading short posts on Facebook and Twitter, and **12** they send quirky photos and videos on Snapchat), the complaints that had always been made about television can seem rather quaint. Those who critiqued television as a dangerous influence on society have since changed to new and, as they would see it, worse targets on the **13** web and are not much interested in television anymore.

— 2 —

Television certainly had its harmful effects on those who watched it for that frankly inconceivable four hours a day. There could be no "couch potatoes" without TVs, and the scourge of reality TV might never have been thrust upon the American viewing public. **14** As aforementioned, shining light in your eyes for many hours at a time can wreak havoc on one of **15** your most important senses: vision.

— 3 —

However, television accomplished some incredible things as well. Drawing on the networks that **16** radio creates throughout the entire country, television provided something truly national for the first time. During the first American performance of The Beatles on *The Ed Sullivan Show*, there was not a single crime committed in the

12
Which choice most closely matches the stylistic pattern established earlier in the sentence?
A) NO CHANGE
B) the sending of quirky photos and videos features prominently on Snapchat),
C) sending quirky photos and videos on Snapchat),
D) they send quirky photos on Snapchat and videos),

13
A) NO CHANGE
B) web,
C) web, they
D) web, the images on the Internet

14
A) NO CHANGE
B) However,
C) That said,
D) Moreover,

15
A) NO CHANGE
B) you're most important senses,
C) you're most important senses;
D) your most important senses;

16
A) NO CHANGE
B) radio created
C) radios' create
D) radio's creation

CONTINUE

United States. **17** Everyone, literally everyone, was watching TV.

— 4 —

A large component of this "big world" was the presence of non-white faces. **18** Especially African Americans, non-white people, who parroted and parodied the patterns of black speech, were represented on the radio by white actors. While African Americans were the most frequently targeted group, Asian Americans and those of all ethnicities were similarly lampooned in the national media. The popularity of television actually ended up forcing these media into a kind of progressivism: the Chinese-American character on *Have Gun Will Travel* **19** and some of the other shows set in the old West would no longer work as racial masquerades. As a result, some of the earliest leading roles for non-white actors and actresses came on television, earlier than in film and theater in many cases.

At this point, the writer is considering adding the following sentence.

> The Beatles had many hits, including "She Loves You" and "I Wanna Hold Your Hand," that continue to influence the course of rock and roll to the present day.

Should the writer make this addition here?

A) Yes, because it helps to explain why the music of The Beatles can help to prevent crime.

B) Yes, because it gives the reader additional context that helps to explain the importance of television.

C) No, because it suggests that television's only function was to broadcast musical performances.

D) No, because it adds a detail that is irrelevant to the paragraph's main focus.

18

A) NO CHANGE

B) For many years, non-white people, especially African Americans, were represented on the radio by white actors, who parroted and parodied the patterns of black speech.

C) African Americans were non-white people especially who for many years parroted by white actors and parodied in speech patterns.

D) White actors parroted especially African Americans from non-white actors in their patterns of black speech, which were parodied for many years.

19

Which choice gives a second supporting example that is most similar to the example already in the sentence?

A) NO CHANGE

B) who was played by Ben Wright on the radio show

C) and even some of the shows that weren't so popular on radio

D) or the African-American character on *The Beulah Show*

CONTINUE →

— 5 —

Television may not play the central role in American culture that it once did, but many of the things that it achieved, both good and bad, remain in the culture today.

— 6 —

This national reach could occasionally lead to conformity and sensationalism, but it also showed **20** many in the American public, just how diverse the American scene had become. People still had to have a certain amount of wealth to travel physically outside of their **21** hometowns. They were usually filled with citizens who had the same basic backgrounds and attitudes. Television could show them just how big the world outside was.

Question 22 asks about the previous passage as a whole.

20

A) NO CHANGE

B) many, in the American public

C) many in the American public

D) many, in the American public,

21

Which choice most effectively combines the sentences at the underlined portion?

A) hometowns: they

B) hometowns, and theirs

C) hometowns with what

D) hometowns, which

Think about the previous passage as a whole as you answer question 22.

22

To make the passage most logical, paragraph 6 should be placed

A) where it is now.

B) before paragraph 2.

C) before paragraph 3.

D) before paragraph 4.

CONTINUE

Questions 23–33 are based on the following passage and supplementary material.

The Noise Is Not for the Birds

Even if you love the vibrant life of the city, you probably still love to come home to a nice, quiet spot. Even the busiest lives need some calm once in a while for some of life's basic, private tasks. In fact, this doesn't only describe human lives. While untouched nature is usually prized for the way it *looks*— 23 there greenery, scurrying animals, and placidity—nature is actually just as much characterized by the way it *sounds*.

24 Thus, when we build highways through thriving natural habitats, we don't just change the way they look. 25 You've certainly been somewhere remote enough that there aren't any cars around, or you've been woken up some morning by the sound of a car horn or a revving engine. Although the sound of the car is the sound of our day-to-day life, that does not change the fact that car traffic is remarkably loud.

23

A) NO CHANGE
B) their
C) it's
D) its

24

A) NO CHANGE
B) Thence,
C) Whereas,
D) This being so,

25

At this point, the writer is considering adding the following sentence.

> We also change the way they sound.

Should the writer make this addition here?

A) Yes, because it reminds the reader of the beauty of birds' songs.
B) Yes, because it completes the idea started in the previous sentence.
C) No, because it shifts the emphasis of the paragraph to sound rather than sight.
D) No, because it disagrees with the thesis developed in the paragraph as a whole.

CONTINUE →

Furthermore, while we have become relatively [26] weakened to the sounds of cars on our "quiet" residential streets, not all animals have. A recent study checked the effect of [27] raising the highway volume on local bird populations. This might seem like an easy study with all the new highway construction going on in the United States all the time, but the researchers [28] at the Intermountain Bird Observatory in Idaho and wanted to study the effects without becoming part of the problem. Instead of building new roads, the researchers opted to produce the *sound* of roads, creating a fake, [29] or, a "phantom," road with 15 pairs of speakers playing the sounds of traffic noise.

A) NO CHANGE

B) inured

C) hip

D) keen

A) NO CHANGE

B) the noise being more on highways

C) increased highway noise

D) highways exhibiting more noise levels

A) NO CHANGE

B) who work at the Intermountain Bird Observatory in Idaho, where they wanted to

C) at the Intermountain Bird Observatory in Idaho wanted to

D) at the Intermountain Bird Observatory in Idaho, they wanted to

A) NO CHANGE

B) or a "phantom," road

C) or a "phantom"; road

D) or a "phantom" road,

CONTINUE

[1] The results were telling. [2] According to the study, the mere *sounds* of 30 traffic, "reduced avian populations by a third and cut species diversity by a significant amount." [3] Birds, it seems, need to spend as much time as possible with their heads down—hunting and pecking, feeding their young, and fattening up for their various migrations. [4] This is bad news for avian life in the deep South, where the Interstate Highway Commission 31 has announced plans to eradicate avian and other wildlife populations between Natchez, Augusta, Savannah, and Knoxville. 32

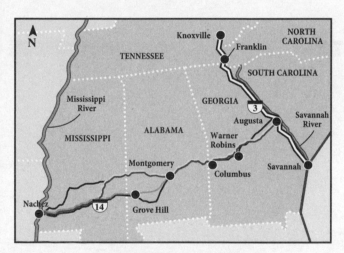

Proposed Interstate Routes

While this study will, the scientists hope, discourage new road construction within the national parks and other forested areas, it can also have effects where the roads are already present. With lower speed limits and rubberized asphalt, 33 the roads won't be quite so noisy, and the native fauna might feel just a little bit freer to roam.

30

A) NO CHANGE

B) traffic reduced

C) traffic, reduced

D) traffic—reduced

31

Which choice offers an accurate interpretation of the data in the figure?

A) NO CHANGE

B) will push avian populations northeast into North Carolina and northwest into western Tennessee.

C) has planned an east-west route from Savannah to Knoxville and a north-south route from Augusta to Natchez.

D) has planned a north-south route from Savannah to Knoxville and an east-west route from Augusta to Natchez.

32

Where is the most logical place in the paragraph to add the following sentence?

When there is so much distraction from outside noise, however, birds are more likely to be looking up than down, casting a cautious eye on their potentially perilous surroundings.

A) After sentence 1

B) After sentence 2

C) After sentence 3

D) After sentence 4

33

A) NO CHANGE

B) there won't be so much noise,

C) they won't be so noisy,

D) there won't be all the noisy roads,

CONTINUE

Questions 34–44 are based on the following passage.

A "Failed" Search for the American Southwest

Sometimes it really *is* about the journey rather than the destination. Francisco Vázquez de Coronado, an early Spanish explorer and **34** conquistador; died believing that he had failed in his mission, but his pursuit of that mission has been just as significant to history as it would have been had he achieved his goal. Coronado's experience is an excellent window into the difficulty of assessing the Spanish explorers, **35** but also we can see the blurring of the line between hero and villain. In much the same way that Columbus is still praised as being the "discoverer" of the United States but reviled for the atrocities he **36** eviscerated against the native populations, Coronado presents a historical challenge.

A) NO CHANGE
B) conquistador
C) conquistador,
D) conquistador—

A) NO CHANGE
B) wherein
C) just as
D) so too

A) NO CHANGE
B) did
C) committed
D) manifested

CONTINUE

Coronado's aims were **37** fewer than noble. He didn't particularly care about making history. He was much more interested in making something **38** else, altogether: money. Coronado, **39** who grew up in a noble family in Spain, came to New Spain (present-day Mexico) when he was 25 years old. Within four years of his arrival, Coronado had become intoxicated by the circulating rumors of the Seven Cities of Gold. **40** They merely lay in wait for someone to claim the bounty, these cities, or so the rumor had it, were richer than any place in the world.

Of course, there were no such places, neither in Cíbola, a city just west of modern-day Albuquerque, nor in Quivira, a town in central Kansas. Coronado's disappointment was absolutely unforgiving and vicious: many fellow travelers died on these expeditions, and **41** many Zuni families in the region were slaughtered as a result of Coronado's greed.

37

A) NO CHANGE
B) less, then
C) less then
D) less than

38

A) NO CHANGE
B) else:
C) else, nevertheless:
D) else, and it was:

39

A) NO CHANGE
B) he grew
C) growing
D) whom grows

40

A) NO CHANGE
B) Merely lying
C) They merely lie
D) While laying merely

41

Which choice provides information that best supports the claim made by this sentence?

A) NO CHANGE
B) the journeys were long and arduous.
C) medical care was very limited at the time.
D) no one stopped to see the sites.

CONTINUE

[1] However, Coronado's journey was not entirely without merit. [2] That's a lot of territory to cover in the middle of the sixteenth century! [3] Notice how far we have traveled in this short essay alone. [4] We started in Spain, then went to Mexico, then to New Mexico, then to Kansas [42] after that. [5] Thus, while Coronado's tactics were vicious and his goals less than noble, he was nonetheless one of the first to provide reliable information on the terrains of vast stretches of the American West. [6] His expedition provided the first European sightings of the Grand Canyon, the Colorado River, and many of the lands along his route. [43]

Though Coronado's expedition may have been fraught with unpleasantness and we may balk at the idea of calling his sightings "discoveries," Coronado's contributions to the course of American history were nonetheless significant. His influence is all around us. [44] While Coronado may not have achieved his stated goal, we have his "failure" to thank for a large swath of the contemporary United States.

42

A) NO CHANGE

B) en route.

C) while we were there.

D) DELETE the underlined portion, and end the sentence with a period.

43

To make this paragraph most logical, sentence 2 should be placed

A) where it is now.

B) before sentence 3.

C) before sentence 4.

D) before sentence 5.

44

At this point, the writer is considering adding the following sentence.

A small island off the coast of San Diego bears his name, as does a high school halfway across the country in Lubbock, Texas.

Should the writer make this addition here?

A) Yes, because it names some of the places of which Coronado was most fond.

B) Yes, because it cites some of the contemporary places that were influenced by Coronado.

C) No, because it disagrees with the paragraph's central claims regarding Coronado's cruelty.

D) No, because it introduces a tangent into the American Southwest that is not further elaborated.

STOP

If you finish before time is called, you may check your work on this section only.
Do not turn to any other section in the test.

No Test Material On This Page

Math Test – No Calculator

25 MINUTES, 20 QUESTIONS

Turn to Section 3 of your answer sheet to answer the questions in this section.

DIRECTIONS

For questions **1-15**, solve each problem, choose the best answer from the choices provided, and fill in the corresponding circle on your answer sheet. For questions **16-20**, solve the problem and enter your answer in the grid on the answer sheet. Please refer to the directions before question 16 on how to enter your answers in the grid. You may use any available space in your test booklet for scratch work.

NOTES

1. The use of a calculator **is not permitted**.
2. All variables and expressions used represent real numbers unless otherwise indicated.
3. Figures provided in this test are drawn to scale unless otherwise indicated.
4. All figures lie in a plane unless otherwise indicated.
5. Unless otherwise indicated, the domain of a given function *f* is the set of all real numbers *x* for which *f(x)* is a real number.

REFERENCE

$A = \pi r^2$
$C = 2\pi r$

$A = \ell w$

$A = \frac{1}{2} bh$

$c^2 = a^2 + b^2$

$2x$ 60° x
30°
$x\sqrt{3}$

s 45° $s\sqrt{2}$
45°
s

Special Right Triangles

$V = \ell wh$

$V = \pi r^2 h$

$V = \frac{4}{3}\pi r^3$

$V = \frac{1}{3}\pi r^2 h$

$V = \frac{1}{3}\ell wh$

The number of degrees of arc in a circle is 360.
The number of radians of arc in a circle is 2π.
The sum of the measures in degrees of the angles of a triangle is 180.

CONTINUE

1

The cost C, in dollars, that a catering company charges to cater a wedding is given by the function $C = 20wt + 300$, where w represents the number of workers catering the wedding and t represents the total time, in hours, it will take to cater the wedding using w workers. Which of the following is the best explanation of the number 20 in the function?

A) A minimum of 20 workers will cater the wedding.

B) The cost of every wedding will increase by $20 per hour.

C) The catering company charges $20 per hour for each worker.

D) There will be 20 guests at the wedding.

2

If $12x + 4 = 20$, what is the value of $6x + 5$?

A) 4

B) 6

C) 10

D) 13

3

$$5x - 4y = 36$$
$$-x - y = 0$$

Which of the ordered pairs (x, y) below is a solution to the system of equations shown above?

A) $(-5, 4)$

B) $(-4, 4)$

C) $(4, -4)$

D) $(5, -4)$

4

In the equation $y - \sqrt{4x^2 + 28} = 0$, $x > 0$ and $y = 8$. What is the value of x?

A) 3

B) 4

C) 5

D) 6

CONTINUE

5

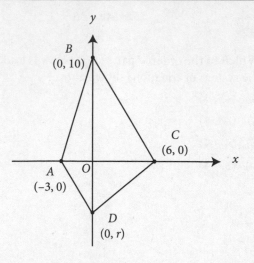

The figure above shows quadrilateral $ABCD$ in the xy-plane. If $\overline{BC}$ is parallel to $\overline{AD}$, what is the value of r?

A) -6

B) -5

C) -3

D) -2

6

Which of the following expressions is equivalent to $16x^6 - 24x^3y^3 + 9y^6$?

A) $(16x^2 - 9y^2)^3$

B) $(16x^3 - 9y^3)^2$

C) $(4x^3 - 3y^3)^2$

D) $(4x - 3y)^6$

7

$$S = 180(n - 2)$$

The measure S, in degrees, of the sum of the angles in a polygon is related to the number of sides, n, of the polygon by the formula above for all $n > 2$. If the sum of the angles of a polygon is greater than $2,000°$, then what is the least number of sides it can have?

A) 11

B) 12

C) 13

D) 14

8

The graph of line k in the xy-plane has a y-intercept of -8 and contains the point $(4, 4)$. The graph of line m contains the points $(1, 5)$ and $(5, -3)$. If lines k and m intersect at the point (s, t), what is the value of $s - t$?

A) 2

B) 3

C) 4

D) 5

CONTINUE

9

$$\left(k^{x^2 + xy}\right)\left(k^{y^2 + xy}\right) = k^{25}$$

In the equation above, $k > 1$ and $x = 3$. What is the positive value of y ?

A) 1

B) 2

C) 4

D) 5

10

$$F = \frac{D}{E - D}$$

A factory tracks quality control by using the formula above to determine a fault rating, F, based on the number of defective parts, D, and the number of acceptable parts, E. Which of the following expresses D in terms of F and E ?

A) $D = \dfrac{E}{1 - F}$

B) $D = \dfrac{E}{1 + F}$

C) $D = \dfrac{FE}{1 - F}$

D) $D = \dfrac{FE}{1 + F}$

11

The graph in the xy-plane of the function g has the property that y is always greater than or equal to –2. Which of the following could be g ?

A) $g(x) = x^2 \quad 3$

B) $g(x) = (x - 3)^2$

C) $g(x) = |x| - 3$

D) $g(x) = (x - 3)^3$

12

Which of the following complex numbers is equivalent to $\dfrac{1 + 10i}{6 - 3i}$? (Note: $i = \sqrt{-1}$)

A) $\dfrac{1}{6} + \dfrac{10i}{3}$

B) $-\dfrac{1}{6} + \dfrac{10i}{3}$

C) $\dfrac{8}{15} + \dfrac{7i}{5}$

D) $-\dfrac{8}{15} + \dfrac{7i}{5}$

CONTINUE

13

The estimated value of a truck declines at an annual rate of 7 percent. If the original value of the truck was $35,000, which of the functions v best models the value of the truck, in dollars, t years later?

A) $v(t) = 0.07(35,000)^t$

B) $v(t) = 0.93(35,000)^t$

C) $v(t) = 35,000(0.07)^t$

D) $v(t) = 35,000(0.93)^t$

14

$$\frac{6x - 1}{x + 4}$$

Which of the following is equivalent to the expression above?

A) $6 - \dfrac{25}{x + 4}$

B) $6 - \dfrac{1}{x + 4}$

C) $6 - \dfrac{1}{4}$

D) $\dfrac{6 - 1}{4}$

15

$$3k^2 - 18k + 12 = 0$$

What is the product of all values of k that satisfy the equation above?

A) 3

B) 4

C) $3\sqrt{5}$

D) $6\sqrt{5}$

CONTINUE

DIRECTIONS

For questions 16-20, solve the problem and enter your answer in the grid, as described below, on the answer sheet.

1. Although not required, it is suggested that you write your answer in the boxes at the top of the columns to help you fill in the circles accurately. You will receive credit only if the circles are filled in correctly.

2. Mark no more than one circle in any column.

3. No question has a negative answer.

4. Some problems may have more than one correct answer. In such cases, grid only one answer.

5. **Mixed numbers** such as $3\frac{1}{2}$ must be gridded as 3.5 or 7/2. (If [3 1 / 2] is entered into the grid, it will be interpreted as $\frac{31}{2}$, not as $3\frac{1}{2}$.)

6. **Decimal Answers:** If you obtain a decimal answer with more digits than the grid can accommodate, it may be either rounded or truncated, but it must fill the entire grid.

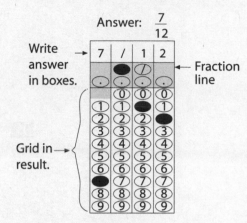

Answer: $\frac{7}{12}$

Write answer in boxes.

Fraction line

Grid in result.

Answer: 2.5

Decimal point

Acceptable ways to grid $\frac{2}{3}$ are:

 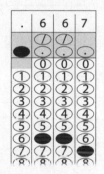

Answer: 201 – either position is correct

NOTE: You may start your answers in any column, space permitting. Columns you don't need to use should be left blank.

CONTINUE

16

In the equation $3(x - 5)^2 + 7 = ax^2 + bx + c$, a, b, and c are constants. If the equation is true for all values of x, what is the value of c ?

17

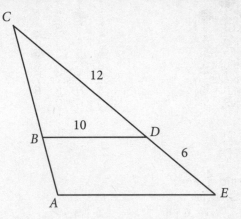

In the figure above, $\overline{BD} \parallel \overline{AE}$. What is the length of $\overline{AE}$?

18

At the end of a card game, Eve has a pile of red and blue chips that is worth $120. If red chips are worth $5 and blue chips are worth $20, and Eve has at least one red chip and at least one blue chip, what is one possible number of red chips Eve has?

19

$$\frac{1}{2}x + ay = 16$$
$$bx + 4y = 48$$

In the system of equations shown above, a and b are constants. If there are infinitely many solutions for this system, what is the value of $a + b$?

CONTINUE

20

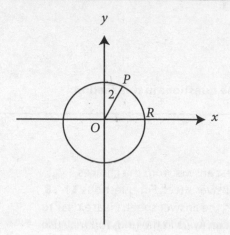

The *xy*-plane above shows the circle with center *O* and radius 2. If the measure of ∠*POR* is $\frac{\pi}{3}$ radians, what is the *x*-coordinate of point *P* ?

STOP
If you finish before time is called, you may check your work on this section only.
Do not turn to any other section in the test.

Math Test – Calculator

55 MINUTES, 38 QUESTIONS

Turn to Section 4 of your answer sheet to answer the questions in this section.

DIRECTIONS

For questions **1-30**, solve each problem, choose the best answer from the choices provided, and fill in the corresponding circle on your answer sheet. For questions **31-38**, solve the problem and enter your answer in the grid on the answer sheet. Please refer to the directions before question 31 on how to enter your answers in the grid. You may use any available space in your test booklet for scratch work.

NOTES

1. The use of a calculator **is permitted**.
2. All variables and expressions used represent real numbers unless otherwise indicated.
3. Figures provided in this test are drawn to scale unless otherwise indicated.
4. All figures lie in a plane unless otherwise indicated.
5. Unless otherwise indicated, the domain of a given function f is the set of all real numbers x for which $f(x)$ is a real number.

REFERENCE

$A = \pi r^2$
$C = 2\pi r$

$A = \ell w$

$A = \frac{1}{2}bh$

$c^2 = a^2 + b^2$

Special Right Triangles

$V = \ell wh$

$V = \pi r^2 h$

$V = \frac{4}{3}\pi r^3$

$V = \frac{1}{3}\pi r^2 h$

$V = \frac{1}{3}\ell wh$

The number of degrees of arc in a circle is 360.
The number of radians of arc in a circle is 2π.
The sum of the measures in degrees of the angles of a triangle is 180.

CONTINUE

1

A contractor creates a mosaic floor pattern in which there are 9 blue tiles for every 80 tiles in total. At this rate, how many blue tiles will there be in a floor pattern of 4,800 tiles?

A) 700

B) 620

C) 540

D) 480

2

$$c = 120 + 75d$$

A couple rents a car for their vacation. When a particular car is rented for d days, the total cost will be c dollars as shown in the equation above. What is the value of d when c is 345 ?

A) 25,995

B) 354

C) 75

D) 3

3

An artist creates prints of her latest painting to sell. The artist earns $50 for each large print she sells and $35 for each small print she sells. Which of the following expressions represents the amount, in dollars, that the artist earns for selling l large prints and s small prints?

A) $50l + 35s$

B) $50l - 35s$

C) $35l + 50s$

D) $35l - 50s$

4

When 6 times a number y is subtracted from 15, the result is 33. What number results when 3 times y is added to 19 ?

A) −3

B) 7

C) 10

D) 28

CONTINUE

Questions 5 and 6 refer to the following information.

A television store's revenue is directly proportional to the number of televisions it sells. The store earns $1,440 in a day in which it sells 6 televisions.

5

The store pays the factory 39% of the money earned from the sale of each television. The rest of the money earned is the store's profit. What is the profit the store makes on a day in which it sells 6 televisions?

A) $390.00

B) $561.60

C) $690.00

D) $878.40

6

How much revenue will the store earn on a day in which it sells 9 televisions?

A) $960

B) $2,160

C) $8,640

D) $12,960

7

A record collector is looking to buy records that cost either $20 or $35 each. Let a be the number of $20 records and b be the number of $35 records. The collector can buy a maximum of 25 records and can spend up to $750. Which of the following systems of inequalities accurately describes this relationship?

A) $\begin{cases} a + b \leq 750 \\ 20a + 35b \leq 25 \end{cases}$

B) $\begin{cases} 20a + 35b \leq 750 \\ a + b \leq 750 \end{cases}$

C) $\begin{cases} \dfrac{a}{20} + \dfrac{b}{35} \leq 750 \\ a + b \leq 25 \end{cases}$

D) $\begin{cases} 20a + 35b \leq 750 \\ a + b \leq 25 \end{cases}$

8

$$y = x^2 - 12x + 35$$

The equation above is a quadratic equation. Which of the following equivalent forms of the equation displays the x-intercepts of the parabola in the xy-plane as constants or coefficients?

A) $y + 1 = (x - 6)^2$

B) $y - 35 = x^2 - 12x$

C) $y = (x - 5)(x - 7)$

D) $y = x(x - 12) + 35$

CONTINUE

9

In a certain quiz game, each player begins with p points, loses 3 points for every question answered incorrectly, and cannot increase his or her score. If a player who answers 15 questions incorrectly has a score of 165, which of the following is the value of p ?

A) 210

B) 180

C) 140

D)   0

10

Number of hours per day Albert expects to devote to typing the document	4
Number of units in the document	21
Number of words Albert types per minute	85
Number of sections in the document	145
Number of pages in the document	725
Number of words in the document	181,235

Albert needs to type a long, prewritten document. The table above shows information about the document, Albert's typing speed, and the number of hours he expects to devote to typing the document each day. If Albert types at the rates provided in the table, which of the following is closest to the number of days Albert would expect to take in order to type the entire document?

A)   9

B)   36

C)   148

D) 2,132

11

At 9:00 A.M. Monday, a trash can with a capacity of 20 cubic feet contains 8 cubic feet of garbage. Each day after Monday, 3 cubic feet of garbage are added to the trash can. If no garbage is removed and d represents the number of days after Monday, which of the following inequalities describes the set of days for which the trash can is full or overflowing?

A) $12 \geq 3d$

B) $8 + 3d \geq 20$

C) $20 - 3 \leq d$

D) $20 \leq 3d$

12

In function m, $m(4) = 6$ and $m(6) = 10$. In function n, $n(6) = 4$ and $n(10) = 2$. What is the value of $m(n(6))$?

A)   2

B)   4

C)   6

D) 10

CONTINUE

13

The circumference of Earth's equator is approximately 40,000 kilometers. Earth rotates completely around its axis in one day. Which of the following is the closest approximation of the average speed, in kilometers per minute, of a point on Earth's equator, as the Earth rotates about its axis?

A) 18

B) 20

C) 28

D) 56

14

A theater owner wanted to determine whether local residents were more interested in seeing operas or symphonies. The theater owner asked 85 people who were in a shopping mall on a Sunday and 5 people declined to respond. Which of the following factors is the greatest flaw in the theater owner's methodology in reaching a reliable conclusion about the local residents' performance-viewing preferences?

A) The size of the sample

B) The location in which the survey was given

C) The population of the area

D) The residents who declined to respond

15

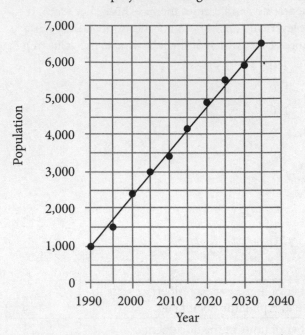

Population of Town T from 1990 projected through 2035

According to the line of best fit in the scatterplot above, which of following best approximates the year in which the population of Town T is projected to reach 5,000 ?

A) 2017

B) 2022

C) 2028

D) 2033

16

The half-life of an unknown isotope is approximately 25% less than that of carbon-14. The half-life of carbon-14 is 5,730 years. Which of the following best approximately the half-life, in years, of the unknown isotope?

A) 1,400

B) 4,300

C) 5,705

D) 7,200

CONTINUE ▶

17

A company's accounting department took a survey of its employees' salaries and found that the mean salary was $80,000 and that the median salary was $45,000. Which of the following could explain the difference between the mean and the median salary in the company?

A) Many of the employees' salaries are between $45,000 and $80,000.

B) The employees have salaries that are close to each other.

C) There are a few employees with salaries that are much lower than the rest.

D) There are a few employees with salaries that are much higher than the rest.

18

Results of Interview for Applicants to College C

	Accepted by College C	Rejected by College C
Completed interview	15,700	34,300
Did not complete interview	9,300	40,700

The table above summarizes the results of the 100,000 applicants to College C. If an accepted student is randomly chosen, what is the probability that the student did <u>not</u> complete an interview?

A) $\dfrac{93}{1,000}$

B) $\dfrac{1}{4}$

C) $\dfrac{93}{250}$

D) $\dfrac{157}{250}$

19

Mathias saves an average of d dollars per month, where $d > 300$. The actual amount he saves per month varies, but is always within $20 of the average amount. If this month Mathias saved k dollars, which of the following inequalities expresses the relationship between k, the amount he saved this month, and d, the average amount he saves per month?

A) $d - k < 20$

B) $d + k < 20$

C) $-20 < d - k < 20$

D) $-20 < d + k < 20$

CONTINUE

Questions 20 and 21 refer to the following information.

The class president chose 200 students at random from each of the junior and senior classes at her high school. Each student was asked how many hours of homework he or she completed in an average school night. The results are shown in the table below.

Number of hours	Junior class	Senior class
1	25	30
2	80	70
3	50	60
4	35	35
5	10	5

There are a total of 600 students in the junior class and 400 students in the senior class.

What is the median number of hours of homework in an average night for all the students surveyed?

A) 2

B) 3

C) 4

D) 5

21

Based on the survey data, which of the following statements accurately compares the expected total number of members of each class who complete four hours of homework?

A) The total number of students who complete four hours of homework in the junior class is 35 more than in the senior class.

B) The total number of students who complete four hours of homework in the senior class is 35 more than in the junior class.

C) The total number of students who complete four hours of homework in the junior class is 200 more than in the senior class.

D) The total number of students who complete four hours of homework is expected to be the same in both classes.

22

The equation of circle P in the xy-plane can be represented as $x^2 + y^2 - 6x + 8y = -9$. What is the radius of circle P ?

A) 2

B) 4

C) 8

D) 16

CONTINUE

Questions 23 and 24 refer to the following information.

$$G = \frac{ab}{d^2}$$

The gravitational force, G, between an object of mass a and an object of mass b is given by the formula above, where d represents the distance between the two objects.

23

Which of the following expressions represents the square of the distance between the two objects in terms of the masses of the objects and the gravitational force between them?

A) $d^2 = \dfrac{Gb}{a}$

B) $d^2 = \dfrac{Ga}{b}$

C) $d^2 = \dfrac{G}{ab}$

D) $d^2 = \dfrac{ab}{G}$

24

Objects k and m have the same masses, respectively, as do objects a and b. If the gravitational force between k and m is 9 times the gravitational force between a and b, then the distance between k and m is what fraction of the distance between a and b ?

A) $\dfrac{1}{243}$

B) $\dfrac{1}{81}$

C) $\dfrac{1}{9}$

D) $\dfrac{1}{3}$

CONTINUE

25

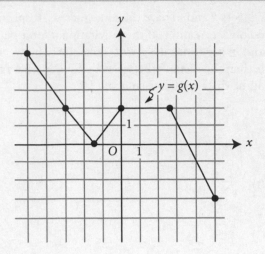

The figure above shows the complete graph of the function g in the xy-plane. Which of the following must be true?

I. $g(-3) = 2$

II. $g(2) = -3$

III. $g\left(\dfrac{1}{2}\right) = g(2)$

A) III only

B) I and II only

C) I and III only

D) I, II, and III

26

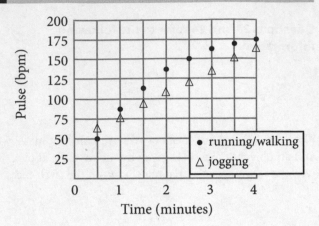

Two athletes have their pulses, in beats per minute (bpm), monitored while they exercise. One athlete alternates brisk running with walking, while the other athlete jogs at a constant pace. The graph above shows the athletes' heart rates at 30-second intervals. Which of the following statements accurately compares the average rates at which the pulses of the two athletes change?

A) In the interval from 1 to 2 minutes, the rate of change of pulse for the athlete who alternates running and walking is of lesser magnitude than the rate of change of pulse for the athlete who jogs only, whereas in the interval from 3 to 4 minutes, the rate of change of pulse for the athlete who jogs only is of lesser magnitude.

B) In the interval from 1 to 2 minutes, the rate of change of pulse for the athlete who jogs only is of lesser magnitude than the rate of change of pulse for the athlete who alternates running and walking, whereas in the interval from 3 to 4 minutes, the rate of change of pulse for the athlete who alternates running and walking is of lesser magnitude.

C) In every 30-second interval, the rate of change of pulse for the athlete who alternates running and walking is of lesser magnitude than it is for the athlete who jogs only.

D) In every 30-second interval, the rate of change of pulse for the athlete who jogs only is of lesser magnitude than it is for the athlete who alternates running and walking.

CONTINUE ▶

27

The graph in the xy-plane of linear function g has an x-intercept at $(s, 0)$ and a y-intercept at $(0, t)$. If $t - s = 0$, $t \neq 0$, and $s \neq 0$, which of the following must be true about the graph of g ?

A) It has a positive slope.

B) It has a negative slope.

C) It has a slope of zero.

D) It has no slope.

28

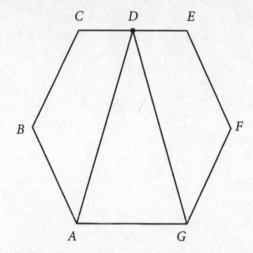

In the figure above, $ABCEFG$ is a regular hexagon and D is the midpoint of $\overline{CE}$. If the area of the hexagon is $864\sqrt{3}$ square feet, what is the area, in square feet, of triangle ADG ?

A) 144

B) 432

C) $288\sqrt{3}$

D) $432\sqrt{3}$

29

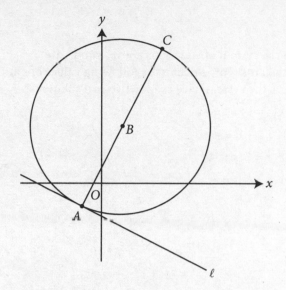

In the xy-plane above, $\overline{AC}$ is the diameter of the circle centered at B, and the coordinates of points A and C are $(-1, -1)$ and $(3, 7)$, respectively. If line ℓ is tangent to the circle at point A, which of the following is an equation of line ℓ ?

A) $y = -\dfrac{1}{2}(x + 3)$

B) $y = -\dfrac{1}{2}x + 3$

C) $y = -2x + 1$

D) $y = -2x - 3$

CONTINUE

$$y = rx^2 + s$$
$$y = -2$$

In the system of equations above, r and s are constants. For which of the following values of r and s does the system have exactly two real solutions?

A) $r = -2, s = -1$

B) $r = -1, s = -2$

C) $r = 2, s = -2$

D) $r = 3, s = 1$

CONTINUE

DIRECTIONS

For questions 31-38, solve the problem and enter your answer in the grid, as described below, on the answer sheet.

1. Although not required, it is suggested that you write your answer in the boxes at the top of the columns to help you fill in the circles accurately. You will receive credit only if the circles are filled in correctly.

2. Mark no more than one circle in any column.

3. No question has a negative answer.

4. Some problems may have more than one correct answer. In such cases, grid only one answer.

5. **Mixed numbers** such as $3\frac{1}{2}$ must be gridded as 3.5 or 7/2. (If  is entered into the grid, it will be interpreted as $\frac{31}{2}$, not as $3\frac{1}{2}$.)

6. **Decimal Answers:** If you obtain a decimal answer with more digits than the grid can accommodate, it may be either rounded or truncated, but it must fill the entire grid.

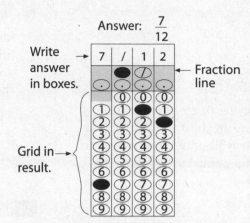

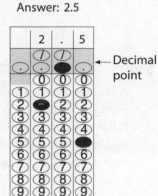

Acceptable ways to grid $\frac{2}{3}$ are:

Answer: 201 – either position is correct

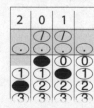

NOTE: You may start your answers in any column, space permitting. Columns you don't need to use should be left blank.

CONTINUE ➡

31

If 560 minutes is equal to *z* hours and 20 minutes, what is the value of *z* ?

32

A climate scientist estimates that a certain state's average snowfall is decreasing by 0.4 inches per year. If the scientist's estimate is accurate, how many years will it take for the average annual snowfall to be 6 inches less than it is now?

33

Dave was charged a fine for returning a number of overdue books to the library. Each week after he incurred the fine, he paid the library a fixed amount until the fine was paid off. The equation $C = 12 - 1.5w$, where $C \geq 0$, models the amount C, in dollars, that Dave owes w weeks after he incurred the fine. According to this model, how much money, in dollars, did Dave initially owe the library? (Disregard the $ sign when gridding in your answer.)

34

$$g(x) = 2x^2 - kx + 14$$

In the xy-plane, the graph of the function above contains the point (4, –2). What is the value of k ?

CONTINUE

35

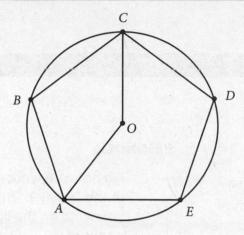

In the figure above, the circle is centered at point O, *ABCDE* is a regular pentagon, and *ABCO* is a quadrilateral. If the length of arc $\overset{\frown}{ABC}$ is 24, what is the circumference of circle O ?

36

Satya ate a breakfast sandwich and an order of fried potatoes and consumed a total of 910 calories. If the breakfast sandwich contained 240 more calories than the fried potatoes, how many calories did the breakfast sandwich contain?

Questions 37 and 38 refer to the following information.

$$P_{t+1} = P_t + 0.3(P_t)\left(1 - \frac{P_t}{C}\right)$$

A certain species of deer on an isolated island has a current population of 4,200. The estimated population of deer next year, P_{t+1}, is related to the population this year, P_t, by the formula above. In this formula, the constant C represents the maximum number of deer the island is capable of supporting.

37

Suppose that environmental conditions on the island changed suddenly, and there was a resultant decrease in the maximum number of deer the island is capable of supporting. If the number of deer increases from 4,200 this year to 4,704 next year, what would be the maximum number of deer the island is capable of supporting?

38

If C = 10,500, and the given formula is accurate, what will the population of deer be 2 years from now? (Round your answer to the nearest whole number.)

STOP

If you finish before time is called, you may check your work on this section only.
Do not turn to any other section in the test.

SAT Essay

DIRECTIONS

The essay gives you an opportunity to show how effectively you can read and comprehend a passage and write an essay analyzing the passage. In your essay you should demonstrate that you have read the passage carefully, present a clear and logical analysis, and use language precisely.

Your essay must be written on the lines provided in your answer sheet booklet; except for the planning page of the answer booklet, you will receive no other paper on which to write. You will have enough space if you write on every line, avoid wide margins, and keep your handwriting to a reasonable size. Remember that people who are not familiar with your handwriting will read what you write. Try to write or print so that what you are writing is legible to those readers.

You have <u>50 minutes</u> to read the passage and write an essay in response to the prompt provided inside this booklet.

REMINDER

— Do not write your essay in this booklet. Only what you write on the lined pages of your answer booklet will be evaluated.

— An off-topic essay will not be evaluated.

CONTINUE →

As you read the passage below, consider how Martin Luther King, Jr. uses

- evidence, such as facts or examples, to support claims.
- reasoning to develop ideas and to connect claims and evidence.
- stylistic or persuasive elements, such as word choice or appeals to emotion, to add power to the ideas expressed.

Adapted from Martin Luther King, Jr.'s "Letter from a Birmingham Jail," written April 16, 1963.

1 My Dear Fellow Clergymen:

2 While confined here in the Birmingham city jail, I came across your recent statement calling my present activities "unwise and untimely." Seldom do I pause to answer criticism of my work and ideas. If I sought to answer all the criticisms that cross my desk, my secretaries would have little time for anything other than such correspondence in the course of the day, and I would have no time for constructive work. But since I feel that you are men of genuine good will and that your criticisms are sincerely set forth, I want to try to answer your statement in what I hope will be patient and reasonable terms.

3 I think I should indicate why I am here in Birmingham, since you have been influenced by the view which argues against "outsiders coming in." I have the honor of serving as president of the Southern Christian Leadership Conference, an organization operating in every southern state, with headquarters in Atlanta, Georgia. We have some eighty five affiliated organizations across the South, and one of them is the Alabama Christian Movement for Human Rights. Frequently we share staff, educational and financial resources with our affiliates. Several months ago the affiliate here in Birmingham asked us to be on call to engage in a nonviolent direct action program if such were deemed necessary. We readily consented, and when the hour came we lived up to our promise. So I, along with several members of my staff, am here because I was invited here. I am here because I have organizational ties here.

4 But more basically, I am in Birmingham because injustice is here. Just as the prophets of the eighth century B.C. left their villages and carried their "thus saith the Lord" far beyond the boundaries of their home towns, and just as the Apostle Paul left his village of Tarsus and carried the gospel of Jesus Christ to the far corners of the Greco Roman world, so am I compelled to carry the gospel of freedom beyond my own home town. Like Paul, I must constantly respond to the Macedonian call for aid.

5 Moreover, I am cognizant of the interrelatedness of all communities and states. I cannot sit idly by in Atlanta and not be concerned about what happens in Birmingham. Injustice anywhere is a threat to justice everywhere. We are caught in an inescapable network of mutuality, tied in a single garment of destiny. Whatever affects one directly, affects all

CONTINUE

indirectly. Never again can we afford to live with the narrow, provincial "outside agitator" idea. Anyone who lives inside the United States can never be considered an outsider anywhere within its bounds.

6   You deplore the demonstrations taking place in Birmingham. But your statement, I am sorry to say, fails to express a similar concern for the conditions that brought about the demonstrations. I am sure that none of you would want to rest content with the superficial kind of social analysis that deals merely with effects and does not grapple with underlying causes. It is unfortunate that demonstrations are taking place in Birmingham, but it is even more unfortunate that the city's white power structure left the Negro community with no alternative…

7   You may well ask: "Why direct action? Why sit-ins, marches and so forth? Isn't negotiation a better path?" You are quite right in calling for negotiation. Indeed, this is the very purpose of direct action. Nonviolent direct action seeks to create such a crisis and foster such a tension that a community which has constantly refused to negotiate is forced to confront the issue. It seeks so to dramatize the issue that it can no longer be ignored. My citing the creation of tension as part of the work of the nonviolent resister may sound rather shocking. But I must confess that I am not afraid of the word "tension." I have earnestly opposed violent tension, but there is a type of constructive, nonviolent tension which is necessary for growth… The purpose of our direct action program is to create a situation so crisis packed that it will inevitably open the door to negotiation. I therefore concur with you in your call for negotiation. Too long has our beloved Southland been bogged down in a tragic effort to live in monologue rather than dialogue.

Write an essay in which you explain how Martin Luther King, Jr. builds an argument in response to the claim that the protests in Birmingham were "unwise and untimely." In your essay, analyze how King uses one or more of the features listed in the box above (or features of your own choice) to strengthen the logic and persuasiveness of his argument. Be sure that your analysis focuses on the most relevant features of the passage.

Your essay should not explain whether you agree with King's claims, but rather explain how King builds an argument to persuade his audience.

END OF TEST

DO NOT RETURN TO A PREVIOUS SECTION.

Completely darken bubbles with a No. 2 pencil. If you make a mistake, be sure to erase mark completely. Erase all stray marks.

1.

YOUR NAME: _____
(Print)
Last   First   M.I.

SIGNATURE: _____   DATE: __/__/__

HOME ADDRESS: _____
(Print)
Number and Street

_____
City   State   Zip Code

PHONE NO.: _____
(Print)

5. YOUR NAME

First 4 letters of last name				FIRST INIT	MID INIT
Ⓐ	Ⓐ	Ⓐ	Ⓐ	Ⓐ	Ⓐ
Ⓑ	Ⓑ	Ⓑ	Ⓑ	Ⓑ	Ⓑ
Ⓒ	Ⓒ	Ⓒ	Ⓒ	Ⓒ	Ⓒ
Ⓓ	Ⓓ	Ⓓ	Ⓓ	Ⓓ	Ⓓ
Ⓔ	Ⓔ	Ⓔ	Ⓔ	Ⓔ	Ⓔ
Ⓕ	Ⓕ	Ⓕ	Ⓕ	Ⓕ	Ⓕ
Ⓖ	Ⓖ	Ⓖ	Ⓖ	Ⓖ	Ⓖ
Ⓗ	Ⓗ	Ⓗ	Ⓗ	Ⓗ	Ⓗ
Ⓘ	Ⓘ	Ⓘ	Ⓘ	Ⓘ	Ⓘ
Ⓙ	Ⓙ	Ⓙ	Ⓙ	Ⓙ	Ⓙ
Ⓚ	Ⓚ	Ⓚ	Ⓚ	Ⓚ	Ⓚ
Ⓛ	Ⓛ	Ⓛ	Ⓛ	Ⓛ	Ⓛ
Ⓜ	Ⓜ	Ⓜ	Ⓜ	Ⓜ	Ⓜ
Ⓝ	Ⓝ	Ⓝ	Ⓝ	Ⓝ	Ⓝ
Ⓞ	Ⓞ	Ⓞ	Ⓞ	Ⓞ	Ⓞ
Ⓟ	Ⓟ	Ⓟ	Ⓟ	Ⓟ	Ⓟ
Ⓠ	Ⓠ	Ⓠ	Ⓠ	Ⓠ	Ⓠ
Ⓡ	Ⓡ	Ⓡ	Ⓡ	Ⓡ	Ⓡ
Ⓢ	Ⓢ	Ⓢ	Ⓢ	Ⓢ	Ⓢ
Ⓣ	Ⓣ	Ⓣ	Ⓣ	Ⓣ	Ⓣ
Ⓤ	Ⓤ	Ⓤ	Ⓤ	Ⓤ	Ⓤ
Ⓥ	Ⓥ	Ⓥ	Ⓥ	Ⓥ	Ⓥ
Ⓦ	Ⓦ	Ⓦ	Ⓦ	Ⓦ	Ⓦ
Ⓧ	Ⓧ	Ⓧ	Ⓧ	Ⓧ	Ⓧ
Ⓨ	Ⓨ	Ⓨ	Ⓨ	Ⓨ	Ⓨ
Ⓩ	Ⓩ	Ⓩ	Ⓩ	Ⓩ	Ⓩ

IMPORTANT: Please fill in these boxes exactly as shown on the back cover of your test book.

2. TEST FORM

6. DATE OF BIRTH

Month	Day		Year	
○ JAN				
○ FEB	⓪	⓪	⓪	⓪
○ MAR	①	①	①	①
○ APR	②	②	②	②
○ MAY	③	③	③	③
○ JUN		④	④	④
○ JUL		⑤	⑤	⑤
○ AUG		⑥	⑥	⑥
○ SEP		⑦	⑦	⑦
○ OCT		⑧	⑧	⑧
○ NOV		⑨	⑨	⑨
○ DEC				

3. TEST CODE   **4. REGISTRATION NUMBER**

⓪	Ⓐ	Ⓙ	⓪	⓪		⓪	⓪	⓪	⓪	⓪	⓪
①	Ⓑ	Ⓚ	①	①		①	①	①	①	①	①
②	Ⓒ	Ⓛ	②	②		②	②	②	②	②	②
③	Ⓓ	Ⓜ	③	③		③	③	③	③	③	③
④	Ⓔ	Ⓝ	④	④		④	④	④	④	④	④
⑤	Ⓕ	Ⓞ	⑤	⑤		⑤	⑤	⑤	⑤	⑤	⑤
⑥	Ⓖ	Ⓟ	⑥	⑥		⑥	⑥	⑥	⑥	⑥	⑥
⑦	Ⓗ	Ⓠ	⑦	⑦		⑦	⑦	⑦	⑦	⑦	⑦
⑧	Ⓘ	Ⓡ	⑧	⑧		⑧	⑧	⑧	⑧	⑧	⑧
⑨			⑨	⑨		⑨	⑨	⑨	⑨	⑨	⑨

7. SEX
○ MALE
○ FEMALE

The **Princeton Review**®

Test ② Start with number 1 for each new section.
If a section has fewer questions than answer spaces, leave the extra answer spaces blank.

Section 1—Reading

1. Ⓐ Ⓑ Ⓒ Ⓓ
2. Ⓐ Ⓑ Ⓒ Ⓓ
3. Ⓐ Ⓑ Ⓒ Ⓓ
4. Ⓐ Ⓑ Ⓒ Ⓓ
5. Ⓐ Ⓑ Ⓒ Ⓓ
6. Ⓐ Ⓑ Ⓒ Ⓓ
7. Ⓐ Ⓑ Ⓒ Ⓓ
8. Ⓐ Ⓑ Ⓒ Ⓓ
9. Ⓐ Ⓑ Ⓒ Ⓓ
10. Ⓐ Ⓑ Ⓒ Ⓓ
11. Ⓐ Ⓑ Ⓒ Ⓓ
12. Ⓐ Ⓑ Ⓒ Ⓓ
13. Ⓐ Ⓑ Ⓒ Ⓓ
14. Ⓐ Ⓑ Ⓒ Ⓓ
15. Ⓐ Ⓑ Ⓒ Ⓓ
16. Ⓐ Ⓑ Ⓒ Ⓓ
17. Ⓐ Ⓑ Ⓒ Ⓓ
18. Ⓐ Ⓑ Ⓒ Ⓓ
19. Ⓐ Ⓑ Ⓒ Ⓓ
20. Ⓐ Ⓑ Ⓒ Ⓓ
21. Ⓐ Ⓑ Ⓒ Ⓓ
22. Ⓐ Ⓑ Ⓒ Ⓓ
23. Ⓐ Ⓑ Ⓒ Ⓓ
24. Ⓐ Ⓑ Ⓒ Ⓓ
25. Ⓐ Ⓑ Ⓒ Ⓓ
26. Ⓐ Ⓑ Ⓒ Ⓓ
27. Ⓐ Ⓑ Ⓒ Ⓓ
28. Ⓐ Ⓑ Ⓒ Ⓓ
29. Ⓐ Ⓑ Ⓒ Ⓓ
30. Ⓐ Ⓑ Ⓒ Ⓓ
31. Ⓐ Ⓑ Ⓒ Ⓓ
32. Ⓐ Ⓑ Ⓒ Ⓓ
33. Ⓐ Ⓑ Ⓒ Ⓓ
34. Ⓐ Ⓑ Ⓒ Ⓓ
35. Ⓐ Ⓑ Ⓒ Ⓓ
36. Ⓐ Ⓑ Ⓒ Ⓓ
37. Ⓐ Ⓑ Ⓒ Ⓓ
38. Ⓐ Ⓑ Ⓒ Ⓓ
39. Ⓐ Ⓑ Ⓒ Ⓓ
40. Ⓐ Ⓑ Ⓒ Ⓓ
41. Ⓐ Ⓑ Ⓒ Ⓓ
42. Ⓐ Ⓑ Ⓒ Ⓓ
43. Ⓐ Ⓑ Ⓒ Ⓓ
44. Ⓐ Ⓑ Ⓒ Ⓓ
45. Ⓐ Ⓑ Ⓒ Ⓓ
46. Ⓐ Ⓑ Ⓒ Ⓓ
47. Ⓐ Ⓑ Ⓒ Ⓓ
48. Ⓐ Ⓑ Ⓒ Ⓓ
49. Ⓐ Ⓑ Ⓒ Ⓓ
50. Ⓐ Ⓑ Ⓒ Ⓓ
51. Ⓐ Ⓑ Ⓒ Ⓓ
52. Ⓐ Ⓑ Ⓒ Ⓓ

Section 2—Writing and Language Skills

1. Ⓐ Ⓑ Ⓒ Ⓓ
2. Ⓐ Ⓑ Ⓒ Ⓓ
3. Ⓐ Ⓑ Ⓒ Ⓓ
4. Ⓐ Ⓑ Ⓒ Ⓓ
5. Ⓐ Ⓑ Ⓒ Ⓓ
6. Ⓐ Ⓑ Ⓒ Ⓓ
7. Ⓐ Ⓑ Ⓒ Ⓓ
8. Ⓐ Ⓑ Ⓒ Ⓓ
9. Ⓐ Ⓑ Ⓒ Ⓓ
10. Ⓐ Ⓑ Ⓒ Ⓓ
11. Ⓐ Ⓑ Ⓒ Ⓓ
12. Ⓐ Ⓑ Ⓒ Ⓓ
13. Ⓐ Ⓑ Ⓒ Ⓓ
14. Ⓐ Ⓑ Ⓒ Ⓓ
15. Ⓐ Ⓑ Ⓒ Ⓓ
16. Ⓐ Ⓑ Ⓒ Ⓓ
17. Ⓐ Ⓑ Ⓒ Ⓓ
18. Ⓐ Ⓑ Ⓒ Ⓓ
19. Ⓐ Ⓑ Ⓒ Ⓓ
20. Ⓐ Ⓑ Ⓒ Ⓓ
21. Ⓐ Ⓑ Ⓒ Ⓓ
22. Ⓐ Ⓑ Ⓒ Ⓓ
23. Ⓐ Ⓑ Ⓒ Ⓓ
24. Ⓐ Ⓑ Ⓒ Ⓓ
25. Ⓐ Ⓑ Ⓒ Ⓓ
26. Ⓐ Ⓑ Ⓒ Ⓓ
27. Ⓐ Ⓑ Ⓒ Ⓓ
28. Ⓐ Ⓑ Ⓒ Ⓓ
29. Ⓐ Ⓑ Ⓒ Ⓓ
30. Ⓐ Ⓑ Ⓒ Ⓓ
31. Ⓐ Ⓑ Ⓒ Ⓓ
32. Ⓐ Ⓑ Ⓒ Ⓓ
33. Ⓐ Ⓑ Ⓒ Ⓓ
34. Ⓐ Ⓑ Ⓒ Ⓓ
35. Ⓐ Ⓑ Ⓒ Ⓓ
36. Ⓐ Ⓑ Ⓒ Ⓓ
37. Ⓐ Ⓑ Ⓒ Ⓓ
38. Ⓐ Ⓑ Ⓒ Ⓓ
39. Ⓐ Ⓑ Ⓒ Ⓓ
40. Ⓐ Ⓑ Ⓒ Ⓓ
41. Ⓐ Ⓑ Ⓒ Ⓓ
42. Ⓐ Ⓑ Ⓒ Ⓓ
43. Ⓐ Ⓑ Ⓒ Ⓓ
44. Ⓐ Ⓑ Ⓒ Ⓓ

The Princeton Review®

Test ➋ Start with number 1 for each new section.
If a section has fewer questions than answer spaces, leave the extra answer spaces blank.

Section 3—Mathematics: No Calculator

1. Ⓐ Ⓑ Ⓒ Ⓓ
2. Ⓐ Ⓑ Ⓒ Ⓓ
3. Ⓐ Ⓑ Ⓒ Ⓓ
4. Ⓐ Ⓑ Ⓒ Ⓓ
5. Ⓐ Ⓑ Ⓒ Ⓓ
6. Ⓐ Ⓑ Ⓒ Ⓓ
7. Ⓐ Ⓑ Ⓒ Ⓓ
8. Ⓐ Ⓑ Ⓒ Ⓓ
9. Ⓐ Ⓑ Ⓒ Ⓓ
10. Ⓐ Ⓑ Ⓒ Ⓓ
11. Ⓐ Ⓑ Ⓒ Ⓓ
12. Ⓐ Ⓑ Ⓒ Ⓓ
13. Ⓐ Ⓑ Ⓒ Ⓓ
14. Ⓐ Ⓑ Ⓒ Ⓓ
15. Ⓐ Ⓑ Ⓒ Ⓓ

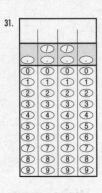
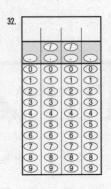

16. 17. 18. 19. 20.

Section 4—Mathematics: Calculator

1. Ⓐ Ⓑ Ⓒ Ⓓ
2. Ⓐ Ⓑ Ⓒ Ⓓ
3. Ⓐ Ⓑ Ⓒ Ⓓ
4. Ⓐ Ⓑ Ⓒ Ⓓ
5. Ⓐ Ⓑ Ⓒ Ⓓ
6. Ⓐ Ⓑ Ⓒ Ⓓ
7. Ⓐ Ⓑ Ⓒ Ⓓ
8. Ⓐ Ⓑ Ⓒ Ⓓ
9. Ⓐ Ⓑ Ⓒ Ⓓ
10. Ⓐ Ⓑ Ⓒ Ⓓ
11. Ⓐ Ⓑ Ⓒ Ⓓ
12. Ⓐ Ⓑ Ⓒ Ⓓ
13. Ⓐ Ⓑ Ⓒ Ⓓ
14. Ⓐ Ⓑ Ⓒ Ⓓ
15. Ⓐ Ⓑ Ⓒ Ⓓ
16. Ⓐ Ⓑ Ⓒ Ⓓ
17. Ⓐ Ⓑ Ⓒ Ⓓ
18. Ⓐ Ⓑ Ⓒ Ⓓ
19. Ⓐ Ⓑ Ⓒ Ⓓ
20. Ⓐ Ⓑ Ⓒ Ⓓ
21. Ⓐ Ⓑ Ⓒ Ⓓ
22. Ⓐ Ⓑ Ⓒ Ⓓ
23. Ⓐ Ⓑ Ⓒ Ⓓ
24. Ⓐ Ⓑ Ⓒ Ⓓ
25. Ⓐ Ⓑ Ⓒ Ⓓ
26. Ⓐ Ⓑ Ⓒ Ⓓ
27. Ⓐ Ⓑ Ⓒ Ⓓ
28. Ⓐ Ⓑ Ⓒ Ⓓ
29. Ⓐ Ⓑ Ⓒ Ⓓ
30. Ⓐ Ⓑ Ⓒ Ⓓ

31. 32. 33. 34. 35.

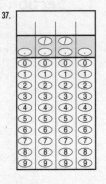

36. 37. 38.

Chapter 6
Practice Test 2:
Answers and
Explanations

PRACTICE TEST 2 ANSWER KEY

Section 1: Reading		Section 2: Writing & Language		Section 3: Math (No Calculator)		Section 4 : Math (Calculator)	
1. D	27. A	1. B	23. D	1. C	11. B	1. C	20. A
2. A	28. A	2. D	24. A	2. D	12. D	2. D	21. A
3. D	29. A	3. B	25. B	3. C	13. D	3. A	22. B
4. C	30. B	4. C	26. B	4. A	14. A	4. C	23. D
5. D	31. A	5. A	27. C	5. B	15. B	5. D	24. D
6. B	32. B	6. D	28. C	6. C	16. 82	6. B	25. C
7. C	33. B	7. D	29. B	7. D	17. 15	7. D	26. B
8. B	34. B	8. B	30. B	8. A	18. 4, 8,	8. C	27. B
9. C	35. D	9. D	31. D	9. B	12, 16,	9. A	28. C
10. A	36. D	10. C	32. C	10. D	or 20	10. A	29. A
11. A	37. A	11. A	33. A		19. $\frac{17}{6}$	11. B	30. A
12. D	38. B	12. C	34. C		or	12. C	31. 9
13. A	39. A	13. A	35. B		2.83	13. C	32. 15
14. C	40. C	14. D	36. C		20. 1	14. B	33. 12
15. C	41. D	15. A	37. D			15. B	34. 12
16. A	42. B	16. B	38. B			16. B	35. 60
17. B	43. D	17. D	39. A			17. D	36. 575
18. A	44. C	18. B	40. B			18. C	37. 7,000
19. A	45. A	19. D	41. A			19. C	38. 5,741
20. A	46. B	20. C	42. D				
21. A	47. C	21. D	43. D				
22. B	48. A	22. D	44. B				
23. B	49. D						
24. D	50. B						
25. C	51. C						
26. C	52. B						

For self-scoring assessment tables, please turn to page 565.

PRACTICE TEST 2 EXPLANATIONS

Section 1: Reading

1. **D**   This question asks for the main idea of the passage. Look for an answer choice that describes the passage in general; beware of answer choices that are true for only part of the passage. Choice (A) mentions *young men*, but the text does not mention their ages, and neither Don Quixote nor Sancho Panza *decide[s] to pretend* that he is entering battle. Choice (B) might— rather generously —describe Don Quixote and his horse, but Sancho Panza is not mentioned, and the giants are not actually there. Choice (C) might initially look good, because the two men do have an argument. However, the text identifies Sancho as Don Quixote's squire. Remember that Mostly Right is All Wrong. Since the two men are not both knights, (C) can be eliminated. Choice (D) includes the battle of the second half of the passage as well as the different perception of reality of the first half (and the very end). Choice (D) is the correct answer.

2. **A**   This question asks about the function of the opening sentence. First, review that sentence: *At this point they came in sight of thirty or forty windmills that are on that plain.* The author tells the reader that these are windmills, not giants, as Don Quixote thinks. Choice (A) mentions the true setting (vs. the setting Don Quixote imagines), which could fit this prediction, so keep it for now. Choice (B) mentions technological advances and their importance, which are not discussed in this passage. The beginning of (C) sounds good in that it describes the field, but the second part of the choice does not match the text. There was no battle. Eliminate (C). Choice (D) says this sentence provides detailed imagery, but there are no details about the windmills, beyond a rough estimate of their number. Thus, (A) has the strongest support and is the correct answer.

3. **D**   This question asks what changes in the main character's focus from paragraph 1 to paragraph 6. Review that part of the text and summarize what happens. For example: "Don Quixote says he's going to attack the giants; Sancho Panza says they're not giants; Don Quixote disagrees." Choose an answer that fits this summary. Choice (A) mentions *recollection* and *prospect*, which do not fit this prediction. Choice (B) mentions *money* and *God*, which do not fit this prediction. Choice (C) contrasts general and specific issues concerning battle, which does not fit this prediction. Choice (D) mentions an *evaluation* (they are giants) and an *argument* (no, they aren't). Choice (D) most strongly matches the prediction and is the correct answer.

4. **C**   This question asks about the effect of the phrase *sweep so evil a breed from off the face of the earth*. First, locate the phrase and read it in context. It occurs at the end of Don Quixote's explanation that he intends to rid the world of these giants. In the next line, Sancho Panza asks, "*What giants?*" Panza's question deflates the inflated heroic tone that Quixote established. So look for an answer choice that supports the idea that Quixote establishes an inflated heroic tone. Choice (A) says the theme is a horror story, which does not fit this prediction. Choice (B) can be eliminated because Don Quixote is not, in fact, a prophet and has not received any

communications from God. Choice (C) could fit, since *grandiose view* matches inflated heroic tone. Choice (D) has no textual support: Quixote is not presented as a religious fanatic. Choice (C) is the correct answer.

5. **D** This question asks how Don Quixote would view his charge into battle. To answer this question, look at what Don Quixote actually says or thinks about this battle. In paragraph 6, he says he plans to *engage them in fierce and unequal combat*. The battle will be *unequal* because there are 30 or 40 of them, and he is only *a single knight*. He also calls the giants *cowards*. Look for an answer choice that fits these parts of the text. Choice (A), *ridiculous*, is what the reader and/or Sancho Panza might think about Don Quixote, not what Don Quixote thinks about himself. Choice (B), *insane*, is an even more extreme interpretation of what the reader and/or Sancho Panza might think. Choice (C), *unexceptional*, does not match the tone of Don Quixote's statement at all. Choice (D), *brave*, fits the prediction. Choice (D) is the correct answer.

6. **B** This question asks how Sancho Panza views Don Quixote. Notice that this is a best evidence question, so Q6 and Q7 can be answered in tandem. Look at the answers for Q7 first. The lines in (7A) show Don Quixote passing a judgment on Sancho Panza, so it cannot help answer Q6. Eliminate (7A). Choice (7B) again shows how Don Quixote views Sancho Panza, so it can be eliminated. Choice (7C) is the only one to actually include Sancho Panza, who cries out that Quixote is about to attack windmills, not giants. Look at the answer choices in Q6 to see if (7C) supports anything. The terms *boss* and *employees* from (6A) are more modern than language Sancho might use, plus Don Quixote never *endangers* Sancho. He actually tells him to stay back if he's frightened. The term *superior* and the phrase *needs looking after* from (6B) fit (7C), so draw a line connecting those answer choices. Sancho definitely does not follow Don Quixote *into battle*, so (6C) can be eliminated. The phrase *who requires help* from (6D) seems right, but Quixote is not portrayed as *a pious man* in the lines from (7C). Now look at (7D). It supports nothing from Q6, so eliminate it. At this point, the only options for correct answer choices are (6B) and (7C.) Choose them! Choices (6B) and (7C) are the correct answers.

7. **C** (See explanation above.)

8. **B** This question asks why Don Quixote does not listen to Sancho Panza's description of the "giants." Panza says they are windmills, and in lines 21–22 Quixote says that Panza is *not used to this business of adventures* and suggests that he might be *afraid*. Choice (A) mentions *eyesight*, which does not fit the prediction. Choice (B) mentions *not as brave*, which could match *afraid*. Keep it for now. Although Don Quixote mentions Friston's schemes, he never indicates whether he believes Sancho also knows about the schemes, so (C) can be eliminated. Choice (D) can be eliminated because Quixote suggests that Panza might start praying, not that he is doing so now. Only (B) has support. Choice (B) is the correct answer.

9. **C** This is a best evidence question, so simply refer back to the lines used to predict the answer to the previous question. Lines 21–22 were used to answer the question, so (C) is the correct answer.

10. **A** This question asks about the main effect of referring to Friston. Use that name as a key word and locate a window. Quixote says that this same Friston *who carried off my study and books* has also *turned these giants into mills in order to rob me of the glory of vanquishing them*. The effect of referring to Friston seems to be to show how Quixote can maintain his delusions in the real world. Even though he can now see that the things he attacked are really windmills, his fanciful view of the world has not changed. Choice (A) mentions that the reader gains insight into how Quixote perceives reality, and this fits, so keep it for now. Choice (B) says mentioning Friston reveals the evil in the world. Since it is unclear whether Friston is even real, and since the author does not say Friston is evil, eliminate (B). Choice (C) may be tempting in that the reader might want a detailed history of how Quixote came to see things, but that history is not present in this passage. Choice (D) again mentions evil as well as how evil results from personal misunderstandings. This has no support. Choice (A) is the correct answer.

11. **A** This question asks about the main idea regarding a problem women have had. Since this is a general question, do it after completing all specific questions. Look for an answer that finds support in several parts of the passage. Choice (A) seems possible, since paragraphs 1, 2, 5, and 7 all explicitly treat the issue of women's right to vote. Choice (B) does not have support in the text. Choice (C) has nothing to do with the text. Choice (D) raises an issue not explicitly discussed in the text. Choice (A) is the correct answer.

12. **D** This question asks what the author means by *grand documents*. Use the given line reference to find the window. The sentence following the one containing this phrase mentions the *Declaration of Independence, the United States Constitution*, and other documents, so choose an answer that means *important documents from U.S. history*. Choice (A) is too literal and too specific. Choice (B) does not match the prediction. Neither does (C). Choice (D) refers to *important legislation* and matches the prediction. Choice (D) is the correct answer.

13. **A** This question asks about a purpose of the Declaration of Independence. Use the lead words *Declaration of Independence* to find a window. The third paragraph says that the Declaration, and other documents, *propose to protect the people in the exercise of their God-given rights*. This fits (A), so keep that answer choice for now. The same paragraph says the opposite of (B), as well as of (C) so both of those answers can be eliminated. There is no support for (D). Choice (A) is the correct answer.

14. **C** This question asks for the best evidence for the answer to Q13. Since the prediction comes from paragraph 3, eliminate answer choices from other paragraphs first. Choice (A) is from paragraph 1. Choices (B) and (C) are both from paragraph 3; keep them for now. Choice (D) is from paragraph 6. Now compare the remaining answer choices. Choice (B) does not contain the phrase used to predict the correct answer to Q13. Choice (C) does contain that phrase. Choice (C) is the correct answer.

15. **C** This is a Vocab-in-Context question, so go back to the text, find the phrase *the exercise* in line 33, and cross it out. Replace it with another word that makes sense in the sentence based

on the context of the passage. Something like *the use* makes sense. Use that prediction to work through the given answers. Choice (A) seems relevant, so keep it for now. Choice (B) makes no sense. Choice (C) fits the prediction exactly. Choice (D) does not make sense. Although (A) might have looked good initially, when compared with (C), (A) loses strength. The people are not doing *an activity* with their rights. They are simply *using* them. Choice (C) is the correct answer.

16. **A**   This question asks for a logical inference regarding the general function of the term *natural right*. Use the given line reference to find the window. The complete phrase is *natural right of all to the ballot*, and the sentence ends with a mention of the *right to vote*. Choice (A) fits this prediction perfectly. Choices (B), (C), and (D) do not fit this prediction. Choice (A) is the correct answer.

17. **B**   This is a Vocab-in-Context question, so go back to the text, find the word *class* in line 59, and cross it out. Replace it with another word that makes sense in the sentence based on the context of the passage. A word like *group* or *part* would make sense, so use those words to work through the answer choices. Choice (A) does not fit the prediction, but (B) does. Choice (C) may seem possible, but is also overly scientific. Choice (D) is another meaning of *classy*. Between (B) and (C), (B) fits the prediction best. Choice (B) is the correct answer.

18. **A**   The question asks what the author concludes about the U.S. government, given the situation described in the text. Notice that the following question is a best evidence question, so questions 18 and 19 can be answered in tandem. Look at the answers for Q19 first. The lines in (19A) mention that the author is accused of the *crime of having voted … without having a lawful right to vote*, so look to see if those words support any answers in Q18. Choice (18A) mentions *laws denying women's suffrage*. Since suffrage means the right to vote, connect those two answers. Next, consider lines for (19B). The speaker quotes selections from the Declaration of Independence about being *created equal* and having *rights* such as *life, liberty, and the pursuit of happiness*. This is not referenced in any choices in Q18, so eliminate (19B). The lines in (19C) refer to the need for revolution when any government becomes repressive. This may weakly support (18D), so connect those two answers. Next, consider lines for (19D). These lines very clearly support (18D), so connect these two answers. Without any support from Q19, (18B) and (18C) can be eliminated. Consider the remaining pairs of answer choices in the context of the passage. While both (18A) and (18D) seem to be something that the author says that the government has done, the question asked what the author says about the government given the situation described in the text. Since that situation is the government unjustly barring women from voting, eliminate (18D) and its support in (19C) and (19D). Choices (18A) and (19A) are the correct answers.

19. **A**   (See explanation above.)

20. **A**   This question asks for the primary contrast in paragraph 7. Scan paragraph 7, and notice that it begins with *the whole people* and then states that *one-half of the people* have been made powerless by *the other half*. Choice (A) involves people and fits the main idea of the entire text.

Choice (B) involves people and a contrast, so keep it for now if you don't see a clear reason to eliminate it. Choices (C) and (D) do not involve people. Now go back to the text to find evidence to best support either (A) or (B). The text does mention rich men and poor men, but the main focus of the paragraph is the contrast between the *one-half of the population* that is *utterly powerless* and *left wholly at the mercy of the other half*. Choice (A) is the correct answer.

21.　**A**　The question asks why it is important to be able to assess the country's water supply. Find and read the window where the passage mentions the Geological Survey. The text states that water supply assessments *are indispensable tools for those involved in water-resources planning and management*, so the correct answer should deal with planning and management. Choice (A) mentions *planning future infrastructure*, so keep it. Choice (B) also uses the words *plan* and *manage*, so keep it for now. Choice (C) mentions researchers assessing data, not *planning* and *management*, so eliminate it. Choice (D) also does not relate to the prediction. Go back to the text now and find evidence to keep or eliminate either (A) or (B). When the two choices are compared, the wording of *all water resources* should stand out as more extreme than the wording in (A). Because there isn't matching extreme wording in the text, (B) can be eliminated. Choice (A) is the correct answer.

22.　**B**　The question asks for the best evidence to support the answer to the previous question. The text cited previously states that water supply assessments *are indispensable tools for those involved in water-resources planning and management*. Find the lines in which this statement is made and select the choice that matches. Choice (B) is the correct answer.

23.　**B**　The question asks why the information in the third paragraph is included. Read above and below the third paragraph to determine how it links the ideas together. Paragraph 2 discusses the importance of assessing water resources. Paragraph 3 mentions how to locate ground water, and paragraph 4 continues to discuss locating ground water with clues from rocks. So paragraph 3 is included because it introduces how a water resource can be found and assessed. Choice (A) mentions a *new method*, which could be tempting but the passage does not specify a method for finding ground water as *new*. Eliminate it. Choice (B) matches because it mentions *finding a natural resource*. Choice (C) does not match since it describes a *need*. Paragraph 3 introduces how a water resource can be found. Eliminate it. Choice (D) mentions a *hydrologic instrument* that is not mentioned in the passage, so eliminate it. Choice (B) is the correct answer.

24.　**D**　This is a Vocab-in-Context question, so go back to the text, find the word *occurrence* in line 32, and cross it out. Replace it with another word that makes sense in the sentence based on the context of the passage. Since the text discusses how to find ground water and the sentence states that *the landscape may offer clues to hydrologists*, the intended meaning of the word must have to do with the *existence* of ground water. Choice (A) does not mean *existence*. Neither does (B) or (C). Choice (D) means *existing* or *occurring*. Choice (D) is the correct answer.

25.　**C**　This is a Vocab-in-Context question, so go back to the text, find the word *penetrated* in line 52, and cross it out. Replace it with another word that makes sense in the sentence based on the context of the passage. The sentence mentions *depth to water* in its description of wells. So wells must be dug underground. The intended meaning of the word is something like *dug into*. Choice (A) does not mean *dug into*. Eliminate it. Choice (B) is similar in meaning to *penetrated*, but does not mean *dug into*. This choice is a trap answer. Eliminate it. Choice (C) means *dug into*. Choice (D) is also similar in meaning to *penetrated* but not similar to the prediction of *dug into*. The correct answer is (C).

26. **C** This question asks what the passage states about the occurrence of ground water. Since much of the passage is about ground water occurrence, this is a general question. Because this is also a paired set of questions, the best evidence question can be answered in tandem with this question. Look at the best evidence answers first and see if any of them support any of the answers for Q26. The lines for (27A) reference how water levels *rise in wet periods and decline in dry periods* and *average about the same as they did in the early part of the twentieth century*, especially in the *humid central and eastern parts of the country*. This supports (26C), so connect those two answers. The lines for (27B) discuss techniques for finding ground water. These lines don't support any of the answer choices for Q26, so (27B) can be eliminated. The lines for (27C) mention using the *landscape* and *hills* to find ground water. Choice (26B) mentions using landscape features to locate water, so connect (27C) and (26B).The lines for (27D) discuss *locating favorable conditions for ground-water development* by mapping the *distribution and positions of the different kinds of rocks*. This evidence does not support any of the choices in question 26. Eliminate it. Look at the remaining pairs of answer choices and use the text to make a decision about which pair is best supported. Choice (26B) is not actually supported by the text, because the *landscape features* mentioned in the text are *hills* and *valleys*. *Existing wells* are not mentioned until later. This eliminates (26B) and (27C). Choices (26C) and (27A) are the correct answers.

27. **A** (See explanation above.)

28. **A** This question asks which hydrologic or geologic layer in the figure holds moisture with molecular attraction. First reference the figure to determine if it describes moisture held by molecular attraction. It does. *Water (not ground water) held by molecular attraction* is labeled by arrows pointing to types of rock above the *water table*. The only two layers depicted above the water table in the figure are the *unsaturated zone* and the *land surface*. Choice (A) is one of those zones. Choice (B) is not depicted above the water table. Eliminate it. Choice (C) is shown both above and below the water table, so it would not hold only moisture with molecular attraction. Eliminate it. Choice (D) is not above the water table, so eliminate it. The correct answer is (A).

29. **A** This question asks which concept is supported by both the passage and the figure. The figure depicts two types of rock orientation which result in differences in ground water. The passage, in paragraph 4, discusses how *positions of the different kinds of rocks* could provide *clues to obtaining useful amounts of ground water*. The correct answer should discuss rock orientation and locating ground water. Choice (A) matches the prediction. Choice (B) is not supported by the figure, so eliminate it. Choice (C) is not supported by the figure either. For (D), while the

passage states that *some sedimentary rocks may extend many miles as aquifers of fairly uniform permeability*, it does not equate *permeability* with rock *position*. Eliminate it. Choice (A) is the correct answer.

30.   **B**   This question asks how the figure depicts the effect of rock orientation on ground water. Reference the figure for information on rock orientation. The figure shows two columns of rocks with different orientations and differences in ground water. Choice (A) mentions *rocks folding or turning*, which is not depicted in the figure. Choice (B) matches the figure. Keep it. Choice (C) mentions a best water indicator, which is not in the figure. Eliminate it. Choice (D) claims the figure shows many miles of aquifer, which it does not. Eliminate it. Choice (B) is the correct answer.

31.   **A**   This question asks about the main idea of the passage, so it should be done after all the specific questions. The passage describes the impact of exports on the global economy, specifically focusing on the banana and its potential impact on the Caribbean. This supports (A). Choice (B) is incorrect because it takes the idea of the passage too far and cannot be proven. Be cautious about answer choices with strong words like *must* or *will*, as these words can make the choice too extreme. Answer choices with strong wording aren't necessarily wrong, but there must be equally strongly-worded support in the passage. This passage does not contain that type of strong wording, so (B) can be eliminated. Eliminate (C) as well because it does not mention exports or bananas. Finally, (D) is incorrect because the Caribbean is not barred from gaining economic independence. Choice (A) is correct.

32.   **B**   This question asks about the main purpose of the second paragraph. Carefully read the second paragraph to determine what's going on in that paragraph. In the first sentence, the author says that the Panama Canal has *so occupied our attention* that we have *overlooked a significant... change taking place*. The paragraph goes on to describe that change. The correct answer will have something to do with a new change in economics or the emergence of the banana as an influential economic player. Choice (A) recycles *the completion of the Panama Canal*, but it is not the main idea of the paragraph, nor is it a true statement based on the passage, so it can be eliminated. Choice (B) matches the prediction, so don't eliminate it. Choice (C) is extreme because the passage never indicates that bananas will *dominate the economy*, and (D) is not the main point of the passage. Both of these choices may be eliminated. Therefore, (B) is correct.

33.   **B**   This is a Vocab-in-Context question. Find the word *exercise* in the passage and cross it out. Use context clues to put in another word that fits the meaning of the passage. The passage mentions the food products having an *influence upon international politics,* so *exercise* could be replaced with something like *exert* or *influence*. While (A), (C), and (D) are all synonyms for *exercise*, based on the context and prediction, (B) is the only answer that works. Choice (B) is the correct answer.

34.   **B**   The question asks for which lines best emphasize the potential importance of the banana as a product. Choice (A) can be eliminated because the lines do not mention bananas. Choice (B)

could work because those lines refer to economists' predictions that Caribbean diplomacy will be determined by the banana crop. Choice (C) does not answer the question, though it seems as though the banana has gained popularity in the United States. A lot of Americans eating bananas doesn't automatically mean bananas play any kind of significant role in the global economy. Eliminate (C). Choice (D) is also off-topic, as it describes how the Caribbean can become self-sustaining with the banana. Therefore, (B) is correct.

35.　**D**　This is a Vocab-in-Context question. Find the word *friendship* in the passage and cross it out. Use context clues to put in another word that fits the meaning of the passage. The passage mentions *near neighbors* and *diplomacy of the Caribbean*, so the missing word must mean something like *positive relations with neighboring countries*. Choices (A) and (B) might be good synonyms for *friendship*, but neither matches the context of the passage. Eliminate both of those choices. *Collusion* does mean working together, but with an illegal or fraudulent goal. This doesn't match the prediction so it can be eliminated. Choice (D) matches the prediction and is the correct answer.

36.　**D**　This question asks for the main idea of the final paragraph. The final paragraph highlights the importance of the Caribbean and the diplomatic importance of exports. Choice (A) is incorrect because it is too literal. While the word *friendship* does show up in the final paragraph, it is not a literal reference to being friends. It's a reference to diplomacy, which is not mentioned in (A). Eliminate (A). Choice (B) is mentioned, but it is not the main point of the paragraph. Choice (C) recycles words, so it might look good at first glance. However, a careful reading of (C) shows that although the words look familiar, they aren't put together in a way that matches the prediction. Eliminate (C). Choice (D) matches the prediction and is the correct answer.

37.　**A**　This question is a general paired question, so look at the next question first to find connections between evidence and the answer choices for this question. Choice (38A) does not support any of the choices in question 37, so eliminate (38A). Choice (38B) supports (37A), so connect those two answer choices. Choice (38C) does not support any of the choices for question 37, so eliminate (38C). Choice (38D) could potentially support (37C) or (37D), so keep these answer choices. Since (37B) is not supported by any of the evidence in question 38, it may be eliminated. Now, look at the question to see which of these pairings answers question 37. The question asks for *potential difficulties* that the author anticipates. Choice (37A) outlines the need for certain technologies to work, which is a potential difficulty. Choices (37C) is extreme and recycles the words in a way that makes the statement untrue. Therefore, eliminate (37C). Choice (37D) is also untrue, so (37D) and (38D) can be eliminated. This leaves (37A) and (38B) as the correct answers.

38.　**B**　(See explanation above.)

39.　**A**　This question asks about data in the tables and ideas in the passage. The correct answer will connect the two. Choice (A) links the idea of the United States importing the majority of the world's bananas with the data showing that the world's banana crop isn't going completely to the United States. Keep (A). Choice (B) may be true based on the text, but there is nothing in the table to support that answer. Eliminate (B). Choice (C) is also true based on the text, but again, does not also connect to the tables, so it can be eliminated. Choice (D) might initially look good, but the tables measure two different things (U.S. Banana Supply and world banana supply), so no trends are indicated. Choice (A) is the correct answer.

40. **C** Simply check the exports from each of these countries to see which shows the greatest increase or decrease in exports to the United States. Jamaica has the greatest difference between those two data points, making (C) correct.

41. **D** Use the chart to answer this question. Choices (A), (B), and (C) are untrue statements according to the chart. From the numbers in the chart, (D) is true because Colombia exported more bananas than Cuba in 1911. Choice (D) is correct.

42. **B** This question asks what Passage 1 says about the caudate. Use this key word to find the window in paragraph 4. The caudate seems to be a brain area that is active during music listening and before the chill response. The next sentence states that *this subregion* is involved in *learning of stimulus-response associations, and in mediating the reinforcing qualities of rewarding stimuli such as food.* Choice (A) suggests that the caudate emerges from study, which makes no sense. Eliminate (A). Choice (B) says the caudate is involved in learning associations, which is strongly supported by the prediction. Choice (C) is deceptive: The caudate activation takes place before the chill response, but it does not cause it. Choice (D) is deceptive: The caudate does not help reinforce qualities of food. Choice (B) is the correct answer.

43. **D** This question asks for the best evidence for the answer to Q42. Since the prediction comes from paragraph 4, eliminate answer choices from other paragraphs first. Choice (A) comes from paragraph 1, and (B) comes from paragraph 3. Both (C) and (D) come from paragraph 4. Choice (C) does not contain the phrases that supported the prediction. Choice (D) is the correct answer.

44. **C** This question asks what the author of Passage 1 says about music. Notice that all four answer choices contain the word *feelings*. Now focus the search for statements the author makes about music and feelings. The text opens asking *Why does music make us feel?* It continues by explaining that music can stimulate certain brain areas, after which we experience certain feelings. Choice (A) says music *may preclude feeling states*. *Preclude* means something like exclude, so (A) is not supported. Choice (B) suggests that feelings cause music, rather than the reverse. Choice (C) fits the prediction well. Choice (D) is deceptive because the individual words in the answer may look familiar, but the answer actually contradicts the text's claim that music is *devoid of … explicit ideas*. Choice (C) is the correct answer.

45. **A** This question is a Vocab-in-Context question, so go back to the text, find the word *betrays*, and cross it out. Now read the complete thought, and insert a word that makes sense based on the

context clues. A word like *expresses* or *shows* would make sense, so use such a word to compare to the answer choices. Choice (A) has a similar meaning, so keep it for now. Choices (B), (C), and (D) are all different meanings of *betray*. Choice (A) is the correct answer.

46. **B** This question asks the main reason the author of Passage 2 refers to coldness. Find the window and read to determine why the author is talking about coldness. *The "coldness" of chills may provide increased motivation for social reunion in the parents.* The correct answer should have something to do with social reunions or families. Choice (A) is deceptive, mentioning the chill effect, but the author is not outlining anything here. Choice (B) is not obviously right, but is also not obviously wrong. Keep it for now. Choice (C) refers to sadness, which is in another part of the passage. Choice (D) is deceptive, since it mentions *piloerection*, but the text says there is no connection, not that one helps trace the other's origin. With three choices eliminated, the correct answer must be what is left. Paragraph 2 is about Panksepp's *evolutionary explanation*, and the description of *coldness* as providing *motivation for social reunion* can be called an illustration. Choice (B) is the correct answer.

47. **C** This question asks what the author of Passage 2 says that Panksepp and Benedek and Kaernbach have in common. Use those names as lead words to locate the relevant parts of the passage. Paragraph 2 states that Panksepp is a *neuroscientist* and shows him as providing an *explanation*. Paragraph 3 says that Benedek and Kaernbach have done *experimental work* that *offers some support for Panksepp's hypothesis* and *lends some support to Panksepp's ideas*. Choice (A) is true for Benedek and Kaernbach, but it is not true for Panksepp. Choice (B) strongly matches Panksepp, and it could weakly match Benedek and Kaernbach. Keep it for now. Choice (C) strongly matches Panksepp in paragraph 2, and Benedek and Kaernbach in paragraph 3. Choice (D) contradicts the passage entirely. Between (B) and (C), (C) has much stronger support in the passage. Choice (C) is the correct answer.

48. **A** This question asks about the effect of the reference to the song "I Will Always Love You." Use the lead words to locate the window. The song is called *a great example*. The previous sentence clarifies that the song is an example of *chills and piloerection* being *associated with sad music*. Choice (A) is very close to this prediction, so keep it. Choice (B) is deceptive, referring to a later part of the paragraph. Choice (C) refers to a researcher mentioned later in the passage. Panksepp is the one who references the song, not Benedek. Choice (D) is deceptive, incorrectly combining terms used in the paragraph (*bleak, repeated*). Choice (A) is the correct answer.

49. **D** This question asks about the main idea of both passages. Passage 1 reports on the findings of Montreal researchers who used brain scan technologies in their experiments. Passage 2 relays a neuroscientist's evolutionary explanation and then reports on the findings of two other researchers who measured physiological responses. Both passages are interested in exploring how music and feelings are connected. Choice (A) mentions methods, but also says the passages focus on *learning* music, which is not the case. Eliminate (A). Choice (B) sets up a false opposition that is not supported in either text. Choice (C) may seem possible, but the use of the word

scientists makes the answer too specific. Eliminate it. Choice (D) says that the passages mean to inform us that neuroscience (the study of the brain) can help us understand responses to music. Since feelings can be responses to music, this fits the prediction. Choice (D) is the correct answer.

50. **B** This question asks about the relationship between the two passages. Think about what is similar and what is different between the passages. Choice (A) attributes the evolutionary explanation to Passage 1, but that is actually in Passage 2, so (A) is flawed. Choice (B) says that Passage 1 considers positive emotions and Passage 2 considers negative emotions in relation to music. This matches the *intense states of excitement … pleasurable stimulus …* and *favorite part* in Passage 1 and *sad … bleak … loss …* and *cries* in Passage 2. Keep (B). Choice (C) contrasts research in Passage 1 to theories in Passage 2. It's true that Passage 1 is about research, but Passage 2 has both theories and research, so that answer doesn't match what's in the text. Eliminate it. Choice (D) correctly states that Passage 1 relies on methods of neuroscience, but then says Passage 2 considers only theoretical work. This is not true, so eliminate (D). Choice (B) is the correct answer.

51. **C** This question asks about a point on which both authors would agree. Although this question asks about both passages, don't forget to POE one passage at a time. Go through the answers considering just Passage 1. Choice (A) is supported, so keep it. Choice (B) might initially look good because those tests are mentioned, but there's no indication that the author thinks those tests are *superior*, so choice (B) can be eliminated. Choice (C) is supported by the text. Choice (D) looks mostly right, because Passage 1 does discuss music and the expression of *positive emotions*, but Passage 1 does not mention anything about *negative emotions*. Eliminate (D). Only (A) and (C) are left. Use Passage 2 to compare the two remaining choices. Although Passage 2 does address *concrete ways* music affects us, there is no acknowledgement in the text about music being *generally abstract*. Eliminate (A). Choice (C) is supported and is the correct answer.

52. **B** This question asks what in Passage 1 best fits a specific part of Passage 2. To tackle this question, start by identifying the exact relevant part of Passage 2. It is an argument attributed to Panksepp. Using the line references provided, locate that argument: *He argues that chills may emerge from brain dynamics associated with the perception of social loss, specifically with separation calls.* Now consider each answer choice to see which one best fits the idea of social loss or separation. Choice (A) is about music being abstract. This does not fit the prediction, so eliminate it. Choice (B) is about music causing a deep reaction. This could fit the prediction, so keep it for now. Choice (C) is about dopamine and some brain areas. It is very specific, and doesn't connect with the ideas of loss in the prediction. Choice (D) talks about sounds functioning as a reward cue. This involves positive emotions, whereas the prediction had a negative emotion. Thus, (D) is not as good a fit for the prediction. If *sound stirs us at our biological roots*, then *sad music* evoking an association with *loss* seems like a good example of being so stirred. Choice (B) is the correct answer.

Section 2: Writing and Language

1. **B** Notice that all four answer choices have essentially the same meaning: *increased, growing, larger spirit of...* all mean roughly the same thing in this context. When this is the case, choose the shortest answer that makes sense in the given context. In this sentence, that answer is (B), which contains all the information the other answers do in the fewest words.

2. **D** While all four choices technically "combine" the sentences, only (D) does so in an effective way. Choices (A) and (C) change the punctuation and some of the words, but this punctuation is not appropriate in context because the first of the two sentences is incomplete. Choice (B) can also be eliminated because it creates awkward combinations such as *moreover for instance* and states, awkwardly, that *swapping jobs is a thing that new workers do now*. Therefore, (D) is correct.

3. **B** The proposed addition helps to clarify business practices in Silicon Valley by explaining how that place is *fast-paced, forward-thinking,* and *occasionally ruthless*. This phrase should be added to the sentence because it enriches the paragraph's description of Silicon Valley and why a business model like Netflix's would be effective there. Choice (B) most effectively captures this reasoning. In addition, check the reasons to find opportunities for POE.

4. **C** Choices (A) and (B) create sentence fragments, so they can be eliminated. Then, since the subject of the remaining verb is the singular noun *Netflix*, the verb too must be singular, making (C) correct.

5. **A** The earlier parts of this sentence mention *visual media* and *home entertainment systems*. In order to make the underlined portion consistent with the earlier parts of the sentence, eliminate (B), which is unnecessarily wordy and (C), which is too specific. Choice (D), *intelligent machines*, may describe something relevant to the sentence, but it does not do so in language consistent with the rest of the sentence, and the term is somewhat broad. Only (A), *computers*, captures the tone of the rest of the sentence without adding unnecessary words or using weird terms.

6. **D** The previous paragraph discusses Netflix's technological innovations. This paragraph discusses Netflix's innovations in the business world. As such, the word or phrase that links the two ideas should indicate some continuation of the discussion. This eliminates (A), which has no obvious relation to either paragraph, and (B), which is not a word. Choice (C) can also be eliminated because it implies a cause-and-effect relationship that is not present in the passage. Only (D), *Furthermore*, appropriately links the two paragraphs.

7. **D** This sentence discusses Netflix's openness about how it conducts business. Choice (A) captures this idea, but it does so in language that is too informal and grammatically incorrect. The sentence is not concerned with Netflix's *rudeness*, eliminating (B). Choice (C) actually contradicts the idea of Netflix's forthrightness. Only (D) effectively sets up the second idea in this sentence.

8. **B** Notice that the underlined word is part of a list. The other parts of the list are *staying late* and *showing loyalty to the company*. As such, the word in the underlined portion should be consistent with *staying* and *showing*. Choices (B) and (D) both contain the word *coming*, which is consistent with the remainder of the list, but (B) is more effective because it does not introduce unnecessary words.

9. **D** When given the option to DELETE the underlined portion, give that option serious consideration: It is often correct. In this case, all of the proposed choices interrupt the idea unnecessarily, so the best option is to delete those words altogether. Choice (D) is therefore the best from among the possible answers.

10. **C** A *premise* is a statement or proposition that provides the basis for a conclusion. While that could potentially work in this context, the word *promise* is much more precise because the passage as a whole is about Netflix's unwillingness to *promise* all the long-term benefits of a typical job. As such, (A) and (B) can be eliminated because they use the wrong word. Then, of the remaining two, (C) is consistent with the given context, which calls for a noun.

11. **A** The passage as a whole is about how Netflix represents a new frontier in how employees interact with the companies for which they work. The passage is not concerned with apocalyptic scenarios like the one described in (B), with helping readers to get jobs at Netflix as in (C), or in losing a job in general as in (D). The most effective restatement of the passage's main claim comes from (A), which refers to Netflix's practices as indicative of a potential *workplace of the future*.

12. **C** The *stylistic pattern established earlier in the sentence* is that of a list. The other two items in this list are *watching six-second videos on Vine* and *reading short posts on Facebook and Twitter*. The format of each of these items is an *-ing* word describing an activity followed by the site on which the activity is conducted. Choices (B) and (C) both follow this format, but (C) adheres more closely to the pattern of the other two items in the list.

13. **A** This sentence is very long, but make sure that there is a good reason to add punctuation. Choices (C) and (D) add commas, but they also add words that create comma splices. Choice (B) adds a comma, but removing the word *and* creates an awkward phrase with no obvious relationship to the rest of the sentence. As such, (A) provides the most effective connection of this part of the sentence with what has come before it.

14. **D** This paragraph is all about TV's *harmful effects*, so this sentence about *shining light in your eyes for many hours at a time* is in keeping with that discussion. Choices (B) and (C) suggest a contrast, so they can be eliminated. Choice (A) suggests that the information has been mentioned before (*aforementioned*), which it has not. Choice (D) is therefore the best answer in that it provides a transition that preserves the continuity of the ideas in the paragraph.

15. **A** This sentence discusses the *senses* belonging to *you*, or *your* senses. Choices (B) and (C) can be eliminated because *you're* is a contraction of *you are*. Then, (D) can be eliminated because it

contains a semicolon, which would require complete ideas both before and after. The single word *vision* is not a complete idea, making (A) the best answer.

16. **B** The sentence and paragraph are in the past tense, so the verb in this underlined portion should be in the past tense as well. This leaves only (B). Choices (C) and (D) are also wrong for introducing apostrophes in text which contains neither possession nor contraction.

17. **D** This paragraph is about television's national reach. It mentions The Beatles, but it is not particularly concerned with The Beatles. As a result, this sentence would add information that is not obviously connected to the paragraph's main focus. Therefore, the sentence should not be added because it is irrelevant to the paragraph's main focus, as (D) states. To help determine "Yes" or "No," check the reasons to use POE.

18. **B** This is a complex sentence, so use the context. The following sentence refers to African Americans as a *targeted group*. The previous sentence refers to a new presence of *non-white faces*, suggesting that *non-white* groups were not represented in quite the same way before. Choices (A) and (C) do not establish the link between the sentences clearly, and while (D) contains all the words the other choices do, it doesn't actually make any sense. As a result, the only choice that correctly positions the parts of the sentence relative to one another is (B).

19. **D** The other example given in this sentence is *the Chinese-American character on* Have Gun Will Travel. Choice (D) gives an example in a similar format and is in fact the only one of the answer choices to provide a second example. The others provide irrelevant information or elaborate on the first example.

20. **C** If there is no specific reason to use commas, don't use them. In this case, setting off the phrase *in the American public* with commas would imply that that information is not necessary to the meaning of the sentence. However, the word *many* is not adequately specific without this information. As such, this phrase should contain no commas at all, as in (C).

21. **D** Choice (A) merely changes the punctuation of the sentences—it does not exactly combine them. It also preserves the ambiguity of the word *they*, which could refer to either *hometowns* or *people*. Choice (B) also preserves this ambiguity. Choice (C) creates a new mistake by introducing words that have no clear role within the sentence. Only (D) correctly links the two parts of the sentence, as the word *which* clearly refers back to the word *hometowns* that precedes it and is offset by a comma.

22. **D** Paragraph 6 begins with *This national reach*, suggesting that the paragraph that precedes it must discuss something about a *national reach*. Paragraph 3 discusses this national reach and how television *provided something truly national for the first time*. Therefore, paragraph 6 should be placed after paragraph 3, or before paragraph 4, as (D) states.

23. **D** The answer choices provide a variety of pronouns, so find the original noun. In this case, the original noun is *nature*, which is singular, thus eliminating (A) and (B). Choice (D) is the

more effective of the remaining choices because it shows possession: *nature's greenery* is *its greenery*, whereas (C) would say *it is greenery*, which doesn't make sense in the context.

24.   **A**   The previous sentence discusses how nature *looks* as well as how it *sounds*. This sentence continues that discussion, introducing the idea that highways don't just change how nature *looks*, they change how it *sounds*. Choices (A) and (D) indicate that continuation, but (A) does so more concisely and precisely, without adding the potentially ambiguous pronoun *this*.

25.   **B**   Everything so far in the passage has taken special care to emphasize how nature *sounds* as well as how it *looks*. This sentence would continue to provide that crucial emphasis, so it should be added here. Choice (B) effectively states the reason: It completes the idea stated in the previous sentence that *when we build highways through thriving natural habitats, we don't just change the way they look*.

26.   **B**   When unsure of what word to use, fill in the blank with a word that makes sense. In this case, something like *accustomed to* would work. Choice (A) certainly does not mean that. Choice (B) does—*inure* means "to grow accustomed to something unpleasant." Choices (C) and (D) don't work in the context at all—*keen* means "eager" and *hip* means "aware" and/or "stylish." Only (B), therefore, works in this context.

27.   **C**   All four choices say essentially say the same thing, so choose the one that does so most concisely and precisely. Choices (B) and (D) add awkward *-ing* constructions, so those choices should be eliminated. Choice (A) makes the highway sound like a radio or stereo system, so that too should be eliminated. Choice (C) works best—it says precisely what the other choices say imprecisely.

28.   **C**   When so many words are changing in the answer choices, ignore the part that stays consistent (*at the Intermountain Bird Observatory in Idaho*), and focus specifically on what is changing. In this case, the word *and* in (A) and the word *who* in (B) create awkward sentence fragments. The word *they* in (D) restates the subject unnecessarily. Choice (C) states the proposed idea most directly without adding new errors.

29.   **B**   In this sentence, the phrase *or a "phantom"* is a rewording or clarification of the word *fake*. The phrase is not necessary to the meaning of the sentence and should therefore be offset with commas, as in (B). Choices (A) and (D) misplace the comma, and (C) uses a semicolon, which cannot work in this context.

30.   **B**   If there is not a good reason to use punctuation marks, don't use them. Nothing is being quoted here, so there is no need for quotation marks, as in (A). No information is being offset as unnecessary, so there is no need for a comma, as in (C). The idea up to and including the word *traffic* is not complete, so a single dash cannot be used, as in (D). Therefore, only (B), which contains no punctuation, can be used.

31. **D** The figure shows proposed highway extensions in the American South. The Interstate High-way Commission has no particular plans to eradicate avian life in these regions, thus eliminating (A) and (B). Then, the route from Savannah to Knoxville goes roughly north-south, and the route from Augusta to Natchez goes roughly east-west, as indicated by the map. Therefore, (D) is correct.

32. **C** The proposed sentence describes what birds do when they are unable to act as they usually would. The word *however* implies a contrast with some previous sentence that describes normal bird behavior. Sentence 3 does so in describing how birds *need to spend as much time as possible with their heads down*. The new sentence describes how highway noise prevents those birds from doing so, so the new sentence would be best placed after sentence 3, as suggested by (C).

33. **A** Notice the modifier at the beginning of this sentence: *With lower speed limits and rubberized asphalt*. This modifier describes *the roads*, which should follow the modifier, thus eliminating (B) and (D). Also, (C) can also be eliminated because the pronoun *they* is ambiguous in the context. Choice (A) places the subject close to its modifier and does so without introducing an ambiguous pronoun.

34. **C** The underlined word is part of a larger phrase, *an early Spanish explorer and conquistador*. With the comma after the word *Coronado*, the passage has already indicated that the phrase should be set off with commas. Choice (C) provides the second comma and does not change the punctuation unnecessarily, as (A) and (D) do, nor remove it, as (B) does.

35. **B** Use POE to eliminate bad answer choices, especially when the choices don't follow an obvious pattern. The phrase *but also* is typically paired with the words *not only*; therefore, because the sentence does not use the phrase *not only*, it should not use *but also* either, eliminating (A). The same pairing happens with the phrase *just as* and *so too*, which are listed separately in (C) and (D) and can both be eliminated. Only (B) works in the context, with the word *wherein* referring back to the word *window*.

36. **C** This question is testing word choice, or idioms. Choices (A) and (D) can be eliminated because the words they contain are not idiomatically consistent with the word *atrocities*. Choice (B) suffers from the same issue, though it is a bit closer in meaning to the correct word, *committed*, as in (C). In short, one *commits atrocities* but does not *do atrocities*.

37. **D** Because the adjective *noble* cannot be counted (one cannot have, for example, five noble), it takes the word *less* rather than the word *fewer*, eliminating (A). Then, because the word *than/then* is being used in a comparison rather than in a sequence, *than* is the correct choice, eliminating (B) and (C). Only (D) remains, which uses the correct forms of each of the words and does not introduce unnecessary punctuation.

38. **B** All four choices contain the word *else* and the colon. Choices (A), (C), and (D) give additional words, but none of these words have a clear, essential role within the passage. As such, (B)

gives the same information as the others and does so in the fewest words. Choice (B) is therefore the best of the available answer choices.

39. **A** Choices (B) and (D) introduce words to the underlined portion, creating awkward sentence fragments that don't make sense. Choice (C) suggests that Coronado was *growing up* in Spain at the moment that he arrived in New Spain, which can't be true. Only (A) remains, therefore, to start the phrase that describes Coronado's upbringing.

40. **B** Choices (A) and (C) begin with the word *They*, which creates a comma splice with the sentence's two ideas: *They lay in wait for someone to claim the bounty* and *these cities were richer than any place in the world*. If these ideas were to remain complete, they would need to be separated by a period or some other kind of Stop punctuation. Choice (D), however, introduces the unnecessary word *While* and breaks up the phrase *lying/laying in wait*. The best of the answer choices is therefore (B), which is concise and fixes the comma splice.

41. **A** The claim made by this sentence is as follows: *Coronado's disappointment was absolutely unforgiving and vicious*. With a specific detail, (A) effectively communicates the *unforgiving and vicious* aspects of Coronado's journey. Choices (B), (C), and (D) may all be true, but none are as specific as the claim made in this sentence.

42. **D** When given the option to DELETE the underlined portion, give that option serious consideration: it is often correct. In this case, all the choices add some redundant or unnecessary detail to the sentence, so it is best to end this sentence at the word *Kansas*, as (D) suggests.

43. **D** Sentence 2 states, *That's a lot of territory to cover in the middle of the sixteenth century!* This sentence thus clearly refers to some previous sentence that describes covering *a lot of territory*. Sentence 4 describes a journey from Mexico to Kansas, the most specific possible referent for the phrase *a lot of territory*. Sentence 2 should therefore be placed before sentence 5, as indicated in (D).

44. **B** The previous sentence says, *His influence is all around us*, but the remainder of the passage does not give any specific instances of where this *influence* can be seen. Therefore, the new sentence should be added to the sentence because it provides examples of Coronado's *influence*. Choice (B) best captures this reasoning. Choice (A) may be true, though the passage does not indicate what Coronado's favorite places were.

Section 3: Math (No Calculator)

1. **C** Use Process of Elimination. The w represents the number of workers, and t represents the total time in hours. Therefore, the 20 must have something to do with the cost of the workers' hourly wage. Eliminate (A) because nothing is mentioned about a minimum number of workers. Eliminate (B) because it is unrelated to the workers. Choice (C) relates to the hourly wage, so keep it, but check (D) just in case. Choice (D) can be eliminated because the number of wedding guests is unrelated to the cost and unrelated to the workers and their time. Choice (C) is correct.

2. **D** Subtract 4 from both sides of the equation to get $12x = 16$. Divide the entire equation by 2 to get $6x = 8$. Therefore, $6x + 5 = 8 + 5 = 13$, which is (D).

3. **C** Plug in the answers, starting with (B). In (B), $x = -4$ and $y = 4$. Plug those values into the first equation to get $5(-4) - 4(4) = 36$. Solve the left side of the equation to get $-20 - 16 = 36$, and $-36 = 36$. Since the values do not work in the first equation, eliminate (B). Next try (C). In (C), $x = 4$, and $y = -4$. Plug those values in the first equation to get $5(4) - 4(-4) = 36$. Solve the left side of the equation to get $20 - (-16) = 36$, and $36 = 36$. Next, try the same numbers in the second equation: $-4 - (-4) = 0$. Solve the left side of the equation to get $-4 + 4 = 0$, and $0 = 0$. The coordinate pair works in both equations, therefore, the correct answer is (C).

4. **A** Plug $y = 8$ into the equation to get $8 - \sqrt{4x^2 + 28} = 0$. Therefore, $\sqrt{4x^2 + 28} = 8$. Plug in the answers to see which value of x works. In (B), $x = 4$, making the square root $\sqrt{4(4)^2 + 28} = \sqrt{4(16) + 28} = \sqrt{92}$, which is not equal to 8. A smaller number is needed, so eliminate (B), (C), and (D). The answer is therefore (A).

5. **B** Parallel lines have the same slope. Since the question asks for the y-coordinate of a point on $\overline{AD}$, which is parallel to $\overline{BC}$, start by finding the slope of $\overline{BC}$. Use the slope formula $\dfrac{y_2 - y_1}{x_2 - x_1}$ to get $\dfrac{10 - 0}{0 - 6} = \dfrac{10}{-6} = \dfrac{5}{-3}$. Now use this slope to find the value of r: $\dfrac{5}{-3} = \dfrac{0 - r}{-3 - 0}$ or $\dfrac{5}{-3} = \dfrac{-r}{-3}$. Therefore, $5 = -r$, so $r = -5$, and the answer is (B).

6. **C** Use bite-sized pieces and Process of Elimination. Focus on just the first term in the expression given, which is $16x^6$. In (A), the first term in the expanded version of the expression would be $(16x^2)^3 = 4,096x^6$. Eliminate (A). In (B), the first term in the expanded version of the expression would be $(16x^3)^2 = 256x^6$. Eliminate (B). In (C), the first term of the expanded expression would be $(4x^3)^2 = 16x^6$. This is correct, so either expand out the rest of (C) or check the first term on the expression in (D) to be sure. The second option is easier: $(4x)^6 = 4,096x^6$, so (C) is correct.

7. **D** When a question asks for the least possible value, plug in the answers, starting with the smallest answer choice. Plug in $n = 11$ from (A) and see if $S > 2,000$ as stated in the question. The equation becomes $S = 180(11 - 9) = 1,620$. This is not greater than 2,000, so eliminate (A). A larger value for n is needed to make the sum of the angles greater than 2,000. Try (C) to get $S = 180(13 - 11) = 1,980$. This is still too small, so (D) must be the correct answer.

8. **A** First, define the equations for both of the lines. The slope-intercept form of a line is $y = mx + b$, where x and y are the coordinates of a point on the line, m is the slope, and b is the y-intercept. Plug in the point $(4, 4)$ and a y-intercept of -8 into the slope-intercept equation to get $4 = (m)(4) - 8$. Solve for m to get $12 = 4m$ and $m = 3$. Therefore,

the equation for line k is $y = 3x - 8$. Next, find the equation of line m. Given two points, use the point-slope formula to find the line: $y - y_1 = m(x - x_1)$. To find the slope, m, use the slope formula $\dfrac{y_2 - y_1}{x_2 - x_1}$. For line m, the slope is $\dfrac{-3-5}{5-1} = \dfrac{-8}{4} = -2$. Therefore, plugging the point $(1, 5)$ into the point-slope formula results in $y - 5 = -2(x - 1)$. Distribute the -2 to get $y - 5 = -2x + 2$. Solve for y to get $y = -2x + 7$. Set the two line equations equal to each other to get $3x - 8 = -2x + 7$. Solve for x to get $5x = 15$, and $x = 3$. Plug $x = 3$ into the equation for line k to get $y = 3(3) - 8 = 1$. Therefore, the point of intersection (s, t) is $(3, 1)$ and $s - t = 3 - 1 = 2$, and the answer is (A).

9. **B** When multiplying variables with the same base and different exponents, add the exponents. The equation becomes $k^{x^2 + xy + y^2 + xy} = k^{25}$. Combine like terms to get $k^{x^2 + 2xy + y^2} = k^{25}$. Therefore, $x^2 + 2xy + y^2 = 25$. Factor the quadratic to get $(x + y)^2 = 25$. Take the square root of both sides to get $x + y = \pm 5$. Substitute 3 for x to get $3 + y = \pm 5$. Since the question asks for the positive value of y, the equation to use is $3 + y = 5$, so $y = 2$, and the correct answer is (B).

10. **D** Plug in. Let $D = 2$ and $E = 5$, so the equation becomes $F = \dfrac{2}{5 - 2} = \dfrac{2}{3}$. Plug these values

for D, E, and F into the answer choices to see which answer works. Choice (A) becomes

$2 = \dfrac{5}{1 - \dfrac{2}{3}}$. Solve the right side of the equation to get $2 = \dfrac{5}{\frac{1}{3}}$, and $2 = 15$. Eliminate (A).

Choice (B) becomes $2 = \dfrac{5}{1 + \dfrac{2}{3}}$. Solve the right side of the equation to get $2 = \dfrac{5}{\frac{5}{3}}$, and

$2 = 3$. Eliminate (B). Choice (C) becomes $2 = \dfrac{\frac{2}{3}(5)}{1 - \dfrac{2}{3}}$. Solve the right side of the equation to

get $2 = \dfrac{\frac{10}{3}}{\frac{1}{3}}$, and $2 = 10$. Eliminate (C). The answer must be (D). And indeed, plugging in the

values gives $2 = \dfrac{\frac{2}{3}(5)}{1 + \dfrac{2}{3}}$. Solving the right side of the equation results in $2 = \dfrac{\frac{10}{3}}{\frac{5}{3}}$, and $2 = 2$.

11. **B** Since calculator use is not allowed on this section, graphing and checking each function is not an option. Plug in instead. Usually, zero is a number to avoid, since it messes things up, but the goal here is to find what must be true, so messing things up helps. If $x = 0$, (A) becomes $0^2 - 3 = -3$. This is not greater than or equal to -2, so eliminate (A). Choice (B) becomes $(0 - 3)^2 = 9$, which is greater than -2, so keep it for now. Choice (C) becomes $|0| - 3 = -3$, and (D) becomes $(0 - 3)^3 = -27$. Neither of these values is greater than -2, so eliminate them and choose (B).

12. **D** When a fraction has imaginary numbers in the denominator, multiply the fraction by the complex conjugate of the denominator. The complex conjugate of $(6 - 3i)$ is $(6 + 3i)$. The original expression becomes $\dfrac{(1 + 10i)(6 + 3i)}{(6 - 3i)(6 + 3i)}$. Use FOIL to multiply it out to get $\dfrac{6 + 3i + 60i + 30i^2}{36 + 18i - 18i - 9i^2}$.

Combine like terms to get $\dfrac{6 + 63i + 30i^2}{36 - 9i^2}$. Since $i = \sqrt{-1}$, $i^2 = -1$. Plug this into the expression, which becomes $\dfrac{6 + 63i + 30(-1)}{36 - 9(-1)} = \dfrac{6 + 63i - 30}{36 + 9} = \dfrac{-24 + 63i}{45}$. Split this into two fractions, as seen in the answer choices, to get $\dfrac{-24}{45} + \dfrac{63i}{45} = \dfrac{-8}{15} + \dfrac{7i}{5}$, which is (D).

13. **D** The decay formula states that $decay = original(1 - r)^t$, where r is the rate of decay and t is time. Therefore, the value of the truck after t years is $35,000(0.93)^t$, which is (D).

14. **A** Rather than trying to do some messy algebraic manipulation, plug in a simple number like $x = 2$. The expression becomes $\dfrac{6(2) - 1}{2 + 4} = \dfrac{11}{6}$. Now plug $x = 2$ into the answer choices to see which one equals $\dfrac{11}{6}$. Choice (A) becomes $6 - \dfrac{25}{2 + 4} = 6 - \dfrac{25}{6} = \dfrac{36}{6} - \dfrac{25}{6} = \dfrac{11}{6}$. That matches, but check the other answer choices to be sure. None of them equals $\dfrac{11}{6}$ when $x = 2$, so the answer is (A).

15. **B** The product of the roots of a quadratic $ax^2 + bx + c = 0$ is $\dfrac{c}{a}$. In the given quadratic, $c = 12$ and $a = 3$, so $\dfrac{12}{3} = 4$. Without this handy trick, another way to solve this is to use the quadratic formula to find the roots, then multiply them together. Either way, the answer is (B).

16. **82** Expand the left side of the equation to get $3(x - 5)(x - 5) + 7$. FOIL the quadratic to get $3(x^2 - 10x + 25) + 7$. Distribute the 3 to get $3x^2 - 30x + 75 + 7 = 3x^2 - 30x + 82$. Therefore, $c = 82$.

17. **15** Because BD and AE are parallel, triangles ACE and BCD are similar triangles (all of their corresponding angles are equal to each other). Therefore, the lengths of their sides are proportional. To solve for the length of $\overline{AE}$, set up the following proportion: $\dfrac{10}{12} = \dfrac{\overline{AE}}{18}$. Cross-multiply to get $12\overline{AE} = 180$. Solve for $\overline{AE}$ to get $\overline{AE} = 15$.

18. **4, 8, 12, 16,** or **20**

Plug in. Start by testing whether a single red chip could work. If Eve has one red chip, then she has $120 − $5 = $115 worth of blue chips, which does not divide by 20 for an integer number of blue chips. If Eve had 2 red chips, she would have 110 worth of blue chips, which still won't work. If Eve had $20 worth of red chips, though, she would have $100 left for exactly 5 blue chips. She would need 4 red chips to equal $20, so 4 is one possible answer. Any number of red chips that gave Eve a multiple of $20 would also work, so 8, 12, 16, and 20 are also acceptable answers.

19. $\dfrac{17}{6}$ or **2.83**

If the system of equations has infinitely many solutions, it means that the two equations are the same line. Therefore, seek to make the two equations look the same. Multiply the top equation by 3 to get $\dfrac{3}{2}x + 3(ay) = 48$. To make the bottom equation the same, it must be true that $b = \dfrac{3}{2}$, and $3a = 4$. Solve for a to get $a = \dfrac{4}{3}$. Therefore, $a + b = \dfrac{4}{3} + \dfrac{3}{2} = \dfrac{17}{6}$.

20. **1**   Convert $\dfrac{\pi}{3}$ radians to degrees by multiplying by $\dfrac{180}{\pi}$. $\dfrac{\pi}{3}\left(\dfrac{180}{\pi}\right) = 60$. Therefore, the angle $POR = 60°$. Next, draw a straight line from P to the x-axis, and mark the angles as follows:

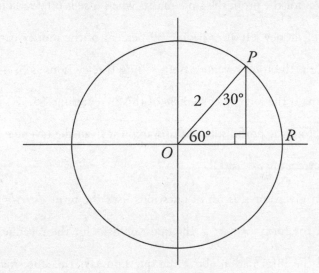

Remember that the sides of a 30-60-90 triangle are in a ratio of $1 : \sqrt{3} : 2$. Given that 2 is opposite the 90° angle, the length opposite the 30° angle is 1, and the x-value of P is therefore also 1.

Section 4: Math (Calculator)

1. **C**   There are 9 blue tiles for every 80 tiles. The question says *at this rate*, so set up a proportion.

Make sure to have like units on the top and like units on the bottom:

$\dfrac{9 \text{ blue}}{80 \text{ total}} = \dfrac{b \text{ blue}}{4{,}800 \text{ total}}$. Cross-multiply to get $80b = 43{,}200$. Divide both sides by 80 to get $b = 540$. The correct answer is (C).

2. **D**   The question asks for the value of d when $c = 345$. Plug this value of c into the equation, $c = 120 + 75d$, to get $345 = 120 + 75d$. Subtract 120 from both sides to get $225 = 75d$. Divide both sides by 75 to get $d = 3$. The correct answer is (D).

3. **A**   The question states that the artist makes \$50 for each large print. Since the artist sells l large prints, she earns a total of $50l$ for all the large prints. The artist also earns \$35 for each small print. Since the artist sells s small prints, she earns a total of $35s$ for all of the small prints. The question asks for the amount she earns for both the l large prints and the s small prints. This is equal to the sum of the two amounts, which is $50l + 35s$. The correct answer is (A).

4. **C**   Translate the first sentence into an equation. The expression *6 times a number y* translates to $6y$. This term *subtracted from 15* translates to $15 - 6y$. The term *the result is 33* translates to $= 33$, so the whole sentence translates to $15 - 6y = 33$. Solve for y. Subtract 15 from both sides to get $-6y = 18$. Divide both sides by -6 to get $y = -3$. The question asks, *What number results when 3 times y is added to 19?* The term *what number* translates to a variable. Use x. The term *results* translates to $=$. The term *3 times y* translates to $3y$. The term *is added to* translates to $+$. Therefore, the question translates to $x = 3y + 19$. Since $y = -3$, plug this into the equation to get $x = 3(-3) + 19 = -9 + 19 = 10$. The correct answer is (C).

5. **D**   The question asks for the profit the store makes when it sells 6 televisions. It also defines profit as the amount of money left after paying 39 percent of the money earned. According to the information given, the total revenues from selling 6 televisions is \$1,440. To determine how much the store paid the factory, take 39% of this by entering $\dfrac{39}{100} \times 1{,}440$ on a calculator to get \$561.60. To find the profit, subtract this amount from the revenue: $\$1{,}440.00 - \$561.60 = \$878.40$. The correct answer is (D).

6. **B**   The information given for this set of questions uses the term *directly proportional*, so set up a proportion in the form $\dfrac{x_1}{y_1} = \dfrac{x_2}{y_2}$. The question asks for the revenue when the store sells 9 televisions, and the information above the question says the store makes a profit of \$1,440 when the store sells 6 televisions. Set up the proportion: $\dfrac{\$1{,}440}{6 \text{ televisions}} = \dfrac{x}{9 \text{ televisions}}$. Be sure to put like units in the numerators and like units in the denominators. Cross-multiply to get $6x = \$12{,}960$. Divide both sides by 6 to get $x = \$2{,}160$. The correct answer is (B).

7. **D**   The question asks for a pair of equations. Use bite-sized pieces to determine each equation. The question says the collector can buy a maximum of 25 records, so the total number of records must be less than or equal to 25. Come up with an expression to determine the total number of records. The number of \$20 records is a and the number of \$35 records is b, so

the total number of records must be $a + b$. Therefore, the correct choice must include the inequality $a + b \leq 25$. Eliminate any choice that does not include this: (A) and (B). The other equation in both remaining answers involves an expression set less than or equal to 750. Find 750 in the problem. The question states that the collector can spend up to $750, so come up with an expression for what the collector spends. To find the cost of the $20 records, multiply the number of these records, a, by 20 to get $20a$. Similarly, to find the total cost of the $35 records multiply b by 35 to get $35b$. Therefore, the total cost of all the records is this sum: $20a + 35b$. This sum must be less than or equal to $750, so the answer must include the inequality $20a + 35b \leq 750$. Eliminate the remaining choice that doesn't include this inequality: (C). Therefore, the correct answer is (D).

8. **C** The x-intercepts, by definition, are the x-coordinates of the points at which $y = 0$, so set $y = 0$ in the equation above to get $0 = x^2 - 12x + 35$. Factor the right side of the equation by finding a pair of numbers with a product of 35 and a sum of -12. This pair is -5 and -7. The factored form of the equation, therefore, is $0 = (x - 5)(x - 7)$. Set both factors equal to 0 to get $x - 5 = 0$ and $x - 7 = 0$. Solve each equation to get $x = 5$ and $x = 7$. Select the answer that includes both the numbers 5 and 7, which is (C). Alternatively, know that the x-intercepts are the same as the solutions. To find the solutions, put in the equation in factored form, which is (C).

9. **A** A player loses 3 points for every question answered incorrectly. If a player answers 15 questions incorrectly, he or she loses $15 \times 3 = 45$ points. If this player has 165 points remaining, he or she must have started with $165 + 45 = 210$ points. Since the player started with k points, k must equal 210. Therefore, the correct answer is (A).

10. **A** Not all the information in the table is relevant. The question asks for the number of days it would take Albert to type the entire document. The table provides the number of pages, sections, and units in the document. However, it does not provide any way to determine the amount of time it would take to type a page, section, or unit, so ignore this information. The table does, however, provide the number of words in the document and the number of words Albert can type per minute. Use the formula: *Amount = Rate × Time*. The amount is 181,235 words, and the rate is 85 words per minute. Set up the equation $181{,}235 = 85t$. Divide both sides by 85 on a calculator to get approximately 2,132 minutes (it's okay to round a bit, since the question asks for the *closest* answer). However, the question asks for days. Each day, Albert expects to devote four hours to typing the document. 2,132 minutes is equal to

$\dfrac{2,132}{60}$ = 35.533 hours. At 4 hours per day, 35.533 hours of typing can be completed in $\dfrac{35.533}{4}$ = 8.88 days. Select the closest choice, which is (A).

11. **B** The capacity of the trash can is 20 cubic feet, and the question asks when the trash can will be full or overflowing. In other words, it asks when the amount of garbage in the trash can is at or above capacity. First, come up with an expression for the amount of garbage in the trash can. Each day 3 cubic feet is added. Therefore, after d days, $3d$ cubic feet has been added. This amount is added to the original amount, which is 8, so the amount of garbage in the trash can after d days is $8 + 3d$. The question asks for when this amount is at or above capacity, which is 20. Therefore, the inequality is $8 + 3d \geq 20$, which is (B).

12. **C** The question asks for the value of $m(n(6))$. For compound functions, start on the inside and work to the outside. The inside is $n(6)$. According to the information in the question, $n(6) = 4$. Therefore $m(n(6)) = m(4)$. According to the information in the question, $m(4) = 6$. Therefore, $m(n(6)) = m(4) = 6$, so the correct answer is (C).

13. **C** The question asks for the average speed in kilometers per minute, so determine distance and time in kilometers and minutes, respectively. The circumference of Earth's equator is about 40,000, so this is the distance. Earth completes a rotation in one day, which is 24 hours. However, the question asks for minutes, so convert hours to minutes with the proportion $\dfrac{1 \text{ hour}}{60 \text{ min}} = \dfrac{24 \text{ hours}}{x \text{ min}}$. Cross-multiply to get $x = 1,440$. To determine speed, divide distance by time to get $\dfrac{40,000 \text{ km}}{1,440 \text{ min}} \approx 28$. The correct answer is (C).

14. **B** The theater owner is trying to determine whether local residents would prefer to see operas or symphonies by surveying people at a mall on a Sunday. Go through each choice and determine which one describes the cause of a flaw in the theater owner's methodology. Choice (A) is the size of the sample. While it's possible that this sample size is too small, there is no information about the area's population to determine whether this is a sufficiently or insufficiently large sample. Eliminate (A). Choice (B) is the location in which the survey was given. The location causes a flaw, because it creates a bias toward people who are likely to visit a shopping mall. Keep (B). Choice (C) is the population of the area. There is no information about the population of the area, so it is impossible to determine whether this creates a problem. Eliminate (C). Choice (D) is the residents who declined to respond. There is no reason to think that this significantly hurts sample size or creates a bias. Eliminate (D). The correct answer is (B).

15. **B** The question asks for the year the population is projected to reach 5,000. Population is expressed by the vertical axis, so find 5,000 on that axis. Trace the line across the graph until reaching the line of best fit. Then, follow downward until reaching the horizontal axis somewhere between 2020 and 2025. The only choice between these two is (B).

16. **B** The half-life of the unknown element is approximately 25% less than that of carbon-14. Take 25% of the half-life of carbon-14, which is $\dfrac{25}{100} \times 5{,}730 = 1{,}432.50$. Since it's 25% *less*, subtract this number from 5,730 to get $5{,}730 - 1432.50 = 4{,}297.50$, which is closest to (B).

17. **D** The question states that the mean salary of the employees is $80,000 and the median salary is $45,000. The mean refers to the average (the sum of the salaries divided by the number of employees), and the median refers to the middle salary when listed in order. If the median is $45,000, there must be an equal number of employees with salaries greater than $45,000 and less than $45,000. If the average is greater than the median, it must mean that the salaries at the top half have a greater effect on the average and the ones at the bottom half, which would happen if a few employees had significantly higher salaries. This is (D). Alternatively, come up with a simple example that describes the situation. For example, there could be three employees with salaries $20,000, $45,000, and $175,000. The median is $45,000 and the mean is $80,000. Go through the choices and eliminate any choice that doesn't describe this situation. Choice (A) says that many employees' salaries are between $45,000 and $80,000. In this case, there are no salaries between $45,000 and $80,000. Eliminate (A). Choice (B) says the employees' salaries are close to each other. In this case, the salaries are far apart from each other. Eliminate (B). Choices (C) and (D) are opposites. Choice (C) says a few salaries are much lower than the rest and (D) says a few salaries are much higher than the rest. In this example, the low salary is much closer to the median than the high salary, so eliminate (C) and pick (D).

18. **C** The question asks for probability, which is $\dfrac{want}{total}$. The question says *an accepted student* is chosen, so the *total* is the number of accepted students, which is $15{,}700 + 9{,}300 = 25{,}000$. The question asks for the probability that *the student did not complete an interview*, so this number represents the *want*. Make sure to only count the students who did not complete an interview and were accepted, which is 9,300. Therefore, the probability is $\dfrac{want}{total} = \dfrac{9{,}300}{25{,}000} = \dfrac{93}{250}$, which is (C).

19. **C** Plug In. Let $d = 400$ and $k = 390$. Plug these values into the answer choices to see which answer works. Choice (A) becomes $400 - 390 < 20$, which is true. Keep (A). Choice (B) becomes $400 + 390 < 20$. This isn't true, so eliminate (B). Choice (C) becomes $-20 < 400 - 390 < 20$. This is also true, so keep (C). Choice (D) becomes $-20 < 400 + 390 < 20$. Eliminate (D). Now plug in some different numbers to try to eliminate (A) or (C). Try $d = 390$ and $k = 400$. Choice (A) becomes $390 - 400 < 20$, and (C) becomes $-20 < 390 - 400 < 20$. Both of these are still true. When that happens, try plugging in some numbers that *don't* work—the correct answer will prove false and an incorrect answer may still be true. Try $d = 400$ and $k = 450$, which don't work because they are more than $20 apart. Choice (A) becomes $400 - 450 < 20$, which is still true, so eliminate it. Choice (C) is false for the numbers that don't work, so it is correct.

20. **A** The median is the middle number when all the numbers are listed in order. However, in this case, there are too many numbers to list them in order. Instead, think in terms of what the middle number would be. Half the numbers should be greater than the median and the other half of the numbers should be less than the median. Since the president polled 200 students each from the junior and senior classes, a total of 400 students were polled. Therefore, in this case, there should be 200 greater than and 200 less the median. Therefore, the median is the average of the 200th and 201st numbers. Find the 200th and 201st numbers in the ordered list. Start with the smallest numbers. In the combined junior and senior classes, there are 25 + 30 = 55 students who complete one hour of homework a night. The median must be greater than this. In the combined junior and senior classes, there are 80 + 70 = 150 students who complete two hours of homework. Therefore, there must be a total of 55 + 150 = 205 students with 1 or 2 hours. Since the tally is greater than 201, the 200th and 201st students must be part of the group of students who complete two hours of homework. Therefore, the average of the 200th and 201st (the median) must be 2. The correct answer is (A).

21. **A** The question asks how to compare the number of students who complete four hours of homework in the two classes. The number in the table for both classes is 35, which would seem to point to (D). However, these numbers do not represent the entirety of the two classes but rather a random sample of 200 from each class. Use proportions to determine the actual expected amounts. Since there are 600 students in the junior class, set up the proportion $\frac{35}{200} = \frac{x}{600}$. Cross-multiply to get $200x = 21{,}000$. Divide both sides by 200 to get $x = 105$ students in the junior class who complete four hours of homework per night. Since there are 400 students in the senior class, set up the proportion $\frac{35}{200} = \frac{x}{400}$. Cross-multiply to get $200x = 14{,}000$. Divide both sides by 200 to get $x = 70$ students in the senior class who complete four hours of homework per night. Therefore, the junior class has $105 - 70 = 35$ more students who complete four hours of homework than does the senior class. The correct answer is (A).

22. **B** The equation of a circle is $(x - h)^2 + (y - k)^2 = r^2$, where r stands for radius. Start by reordering the equation to get $x^2 - 6x + y^2 + 8y = -9$. To solve for the radius, it is necessary to complete the squares. Remember what gets added to one side of the equation must be added to the other: $(x^2 - 6x + 9) + (y^2 + 8y + 16) = -9 + 9 + 16$. Therefore, $r^2 = -9 + 9 + 16 = 16$, and $r = 4$, which is (B).

23. **D** Solve the equation for d^2. First multiply both sides of the equation by d^2 to get $Gd^2 = ab$. Then divide by G to get $d^2 = \frac{ab}{G}$. Therefore, (D) is correct.

24. **D** Start by plugging in the same mass for k, m, a, and b. Let $k = m = a = b = 2$. The gravitational force between k and m is 9 times the force between a and b, so plug in $G_{km} = 81$ and $G_{ab} = 9$. Square numbers will work well here, since the distance is squared in the formula. Use these values in the formula to find the distance between the given objects. The gravitational force for k and m becomes $81 = \dfrac{(2)(2)}{(d_{km})^2}$, so $81(d_{km})^2 = 4$, and $(d_{km})^2 = \dfrac{4}{81}$. Take the square root of both sides to get $d_{km} = \dfrac{2}{9}$.

Follow the same steps to find the gravitational force for a and b: $9 = \dfrac{(2)(2)}{(d_{ab})^2}$, then $9(d_{ab})^2 = 4$, so $(d_{ab})^2 = \dfrac{4}{9}$, and $d_{ab} = \dfrac{2}{3}$. Now make the fraction: $\dfrac{d_{km}}{d_{ab}} = \dfrac{\frac{2}{9}}{\frac{2}{3}} = \dfrac{2}{9} \times \dfrac{3}{2} = \dfrac{1}{3}$, which is (D).

25. **C** Remember that $f(x)$ or $g(x) = y$. The graph shows that when the x-value is –3, the y-value is 2. Therefore, Statement (I) is true. Eliminate (A). The graph shows that when the x-value is 2, the y-value is 2. Therefore, Statement (II) is false. Eliminate (B) and (D). The correct answer is therefore (C).

26. **B** Use Process of Elimination. The graph of the athlete who only jogs is linear, which is to say the rate of change is consistent throughout time, while the rate of change for the athlete who alternates running/walking is represented by a curve—it flattens out during minutes 3 and 4. Based on this, eliminate (C) and (D) since the rate of change is not consistent for the running/walking athlete. Eliminate (A) because the rate of change is greater for the athlete who jogs during minutes 3 and 4. The correct answer is therefore (B).

27. **B** Plug in values for s and t that make the statement $t - s = 0$ true, such as $t = 5$ and $s = 5$. Therefore, the points (0, 5) and (5, 0) are on the line. The answers all refer to the slope of the line, so plug these points into the slope formula: $\dfrac{y_2 - y_1}{x_2 - x_1}$. This becomes $\dfrac{0 - 5}{5 - 0} = \dfrac{-5}{5} = -1$, making (B) the correct answer.

28. **C** Rather than trying to remember the formula for the area of a hexagon, ignore triangle ADG for now and divide the hexagon up into triangles, like this:

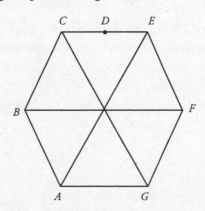

Because the hexagon is a regular one, each of these six triangles is the same. The area of each triangle is $\frac{1}{6}$ of the hexagon, or $144\sqrt{3}$. Each internal angle in a regular hexagon is 120°, so each triangle is equilateral. Use this information to find the length of a side of the hexagon. Isolate one triangle to work with, and divide it in half to form two 30°-60°-90° triangles.

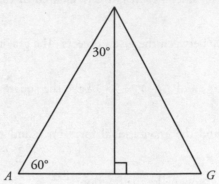

To more easily use the relationships of the 30°-60°-90° triangle's sides, label $\overline{AG}$ as $2x$, so the height of the equilateral triangle is $x\sqrt{3}$.

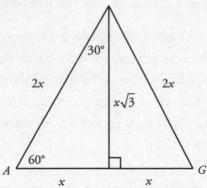

The area of a triangle is $A = \frac{1}{2}bh$, so plug the information into the formula to get $144\sqrt{3} = \frac{1}{2}(2x)(x\sqrt{3})$. Simplify the right side to get $144\sqrt{3} = x^2\sqrt{3}$, then divide both sides by $\sqrt{3}$ to get $144 = x^2$. This means that $x = 12$, and $\overline{AG} = 2x = 24$. This is the base of triangle ADG.

To find the height, go back to the hexagon divided into equilateral triangles. The height of each equilateral triangle is $x\sqrt{3}$ or $12\sqrt{3}$, and the height of triangle ADG is equal to 2 of these heights, or $24\sqrt{3}$.

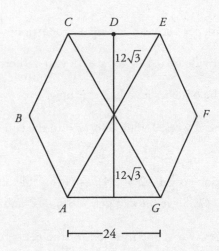

Plug these values into the area formula to get $A = \frac{1}{2}(24)\left(24\sqrt{3}\right) = 288\sqrt{3}$, which is (C). Another way to approach this question is to ballpark—the area of triangle ADG is about one-third of the area of the hexagon. Dividing $864\sqrt{3}$ by 3 results in $288\sqrt{3}$, which is—not just approximately—(C).

29. **A** Start by using Process of Elimination. The diagram shows that line l has a negative slope and a negative y-intercept. All the answers have lines with negative slopes, but only (A) and (D) have negative y-intercepts. Eliminate (B) and (C). Since line l is tangent to the circle at point A, line l is perpendicular to the line containing $\overline{AC}$. Perpendicular lines have slopes that are opposite reciprocals, so find the slope of $\overline{AC}$. The slope formula is $\dfrac{y_2 - y_1}{x_2 - x_1}$, which becomes $\dfrac{7 - (-1)}{3 - (-1)} = \dfrac{8}{4} = 2$ for $\overline{AC}$. Therefore, the slope of line l is $-\dfrac{1}{2}$, so (A) is the answer.

30. **A** The solutions to a system of equations are the points the equations share. The line $y = -2$ is the straightforward equation, so y must be -2 in the other equation. Plug the values given in each answer choice for r and s, along with -2 for y, into the first equation, and solve for x. The answer that yields two real solutions for x will be the correct answer. Choice (A) becomes $-2 = -2x^2 - 1$. Add 1 to both sides to get $-1 = -2x^2$. Divide both sides by -2 to get $\frac{1}{2} = x^2$. Take the square root of both sides of the equation to get $\pm\sqrt{\dfrac{1}{2}} = x$. Therefore, (A) has two real solutions: $\left(-\sqrt{\dfrac{1}{2}}, -2\right)$ and $\left(\sqrt{\dfrac{1}{2}}, -2\right)$, so (A) is the correct answer.

31. **9** There are 60 minutes in an hour. To convert minutes into hours, divide the number of minutes by 60. $\dfrac{560}{60} = 9.\overline{3}$ or nine and one-third hours. Therefore, 560 minutes is equal to 9 hours and 20 minutes, and $z = 9$.

32. **15** The rate of decrease is 0.4 inches per year. Set up a proportion: $\dfrac{0.4 \text{ inches}}{1 \text{ year}} = \dfrac{6 \text{ inches}}{x}$. Cross-multiply to get $6 = 0.4x$, then divide by 0.4 to get $x = 15$ years. Therefore, it will take 15 years for the average annual snowfall to be 6 inches less than it is now.

33. **12** Dave incurred the initial fine at week 0. Plug 0 for w into the equation to get $C = 12 - 1.5(0)$. Solve for C to get $C = 12 - 0 = 12$.

34. **12** Plug $(4, -2)$ into the function to get $-2 = 2(4)^2 - k(4) + 14$. Simplify the equation to get $-2 = 32 - 4k + 14$, and $-2 = 46 - 4k$. Solve for k to get $-48 = -4k$, and $k = 12$.

35. **60** Because the angle COA faces two of the five sides of the pentagon, angle COA is $\dfrac{2}{5}$ of the circle. The length of the arc made by this angle is 24, so set up an equation: $24 = \dfrac{2}{5} \times circumference$. Multiply both sides by $\dfrac{5}{2}$ to get $circumference = 60$.

36. **575** Let b represent the number of calories in the breakfast sandwich and f represent the number of calories in the fried potatoes. The information in the question can then be translated into the following equations: $b + f = 910$ and $b = f + 240$. Solve the second equation for f to get $f = b - 240$. Plug this value for f into the first equation to get $b + b - 240 = 910$. Solve for b to get $2b - 240 = 910$, $2b = 1,150$, and $b = 575$.

37. **7,000** According to the question, $P_t = 4,200$ and $P_{t+1} = 4,704$. Plug these values into the equation to get $4,704 = 4,200 + 0.3(4,200)\left(1 - \dfrac{4,200}{C}\right)$. Simplify the right side of the equation to get $4,704 = 4,200 + 1,260\left(1 - \dfrac{4,200}{C}\right)$. Subtract 4,200 from both sides of the equation to get $504 = 1,260\left(1 - \dfrac{4,200}{C}\right)$. Divide the equation by 1,260 to get $0.4 = 1 - \dfrac{4,200}{C}$. Solve for C to get $-0.6 = -\dfrac{4,200}{C}$, $-0.6C = -4,200$, and $C = 7,000$.

38. **5,741** According to the question, $C = 10,500$ and $P_t = 4,200$. Therefore, $P_{t+1} = 4,200 + 0.3(4,200)\left(1 - \dfrac{4,200}{10,500}\right)$. Solve the equation to get $P_{t+1} = 4,200 + 1,260(1 - 0.4) = 4,200 + 756 = 4,956$. That's the deer population after one year, but the question asks for the population after two years, so do it again. Plug 4,956 into the equation as the new P_t to get the deer population two years from now: $P_{t+1} = 4,956 + 0.3(4,956)\left(1 - \dfrac{4,956}{10,500}\right)$. Solve the equation to get $P_{t+1} = 4,956 + 1,486.8(1 - 0.472) = 4,956 + 785.03 \approx 5,741$. Only round at the last step to make sure the answer is as accurate as possible.

Chapter 7
Practice Test 3

Reading Test

65 MINUTES, 52 QUESTIONS

Turn to Section 1 of your answer sheet to answer the questions in this section.

DIRECTIONS

Each passage or pair of passages below is followed by a number of questions. After reading each passage or pair, choose the best answer to each question based on what is stated or implied in the passage or passages and in any accompanying graphics (such as a table or graph).

Questions 1–10 are based on the following passage.

This passage is adapted from Oscar Wilde, "Lord Arthur Savile's Crime." Originally published in 1887.

It was Lady Windermere's last reception before Easter, and Bentinck House was even more crowded than usual. Six Cabinet Ministers had come on from
Line the Speaker's Levée in their stars and ribands, all the
5 pretty women wore their smartest dresses, and at the end of the picture-gallery stood the Princess Sophia of Carlsrühe, a heavy Tartar-looking lady, with tiny black eyes and wonderful emeralds, talking bad French at the top of her voice, and laughing immoderately
10 at everything that was said to her. It was certainly a wonderful medley of people. Gorgeous peeresses chatted affably to violent Radicals, popular preachers brushed coat-tails with eminent sceptics, a perfect bevy of bishops kept following a stout prima-donna from
15 room to room, on the staircase stood several Royal Academicians, disguised as artists, and it was said that at one time the supper-room was absolutely crammed with geniuses. In fact, it was one of Lady Windermere's best nights, and the Princess stayed till nearly half-past
20 eleven.

As soon as she had gone, Lady Windermere returned to the picture-gallery, where a celebrated political economist was solemnly explaining the scientific theory of music to an indignant virtuoso
25 from Hungary, and began to talk to the Duchess of Paisley. Lady Windermere looked wonderfully beautiful with her grand ivory throat, her large blue forget-me-not eyes, and her heavy coils of golden hair. *Or pur* ("pure gold") they were—not
30 that pale straw colour that nowadays usurps the gracious name of gold, but such gold as is woven into sunbeams or hidden in strange amber; and they gave to her face something of the frame of a saint, with not a little of the fascination of a sinner. She was
35 a curious psychological study. Early in life she had discovered the important truth that nothing looks so like innocence as an indiscretion; and by a series of reckless escapades, half of them quite harmless, she had acquired all the privileges of a personality. She had
40 more than once changed her husband; indeed, Debrett credits her with three marriages; but as she had never changed her lover, the world had long ago ceased to talk scandal about her. She was now forty years of age, childless, and with that inordinate passion for pleasure
45 which is the secret of remaining young.

Suddenly she looked eagerly round the room, and said, in her clear contralto voice, 'Where is my chiromantist?'

'Your what, Gladys?' exclaimed the Duchess, giving
50 an involuntary start.

'My chiromantist, Duchess; I can't live without him at present.'

'Dear Gladys! you are always so original,' murmured the Duchess, trying to remember what
55 a chiromantist really was, and hoping it was not the same as a chiropodist.

'He comes to see my hand twice a week regularly,' continued Lady Windermere, 'and is most interesting about it.'

CONTINUE →

60 'Good heavens!' said the Duchess to herself, 'he is a
sort of chiropodist after all. How very dreadful. I hope
he is a foreigner at any rate. It wouldn't be quite so bad
then.'

'I must certainly introduce him to you.'

65 'Introduce him!' cried the Duchess; 'you don't mean
to say he is here?' and she began looking about for a
small tortoise-shell fan and a very tattered lace shawl,
so as to be ready to go at a moment's notice.

'Of course he is here; I would not dream of giving
70 a party without him. He tells me I have a pure psychic
hand, and that if my thumb had been the least little bit
shorter, I should have been a confirmed pessimist, and
gone into a convent.'

'Oh, I see!' said the Duchess, feeling very much
75 relieved; 'he tells fortunes, I suppose?'

'And misfortunes, too,' answered Lady Windermere,
'any amount of them. Next year, for instance, I am in
great danger, both by land and sea, so I am going to
live in a balloon, and draw up my dinner in a basket
80 every evening. It is all written down on my little finger,
or on the palm of my hand, I forget which.'

1

Which choice best summarizes the passage?

A) A woman tries to introduce a guest to the practice
   of chiromancy.

B) A woman hosts a large party and engages another
   woman in conversation.

C) A detailed description of a party and its host.

D) A woman hosts her last party before fleeing
   danger.

2

As used in line 5, "smartest" most nearly means

A) most fashionable.

B) most clever.

C) most painful.

D) brightest.

3

The passage most clearly implies that Lady
Windermere is

A) nearing the end of her hostessing days.

B) uninterested in discussions of political economy.

C) less gracious than the Duchess of Paisley.

D) less serious about fortune-telling than she claims.

4

Which choice provides the best evidence for the
answer to the preceding question?

A) Lines 1–3 ("It was . . . usual")

B) Lines 46–48 ("Suddenly . . . chiromantist")

C) Lines 69–70 ("Of course . . . him")

D) Lines 78–81 ("I am . . . which")

5

The description of "gorgeous peeresses … violent
Radicals, popular preachers … eminent sceptics"
and "a perfect bevy of bishops" (lines 11-14) mainly
serves to

A) contrast political and artistic types of people.

B) illustrate the variety of people attending the
   reception.

C) compare the women to the men.

D) underscore the discrepancy between social classes.

6

As used in line 50, the word "start" most nearly means

A) opening.

B) commencement.

C) twitch.

D) procedure.

CONTINUE

7

The narrator indicates that Princess Sophia, the Radicals, and the Royal Academicians are

A) violent, yet disguised.

B) as immoderate as the other guests.

C) more popular than those who had not been invited.

D) an interesting combination of different types of people.

8

The narrator implies that Lady Windermere will

A) be unable to live without her chiromantist.

B) relocate to a hot-air balloon.

C) get another divorce.

D) enjoy her reception.

9

As presented in the passage, the Duchess of Paisley is best described as

A) innocent but indiscreet.

B) proper but curious.

C) youthful but experienced.

D) saintly but sinful.

10

Which choice provides the best evidence for the answer to the preceding question?

A) Lines 32–34 ("and they . . . sinner")

B) Lines 35–37 ("Early in . . . indiscretion")

C) Lines 60–63 ("Good heavens . . . then")

D) Lines 65–68 ("Introduce him . . . notice")

CONTINUE

Questions 11-20 are based on the following passage and supplementary material.

This passage is adapted from Michael W. Kraus and Bennett Callaghan, "Noblesse Oblige? Social Status and Economic Inequality Maintenance among Politicians." ©2014 by Public Library of Science.

The United States is in the midst of unprecedented levels of economic inequality. These large scale economic disparities place the most strain on those at the bottom of the social hierarchy—poor and working
5   class families—who must contend with increased poverty, unemployment, problems with health and social support, and homelessness. Americans have few options to combat economic inequality, but they can turn to the democratic system to enact social and
10 fiscal policies that protect individuals from growing wealth disparities. Given that political participation is one of the only avenues available for individuals to combat this economic trend, investigations into the factors that predict whether politicians will support the
15 reduction or increase of economic inequality remain an important area of research.

Social status is broadly defined as the rank-based value of individuals, and can be measured by one's leadership role in organizations, by assessing levels of
20 socioeconomic status (SES; e.g., occupation prestige, annual income), or by one's membership in one or more social categories—such as one's race or gender. However social status is measured, most research finds that higher status confers greater benefits than
25 lower status. For example, when compared to high SES individuals, men, and European Americans, lower status individuals (i.e., low SES individuals, women, and African Americans) experience stereotype threat —anxiety about confirming negative stereotypes about
30 their low status group— that impedes their academic performance. In general, individuals belonging to higher status positions in society benefit from greater access to material and social resources, increased workplace opportunities, and reduced discrimination
35 based on their social status. High status individuals also tend to hold public office more than their low status counterparts, and as a result, have unique access to decision-making power on matters related to economic policy and wealth distribution.

40 Status disparities force high status individuals to explain why they hold a potentially unfair advantage in society relative to their low status counterparts. Recent research indicates that when faced with explaining their elevated social positions, high status individuals
45 endorse meritocratic beliefs. Specifically, high status individuals, motivated to maintain their elevated social positions and the benefits they bestow, are particularly likely to explain their many social advantages in terms of a fair application of effort, talent, and skill.

50 Several lines of empirical evidence suggest that high status individuals endorse meritocratic beliefs more than their low status counterparts. For instance, people with higher status are happier when they believe that positive outcomes in society are based on
55 merit and high-performing members of a group are more likely to advocate dividing resources based solely on merit. In a recent online survey, individuals with higher income and who subjectively ranked themselves higher in the social class hierarchy in society—
60 using rungs of a ladder based on ascending levels of education, income, and occupation status—reported a greater belief that the world is fair and that society's structure is based on merit than did their lower status counterparts.

65 The present research aligns with mounting evidence suggesting that an individual's social status is a reliable predictor of support for economic inequality in society. That social status predicts support for economic inequality among members of
70 Congress—individuals with direct access to creating and implementing policies that shape the future of economic inequality in the US—is a potentially important piece of information for US citizens to consider in future elections.

CONTINUE

Panel A

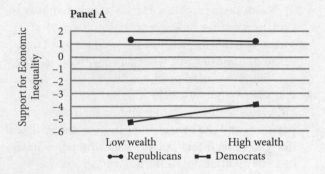

Panel B

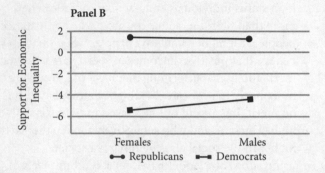

Relationships between social status and the tendency to sponsor legislation supporting economic inequality

11

What function does the first paragraph (lines 1-16) serve in the passage as a whole?

A) It advocates embracing the trend supported by subsequent research in following paragraphs.

B) It illustrates a practice favored by the authors that should be implemented according to correlational research.

C) It acknowledges that a discrepancy exists and offers solutions to the problem based on research results.

D) It gives an overview of a discrepancy and indicates why research on that discrepancy might be important.

12

Which choice do the authors explicitly cite as an advantage of individuals with higher socioeconomic status?

A) Stereotype threat

B) Increased workplace opportunities

C) Political activism

D) Discrimination

13

Which choice provides the best evidence for the answer to the previous question?

A) Lines 23–25 ("However social . . . status")

B) Lines 25–31 ("For example . . . performance")

C) Lines 31–35 ("In general . . . status")

D) Lines 40–42 ("Status disparities . . . counterparts")

14

The central idea of the third paragraph (lines 40-49) is that

A) some individuals with higher socioeconomic status cite reasons other than SES for their perceived advantage.

B) the world is fair and society's structure is based on merit for both high and low SES individuals.

C) individuals of high socioeconomic status seek to keep those of lower socioeconomic status from succeeding.

D) SES predicts social inequality in most societies.

CONTINUE

15

Which choice provides the best evidence for the answer to the previous question?

A) Lines 35–39 ("High status . . . distribution")

B) Lines 40–42 ("Status disparities . . . counterparts")

C) Lines 42–45 ("Recent research . . . beliefs")

D) Lines 57–64 ("In a . . . counterparts")

16

As used in line 47, "bestow" most nearly means

A) withhold.

B) grant.

C) earn.

D) promote.

17

As used in line 65, "aligns" most nearly means

A) arranges.

B) straightens.

C) agrees.

D) focuses.

18

Which choice best supports the conclusion that an individual's social status is a reliable predictor of support for economic inequality in society?

A) Lines 35–39 ("High status . . . distribution")

B) Lines 50–52 ("Several lines . . . counterparts")

C) Lines 57–59 ("In a . . . society")

D) Lines 68–74 ("That social . . . elections")

19

Which choice is supported by the data in the figure?

A) Males are slightly less likely to sponsor legislation supporting economic inequality than females.

B) The number of individuals polled who identify as low SES is higher than the number of individuals who identify as high SES.

C) The number of Republicans endorsing legislation that supports economic inequality and the number of Democrats supporting such legislation is roughly the same.

D) A female Democrat self-reporting a lower wealth status is most likely to vote for legislation reducing economic inequality.

20

Taken together, the two figures suggest that most people who are likely to sponsor legislation supporting economic inequality

A) are employed and have upward mobility with increased work opportunities.

B) are from all socioeconomic backgrounds and social categories.

C) are Democrats who identify as female and low wealth.

D) are Republicans, regardless of gender.

CONTINUE

Questions 21–30 are based on the following passage.

This passage is adapted from PLoS, "No Rest for the Weary: Migrating Songbirds Keep Their Wits without Sleep." ©2004 by Public Library of Science.

Every spring and fall, billions of songbirds fly thousands of miles between their summer breeding grounds in North America and their wintering
Line grounds in the more hospitable climates of southern
5 California, Mexico, and Central and South America. While some birds fly during the day, most, including the white-crowned sparrow, fly under cover of night. Many aspects of this remarkable voyage remain obscure, especially if, and how, nocturnal migrators get
10 any sleep at night.

A tracking study of the Swainson's thrush found that the roughly seven-inch birds flew up to seven hours straight on six of seven nights, racking up over 930 miles. While the study didn't track their daytime
15 behavior, the birds' migratory pace—as well as the increased activity required to sustain migrations— suggests little time for sleep. Yet field observations indicate that presumably sleep-deprived fliers appear no worse for wear, foraging, navigating, and avoiding
20 predators with aplomb. Researchers are left trying to reconcile this observation with the vast body of evidence linking sleep deprivation to impaired neurobehavioral and physiological function. How do songbirds cope with so little sleep? Do they take power
25 naps? Have they taken "sleep walking" to new heights? Or have they managed to selectively short-circuit the adverse effects of sleep deprivation during migratory stints?

To investigate these questions, Ruth Benca and
30 colleagues studied cognitive and sleep behaviors in captive white-crowned sparrows over the course of a year. The sparrows fly nearly 2,700 miles twice a year between their Alaska and southern California homes. In laboratory cages, the birds' migratory instincts
35 manifest as increased restlessness at night during the migratory season, with lots of hopping around and wing flapping.

Niels Rattenborg et al. characterized the birds' activity levels with motion-detection measurements
40 and video recordings, and placed sensors on their brains to monitor their seasonal sleep patterns. The brain recordings showed a marked seasonal difference in both the amount and type of sleep during a 24- hour period. Cognitive tests—birds performed a task

45 that involved pecking a key in exchange for seed— revealed that birds in the nonmigrating state suffered cognitive deficits when sleep-deprived but displayed an "unprecedented" ability to maintain cognitive function in the face of ongoing sleep loss in the migratory state.

50 These results suggest that wild songbirds drastically reduce sleep time during migration, though Benca and colleagues concede it's impossible to know for sure without recording the birds in action. Such an ability to temporarily circumvent the need for sleep, however,
55 could prove useful for humans in situations that demand continuous performance.

Whatever the mechanism, the unprecedented imperviousness of migrating songbirds to sleep deprivation, the authors conclude, clearly warrants
60 further testing. But it also raises interesting questions about the role of sleep, which recent studies suggest is required to incorporate novel perceptions into the brain's memory banks. If this is true, how do songbirds consolidate memories of migratory events with so little
65 sleep?

Understanding the mechanisms that power the sleepless flight of songbirds promises to unravel one of the longstanding mysteries of their improbable journey. It may also shed light on the origins of sleep-
70 related seasonal disorders and the much-debated role of sleep itself.

21

Which choice best reflects the overall sequence of events in the passage?

A) A phenomenon is observed and a series of experiments seek to explain it, yet further research is necessary to fully understand the data found.

B) An anomaly is observed and recorded; the results are analyzed and declared inconclusive.

C) A new discovery revolutionizes a current theory, disproving old assumptions, and a new hypothesis is formed.

D) An unexpected finding arises during a study, spawning a secondary study; both studies are interpreted and summarized.

CONTINUE ➡

22

As used in line 21, "reconcile" most nearly means

A) reunite.

B) appease.

C) clarify.

D) integrate.

23

Which statement best captures Ruth Benca's central assumption in setting up her research?

A) The acquisition of sleepwalking from their evolutionary ancestors allows songbirds to travel great distances while migrating.

B) The tendency for songbirds to hop and flap their wings indicates their tendency towards migration.

C) Songbirds in a controlled research setting will be less likely to exhibit migration behavior than those in the wild.

D) Songbirds' ability to fly long distances without sleeping has little effect on their cognitive abilities.

24

Which choice provides the best evidence for the answer to the previous question?

A) Lines 11–14 ("A tracking . . . miles")

B) Lines 14–17 ("While the . . . sleep")

C) Lines 17–20 ("Yet field . . . aplomb")

D) Lines 34–37 ("In laboratory . . . flapping")

25

In the fourth paragraph (lines 38–49), the results of Niels Rattenborg's findings mainly serve to

A) show how unexpected results can upset an entire hypothesis.

B) reinforce the findings of Ruth Benca's laboratory research and previous field observations.

C) introduce a component of previous research on the songbirds' migration patterns.

D) underscore certain differences between other researchers and Benca's research.

26

After researchers noted the "'unprecedented' ability to maintain cognitive function" during migratory state, (line 48), they

A) concluded that it was impossible to know how the birds maintain normal levels of cognition during migratory seasons.

B) acknowledge that the correlation raises other questions about how the birds function during migration.

C) observed the birds' cognitive deficits when sleep-deprived in a nonmigratory state.

D) consulted other researchers in the field to compare their results.

27

The passage identifies which of the following as a factor necessitating that the team of researchers concede that further research is necessary?

A) The speed at which the birds flapped and hopped

B) The birds' increased activity levels

C) The controlled environment of the study

D) The decreased cognitive levels during sleep deprived, nonmigratory states

28

As used in line 68, "improbable" most nearly means

A) dubious.

B) unconvincing.

C) remarkable.

D) supposed.

CONTINUE

What can reasonably be inferred about songbirds from the passage?

A) Their activity levels may correlate to migratory seasons.

B) Their activity levels while migrating are similar to those of sleepwalkers.

C) Their mechanisms of migration are impossible to fully understand.

D) Their cognition and memories increase during migration.

Which choice provides the best evidence for the answer to the previous question?

A) Line 25 ("Have they . . . heights")

B) Lines 34–37 ("In laboratory . . . flapping")

C) Lines 50–53 ("These results . . . action")

D) Lines 60–63 ("But it . . . banks")

CONTINUE

Questions 31–41 are based on the following passages.

Passage 1 is adapted from Carol Boston, "High School Report Cards. ERIC Digest." Originally published 2003. Passage 2 is adapted from Winnie Hu, "Report Cards Give up A's and B's for 4s and 3s." Originally published 2009.

Passage 1

Most states have embraced standards-based education, a process that requires them to identify what specific knowledge and skills students are
Line expected to master at each grade level and then align
5 curriculum, teaching, and testing with those standards. Some schools are now experimenting with changes in their report cards to better reflect student progress toward achieving the standards.

Rather than the familiar A through F in each
10 subject, standards-based report cards might feature numbers or phrases that represent whether students have reached, exceeded, or not yet met various specific performance expectations. As an example, a third-grade mathematics grade might include a number or
15 phrase that would denote whether students exceed, meet, approach, or begin to achieve standards in comparing, adding, and subtracting fractions and identifying place values. Such a report card actually provides more detailed, specific information than a
20 traditional grade, though parents and students may find the change disconcerting, and concerns have been expressed about how colleges might evaluate report cards that don't show traditional grade point averages (Manzo, 2001).

25 Report cards that combine traditional grades and information about progress toward standards are also an option. Wiggins (1994) advocates a performance-based report card that plots overall student achievement against norms and standards,
30 identifies strengths and weaknesses in specific areas, and also includes teacher judgments about students' academic progress, growth, intellectual character, and work habits. Marzano (1998) shows an example report card that includes a transcript indicating how many
35 times each standard has been assessed, the average score obtained, as well as the highest, lowest, and most recent scores.

Passage 2

Thomas R. Guskey, a professor at Georgetown College in Kentucky and an author of *Developing*
40 *Standards-Based Report Cards*, a book that is soon to be released, said the new approach was more accurate, because it measures each student against a stated set of criteria, rather than grading on a curve, which compares members of a class with one another. "The
45 dilemma with that system is you really don't know whether anybody has learned anything. They could all have done miserably, just some less miserably than others."

The executive director of the National Association
50 of Secondary School Principals, Gerald Tirozzi—who supports standards-based report cards—said that many educators and parents were far from ready to scrap letter grades, especially for older students, in part because they worry about the ripple effects on
55 things like the honor roll and class rank. "I think the present grading system—A, B, C, D, F—is ingrained in us," Mr. Tirozzi said. "It's the language which college admissions officers understand; it's the language which parents understand."

60 Outside San Francisco, the San Mateo-Foster City district delayed plans to expand standards-based report cards to its four middle schools from its elementary schools, where they have been used since 2006, after parents packed school board meetings and
65 collected more than 500 signatures in opposition.

Addressing these parental complaints, Pelham district officials said they planned to change the system next year to use benchmarks for each marking period—rather than a year-end standard—to give
70 more timely snapshots of students' progress (and allow many more students to earn 4's from the beginning). They also plan to bring back teacher comments, and are looking for ways to recognize student effort and attitude.

CONTINUE ▶

31

As used in line 10, "feature" most nearly means

A) present.

B) attribute.

C) report.

D) promote.

32

It can be inferred that the author of Passage 1 believes that a standards-based report card

A) will be challenging for colleges and universities to evaluate.

B) provides a more specific way for teachers to evaluate students.

C) is unnecessarily complicated compared to a traditional report card.

D) is more effective for a student in third grade than a student in high school.

33

Which choice provides the best evidence for the answer to the previous question?

A) Lines 6–8 ("Some schools . . . standards")

B) Lines 9–13 ("Rather than . . . expectations")

C) Lines 13–18 ("As an . . . values")

D) Lines 18–23 ("Such a . . . averages")

34

According to the author of Passage 2, the use of standards-based report cards in elementary schools

A) led to plans for expansion into higher grades.

B) encountered much resistance.

C) has proven more accurate than other systems.

D) has been successfully implemented.

35

As used in line 53, "scrap" most nearly means

A) save.

B) fragment.

C) discard.

D) detach.

36

Passage 2 states that the new approach to grading

A) introduces a dilemma into the system.

B) does not truly measure whether learning has occurred.

C) is supported by experts in educational theory.

D) does not compare members of a class to each other.

37

Which choice provides the best evidence for the answer to the previous question?

A) Lines 38–44 ("Thomas R. Guskey . . . another")

B) Lines 44–46 ("The dilemma . . . anything")

C) Lines 46–48 ("They could . . . others")

D) Lines 72–74 ("They also . . . attitude")

38

The author of Passage 2 includes the quote by Thomas Guskey (lines 44-48) in order to address which concern not mentioned in Passage 1?

A) Colleges might favor traditional report cards over standards-based report cards.

B) Students might be disconcerted by a change from letter grades to number grades.

C) Student learning might be less accurately measured on a curve than by set criteria.

D) Traditional report cards might not provide information as specific as that in a standards-based report card.

CONTINUE ▶

39

Which best describes the overall relationship between Passage 1 and Passage 2?

A) Passage 2 examines different responses to the argument presented in Passage 1.

B) Passage 2 strongly challenges the point of view in Passage 1.

C) Passage 2 draws alternative conclusions from the evidence presented in Passage 1.

D) Passage 2 elaborates on the proposal presented in Passage 1.

40

The authors of both passages would most likely agree with which of the following statements about standards-based report cards?

A) Parental insistence on including traditional information has helped to improve the new system.

B) Despite encountering some resistance, standards-based report cards may provide more information than do previous systems.

C) Standards-based report cards remove the flawed system of grading on a curve.

D) Although concerns are understandable, standards-based report cards are superior to the alternatives.

41

How would the author of Passage 1 most likely respond to the points made in the final paragraph (lines 66–74) of Passage 2?

A) The author of Passage 1 would sympathize with the parental worries.

B) The author of Passage 1 would caution against the use of benchmarks.

C) The author of Passage 1 would agree with the proposed changes.

D) The author of Passage 1 would insist that intellectual character be included.

CONTINUE

Questions 42–52 are based on the following passage and supplementary material.

This passage is adapted from Nadav S. Bar, Sigurd Skogestad, Jose M. Marçal, Nachum Ulanovsky, and Yossi Yovel, "A Sensory-Motor Control Model of Animal Flight Explains Why Bats Fly Differently in Light Versus Dark", published 2015 by Public Library of Science. A series of flight experiments are performed with live and simulated bats.

Animal flight requires fine motor control. However, it is unknown how flying animals rapidly transform noisy sensory information into adequate
Line motor commands. Here we developed a sensorimotor
5 control model that explains vertebrate flight guidance with high fidelity. This simple model accurately reconstructed complex trajectories of bats flying in the dark.

To test our model, we used behavioral data
10 from Egyptian fruit bats (*Rousettus aegyptiacus*)—flying mammals that possess an advanced biosonar (echolocation) system, as well as an excellent visual system. We found that a simple model, which considers only the angle-to-target and its derivative,
15 was able to reconstruct complex, several-meter-long flight trajectories very accurately—with an average error of only 14.6 cm.

In reality, however, all organisms have sensory errors. To assess the effect of this sensory noise,
20 we tested two models of angle-dependent additive Gaussian noise, which mimic the sensory errors found in the auditory system of several vertebrates. As expected, sensory noise had strong implications for the convergence of the model: in many trials, adding the
25 noise resulted in increased maneuvering errors, and oftentimes led to complete failure to converge.

We therefore hypothesized that the bat must use a noise-suppression strategy and integrate (average) over several sensory measurements to overcome the
30 noise. An exponentially decaying integrator, which only takes into account the three to four most recent measurements, was found to outperform uniform and linearly decaying integrators. This simple exponential integrator exhibited successful noise suppression
35 and reproduced the bat's flight trajectories with high fidelity.

An important prediction of our model is that sensory noise determines motor performance. To test this hypothesis, we conducted new experiments in
40 which the same individual bats (five of the six bats) flew under a light level that is considered optimal for bat vision (1 lux), while performing the same landing task. We found that, as we hypothesized, the simulated bat exhibited significantly larger gain parameters in
45 light versus dark. Further, the simulated bat exerted significantly stronger forces when flying in the light. Moreover, flight trajectories in light conditions were more direct than in darkness, as quantified by their higher straightness index.
50 Taken together, these results imply the surprising conclusion that the highly curved flight trajectories often exhibited by bats in the dark are due to sensory limitations—not motor limitations.

The Effect of Noise on Sensorimotor Control

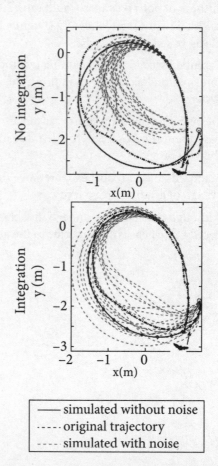

The figure above indicates the results of the experiments described in the 3rd and 4th paragraphs of the passage.

CONTINUE

42

The words "must," "exhibited," and "reproduced" in the fourth paragraph (lines 27-36) have what impact on the tone of the paragraph?

A) They display a hopeful tone that demonstrates the authors want the reader to agree with their uncertain results.

B) They display a confident tone that demonstrates the authors have faith in some elements of their conclusions.

C) They display an argumentative tone that demonstrates the authors disagree with researchers who conclude that bats do not use a noise-suppression strategy.

D) They display a commanding tone that demonstrates the authors desire to instruct others in the reproduction of simulated bat trajectories.

43

In line 49, the passage indicates that particular experiments resulted in a "higher straightness index." According to the passage, which of the following choices represents the theory these experiments were performed in order to verify?

A) In order to maintain experimental control conditions, it is vital to use the same bats in both the original and later experiments.

B) Inaccurate perceptions caused by common sensory errors have a significant detrimental impact on physical movements and coordination.

C) Mathematical models designed to test average measurements should always avoid uniform or linearly decaying integrators.

D) Bats which fly under light conditions that differ significantly from 1 lux, either brighter or darker, will not likely demonstrate optimal gain parameters.

44

Which choice provides the best evidence for the answer to the previous question?

A) Lines 30–33 ("An exponentially . . . integrators")

B) Lines 37–38 ("An important . . . performance")

C) Lines 38–43 ("To test . . . task")

D) Lines 43–45 ("We found . . . dark")

45

It can be inferred from the passage that including a simple exponential integrator countered what inaccuracy in the described experiments?

A) It can replace information the bats lose when they fly.

B) It accounted for sub-optimal light conditions.

C) It combined sensory input data for more accurate predictions.

D) It increased errors due to sensory noise.

46

Which choice provides the best evidence for the answer to the previous question?

A) Line 1 ("Animal flight . . . control")

B) Lines 6–8 ("This simple . . . dark")

C) Lines 33–36 ("This simple . . . fidelity")

D) Lines 50–53 ("Taken together . . . limitations")

47

As used in line 36, "fidelity" most nearly means

A) an accurate reproduction of the significant details.

B) a consistent performance of lower quality.

C) a complete perfection in all areas.

D) a rough, approximate similarity.

48

The main purpose of the fourth paragraph (lines 27–36) is to

A) describe a theory and experimental verification regarding the method a bat uses to handle imperfect perception.

B) suggest a trial in which three to four measurements are taken of several vertebrates to assess noise reduction.

C) introduce the probable pitfalls of the earlier theory briefly summarized in the following paragraph (lines 37–49).

D) detail the resulting data of a test that supports the authors' claim involving the accuracy of uniform integrators as applied to bat trajectories.

49

The authors assume that highly curved flight trajectories

A) are atypical of the *Rousettus aegyptiacus*.

B) never straighten for any brief period of time.

C) were not replaced by significantly straighter trajectories by bats flying in bright light.

D) were caused by physical limitations of the bat.

50

Based on the data in the figure, what is the best description of whether simulated trajectories with noise and a noise-suppression strategy reached the target?

A) All of the many trajectories reached the target.

B) The single trajectory smoothly reached the target.

C) The single trajectory wobbled, but reached the target.

D) None of the many trajectories reached the target.

51

Based on the data in the figure, which of the following trajectories most nearly matched the original trajectory?

A) The simulated trajectory with no noise and no integration

B) The simulated trajectory with no noise and integration

C) The simulated trajectory with noise and integration

D) The simulated trajectory with noise and no integration

52

Is the claim made by the authors that bat flight trajectories under optimal light conditions are more direct supported by the information in the figure?

A) Yes, because the simulated trajectories most nearly like the original trajectory are some of the 30 of those trajectories that included both noise and integration.

B) Yes, because the simulations with and without integration demonstrate that sensory noise caused bats to develop a compensating factor.

C) No, because they do not provide comparative data regarding the flights under optimal light conditions.

D) No, because the simulations with and without integration fail to clarify whether noise was a causal factor.

STOP

If you finish before time is called, you may check your work on this section only.
Do not turn to any other section in the test.

No Test Material On This Page

Writing and Language Test

35 MINUTES, 44 QUESTIONS

Turn to Section 2 of your answer sheet to answer the questions in this section.

DIRECTIONS

Each passage below is accompanied by a number of questions. For some questions, you will consider how the passage might be revised to improve the expression of ideas. For other questions, you will consider how the passage might be edited to correct errors in sentence structure, usage, or punctuation. A passage or a question may be accompanied by one or more graphics (such as a table or graph) that you will consider as you make revising and editing decisions.

Some questions will direct you to an underlined portion of a passage. Other questions will direct you to a location in a passage or ask you to think about the passage as a whole.

After reading each passage, choose the answer to each question that most effectively improves the quality of writing in the passage or that makes the passage conform to the conventions of standard written English. Many questions include a "NO CHANGE" option. Choose that option if you think the best choice is to leave the relevant portion of the passage as it is.

Questions 1–11 are based on the following passage.

The Agents of the FDA

When you go to the grocery store, **1** can't it be fun to go with your friends and family? Why do you trust the chicken that you buy from the grocery store more than the chicken you could buy off the back of some guy's truck? Beyond common sense, the answer is pretty simple: the Food and Drug Administration, or FDA. The **2** agency's beginnings came in 1906, when politicians and consumer

1

Which choice provides the most appropriate introduction to the passage?

A) NO CHANGE

B) which way do you take when you drive or walk?

C) how is it possible to buy only the things that you need?

D) how do you know what you're buying is safe?

2

A) NO CHANGE

B) agency's beginning's

C) agencies beginnings

D) agencies' beginnings'

CONTINUE

advocates began to realize how harmful unregulated food, cosmetics, and drugs could be. The FDA **3** for we know it today was formally created in 1930.

The FDA is everywhere in American culture. **4** In fact, the FDA regulates nearly $1 trillion worth of American consumer goods. This $1 trillion constitutes approximately 25% of all that is bought and sold in the United States. A large portion of this money is devoted to goods imported into the U.S. The FDA operates on a budget of nearly $5 billion a year, much of which is generated by user fees, **5** which come primarily from pharmaceutical companies, whose drugs require FDA approval.

3

A) NO CHANGE

B) how

C) as

D) DELETE the underlined portion.

4

In context, which choice best combines the underlined sentences?

A) In fact, the FDA regulates nearly $1 trillion worth of American consumer goods, approximately 25% of all that is bought and sold in the United States.

B) The FDA, in fact, which regulates nearly $1 trillion worth of American consumer goods, moreover regulates what amounts to 25% of all that is bought and sold.

C) A quarter of all that is bought and sold in the United States, which amounts to $1 trillion dollars approximately, is approved in some way by the FDA.

D) The $1 trillion dollars of goods in the United States, the same goods that constitute 25% of United States trade, are regulated by the FDA.

5

A) NO CHANGE

B) thus coming

C) those come

D) they come

CONTINUE

6 Still, while many people are familiar with the FDA's warning labels and health warnings, few know who actually *works* there. After all, an "agency" requires some agents, and the FDA must be a huge operation with all the food and pharmaceutical drugs needed in a population of hundreds of millions. The FDA is certainly large: **7** you've almost certainly seen its approvals on some of the products you use.

While the largest group of FDA employees comprises consumer safety officers, the central work of the FDA is conducted by scientists. **8** Relying on scientists makes sense, since the science of acceptable food is something most of us never think about. But how is it possible to know whether a type of food is safe for general consumption?

A) NO CHANGE

B) Stunningly,

C) Therefore,

D) For safety's sake,

Which choice best supports the statement made in the first part of the sentence?

A) NO CHANGE

B) it has played a large role in reducing the amount of tobacco use in the United States.

C) Teddy and Franklin Roosevelt were proud of it, and you should be, too.

D) it has over 200 offices in the United States and employs many thousands of people.

At this point, the writer is considering adding the following sentence.

> The FDA employs nearly 1,000 chemists, 500 biologists, 300 pharmacologists, 40 epidemiologists, and many, many more.

Should the writer make this addition here?

A) Yes, because it lists the employment statistics for the FDA last year.

B) Yes, because it gives some data that will be elaborated upon later in the paragraph.

C) No, because it interrupts the paragraph's discussion of consumer safety officers.

D) No, because it does not account for the non-scientists who work at the FDA.

CONTINUE

How can one possibly be confident that a packaged good on a supermarket shelf will be safe **9** with confidence? This can't be a matter of taste: it must be a matter of chemistry, **10** biology, and a matter of physics. The average consumer simply does not have the knowledge to be able to assess the quality of food. The same goes for drugs. Imagine you were taking five prescription drugs at once—if the pills got mixed up, what would you do?

In short, the FDA is omnipresent in American life, even if it is a bit hidden. The truly remarkable thing about the FDA, other than its high rates of success, **11** are being the collection of expertise it has amassed among its workforce. Perhaps no other government agency requires such an incredible amount of brainpower on the cutting edge of scientific thought.

9

A) NO CHANGE

B) certainly?

C) with sureness?

D) DELETE the underlined portion and end the sentence with a question mark.

10

A) NO CHANGE

B) biology, including some

C) biology, and

D) biological sciences, and

11

A) NO CHANGE

B) have had

C) is

D) are

CONTINUE

Questions 12–22 are based on the following passage.

Drop the Puck!

For anyone aspiring to play ice hockey professionally, the National Hockey League (NHL) represents the pinnacle of hockey greatness in North America, if not the world. But how did the NHL rise to these remarkable ranks?

The story begins with that elusive trophy: the Stanley Cup. In many ways, this goal is as old as the history of professional hockey **12** its self. It was commissioned in 1892 as the Dominion Hockey Challenge Cup and was given to Canada's top-ranking amateur team each year. The name was later changed to commemorate the contributions of then-Governor General of Canada, Lord Stanley of Preston, **13** who did a great deal to grow the sport in the country.

12

A) NO CHANGE

B) themselves

C) itself

D) himself

13

Which choice provides the most logical conclusion to the sentence?

A) NO CHANGE

B) who was born in London and educated at Eton and Sandhurst.

C) who served as Governor General under British Queen Victoria.

D) DELETE the underlined portion and end the sentence with a period after the word *Preston*.

CONTINUE →

One of the early contenders for this prize was the National Hockey Association (NHA). When the NHA folded in 1917, it was replaced by the NHL that same year. Despite the name change, the NHL followed from the NHA in just about every way. Just as the NHA had before, **14** also competing annually for the Stanley Cup. This competition came against a variety of other professional and amateur teams and leagues, most notably the Pacific Coast Hockey Association (PCHA), which had formalized its relations with the NHA in 1915. The Boston Bruins, established in **15** 1924; they began the NHL's expansion into the United States.

By 1926, however, all other competing leagues had folded or merged, and the only remaining league was the NHL. **16** While other leagues and teams have issued challenges for the Cup, no non-NHL team has played for the Cup since that time. The NHL's sole dominion over Lord Stanley's Cup also symbolized its **17** supremacy in the world of professional hockey.

14

A) NO CHANGE
B) so too did the NHL compete
C) so too competed
D) so too was competing

15

A) NO CHANGE
B) 1924,
C) 1924. They
D) 1924:

16

The writer is considering deleting the previous sentence. Should the writer make this change?

A) Yes, because it breaks with the logical flow of the previous paragraph.
B) Yes, because it provides a topic sentence that would be better placed elsewhere in the passage.
C) No, because it contains the central argument of the passage as a whole.
D) No, because it provides a logical introduction and relevant information for this paragraph.

17

Which choice best maintains the tone established in the passage?

A) NO CHANGE
B) awesomeness
C) formality
D) swagger

CONTINUE

This high position was firmly cemented in the 1940s when the "Original Six" NHL franchises competed with one another each year. **18** There were two Canadian teams that were especially ascendant, even dominant, and many of the players from the era are still considered all-time greats. The league has only continued to expand. Six more teams were added during the first expansion of 1967. Today, the league has 30 teams. **19**

18

A) NO CHANGE

B) Ascendant, even dominant, were the Canadian teams especially,

C) Canadian teams were especially ascendant, even dominant,

D) Canadian teams especially were dominant,

19

Which choice most logically follows the previous sentence?

A) There are even plans to expand the league to 32, with teams in Las Vegas and Quebec City.

B) My personal favorite team is the Philadelphia Flyers, who were part of the 1967 expansion.

C) Many of the "Original Six" teams have won the Stanley Cup in recent years.

D) It can seem a little bit odd to have hockey teams in places with no natural ice, but that's the way it goes.

CONTINUE

Since the early days of professional **20** hockey, but other leagues have come and gone. There are other **21** leagues. These, however, are "minor leagues," where young players develop the skills necessary for NHL play, or where players spend whole careers waiting for their chance at the big leagues. Still, while the NHL, made up of players from all over the world, **22** hold the sway that it does, the short history given here provides the important reminder that leagues come and go. The only thing that remains, the only unadulterated constant, is the passion both men and women have for the game.

A) NO CHANGE

B) hockey,

C) hockey;

D) hockey:

The writer is considering revising the underlined portion of the sentence to read:

leagues, such as the AHL, OHL, and QMJHL.

Should the writer add this information here?

A) Yes, because it lays the groundwork for the shift in this paragraph's focus.

B) Yes, because it provides examples of some current leagues other than the NHL.

C) No, because it suggests that the NHL is not such an important league after all.

D) No, because it provides details that should be given earlier in the passage.

A) NO CHANGE

B) holds the sway that they do,

C) hold the sway that they do,

D) holds the sway that it does,

CONTINUE

Questions 23–33 are based on the following passage and supplementary material.

Is Sitting the New Smoking?

[1] Health scientists have a new warning: "Sitting is the new smoking." [2] However, excessive sitting and stillness, particularly when it is interruptedly sedentary, can have terrible consequences for health. [3] Indeed, now that many Americans have accepted the health risks of smoking and **23** puffed away from that deadly pastime, researchers worry that the sedentary lifestyle of many Americans may have replaced smoking as a national health risk. [4] This may sound odd because everyone has to sit at some point, whether at a job, in class, or in a car. **24**

25 Nearly 20 studies conducted in about as many years have confirmed this grim conclusion, and these studies have covered over 800,000 people overall. While this number does not cover the entire population, it is safely representative as a sample. In one study, researchers found a 46 percent increase in deaths from any cause among people who sat for more than four hours a day while watching television, **26** which is as compared to people who sat for only two. Other studies found links between excessive sitting and obesity, diabetes, and heart problems.

23

A) NO CHANGE
B) run
C) fired
D) veered

24

To make this paragraph most logical, sentence 4 should be placed

A) where it is now.
B) at the beginning of the paragraph.
C) before sentence 2.
D) before sentence 3.

25

Which choice most effectively combines the underlined sentences?

A) 800,000 is safely representative of the entire population, and that's precisely the number that nearly twenty studies used to confirm the grim conclusion that was mentioned above.
B) 20 tests used 800,000 subjects over the course of twenty or so years to confirm the grim conclusion and did so with a representative sample that was safe.
C) Nearly 20 studies conducted in about as many years have confirmed this grim conclusion, and these studies have covered over 800,000 people overall, a safely representative sample.
D) 800,000 people were safe from the grim conclusion of representative samples, as they were the 20 experiments of people in their 20s.

26

A) NO CHANGE
B) having
C) this is
D) DELETE the underlined portion.

CONTINUE

The problem, it seems, is that the human body has not evolved for this kind of idleness. Consider our primate **27** ancestors for example, if they were not incredibly active at all times, they would not have survived. Even many humans throughout history had to live actively—not just as hunters, but as farmers or machinists. Now, as most white-collar jobs involve sitting at a desk, human bodies aren't sure what to do with all the free time. And there is a lot of it, with some estimates showing that the average American is upright and active **28** for only 8 hours of a day. This data shows that the sitting epidemic is not restricted to the workplace: **29** standing desks have become increasingly popular in the American workplace.

How Sedentary is the Typical American Each Day?

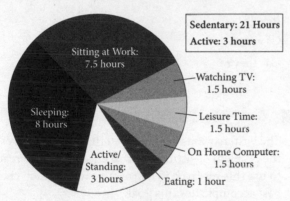

Sedentary: 21 Hours
Active: 3 hours

Sitting at Work: 7.5 hours
Watching TV: 1.5 hours
Leisure Time: 1.5 hours
On Home Computer: 1.5 hours
Sleeping: 8 hours
Active/Standing: 3 hours
Eating: 1 hour

27

A) NO CHANGE
B) ancestors. For example,
C) ancestors, for example,
D) ancestors, for example:

28

Which choice offers an accurate interpretation of the data in the graph?

A) NO CHANGE
B) for only 3 hours of the 24-hour day.
C) for nearly one third of an average day.
D) for less than an hour a day.

29

Which choices offers an accurate interpretation of the data in the graph?

A) NO CHANGE
B) the sitting done at work accounts for more than half of all sitting on an average day.
C) the average American also eats far too much, sometimes for hours at a time.
D) less than half of all sitting during an average day is done at work.

CONTINUE

There may be a message of hope in this news, however. For one, this research suggests that much of the American obesity epidemic could be solved with a change in sitting habits rather than a change in eating habits. More walking (not to mention more running, biking, or other strenuous activity) can reduce weights significantly over time.

Also, the mantra that "sitting is the new smoking" may not apply to those **30** that, of all things, fidget. Researchers in the U.K. tracked the habits of nearly 13,000 women over the course of 12 years. In controlling for other factors, they found that the women who fidgeted—who moved their hands and feet in small, seemingly negligible ways—were less at risk for the perils of sitting than those who **31** sit perfectly still. The leader of the study, Janet Cade, says that fidgeting may not help with body-mass index, but it could improve metabolism.

Thus, while sitting is not likely to come with a warning label, we can see some of **32** their detrimental effects. We can also see, however, how easy those detrimental effects are to counteract. Perhaps you can't avoid sitting down on the job, but you can do yourself all kinds of favors by standing up, stretching out, or tapping your toes. **33** You don't have to take this national health threat sitting down.

30

A) NO CHANGE

B) who

C) we

D) which

31

A) NO CHANGE

B) went

C) are

D) sat

32

A) NO CHANGE

B) its

C) it's

D) they're

33

The writers wants a conclusion that acknowledges the problem of sitting but also encourages the reader to use this research in a proactive way. Which choice best accomplishes this goal?

A) NO CHANGE

B) You should also really go to the gym once in a while.

C) You might consider applying for a job that allows you to go outside sometimes.

D) There's not all that much you can do, frankly.

CONTINUE

Questions 34–44 are based on the following passage.

It's So Rustic It's Chic

For many people, "fashion"—the latest lines of shoes, suits, dresses, or **34** furniture; refers to new things. Increasingly, however, the new things are considered *less* fashionable than the old ones. Granted, "retro" has been popular for a long time, as people have sported the clothes and **35** furnished their homes with the knick-knacks of yesteryear. The newest style of all is both newer and older than mere "retro." This new style, rustic chic, rooted in the various attempts by the stylish to glorify old things, **36** seeks to take its proponents back even further to… well, no one's quite sure.

34

A) NO CHANGE
B) furniture
C) furniture,
D) furniture—

35

A) NO CHANGE
B) have furnished
C) furnish
D) furnishing

36

A) NO CHANGE
B) has sought
C) seek
D) seeking

CONTINUE

Poking fun at this trend, the creators of a popular comedy [37] show IFC's *Portlandia*, changed their early theme song "The Dream of the '90s is Alive in Portland." Back-dropped by men riding nineteenth-century bicycles, chipping their own ice, curing their own meats, and coiffing their handlebar [38] mustaches; these parts of the song jokes that the dream of the 1890s is alive in Portland. In fact, this joke is rooted in reality. Go into many coffee shops, restaurants, clothing stores, and furniture stores, and [39] the results may surprise you; salvaged furniture repainted in such a way that its age shows, handmade goods from artisans and craftspeople, and facial-hair configurations last seen on William Howard Taft.

This concept of rustic chic may seem a little odd. First, there's the question of economics. [40] Why, for instance, would anyone want to pay good money for a piece of furniture that is not only out of style but shows its signs of age? Or why would someone want to pay *more* money for something that is worn and broken than for something that is new?

37

A) NO CHANGE
B) show, IFC's *Portlandia*,
C) show, IFC's, *Portlandia*
D) show, IFC's, *Portlandia*,

38

A) NO CHANGE
B) mustaches, the song
C) mustaches. These parts of the song
D) mustaches. The song

39

Which choice most effectively sets up the examples that follow?
A) NO CHANGE
B) you'll notice something peculiar:
C) you'll see the look of yesteryear:
D) everything will be curiously expensive;

40

At this point, the writer is considering adding the following sentence.

The effect of rustic chic on the American gross domestic product is yet to be determined.

Should the writer make this addition here?
A) Yes, because it adds a note of economic seriousness to the passage.
B) Yes, because the passage goes on to describe the global economy.
C) No, because it is not relevant to the main focus of the passage.
D) No, because it contradicts information given in the following paragraph.

CONTINUE

Moreover, rustic chic is difficult to understand because it does not have a clear **41** interest. At least we know that hippies are trying to dress like people from the 1960s and flappers are trying to dress like people from the 1920s. How about people who are interested in the rustic chic aesthetic? When people plan barn weddings, they do so because they want to get married like "they" did. **42** Why do you think people are getting married later now?

[1] These questions may be unanswerable, but that does not mean that we cannot speculate as to why rustic chic has become such a popular style. [2] Wear the clothes that men and women did *before* the existence of the fashion industry. [3] The simple answer would seem to be this: people want authenticity, so they want to free themselves of all the things that would seem to have created our contemporary, inauthentic world. [4] Have corporations ruined everything? [5] Buy from individual sellers and farmers. [6] Has the fashion industry ruined everything? **43**

In a culture wherein advertisements tell us every day to be ourselves, many have found that command to be restricting rather than liberating. Truly being yourself is the work of a lifetime. Even so, rustic chic provides one way to **44** prevent the capitalist system from turning us all into drones, though depending on whose side you're on, you might just think of it as more clutter.

41

A) NO CHANGE

B) choice.

C) fashion.

D) referent.

42

The writer wants to link this paragraph with the ideas that follow. Which choices best accomplishes this goal?

A) NO CHANGE

B) But who are "they"?

C) As it was famously said, "There's no accounting for the public's taste."

D) It's one thing to have a beard, but who actually likes mustaches?

43

To make this paragraph most logical, sentence 2 should be placed

A) where it is now.

B) after sentence 4.

C) after sentence 5.

D) after sentence 6.

44

A) NO CHANGE

B) reduce some of the clutter of contemporary life,

C) halt the military-industrial complex of today,

D) go off the grid and live a pure life,

STOP

If you finish before time is called, you may check your work on this section only.
Do not turn to any other section in the test.

Math Test – No Calculator

25 MINUTES, 20 QUESTIONS

Turn to Section 3 of your answer sheet to answer the questions in this section.

DIRECTIONS

For questions **1-15**, solve each problem, choose the best answer from the choices provided, and fill in the corresponding circle on your answer sheet. For questions **16-20**, solve the problem and enter your answer in the grid on the answer sheet. Please refer to the directions before question 16 on how to enter your answers in the grid. You may use any available space in your test booklet for scratch work.

NOTES

1. The use of a calculator **is not permitted**.
2. All variables and expressions used represent real numbers unless otherwise indicated.
3. Figures provided in this test are drawn to scale unless otherwise indicated.
4. All figures lie in a plane unless otherwise indicated.
5. Unless otherwise indicated, the domain of a given function f is the set of all real numbers x for which $f(x)$ is a real number.

REFERENCE

$A = \pi r^2$
$C = 2\pi r$
$\quad A = \ell w \quad$
$A = \frac{1}{2}bh$
$\quad c^2 = a^2 + b^2 \quad$
Special Right Triangles

$V = \ell wh \qquad V = \pi r^2 h \qquad V = \frac{4}{3}\pi r^3 \qquad V = \frac{1}{3}\pi r^2 h \qquad V = \frac{1}{3}\ell wh$

The number of degrees of arc in a circle is 360.
The number of radians of arc in a circle is 2π.
The sum of the measures in degrees of the angles of a triangle is 180.

CONTINUE

1

If $4s = 28$, what is the value of $8s + 13$?

A) 7

B) 56

C) 69

D) 84

2

Which of the following is equal to $b^{\frac{3}{4}}$, for all values of b ?

A) $\sqrt[4]{b^3}$

B) $\sqrt[4]{\dfrac{1}{b^3}}$

C) $\sqrt[4]{\dfrac{1}{b^4}}$

D) $\sqrt[4]{b^4}$

3

A landscaper will sod p plots of land with the same dimensions with a particular type of grass. The landscaper charges based on the equation $Cost = pGlw$, where p is the number of plots, G is a constant in dollars per square meter, l is the length of a plot in meters, and w is the width of a plot in meters. If the customers asks the landscaper to use a cheaper type of grass for sodding, the value of which of the following would change?

A) p

B) G

C) l

D) w

4

$$3x + 2y = -21$$
$$5x + 6y = -35$$

If (x, y) is a solution to the system of equations above, what is $x + y$?

A) −14

B) −7

C) 14

D) 56

CONTINUE

5

The number of countries that were members of the European Union in 2008 was three times the number of countries in the European Union in 1974. If the European Union had 27 members in 2008 and m members in 1974, which of the following equations is true?

A) $m + 27 = 3$

B) $\dfrac{m}{3} = 27$

C) $3m = 27$

D) $27m = 3$

6

If $\dfrac{7}{y} = \dfrac{17}{y + 30}$, what is the value of $\dfrac{y}{7}$?

A) $\dfrac{1}{3}$

B) 3

C) 7

D) 21

7

$$cx - 6y = 8$$
$$3x - 7y = 5$$

In the system of equations shown above, c is a constant and x and y are variables. For what value of c will the system of equations have no solution?

A) $\dfrac{24}{5}$

B) $\dfrac{18}{7}$

C) $-\dfrac{18}{7}$

D) $-\dfrac{24}{5}$

8

x	$g(x)$
0	2
1	5
3	−1
7	0

The function g is defined by a polynomial. Some of the values of x and $g(x)$ are shown in the table above. Which of the following must be a factor of $g(x)$?

A) $x - 1$

B) $x - 2$

C) $x - 3$

D) $x - 7$

CONTINUE

9

The line $y = cx + 6$, where c is constant, is graphed in the xy-plane. If the point (r, s) lies on the line, where $r \neq 0$ and $s \neq 0$, which is the slope of the line in terms of r and s ?

A) $\dfrac{r - 6}{s}$

B) $\dfrac{6 - s}{r}$

C) $\dfrac{6 - r}{s}$

D) $\dfrac{s - 6}{r}$

10

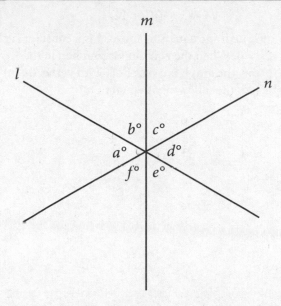

Note: Figure not drawn to scale.

In the figure above, lines l, m, and n intersect at a single point. If $a + b = c + d$, which of the following must be true?

    I. $b = c$

    II. $e = f$

    III. $a = e$

A) I and II only

B) II and III only

C) I and III only

D) I, II, and III

CONTINUE

11

$$y = k(x - 4)(x + 12)$$

In the quadratic equation above, k is a constant such that $k \neq 0$. When the equation is graphed in the xy-plane, the graph is a parabola with vertex (m, n). Which of the following is equal to n ?

A) $-24k$

B) $-36k$

C) $-48k$

D) $-64k$

12

In the xy-plane, a parabola defined by the equation $y = (x - 8)^2$ intersects the line defined by the equation $y = 36$ at two points, P and Q. What is the length of $\overline{PQ}$?

A) 8

B) 10

C) 12

D) 14

13

$$F(C) = \frac{9}{5}C + 32$$

The function above describes the relationship between temperatures measured in degrees Fahrenheit, F, and in degrees Celsius, C. Based on the function, which of the following must be true?

   I.   A temperature decrease of 1.8 degrees Celsius is equivalent to a temperature decrease of 1 degree Fahrenheit.

   II. A temperature decrease of 1 degree Celsius is equivalent to a temperature decrease of $\frac{9}{5}$ degrees Fahrenheit.

   III. A temperature decrease of $\frac{5}{9}$ degrees Fahrenheit is equivalent to a temperature decrease of 1 degree Celsius.

A) I only

B) II only

C) II and III only

D) I, II, and III

CONTINUE

14

$$\frac{80x^2 + 84x - 13}{kx - 4} = -16x - 4 - \frac{29}{kx - 4}$$

The equation above is true for all $x \neq \dfrac{4}{k}$, where k is a constant. What is the value of k ?

A) −5

B) −2

C) 2

D) 5

15

What are the solutions to $5x^2 + 30x + 15 = 0$?

A) $x = -2 \pm 2\sqrt{6}$

B) $x = -2 \pm \sqrt{6}$

C) $x = -3 \pm \dfrac{\sqrt{60}}{10}$

D) $x = -3 \pm \sqrt{6}$

CONTINUE

DIRECTIONS

For questions 16-20, solve the problem and enter your answer in the grid, as described below, on the answer sheet.

1. Although not required, it is suggested that you write your answer in the boxes at the top of the columns to help you fill in the circles accurately. You will receive credit only if the circles are filled in correctly.

2. Mark no more than one circle in any column.

3. No question has a negative answer.

4. Some problems may have more than one correct answer. In such cases, grid only one answer.

5. **Mixed numbers** such as $3\frac{1}{2}$ must be gridded as 3.5 or 7/2. (If [3 1 / 2] is entered into the grid, it will be interpreted as $\frac{31}{2}$, not as $3\frac{1}{2}$.)

6. **Decimal Answers:** If you obtain a decimal answer with more digits than the grid can accommodate, it may be either rounded or truncated, but it must fill the entire grid.

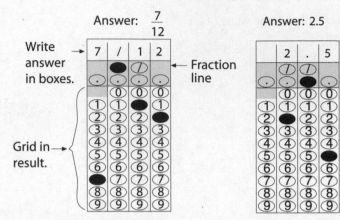

Answer: $\frac{7}{12}$

Write answer in boxes. → Fraction line

Grid in → result.

Answer: 2.5 ← Decimal point

Acceptable ways to grid $\frac{2}{3}$ are:

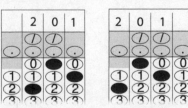

Answer: 201 – either position is correct

NOTE: You may start your answers in any column, space permitting. Columns you don't need to use should be left blank.

CONTINUE →

16

If $\dfrac{21}{25}z - \dfrac{16}{25}z = \dfrac{1}{2} + \dfrac{3}{10}$, what is the value of z?

17

$$y^3(y^2 - 10) = -9y$$

If $y > 0$, what is one possible solution to the equation above?

18

At a music school, each long session lasts twenty minutes longer than each short session. If 3 long sessions and 4 short sessions last a total of 270 minutes, how many minutes does a long session last?

19

In triangle UVW, the measure of $\angle U$ is 90°, $WV = 39$, and $UV = 36$. Triangle XYZ is similar to triangle UVW, where $\angle X$, $\angle Y$, and $\angle Z$ correspond to $\angle U$, $\angle V$, and $\angle W$, respectively. If each side of triangle XYZ is $\dfrac{3}{5}$ the length of its corresponding side of triangle UVW, what is the value of $\cos Z$?

CONTINUE

20

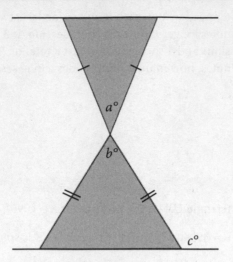

Note: Figure not drawn to scale.

Two isosceles triangles are shown above. If
$b = 180 - 4a$ and $a = 35$, what is the value of c ?

STOP
If you finish before time is called, you may check your work on this section only.
Do not turn to any other section in the test.

230 | 6 Practice Tests for the SAT

No Test Material On This Page

Math Test – Calculator

55 MINUTES, 38 QUESTIONS

Turn to Section 4 of your answer sheet to answer the questions in this section.

DIRECTIONS

For questions **1-30**, solve each problem, choose the best answer from the choices provided, and fill in the corresponding circle on your answer sheet. For questions **31-38**, solve the problem and enter your answer in the grid on the answer sheet. Please refer to the directions before question 31 on how to enter your answers in the grid. You may use any available space in your test booklet for scratch work.

NOTES

1. The use of a calculator **is permitted**.
2. All variables and expressions used represent real numbers unless otherwise indicated.
3. Figures provided in this test are drawn to scale unless otherwise indicated.
4. All figures lie in a plane unless otherwise indicated.
5. Unless otherwise indicated, the domain of a given function *f* is the set of all real numbers *x* for which *f(x)* is a real number.

REFERENCE

$A = \pi r^2$
$C = 2\pi r$

$A = \ell w$

$A = \frac{1}{2} bh$

$c^2 = a^2 + b^2$

Special Right Triangles

$V = \ell wh$

$V = \pi r^2 h$

$V = \frac{4}{3} \pi r^3$

$V = \frac{1}{3}\pi r^2 h$

$V = \frac{1}{3}\ell wh$

The number of degrees of arc in a circle is 360.
The number of radians of arc in a circle is 2π.
The sum of the measures in degrees of the angles of a triangle is 180.

CONTINUE

1

| Species | Eye color | | Total |
	Yellow	Brown	
Grey wolf	16	2	18
Coyote	7	5	12
Total	23	7	30

The table above shows the distribution by species and eye color for the 30 canids living in a nature conservancy. If one canid is selected at random, what is the probability that it will be either a grey wolf with yellow eyes or a coyote with brown eyes?

A) $\frac{11}{30}$

B) $\frac{17}{30}$

C) $\frac{21}{30}$

D) $\frac{23}{30}$

2

The graph below shows U.S. military spending, in billions of dollars, each year from 1992 through 2006.

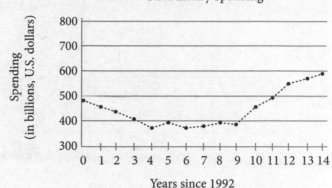

U.S. Military Spending

Years since 1992

Based on the graph, which of the following best describes the overall trend in U.S. military spending from 1992 through 2006 ?

A) Spending generally decreased in every year since 1992.

B) Spending generally increased in every year since 1992.

C) Spending generally remained constant in every year from 1992 through 2006.

D) Spending decreased until 1996 and increased after 2001.

CONTINUE

3

Eddie's Bike Ride

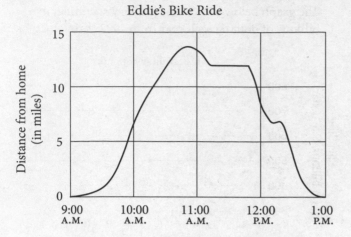

The graph above represents Eddie's distance from home during a 4-hour bike ride. He stopped for 40 minutes during his bike ride to repair a flat tire. According to the graph, which of the following is nearest to the time he finished repairing his flat tire and continued on his ride?

A) 11:10 A.M.

B) 11:50 A.M.

C) 12:10 P.M.

D) 12:50 P.M.

4

At the Acme automobile factory, approximately 4 percent of male employees and 6 percent of female employees received performance bonuses last month. If there were 648 male employees and 519 female employees at the Acme automobile factory last month, which of the following is closest to the total number of male and female employees at the Acme automobile factory who received performance bonuses last month?

A) 26

B) 31

C) 57

D) 113

5

What is the sum of the polynomials $4x^2 + 3x - 2$ and $2x^2 - 8x + 9$?

A) $6x^2 - 5x - 7$

B) $6x^2 - 5x + 7$

C) $6x^4 - 5x - 7$

D) $6x^4 - 5x + 7$

CONTINUE

6

k	1	2	3	4	5
$g(k)$	–3	1	5	9	13

The table above shows selected values of the linear function g. Which of the following best defines g ?

A) $g(k) = k - 1$

B) $g(k) = 2k - 4$

C) $g(k) = 3k - 5$

D) $g(k) = 4k - 7$

7

The total annual rainfall, in inches, in Brown County from 2005 to 2015 can be modeled by the equation $y = -0.14x + 7.8$, where x is the number of years since 2005 and y is the total annual rainfall. Which of the following best describes the meaning of the number -0.14 in the equation?

A) The total annual rainfall in 2005

B) The total annual rainfall in 2015

C) The estimated difference between the total rainfall in 2005 and the total rainfall in 2015

D) The estimated decrease in the average rainfall per year from 2005 to 2015

8

An insect crawls 30 inches in 16.3 minutes. If the insect continues to crawl at the same rate, approximately how many inches will it crawl in 6 hours?

A) 200

B) 300

C) 650

D) 960

CONTINUE

9

$$\frac{8}{5}v = \frac{7}{4}$$

In the equation above, what is the value of v?

A) $\dfrac{56}{20}$

B) $\dfrac{35}{32}$

C) $\dfrac{32}{35}$

D) $\dfrac{20}{56}$

10

The function g has four distinct zeros. Which of the following could be the complete graph of g in the xy-plane?

A)

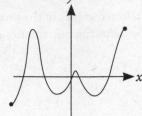

B)

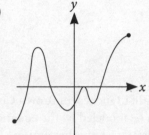

C)

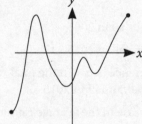

D)

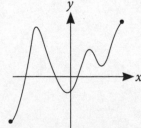

CONTINUE

Questions 11 and 12 refer to the following information.

Substance	Specific heat capacity $\left(\dfrac{J}{g}\right)$
Aluminum	0.90
Copper	0.39
Glass	0.67
Gold	0.13
Olive oil	1.79
Porcelain	1.08
Rubber	1.25
Water	4.18

The chart above gives approximations for the specific heat capacity, in joules per gram $\left(\dfrac{J}{g}\right)$, for eight common substances. The heat energy required to raise the temperature of a substance by 1° Celsius can be represented by the expression $Q = mC$, where Q is heat energy measured in joules (J), m is the mass of the substance measured in grams (g), and C is the specific heat capacity measured in $\dfrac{J}{g}$.

11

A piece of copper has a mass of 75 grams. How much heat energy, in joules, is needed to raise the temperature of the piece of copper by 1° Celsius?

A) 29.25

B) 50.25

C) 111.95

D) 192.30

12

A piece of porcelain requires 80 joules of heat energy to raise its temperature by 1° Celsius. If a piece of another substance with the same mass requires approximately 67 joules of heat energy to raise its temperature by 1° Celsius, the piece could be composed of which substance?

A) Aluminum

B) Glass

C) Olive oil

D) Rubber

CONTINUE

13

A medical study was conducted in order to determine whether product K could help people with hearing loss improve their hearing. The administrators of the study selected 200 subjects at random from a large group of people who had severe hearing loss. Half of the subjects were randomly assigned to be given product K and half were not. The resulting data demonstrated that subjects who were given product K had significantly improved hearing compared to those who were not given product K. Based on this study, which of the following conclusions is most appropriate?

A) Product K will enable all people who take it to significantly improve their hearing.

B) Product K is more effective than all other hearing-improvement products.

C) Product K will help people significantly improve their hearing.

D) Product K is likely to help people with severe hearing loss improve their hearing.

14

A car accelerates for t seconds at a constant rate of a meters per second squared $\left(\dfrac{m}{s^2}\right)$ until it reaches a velocity of v meters per second. The distance in meters the car travels is given by $d = vt - \dfrac{1}{2}at^2$. Which of the following gives a in terms of v, d, and t ?

A) $a = 2\left(v - \dfrac{d}{t}\right)$

B) $a = 2\left(v + \dfrac{d}{t}\right)$

C) $a = 2\left(\dfrac{v}{t} - \dfrac{d}{t^2}\right)$

D) $a = 2\left(\dfrac{v}{t} + \dfrac{d}{t^2}\right)$

15

A certain type of ribbon costs $0.15 per inch. Which of the equations below gives the total price, p, in dollars, for y yards of ribbon? (1 yard = 36 inches)

A) $p = 0.15y + 36$

B) $p = 0.15(36y)$

C) $p = \dfrac{0.15y}{36}$

D) $p = \dfrac{36y}{0.15}$

CONTINUE

Questions 16 and 17 refer to the following information.

$$C(q) = 60q + 300$$

$$R(q) = 75q$$

The cost of producing a product and the revenue earned from selling a product are functions of the number of units sold. The functions shown above are the estimated cost and revenue functions for a certain product. The function $C(q)$ gives the total cost, in dollars, of producing a quantity of q units of the product, and the function $R(q)$ gives the total revenue, in dollars, earned from selling a quantity of q units of the product.

16

How will the total cost of producing q units change if the quantity is decreased by 20 units?

A) The total cost will decrease by $1,200.

B) The total cost will decrease by $320.

C) The total cost will decrease by $20.

D) The total cost will increase by $1,200.

17

At what quantity will the cost of producing q units equal the revenue earned from selling q units?

A) 2

B) 15

C) 20

D) 45

18

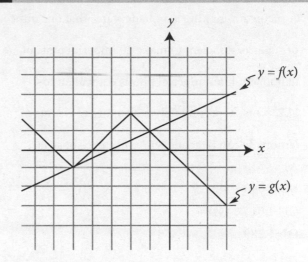

The figure above shows the graphs of the functions f and g in the xy-plane. For which of the following values of x is it true that $f(x) + g(x) = 1$?

A) −5

B) −4

C) −3

D) −2

19

Of the four types of depreciation shown below, which one would yield exponential decay in the value of an item?

A) The item loses 5% of its initial value in each successive year.

B) The item loses 6% of its current value in each successive year.

C) The value of the item decreases by $50 in each successive year.

D) The value of the item decreases by $60 in each successive year.

CONTINUE

20

A recipe for making lemonade states that one ounce of sugar is sufficient to make 30 imperial pints of lemonade. If an imperial pint is equivalent to $1\frac{1}{4}$ U.S. pints, approximately how many U.S. pints of lemonade can be made with 17 ounces of sugar?

A)   515

B)   640

C) 1,015

D) 1,280

21

Horizontal Distance versus Vertical Distance

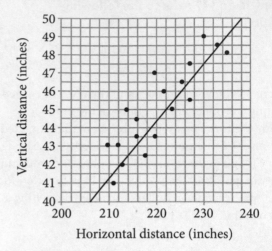

For a physics experiment, Hussain made 18 long jumps, and his classmates recorded the results. The scatterplot above shows both the vertical and horizontal distance of each jump. A line of best fit for the data is also shown. For the jump with a horizontal distance of 230 inches, the vertical distance was approximately how many inches more than the distance predicted by the line of best fit?

A) 1.5

B) 3

C) 4.5

D) 6

22

Mrs. Warren has b boxes of Girl Scout cookies that she wants to distribute to the members of her troop. If she gives each girl 4 boxes, she will have 11 boxes left over. If she wanted to give each student 5 boxes, she would need an additional 12 boxes. How many girls are in Mrs. Warren's Girl Scout troop?

A) 12

B) 23

C) 27

D) 32

23

When three numbers are added together, the result is 665. The largest number is one-third more than the sum of the other two numbers. What is the value of the largest number?

A) 95

B) 245

C) 350

D) 380

24

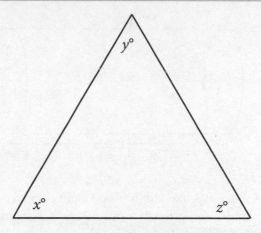

Note: Figure not drawn to scale.

In the triangle shown above, $\cos(x°) = \sin(z°)$. If $x = 3j - 19$ and $z = 5j - 15$, what is the value of j ?

A) 8.5

B) 15.5

C) 34.5

D) 51.5

25

The length of a rectangle is decreased by 25 percent, and the width of the rectangle is increased by k percent. If the area of the rectangle increases by 5 percent, what is the value of k ?

A) 25

B) 30

C) 35

D) 40

CONTINUE

26

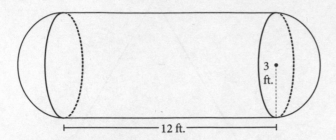

A space capsule is built from a right circular cylinder and two halves of a sphere with internal measurements as shown in the figure above. Which of the following is closest to the volume, in cubic feet, of the capsule?

A) 339.9

B) 396.3

C) 452.4

D) 565.6

27

The graph of line ℓ in the xy-plane passes through the origin and the points $(p, 4)$ and $(9, p)$. Which of the following is a possible value for p ?

A) −6

B) −3

C) 0

D) 12

28

	Decaffeinated	Caffeinated
Tea		
Coffee		
Total	28	116

The partially completed table above shows all the drinks that were sold on one day at a coffee shop. The shop sold 3 times as many cups of caffeinated tea as it did decaffeinated tea, and it sold 5 times as many cups of caffeinated coffee as it did decaffeinated coffee. If 28 cups of decaffeinated beverages and 116 cups of caffeinated beverages were sold, and one cup is selected at random out of all the caffeinated beverages that were sold, which of the following is closest to the probability that this cup contains coffee?

A) 0.508

B) 0.583

C) 0.672

D) 0.690

CONTINUE

29

$$4x + j = 7x - 9$$
$$4y + k = 7y - 9$$

In the system of equations shown above, j and k are constants, and j is k plus $\dfrac{3}{2}$. Which of the following must be true?

A) x is y minus $\dfrac{1}{2}$

B) x is y plus $\dfrac{1}{2}$

C) x is y minus $\dfrac{3}{2}$

D) x is y plus $\dfrac{9}{2}$

30

Banerji currently owns 6,500 baseball cards. He is gradually selling his collection and estimates that the number of cards he owns will decrease by 20 percent every 6 months. Which of the following expressions best models Banerji's estimate of the number of baseball cards he will own m months from now?

A) $6{,}500(0.2)^{\frac{m}{6}}$

B) $6{,}500(0.2)^{6m}$

C) $6{,}500(0.8)^{\frac{m}{6}}$

D) $6{,}500(0.8)^{6m}$

CONTINUE ▶

DIRECTIONS

For questions 31-38, solve the problem and enter your answer in the grid, as described below, on the answer sheet.

1. Although not required, it is suggested that you write your answer in the boxes at the top of the columns to help you fill in the circles accurately. You will receive credit only if the circles are filled in correctly.

2. Mark no more than one circle in any column.

3. No question has a negative answer.

4. Some problems may have more than one correct answer. In such cases, grid only one answer.

5. **Mixed numbers** such as $3\frac{1}{2}$ must be gridded as 3.5 or 7/2. (If $\boxed{3\,1\,/\,2}$ is entered into the grid, it will be interpreted as $\frac{31}{2}$, not as $3\frac{1}{2}$.)

6. **Decimal Answers:** If you obtain a decimal answer with more digits than the grid can accommodate, it may be either rounded or truncated, but it must fill the entire grid.

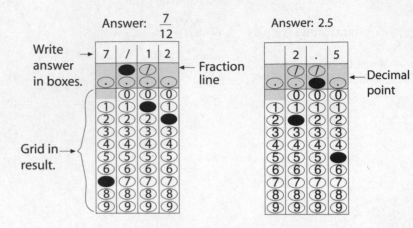

Acceptable ways to grid $\frac{2}{3}$ are:

Answer: 201 – either position is correct

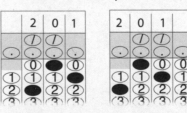

NOTE: You may start your answers in any column, space permitting. Columns you don't need to use should be left blank.

CONTINUE ➜

31

If the expression $(6x^2 - 7x + 5) - 3(x^2 - 5x + 4)$ is written in the form $ax^2 + bx + c$, what is the value of a?

32

At a grocery store, potatoes are \$0.30 each, and onions are \$0.50 each. If Emeril plans to spend at least \$2.00 but no more than \$2.50 on p potatoes and 1 onion, what is one possible value for p?

33

Height of 12 infants in Mrs. Graham's daycare program

Student	Height	Student	Height
Angela	25	Letitia	22
Benjamin	22	Moishe	26
Charles	23	Nancy	30
Denise	27	Sasha	21
Elaine	24	Tormund	27
Johanna	30	Walter	25

The table above shows the heights, in inches, of 12 infants between the ages of 3 months and 6 months. According to the table, what is the mean height, in inches, of these infants? (Round your answer to the nearest tenth.)

34

In a certain course, students take 8 exams that are graded on a scale from 0 to 100, inclusive. Jacob received an average score of 65 on his first 4 exams. What is the lowest score he can receive on his 5th exam and still be able to score an average of 75 for all 8 exams?

CONTINUE

35

$$y \leq 20x + 3{,}500$$
$$y \leq -8x$$

The graph in the xy-plane of the solution set of the system of inequalities above contains the point (j, k). What is the greatest possible value of k ?

36

In the circle centered at P, the measure of central angle QPR is $\dfrac{7\pi}{6}$ radians. The length of the arc defined by central angle QPR is what fraction of the circumference of the circle?

Questions 37 and 38 refer to the following information.

According to a well-known statistics theorem, if patients enter a medical clinic at a rate of m patients per minute and each stays at the clinic an average of W minutes, the average number of patients, L, in the clinic at any point in time is given by $L = mW$.

The manager of the Kind Care clinic estimates that when the clinic is open, an average of 4 patients per minute enter the clinic and that on average, each of them stays 45 minutes. The manager uses the above theorem to estimate that at any point in time, there are 180 patients in the clinic.

37

A rival clinic, the Speedy Care clinic, recently opened across the street. The manager of this clinic estimates that, when the clinic is open, an average of 324 patients per <u>hour</u> enter the clinic and that, on average, each of them stays 40 minutes. The average number of patients in the Speedy Care clinic at any point in time is what percent greater than the average number of patients in the Kind Care clinic at any point in time? (Note: Disregard the percent sign when gridding in your answer. For example, if your answer is 38.4%, enter 38.4)

CONTINUE

38

The theorem above may be applied to any part of the clinic, such as the waiting room or a particular office. The manager observes that, when the clinic is open, approximately 36 patients per hour are being treated by a doctor, and that each of these patients spends an average of 15 minutes with his or her doctor. At any time when the clinic is open, approximately how many patients, on average, are being treated by a doctor at the Kind Care clinic?

▲

STOP
If you finish before time is called, you may check your work on this section only.
Do not turn to any other section in the test.

SAT Essay

DIRECTIONS

The essay gives you an opportunity to show how effectively you can read and comprehend a passage and write an essay analyzing the passage. In your essay you should demonstrate that you have read the passage carefully, present a clear and logical analysis, and use language precisely.

Your essay must be written on the lines provided in your answer sheet booklet; except for the planning page of the answer booklet, you will receive no other paper on which to write. You will have enough space if you write on every line, avoid wide margins, and keep your handwriting to a reasonable size. Remember that people who are not familiar with your handwriting will read what you write. Try to write or print so that what you are writing is legible to those readers.

You have <u>50 minutes</u> to read the passage and write an essay in response to the prompt provided inside this booklet.

REMINDER

— Do not write your essay in this booklet. Only what you write on the lined pages of your answer booklet will be evaluated.

— An off-topic essay will not be evaluated.

CONTINUE ➡

As you read the passage below, consider how Stiffler and Dubrow use

- evidence, such as facts or examples, to support claims.
- reasoning to develop ideas and to connect claims and evidence.
- stylistic or persuasive elements, such as word choice or appeals to emotion, to add power to the ideas expressed.

Excerpted from Lisa Stiffler and Aaron Dubrow, "Benefits and Risks of the 'Internet of Things.'" © 2015 by National Science Foundation. Originally posted online on October 23, 2015.

1   Technology publications call 2015 "the year of the car hack."

2   This summer at DEF CON—one of the world's largest computer-hacker conferences—attendees tested the vulnerability of car computer systems at the first "Car Hacking Village." Members of Congress recently introduced the SPY Car Act, aimed at strengthening security in modern cars.

3   In other words, the rest of the world is catching up to the University of Washington's (UW) Security and Privacy Research Lab. Four years ago, with support from the National Science Foundation (NSF), the lab in the UW's Department of Computer Science & Engineering co-led an effort that first exposed weaknesses in car computer systems and demonstrated that hackers could remotely control a vehicle's brakes, door locks and other functions.

4   "We like to look in the places that no one else is looking yet," said computer science and engineering associate professor Yoshi Kohno, who founded the security lab. "You open that area up, and once people start to show up, you move on to the next thing."

5   That trailblazing strategy has put the lab, which Kohno runs jointly with assistant professor Franziska Roesner, at the forefront of computer security and privacy. The UW engineers are international leaders in addressing problems others haven't considered and helping guide the direction of the entire field. Their findings have driven security improvements in cars, medical devices, electronic voting machines and online browsing.

6   The lab's work is increasingly influential as computers are installed in countless everyday devices, making users' lives better and easier, but also putting them at risk for identity theft and even physical harm. This year alone, more than 530 security breaches have compromised more than 140 million records kept by credit card and insurance companies, hospitals, government agencies and others.

7   To combat these and other cyber threats, Kohno and Roesner investigate ways that people can co-opt a computerized product or use online information, warping it into something never intended. Take the car example: The UW researchers, in partnership with alumni Alexei Czeskis and Karl Koscher and computer scientists from the University of California

CONTINUE →

at San Diego, were curious about the security of modern vehicles and their computerized systems. So the teams at each university bought cars and plugged their computers into the vehicles' computers to see if they could decode, and ultimately hijack, the cars' software. They did it by listening as the computer systems talked to each other.

8 "If I go to a foreign country and try to learn the language, one of the best ways to do this is to eavesdrop," Kohno said. Then, he said, you "try to repeat things, and see if you get the same reaction."

9 Once the engineers figured out how to talk to the cars' computers and manipulate their functions while plugged in, they moved to the next phase: controlling the cars remotely...

10 "We were surprised by how easy some things were" when it came to commandeering the vehicles, Roesner said. But up to that point, the carmakers hadn't thought to install systems that would make it difficult.

11 That's no longer the case. The car hacking experiments caught the attention of the National Highway Traffic Safety Administration, and the Society of Automotive Engineers created a cybersecurity taskforce. The federal car safety legislation can likewise be traced to the work by the UW lab. While the car hacking work garnered the most public attention, the lab has identified other important security weaknesses...

12 With Kohno's and Roesner's help, many of the UW Computer Science & Engineering students will graduate with a better understanding of risks posed by hackers. Professors there teach an undergraduate course in security and privacy that fills up almost instantly and has a waiting list of a dozen or more.

13 The course essentially turns traditional software development on its head by taking a finished product that works one way and asking how it could be twisted, potentially for nefarious purposes. "It's kind of a surprising mind switch," Roesner said. But, she added, it's important for students to grasp if the industry is going to get a handle on security threats.

14 "In order to build secure systems," she said, "you have to understand how to break them."

Write an essay in which you explain how Stiffler and Dubrow build an argument to advocate for the importance of research that includes hacking into systems. In your essay, analyze how Stiffler and Dubrow use one or more of the features listed in the box above (or features of your own choice) to strengthen the logic and persuasiveness of their argument. Be sure that your analysis focuses on the most relevant features of the passage.

Your essay should not explain whether you agree with the authors' claims, but rather explain how Stiffler and Dubrow build an argument to persuade their audience.

END OF TEST

DO NOT RETURN TO A PREVIOUS SECTION.

Completely darken bubbles with a No. 2 pencil. If you make a mistake, be sure to erase mark completely. Erase all stray marks.

1.

YOUR NAME: _____
(Print)   Last   First   M.I.

SIGNATURE: _____   DATE: __/__/__

HOME ADDRESS: _____
(Print)   Number and Street

_____
City   State   Zip Code

PHONE NO.: _____
(Print)

5. YOUR NAME

First 4 letters of last name				FIRST INIT	MID INIT
Ⓐ	Ⓐ	Ⓐ	Ⓐ	Ⓐ	Ⓐ
Ⓑ	Ⓑ	Ⓑ	Ⓑ	Ⓑ	Ⓑ
Ⓒ	Ⓒ	Ⓒ	Ⓒ	Ⓒ	Ⓒ
Ⓓ	Ⓓ	Ⓓ	Ⓓ	Ⓓ	Ⓓ
Ⓔ	Ⓔ	Ⓔ	Ⓔ	Ⓔ	Ⓔ
Ⓕ	Ⓕ	Ⓕ	Ⓕ	Ⓕ	Ⓕ
Ⓖ	Ⓖ	Ⓖ	Ⓖ	Ⓖ	Ⓖ
Ⓗ	Ⓗ	Ⓗ	Ⓗ	Ⓗ	Ⓗ
Ⓘ	Ⓘ	Ⓘ	Ⓘ	Ⓘ	Ⓘ
Ⓙ	Ⓙ	Ⓙ	Ⓙ	Ⓙ	Ⓙ
Ⓚ	Ⓚ	Ⓚ	Ⓚ	Ⓚ	Ⓚ
Ⓛ	Ⓛ	Ⓛ	Ⓛ	Ⓛ	Ⓛ
Ⓜ	Ⓜ	Ⓜ	Ⓜ	Ⓜ	Ⓜ
Ⓝ	Ⓝ	Ⓝ	Ⓝ	Ⓝ	Ⓝ
Ⓞ	Ⓞ	Ⓞ	Ⓞ	Ⓞ	Ⓞ
Ⓟ	Ⓟ	Ⓟ	Ⓟ	Ⓟ	Ⓟ
Ⓠ	Ⓠ	Ⓠ	Ⓠ	Ⓠ	Ⓠ
Ⓡ	Ⓡ	Ⓡ	Ⓡ	Ⓡ	Ⓡ
Ⓢ	Ⓢ	Ⓢ	Ⓢ	Ⓢ	Ⓢ
Ⓣ	Ⓣ	Ⓣ	Ⓣ	Ⓣ	Ⓣ
Ⓤ	Ⓤ	Ⓤ	Ⓤ	Ⓤ	Ⓤ
Ⓥ	Ⓥ	Ⓥ	Ⓥ	Ⓥ	Ⓥ
Ⓦ	Ⓦ	Ⓦ	Ⓦ	Ⓦ	Ⓦ
Ⓧ	Ⓧ	Ⓧ	Ⓧ	Ⓧ	Ⓧ
Ⓨ	Ⓨ	Ⓨ	Ⓨ	Ⓨ	Ⓨ
Ⓩ	Ⓩ	Ⓩ	Ⓩ	Ⓩ	Ⓩ

IMPORTANT: Please fill in these boxes exactly as shown on the back cover of your test book.

2. TEST FORM

_____

6. DATE OF BIRTH

Month		Day		Year	
○ JAN					
○ FEB	⓪	⓪	⓪	⓪	
○ MAR	①	①	①	①	
○ APR	②	②	②	②	
○ MAY	③	③	③	③	
○ JUN		④	④	④	
○ JUL		⑤	⑤	⑤	
○ AUG		⑥	⑥	⑥	
○ SEP		⑦	⑦	⑦	
○ OCT		⑧	⑧	⑧	
○ NOV		⑨	⑨	⑨	
○ DEC					

3. TEST CODE

⓪	Ⓐ	Ⓙ	⓪
①	Ⓑ	Ⓚ	①
②	Ⓒ	Ⓛ	②
③	Ⓓ	Ⓜ	③
④	Ⓔ	Ⓝ	④
⑤	Ⓕ	Ⓞ	⑤
⑥	Ⓖ	Ⓟ	⑥
⑦	Ⓗ	Ⓠ	⑦
⑧	Ⓘ	Ⓡ	⑧
⑨			⑨

4. REGISTRATION NUMBER

⓪	⓪	⓪	⓪	⓪	⓪	⓪	⓪
①	①	①	①	①	①	①	①
②	②	②	②	②	②	②	②
③	③	③	③	③	③	③	③
④	④	④	④	④	④	④	④
⑤	⑤	⑤	⑤	⑤	⑤	⑤	⑤
⑥	⑥	⑥	⑥	⑥	⑥	⑥	⑥
⑦	⑦	⑦	⑦	⑦	⑦	⑦	⑦
⑧	⑧	⑧	⑧	⑧	⑧	⑧	⑧
⑨	⑨	⑨	⑨	⑨	⑨	⑨	⑨

7. SEX

○ MALE
○ FEMALE

The **Princeton Review**®

Test ③ Start with number 1 for each new section.
If a section has fewer questions than answer spaces, leave the extra answer spaces blank.

Section 1—Reading

1. Ⓐ Ⓑ Ⓒ Ⓓ
2. Ⓐ Ⓑ Ⓒ Ⓓ
3. Ⓐ Ⓑ Ⓒ Ⓓ
4. Ⓐ Ⓑ Ⓒ Ⓓ
5. Ⓐ Ⓑ Ⓒ Ⓓ
6. Ⓐ Ⓑ Ⓒ Ⓓ
7. Ⓐ Ⓑ Ⓒ Ⓓ
8. Ⓐ Ⓑ Ⓒ Ⓓ
9. Ⓐ Ⓑ Ⓒ Ⓓ
10. Ⓐ Ⓑ Ⓒ Ⓓ
11. Ⓐ Ⓑ Ⓒ Ⓓ
12. Ⓐ Ⓑ Ⓒ Ⓓ
13. Ⓐ Ⓑ Ⓒ Ⓓ
14. Ⓐ Ⓑ Ⓒ Ⓓ
15. Ⓐ Ⓑ Ⓒ Ⓓ
16. Ⓐ Ⓑ Ⓒ Ⓓ
17. Ⓐ Ⓑ Ⓒ Ⓓ
18. Ⓐ Ⓑ Ⓒ Ⓓ
19. Ⓐ Ⓑ Ⓒ Ⓓ
20. Ⓐ Ⓑ Ⓒ Ⓓ
21. Ⓐ Ⓑ Ⓒ Ⓓ
22. Ⓐ Ⓑ Ⓒ Ⓓ
23. Ⓐ Ⓑ Ⓒ Ⓓ
24. Ⓐ Ⓑ Ⓒ Ⓓ
25. Ⓐ Ⓑ Ⓒ Ⓓ
26. Ⓐ Ⓑ Ⓒ Ⓓ
27. Ⓐ Ⓑ Ⓒ Ⓓ
28. Ⓐ Ⓑ Ⓒ Ⓓ
29. Ⓐ Ⓑ Ⓒ Ⓓ
30. Ⓐ Ⓑ Ⓒ Ⓓ
31. Ⓐ Ⓑ Ⓒ Ⓓ
32. Ⓐ Ⓑ Ⓒ Ⓓ
33. Ⓐ Ⓑ Ⓒ Ⓓ
34. Ⓐ Ⓑ Ⓒ Ⓓ
35. Ⓐ Ⓑ Ⓒ Ⓓ
36. Ⓐ Ⓑ Ⓒ Ⓓ
37. Ⓐ Ⓑ Ⓒ Ⓓ
38. Ⓐ Ⓑ Ⓒ Ⓓ
39. Ⓐ Ⓑ Ⓒ Ⓓ
40. Ⓐ Ⓑ Ⓒ Ⓓ
41. Ⓐ Ⓑ Ⓒ Ⓓ
42. Ⓐ Ⓑ Ⓒ Ⓓ
43. Ⓐ Ⓑ Ⓒ Ⓓ
44. Ⓐ Ⓑ Ⓒ Ⓓ
45. Ⓐ Ⓑ Ⓒ Ⓓ
46. Ⓐ Ⓑ Ⓒ Ⓓ
47. Ⓐ Ⓑ Ⓒ Ⓓ
48. Ⓐ Ⓑ Ⓒ Ⓓ
49. Ⓐ Ⓑ Ⓒ Ⓓ
50. Ⓐ Ⓑ Ⓒ Ⓓ
51. Ⓐ Ⓑ Ⓒ Ⓓ
52. Ⓐ Ⓑ Ⓒ Ⓓ

Section 2—Writing and Language Skills

1. Ⓐ Ⓑ Ⓒ Ⓓ
2. Ⓐ Ⓑ Ⓒ Ⓓ
3. Ⓐ Ⓑ Ⓒ Ⓓ
4. Ⓐ Ⓑ Ⓒ Ⓓ
5. Ⓐ Ⓑ Ⓒ Ⓓ
6. Ⓐ Ⓑ Ⓒ Ⓓ
7. Ⓐ Ⓑ Ⓒ Ⓓ
8. Ⓐ Ⓑ Ⓒ Ⓓ
9. Ⓐ Ⓑ Ⓒ Ⓓ
10. Ⓐ Ⓑ Ⓒ Ⓓ
11. Ⓐ Ⓑ Ⓒ Ⓓ
12. Ⓐ Ⓑ Ⓒ Ⓓ
13. Ⓐ Ⓑ Ⓒ Ⓓ
14. Ⓐ Ⓑ Ⓒ Ⓓ
15. Ⓐ Ⓑ Ⓒ Ⓓ
16. Ⓐ Ⓑ Ⓒ Ⓓ
17. Ⓐ Ⓑ Ⓒ Ⓓ
18. Ⓐ Ⓑ Ⓒ Ⓓ
19. Ⓐ Ⓑ Ⓒ Ⓓ
20. Ⓐ Ⓑ Ⓒ Ⓓ
21. Ⓐ Ⓑ Ⓒ Ⓓ
22. Ⓐ Ⓑ Ⓒ Ⓓ
23. Ⓐ Ⓑ Ⓒ Ⓓ
24. Ⓐ Ⓑ Ⓒ Ⓓ
25. Ⓐ Ⓑ Ⓒ Ⓓ
26. Ⓐ Ⓑ Ⓒ Ⓓ
27. Ⓐ Ⓑ Ⓒ Ⓓ
28. Ⓐ Ⓑ Ⓒ Ⓓ
29. Ⓐ Ⓑ Ⓒ Ⓓ
30. Ⓐ Ⓑ Ⓒ Ⓓ
31. Ⓐ Ⓑ Ⓒ Ⓓ
32. Ⓐ Ⓑ Ⓒ Ⓓ
33. Ⓐ Ⓑ Ⓒ Ⓓ
34. Ⓐ Ⓑ Ⓒ Ⓓ
35. Ⓐ Ⓑ Ⓒ Ⓓ
36. Ⓐ Ⓑ Ⓒ Ⓓ
37. Ⓐ Ⓑ Ⓒ Ⓓ
38. Ⓐ Ⓑ Ⓒ Ⓓ
39. Ⓐ Ⓑ Ⓒ Ⓓ
40. Ⓐ Ⓑ Ⓒ Ⓓ
41. Ⓐ Ⓑ Ⓒ Ⓓ
42. Ⓐ Ⓑ Ⓒ Ⓓ
43. Ⓐ Ⓑ Ⓒ Ⓓ
44. Ⓐ Ⓑ Ⓒ Ⓓ

Test 3 Start with number 1 for each new section.
If a section has fewer questions than answer spaces, leave the extra answer spaces blank.

Section 3—Mathematics: No Calculator

1. Ⓐ Ⓑ Ⓒ Ⓓ
2. Ⓐ Ⓑ Ⓒ Ⓓ
3. Ⓐ Ⓑ Ⓒ Ⓓ
4. Ⓐ Ⓑ Ⓒ Ⓓ
5. Ⓐ Ⓑ Ⓒ Ⓓ
6. Ⓐ Ⓑ Ⓒ Ⓓ
7. Ⓐ Ⓑ Ⓒ Ⓓ
8. Ⓐ Ⓑ Ⓒ Ⓓ
9. Ⓐ Ⓑ Ⓒ Ⓓ
10. Ⓐ Ⓑ Ⓒ Ⓓ
11. Ⓐ Ⓑ Ⓒ Ⓓ
12. Ⓐ Ⓑ Ⓒ Ⓓ
13. Ⓐ Ⓑ Ⓒ Ⓓ
14. Ⓐ Ⓑ Ⓒ Ⓓ
15. Ⓐ Ⓑ Ⓒ Ⓓ

16.  17. 18. 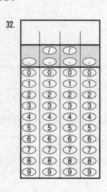 19. 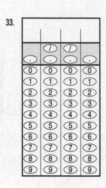 20.

Section 4—Mathematics: Calculator

1. Ⓐ Ⓑ Ⓒ Ⓓ
2. Ⓐ Ⓑ Ⓒ Ⓓ
3. Ⓐ Ⓑ Ⓒ Ⓓ
4. Ⓐ Ⓑ Ⓒ Ⓓ
5. Ⓐ Ⓑ Ⓒ Ⓓ
6. Ⓐ Ⓑ Ⓒ Ⓓ
7. Ⓐ Ⓑ Ⓒ Ⓓ
8. Ⓐ Ⓑ Ⓒ Ⓓ
9. Ⓐ Ⓑ Ⓒ Ⓓ
10. Ⓐ Ⓑ Ⓒ Ⓓ
11. Ⓐ Ⓑ Ⓒ Ⓓ
12. Ⓐ Ⓑ Ⓒ Ⓓ
13. Ⓐ Ⓑ Ⓒ Ⓓ
14. Ⓐ Ⓑ Ⓒ Ⓓ
15. Ⓐ Ⓑ Ⓒ Ⓓ
16. Ⓐ Ⓑ Ⓒ Ⓓ
17. Ⓐ Ⓑ Ⓒ Ⓓ
18. Ⓐ Ⓑ Ⓒ Ⓓ
19. Ⓐ Ⓑ Ⓒ Ⓓ
20. Ⓐ Ⓑ Ⓒ Ⓓ
21. Ⓐ Ⓑ Ⓒ Ⓓ
22. Ⓐ Ⓑ Ⓒ Ⓓ
23. Ⓐ Ⓑ Ⓒ Ⓓ
24. Ⓐ Ⓑ Ⓒ Ⓓ
25. Ⓐ Ⓑ Ⓒ Ⓓ
26. Ⓐ Ⓑ Ⓒ Ⓓ
27. Ⓐ Ⓑ Ⓒ Ⓓ
28. Ⓐ Ⓑ Ⓒ Ⓓ
29. Ⓐ Ⓑ Ⓒ Ⓓ
30. Ⓐ Ⓑ Ⓒ Ⓓ

31. 32. 33. 34. 35.

36. 37. 38.

Chapter 8
Practice Test 3:
Answers and
Explanations

PRACTICE TEST 3 ANSWER KEY

Section 1:
Reading

1.	B	27.	C
2.	A	28.	C
3.	D	29.	A
4.	D	30.	B
5.	B	31.	A
6.	C	32.	B
7.	D	33.	D
8.	D	34.	A
9.	B	35.	C
10.	D	36.	D
11.	D	37.	A
12.	B	38.	C
13.	C	39.	D
14.	A	40.	B
15.	C	41.	C
16.	B	42.	B
17.	C	43.	B
18.	A	44.	B
19.	D	45.	C
20.	D	46.	C
21.	A	47.	A
22.	D	48.	A
23.	D	49.	D
24.	C	50.	A
25.	B	51.	C
26.	B	52.	C

Section 2:
Writing & Language

1.	D	23.	D
2.	A	24.	C
3.	C	25.	C
4.	A	26.	D
5.	A	27.	D
6.	A	28.	B
7.	D	29.	D
8.	B	30.	B
9.	D	31.	D
10.	C	32.	B
11.	C	33.	A
12.	C	34.	D
13.	A	35.	A
14.	B	36.	A
15.	B	37.	B
16.	D	38.	B
17.	A	39.	C
18.	D	40.	C
19.	A	41.	D
20.	B	42.	B
21.	B	43.	D
22.	D	44.	B

Section 3:
Math (No Calculator)

1.	C	11.	D
2.	A	12.	C
3.	B	13.	B
4.	B	14.	A
5.	C	15.	D
6.	B	16.	4
7.	B	17.	1 or 3
8.	D	18.	50
9.	D	19.	$\frac{5}{13}$
10.	A	20.	110

Section 4 :
Math (Calculator)

1.	C	20.	B
2.	D	21.	A
3.	B	22.	B
4.	C	23.	D
5.	B	24.	B
6.	D	25.	D
7.	D	26.	C
8.	C	27.	A
9.	B	28.	D
10.	B	29.	B
11.	A	30.	C
12.	A	31.	3
13.	D	32.	5 or 6
14.	C	33.	25.2
15.	B	34.	40
16.	A	35.	1,000
17.	C	36.	$\frac{7}{12}$ or .583
18.	C		
19.	B	37.	20
		38.	9

For self-scoring assessment tables, please turn to page 565.

PRACTICE TEST 3 EXPLANATIONS

Section 1: Reading

1. **B** This question asks for the best summary of the passage. Look for an answer choice that matches the passage as a whole; eliminate answer choices that are true but too specific. The first paragraph describes the party, the second paragraph gives the back story of the woman Lady Windermere is talking to, and the rest of the text relates their conversation. Choice (A) is true, but only refers to the last part of the text. Eliminate (A). Choice (B) could be true, as it reflects all three parts of the text. Keep (B) for now. Choice (C) is true, but only refers to the first part of the text. Eliminate (C). Choice (D) is both false and deceptive: This is her last reception before Easter, not her last reception ever, and she only jokingly refers to the need to flee danger. Eliminate (D). Choice (B) is the correct answer.

2. **A** This question asks for the meaning of *smartest* in context. So find the word in context: *all the pretty women wore their smartest dresses*. Here, *smartest* has to do with a nice appearance. Choice (A), *most fashionable*, is possible; keep it for now. Choice (B), *most clever*, is another meaning of *smartest*. Eliminate (B). Choice (C), *most painful*, recalls another meaning of the verb 'to smart'. Eliminate (C). Choice (D), *brightest*, could be about appearance, so keep it for now. Compare the remaining answer choices: *most fashionable* is appropriately general, while *brightest* does not work in this context. Eliminate (D). Choice (A) is the correct answer.

3. **D** This question is a general question followed by a best evidence question, so the Parallel POE strategy will work nicely here. Look at the answers for Q4 first and decide if any of them connect with the answers for Q3. Choice (4A) references Lady Windermere's *last reception before Easter*, which could initially connect to (3A). Draw a line between them. Choice (4B) does not support any of the answers for Q3, so eliminate it. Choice (4C) supports the idea that Lady Windermere is serious about the fortune-teller, which is not an idea presented in Q3, so eliminate (4C). Choice (4D) shows Lady Windermere's off-hand response to the Duchess's question about the chiromantist's fortunes. Her response is definitely not serious, so (4A) could connect with (3D). Without support from Q4, (3B) and (3C) can also be eliminated. Read the remaining pairs closely, looking for the one that best answers the question. Notice that (3A) says Lady Windermere is *nearing the end of her hostessing days*, while the text simply says it's the *last reception before Easter*. These two answers don't accurately support each other, so you can eliminate them. This leaves (3D) and (4D) as the correct answers.

4. **D** (See explanation above.)

5. **B** This question asks about the purpose of the description of *gorgeous peeresses … violent Radicals, popular preachers … eminent sceptics* and *a perfect bevy of bishops*. Look for that description in context. It is located in paragraph 1, following this sentence: *It was certainly a wonderful*

medley of people. Medley means *blend*, and so the description seems to support the claim that it was a wonderful mix of people. Choice (A) could be true, since political and artistic types are indeed two different groups. Choice (B) is even better, since the phrase *variety of people* can refer to *peeresses, Radicals, preachers, sceptics, and bishops*. Eliminate (A) for being too narrow in scope. Choice (C) is also narrow in scope, reducing the list to women and men, which is not the point of the description. Eliminate (C). Choice (D) can be eliminated because there is no explicit difference set up between any classes in the text. Choice (B) is the correct answer.

6. **C**   This is a Vocab-in-Context question, so return to the text, find the word in question, and cross it out. Then use the surrounding text to fill in another word that fits the context. The Duchess is showing that she is surprised by something. *Start* must mean something that shows surprise. Choices (A), *opening*, and (B), *commencement*, refer to another meaning of start. Eliminate (A) and (B). Choice (C), *twitch*, refers to a movement that one might make when surprised, so keep it for now. Choice (D), *procedure*, is irrelevant, so eliminate (D). Choice (C) is the correct answer.

7. **D**   This question asks what the narrator indicates about Princess Sophia, the Radicals, and the Royal Academicians. Find where they are mentioned, and see what the narrator actually says about them. They are mentioned in the middle of the first paragraph, which is describing the lively party with its different guests. Choice (A) could fit the Radicals, who are explicitly called violent, but the Royal Academicians are the ones who are disguised; the princess is neither violent nor disguised. Eliminate (A). Choice (B) fits the princess's laughter, but not necessarily anything else about her, and does not fit the Radicals or the Royal Academicians. Eliminate (B). Choice (C) could be true, but the text doesn't say so, so we don't know this. Choice (D) fits and has textual support in the sentence: *It was certainly a wonderful medley of people.* Choice (D) is the correct answer.

8. **D**   This question asks what the narrator implies about Lady Windermere. To answer an inference question, look for what the narrator actually says about her. Choice (A) is in the text, but it is something Lady Windermere jokes about herself. It's not something the narrator says. Eliminate (A). Choice (B) again corresponds to a joke Lady Windermere makes rather than something the narrator says. Eliminate (B). Choice (C) could be true, but the text says nothing about this, so it has no support. Although Lady Windermere has been married several times, there is no indication that she will get another divorce. Eliminate (C). Choice (D) is supported by lines 18–19: *In fact, it was one of Lady Windermere's best nights.* Since this is the only answer choice with textual support, select it. Choice (D) is the correct answer.

9. **B**   This question asks how the Duchess of Paisley is described in the passage. Be sure to read for descriptions of the Duchess, not Lady Windermere. Because Q10 is a best evidence question, those answer choices can be considered in tandem with Q9 using Parallel POE. First consider (10A). Although those lines might initially seem to support (9D), that description is of Lady Windermere, not the Duchess. Eliminate (10A). Choice (10B) also describes Lady Windermere,

rather than the Duchess, so eliminate that answer. Choice (10C) is relevant to the Duchess, but the lines do not support anything from Q9. Eliminate (10C). Choice (10D) supports (9B). Because (9B) is the only answer in Q9 that has any support from Q10, eliminate (9A), (9C), and (9D). The correct answers are (9B) and (10D).

10. **D** (See explanation above.)

11. **D** This question asks how the first paragraph fits in with the rest of the passage. The opening paragraph gives an overview of the growing disparity between individuals of high and low SES. Eliminate (A) and (B), since neither mentions a disparity or discrepancy. Choice (C) does acknowledge a discrepancy, but there are no solutions offered throughout the course of the passage, making this choice incorrect. Choice (D) is correct because it highlights the discrepancy and mentions the research that permeates the rest of the passage.

12. **B** The question refers to advantages to higher SES. Look for clues in the question and try to locate the correct window. The advantages of higher SES are included in the second paragraph, which explicitly states that *individuals belonging to higher status positions in society benefit from greater access to material and social resources, increased workplace opportunities,* supporting (B). Choices (A) and (D) are incorrect because *stereotype threat* and *discrimination* are hindrances, not advantages. Similarly, Choice (C) is incorrect because *political activism* may manifest in any individuals, regardless of SES or social category. Choice (B) is correct.

13. **C** This is a specific paired question, so locate the sentence that gave the answer in the previous question. The prediction for question 12 came from lines 31–34. Therefore, (C) is correct.

14. **A** The question asks for the function of the third paragraph, which is to explain the viewpoint of individuals of a higher socioeconomic status. These individuals attribute their successes to other aspects of life such as education and achievement based on merit. This fits (A), which states that these individuals cite reasons other than SES for their success. Choice (B) states that there is equal opportunity for both high and low SES, which contradicts the passage. Choice (C) is extreme and offensive, implying that the high SES individuals purposely repress those less fortunate, and (D) is too strong and over encompassing as well. Choice (A) is correct.

15. **C** This is a specific paired question, so locate the sentence that gave the answer in the previous question. The prediction for question 14 came from 42–45. Therefore, (C) is correct.

16. **B** This is a Vocab-in-Context question, so go back to line 47, find the word *bestow,* and cross it out. Then use the surrounding text to put in another word that makes sense based on the context. This part of the text talks about the *benefits* of *elevated social positions.* Something like *give* would also work in the sentence. Eliminate (A) because it's the opposite of *give.* Choice (B) might work, so hang on to it. Choice (C) might initially look attractive, but a closer reading of the window shows that these individuals try to explain their benefits as something earned, but they actually aren't. Eliminate (C). Choice (D) does not match the prediction. Choice (B) is the correct answer.

17. **C** This is a Vocab-in-Context question, so go back to line 65, find the word *aligns*, and cross it out. Then use the surrounding text to put in another word that makes sense based on the context. The text talks about the *present research* doing something with *mounting evidence* about *reliable predictors*. The missing word must mean something like *agree*. Now use the prediction to go through the answer choices and eliminate anything that doesn't match the prediction. Choice (A) can be eliminated because *arranges* has nothing to do with *agrees*. Choice (B) does not match the prediction and can be eliminated. Choice (C) matches the prediction. Keep it. Choice (D) can be eliminated, leaving (C) as the correct answer.

18. **A** This question asks about *supporting a conclusion* mentioned at the end of the passage. The correct answer must provide details that strengthen the conclusion that *social status is a reliable predictor of economic inequality*. Choice (A) talks about how *high status individuals* are more likely to *hold public office*, giving them *decision-making power on matters related to economic policy*. That connects strongly to the conclusion, so don't eliminate (A). Choice (B) states how individuals of different socioeconomic statuses perceive themselves, but does not support those differences predicting inequality. Eliminate (B). Choice (C) outlines a self-reflective study, not necessarily related to the inequality that exists between the two groups, making it incorrect as well. Choice (D) might initially look good because it mentions *social status predicts support for inequality*, but a closer reading of the text reveals that the conclusion itself is used as support for a call to action in this part of the text. Choice (D) can be eliminated. Choice (A) is correct.

19. **D** This question asks about data in the figure. Go straight to the figure and use the data points to POE. Find precise data points on the figure to support keeping or eliminating answer choices. Choice (A) can be eliminated because Panel B shows clearly that Democratic males are more likely to support the legislation that their female counterparts. Choices (B) and (C) are both incorrect because no information is given about the number of individuals who answered the polls to obtain this data. Choice (D) is supported by both Panel A and Panel B, making it the correct answer.

20. **D** The figures show an elected official's tendency to support or not support legislation supporting economic inequality, so a positive number would be more likely to support while a negative number would be less likely to support such legislation. Consistently, Republicans are in the positive range while the Democrats are in the negative range, supporting (D). Choice (A) is incorrect because, while it may be true based on the passage, it is not supported by the figures. Several socioeconomic and social categories are mentioned in these figures, but they are not equally supporting or opposing such legislation. Choice (C) is also incorrect because Democratic females and individuals with low wealth are the most likely to *oppose* such legislation, not support it. Choice (D) is correct.

21. **A** This is a general question about the sequence of events in the passage, so save it until after the specific questions are answered. The passage begins with the songbirds' migration and then discusses experiments about the migration that provided some information but left other ques-

tions unanswered. Choice (A) works because the observed phenomenon is the birds' nocturnal migration and decreased sleep need during migratory states. There is more research to be done since the lab is a controlled environment and migration happens in the wild. Choice (B) is partially true, but the portion about inconclusive results makes it incorrect, since the study did reveal strong findings. Choice (C) is incorrect because nothing is revolutionized or disproved. Similarly, (D) is incorrect because there is never a second study mentioned in the passage. Therefore, (A) is correct.

22. **D** This is a Vocab-in-Context question, so go back to line 21, find the word *reconcile*, and cross it out. Then use the surrounding text to put in another word that makes sense based on the context of the passage. This part of the text talks about researchers trying to bring together conflicting observations that *sleep-deprived fliers appear no worse for wear* and that there's *evidence linking sleep deprivation to impaired neurobehavioral and physiological function*. The missing word must mean something like *bring together* or *make fit*. Choices (A) and (B) are both definitions of *reconcile*, but neither works in this context. Eliminate both of those answers. Choice (C) might initially sound good, because *clarify* might help researchers figure out the disparity between the observations, but it doesn't fit the context of needing to *bring together* the theories. Choice (D), *integrate*, does mean *bring together*. Choice (D) is the correct answer.

23. **D** This is a best evidence question, so it can be done in tandem with Q24. Consider the answer choices for Q24 and see if they support any of the answer choices for Q23. If the lines in Q24 don't support any of the answers to Q23, they can be eliminated. The lines in (24A) refer to the many miles the birds travel, which might initially look good for (23A) or (23D), but because those lines don't say anything about sleep, they don't actually support either of those answers. Choice (24A) can be eliminated. Choice (24B) mentions both the distance the birds flew as well as the birds having *little time for sleep*. This could support (23A), except (23A) mentions the birds' *evolutionary ancestors*. That idea isn't mentioned anywhere, so eliminate (24B). Choice (24C) could connect with (23D), so draw a line connecting those two answer choices. Choice (24D) connects with (23B), so draw a line connecting those two answer choices. Without support from Q24, (23A) and (23C) can be eliminated. The question asks about Benca's *central assumption in setting up her research*, which was about the birds sleeping while they migrate. While the birds' behavior in the lab cages is in the passage, it is not the central assumption. Eliminate (23B) and (24D). This leaves (23D) and (24C) as the correct answers.

24. **C** (See explanation above.)

25. **B** This question asks about Neils Rattenborg's findings and what they serve to do. Carefully read the fourth paragraph to see what Rattenborg found. His tests found that birds in the *nonmigrating state suffered cognitive deficits when sleep-deprived* but were able to *maintain cognitive function* when faced with *ongoing sleep loss in the migratory state*. These findings dovetail nicely with what Benca observed in the field. Eliminate any answers that have nothing to do with this prediction. Choice (A) can be eliminated because the results support the hypothesis rather

than upset it. Choice (B) is almost exactly what the prediction is, so keep it. Choice (C) can be eliminated, because no previous research was introduced. Choice (D) can be eliminated because there are no differences that are underscored. This leaves (B), which is the correct answer.

26. **B** Use the line reference to find the window for this question. Since the researchers noticed an *unprecedented ability to maintain cognitive function* during migratory states, they were able to draw a correlation between migratory states and decreased sleep without suffering cognitive deficits. The passage goes on to say that *Benca and colleagues concede it's impossible to know for sure without recording the birds in action.* The answer must have something to do with conceding a lack of information. Choice (A) might initially look good because it contains the word *impossible*, but that answer choice is too extreme. It's not impossible to know, just impossible to know without additional information. Eliminate (A). Choice (B) is a good paraphrase of the prediction, so keep it. Choice (C) can be eliminated because that observation happened before, not after. Choice (D) is not mentioned anywhere in the text. Choice (B) is the correct answer.

27. **C** This question asks about the factor that would necessitate further research. Using chronology, the answer to this question must come after the noted results from the research, so look around lines 50–56. The text says that the additional answers to the cognition question would be *impossible to know for sure without recording the birds in action.* The study tested the birds in a lab setting, so further research must require birds actually flying and migrating. Choice (C) is the only answer that addresses this and is the correct answer.

28. **C** This is a Vocab-in-Context question, so go back to line 68, find the word *improbable*, and cross it out. Then use the surrounding text to put in another word that makes sense based on the context of the passage. This part of the text talks about the *longstanding mysteries* of the *sleepless flight* of the migrating birds. The missing word must mean something like *mysterious* or *amazing*. Choices (A), (B), and (D) could be possible meanings for *improbable* in other contexts, but only (C), *remarkable*, fits the context of the passage. Choice (C) is the correct answer.

29. **A** This is a general question that comes at the end of the set of questions. After answering all the other questions, POE is very straightforward for the general questions. Go straight to the answers and see what can be eliminated about the songbirds based on the answers to prior questions. Choice (A) is exactly what many of the previous questions have been about, so don't eliminate it. Choice (B) is irrelevant—no mention of actual sleepwalkers occurred within the passage. Choice (C) might look good because of the word *impossible*, but the mechanisms are not actually *impossible to understand*, so (C) can be eliminated. Choice (D) is never mentioned, so eliminate it. This leaves (A) as the correct answer.

30. **B** This question asks about the best evidence to support the previous question, so simply eliminate any answer choices that don't support *activity levels correlating to migratory seasons.* Choice (A) is a rhetorical question introducing a question. Eliminate it. Choice (B) describes behavior

of songbirds. If there isn't a clear reason to eliminate an answer choice, keep it for now. Choice (C) mentions the birds' reduced sleep time, but that doesn't address the *activity level*. Choice (D) is irrelevant to Q29. Eliminate it. This leaves (B), which directly connects birds' activity levels (*hopping and wing flapping*) with *migratory seasons*. Choice (B) is the correct answer.

31.   **A**   This is a Vocab-in-Context question, so go back to line 68, find the word *feature*, and cross it out. Then use the surrounding text to put in another word that makes sense based on the context of the passage. Words like *have*, *give*, or *show* could work. Notice that the word is used as a verb. Choice (A), *present*, might look like the noun, but as a verb, it matches the prediction, so keep it. Choice (B), *attribute*, does not fit the prediction, so eliminate it. Choice (C), *report*, matches the prediction, so keep it. Choice (D), *promote*, does not fit the prediction, so eliminate it. Consider the remaining answer choices, (A) and (C). *Report* means to tell, to convey information; *present* more generally means to give or to show. Although these might initially seem very close, the report cards are not reporting the phrases. They are using the phrases to communicate performance expectations. Eliminate (C) and choose (A), which is the correct answer.

32.   **B**   This question asks for a reasonable inference about what the authors of Passage 1 believe about a standards-based report card. So look and see what they actually say about that topic. Paragraph two contains descriptions corresponding to the authors' claims, as opposed to reports about how other people think or feel about the new report cards: *Such a report card actually provides more detailed, specific information than a traditional grade....* Choice (A) is not necessarily an opinion of the authors, who report that *concerns have been expressed about how colleges might evaluate* these report cards. But whose concerns? We don't know, so eliminate (A). Choice (B) fits the prediction, so keep it. Choice (C) refers to an opinion not mentioned anywhere in the text; eliminate it. Choice (D) is deceptive; it compares third-graders and high-schoolers, both of whom are mentioned in the text, but who are not compared along the lines of this choice; eliminate (D). Select the remaining answer choice, (B), which is the correct answer.

33.   **D**   This question asks for the best evidence for the answer to Q32. Since the phrase *Such a report card actually provides more detailed, specific information than a traditional grade...* supported that answer, look for it in the answer choices here. Choice (A) is from the wrong paragraph; eliminate it; (B) and (C) are from the right paragraph, but do not contain the predicted phrase; eliminate them. Choice (D) fits the prediction and is the correct answer.

34.   **A**   This question asks what the author of Passage 2 says about the use of standards-based report cards in elementary schools. Since it is not clear from what part of the passage the answer will come, this question can be answered later. But then look for discussion of elementary schools in particular. There is no mention of elementary schools until paragraph 3, and elementary schools are not mentioned again in paragraph 4, so the correct answer has to be a restatement of something said in paragraph 3. Choice (A) matches paragraph 3's mention of *plans to expand*

standards-based report cards to its four middle schools from its elementary schools, where they have been used since 2006, even though the paragraph is about the delay of such plans. Keep it for now. Choice (B) is deceptive, because it matches the resistance encountered to instituting the report cards in the middle school, rather than the elementary school. Eliminate (B). Choice (C) is too strong: There is no comparison between the standards-based report cards and other systems in Passage 2. Eliminate (C). Choice (D) goes too far. We know that they have been implemented, but the text does not specify whether they have been successfully implemented in grade schools. Eliminate (D). Choice (A) is the correct answer.

35.　**C**　This is a Vocab-in-Context question, so go back to line 53, find the word *scrap*, and cross it out. Then use the surrounding text to put in another word that makes sense based on the context of the passage. Words like *get rid of* would work. Choices (A), *save*, (B), *fragment*, and (D), *detach*, do not fit this prediction, although they do recall the noun form meanings of the word *scrap*. Only (C), *discard*, fits the prediction and is therefore the correct answer.

36.　**D**　This question asks what Passage 2 states about the new approach to grading. Notice that Q37 is a best evidence question, so Q36 and Q37 can be answered in tandem. First, read over the answer choices to Q36. Next, look at the answer choices to Q37 to see whether they provide support for anything in Q36. Choice (37A) refers to a contrast between the new approach's criterion-based grading vs. grading on a curve. This supports (36D), so draw a line connecting them. Choice (37B) is deceptive: it refers to a dilemma, which would seem to support (36A), but the dilemma refers to the old, curve system, not the new one. Eliminate (37B). Choice (37C) again refers to the inferiority of the old, curve system. Eliminate (37C). Choice (37D) refers to plans to bring back teacher comments, and to recognize student effort and attitude. This does not support anything in Q36, so eliminate it. Since the only remaining choice in Q37 is (37A), select that answer and the answer it connects to, (36D). Both of these are the correct answers.

37.　**A**　(See explanation above.)

38.　**C**　This question asks why the author of Passage 2 uses a particular quote. It also asks what concern Passage 2 thereby addresses that Passage 1 does not address. First, locate the quote in context and predict an answer based on the text. In Passage 2, the quote in question describes a weakness of the older system of grading on a curve. So look for an answer choice that addresses this issue. Choices (A), (B), and (D) do not fit this specific prediction, but (C) does match it. Eliminate (A), (B), and (D). Since the concern about grading on a curve is indeed not mentioned in Passage 1, select (C), which is the correct answer.

39.　**D**　This question asks about the general relationship between Passage 1 and Passage 2. Answer it only after answering the specific questions about Passage 1 only and Passage 2 only. First, consider the tone and opinions of both passages. Both of them report on new report cards, and have a neutral-to-positive tone. Eliminate answer choices that misrepresent these facts. Choice (A) indicates a match in tone, but Passage 1 does not contain an argument, and Passage 2 does not contain responses to that argument. Eliminate (A). Choice (B) is completely wrong in tone, so eliminate (B). Choice (C) could match in tone, but there are no alternative conclusions drawn in one passage vs. the other. Eliminate (C). Choice (D) matches in tone, and Passage 2 does contain further information about the new report cards, so select (D), which is the correct answer.

40. **B** This question asks what the authors of both passages would likely agree on regarding standards-based report cards. To answer it, consider what the authors of both passages actually say about these report cards, and base the prediction on that evidence. Choice (A) references *parental insistence*, which sounds something like the parental complaints mentioned in Passage 2. But the only thing Passage 1 says about parents is that they *may find the change disconcerting*. Because Passage 1 provides no evidence about possible agreement with Passage 2 on this point, (A) can be eliminated. Choice (B) references *some resistance*, which both Passages 1 and 2 also do, and (B) states that the new report cards may provide more information than previous systems; both Passages 1 and 2 also do this. Since both passages state these things explicitly, it is reasonable to assume that both authors would agree on this point. Keep (B), but also keep checking, in case something better comes along. Choice (C) references *grading on a curve*, which is not mentioned in Passage 1, so eliminate (C) on that basis. Also, we do not know whether the new report cards *remove* the other system, so (C) is wrong on that count as well. Choice (D) sounds reasonable up to the comma, but the claim that the new report cards are *superior* to alternatives is not supported by statements in either passage. Eliminate (D). Select (B), which is the correct answer.

41. **C** This question asks how the author of Passage 1 would most likely respond to points made in the final paragraph of Passage 2. To answer this question, first review the final paragraph of Passage 2, which talks about responding to parental complaints by introducing benchmarks for each marking period, bringing back teacher comments, and looking for ways to recognize student effort and attitude. Then consider what the author of Passage 1 actually says that is relevant to these points. In the second paragraph of Passage 1, the author states that a standards-based report card provides more information than does a traditional report card, which shows clear support for the new system. But in the third paragraph of Passage 1, the author also shows support for report cards *that combine traditional grades and information about progress toward standards* and cites a researcher who supports including *teacher judgments about students' academic progress, growth, intellectual character, and work habits*. Based on this evidence, it seems the author of Passage 1 would support the changes mentioned in the fourth paragraph of Passage 2. Choice (A) could be true, but there isn't strong textual support for such sympathy. Keep (A) for now, just in case. Choice (B) can be eliminated: The author of Passage 1 would likely support the use of benchmarks, not oppose it. Choice (C) looks good, as it fits the evidence-based prediction made above, so keep it, and eliminate (A), as (C) is better. Choice (D) is too strong: The author of Passage 1 cites an author who supports including intellectual character. This is not the same thing as the author of Passage 1 *insisting* that this factor be included. Eliminate (D). Select (C), which is the correct answer.

42. **B** This question asks about the impact of the words *must, exhibited,* and *reproduced* on the tone of the paragraph. Look for specific evidence in the text indicating the authors' goal of the paragraph. The paragraph is informational—the authors give straightforward information about a hypothesis and the observed results of the experiments. Choice (A) can be eliminated because the authors aren't *hopeful* or trying to convince readers of *uncertain results*. Choice (B) goes along with the prediction based on the text, so don't eliminate it. Choice (C) can be eliminated because the authors are straightforward but not argumentative. Choice (D) does not work because there is no indication that the authors want to *instruct others in the reproduction of simulated bat trajectories*. Choice (B) is the correct answer.

43. **B** This question mentions the key phrase *higher straightness index*, but that phrase is not actually a main part of the question. The question asks about the theory *experiments were performed in order to verify*. Use the key phrase to locate the necessary information in the passage. The experiments in the passage are about testing bats' *flight guidance* and *ability to fly in the dark*. Specifically, as written in paragraph 5, the theory is that *sensory noise determines motor performance*. Choice (A) does not address the issue of sensory noise. It may initially look attractive because the passage does mention using the same bats, but this answer does not address the theory the researchers are working on. Eliminate (A). Choice (B) looks good. It's a scientific paraphrase of the prediction. Keep it. Choice (C) has some words that look familiar from the text, but the words do not come together to say anything close to the prediction. Eliminate (C). Choice (D) can be eliminated because the text states that bats flew better in the light than they did in the dark. Also, the theory was about general sensory noise, not light vs. dark specifically. Choice (B) is the correct answer.

44. **B** This is a best evidence question. Simply look at the line used to support the answer to the previous question. Choice (D) may initially look attractive, but it can be eliminated for the same reason (D) was eliminated in the previous question. Light vs. dark was an experiment to test the theory, not the theory itself. Choice (C) can be eliminated for the same reason. It addresses the specifics of the experiment rather than the theory behind the experiment. The actual theory was about the sensory noise and motor performance. Choice (B) is the correct answer.

45. **C** This question asks about the role of the *single exponential integrator*. Read the window to determine what the integrator does. According to the text, the integrator is a *noise-suppression strategy* used by the bats used to *overcome the [sensory] noise*. Choice (A) can be eliminated because information is not lost. Choice (B) can be eliminated because it's too specific. The integrator deals with all sensory noise, not just *sub-optimal light*. Choice (C) can be kept because it's a solid rewording of the prediction. Choice (D) can be eliminated because it's the opposite of the prediction. Choice (C) is the best answer.

46. **C** This is a best evidence question. Consider the line(s) used to answer the previous question. Choice (C) is the correct answer.

47.	**A**	This is a Vocab-in-Context question. Go back to the text, find the word *fidelity*, and use the context to determine another word or phrase that would fit in place of *fidelity*. Something like *reproduced accurately* or *came closer than before* would work, based on the context. Choice (A) could work, so keep it. Choice (B) can be eliminated because the results were not *lower quality*. Choice (C) can be eliminated because there is no evidence of *complete perfection*. Choice (D) might look okay on its own, but when compared with (A), choice (A) is better, because the correct answer should be as close to *really accurate* as possible. The *reproduction of details* matches the text's description that the integrator *reproduced…trajectories with high fidelity*. Choice (A) is the correct answer.

48.	**A**	This question asks about the *main purpose* of the fourth paragraph. Read the paragraph to determine what the main idea is. The researchers hypothesized that the bat were using *a noise-suppression strategy…to overcome the noise*. Then they determined this strategy was the *simple exponential integrator*. Choice (A) completely describes this, so keep it. Choice (B) is deceptive, using several words and phrases from the text without actually matching the prediction. Eliminate it. No *pitfalls of a theory* are mentioned, so eliminate (C). Choice (D) does not match the text since the authors found the simple exponential integrator outperformed the uniform integrator. Choice (A) is the correct answer.

49.	**D**	This question asks about the assumption made about *highly curved flight trajectories*. In the final sentence of the passage, the authors summarize their findings as a *surprising conclusion* that the curved trajectories *are due to sensory limitations—not motor limitations*. Therefore, the flight patterns are a result of a limitation the bat deals with. Choice (A) can be eliminated, because the trajectories were normal for bats with the introduction of sensory noise. Choice (B) can be eliminated because it's too extreme and not supported by the text. Choice (C) doesn't make sense. The researchers compared flight trajectories of bats in light and dark, but no flight trajectory replaced another one. Choice (D) matches the prediction because the authors were surprised that sensory limitations rather than motor limitations caused the curved trajectory, so they must have previously thought the curved trajectories were caused by the physicality of the bat. Choice (D) is the correct answer.

50.	**A**	This question asks about a simulated trajectory with noise and integration. Look at the second graphic. The lines that represent *simulated trajectory with noise* are the gray lines. There are many of them, so eliminate (B) and (C). In the Integration graphic, all the lines reach the target, so (A) is the correct answer.

51.	**C**	This question asks about the trajectory that most nearly *matches the original trajectory*. The *original trajectory* line is the dotted black line. Find the line that most closely follows that one. The *Integration* lines are all much closer to the original trajectory than any of the *No Integration* lines, so eliminate (A) and (D). Look to see which line most closely lines up with the *original trajectory* line in the *Integration* graphic. It's one of the gray lines, which are *simulated with noise*. Choice (C) is the correct answer.

52. **C** There is no evidence in the figure to show *optimal light conditions*. Eliminate (A) and (B). Choice (C) addresses the lack of information about optimal light conditions in the figure. Keep it. Choice (D) does not address optimal light specifically. Eliminate (D). Choice (C) is the correct answer.

Section 2: Writing and Language

1. **D** The passage as a whole is about the FDA's role in ensuring that the goods we buy are safe for use. It does not concern family activities, as in (A), directions, as in (B), or family budgets, as in (C). The only appropriate introduction comes from (D), which addresses food safety.

2. **A** There are only two reasons to use an apostrophe: possession and contraction. The word *beginnings* does not fit within either of these categories, so there should be no apostrophe on this word. This eliminates (B) and (D). These *beginnings*, however, belong to the *agency*, so they should be described as the *agency's beginnings*, as in (A).

3. **C** When given the option to DELETE, give that option special consideration because it is often correct. In this case, however, the deletion of the word breaks up the commonly used phrase *as we know it* and makes the sentence incomplete. Eliminate (D). Choice (A) also makes the sentence incomplete, so eliminate it. The only choice that correctly completes the phrase, *as we know it,* is (C).

4. **A** Use POE! Choice (B) is not an effective combination as it repeats the word *regulates* and uses too many commas. Choice (C) is not effective because it uses the passive voice awkwardly. Choice (D) also uses a passive construction and refers to *the $1 trillion dollars of goods* as if that amount has been cited previously in the passage. Choice (A) is the only effective combination that does not introduce new errors.

5. **A** While (A), (C), and (D) all seem to say roughly the same thing, notice that (C) and (D) contain subjects and verbs. The introduction of subjects and verbs into the underlined portions of (C) and (D) creates a comma splice within the sentence by separating two complete ideas with only a comma. The use of the word *thus* in (B) implies a cause and effect in the sentence where none is actually present. Only (A) remains, with the word *which* referring back to *fees* and creating a dependent idea.

6. **A** This paragraph marks a shift in tone, referring to the FDA's hidden role in our lives. The only one of the answer choices that effectively signals this shift is (A). Choices (B) and (D) are irrelevant in the context, and (C) suggests a continuation rather than a shift. Therefore, (A) is correct.

7. **D** The statement made in the first part of the sentence is the following: *The FDA is certainly large.* Therefore, a supporting statement should give some evidence of the FDA's large size. While (B)

uses the word *large*, it does so to describe the FDA's role in regulating the tobacco industry, not to describe the actual size of the agency. Choice (B) is irrelevant to the passage, as is (C). The best answer is (D), which lists some numbers that demonstrate the vast size of the FDA.

8. **B**   The previous sentence refers to *consumer safety officers* but suggests that the bulk of the FDA's work is done by *scientists*. The sentence given in the question would help to elaborate upon that point by breaking down the number of scientists the FDA employs. The latter part of the paragraph actually goes on to describe some of the work of these various scientists. Choices (A) and (C) can be eliminated because the reasons are incorrect. Since the rest of the paragraph is concerned with scientists, not *non-scientists*, (D) can be eliminated as well. The sentence should be added for the reason given in (B).

9. **D**   When given the option to DELETE, give that option special consideration because it is often correct. The information in (A), (B), and (C) is already given in the non-underlined portion of the sentence by way of the word *confidence*. Therefore, the best option is to DELETE this underlined portion altogether because none of the proposed choices add anything substantive to the sentence.

10. **C**   Make the items in a list consistent with one another. In this case, that list consists of the single-word names for various sciences: *chemistry, biology, and physics*. Choices (A), (B), and (D) all add unnecessary words to this list.

11. **C**   When there are verbs changing in the answer choices, find the subject. Here, the subject is *thing*, which is singular. Choices (A), (B), and (D) can all be eliminated because they contain plural verbs. The only singular verb in the list comes in (C), which is therefore the correct answer.

12. **C**   The pronoun in question refers to the noun *hockey*. This noun is neither a *them* nor a *he*, so (B) and (D) can be eliminated. Then, (A) can also be eliminated because it refers to the *self* of hockey rather than using the pronoun and conventional expression *itself*. Choice (C) provides the best answer in the context.

13. **A**   This sentence has not yet indicated why the Cup should be named after Lord Stanley of Preston, so the underlined portion should provide that information. Choices (B) and (C) may be true, but they do not explain why the Cup is named after Stanley and stray from the main idea of the passage. Choice (D) is worth considering, but this answer would delete a crucial piece of information. Therefore, the best answer is (A), which explains Lord Stanley's importance to the game of hockey.

14. **B**   This question is testing knowledge of the idiom *just as...so too*. Because these words need to exist in this pair, (A) can be eliminated. Of the remaining answer choices, only choice (B) mentions the NHL, which is needed to establish the movement from the NHA to the NHL that this sentence describes.

15. **B** The underlined portion contains Stop punctuation, so do the vertical line test. The first part of the sentence is not complete, so eliminate (A) and (C). Choice (D) has a colon, which is Half-Stop punctuation and also requires a complete idea before it. Eliminate (D). The phrase *established in 1924* is unnecessary to the meaning of the sentence, as implied by the comma after the word *Bruins*. Therefore, that phrase should be set off in a way consistent with the punctuation in the non-underlined portion. In this case, that punctuation is a comma, so the correct answer must be (B).

16. **D** This sentence has a clear marker, *1926*, which places it in a consistent timeframe at this point in the passage. Eliminate (A) and (B). The sentence also contains relevant information that helps to develop the story about the emergence of the NHL. Eliminate (C), as the sentence contributes to the story of the emergence of the NHL but does not contain the entirety of the argument. The sentence does provide a logical introduction to the paragraph as well as relevant information, so (D) is the best answer.

17. **A** The phrase *sole dominion* earlier in the passage suggests that the NHL has risen to a high position. Choice (A) effectively captures that high position. Choices (B) and (D) are too informal (i.e., they do not "maintain the tone established in the passage"), and (C) is irrelevant to the passage's meaning.

18. **D** All four of these answer choices say similar things, but some do so in fewer words. Eliminate extra words when possible. In this case, *ascendant* and *dominant* are redundant, so any answer choices that include both of them can be eliminated. This leaves only (D), which contains all the same information as the other choices in the fewest words.

19. **A** The previous sentence states, *Today, the league has 30 teams.* This is a continuation of the discussion of the league's expansion from six teams. The next sentence should therefore continue the discussion of expansion. Choices (B) and (D) are not relevant to that discussion and can be eliminated. Choice (C) discusses the league's *"Original Six" teams* but is out of place in the paragraph. Therefore, the best answer is (A), which discusses the league's plans to continue expanding.

20. **B** Note the idea before the punctuation: *Since the early days of professional hockey.* This idea is incomplete, so it cannot be followed by the punctuation given in (A), (C), or (D). Semicolons require complete ideas on both sides. Colons require complete ideas beforehand, and the combination of a comma plus one of the coordinating conjunctions (for, and, nor, but, or, yet, so) requires a complete idea on both sides of the combination. Only (B) remains.

21. **B** As it is, this sentence says merely, *There are other leagues.* This information is already given in the previous sentence, so this sentence must say something new. The proposed addition would help it to do so while adding relevant specificity to an otherwise too-general sentence. Eliminate (C) and (D) as they do not reflect the need for the additional information. Choice (A) incorrectly states that the paragraph changes focus. Eliminate (A) and choose (B), which accurately reflects the fact that the proposed revision adds relevant information.

22. **D** There are two main changes in the answer choices here: *hold/holds* and *it/they*. Both the verb *hold/holds* and the pronoun *it/they* need to be consistent with other information in the sentence. The subject of the verb is *the NHL*, which is singular and therefore requires the singular verb *holds*. Eliminate (A) and (C). The referent for the pronoun is also *the NHL*, which requires the singular pronoun *it*. Therefore, (D) is correct.

23. **D** The word in the underlined portion should mean something like *turned*, describing how people *accepted the health risks of smoking* and then went *away from the deadly pastime*. Choices (A) and (C) might seem to be appealing because they appear to play off what one does with a cigarette, but they do not effectively signal that many Americans have abandoned the pastime. Between (B) and (D), choice (D) better reflects the sense of turning away from the behavior, while (B) suggests an urgency that is not fully supported by the passage. Eliminate (B) and choose (D).

24. **C** Sentence 4 starts with the idea that *This may sound odd because everyone has to sit at some point.* Therefore, the sentence that precedes it should contain information about how sitting is dangerous or unnatural. Sentence 1 contains the scientists' dictum that *Sitting is the new smoking*, so sentence 4 would follow logically from this idea. Additionally, sentences 1 and 2 are not contrasting ideas, but sentence 2 begins with the word *however*. Something needs to be inserted between sentences 1 and 2 for the non-underlined portion to make sense. Therefore, sentence 4 would best be placed before sentence 2, making (C) correct.

25. **C** Use POE! Choice (A) can be eliminated because it suggests that 800,000 was the target number for a representative sample, whereas the initial sentences indicate that it was merely the number of initial test subjects. Choice (B) reuses the word *safe* in a way that does not make sense in the context. Choice (D) refers to *people in their 20s*, which is not part of the initial sentences. Only (C) remains, which effectively combines the sentences by shortening them while preserving the initial meaning.

26. **D** When given the option to DELETE, give that option serious consideration: it is often correct. In this case, none of the proposed words in the underlined portion add to the sentence in a substantive way, so the best option is to DELETE them altogether, as in (D).

27. **D** Although it may not look like one at first glance, the idea *Consider our primate ancestors, for example* is in fact complete, so it should be set off from the next complete idea: *If they were not incredibly active at all times, they would not have survived.* Choices (A) and (C) do not have sufficient punctuation to separate two complete ideas. Choice (B) contains appropriate punctuation, but it attaches the *for example* to the wrong idea. Choice (D) is therefore the best possible answer in the context.

28. **B** Read the graph carefully. It estimates that the average human is "Active/Standing" for 3 hours a day, as (B) indicates. Keep (B), but check the other answer choices. Choice (A) incorrect states this number as 8. Choice (C) misreads 3 hours as one-third of the 24 hours in a day. Choice (D) is not supported. Eliminate (A), (C), and (D) and choose (B).

29. **D** Read the graph carefully, and make sure that the information in the answers is supported. Choices (A) and (C) are not addressed in the graph, so eliminate them. Also, eliminate (B), which gives incorrect information based on the graph. Only (D) is supported, as only 7.5 of the 21 sitting hours in a day are done at work.

30. **B** The underlined word refers directly back to *those*, or those people who fidget. Therefore, (A) and (D) can be eliminated because they are not used to refer to people in this context. Choice (C) can also be eliminated because the word *we* is not used in this part of the passage. Choice (B) correctly refers to *those*.

31. **D** This sentence is in the past tense, as indicated by the earlier verb *were*. The need for past tense eliminates (A) and (C). Choice (B) can also be eliminated because the word *went* does not make sense in the given context. Choice (D) is the best answer, as it contains the correct meaning and tense.

32. **B** The underlined pronoun is a substitute for the word *sitting*. The phrase as a whole is concerned with the *detrimental effects of sitting*. Choices (A) and (D) can be eliminated because they are plural, while *sitting* is singular. Choice (C) can also be eliminated because it gives the contraction *it is*, while this sentence requires a possessive pronoun. Therefore, (B) is correct.

33. **A** Read the question carefully. It wants a conclusion that *acknowledges the problem of sitting but also encourages the reader to use this research in a proactive way*. Choices (B) and (C) do not acknowledge the problem of sitting, and (D) is not encouraging. Choice (A) contains both elements and is therefore the correct answer.

34. **D** The underlined portion contains Stop punctuation, so use the vertical line test. The first part of the sentence is incomplete, so eliminate (A). The phrase *the latest lines of shoes, suits, dresses, or furniture* is offset as unnecessary information, indicated by the dash after the word *fashion*. Keep the punctuation consistent by inserting another dash after the word *furniture*, as in (D).

35. **A** This word is part of a short list with the phrase *sported the clothes*. Keep this part of the list consistent. The underlined word should be consistent with the word *sported*, as in the word *furnished* in (A). Choice (B) also contains the word *furnished*, but it contains the unnecessary word *have*.

36. **A** The previous sentence is in the present tense, referring to *the newest style*. Because the sentence containing the underlined portion continues the discussion of that style, it should also be in the present tense, eliminating (B). Choice (D) would create a sentence fragment, so eliminate it. In order to choose between (A) and (C), find the subject of the verb. The subject is *style*, which is singular and therefore requires the singular verb *seeks*, given in (A).

37. **B** Because the information *IFC's Portlandia* is not essential to the completeness of the sentence, it should be offset with a pair of commas, thus eliminating (A) and (C). Choice (D) can also be

eliminated because it contains an unnecessary comma after the word *IFC's*. Only (B) has the proper number of commas.

38. **B** The idea before the punctuation (*Back-dropped by…mustaches*) is incomplete, so it cannot be followed by a semicolon or a period, eliminating (A), (C), and (D). Choice (B) is the only choice that correctly punctuates the first part of the sentence, regardless of what follows that punctuation.

39. **C** This sentence gives some examples of the "rustic chic" style, which is interested in using older styles. The underlined portion should therefore contain some mention of these older styles, as only (C) does. Choices (A) and (D) refer to examples of the rustic chic style as *results* and *expensive*, both of which are irrelevant. Choice (B) may be tempting, but it's referring to examples of the rustic chic style as *peculiar* before discussing the peculiarity of these items. This concept is elaborated on in the next paragraph, not this one, so (B) is not the best answer.

40. **C** While the previous sentence mentions economics, it is not doing so in a way that is literally concerned with rustic chic's influence on the global economy. The idea should therefore not be added, thus eliminating (A) and (B). Choice (D) can also be eliminated because the proposed sentence does not contradict other information in the passage. Only (C) remains as the correct answer.

41. **D** Use POE. Choice (A) can be eliminated because rustic chic has clearly generated *interest*, as the passage indicates throughout. Choice (B) can be eliminated because there is no discussion of rustic chic being a *choice*. Choice (C) can be eliminated because rustic chic *is a fashion*. Choice (D) correctly suggests that rustic chic can be confusing because it does not refer back to a clear or specific moment in history.

42. **B** As indicated by the topic sentence of this paragraph, rustic chic is a popular historically-minded style even though it does not refer back to a specific historical period. The sentence in the underlined portion should contain some indication of this lack of specificity, as (B) does. Additionally, (B) helps the preceding sentence make sense because it gives a context of what is meant by *"they."* Choices (A), (C), and (D) may have merit in other contexts, but they are not relevant here.

43. **D** Sentence 2 contains a directive that has something to do with the fashion industry. This directive is best used as an answer to the question posed in sentence 6. Placing sentence 2 after sentence 6 would also continue a pattern established by sentences 4 and 5. Sentence 2 is therefore best placed after sentence 6, as (D) indicates.

44. **B** Use POE. Choices (A), (C), and (D) may be attractive choices in other contexts, but in this essay, they are far too grandiose and negative to fit. Only (B) works because it contains the proper tone, and it matches with the mention of *clutter* at the end of the sentence.

Section 3: Math (No Calculator)

1. **C** The question asks for the value of $8s + 13$, so determine the value of s. Since $4s = 28$, divide both sides by 4 to get $s = 7$. Therefore, $8s + 13 = 8(7) + 13 = 56 + 13 = 69$. Alternatively, since $4s = 28$, $8s = 2(4s) = 2(28) = 56$. Therefore, $8s + 13 = 56 + 13 = 69$. Using either method, the answer is (C).

2. **A** The question asks which choice is equal to $b^{\frac{3}{4}}$. By rule, fractional exponents express roots. Let the denominator of the fraction equal the root taken. Since the denominator is 4, take the 4th root. The numerator of the fraction remains as the exponent. Therefore, $b^{\frac{3}{4}} = \sqrt[4]{b^3}$, which is (A).

3. **B** The question asks for the value that will change if a cheaper type of grass is used. The only thing that has changed is that the customer has asked for a cheaper type of grass. A cheaper type of grass does not change the number of plots, the length of a plot, or the width of any plot, so the values p, l, and w do not change. Eliminate (A), (C), and (D). Only (B) remains. Alternatively, note that it is only the price that changes and the only value whose units involve dollars is G, so this must be the value that changes. The answer is (B).

4. **B** When there is a system of equations, stack and add or subtract the two equations to get an equation. The goal is to find an equation in which the coefficients on x and y are the same as in the expression the question asks for the value of. In this case, since the question asks for $x + y$, the coefficients on x and y should be equal. Stack and add the two equations to get $8x + 8y = -56$. Divide both sides by 8 to get $x + y = -7$. The answer is (B).

5. **C** The question says that the number of countries in the European Union in 2008 was three times the number of countries in 1974. Translate this into an equation. Since the question says that the European Union had 27 members in 2008, translate *the number of countries in the European Union in 2008* to 27. Translate *was* to =. Translate *three times* to 3( ), leaving room between the parentheses for whatever follows in the sentence. What follows is *the number of countries in the European Union in 1974*, which the question later says is m. Therefore the sentence translates to $27 = 3(m)$, or $3m = 27$, which is (C).

6. **B** The question asks for $\dfrac{y}{7}$, so solve for y. Since $\dfrac{7}{y} = \dfrac{17}{y + 30}$, cross-multiply to get $7(y + 30) = 17y$. Distribute the 7 to get $7y + 210 = 17y$. Subtract $7y$ from both sides to get $210 = 10y$. Divide both sides by 10 to get $21 = y$. Therefore, $\dfrac{y}{7} = \dfrac{21}{7} = 3$, which is (B).

7. **B** Since there are no exponents on x or y in either equation, the equations are linear. A system of linear equations has no solution if the two lines represented by the equations are parallel. Two lines are parallel when they have the same slope. To determine the slope of the lines, get each line in slope-intercept form: $y = mx + b$. Start with the second equation, $3x - 7y = 5$. Subtract

$3x$ from both sides to get $-7y = -3x + 5$. Divide both sides by -7 to get $y = \frac{3}{7}x - \frac{5}{7}$. In slope-intercept form, the slope is equal to m, so the slope of this line is $\frac{3}{7}$. Now get the slope of the other line, $cx - 6y = 8$. Subtract cx from both sides to get $-6y = -cx + 8$. Divide both sides by -6 to get $y = \frac{c}{6}x - \frac{8}{6}$, so the slope of this line is $\frac{c}{6}$. Since these two slopes have to be equal, set $\frac{3}{7} = \frac{c}{6}$. Cross-multiply to get $7c = 18$. Divide both sides by 7 to get $c = \frac{18}{7}$. The answer is (B).

8. **D**   A factor of a polynomial is used to find a solution, or a value of x for which the corresponding value of the function is 0. When a function in factored form is set equal to 0, each factor can be set equal to 0 to get each solution. Since, according to the table, $g(7) = 0$, $x = 7$ is one solution of g. Therefore, it must also be the solution to an equation made by setting one of the factors equal to 0. To find this factor, get the equation $x = 7$ into the form of an equation with one side equal to 0. Subtract 7 from both sides to get $x - 7 = 0$. Therefore, $x - 7$ is one of the factors of g, and the answer is (D).

9. **D**   A line whose equation is in the form $y = mx + b$ has slope m and y-intercept b. In the equation $y = cx + 6$, the slope is c. Plug the point (r, s) into the equation to get $s = cr + 6$. To find the slope, solve for c. First, subtract 6 from both sides to get $s - 6 = cr$. Now, divide both sides by r to get $c = \frac{s - 6}{r}$. The correct answer is (D).

10. **A**   The question asks for pairs of congruent angles. Start with the vertical angles. Vertical angles are non-adjacent angles formed by intersecting lines. The pairs of vertical angles in this figure are $a°$ and $d°$, $b°$ and $e°$, and $c°$ and $f°$. Since vertical angles are always congruent, $a = d$, $b = e$, and $c = f$. The question also states that $a + b = c + d$. Since $a = d$, it must also be the case that $b = c$. This shows that Statement (I) is true, so (B) can be eliminated. Since $b = c$, $b = e$, and $c = f$, then e must also equal f. Statement (II) is true, so eliminate (C). Statement (III) says that $a = e$. It has been determined that $b = c = e = f$ and that $a = d$, but so far nothing has shown that $a = e$. To be sure, plug in for e. Let $e = 30$. If $e = 30$, then $b = c = f = 30$, so $b + c + e + f = 30 + 30 + 30 + 30 = 120$. Since $a + b + c + d + e + f = 360$, then $a + d + 120 = 360$ and $a + d = 240$. Since $a = d$, then a and d are both equal to 120. Therefore, $a \neq e$. Cross off (III) and eliminate (D). The answer is (A).

11. **D**   The graph asks for the y-coordinate of the vertex, which is the point of the parabola on the axis of symmetry. Therefore, the axis of symmetry is the line $x = m$. To determine the value of m, find a pair of points with the same y-coordinate, and get the midpoint of the segment between them. To make this easy, let $y = 0$ to get $0 = k(x - 4)(x + 12)$. Set each factor equal to 0 to get $k = 0$, $x - 4 = 0$, and $x + 12 = 0$. Since the question says $k \neq 0$, reject the first equation. Solve

the second equation, $x - 4 = 0$, by adding 4 to both sides to get $x = 4$. Solve the third equation, $x + 12 = 0$, by subtracting 12 from both sides to get $x = -12$. Therefore, the points $(4, 0)$ and $(-12, 0)$ are on the parabola. The midpoint of $(4, 0)$ and $(-12, 0)$ is $\left(\dfrac{4 + (-12)}{2}, 0\right) = \left(\dfrac{-8}{2}, 0\right) = (-4, 0)$. Therefore, $m = -4$. Since (m, n) is a point on the parabola, $n = k(m - 4)(m + 12)$. To find n, plug in $m = -4$ to get $n = k(-4 - 4)(-4 + 12) = k(-8)(8) = -64k$. Another option would be to plug in for k to get a quadratic, then complete the square on the x-terms to get the equation into the vertex form. Either way, the correct answer is (D).

12. **C** The question asks about points of intersection. Points of intersection are solutions to both equations. Since $y = (x - 8)^2$ and $y = 36$, set $(x - 8)^2 = 36$. To solve, take the square root of both sides to get $x - 8 = \pm 6$. Always remember to use $\pm$ when taking the square root of both sides of an equation. Consider both possible equations. If $x - 8 = 6$, add 8 to both sides to get $x = 14$. If $x - 8 = -6$, add 8 to both sides to get $x = 2$. Therefore, points P and Q are at coordinates $(2, 36)$ and $(14, 36)$. Since the endpoints of PQ share y-coordinates, the length of the segment is the difference in the x-coordinates of the endpoints. Therefore, $\overline{PQ} = 14 - 2 = 12$. The correct answer is (C).

13. **B** The question statements refer to equivalent decreases in Celsius and Fahrenheit. Test each of these statements by plugging in an example. Statement (I) refers to a decrease of 1.8 degrees Celsius. Use a simple example of such a decrease. Try $C = 1.8$ and $C = 0$. Since the formula includes fractions, convert 1.8 into a fraction in order to do the arithmetic. $\dfrac{1.8}{1.0} = \dfrac{18}{10} = \dfrac{9}{5}$, so $1.8 = \dfrac{9}{5}$. If $C = \dfrac{9}{5}$, then $F\left(\dfrac{9}{5}\right) = \dfrac{9}{5}\left(\dfrac{9}{5}\right) + 32 = \dfrac{81}{25} + 32 = 3\dfrac{6}{25} + 32 = 35\dfrac{6}{25}$. If $C = 0$, then $F(0) = \dfrac{9}{5}(0) + 32 = 32$. Since this is a decrease of more than 1, cross out (I) and eliminate any choice that includes (I): (A) and (D). Now look at the remaining choices. Since both remaining choices include (II), (II) must be true, so test (III) only. Statement (III) refers to a decrease of $\dfrac{5}{9}$ degrees Fahrenheit. Pick two easy values for F with a difference of $\dfrac{5}{9}$. $F = \dfrac{5}{9}$ and $F = 0$ might appear easy, but the first step to solving will be to subtract 32, which is not convenient with $F = \dfrac{5}{9}$. Instead, use $F = 32\dfrac{5}{9}$ and $F = 32$. If $F = 32\dfrac{5}{9}$, then $32\dfrac{5}{9} = \dfrac{9}{5}C + 32$. Subtract

32 from both sides to get $\frac{5}{9} = \frac{9}{5}C$. Multiply both sides by $\frac{5}{9}$ to get $\frac{25}{81} = C$. If $F = 32$, then

$32 = \frac{9}{5}C + 32$. Subtract 32 from both sides to get $0 = \frac{9}{5}C$. Multiply both sides by $\frac{5}{9}$ to get

$0 = C$. Since this a decrease of less than 1, cross off (III) and eliminate (C). The answer is (B).

14. **A** This is a complicated algebra question, so look for a way to plug in. Since no calcula-

tor is allowed on this section, it is especially important to plug in an easy number. Try

$x = 1$. If $x = 1$, then $\dfrac{80(1)^2 + 84(1) - 13}{k(1) - 4} = -16(1) - 4 - \dfrac{29}{k(1) - 4}$. Simplify to get

$\dfrac{80 + 84 - 13}{k - 4} = -16 - 4 - \dfrac{29}{k - 4}$ and $\dfrac{151}{k - 4} = -20 - \dfrac{29}{k - 4}$. Add $\dfrac{29}{k - 4}$ to both sides to get

$\dfrac{151}{k - 4} + \dfrac{29}{k - 4} = -20$. Since the fractions on the right have the same denominator, add both

the numerators to get $\dfrac{180}{k - 4} = -20$. Multiply both sides by $(k - 4)$ to get $180 = -20(k - 4)$.

Distribute on the right side to get $180 = -20k + 80$. Subtract 80 from both sides to get

$100 = -20k$. Divide both sides by -20 to get $k = -5$, which is (A).

15. **D** To find the solutions to a quadratic equation, the first option is to factor. First, since 5

is a factor of each term, factor 5 to get $5(x^2 + 6x + 3) = 0$. Divide both sides by 5 to get

$x^2 + 6x + 3 = 0$. However, as the answer choices hint, factoring this equation further will be

difficult, so use the quadratic formula: $x = \dfrac{-b \pm \sqrt{b^2 - 4ac}}{2a}$. The standard form of a qua-

dratic equation is $ax^2 + bx + c = 0$, so $a = 1$, $b = 6$, and $c = 3$. Therefore, $x = \dfrac{-b \pm \sqrt{b^2 - 4ac}}{2a}$

$= \dfrac{-6 \pm \sqrt{6^2 - 4(1)(3)}}{2(1)} = \dfrac{-6 \pm \sqrt{36 - 12}}{2} = \dfrac{-6 \pm \sqrt{24}}{2}$. Simplify the square root by finding a

perfect square factor. Since $24 = 4 \times 6$, $\sqrt{24} = \sqrt{4} \times \sqrt{6} = 2\sqrt{6}$, so $x = \dfrac{-6 \pm 2\sqrt{6}}{2}$. Simplify

the fraction by dividing both terms in the numerator by 2 to get $x = -3 \pm \sqrt{6}$. The correct

answer is (D).

16. **4** To solve this equation, start by simplifying like terms on the left side. Since the denominators

are the same, subtract the numerators to get $\dfrac{5}{25}z = \dfrac{1}{2} + \dfrac{3}{10}$. Simplify the fraction on the left side of the equation to get $\frac{1}{5}z = \frac{1}{2} + \frac{3}{10}$. Now eliminate the fractions by multiplying both sides by a common multiple of all three denominators, such as 10. The result is $2z = 5 + 3$.

Simplify the right side to get $2z = 8$. Divide both sides by 2 to get $z = 4$. The answer is 4.

17. **1 or 3** To solve a polynomial, get one side of the equation equal to 0. To do that in this case, add $9y$ to both sides to get $y^3(y^2 - 10) + 9y = 0$. Distribute y^3 to get $y^5 - 10y^3 + 9y = 0$. Since each term on the left includes y, factor y to get $y(y^4 - 10y^2 + 9) = 0$. Now factor $(y^4 - 10y^2 + 9)$. Notice that this resembles a quadratic of the form $ax^2 + bx + c$ but with the exponents doubled. It can be factored the same way. The quadratic $(y^2 - 10y + 9)$ factors to $(y - 9)(y - 1)$, so $(y^4 - 10y^2 + 9)$ factors to $(y^2 - 9)(y^2 - 1)$. Notice that each of these factors is a difference of squares, so $(y^2 - 9)$ = $(y - 3)(y + 3)$ and $(y^2 - 1) = (y - 1)(y + 1)$. Therefore, the equation $y(y^4 - 10y^2 + 9) = 0$ factors to $y(y - 3)(y + 3)(y - 1)(y + 1) = 0$. Set each of these factors equal to 0 to get $y = 0$, $y - 3 = 0$, $y + 3 = 0$, $y - 1 = 0$, and $y + 1 = 0$. Solve these equations to get $y = 0$, $y = 3$, $y = -3$, $y = 1$, and $y = -1$, respectively. Since the question specifies that $y > 0$, the only remaining possible solutions are $y = 3$ and $y = 1$. Grid in either of these two answers.

18. **50** To solve this problem, translate each statement into an equation. Let L represent the length of a long session and S represent the length of a short session. Each long session lasts 20 minutes longer than each short session. *Each long session* translates to L. The word *lasts* is the main verb of the sentence, so it translates to =. The phrase *20 minutes longer* translates to ___ + 20, leaving room on the left for whatever follows. What follows is *each short session*, which translates to S. Therefore, the first sentence translates to $L = S + 20$. Now translate the second sentence. The term *3 long sessions* translates to $3L$. The word *and* translates to +. The term *4 short sessions* translates to $4S$. The term *last a total of* translates to =. Therefore, the second sentence translates to $3L + 4S = 270$. To solve this system of equations, substitute $L = S + 20$ into the second equation to get $3(S + 20) + 4S = 270$. Distribute 3 to get $3S + 60 + 4S = 270$. Combine like terms to get $7S + 60 = 270$. Subtract 60 from both sides to get $7S = 210$. Divide both sides by 7 to get $S = 30$. This is not the answer. Don't forget to read the question, which asks for the length of a *long* session. Since $L = S + 20$, $L = 30 + 20 = 50$. The answer is 50.

19. $\frac{5}{13}$ The question asks for the value of $\cos Z$. By definition, corresponding angles in similar triangles are congruent. Since $\angle Z$ corresponds to $\angle W$ in a similar triangle, $\angle Z$ is congruent to $\angle W$. Since congruent angles have equal cosines, $\cos Z = \cos W$. Therefore, this question can be answered by ignoring triangle XYZ and working exclusively in triangle UVW to determine the value of $\cos W$, and thus the value of $\cos Z$. Draw triangle UVW, filling in $WV = 39$ and $UV = 36$.

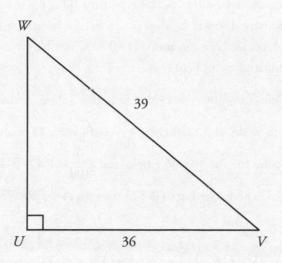

By definition, $\cos W = \dfrac{adj}{hyp}$. The hypotenuse is 39, but the adjacent side isn't given. The adjacent side can be solved for using the Pythagorean Theorem, but this is difficult with numbers this large and no calculator. Instead, look for a Pythagorean triple. The ratio 36:39, can be reduced by a factor of 3 to 12:13, so this is a 5:12:13 right triangle. Therefore the missing side, $\overline{UW}$, must have a length of 3 × 5 = 15. Thus, the adjacent side is 15, and $\cos W = \dfrac{adj}{hyp} = \dfrac{15}{39} = \dfrac{5}{13}$. The answer is $\dfrac{5}{13}$.

20. **110**   Start with the equation $b = 180 - 4a$. Since $a = 35$, $b = 180 - 4(35) = 180 - 140 = 40$. Therefore, the two base angles of the lower triangle have a sum of $180° - 40° = 140°$. Since the two base angles are opposite equal sides, they must be equal, so each is 70°. The angle with measure c combines with the base angle on the right to form a straight angle. Therefore, $70° + c° = 180°$, and $c = 110$. The answer is 110.

Section 4: Math (Calculator)

1. **C**   The probability of selecting a grey wolf with yellow eyes is $\dfrac{16}{30}$, and the probability of selecting coyote with brown eyes is $\dfrac{5}{30}$. Therefore, the probability of selecting one or the other is $\dfrac{16}{30} + \dfrac{5}{30} = \dfrac{21}{30}$, so (C) is correct.

2. **D**   Use Process of Elimination. From 1992 to 1996 the graph shows a downward slope, which indicates a decrease in military spending. Therefore, eliminate (B) and (C). In 2001 the graph shows an upward slope, which indicates an increase in military spending. Eliminate (A). Choice (D) is correct.

3. **B** During the 40 minutes that Eddie stops to repair his bike, his distance does not change. On the graph, this time period would be shown as a flat horizontal line. The only flat horizontal portion of the graph occurs between about 11:10 A.M., just before noon. So, he finished repairing his bike just before noon, and (B) is correct.

4. **C** Use bite-sized pieces to carefully tackle this one step at a time. Translate "4 percent" of the 648 male employees into math and calculate: $\frac{4}{100}(648) = 25.92$ male employees who received bonuses. Do the same for the female employees: $\frac{6}{100}(519) = 31.14$ female employees who received bonuses. Add these together to get $25.92 + 31.14 = 57.06$. This is closest to (C), so (C) is correct.

5. **B** Use bite-sized pieces. Start by adding the x^2 terms: $4x^2 + 2x^2 = 6x^2$. Eliminate (C) and (D). Next, since the x terms are the same in the remaining answers, add the constants: $-2 + 9 = 7$. Eliminate (A). Therefore, the correct answer is (B).

6. **D** Plug in. According to the table, when $k = 1$, $g(k) = -3$. Plug in 1 for k in the answers and eliminate any answers that do not return a value of -3. Choice (A) becomes $1 - 1 = 0$. Eliminate (A). Choice (B) becomes $2(1) - 4 = -2$. Eliminate (B). Choice (C) becomes $3(1) - 5 = -2$. Eliminate (C). Choice (D) becomes $4(1) - 7 = -3$. Therefore, the correct answer is (D).

7. **D** Use Process of Elimination. Since x represents the number of years since 2005, the -0.14 must somehow be related to the number of years. Eliminate (A) and (B) since the question states that y represents the rainfall in any given year. Choice (C) would be represented by the y value for 2005 minus the y value for 2015, so eliminate (C). The correct answer is (D).

8. **C** There are $60(6) = 360$ minutes in 6 hours. To calculate the distance the insect crawls, set up the following proportion: $\frac{30 \text{ inches}}{16.3 \text{ min}} = \frac{x}{360 \text{ min}}$. Cross-multiply: $16.3x = 30(360)$. Solve for x, resulting in $16.3x = 10,800$ and $x = 662.577$. The question asks for an *approximate* answer, so choose the closest answer, which is (C).

9. **B** To isolate v, multiply both sides of the equation by $\frac{5}{8}$, resulting in $v = \frac{7}{4} \times \frac{5}{8} = \frac{35}{32}$. Choice (B) is correct.

10. **B** The term *zero* means an x-intercept (a point where the curve crosses the x-axis. The only graph showing a curve that crosses the x-axis 4 times is (B), so (B) is correct.

11. **A** According the information given, $Q = mC$ where $C = \frac{J}{g}$. The chart shows that the heat capacity $\left(\frac{J}{g}\right)$ for copper is 0.39, and the mass is 75. Therefore, $Q = 75(0.39) = 29.25$, which matches (A).

12. **A** According to the information given, $Q = mC$. The table indicates that for porcelain, $C = 1.08$. Find the mass of the porcelain by plugging in 80 for Q and 1.08 for C, resulting in $80 = m(1.08)$. Solve for m to get $m \approx 74$. To find the unknown substance, plug in 67 for Q and 74 for m, resulting in $67 = 74C$. Solve for C to get $C \approx 0.9054$. This approximates the value given for aluminum in the chart. Choice (A) is correct.

13. **D** Use Process of Elimination. The study was done on 200 people with severe hearing loss. Eliminate (A) because the study population doesn't deal with all people; it only deals with people who have severe hearing loss. Because no other hearing-improvement products were mentioned in the question, eliminate (B). In comparing (C) and (D), (C) is too broad, because it applies to people generally, rather than just to the people with severe hearing loss who were studied. Therefore, eliminate (C) and choose (D).

14. **C** Since the problem asks for an expression for a, rearrange the formula so that a is alone on one side. First, subtract vt from both sides, resulting in $d - vt = -\frac{1}{2}at^2$. Next, multiply both sides by -2, resulting in $-2(d - vt) = at^2$, then divide both sides by t^2, resulting in $\frac{-2(d - vt)}{t^2} = a$. To make the equation look like the answer choices, flip it around so the a is on the left and apply the t^2 in the denominator to each part of the binomial in the parentheses. The equation becomes $a = -2\left(\frac{d}{t^2} - \frac{vt}{t^2}\right)$, and the second fraction can be reduced, resulting in $a = -2\left(\frac{d}{t^2} - \frac{v}{t}\right)$. Finally, apply the negative sign in front of the 2 to the terms in the parentheses and switch their order: $a = 2\left(\frac{v}{t} - \frac{d}{t^2}\right)$, which matches (C).

15. **B** The ribbon costs $0.15(36) = \$5.40$ per yard. There are variables in the answer choices, so plug in. If $y = 2$, then $p = 2(5.40) = 10.80$. Plug 2 in for y in the answers to see which answer returns a value of 10.80. Choice (A) becomes $0.15(2) + 36 = 36.30$. Eliminate (A). Choice (B) becomes $0.15(36)(2) = 10.8$. Keep (B), but check (C) and (D) just in case. Choice (C) becomes $\frac{0.15(2)}{36} \approx 0.008$. Eliminate (C). Choice (D) becomes $\frac{36(2)}{0.15} = 480$. Eliminate (D). Choice (B) is correct.

16. **A** There are variables in the answer choices, so plug in. If $q = 40$, then $C = 60(40) + 300 = 2,700$. Now decrease q by 20 units: if $q = 20$, then $C = 60(20) + 300 = 1,500$. $2,700 - 1,500 = 1,200$. Choice (A) is correct.

17. **C** To find the quantity at which revenues will equal costs, set the equations equal to each other: $60q + 300 = 75q$. Subtract $60q$ from each side to get $300 = 15q$, and $q = 20$, which matches (C).

18.   **C**   Look up the values for $f(x)$ and $g(x)$ for each of the x-values in the answer choices and see which pair adds up to 1. For (A), $f(-5) = -1$ and $g(-5) = -1$, and the sum of these values is -2. Eliminate (A). For (B), $f(-4)$ is a small negative number and $g(-4) = 0$, and the sum of these values is negative, so eliminate (B). For (C), $f(-3) = 0$ and $g(-3) = 1$, and the sum of these values is 1. Therefore, (C) is correct.

19.   **B**   Exponential decay provides increasingly greater or smaller changes in values as time progresses. Plug in to see what would happen in each situation. Let the initial value of the item equal $100. For (A), the item would lose $100 \times 0.05 = \$5$ every year. Eliminate (A), because the amount of value the item loses would be the same every year. For (B), the item would lose $100 \times 0.06 = \$6$ the first year. Therefore, the new item value would be $100 - 6 = \$94$. The second year, the item would lose $94 \times 0.06 = \$5.64$, and the new item value would be $94 - 5.64 = \$88.36$. Each successive year, the loss would be less than the loss the year before. This is an exponential decay; therefore, the correct answer is (B).

20.   **B**   First, calculate the number of imperial pints that can be made with 17 ounces of sugar. Set up

the following proportion: $\dfrac{1 \text{ ounce}}{30 \text{ I. pints}} = \dfrac{17 \text{ ounces}}{x}$. Cross-multiply to get $x = 510$ imperial pints.

Next, calculate the number of U.S. pints that are equivalent to 510 imperial pints by setting up

the following proportion: $\dfrac{1 \text{ I. pint}}{1\frac{1}{4} \text{ U.S. pints}} = \dfrac{510 \text{ I. pints}}{x}$. Simplify the left side of the equation to

$\dfrac{1}{\frac{5}{4}} = \dfrac{510}{x}$, or $\dfrac{4}{5} = \dfrac{510}{x}$. Cross-multiply, resulting in $4x = 2{,}550$. Solve for x to get $x = 637.5$. The

closest approximation for 637.5 is 640. Choice (B) is correct.

21.   **A**   The actual plotted point at 230 inches is 49 yards. However, the line of best fit at 230 inches equals 47.5 inches. $49 - 47.5 = 1.5$. Therefore, (A) is correct.

22.   **B**   The question asks for a specific amount, so plug in the answers. Start with (B). If there are 23 girls in the troop, then Mrs. Warren currently has $23(4) + 11 = 103$ boxes. If she were to give 5 boxes to each girl, she would need $23(5) = 115$. Therefore, she is $115 - 103 = 12$ boxes short. Since this matches the information given in the problem, the correct answer is (B).

23.   **D**   Let l = the largest number and s = the sum of the other two numbers. According to the question, $l = \dfrac{4}{3}s$. Divide both sides by $\dfrac{4}{3}$ to get $\dfrac{3}{4}l = s$. Plug in the answers, starting with (B). If the largest number is 245, the sum of the other two numbers is $\dfrac{3}{4}(245) = 183.75$. The sum of all three numbers would be $245 + 183.75 = 428.75$. Eliminate both (A) and (B) because these values

are too small. Try (C). If the largest number is 350, then the sum of the other two numbers is $\frac{3}{4}(350) = 262.5$, and the sum of all three numbers is $350 + 262.5 = 612.5$. Eliminate (C). Since only (D) remains, it must be the correct answer.

24. **B** When the question asks for a specific value, plug in the answers. Start with (B) and make $j - 15.5$. The value of x would then be $3(15.5) - 19 = 27.5$, and the value of z would be $5(15.5) - 15 = 62.5$. Now use a calculator to check to if $\cos(27.5°) = \sin(62.5°)$. Both equal 0.887, so (B) is correct.

25. **D** First, plug in a length and a width for the rectangle. Let, $l = 12$ and $w = 10$. The area of this rectangle can be calculated as $A = lw = (12)(10) = 120$. In the new rectangle, the length is reduced by 25% or $\frac{1}{4}$, making the new length $12 - \left(\frac{1}{4}\right)(12) = 9$. The area of 120 is increased by 5%, so the new area is $120 + \left(\frac{5}{100}\right)(120) = 120 + 6 = 126$. Plug these new numbers into the area formula to get $126 = 9w$, then divide both sides by 9 to get $w = 14$. The width increased from 10 to 14, but the question asks for the percent increase, which is calculated as $\frac{difference}{original} \times 100$. In this case, that value is $\frac{14 - 10}{10}(100) = \frac{4}{10}(100) = 40$, so $k = 40\%$, and the correct answer is (D).

26. **C** The formula for the volume of a cylinder is $V = \pi r^2 h$. For the figure shown, $r = 3$ and $h = 12$. The volume of the cylinder portion of the capsule is $V = \pi(3^2)(12) = 108\pi$. The two ends of the capsule make up one complete sphere. The formula for the volume of a sphere is $V = \frac{4}{3}\pi r^3$. Again, $r = 3$. Therefore, the volume of spherical portion of the capsule is $V = \frac{4}{3}\pi(3)^3 = 36\pi$. The volume of the entire figure is $108\pi + 36\pi = 144\pi \approx 452.4$. The correct answer is (C).

27. **A** Given two points on a line, the slope is calculated as $\frac{y_2 - y_1}{x_2 - x_1}$. Use the points $(0, 0)$ and $(p, 4)$ to find the slope of the line: $\frac{4 - 0}{p - 0} = \frac{4}{p}$. Next, use the points $(0, 0)$ and $(9, p)$ to find the slope of the line: $\frac{p - 0}{9 - 0} = \frac{p}{9}$. Set the two expressions equal to each other to get $\frac{4}{p} = \frac{p}{9}$. Cross-multiply to get $p^2 = 36$. Solve for p to get $p = \pm 6$. Only the -6 value appears in the answers, therefore (A) is correct.

28. **D** To fill in the table, write a system of equations using the information given. Call the number of decaffeinated teas x, so the number of caffeinated teas is $3x$. Call the number to decaffeinated coffees y, so the number of caffeinated coffees is $5y$. The two equations that can be written from this information and the table are $x + y = 28$ and $3x + 5y = 116$. When dealing with systems of equations, look for a way to stack and add the equations to eliminate one variable and solve for another.

To do this, multiply the first equation, $x + y = 28$, by -3 to get $-3x -3y = -84$. Now stack and add the equations:

$$3x + 5y = 116$$
$$\underline{-3x - 3y = -84}$$
$$2y = 32$$

Divide by 2 to get $y = 16$. This means that $x = 28 - y = 28 - 16 = 12$. Use these values to fill in the chart.

	Decaffeinated	Caffeinated
Tea	$x = 12$	$3x = 36$
Coffee	$y = 16$	$5y = 80$
Total	28	116

Now find the probability that a caffeinated beverage chosen at random is a coffee. Divide the number of caffeinated coffees, 80, by the total number of caffeinated beverages, 116, to get a probability of 0.69. Choice (D) is correct.

29. **B** Start by consolidating like terms. The top equation becomes $j = 3x - 9$, and the bottom equation becomes $k = 3y - 9$. In the first equation, replace j with $k + 1.5$ to get $k + 1.5 = 3x - 9$. Solve this equation for k to get $k = 3x - 10.5$. Set the two equations equal to each other to get $3y - 9 = 3x - 10.5$. Add 10.5 to both sides to get $3y + 1.5 = 3x$. Divide the entire equation by 3 to get $y + 0.5 = x$. Choice (B) is correct. Another approach would be to plug in numbers for j and k then solve for x and y.

30. **C** The fastest way to solve this is to use the decay formula: *final amount = original amount* $(1 - r)^t$. In this case, the *original amount* $= 6,500$ and the $r = 0.2$. The *final amount* $= 6,500(1 - 0.2)^t = 6,500(0.8)^t$. Eliminate (A) and (B). Next, plug in a value for m. If $m = 12$, then because the value of the baseball cards decreases every 6 months, $t = \dfrac{12}{6} = 2$. This matches (C). Of course, this question can also be solved without the formula, though not as quickly. Pick a value for m that will make the number of baseball cards easy to calculate, such as $m = 6$. Banerji starts with 6,500 cards, and he will sell off 20% of them in those 6 months. Calculate 20% of 6,500, which is 1,300, then subtract that from 6,500 to get 5,200 cards. This is the target value. Plug in $m = 6$ in each of the answer choices to see which one equals 5,200. Only (C) matches this target value.

31. **3** Start by distributing the negative three to get $6x^2 - 7x + 5 - 3x^2 + 15x - 12$. Combine like terms to get $3x^2 + 8x - 7$. Therefore, $a = 3$.

32. **5 or 6** One onion costs $0.50. Subtract that from the total amounts that Emeril might spend to find that he can spend between $1.50 and $2 on potatoes. If he spends $1.50 on potatoes that cost $0.30 each, he can buy 5 potatoes. If he spends closer to $2.00 on potatoes, he can get 6 for $1.80. He can't get 7 potatoes, as that would put him over his $2 potato budget, so Emeril can get 5 or 6 potatoes.

33. **25.2** The mean of a list is the total divided by the number of items in the list. Here, the total of all the heights is 302, and there are 12 infants in the program. $\frac{302}{12} = 25.1\overline{6}$. Rounded to the nearest tenth, this becomes 25.2.

34. **40** For an average score of 75 on all 8 exams, Jacob needs to score a total of 75 × 8 = 600 points. Over the first 4 exams, he has already scored 65 × 4 = 260 points. To find the minimum score allowable for the 5th exam, maximize the scores on all of the other remaining exams. The most he can score on an exam is 100. If he got 100 on the 6th, 7th, and 8th exams that would be a total of 300 points. Add this to his current points: 300 + 260 = 560 points, which means that on the 5th test, he would need to score a minimum of 600 − 560 = 40.

35. **1,000** Draw a rough sketch of the graph of this system of inequalities to figure out what is going on here. It would look something like this:

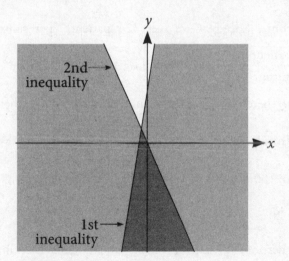

The area included in both inequalities represents the solution to the system. The question asks for the greatest value of k, which is the y-coordinate, so it would happen as close to the top of the graph as possible. For the area of overlap representing the solution, this happens at the point of intersection of the two lines. Find this point of intersection by setting the two equations $y = 20x + 3,500$ and $y = -8x$ equal to each other to get $20x + 3,500 = -8x$. Add $8x$ to both sides to get $28x + 3,500 = 0$, then subtract 3,500 from both sides to get $28x = -3,500$. Dividing both sides by 28 results in $x = -125$. This is the value for j, and it can be plugged back into either equation to get the value of k, the y-coordinate at that point. Use the easier equation, $y = -8x$ to get $k = -8(-125) = 1,000$.

36. $\dfrac{7}{12}$ or .583

There is a proportional relationship between the arc length, degree measure, and area of a section of a circle formed by two radii. For this question, the important aspects of the circle are the given angle measure of $\dfrac{7\pi}{6}$ radians and the arc the question asks about. Set up a proportion: $\dfrac{\text{arc}}{\text{circumference}} = \dfrac{\text{angle measure}}{\text{total radians}}$. This fractional part of the circumference in the first part of the proportion is what the question is asking for, so focus on the second part. The angle measure is given, and the total number of radians in a circle is 2π. Fill in the second fraction to get $\dfrac{\text{arc}}{\text{circumference}} = \dfrac{\frac{7\pi}{6}}{2\pi}$. Dividing by a number is the same as multiplying by the reciprocal of the number, so the second fraction becomes $\dfrac{7\pi}{6} \times \dfrac{1}{2\pi} = \dfrac{7}{12}$.

37. **20** Start by calculating the average number of patients in the Kind Care clinic. According to the information provided, $m = 4$ and $W = 45$. Therefore, Kind Care has an average of $4(45) = 180$ patients in their clinic. Speedy Care sees 324 patients "per hour," so set up a proportion: $\dfrac{324 \text{ patients}}{60 \text{ minutes}} = \dfrac{m \text{ patients}}{1 \text{ minute}}$. Cross-multiply to get $60m = 324$, then divide by 60 to get $m = 5.4$ patients per minute. Therefore, the average number of patients in their clinic can be calculated as $L = 5.4(40) = 216$. To calculate a "percent greater than," use the following formula percent change formula: $\dfrac{\textit{difference}}{\textit{original}} \times 100$. In this case, the smaller number is the original, so the percent change is $\dfrac{216 - 180}{180} \times 100 = 20$.

38. **9** According to the question, the rate at which patients enter the clinic is defined as m patients per minute. This question gives the rate of 36 patients "per hour," so set up a proportion: $\dfrac{36 \text{ patients}}{60 \text{ minutes}} = \dfrac{m \text{ patients}}{1 \text{ minute}}$. Cross-multiply to get $60m = 36$, then divide by 60 to get $m = 0.6$ patients per minute. Each stays with the doctor an average of 15 minutes, so to find the average number of patients being treated, L, use the formula to get $L = (0.6)(15) = 9$.

Chapter 9
Practice Test 4

Reading Test

65 MINUTES, 52 QUESTIONS

Turn to Section 1 of your answer sheet to answer the questions in this section.

DIRECTIONS

Each passage or pair of passages below is followed by a number of questions. After reading each passage or pair, choose the best answer to each question based on what is stated or implied in the passage or passages and in any accompanying graphics (such as a table or graph).

Questions 1–10 are based on the following passage.

This passage is adapted from Ayn Rand, *Anthem*. © 1938. The protagonist, a street sweeper named Equality 7-2521, lives in a society in which the word "I" is forbidden.

Note: Because the word "I" is forbidden in this society, the narrator refers to himself as "we."

And as we all undress at night, in the dim light of the candles, our brothers are silent, for they dare not speak the thoughts of their minds. For all must agree
Line with all, and they cannot know if their thoughts are the
5 thoughts of all, and so they fear to speak. And they are glad when the candles are blown for the night. But we, Equality 7-2521, look through the window upon the sky, and there is peace in the sky, and cleanliness, and dignity. And beyond the City there lies the plain, and
10 beyond the plain, black upon the black sky, there lies the Uncharted Forest. We do not wish to look upon the Uncharted Forest. We do not wish to think of it. But ever do our eyes return to that black patch upon the sky. Men never enter the Uncharted Forest, for there is
15 no power to explore it and no path to lead among its ancient trees which stand as guards of fearful secrets. It is whispered that once or twice in a hundred years, one among the men of the City escape alone and run to the Uncharted Forest, without call or reason. These
20 men do not return. They perish from hunger and from the claws of the wild beasts which roam the Forest. But our Councils say that this is only a legend. We have heard that there are many Uncharted Forests over the land, among the Cities. And it is whispered that
25 they have grown over the ruins of many cities of the

Unmentionable Times. The trees have swallowed the ruins, and the bones under the ruins, and all the things which perished. And as we look upon the Uncharted Forest far in the night, we think of the secrets of the
30 Unmentionable Times. And we wonder how it came to pass that these secrets were lost to the world.

We have heard the legends of the great fighting, in which many men fought on one side and only a few on the other. These few were the Evil Ones and they were
35 conquered. Then great fires raged over the land. And in these fires the Evil Ones and all the things made by the Evil Ones were burned. And the fire which is called the Dawn of the Great Rebirth, was the Script Fire where all the scripts of the Evil Ones were burned, and with them
40 all the words of the Evil Ones. The words of the Evil Ones... The words of the Unmentionable Times... What are the words which we have lost? May the Council have mercy upon us! We had no wish to write such a question, and we knew not what we were doing till we
45 had written it. We shall not ask this question and we shall not think it. We shall not call death upon our head.

And yet . . . And yet . . . There is some word, one single word which is not in the language of men, but which had been. And this is the Unspeakable Word,
50 which no men may speak nor hear. But sometimes, and it is rare, sometimes, somewhere, one among men find that word. They find it upon scraps of old manuscripts or cut into the fragments of ancient stones. But when they speak it they are put to death.
55 There is no crime punished by death in this world, save this one crime of speaking the Unspeakable Word.

CONTINUE ▶

1

In the passage, the narrator's focus shifts from

A) fear of exploring frontiers to preparation for it.

B) disquiet about the unknown to curiosity about it.

C) acknowledgement of an ancient city to dismissal of it.

D) repetition of the Council's rules to acceptance of them.

2

Which choice provides the best evidence for the answer to the previous question?

A) Lines 1–3 ("And as . . . minds")

B) Line 22 ("But our . . . legend")

C) Lines 35–37 ("And in . . . burned")

D) Lines 47–49 ("And yet . . . been")

3

As used in lines 3–4, "all must agree with all" most nearly means

A) truth is true.

B) language must be accurate.

C) thought must be uniform.

D) words match their meaning.

4

The sentence in lines 12–14 ("But ever . . . sky") mainly serves to

A) confirm that the narrator's job is to guard against outside threats.

B) show that some people find an object of mystery to be of recurring interest.

C) indicate that members of the narrator's society know everyone keeps looking at the horizon.

D) illustrate a repeated action stemming from a confusion about an unexplainable phenomenon.

5

The narrator states that a person who wished to navigate the Uncharted Forest would find

A) no source of electricity.

B) it impossible to locate objects within.

C) answers to many long-forgotten questions.

D) no clear trail through.

6

Which choice provides the best evidence for the answer to the previous question?

A) Lines 14–16 ("Men never . . . secrets")

B) Lines 20–21 ("They perish . . . Forest")

C) Lines 26–28 ("The trees . . . perished")

D) Lines 37–40 ("And the . . . Ones")

7

Which of the following most accurately expresses the narrator's perspective about exploring the secrets of the past?

A) Compelling but dangerous

B) Easily pursuable but illegal

C) Unavoidable but unexpectedly challenging

D) Appealing but inauthentic

8

The statement the narrator makes in lines 26–28 ("The trees . . . perished") can be most clearly inferred to mean that

A) people who ask questions in the narrator's society are banished to the Forest.

B) the trees grew in the streets of cities in the Unmentionable Times.

C) the visible traces of the past have been completely obscured.

D) the city buries its dead in the Forest.

CONTINUE

As used in lines 30–31, "how it came to pass" most nearly means

A) what crossed each other.

B) what went in circles.

C) what happened historically.

D) how time elapsed.

As used in line 39, "scripts" most nearly means

A) clothes.

B) habits.

C) screenplays.

D) writings.

CONTINUE ➤

Questions 11-21 are based on the following passage and supplementary material.

The following excerpt is from The Economist, "Bring on the Hipsters: Gentrification Is Good for the Poor," © 2015 by The Economist.

In an old bar on U Street in Washington, DC—a place that was once a centre of black life and is now an inferno of hipsterdom—Jay, the bartender, is talking
Line about how the area has changed over the past decade
5 or so. "They ain't got barmen any more," he says, with a grin. "They got mixologists." What happens in Washington, he explains, is that young white professionals move in, bars open, "and then you know that all the bodegas and liquor stores on every corner,
10 they ain't got long either."

Such gentrification obsesses the *bien-pensants*. In November the *New York Times* instructed its journalists to stop comparing everywhere to gentrified Brooklyn. A *Saturday Night Live* sketch showed a
15 young man in a tough neighborhood talking about his "bitches"—only to reveal that he runs a dog-walking business, and even knits matching sweaters for his bitches. In Philadelphia and San Francisco, presumed gentrifiers have been the target of protests and attacks.
20 Elsewhere, the term is used as an insult ("I would hate to be a gentrifier," says one young professional in Detroit). Yet the evidence suggests that gentrification is both rare and, on balance, a good thing.

The case against it is simple. Newcomers with
25 more money supposedly crowd out older residents. In Washington, according to a study by *Governing* magazine, 52% of census tracts that were poor in 2000 have since gentrified—more than in any other city bar Portland, Oregon. Young, mostly white singletons have
30 crowded into a district once built for families. Over the same period, housing in Washington has become vastly more expensive. And many black residents have left: between 1990 and 2010, the number of African-Americans in the District declined by almost 100,000,
35 falling from 66% of the population to 51%.

In New York and San Francisco, which both have rent-control rules, soaring property prices create an incentive for property owners to get rid of their tenants. Stories abound of unscrupulous developers
40 buying up rent-controlled properties and then using

legal loopholes or trickery to force residents to leave. Letting a building deteriorate so much that it can be knocked down is one tactic; bribing building inspectors to evict tenants illegally is another.

45 Yet there is little evidence that gentrification is responsible for displacing the poor or minorities. Black people were moving out of Washington in the 1980s, long before most parts of the city began gentrifying. In cities like Detroit, where gentrifiers are few and far
50 between and housing costs almost nothing, they are still leaving. One 2008 study of census data found "no evidence of displacement of low-income non-white households in gentrifying neighborhoods". They did find, however, that the average income of black people
55 with high-school diplomas in gentrifying areas soared.

Gentrifiers can make life better for locals in plenty of ways, argues Stuart Butler of the Brookings Institution, a think-tank. When professionals move to an area, "they know how to get things done". They
60 put pressure on schools, the police and the city to improve. As property prices increase, rents go up—but that also generates more property-tax revenue, helping to improve local services. In many cities, zoning laws force developers to build subsidized housing for the
65 poor as well as pricey pads for well-off newcomers, which means that rising house prices can help to create more subsidized housing, not less.

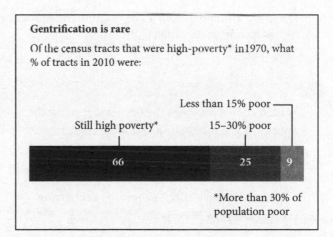

Gentrification is rare

Of the census tracts that were high-poverty* in 1970, what % of tracts in 2010 were:

Less than 15% poor

Still high poverty*   15–30% poor

| 66 | 25 | 9 |

*More than 30% of population poor

CONTINUE

The bigger problem for most American cities, says Mr. Butler, is not gentrification but the opposite: the
70 concentration of poverty. Of neighborhoods that were more than 30% poor in 1970, just 9% are now less poor than the national average (see chart), according to the City Observatory, a think-tank. In Chicago, yuppies can easily buy coffee and vinyl records in northern
75 neighborhoods such as Wicker Park. But the South Side, where racist housing policies created a ghetto in the 1950s and 1960s, remains violent and poor. In Brooklyn the most famously gentrified district, Williamsburg, was never all that poor in the first place.
80 However annoying they may be, hipsters help the poor. Their vintage shops and craft-beer bars generate jobs and taxes. So if you see a bearded intruder on a fixed-gear bike in your neighborhood, welcome him.

11

According to the passage, which choice best describes the case against gentrification?

A) New establishments catering to professionals threaten existing neighborhood stores.

B) As professionals move into neighborhoods, they displace previous residents.

C) Small businesses moving into the neighborhoods can create positive economic benefits for the area.

D) Discriminatory policies have led to the formation of minority-dominated ghettos.

12

Which choice provides the best evidence for the answer to the previous question?

A) Lines 5–6 ("They ain't . . . mixologists")

B) Lines 24–25 ("Newcomers with . . . residents")

C) Lines 46–48 ("Black people . . . gentrifying")

D) Lines 81–82 ("Their vintage . . . taxes")

13

According to the passage, members of which demographic moved into census tracts that were poor in 2000?

A) White singletons

B) Established families

C) African-Americans

D) Older residents

14

In line 37, "soaring" is closest in meaning to

A) flying.

B) suffering.

C) floating.

D) rising.

15

Which choice best summarizes the fifth paragraph of the passage (lines 45–55)?

A) Gentrification can lead to an increase in income for minority high-school graduates.

B) Minorities have been leaving cities like Washington and Detroit for decades.

C) Residents of poor minority households can be displaced by things other than gentrification.

D) Minorities have been profiting from gentrification in Washington and Detroit.

CONTINUE

16

The passage implies that gentrifiers moving into communities

A) cause property values to decrease to prohibitive levels.

B) put pressure on local police to remove low-income residents.

C) always crowd out older, established residents.

D) can effect positive change in their communities.

17

Which choice provides the best evidence for the answer to the previous question?

A) Lines 45–46 ("Yet there . . . minorities")

B) Lines 53–55 ("They did . . . soared")

C) Lines 61–63 ("As property . . . services")

D) Lines 68–70 ("The bigger . . . poverty")

18

As used in line 62 , "generates" is closest in meaning to

A) powers.

B) ages.

C) creates.

D) increases.

19

The author of the passage would most likely consider the information in the chart to be

A) clear evidence to support an expert's opinion.

B) definitive proof for the main argument in the passage.

C) ambiguous data provided by a think-tank.

D) too limited to be useful.

20

According to the chart, most high-poverty census tracts in 1970 were characterized by

A) high poverty in 2010.

B) 15%–30% poverty in 2010.

C) less than 15% poverty in 2010.

D) increased poverty in 2010.

21

The chart suggests which of the following about poor areas?

A) One-tenth of gentrified areas have the lowest number of poor people.

B) One-fourth of poor areas might become gentrified.

C) One-third of poor areas might become gentrified.

D) Two-thirds of high-poverty areas may remain impoverished.

CONTINUE

Questions 22–32 are based on the following passage and supplementary material.

This passage is adapted from Schmitt et al., "Identifying the Volcanic Eruption Depicted in a Neolithic Painting at Çatalhöyük, Central Anatolia, Turkey." © 2014 by PLOS ONE.

A mural excavated at the Neolithic Çatalhöyük site (Central Anatolia, Turkey) has been interpreted as the oldest known map. Dating to around 6600 B.C.E.,

Line 5 it putatively depicts an explosive summit eruption of the Hasan Dağı twin-peaks volcano located about 130 km northeast of Çatalhöyük, and a birds-eye view of a town plan in the foreground. This interpretation, however, has remained controversial not least because independent evidence for a contemporaneous

10 explosive volcanic eruption of Hasan Dağı has been lacking.

Here, we document the presence of andesitic pumice veneer on the summit of Hasan Dağı, which we dated using (U-Th)/He zircon geochronology.

15 Collectively, our results reveal protracted intrusive activity at Hasan Dağı punctuated by explosive venting, and provide the first radiometric ages for a Holocene explosive eruption which was most likely witnessed by humans in the area. Geologic and

20 geochronologic lines of evidence thus support previous interpretations that residents of Çatalhöyük artistically represented an explosive eruption of Hasan Dağı volcano.

Starting from the discovery of the Neolithic

25 settlement of Çatalhöyük in the early 1960s by British archaeologist James Mellaart, the excavations at this location have provided unique insights into the living conditions of humans at the transition from hunter-gatherer to settled agriculture societies.

30 One outstanding find is a mural from level VII of Çatalhöyük famously described by its discoverer as depicting a volcanic eruption.

Similar interpretations, differing in detail, have been put forward since then, implicating this painting

35 not only as the oldest depiction of a volcanic eruption, but as a contender for being the first graphical representation of a landscape or a map. Detailed volcanological interpretations of the painting include reconstructions of the eruptive style with the summit

40 region showing "falling volcanic 'bombs' or large semiliquid lava." According to these interpreters, the most likely candidate for the erupting volcano depicted in the upper register of the painting is the twin-peak

volcano of Hasan Dağı, located about 130 km NE of
45 Çatalhöyük.

This view, however, has been contested, largely because of the extraordinary age of the mural, and the absence of any other landscape art or map until much later in history. The depiction of a leopard skin

50 underlain by geometric patterns has been proposed instead.

A testable prediction of the volcanic eruption hypothesis for the Çatalhöyük mural is a geologic record of an eruption that would fall into, or briefly

55 predate, the time when the Çatalhöyük mural was painted.

Protracted periods of oral tradition over 250 generations have been proposed for prehistoric native North American myths following the Mount Mazama

60 eruption at around 5700 B.C.E. For the Çatalhöyük map (and volcano) hypothesis to be plausible, however, we surmise that a brief line of oral tradition, or even an eyewitness portrayal, is perhaps more likely than tradition of a myth that detached itself from its

65 inspiration in the physical world. This is not to say that realism must prevail in Neolithic art, but many of the apparent details can be reasonably expected to become lost or obscured during a long period of oral tradition. A tradition that predated the settlement of Çatalhöyük

70 thus appears very unlikely, and hence we would predict a time period for the eruption between 7400 and 6600 B.C.E. based on the ^{14}C chronology of the Çatalhöyük cultural strata.

Neither proponents nor opponents of the "volcano"

75 hypothesis for the Çatalhöyük painting have thus far scrutinized if and when such a volcanic eruption might have occurred. The radiometric age, and the following geologic evidence, corroborates the "volcano" hypothesis.

CONTINUE ➤

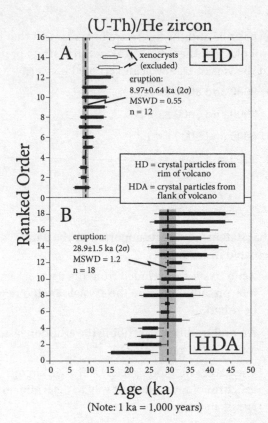

(U-Th)/He zircon

Figure 1: This table shows the (U-Th)/He zircon dated ages of sample particles removed from the rim and the flank of the Hasan Dağı volcano.

The main purpose of the passage is to

A) describe periods in Turkey's ancient geologic history.

B) explain the ways scientists use radiometric aging.

C) describe opposing views regarding an ancient mural and cautiously endorse one view.

D) explain how andesitic pumice veneer forms after volcanic eruptions.

23

Over the course of the passage, the focus shifts from

A) an explanation of a theory to a response to criticism of this theory.

B) a depiction of an event to its proof in oral history.

C) the use of (U-Th)/He zircon geochronology to a new method.

D) the use of radiometric aging to an examination of andesitic pumice veneer.

Which choice provides the best evidence for the answer to the previous question?

A) Lines 12–14 ("Here, we . . . geochronology")

B) Lines 46–49 ("This view . . . history")

C) Lines 60–65 ("For the . . . world")

D) Lines 77–79 ("The radiometric . . . hypothesis")

25

The author uses the phrase "it putatively depicts" (line 4) most likely to

A) detail the hands-on nature of the work done by those who study science.

B) emphasize the fact that scientists must always question theories.

C) underscore the need for clarification of the work of scientists.

D) bolster the idea that the evidence to support the claim is imperfect.

Where does the author indicate the Neolithic volcanic eruption most probably was located?

A) Near Central Anatolia, in Turkey

B) In the British Isles

C) In the Middle East

D) In the central region of North America

CONTINUE

27

Which choice provides the best evidence for the answer to the previous question?

A) Lines 1–6 ("A mural . . . Çatalhöyük")

B) Lines 24–29 ("Starting from . . . societies")

C) Lines 57–60 ("Protracted periods . . . B.C.E.")

D) Lines 60–65 ("For the . . . world")

28

As used in line 65, the phrase "This is not to say" implies that

A) the lost details are crucial for proving the truth.

B) oral traditions describe stories but not real events.

C) the scientists don't expect the mural to be completely true to life.

D) Neolithic artists used realism to portray the natural world.

29

Which choice best supports the claim that the mural was painted near the time of the volcanic eruption?

A) Lines 7–11 ("This interpretation . . . lacking")

B) Lines 49–51 ("The depiction . . . instead")

C) Lines 65–68 ("This is . . . tradition")

D) Lines 74–77 ("Neither proponents . . . occurred")

30

According to the data, the youngest Holocene eruption age for Hasan Dağı is approximately

A) 1.2 ka.

B) 8.97 ka.

C) 18 ka.

D) 28.9 ka.

31

The passage and the figure are in agreement that the chronology of the Çatalhöyük cultural strata predicts that the Hasan Dağı volcano erupted between

A) 9000 and 8000 B.C.E.

B) 7000 and 6000 B.C.E.

C) 6000 and 5000 B.C.E.

D) 4500 and 3500 B.C.E.

32

What statement is best supported by the data presented in the figure?

A) Xenocrysts are excluded from the data interpretation because the crystals are too new to be useful.

B) An oral tradition describing the eruption lasted for over 250 generations.

C) The dating method called (U-Th)/He zircon geochronology is the best way to determine the age of an artifact.

D) Particles on the rim of a volcano are more likely to be from recent eruptions than particles on the flank of the volcano.

CONTINUE

Questions 33–42 are based on the following passages.

Passage 1 is excerpted from Edmund Burke, *Reflections on the Revolution in France.* Originally published in 1790. Passage 2 is excerpted from Thomas Paine, *Common Sense.* Originally published in 1776.

Passage 1

A few years ago I should be ashamed to overload a matter so capable of supporting itself by the then unnecessary support of any argument; but this seditious, unconstitutional doctrine is now publicly
5 taught, avowed, and printed.

The people of England will not ape the fashions they have never tried, nor go back to those which they have found mischievous on trial. They look upon the legal hereditary succession of their crown as among
10 their rights, not as among their wrongs; as a benefit, not as a grievance; as a security for their liberty, not as a badge of servitude. They look on the frame of their commonwealth, *such as it stands*, to be of inestimable value; and they conceive the undisturbed succession of
15 the crown to be a pledge of the stability and perpetuity of all the other members of our Constitution.

I shall beg leave, before I go any further, to take notice of some paltry artifices which the abettors of election as the only lawful title to the crown are
20 ready to employ, in order to render the support of the just principles of our Constitution a task somewhat invidious. These sophisters substitute a fictitious cause, and feigned personages, in whose favor they suppose you engaged, whenever you defend the inheritable
25 nature of the crown. It is common with them to dispute as if they were in a conflict with some of those exploded fanatics of slavery who formerly maintained, what I believe no creature now maintains, "that the crown is held by divine, hereditary, and indefeasible
30 right."

These old fanatics of single arbitrary power dogmatized as if hereditary royalty was the only lawful government in the world, just as our new fanatics of popular arbitrary power maintain that a popular
35 election is the sole lawful source of authority. The old prerogative enthusiasts, it is true, did speculate foolishly, and perhaps impiously too, as if monarchy had more of a divine sanction than any other mode of government; and as if a right to govern by inheritance
40 were in strictness *indefeasible* in every person who should be found in the succession to a throne, and under every circumstance, which no civil or political right can be.

Passage 2

But it is not so much the absurdity as the evil of
45 hereditary succession which concerns mankind. Did it ensure a race of good and wise men it would have the seal of divine authority, but as it opens a door to the FOOLISH, the WICKED, and the IMPROPER, it hath in it the nature of oppression. Men who look upon
50 themselves born to reign, and others to obey, soon grow insolent; selected from the rest of mankind their minds are early poisoned by importance; and the world they act in differs so materially from the world at large, that they have but little opportunity of knowing its true
55 interests, and when they succeed to the government are frequently the most ignorant and unfit of any throughout the dominions. Another evil which attends hereditary succession is, that the throne is subject to be possessed by a minor at any age; all which time the
60 regency, acting under the cover of a king, have every opportunity and inducement to betray their trust. The same national misfortune happens, when a king worn out with age and infirmity, enters the last stage of human weakness. In both these cases the public
65 becomes a prey to every miscreant, who can tamper successfully with the follies either of age or infancy.

The most plausible plea, which hath ever been offered in favour of hereditary succession, is, that it preserves a nation from civil wars; and were this true,
70 it would be weighty; whereas, it is the most barefaced falsity ever imposed upon mankind. The whole history of England disowns the fact. Thirty kings and two minors have reigned in that distracted kingdom since the conquest, in which time there have been
75 (including the Revolution) no less than eight civil wars and nineteen rebellions. Wherefore instead of making for peace, it makes against it, and destroys the very foundation it seems to stand on. ... In short, monarchy and succession have laid (not this or that kingdom
80 only) but the world in blood and ashes.

33

In Passage 1, Burke indicates that the argument of those who support elected leaders is characterized by its

A) weakness and dishonesty

B) universality and fanaticism

C) antiquity and irrelevance

D) hypocrisy and innovation

34

As used in line 1, "overload" most nearly means

A) burden excessively.

B) cause to burst.

C) express emotionally.

D) short circuit.

35

As used in line 20, "employ" most nearly means

A) hire.

B) utilize.

C) reimburse.

D) work.

36

Passage 2 most strongly suggests that Paine believes leaderships by right of birth to be

A) illegitimate failures that cause devastating results.

B) useful means by which to avoid dangerously inferior governance.

C) complicated and passionate methods for expressing opinions.

D) valuable despite some historical setbacks.

37

In response to Burke's statement in lines 22–25 ("These sophisters . . . crown"), what would Paine most likely say?

A) He would indicate that it is important to address all possible reasons for supporting an unjust cause.

B) He would state that the argument against the divine right to rule is less important than the tendencies of rulers to arbitrarily provide favors to their supporters.

C) He would clarify that the argument against an accepted form of rule is based on results, not redirection.

D) He would deny that the old belief in an inherently granted right to rule a state has completely disappeared.

38

Which choice provides the best evidence for the answer to the previous question?

A) Lines 49–51 ("Men who . . . insolent")

B) Lines 57–59 ("Another evil . . . age")

C) Lines 67–69 ("The most . . . wars")

D) Lines 71–72 ("The whole . . . fact")

39

Which of the following types of responses would Burke most likely make to Paine's statements in the final paragraph of Passage 2?

A) One of disagreement, because conflicts do not necessarily indicate an unstable structure.

B) One of agreement, because civil wars are a burden on a nation.

C) One of acceptance, because excessive violence demonstrates a failure of a system.

D) One of doubt, because Paine failed to provide details and dates of the wars and rebellions he cites.

CONTINUE ➡

40

Which choice provides the best evidence for the answer to the previous question?

A) Lines 6–8 ("The people . . . trial")

B) Lines 12–16 ("They look . . . Constitution")

C) Lines 31–35 ("These old . . . authority")

D) Lines 35–39 ("The old . . . government")

41

Which choice best states the relationship between the two passages?

A) Passage 2 underscores the concerns raised by Passage 1.

B) Passage 2 argues a point dismissed by Passage 1.

C) Passage 2 presents another method for resolving the issues delineated in Passage 1.

D) Passage 2 expands on the main position expressed and advocated in Passage 1.

42

The main purpose of both passages is to

A) evaluate the various benefits of parliamentary forms of government.

B) seek compromise on a passionately debated issue of importance.

C) reject an opposing view and a particular position.

D) prove that history is based on false beliefs.

CONTINUE

Questions 43–52 are based on the following passage.

This passage is excerpted from Heidi Ledford, "Where Could the First CRISPR Baby Be Born?" © 2015 by Nature.

They are meeting in China; they are meeting in the United Kingdom; and they met in the United States last week. Around the world, scientists are gathering to discuss the promise and perils of editing the genome of a human embryo. Should it be allowed—and if so, under what circumstances?

The meetings have been prompted by an explosion of interest in the powerful technology known as CRISPR/Cas9, which has brought unprecedented ease and precision to genetic engineering. This tool, and others like it, could be used to manipulate the DNA of embryos in a dish to learn about the earliest stages of human development. In theory, genome editing could also be used to 'fix' the mutations responsible for heritable human diseases. If done in embryos, this could prevent such diseases from being passed on.

The prospects have prompted widespread concern and discussion among scientists, ethicists and patients. Fears loom that if genome editing becomes acceptable in the clinic to stave off disease, it will inevitably come to be used to introduce, enhance or eliminate traits for non-medical reasons. Ethicists are concerned that unequal access to such technologies could lead to genetic classism. And targeted changes to a person's genome would be passed on for generations, through the germ line (sperm and eggs), fueling fears that embryo editing could have lasting, unintended consequences.

Adding to these concerns, the regulations in many countries have not kept pace with the science.

Nature has tried to capture a snapshot of the legal landscape by querying experts and government agencies in 12 countries with histories of well-funded biological research. The responses reveal a wide range of approaches. In some countries, experimenting with human embryos at all would be a criminal offense, whereas in others, almost anything would be permissible.

Concerns over the manipulation of human embryos are nothing new. Rosario Isasi, a legal scholar at McGill University in Montreal, Canada, points to two key waves of legislation over the years: one sparked by concerns about the derivation of embryonic stem cells, which was largely deemed acceptable; the other about reproductive cloning, which was largely prohibited for safety reasons.

But the research has already begun, and more is coming. Scientists in China announced in April that they had used CRISPR to alter the genomes of human embryos, albeit ones incapable of producing a live baby (P. Liang, *et al.* Protein Cell 6, 363-372; 2015). Xiao-Jiang Li, a neuroscientist at Emory University in Atlanta, Georgia, who has used the technique in monkeys, says he has heard rumours that several other Chinese laboratories are already doing such experiments. And in September, developmental biologist Kathy Niakan of the Francis Crick Institute in London applied to the UK Human Fertilisation and Embryology Authority for permission to use the technique to study errors in embryo development that can contribute to infertility and miscarriage. No one so far has declared an interest in producing live babies with edited genomes, and initial experiments would suggest that it is not yet safe. But some suspect that it is only a matter of time.

Tetsuya Ishii, a bioethicist at Hokkaido University in Sapporo, Japan, spent nearly a year analysing relevant legislation and guidelines in 39 countries, and found that 29 have rules that could be interpreted as restricting genome editing for clinical use (M. Araki and T. Ishii Reprod. Biol. Endocrinol. 12, 108; 2014). Ishii predicts that countries with high rates of *in vitro* fertilization will be the first to attempt clinical applications. Japan, he says, has one of the highest numbers of fertility clinics in the world, and has no enforceable rules on germline modification. The same is true for India.

Guoping Feng, a neuroscientist at the Massachusetts Institute of Technology in Cambridge, hopes that with improvement, the technique could eventually be used to prevent genetic disease. But he argues that it is much too soon to be trying it in the clinic. "Now is not the time to do human-embryo manipulation," he says. "If we do the wrong thing, we can send the wrong message to the public—and then the public will not support scientific research anymore."

CONTINUE

43

The primary purpose of the passage is to

A) evaluate the findings of a long-term study.

B) present the background of a scientific discovery.

C) evaluate competing theories in a scientific field.

D) explain the prospects of a developing branch of science.

44

The author's attitude toward CRISPR/Cas9 technology is best described as one of

A) unconcerned ambivalence.

B) cautious optimism.

C) restrained fear.

D) unqualified exuberance.

45

As used in line 13, "editing" most nearly means

A) abridging.

B) altering.

C) revising.

D) polishing.

46

What does the author suggest about the prospects of human embryo editing?

A) They are limited by the expensive nature of monkey testing.

B) They are focused only on producing live babies with edited genomes.

C) They are not yet ready to be used on humans for ethical reasons.

D) They are ready for clinical trials in most countries.

47

Which choice provides the best evidence for the answer to the previous question?

A) Lines 13–16 ("In theory . . . on")

B) Lines 17–18 ("The prospects . . . patients")

C) Lines 35–38 ("In some . . . permissible")

D) Lines 52–56 ("Xiao-Jiang Li . . . experiments")

48

According to the passage, which of the following is true of CRISPR technology?

A) It is being researched at well-funded institutions.

B) It stems from months of previous genetic modification research.

C) It reduces the risk of passing on genetic mutations responsible for heritable diseases.

D) It has been used already in the United States.

49

Which choice provides the best evidence for the answer to the previous question?

A) Lines 13–16 ("In theory . . . on")

B) Lines 29–30 ("Adding to . . . science")

C) Lines 52–56 ("Xiao-Jiang Li . . . experiments")

D) Lines 74–77 ("Japan, he . . . India")

50

Which of the following does the author suggest about the "*in vitro* fertilization" mentioned in line 73?

A) Some human embryos have been genetically altered in China.

B) Japan will become the first country to produce a genetically mutated human.

C) It may be one of the first clinical applications of genetic editing in humans.

D) It will be the future of heritable disease prevention.

CONTINUE

51

The phrase "much too soon" (line 82) most directly suggests that

A) human genome editing has potential but is not yet ready for human trials.

B) human genome editing will soon be a valuable asset to heritable disease prevention.

C) human genome editing will prove to be financially insupportable.

D) human genome editing will be an inevitable failure that should not be attempted.

The most likely purpose of the quotations from Guoping Feng in lines 83–87 is to

A) reinforce an earlier point.

B) clarify an abstract concept.

C) define a theory.

D) refute a new hypothesis.

STOP
**If you finish before time is called, you may check your work on this section only.
Do not turn to any other section in the test.**

No Test Material On This Page

Writing and Language Test

35 MINUTES, 44 QUESTIONS

Turn to Section 2 of your answer sheet to answer the questions in this section.

Each passage below is accompanied by a number of questions. For some questions, you will consider how the passage might be revised to improve the expression of ideas. For other questions, you will consider how the passage might be edited to correct errors in sentence structure, usage, or punctuation. A passage or a question may be accompanied by one or more graphics (such as a table or graph) that you will consider as you make revising and editing decisions.

Some questions will direct you to an underlined portion of a passage. Other questions will direct you to a location in a passage or ask you to think about the passage as a whole.

After reading each passage, choose the answer to each question that most effectively improves the quality of writing in the passage or that makes the passage conform to the conventions of standard written English. Many questions include a "NO CHANGE" option. Choose that option if you think the best choice is to leave the relevant portion of the passage as it is.

Questions 1–11 are based on the following passage.

The New American Renaissance

Since 1970 or so, the shape of the humanities has changed significantly. Before that time, it was rare to read books, look at paintings, or **1** watch plays by anyone other than white male European-American artists. While a bias still remains, there is no question that the canon, the group of accepted "classic" **2** works; has become much

1
A) NO CHANGE
B) rarer still was watching
C) to watch
D) DELETE the underlined portion.

2
A) NO CHANGE
B) works—
C) works
D) works,

CONTINUE

more diverse. Still, in the United States, some groups have been **3** more vocal than others. There is no better example of such a marginalization than that of Native Americans.

Each century has had its figures—William Apess was a minister and autobiographer in the nineteenth century and Zitkala-Sa was a story writer and memoirist in the early twentieth. Still, these figures were never able to reach audiences as broad as those of their white contemporaries. Today, however, as the reclamation of heritage gains more traction, this public marginalization may be changing.

Literary critic Kenneth Lincoln identifies the change and **4** outlined a kind of historical timeline in his 1983 book *Native American Renaissance*. Throughout the nineteenth century, Native Americans were systematically eradicated throughout all parts of the growing United States. Much of their **5** repartee with white Americans came in the form of military campaigns. When the wars subsided, the American government started a similarly cruel program of assimilation, **6** often this involved the movement of Native American children from their homes to "Indian schools" that sought to remove any trace of tribal inheritance.

3

Which choice most effectively sets up the information that follows?

A) NO CHANGE

B) successful despite the obstacles.

C) forced to stay on the periphery.

D) content to stay out of the public eye.

4

A) NO CHANGE

B) outlining

C) was outlining

D) outlines

5

A) NO CHANGE

B) contact

C) chatting

D) badinage

6

A) NO CHANGE

B) it often involved

C) this type of thing often involved

D) often involving

CONTINUE

7 There were lots of anti-war demonstrations in the 1960s and 1970s, an era of cultural reclamation, when the emphasis on "melting-pot"-style assimilation shifted toward an attitude of "multicultural society." 8 At this time, people from all races began to think it possible to live in the United States while at the same time identifying with a particular racial group. Around this time, after many of the "Indian schools" had closed, Native American children could gain English-language education closer to home. 9 Nevertheless, they could continue to identify with their cultural heritage while gaining an "American" education.

Which choice connects the sentence with the previous paragraph?

A) NO CHANGE

B) Kenneth Lincoln was just a young man

C) This practice of assimilation had begun to change

D) Many important things happened

At this point, the writer is considering adding the following sentence.

> This was not always the case as many groups have been marginalized throughout American history.

Should the writer make this addition here?

A) Yes, because it gives an important reminder that the United States is always changing.

B) Yes, because it shows that Native American writers have not always been popular.

C) No, because it makes a historical claim that the passage contradicts.

D) No, because it repeats information from earlier in the passage that is already implied in this paragraph.

A) NO CHANGE

B) And,

C) Because,

D) Moreover,

CONTINUE

This shift led to more Native Americans attending colleges and universities, and more empathetic attitudes among the literary establishment allowed more **10** of them space for publication of poetry and fiction. **11** The result was an efflorescence of Native American writers, particularly in the 1970s and 1980s. During this period, writers like Leslie Marmon Silko, Gerald Vizenor, and Paula Gunn Allen became popular. These writers are now among the most respected in the country, and they have influenced countless others. While the literary establishment may have been centuries late in acknowledging the significant contributions that Native American culture can make to the world, we should nonetheless be glad that this influence is finally more widely available.

10

A) NO CHANGE

B) Native American writers

C) of these

D) from it

11

Which choice most effectively combines the underlined sentences?

A) Particularly in the 1970s and 1980s, writers like Leslie Marmon Silko, Gerald Vizenor, and Paula Gunn Allen became popular, a resultant efflorescence of Native American writers.

B) The result was an efflorescence of Native American writers, particularly in the 1970s and 1980s; in these decades, popularity was earned for writers including Leslie Marmon Silko, Gerald Vizenor, an Paula Gunn Allen.

C) Leslie Marmon Silko, Gerald Vizenor, and Paula Gunn Allen were three of the writers who became popular in this period of the 1970s and 1980s amid the resulting efflorescence of Native American writers.

D) The result, particularly in the 1970s and 1980s, was an efflorescence of Native American writers including Leslie Marmon Silko, Gerald Vizenor, and Paula Gunn Allen.

CONTINUE

Questions 12–22 are based on the following passage.

Make Like a Tree and Change Leaves

Anyone who lives in the Mid-Atlantic or New England **12** knows the flowering of spring and the lush greens of summer. The four seasons in these areas are most evident in the look of the trees. This is never more true than **13** when people are in the case of fall, when the trees are covered with beautiful swatches of red, yellow, and orange as the leaves change color. For many, this fall foliage represents the Northeast in **14** the state in which it is most pure.

People in this region have taken to the idea. Now, foliage tourism is as much a part of the region as beach season is for those on the coast. Many business **15** owners including, restaurant owners, hoteliers, and farmers, throughout the region depend on a boom in October and November.

12

A) NO CHANGE
B) bodes
C) foretells
D) indicates

13

A) NO CHANGE
B) considering
C) with the consideration
D) DELETE the underlined portion.

14

A) NO CHANGE
B) its purest state.
C) which it is in the purest possible state.
D) the state of purity rather than impurity.

15

A) NO CHANGE
B) owners, including
C) owners, including,
D) owners including:

CONTINUE

However, there is a problem. Except in very odd circumstances, it will *always* be beach season in July and August. Foliage season, however, is a bit more difficult to predict. It is clear, **16** for instance, that the leaves tend to change in the last few months of the year, but when they change and how vivid their colors will be has long remained a mystery. Of course, many people would certainly like to know the cause. **17** Because of it, fall without the foliage is like a whole season of rainy beach days, at least from a tourism perspective.

A recent study published in *Proceedings of the National Academy of Sciences* has begun to uncover some of the factors behind the change. Scientists **18** have long known that climate conditions influence the changing of the leaves, but no one has ever been sure which aspect of the weather to privilege—moisture, temperature, frost, etc. **19** No previous explanation has been able to say why in one year the leaves were still a vibrant yellow on the first of November while the next year they had all fallen already.

16

A) NO CHANGE
B) nevertheless,
C) for all that,
D) on the other hand,

17

A) NO CHANGE
B) Subsequently,
C) After all,
D) Additionally,

18

A) NO CHANGE
B) long knows
C) long know
D) are long knowing

19

At this point, the writer is considering adding the following sentence.

> The Mount Washington Observatory reports that the average rainfall in the New Hampshire region is approximately 6-9 inches, depending on the month.

Should the writer make this addition here?

A) Yes, because it provides support for the passage's main claim that fall foliage can now be accurately predicted.

B) Yes, because it adds an important detail regarding the expected moisture levels in one region.

C) No, because it introduces the work of an organization that is not discussed elsewhere in the passage.

D) No, because it is not relevant to the paragraph's description of the general factors that influence fall foliage.

CONTINUE ➡

The answer, it seems, is that [20] their is different factors in different places. This group of scientists analyzed two different New England ecosystems, one along the coast and one in the highlands. They found that both reacted to frosts in the fall, but only the highlands reacted to frosts in the spring. [21]

Combining these findings with climate-change predictions for the next century, [22] having suggested that the changes will come later in the year for the highlands and perhaps a bit earlier for the coasts. Should these predictions turn out to be true, it could be a major boon for the tourism industry in these areas and for the tourists who visit them.

20

A) NO CHANGE

B) their's

C) their are

D) there are

21

At this point, the writer wants to add another detail that adds to the findings described in this paragraph. Which choice most effectively accomplishes this goal?

A) The forests along the coast, perhaps not surprisingly, were particularly sensitive to rain and other types of moisture.

B) The leaves fall from the trees after they have changed, thus giving the name "fall" to the season.

C) Except for the ocean breezes, temperatures along the water tend to be a bit higher than in the mountains.

D) The leaves do not change color in the same way in the spring, but the blossoms of the trees create their own kind of beauty.

22

A) NO CHANGE

B) to suggest

C) suggesting

D) the researchers suggest

CONTINUE →

Questions 23–33 are based on the following passage and supplementary material.

(Almost) The Fifty-First State

When people refer to the "fifty-first state," they are usually referring to Puerto Rico or one of the contemporary U.S. holdings outside the fifty states. What many don't realize, however, is that the idea of extra states, particularly within U.S. borders, **23** is mainly the concern of academics. One early case is the state of Franklin. On a modern map, the state of Franklin would be bound by Tennessee to the west and south, Virginia to the north, and North Carolina to the southeast. **24**

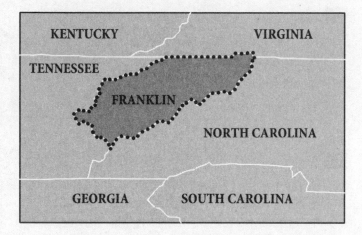

North Carolina, one of the original thirteen colonies, offered a few of its westernmost counties to the federal **25** government as payment for debts; those that had been incurred—for manpower and ammunition—during the Revolutionary War. As Congress decided what to do with the land, the North Carolinian legislature decided that the western counties were too valuable to let go, and the state soon retracted **26** it's offer of its' western counties.

23

Which choice most effectively completes the contrast in the sentence and is consistent with the information in the rest of the passage?

A) NO CHANGE

B) presents a fun historical challenge.

C) is actually quite an old idea.

D) is rather outdated in this day and age.

24

The writer wants the information in the passage to correspond as closely as possible with the information in the map. Given that goal and assuming that the rest of the previous sentence would remain unchanged, in which sequence should the three state names be discussed?

A) NO CHANGE

B) Virginia, Tennessee, North Carolina

C) North Carolina, Virginia, Tennessee

D) North Carolina, Tennessee, Virginia

25

A) NO CHANGE

B) government as payment for debts:

C) government as payment for debts

D) government-as payment for debts,

26

A) NO CHANGE

B) it's offer of its

C) its offer of it's

D) its offer of its

In the meantime, though, the counties in the northwest corner of the state had been developing a kind of regional identity. The three counties now called the State of Franklin **27** having been attempted to secede from North Carolina. Encouraged by the new federal government's quick creation of states from ceded lands, the three counties issued a declaration of **28** independence, yet their independence was rooted in particular in their distance from North Carolina's state capital.

[1] The secession was not recognized by Congress, and John Sevier and the leaders of the Franklin movement eventually took oaths of allegiance to the state of North Carolina. [2] This time, Congress acted quickly and accepted North Carolina's offer, interested as it was in pushing statehood further west from the thirteen colonies along the Atlantic coast. [3] Sevier and others led the administration of the ceded territories. [4] These territories were eventually granted statehood in 1796, though this time as something more recognizable—as the northeastern **29** boarder to the modern-day state of Tennessee. **30**

27

A) NO CHANGE

B) was attempting

C) were attempting

D) is attempting

28

A) NO CHANGE

B) independence, which

C) independence. Independence

D) independence, and independence

29

A) NO CHANGE

B) boarder from

C) border to

D) broader than

30

To improve the cohesion and flow of this paragraph, the writer wants to add the following sentence.

> In 1789, however, North Carolina renewed its offer of the western counties to the federal government.

The sentence would most logically be placed after

A) sentence 1.

B) sentence 2.

C) sentence 3.

D) sentence 4.

CONTINUE ▶

Today, Franklin is a distant memory, but its short-lived history provides a unique look into some of the early machinations of the newly formed American government. The contemporary fifty states may seem like they have always existed, but that is certainly not the case—just as national borders are artificial creations, **31** so too are state borders, and as such, they are always subject to change. It may have been nearly 150 years since a state, West Virginia, was carved out of another existing state, Virginia, but that does not mean that the map as it is drawn now will forever be so. The State of Franklin may be a mere historical **32** curiosity to some, but to others, it is a reminder that even a powerful, federally oriented nation is **33** usually made up of 50 or so states.

31

A) NO CHANGE

B) being

C) but also are

D) the same can be said of

32

The writer wants to convey an attitude of genuine interest and to avoid the appearance of mockery. Which choice best accomplishes this goal?

A) NO CHANGE

B) stumper

C) thing

D) mind-blower

33

Which choice most effectively concludes the sentence and paragraph?

A) NO CHANGE

B) very important in the world and in history.

C) a living, breathing thing, ever subject to change.

D) home to many things of historical interest.

CONTINUE

Questions 34–44 are based on the following passage.

What's So Civil About Engineers Anyway?

No matter where you live, you see their work everywhere. Whether you cross a bridge or drive on a highway, you [34] see the work of civil engineers. Civil engineering as a profession is centuries old and has long been necessary for the functioning of modern government. [35] As long as people need to get to school or work, civil engineers will continue to be [36] foundations of modern societies.

CONTINUE

[34]

A) NO CHANGE

B) saw

C) have been seeing

D) sees

[35]

At this point, the writer is considering adding the following sentence.

> Few governments in the modern world could function without the work of civil engineers.

Should the writer make this addition here?

A) Yes, because it supports the information contained in the following paragraph.

B) Yes, because it provides an important reminder that governments are not made up of politicians alone.

C) No, because it is a mere restatement of an idea expressed in the previous sentence.

D) No, because it is a digression from the main point of the paragraph.

[36]

A) NO CHANGE

B) cornerstones

C) pillars

D) manipulators

The American Society of Civil Engineers defines the profession as "the design and maintenance of public works such as roads, bridges, water, and energy systems as well as public facilities like ports, railways, and airports." **37** In other words, civil engineers design and maintain the components of energy and transportation systems in the modern world. The projects can be **38** large—like the Hoover Dam, the Holland Tunnel, or the interstate system that covers the whole country—or small—like local roads and power stations. Civil engineers see these projects through from start to finish: from the earliest stages of design and analysis to the final stages of completion and beyond.

37

A) NO CHANGE

B) On the other hand,

C) Nonetheless,

D) In the abstract,

38

A) NO CHANGE

B) large; like the Hoover Dam, the Holland Tunnel, or the interstate system that covers the whole country;

C) large: like the Hoover Dam, the Holland Tunnel, or the interstate system that covers the whole country,

D) large: like the Hoover Dam, the Holland Tunnel, or the interstate system that covers the whole country—

CONTINUE

[1] Civil engineers collaborate on large projects. [2] Their backgrounds tend to **39** vary—however, specialties can range from architecture to environmental engineering, from ecology to urban planning. [3] Those who want a greener country draw on the expertise of civil engineers in designing windmills and other sustainable sources of energy. [4] Environmental engineering has been particularly popular of late on both sides of the environmental debate. [5] Those who are less concerned with long-term energy sources have drawn on the help of civil engineers in mining oil and gas and in **40** creating delivery mechanisms that they make to get those resources all over the country. **41**

39

A) NO CHANGE

B) vary however specialties

C) vary, however, specialties

D) vary, however. Specialties

40

A) NO CHANGE

B) creating delivery mechanisms

C) creating delivery mechanisms by making them

D) fabricating and making mechanisms for delivery

41

To make this paragraph most logical, sentence 3 should be

A) placed where it is now.

B) placed after sentence 4.

C) placed after sentence 5.

D) DELETED from the paragraph.

CONTINUE

In either case, civil engineering is a fascinating field, and it is **42** full of interesting people. The Bureau of Labor Statistics predicts that the field will grow by nearly 20% between 2012 and 2022. The field offers incredible job security—regardless of changes in political power, civil engineering will continue to occupy a central place in the world. With every new development in energy or transportation, a civil engineer faces a new set of problems that **43** they have to solve for the country to reap the full benefits of these developments.

44 Should you so choose the work of civil engineering it may not have the glory of political leadership, but it certainly does present opportunities to make a tangible difference in the city, state, or country in which you live. The work of civil engineers is always about the future. After all, it wouldn't make sense to build a bridge if it were only meant to stand for your own lifetime. The work of civil engineers is a gift to future generations in a way that few other types of work can be.

42

Which choice results in a sentence that best supports the point developed in this paragraph?

A) NO CHANGE

B) very complicated.

C) constantly growing.

D) difficult to describe.

43

A) NO CHANGE

B) they must solve

C) all of them really have to solve

D) he or she must solve

44

A) NO CHANGE

B) The career they call civil engineering

C) Civil engineering

D) Opting for a career in civil engineering

STOP
**If you finish before time is called, you may check your work on this section only.
Do not turn to any other section in the test.**

Math Test – No Calculator

25 MINUTES, 20 QUESTIONS

Turn to Section 3 of your answer sheet to answer the questions in this section.

DIRECTIONS

For questions **1-15**, solve each problem, choose the best answer from the choices provided, and fill in the corresponding circle on your answer sheet. For questions **16-20**, solve the problem and enter your answer in the grid on the answer sheet. Please refer to the directions before question 16 on how to enter your answers in the grid. You may use any available space in your test booklet for scratch work.

NOTES

1. The use of a calculator **is not permitted**.
2. All variables and expressions used represent real numbers unless otherwise indicated.
3. Figures provided in this test are drawn to scale unless otherwise indicated.
4. All figures lie in a plane unless otherwise indicated.
5. Unless otherwise indicated, the domain of a given function f is the set of all real numbers x for which $f(x)$ is a real number.

REFERENCE

$A = \pi r^2$
$C = 2\pi r$

$A = \ell w$

$A = \frac{1}{2}bh$

$c^2 = a^2 + b^2$

Special Right Triangles

$V = \ell wh$

$V = \pi r^2 h$

$V = \frac{4}{3}\pi r^3$

$V = \frac{1}{3}\pi r^2 h$

$V = \frac{1}{3}\ell wh$

The number of degrees of arc in a circle is 360.
The number of radians of arc in a circle is 2π.
The sum of the measures in degrees of the angles of a triangle is 180.

CONTINUE

1

In the function $g(x) = \frac{5}{3}x + k$, k is a constant. If $g(9) - 12$, what is the value of $g(-3)$?

A) −12

B) −8

C) −3

D) 2

2

$$3(k + 2) = h$$

$$\frac{h}{k} = 5$$

If the solution set to the system of equations shown above is (h, k), what is the value of k ?

A) 1

B) 3

C) 6

D) 15

3

Which of the following expressions is equal to 1 for some value of y ?

A) $|2 - y| + 2$

B) $|y - 2| + 2$

C) $|y + 2| + 2$

D) $|2 - y| - 2$

4

If $\frac{x + y}{x}$ is equal to $\frac{6}{5}$, which of the following is true?

A) $\frac{y}{x} = \frac{1}{5}$

B) $\frac{y}{x} = \frac{11}{5}$

C) $\frac{x + y}{x} = \frac{1}{5}$

D) $\frac{x - 2y}{x} = -\frac{1}{5}$

CONTINUE

5

$$g(x) = -4x - 7$$

The function g is shown above. Which of the following is equal to $g(-2x)$?

A) $8x - 7$

B) $8x + 7$

C) $8x^2 - 21x$

D) $-8x - 7$

6

Which of the following expressions is equivalent to $4(3x - 2)(5x - 2)$?

A) $12x$

B) $7x^2 + 15x$

C) $60x^2 + 16x$

D) $60x^2 - 64x + 16$

7

If $k = 1$, which of the following is the solution set for

$x - 7 = \sqrt{x - k}$?

A) $\{1\}$

B) $\{5\}$

C) $\{10\}$

D) $\{5, 10\}$

8

While preparing for a weightlifting competition, Alexei plans a training program in which his heaviest lift of each day increases by a constant amount. If Alexei's training program requires that his heaviest lift on day 6 is 180 pounds and his heaviest lift on day 24 is 225 pounds, which of the following most accurately describes how the amount Alexei lifts changes from day 6 to day 24 in his training program?

A) Alexei increases the weight of his heaviest lift by 2 pounds every 5 days.

B) Alexei increases the weight of his heaviest lift by 2 pounds per day.

C) Alexei increases the weight of his heaviest lift by 2.5 pounds per day.

D) Alexei increases the weight of his heaviest lift by 5 pounds per day.

CONTINUE

9

$$y = -4x - 6$$

Which of the following is the equation of a line that is parallel to the line with the equation shown above?

A) $4x - y = 9$

B) $4x + 2y = 8$

C) $6x + 3y = 12$

D) $12x + 3y = 10$

10

$$y = (x - 7)(3x + 4)$$

$$x = 3y - 1$$

The solution set for the system of equations shown above contains how many ordered pairs?

A) Infinitely many

B) 2

C) 1

D) 0

11

Peggie and Joan each purchased a bouquet of flowers from a florist. The price of Peggie's bouquet was d dollars, and the price of Joan's bouquet was $4 less than the price of Peggie's bouquet. If Peggie and Joan split the cost of the bouquets equally, and each paid 15% sales tax on her share, which of the following expressions gives the amount, in dollars, that each of them paid?

A) $1.15d - 2.3$

B) $2d - 1.15$

C) $2.15d - 2$

D) $2.3d - 4.6$

12

$$\frac{z - 3}{z + 3} = 8$$

What is the value of z in the equation above?

A) $-\dfrac{27}{7}$

B) $-\dfrac{7}{2}$

C) -3

D) $-\dfrac{21}{9}$

CONTINUE

13

In the quadratic equation $x^2 - 3t = \dfrac{v}{3}x$, t and v are constants. What are the solutions for x ?

A) $x = \dfrac{v}{3} \pm \dfrac{\sqrt{v^2 + 4t}}{3}$

B) $x = \dfrac{v}{3} \pm \dfrac{\sqrt{v^2 + 36t}}{6}$

C) $x = \dfrac{v}{6} \pm \dfrac{\sqrt{v^2 + 108t}}{6}$

D) $x = \dfrac{v}{6} \pm \dfrac{\sqrt{v^2 + 4t}}{6}$

14

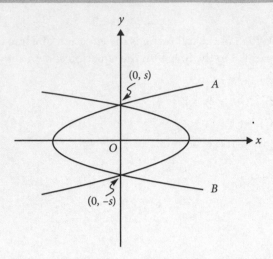

Two equations A and B, defined by $x = 18y^2 - 2$ and $x = -18y^2 + 2$ respectively, are graphed in the xy-plane above. The graphs of A and B intersect at the points $(0, s)$ and $(0, -s)$. What is the value of s ?

A) 3

B) 1

C) $\dfrac{1}{3}$

D) $\dfrac{1}{9}$

CONTINUE

15

In the equation $\dfrac{18 + i}{4 + 3i} = a + bi$, where a and b are real numbers, what is the value of a?

(Note: $i = \sqrt{-1}$)

A)   2

B)   3

C) $\dfrac{18}{4}$

D) $\dfrac{11}{2}$

CONTINUE

DIRECTIONS

For questions 16-20, solve the problem and enter your answer in the grid, as described below, on the answer sheet.

1. Although not required, it is suggested that you write your answer in the boxes at the top of the columns to help you fill in the circles accurately. You will receive credit only if the circles are filled in correctly.

2. Mark no more than one circle in any column.

3. No question has a negative answer.

4. Some problems may have more than one correct answer. In such cases, grid only one answer.

5. **Mixed numbers** such as $3\frac{1}{2}$ must be gridded as 3.5 or 7/2. (If $\boxed{3\ 1\ /\ 2}$ is entered into the grid, it will be interpreted as $\frac{31}{2}$, not as $3\frac{1}{2}$.)

6. **Decimal Answers:** If you obtain a decimal answer with more digits than the grid can accommodate, it may be either rounded or truncated, but it must fill the entire grid.

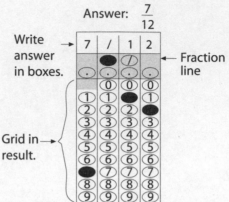

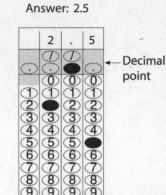

Acceptable ways to grid $\frac{2}{3}$ are:

Answer: 201 – either position is correct

 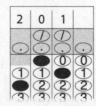

NOTE: You may start your answers in any column, space permitting. Columns you don't need to use should be left blank.

CONTINUE →

16

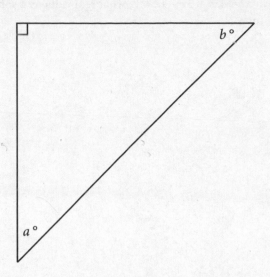

In the triangle above, the cosine of $a°$ is 0.625. What is the sine of $b°$?

17

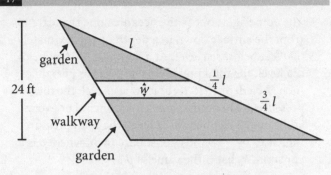

Bridget owns a triangular patch of land. She decides to convert it into a garden with a paved walkway, as shown above. The long sides of the walkway are parallel to each other and to the base of the triangular patch of land. What is the width, w, in feet, of the walkway?

18

$$8x - 5y = 27$$

$$5x + 10y = 30$$

The solution set of the system of equations above is (x, y). What is the value of y ?

19

The epipelagic zone is the oceanic zone that extends from the surface down to a depth of approximately 650 feet below sea level. At a depth of 170 feet below sea level, the total pressure is 90 pounds per square inch. At a depth 215 feet below sea level, the total pressure is 110 pounds per square inch. For every additional 5 feet below sea level, the total pressure increases by p pounds per square inch, where p is a constant. What is the value of p ?

20

If $x^3 - 4x^2 + 3x - 12 = 0$, what real value is a solution for x ?

STOP

If you finish before time is called, you may check your work on this section only.
Do not turn to any other section in the test.

No Test Material On This Page

Math Test – Calculator

55 MINUTES, 38 QUESTIONS

Turn to Section 4 of your answer sheet to answer the questions in this section.

DIRECTIONS

For questions **1-30**, solve each problem, choose the best answer from the choices provided, and fill in the corresponding circle on your answer sheet. For questions **31-38**, solve the problem and enter your answer in the grid on the answer sheet. Please refer to the directions before question 31 on how to enter your answers in the grid. You may use any available space in your test booklet for scratch work.

NOTES

1. The use of a calculator **is permitted**.
2. All variables and expressions used represent real numbers unless otherwise indicated.
3. Figures provided in this test are drawn to scale unless otherwise indicated.
4. All figures lie in a plane unless otherwise indicated.
5. Unless otherwise indicated, the domain of a given function f is the set of all real numbers x for which $f(x)$ is a real number.

REFERENCE

$$A = \pi r^2$$
$$C = 2\pi r$$

$$A = \ell w$$

$$A = \tfrac{1}{2} bh$$

$$c^2 = a^2 + b^2$$

Special Right Triangles

$$V = \ell wh$$

$$V = \pi r^2 h$$

$$V = \tfrac{4}{3}\pi r^3$$

$$V = \tfrac{1}{3}\pi r^2 h$$

$$V = \tfrac{1}{3}\ell wh$$

The number of degrees of arc in a circle is 360.
The number of radians of arc in a circle is 2π.
The sum of the measures in degrees of the angles of a triangle is 180.

CONTINUE

1

To make the high school football team, Walter must be able to run a 40-yard dash in under 6 seconds. Walter currently runs the 40-yard dash in 7.2 seconds, and believes that with training he can reduce his time by 0.2 seconds per week. Which of the following represents the number of seconds in which Walter believes he will be able to run the 40-yard dash w weeks from now?

A) $0.2 - 7.2w$

B) $6.0 - 0.2w$

C) $7.2 + 0.2w$

D) $7.2 - 0.2w$

2

A piece of yarn 4 yards long is cut in half, and each half is cut into fourths. What is the length, in inches, of each of the pieces of yarn? (1 yard = 36 inches)

A)   8

B) 18

C) 24

D) 36

3

A ride-sharing service charges a base fee of $2.40 per ride. The cost of gas is included in the base fee, but there is an additional charge of $0.30 per mile. For one ride, Edward paid $3.60. How many miles long was Edward's ride?

A) 2

B) 3

C) 4

D) 5

4

Yesterday Tiki cycled 13 fewer miles than Irina. If the two of them cycled a total of 51 miles yesterday, how many miles did Irina cycle?

A) 19

B) 32

C) 38

D) 64

CONTINUE

5

The resistance of a circuit is equal to the voltage applied to the circuit divided by the number of amps flowing through the circuit. How many amps are flowing through a circuit with a resistance of 9 ohms if 54 volts are applied to the circuit?

A) 486

B) 45

C) 6

D) 0.167

6

Florence interviewed a random sample of her first-year classmates in medical school to determine the statistical distribution of blood types among the students. Of the 75 students she interviewed, 38.7% had O-positive blood type. Based on this result, about how many of the 265 students in Florence's first-year class would be expected to have O-positive blood type?

A) 40

B) 80

C) 100

D) 110

CONTINUE

Number of Viewers by Favorite Television Network

| Network | Age (years) | | | | | Total |
	18-24	25-34	35-44	45-64	65 and older	
A	3,729	11,471	12,758	4,164	3,284	35,406
B	5,731	19,879	23,480	7,999	5,466	62,555
C	3,798	12,360	15,252	4,643	3,685	39,738
D	2,984	8,975	12,084	3,676	3,053	30,772
Total	16,242	52,685	63,574	20,482	15,488	168,471

A survey asked television viewers to name their one favorite network A, B, C, or D. The table above displays the number of surveyed viewers, categorized by age group and favorite network. According to the table, if a viewer who was 35 to 64 years old at the time of the survey is chosen at random, which of the following is nearest to the probability that the viewer preferred network D ?

A) 0.20

B) 0.35

C) 0.50

D) 0.75

CONTINUE

8

Custom Furniture Made in 2015

Wood species	Furniture type				
	Beds	Chairs	Desks	Tables	Total
Cherry	9	7	0	15	31
Maple	12	6	9	0	27
Walnut	3	1	11	2	17
Total	24	14	20	17	75

The table above shows the 75 pieces of furniture that a custom furniture maker made in 2015, categorized by furniture type and wood species. What proportion of the furniture pieces are desks made of maple?

A) $\dfrac{2}{25}$

B) $\dfrac{3}{25}$

C) $\dfrac{4}{15}$

D) $\dfrac{9}{25}$

9

The graph of line m in the xy-plane passes through Quadrants I, II, and III, but not Quadrant IV. Which of the following must be true about the slope of line m?

A) It is positive.

B) It is negative.

C) It is undefined.

D) It is zero.

10

The graph of the function g in the xy-plane has x-intercepts at –2, 2, and 5. Which of the following could be the function g?

A) $g(x) = (x - 2)^2(x - 5)$

B) $g(x) = (x - 2)(x + 2)(x + 5)$

C) $g(x) = (x + 2)^2(x + 5)$

D) $g(x) = (x - 5)(x - 2)(x + 2)$

CONTINUE

Of the points labeled *P*, *Q*, *R*, and *S*, which point represents the species whose ratio of brain weight to body weight is the least?

A) *P*

B) *Q*

C) *R*

D) *S*

Questions 11 and 12 refer to the following information.

Body weight versus brain weight

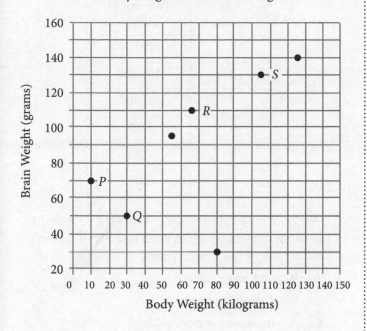

A researcher at a university made the scatterplot above to illustrate the relationship between the body weight and brain weight of 9 species of animals.

What is the brain weight, in grams, of the animal that has the greatest body weight?

A) 70

B) 125

C) 140

D) 160

CONTINUE

13

Which of the scatterplots below illustrates a relationship that is best modeled by the function $f(x) = \left(\dfrac{j}{x}\right)^k$, where j is a positive constant and k is a constant less than -1 ?

A)

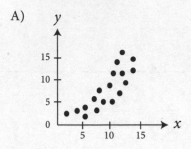

B)

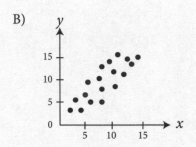

C)

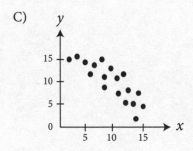

D)

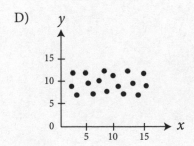

14

The estimated number of bacteria in a laboratory culture over a span of 10 hours is shown in the table below.

Time (hours)	Number of bacteria
0	1,000,000
2	100,000
4	10,000
6	1,000
8	100
10	10

Which of the following is true about the relationship between time and the estimated number of bacteria during the 10-hour time span?

A) It is increasing linearly.

B) It is decreasing linearly.

C) It is increasing exponentially.

D) It is decreasing exponentially.

CONTINUE

15

The expression $20,000\left(1 + \dfrac{p}{400}\right)^4$ shows the value, in dollars, one year after purchase, of a savings bond that has an initial value of $20,000 and that pays an interest rate of p percent, compounded quarterly. If Roger purchased a bond that pays an interest rate of 4 percent and Pete purchased a bond that pays an interest rate of 6 percent, which of the following expressions represents how much more Pete earned than Roger earned, after one year?

A) $20,000\left(1 + \dfrac{6-4}{400}\right)^4$

B) $20,000\left(1 + \dfrac{\frac{6}{4}}{400}\right)^4$

C) $20,000\left(1 + \dfrac{6}{400}\right)^4 - 20,000\left(1 + \dfrac{4}{400}\right)^4$

D) $\dfrac{20,000\left(1 + \dfrac{6}{400}\right)^4}{20,000\left(1 + \dfrac{4}{400}\right)^4}$

Questions 16 and 17 refer to the following information.

Stella is planning a vacation and deciding which travel package to purchase. The table below shows the cost of airfare, hotel, and car rental for three different travel packages.

Travel package	Cost of airfare, A (in dollars)	Cost of hotel, H (in dollars per day)	Cost of car rental, R (in dollars per day)
P	400	85	60
Q	550	75	50
R	500	80	70

The total cost, $f(x)$, of a travel package for x days is given by the function $f(x) = A + H(x-1) + Rx$, where $x \geq 2$.

16

If the relationship between the total cost, $f(x)$, of airfare, hotel, and car rental with travel package R and the number of days, x, for the package is graphed in the xy-plane, the slope of the graph represents which of the following?

A) The combined daily cost of the hotel and car rental

B) The daily cost of the hotel

C) The daily cost of car rental

D) The total cost of airfare

CONTINUE

17

For how many days, x, will the total cost of travel package Q be less than or equal to the total cost of travel package P?

A) $x \leq 8$

B) $x \geq 8$

C) $x \leq 9.4$

D) $x \geq 9.4$

18

A well-known projection known as Moore's law states that the maximum number of transistors that can be placed on an integrated circuit doubles every two years. Which of the following graphs is an accurate representation of Moore's law? (Note: In each graph below, O represents $(0, 0)$.)

A)

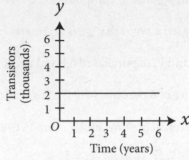

B)

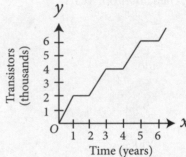

C)

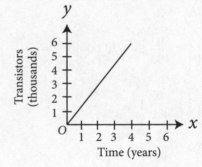

D)

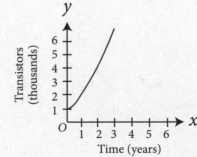

CONTINUE

19

Bob has a number of identical right circular cylindrical buckets, each with an inside diameter of 1 foot. He pours oil from a 55-gallon drum into each bucket until it is full. If the height of the oil in each bucket is approximately 1.5 feet, what is the greatest number of full buckets Bob can pour from one 55-gallon drum of oil? (Note: There are 0.133 cubic feet in 1 gallon.)

A) 6

B) 7

C) 9

D) 10

20

If $2x + 5 \leq 9$, what is the greatest possible value of $2x - 5$?

A) −3

B) −1

C) 0

D) 2

21

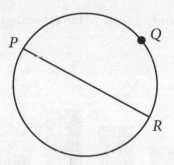

In the figure above, $\overline{PR}$ is a diameter. If the length of arc $\overset{\frown}{PQR}$ is 18π, what is the length of $\overline{PR}$?

A) 6

B) 12

C) 18

D) 36

CONTINUE

Questions 22 and 23 refer to the following information.

Average Temperature

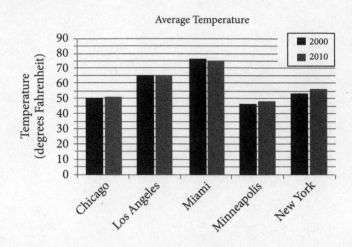

The bar graph above shows the average temperature in degrees Fahrenheit for five select cities in 2000 and 2010.

22

In a scatterplot of this data where the average temperature of each city in the year 2000 is plotted along the x-axis and the average in the year 2010 is plotted along the y-axis, how many data points would be below the line $y = x$?

A) 1

B) 2

C) 3

D) 4

23

Of the following, which best approximates the percent increase in the average temperature of New York from 2000 to 2010 ?

A) 0.5%

B) 1%

C) 6%

D) 12%

CONTINUE

24

The tables below show the distribution of scores of recent quizzes in English and Physics given to the same 33 students of a particular class.

English Quiz

Score	Frequency
1	5
2	7
3	8
4	7
5	6

Physics Quiz

Score	Frequency
1	1
2	2
3	3
4	22
5	5

Which of the following is true about the data provided for the 33 students?

A) The standard deviation of the scores on the English quiz is larger.

B) The standard deviation of scores on the Physics quiz is larger.

C) The standard deviation of the scores on the English quiz is the same as that of the Physics quiz.

D) The standard deviation for the scores on the two quizzes cannot be calculated from the data provided.

25

Let a and b be numbers such that $b < a < -b$. Which of the following must be true?

    I. $a < 0$

    II. $b < 0$

    III. $a < |b|$

A) I only

B) III only

C) I and II only

D) II and III only

CONTINUE

26

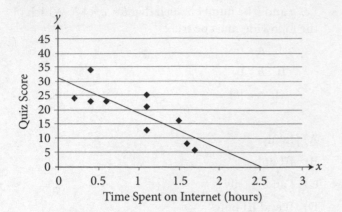

The scatterplot above shows scores on a recent quiz in a particular class and the number of hours the student spent on the Internet the day before. The line of best fit is also shown and can be described as $y = -12.408x + 31$. Which of the following best describes how the number 31 in the equation relates to the scatterplot?

A) On the quiz, even students who spend very little time on the Internet are unlikely to score above 31 on the quiz.

B) On the quiz, even students who spend very little time on the Internet never score above 31 on the quiz.

C) On the quiz, the lowest score was about 31% of the highest score.

D) On the quiz, the highest score on the test was 31.

27

$$r(x) = 3x^3 + 24x^2 + 21x$$

$$s(x) = x^2 + 8x + 7$$

The polynomials $r(x)$ and $s(x)$ are defined above. Which of the following polynomials is divisible by $3x + 4$?

A) $a(x) = r(x) + s(x)$

B) $b(x) = r(x) + 2s(x)$

C) $c(x) = r(x) + 4s(x)$

D) $d(x) = 2r(x) + 4s(x)$

28

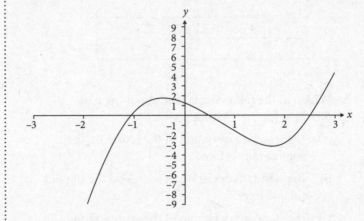

The function $g(x) = x^3 - 2x^2 - 2x + \dfrac{4}{3}$ is graphed in the

xy-plane above. If c is a constant such that $g(x) = c$ has

one real solution, which of the following could be the

value of c ?

A)   3

B)   1

C)   0

D)   −1

CONTINUE

29

$$g(x) = (x - 10)(x + 4)$$

Which of the following is an equivalent of the function g shown above in which the minimum value of g appears as a constant or coefficient?

A) $g(x) = (x + 3)^2 - 31$

B) $g(x) = (x - 3)^2 - 49$

C) $g(x) = x^2 - 6x - 40$

D) $g(x) = x^2 - 40$

30

If a is the average (arithmetic mean) of $4x$ and 7, b is the average of $5x$ and 6, and c is the average of $3x$ and 11, what is the average of a, b, and c, in terms of x?

A) $x + 4$

B) $x + 8$

C) $2x + 4$

D) $4x + 8$

CONTINUE

DIRECTIONS

For questions 31-38, solve the problem and enter your answer in the grid, as described below, on the answer sheet.

1. Although not required, it is suggested that you write your answer in the boxes at the top of the columns to help you fill in the circles accurately. You will receive credit only if the circles are filled in correctly.

2. Mark no more than one circle in any column.

3. No question has a negative answer.

4. Some problems may have more than one correct answer. In such cases, grid only one answer.

5. **Mixed numbers** such as $3\frac{1}{2}$ must be gridded as 3.5 or 7/2. (If 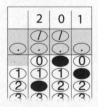 is entered into the grid, it will be interpreted as $\frac{31}{2}$, not as $3\frac{1}{2}$.)

6. **Decimal Answers:** If you obtain a decimal answer with more digits than the grid can accommodate, it may be either rounded or truncated, but it must fill the entire grid.

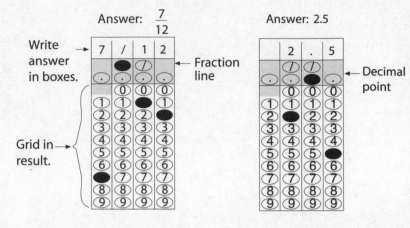

Answer: $\frac{7}{12}$

Write answer in boxes. ← Fraction line

Grid in result.

Answer: 2.5 ← Decimal point

Acceptable ways to grid $\frac{2}{3}$ are:

Answer: 201 – either position is correct

NOTE: You may start your answers in any column, space permitting. Columns you don't need to use should be left blank.

CONTINUE ➤

31

The target heart rate during moderate activity R, in beats per minute, for an adult who is y years old can be estimated using the equation $R = \dfrac{3(220 - y)}{5}$. According to this estimate, for every increase of 2 years in age, by how many beats per minute will the target heart rate for adults engaged in moderate activity decrease?

32

At 1:00 P.M., a truck driver is 200 miles into a long journey to make a delivery. The driver continues on the journey and travels at an average speed of 60 miles per hour. How many total miles into the journey will the driver be at 8:00 P.M.?

33

$$d = \frac{1}{2}at^2$$

The displacement d of an object in a vacuum, starting from rest with an acceleration a can be found using the formula above, where t is the time the object has been moving. A physics student uses the formula to determine the displacement of an object in a vacuum accelerating from rest for time t and an object with the same acceleration from rest for time $2.5t$. What is the ratio of the displacement of the object that accelerated for more time to the displacement of the object that accelerated for less time?

34

The *deben*, an ancient Egyptian unit of weight, is approximately equal to 3.21 ounces. It is also equivalent to 12 smaller Egyptian units called *shematies*. Based on these relationships, 488 shematies is equal to how many <u>pounds</u>, to the nearest hundredth? (16 ounces = 1 pound)

CONTINUE

35

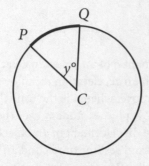

Note: Figure not drawn to scale.

The circle above has center C and has a radius of 20. If the length of arc $\overset{\frown}{PQ}$ (shown in bold) is between 15 and 16, what is one possible <u>integer</u> value of y?

36

A toy store keeps marbles in the closet of its stock room. In the closet, 230 marbles are blue and 370 marbles are red. If 110 red marbles are added, how many blue marbles must be added to the closet so that $\frac{2}{5}$ of the marbles in the closet are blue?

Questions 37 and 38 refer to the following information.

A CD account contains \$5,400 today. The account earns an annual interest of 7% for each of the next four years. The bank uses the equation $A = 5,400(r)^y$ to determine the amount of money in the account, A, after y years if no other deposits or withdrawals are made.

37

What numerical value should the bank use for r?

38

To the nearest dollar, how much money will be in the CD account at the end of the four years? (Note: Disregard the \$ sign when gridding your answer.)

STOP
If you finish before time is called, you may check your work on this section only.
Do not turn to any other section in the test.

No Test Material On This Page

SAT Essay

DIRECTIONS

The essay gives you an opportunity to show how effectively you can read and comprehend a passage and write an essay analyzing the passage. In your essay you should demonstrate that you have read the passage carefully, present a clear and logical analysis, and use language precisely.

Your essay must be written on the lines provided in your answer sheet booklet; except for the planning page of the answer booklet, you will receive no other paper on which to write. You will have enough space if you write on every line, avoid wide margins, and keep your handwriting to a reasonable size. Remember that people who are not familiar with your handwriting will read what you write. Try to write or print so that what you are writing is legible to those readers.

You have <u>50 minutes</u> to read the passage and write an essay in response to the prompt provided inside this booklet.

REMINDER

— Do not write your essay in this booklet. Only what you write on the lined pages of your answer booklet will be evaluated.

— An off-topic essay will not be evaluated.

CONTINUE →

As you read the passage below, consider how President Obama uses

- evidence, such as facts or examples, to support claims.
- reasoning to develop ideas and to connect claims and evidence.
- stylistic or persuasive elements, such as word choice or appeals to emotion, to add power to the ideas expressed.

Excerpted from a speech given by President Barack Obama at the First Session of COP21, the United Nations Climate Change conference. The speech was delivered at Le Bourget in Paris, France on November 30, 2015.

1   President Hollande, Mr. Secretary General, fellow leaders. We have come to Paris to show our resolve...

2   Nearly 200 nations have assembled here this week—a declaration that for all the challenges we face, the growing threat of climate change could define the contours of this century more dramatically than any other. What should give us hope that this is a turning point, that this is the moment we finally determined we would save our planet, is the fact that our nations share a sense of urgency about this challenge and a growing realization that it is within our power to do something about it.

3   Our understanding of the ways human beings disrupt the climate advances by the day. Fourteen of the fifteen warmest years on record have occurred since the year 2000—and 2015 is on pace to be the warmest year of all. No nation—large or small, wealthy or poor— is immune to what this means.

4   This summer, I saw the effects of climate change firsthand in our northernmost state, Alaska, where the sea is already swallowing villages and eroding shorelines; where permafrost thaws and the tundra burns; where glaciers are melting at a pace unprecedented in modern times. And it was a preview of one possible future—a glimpse of our children's fate if the climate keeps changing faster than our efforts to address it. Submerged countries. Abandoned cities. Fields that no longer grow. Political disruptions that trigger new conflict, and even more floods of desperate peoples seeking the sanctuary of nations not their own.

5   That future is not one of strong economies, nor is it one where fragile states can find their footing. That future is one that we have the power to change. Right here. Right now. But only if we rise to this moment. As one of America's governors has said, "We are the first generation to feel the impact of climate change, and the last generation that can do something about it."

6   I've come here personally, as the leader of the world's largest economy and the second-largest emitter, to say that the United States of America not only recognizes our role in creating this problem, we embrace our responsibility to do something about it.

CONTINUE ▶

7   Over the last seven years, we've made ambitious investments in clean energy, and ambitious reductions in our carbon emissions. We've multiplied wind power threefold, and solar power more than twentyfold, helping create parts of America where these clean power sources are finally cheaper than dirtier, conventional power. We've invested in energy efficiency in every way imaginable. We've said no to infrastructure that would pull high-carbon fossil fuels from the ground, and we've said yes to the first-ever set of national standards limiting the amount of carbon pollution our power plants can release into the sky.

8   The advances we've made have helped drive our economic output to all-time highs, and drive our carbon pollution to its lowest levels in nearly two decades...

9   And, my fellow leaders, accepting this challenge will not reward us with moments of victory that are clear or quick. Our progress will be measured differently—in the suffering that is averted, and a planet that's preserved. And that's what's always made this so hard. Our generation may not even live to see the full realization of what we do here. But the knowledge that the next generation will be better off for what we do here—can we imagine a more worthy reward than that? Passing that on to our children and our grandchildren, so that when they look back and they see what we did here in Paris, they can take pride in our achievement.

10   Let that be the common purpose here in Paris. A world that is worthy of our children. A world that is marked not by conflict, but by cooperation; and not by human suffering, but by human progress. A world that's safer, and more prosperous, and more secure, and more free than the one that we inherited.

11   Let's get to work. Thank you very much. (Applause.)

Write an essay in which you explain how President Obama builds an argument to advocate for world efforts to combat climate change. In your essay, analyze how Obama uses one or more of the features listed in the box above (or features of your own choice) to strengthen the logic and persuasiveness of his argument. Be sure that your analysis focuses on the most relevant features of the passage.

Your essay should not explain whether you agree with Obama's claims, but rather explain how Obama builds an argument to persuade his audience.

END OF TEST

DO NOT RETURN TO A PREVIOUS SECTION.

The **Princeton Review**®

Completely darken bubbles with a No. 2 pencil. If you make a mistake, be sure to erase mark completely. Erase all stray marks.

1.

YOUR NAME: _____
(Print)   Last   First   M.I.

SIGNATURE: _____   DATE: __ / __ / __

HOME ADDRESS: _____
(Print)   Number and Street

_____
City   State   Zip Code

PHONE NO.: _____
(Print)

IMPORTANT: Please fill in these boxes exactly as shown on the back cover of your test book.

2. TEST FORM

6. DATE OF BIRTH

Month	Day	Year
○ JAN		
○ FEB	⓪ ⓪	⓪ ⓪
○ MAR	① ①	① ①
○ APR	② ②	② ②
○ MAY	③ ③	③ ③
○ JUN	④ ④	④
○ JUL	⑤ ⑤	⑤
○ AUG	⑥ ⑥	⑥
○ SEP	⑦ ⑦	⑦
○ OCT	⑧ ⑧	⑧
○ NOV	⑨ ⑨	⑨
○ DEC		

3. TEST CODE

⓪ Ⓐ Ⓙ ⓪ ⓪
① Ⓑ Ⓚ ① ①
② Ⓒ Ⓛ ② ②
③ Ⓓ Ⓜ ③ ③
④ Ⓔ Ⓝ ④ ④
⑤ Ⓕ Ⓞ ⑤ ⑤
⑥ Ⓖ Ⓟ ⑥ ⑥
⑦ Ⓗ Ⓠ ⑦ ⑦
⑧ Ⓘ Ⓡ ⑧ ⑧
⑨ ⑨ ⑨

4. REGISTRATION NUMBER

⓪ ⓪ ⓪ ⓪ ⓪ ⓪ ⓪
① ① ① ① ① ① ①
② ② ② ② ② ② ②
③ ③ ③ ③ ③ ③ ③
④ ④ ④ ④ ④ ④ ④
⑤ ⑤ ⑤ ⑤ ⑤ ⑤ ⑤
⑥ ⑥ ⑥ ⑥ ⑥ ⑥ ⑥
⑦ ⑦ ⑦ ⑦ ⑦ ⑦ ⑦
⑧ ⑧ ⑧ ⑧ ⑧ ⑧ ⑧
⑨ ⑨ ⑨ ⑨ ⑨ ⑨ ⑨

7. SEX
○ MALE
○ FEMALE

The **Princeton Review**®

5. YOUR NAME

First 4 letters of last name				FIRST INIT	MID INIT

(Columns of bubbles A through Z for each letter position, FIRST INIT, and MID INIT)

Ⓐ Ⓑ Ⓒ Ⓓ Ⓔ Ⓕ Ⓖ Ⓗ Ⓘ Ⓙ Ⓚ Ⓛ Ⓜ Ⓝ Ⓞ Ⓟ Ⓠ Ⓡ Ⓢ Ⓣ Ⓤ Ⓥ Ⓦ Ⓧ Ⓨ Ⓩ

Test ④   Start with number 1 for each new section.
If a section has fewer questions than answer spaces, leave the extra answer spaces blank.

Section 1—Reading

1. Ⓐ Ⓑ Ⓒ Ⓓ
2. Ⓐ Ⓑ Ⓒ Ⓓ
3. Ⓐ Ⓑ Ⓒ Ⓓ
4. Ⓐ Ⓑ Ⓒ Ⓓ
5. Ⓐ Ⓑ Ⓒ Ⓓ
6. Ⓐ Ⓑ Ⓒ Ⓓ
7. Ⓐ Ⓑ Ⓒ Ⓓ
8. Ⓐ Ⓑ Ⓒ Ⓓ
9. Ⓐ Ⓑ Ⓒ Ⓓ
10. Ⓐ Ⓑ Ⓒ Ⓓ
11. Ⓐ Ⓑ Ⓒ Ⓓ
12. Ⓐ Ⓑ Ⓒ Ⓓ
13. Ⓐ Ⓑ Ⓒ Ⓓ
14. Ⓐ Ⓑ Ⓒ Ⓓ
15. Ⓐ Ⓑ Ⓒ Ⓓ
16. Ⓐ Ⓑ Ⓒ Ⓓ
17. Ⓐ Ⓑ Ⓒ Ⓓ
18. Ⓐ Ⓑ Ⓒ Ⓓ
19. Ⓐ Ⓑ Ⓒ Ⓓ
20. Ⓐ Ⓑ Ⓒ Ⓓ
21. Ⓐ Ⓑ Ⓒ Ⓓ
22. Ⓐ Ⓑ Ⓒ Ⓓ
23. Ⓐ Ⓑ Ⓒ Ⓓ
24. Ⓐ Ⓑ Ⓒ Ⓓ
25. Ⓐ Ⓑ Ⓒ Ⓓ
26. Ⓐ Ⓑ Ⓒ Ⓓ
27. Ⓐ Ⓑ Ⓒ Ⓓ
28. Ⓐ Ⓑ Ⓒ Ⓓ
29. Ⓐ Ⓑ Ⓒ Ⓓ
30. Ⓐ Ⓑ Ⓒ Ⓓ
31. Ⓐ Ⓑ Ⓒ Ⓓ
32. Ⓐ Ⓑ Ⓒ Ⓓ
33. Ⓐ Ⓑ Ⓒ Ⓓ
34. Ⓐ Ⓑ Ⓒ Ⓓ
35. Ⓐ Ⓑ Ⓒ Ⓓ
36. Ⓐ Ⓑ Ⓒ Ⓓ
37. Ⓐ Ⓑ Ⓒ Ⓓ
38. Ⓐ Ⓑ Ⓒ Ⓓ
39. Ⓐ Ⓑ Ⓒ Ⓓ
40. Ⓐ Ⓑ Ⓒ Ⓓ
41. Ⓐ Ⓑ Ⓒ Ⓓ
42. Ⓐ Ⓑ Ⓒ Ⓓ
43. Ⓐ Ⓑ Ⓒ Ⓓ
44. Ⓐ Ⓑ Ⓒ Ⓓ
45. Ⓐ Ⓑ Ⓒ Ⓓ
46. Ⓐ Ⓑ Ⓒ Ⓓ
47. Ⓐ Ⓑ Ⓒ Ⓓ
48. Ⓐ Ⓑ Ⓒ Ⓓ
49. Ⓐ Ⓑ Ⓒ Ⓓ
50. Ⓐ Ⓑ Ⓒ Ⓓ
51. Ⓐ Ⓑ Ⓒ Ⓓ
52. Ⓐ Ⓑ Ⓒ Ⓓ

Section 2—Writing and Language Skills

1. Ⓐ Ⓑ Ⓒ Ⓓ
2. Ⓐ Ⓑ Ⓒ Ⓓ
3. Ⓐ Ⓑ Ⓒ Ⓓ
4. Ⓐ Ⓑ Ⓒ Ⓓ
5. Ⓐ Ⓑ Ⓒ Ⓓ
6. Ⓐ Ⓑ Ⓒ Ⓓ
7. Ⓐ Ⓑ Ⓒ Ⓓ
8. Ⓐ Ⓑ Ⓒ Ⓓ
9. Ⓐ Ⓑ Ⓒ Ⓓ
10. Ⓐ Ⓑ Ⓒ Ⓓ
11. Ⓐ Ⓑ Ⓒ Ⓓ
12. Ⓐ Ⓑ Ⓒ Ⓓ
13. Ⓐ Ⓑ Ⓒ Ⓓ
14. Ⓐ Ⓑ Ⓒ Ⓓ
15. Ⓐ Ⓑ Ⓒ Ⓓ
16. Ⓐ Ⓑ Ⓒ Ⓓ
17. Ⓐ Ⓑ Ⓒ Ⓓ
18. Ⓐ Ⓑ Ⓒ Ⓓ
19. Ⓐ Ⓑ Ⓒ Ⓓ
20. Ⓐ Ⓑ Ⓒ Ⓓ
21. Ⓐ Ⓑ Ⓒ Ⓓ
22. Ⓐ Ⓑ Ⓒ Ⓓ
23. Ⓐ Ⓑ Ⓒ Ⓓ
24. Ⓐ Ⓑ Ⓒ Ⓓ
25. Ⓐ Ⓑ Ⓒ Ⓓ
26. Ⓐ Ⓑ Ⓒ Ⓓ
27. Ⓐ Ⓑ Ⓒ Ⓓ
28. Ⓐ Ⓑ Ⓒ Ⓓ
29. Ⓐ Ⓑ Ⓒ Ⓓ
30. Ⓐ Ⓑ Ⓒ Ⓓ
31. Ⓐ Ⓑ Ⓒ Ⓓ
32. Ⓐ Ⓑ Ⓒ Ⓓ
33. Ⓐ Ⓑ Ⓒ Ⓓ
34. Ⓐ Ⓑ Ⓒ Ⓓ
35. Ⓐ Ⓑ Ⓒ Ⓓ
36. Ⓐ Ⓑ Ⓒ Ⓓ
37. Ⓐ Ⓑ Ⓒ Ⓓ
38. Ⓐ Ⓑ Ⓒ Ⓓ
39. Ⓐ Ⓑ Ⓒ Ⓓ
40. Ⓐ Ⓑ Ⓒ Ⓓ
41. Ⓐ Ⓑ Ⓒ Ⓓ
42. Ⓐ Ⓑ Ⓒ Ⓓ
43. Ⓐ Ⓑ Ⓒ Ⓓ
44. Ⓐ Ⓑ Ⓒ Ⓓ

Test 4

Start with number 1 for each new section.
If a section has fewer questions than answer spaces, leave the extra answer spaces blank.

Section 3—Mathematics: No Calculator

1. Ⓐ Ⓑ Ⓒ Ⓓ
2. Ⓐ Ⓑ Ⓒ Ⓓ
3. Ⓐ Ⓑ Ⓒ Ⓓ
4. Ⓐ Ⓑ Ⓒ Ⓓ
5. Ⓐ Ⓑ Ⓒ Ⓓ
6. Ⓐ Ⓑ Ⓒ Ⓓ
7. Ⓐ Ⓑ Ⓒ Ⓓ
8. Ⓐ Ⓑ Ⓒ Ⓓ
9. Ⓐ Ⓑ Ⓒ Ⓓ
10. Ⓐ Ⓑ Ⓒ Ⓓ
11. Ⓐ Ⓑ Ⓒ Ⓓ
12. Ⓐ Ⓑ Ⓒ Ⓓ
13. Ⓐ Ⓑ Ⓒ Ⓓ
14. Ⓐ Ⓑ Ⓒ Ⓓ
15. Ⓐ Ⓑ Ⓒ Ⓓ

16. 17. 18. 19. 20.

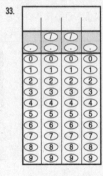

Section 4—Mathematics: Calculator

1. Ⓐ Ⓑ Ⓒ Ⓓ
2. Ⓐ Ⓑ Ⓒ Ⓓ
3. Ⓐ Ⓑ Ⓒ Ⓓ
4. Ⓐ Ⓑ Ⓒ Ⓓ
5. Ⓐ Ⓑ Ⓒ Ⓓ
6. Ⓐ Ⓑ Ⓒ Ⓓ
7. Ⓐ Ⓑ Ⓒ Ⓓ
8. Ⓐ Ⓑ Ⓒ Ⓓ
9. Ⓐ Ⓑ Ⓒ Ⓓ
10. Ⓐ Ⓑ Ⓒ Ⓓ
11. Ⓐ Ⓑ Ⓒ Ⓓ
12. Ⓐ Ⓑ Ⓒ Ⓓ
13. Ⓐ Ⓑ Ⓒ Ⓓ
14. Ⓐ Ⓑ Ⓒ Ⓓ
15. Ⓐ Ⓑ Ⓒ Ⓓ
16. Ⓐ Ⓑ Ⓒ Ⓓ
17. Ⓐ Ⓑ Ⓒ Ⓓ
18. Ⓐ Ⓑ Ⓒ Ⓓ
19. Ⓐ Ⓑ Ⓒ Ⓓ
20. Ⓐ Ⓑ Ⓒ Ⓓ
21. Ⓐ Ⓑ Ⓒ Ⓓ
22. Ⓐ Ⓑ Ⓒ Ⓓ
23. Ⓐ Ⓑ Ⓒ Ⓓ
24. Ⓐ Ⓑ Ⓒ Ⓓ
25. Ⓐ Ⓑ Ⓒ Ⓓ
26. Ⓐ Ⓑ Ⓒ Ⓓ
27. Ⓐ Ⓑ Ⓒ Ⓓ
28. Ⓐ Ⓑ Ⓒ Ⓓ
29. Ⓐ Ⓑ Ⓒ Ⓓ
30. Ⓐ Ⓑ Ⓒ Ⓓ

31. 32. 33. 34. 35.

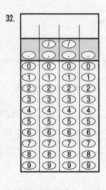

36. 37. 38.

Chapter 10
Practice Test 4:
Answers and
Explanations

PRACTICE TEST 4 ANSWER KEY

Section 1: Reading

1.	B	27.	A
2.	D	28.	C
3.	C	29.	C
4.	B	30.	B
5.	D	31.	B
6.	A	32.	D
7.	A	33.	A
8.	C	34.	A
9.	C	35.	B
10.	D	36.	A
11.	B	37.	C
12.	B	38.	D
13.	A	39.	A
14.	D	40.	B
15.	C	41.	B
16.	D	42.	C
17.	C	43.	D
18.	C	44.	B
19.	A	45.	B
20.	A	46.	C
21.	D	47.	B
22.	C	48.	D
23.	A	49.	C
24.	B	50.	C
25.	D	51.	A
26.	A	52.	A

Section 2: Writing & Language

1.	A	23.	C
2.	D	24.	A
3.	C	25.	B
4.	D	26.	D
5.	B	27.	C
6.	D	28.	B
7.	C	29.	C
8.	D	30.	A
9.	D	31.	A
10.	B	32.	A
11.	D	33.	C
12.	A	34.	A
13.	D	35.	C
14.	B	36.	B
15.	B	37.	A
16.	A	38.	A
17.	C	39.	D
18.	A	40.	B
19.	D	41.	B
20.	D	42.	C
21.	A	43.	D
22.	D	44.	C

Section 3: Math (No Calculator)

1.	B
2.	B
3.	D
4.	A
5.	A
6.	D
7.	C
8.	C
9.	D
10.	B
11.	A
12.	A
13.	C
14.	C
15.	B
16.	$\frac{5}{8}$ or .625
17.	3
18.	1
19.	$\frac{20}{9}$ or 2.22
20.	4

Section 4: Math (Calculator)

1.	D	20.	B
2.	B	21.	D
3.	C	22.	A
4.	B	23.	C
5.	C	24.	A
6.	C	25.	D
7.	A	26.	A
8.	B	27.	C
9.	A	28.	A
10.	D	29.	B
11.	C	30.	C
12.	D	31.	1.2
13.	A	32.	620
14.	D	33.	$\frac{25}{4}$, $\frac{50}{8}$, or 6.25
15.	C		
16.	A		
17.	B		
18.	D	34.	8.16
19.	A	35.	43, 44, or 45
		36.	90
		37.	1.07
		38.	7,078

For self-scoring assessment tables, please turn to page 565.

PRACTICE TEST 4 EXPLANATIONS

Section 1: Reading

1. **B** This is a general question that asks about the narrator's shift in focus through the passage. Save this question until the end of the set, because the big picture will be clearer after all the specific questions have been answered. At the beginning of the passage, the narrator is uneasy about the Uncharted Forest, but as the passage progresses he begins to say things like, *And we wonder*, or *We shall not ask this question... and yet...*. Eliminate (A) because the narrator never prepares to explore a frontier. Choice (B) refers to a shift from *disquiet* to *curiosity*, which can be supported with the text. Keep (B). Choice (C) might look good initally, because the narrator does acknowledge the ancient city. He never *dismisses* it, though, so eliminate (C). Choice (D) can be eliminated because, although the narrator mentions the Council's rules, there's no shift from *repetition... to acceptance*. Choice (B) is the correct answer.

2. **D** This is a best evidence question, so consider the lines used to predict the answer to the previous question. The correct answer to this question should support *a shift* in the narrator's focus. Choice (A) can be eliminated because those lines don't refer to the narrator's focus. Choice (B) could refer to the *disquiet about the unknown*, but there's no support for a shift. Eliminate (B). Choice (C) does not refer to the narrator at all, so eliminate it. Choice (D) contains the phrase *and yet,* which indicates a change. In context, the lines show the narrator shifting from *we shall not ask this question* to wondering about that very question. This supports the answer to Q1. Choice (D) is the correct answer.

3. **C** This question asks about the meaning of the phrase *all must agree with all* in the context of the passage. Find evidence in the text to predict the answer. The text further explains the brothers are silent because they don't know if their *thoughts are the thoughts of all*. The phrase must mean something like *all in agreement*. Choice (A) can be eliminated because there's nothing in the text about whether the thoughts are actually true or not. Choices (B) and (D) can be eliminated for similar reasons because the text never talks about the accuracy or meaning of language. The brothers must simply agree, regardless of the truth. Choice (C), *thought must be uniform,* matches the prediction. Choice (C) is the right answer.

4. **B** This question asks about the role of the indicated sentence, so find evidence in the text to explain the function of the sentence. Before the sentence, the narrator mentions the *Uncharted Forest* and says *we do not wish to look upon…we do not wish to think of it. But ever do our eyes return to that black patch*. The *but* indicates a contrast, showing that even though the narrator may not wish to think about it, he definitely does. After the indicated sentence, the narrator provides evidence that the people know very little about the Uncharted Forest, and the only things he has heard have been dismissed as legend. Choice (A) can be eliminated because there is no indication that the Forest is an immediate threat or that the narrator's job is to guard anything. Choice (B)

matches the prediction, so don't eliminate it. Choice (C) does match the part that the narrator keeps looking at the horizon, but it doesn't address *why* he is looking in that direction. Eliminate (C). Choice (D) might initially look good because there is a repeated action and something unexplainable, but there's nothing in the text to support *confusion*. Eliminate (D). This leaves (B), which is supported by the text and is the correct answer.

5. **D**   This question asks about a *person who wished to navigate the Uncharted Forest*. Find the reference and read the window. In the middle of the second paragraph, the narrator says *Men never enter the Uncharted Forest, for there is no power to explore it and no path to lead among its ancient trees*. The narrator is pretty clear that anyone wishing to navigate the Uncharted Forest is going to have a lot of trouble because there's no path, or map, or any good way to get through it. Choices (A) and (C) can be eliminated immediately because they have nothing to do with the prediction. Choice (B) doesn't quite match the prediction because the text focuses on the men getting lost in the Forest rather than on objects already lost in the woods. Eliminate (B). Choice (D) is the correct answer.

6. **A**   These are the lines used to answer the previous question. Choice (A) is the correct answer.

7. **A**   This question asks about the narrator's view of the secrets of the past. He knows the secrets exist, but he doesn't know the secrets themselves. He pays attention and wonders about the legends and stories. He equates seeking answers to the questions with *calling death upon our head*. The narrator is fascinated by the secrets of the past but also afraid of this curiosity because it is forbidden. Choice (A) matches this prediction, so keep it. Choice (B) can be eliminated because the text makes it clear that the answers to the secrets are not *easily pursuable*. Choice (C) does not match the prediction because the narrator is doing a very good job of avoiding exploring the secrets. Choice (D) can be eliminated because there is no mention of authenticity in the text. Choice (A) is the correct answer.

8. **C**   This question asks about the inference that can be made from the given line. Find the line and carefully read the window around it to determine what clues are in the text about the meaning of the line. The Uncharted Forests have *grown over the ruins of many cities* and the *trees have swallowed…all things which perished*. The narrator means that anything that existed in the ancient cities is now covered up and destroyed by the growth of the Forests. Choice (A) can be eliminated because there's no stated connection in these lines between people in the narrator's society and the ancient cities. Choice (B) can be eliminated because the trees mentioned in the lines are covering the ancient cities, not living within them. Choice (C) matches the prediction, so don't eliminate it. Choice (D) can be eliminated because the text indicates that the Forest is forbidden, and there is no evidence that the Forest is used for any literal purpose. Choice (C) is the correct answer.

9. **C**   This is a Vocab-in-Context question, so go back to the text, find the phrase *how it came to pass* in lines 30–31, and cross it out. Replace it with another phrase that makes sense in the sentence based on the context of the passage. The phrase means something like *what happened*

back then. Choices (A) and (B) can be eliminated because nothing is crossing anything else or going in a circle. Choice (C) matches the prediction. Choice (D) might initially look good because it connects to the passage of time, but the original phrase refers to what actually happened in the past, not how time moved from the past to the present. Choice (C) is the correct answer.

10. **D** This is a Vocab-in-Context question, so go back to the text, find the word *scripts* in line 39, and cross it out. Replace it with another word that makes sense in the sentence based on the context of the passage. The author refers to the *words of the Unmentionable Times*, so *scripts* must have to do with something written. Eliminate (A) and (B). There is no evidence in the text that the words are specifically screenplays, or even that there are movies at all, so (C) can be eliminated. Choice (D) is the correct answer.

11. **B** This question asks about the *case against gentrification* according to the passage. Notice that the next question is a best evidence question, so these two can be done in tandem. This is an efficient way to look for evidence in the text if there isn't a given line reference. Consider the answers for Q12 first to see if they support any of the answers in Q11. Choice (12A) is a quote from a bartender that *barmen* are now *mixologists*. That doesn't support any of the answers for Q11, so eliminate it. Choice (12B) talks about how the *newcomers crowd out older residents*, which is a direct paraphrase of (11B). Draw a line connecting those two answer choices. Choice (12C) does not support any of the answers to Q11, so it can be eliminated. Choice (12D) supports (11C), so connect those two answers. Because neither (11A) nor (11D) has support in Q12, those two answers can also be eliminated. Return to the question. It asks about a case *against* gentrification. While the (11C)/(12D) pair may be true, it provides a case *for* gentrification, so it can be eliminated. This leaves (11B) and (12B), which support each other and answer the question. Choices (11B) and (12B) are the correct answers.

12. **B** (See explanation above.)

13. **A** This question asks who moved into census tracts that were poor in 2000. Look for the year 2000, find it in paragraph three, and read the following: *In Washington, according to a study by Governing magazine, 52% of census tracts that were poor in 2000 have since gentrified—more than in any other city bar Portland, Oregon. Young, mostly white singletons have crowded into a district once built for families.* According to this evidence, the correct answer would be white singletons. Choose (A), and eliminate (B), (C), and (D). The correct answer is (A).

14. **D** This is a Vocab-in-Context question, so go back to the text, find the word *soaring* in line 37, and cross it out. Replace it with another word that makes sense in the sentence based on the context of the passage. Since it's prices doing the *soaring*, a word like *increasing* would make sense. Compare this prediction to the four answer choices: neither (A), (B), nor (C) fits the prediction, although two of them could mean *soaring* in another context. Choice (D), *rising*, fits the prediction perfectly. Choice (D) is the correct answer.

15. **C** This question asks for the best summary of paragraph five. So read paragraph five, and then summarize the text before looking at the answer choices. This paragraph starts with a claim (*Yet there is little evidence that gentrification is responsible for displacing the poor or minorities*) and continues with three bits of evidence to support that claim. The paragraph concludes by noting that minorities' incomes in gentrified areas have soared. So the best summary of the paragraph will be one that conveys the idea that when poor minority populations leave cities, it's not always because of gentrification. Choice (A) is true, but too specific. This is a common trap for main idea questions. Choice (B) is deceptive: It mentions two cities that are in the paragraph, but tells a negative story rather than counters a negative story. Choice (C) fits the prediction that gentrification is not always the reason certain populations leave cities, so keep it. Choice (D) might look good initially because of the final sentence of the paragraph. However, there is only one detail in the paragraph that fits this story of profit, namely the detail about average incomes soaring, so (D) is too broad. Choice (C), on the other hand, fits the paragraph's opening claim as well as its overall purpose. Choice (C) is the correct answer.

16. **D** This question asks what the passage implies about gentrifiers moving into communities. Notice that Q17 is a best evidence question, so Q16 and Q17 can be answered in tandem. First, read over the answer choices to Q16. Next, look at the answer choices to Q17 to see whether they provide support for anything in Q16. Choice (17A) refers to text that implies that gentrifiers are not responsible for displacing the poor or minorities. This does not fit any of the answer choices in Q16, so eliminate (17A). Choice (17B) refers to text that discusses the increase in incomes of black people with high-school diplomas. This choice supports the idea that gentrification can be good, which (16D) indicates, so connect (17B) to (16D). Choice (17C) refers to text that discusses how the effects of gentrification include improving local services. This choice also supports the idea that gentrification can be good, which (16D) indicates, so connect (17C) to (16D). Choice (17D) refers to text that states that gentrification is not a problem, and that turns attention to another problem. This does not fit any of the answer choices in Q16, so eliminate (17D). At this point, the only answer choice with support in Q16 is (16D), so eliminate (16A), (16B), and (16C). Choice (16D) has two answers from Q17 connected to it, so go back to the text to see which one is most closely connected to the benefits of genetrifiers moving into communities. While (17B) is a positive thing, it's not directly connected to gentrifiers moving in. Choice (17C) is, however. Choices (16D) and (17C) are the correct answers.

17. **C** (See explanation above.)

18. **C** This is a Vocab-in-Context question, so go back to the text, find the word *generates* in line 62, and cross it out. Replace it with another word that makes sense in the sentence based on the context of the passage. A word like *makes* would make sense. Compare this prediction to the four answer choices. Neither (A), *powers*, (B), *ages*, nor (D), *increases*, means *makes*. Eliminate them. Choice (C), *creates*, means *makes*, so select it. The correct answer is (C).

19. **A** This question asks about the information in the chart and how the author would consider it. Go back to the chart and look at how the information in the chart fits with the passage. The chart has information about the change in poverty levels in certain census tracts from 1970 to 2010. It shows that a majority of the tracts remained in high poverty over that time span. Look above or below the chart in the passage to get information about the context of the information. The passage says that *Stuart Butler of the Brookings Institution, a think-tank...* says the bigger problem for most American cities is *the concentration of poverty*. The statistics in the chart support this idea. The correct answer to this question should be something like *support Butler's idea*. Choice (A) looks solid according to the prediction, so keep it. Choice (B) does mention *proof*, but the main argument in this passage is about gentrification, not poverty levels, so (B) can be eliminated. Choice (C) throws in the attractive phrase *think-tank,* but the data is not *ambiguous*. Eliminate (C). Choice (D) can be eliminated because Butler uses the data, so it is useful. Choice (A) is the correct answer.

20. **A** This question asks what the chart says about most high-poverty census tracts in 1970. So look at the chart. All data presented there concern high-poverty census tracts, so what is true about *most* of them? Sixty-six percent are listed as *still high poverty*, so the correct answer will fit this prediction. Choice (A) fits, so keep it. Choices (B) and (C) are both on the chart, but do not show *most* of the high poverty tracts. Eliminate these two answer choices. Consider (D) carefully. The percentage of *high poverty tracts* in 2010 was 66% of what it was in 1970, so the level of high poverty did not increase. Eliminate (D). Choice (A) is the correct answer.

21. **D** This question asks what the chart suggests about poor areas. Since the answer choices all contain fractions, the correct answer will match the numbers as well as the concepts presented in the chart. Choice (A) refers to the number of poor people. The chart does not give information about the numbers, so eliminate (A). Choices (B) and (C) both describe what might happen in the future; the chart compares areas from 1970 to 2010. Thus both (B) and (C) are out of scope; eliminate them. Choice (D) refers to 2/3 of high-poverty areas, which fits the 66% in the graph, and (D) says that they *may remain impoverished*, which is also what the graph indicates. Choice (D) is the correct answer.

22. **C** This question asks about the main purpose of the passage, so don't answer it until after the other questions. The main purpose of the passage is to discuss how the authors investigated whether an ancient mural in Turkey depicts an actual eruption by proving that there was an eruption nearby at approximately the same time. Choice (A) can be eliminated because the passage doesn't discuss multiple geologic ages. Choice (B) can be eliminated because although the passage mentions radiometric aging, it never explains the ways in which it was used. It's also not the main idea. Choice (C) closely matches the prediction, so keep it. Choice (D) similarly doesn't explain how the pumice veneer forms nor is this the main idea, so this answer can be eliminated. Choice (C) is the correct answer.

23. **A** This question is a general question so answer it at the end of the question set. The passage primarily focuses on whether the mural could be a depiction of a real volcano and how the authors set about proving this, but the fifth paragraph states *This view, however, has been contested, largely because of the extraordinary age of the mural, and the absence of any other landscape art or map until much later in history. The depiction of a leopard skin underlain by geometric patterns has been proposed instead.* This is a criticism of the theory that the passage addresses. Choice (A) is a good description of this prediction, so don't eliminate it. Choice (B) might initially look good, since it addresses the idea that the volcano was depicted, but the discussion of oral history doesn't provide any sort of proof of the mural's purpose. This answer can be eliminated. Choice (C) uses complex words from the passage that may look attractive, but the passage doesn't shift from one aging method to another. Eliminate it. Choice (D) also uses scientific wording to make the answer possibly look good, but the content of the answer choice doesn't match the prediction because radiometric aging is mentioned throughout. Choice (A) is the correct answer.

24. **B** This is a best evidence question, so simply look at the lines used to answer the previous question. Choice (B) contains the line used to show the shift to a new focus: *This view, however, has been contested…*. Choice (B) is the correct answer.

25. **D** This question asks about the phrase *it putatively depicts* in the context of the passage. The context reveals that it's not clear whether the mural shows an actual volcano or not, since no research has been done to determine whether it's even possible that someone during that time could have witnessed an eruption. Another word or phrase that could go into the passage here might be *possibly* or *theoretically*. Choice (A) describes what scientists do and has nothing to do with the doubt relayed, so it can be eliminated. Choices (B) and (C) are closer in that they mention the need for clarification and certainty that scientists rely upon, but they're both too general. Choice (B) says theories must *always* be questioned, but the text only discusses one theory. Choice (C) refers to *the work of scientists*, which is again too broad. Only (D) addresses the idea that this specific claim does not have enough evidence to be proven with a reasonable amount of satisfaction. Choice (D) is the correct answer.

26. **A** The passage states that the mural was found at the *Neolithic Çatalhöyük site (Central Anatolia, Turkey) and appears to show an eruption of the Hasan Daği twin-peaks volcano located about 130 km northeast of Çatalhöyük*. Choice (A) is the correct answer.

27. **A** Refer to the lines used to answer the previous question. Choice (A) is the correct answer.

28. **C** This question asks about the meaning of the phrase *This is not to say* in the context of the passage. Prior to this sentence the passage states *For the Çatalhöyük map (and volcano) hypothesis to be plausible, however, we surmise that a brief line of oral tradition, or even an eyewitness portrayal, is perhaps more likely than tradition of a myth that detached itself from its inspiration in the physical world*. Basically, for the map to be somewhat accurate, someone would have to have seen the eruption himself or the description could only have been relayed a couple times.

This is not to say clarifies that they wouldn't expect a Neolithic map to be completely accurate, but it should have details specific to that type of volcano. Choice (A) can be eliminated because it isn't stated that details were lost, nor does the passage state that details from the mural are crucial for proving the truth. Choice (B) is tempting since this sentence is near the discussion of oral histories, but the passage doesn't say that oral histories don't describe real events. Choice (C) closely matches the prediction, so don't eliminate it. Choice (D) is the opposite of the prediction, since the passage says *realism must not prevail in Neolithic art*, meaning that it wasn't important to the scientists that the drawing be realistic. Choice (C) is the correct answer.

29. **C** Although this question might initially look like a best evidence paired question, notice that the lines in the answers are all answers for this question. The question asks about evidence that supports the claim the *mural was painted near the time of the volcanic eruption*, so find evidence in the passage to support that. It would also be efficient to work backwards, using the lines given in the answers. Choice (A) does address the volcanic eruption, but it does not connect the eruption to the mural at all. Eliminate (A). Choice (B) has nothing to do with the volcano or the mural, so it can be eliminated. Choice (C) does connect time with accuracy, saying *but many of the apparent details can be reasonably expected to become lost or obscured during a long period of oral tradition.* That is, if the eruption happened and was described over many generations, the truth about the details would gradually change. Thus, the eruption must have happened close to the time of the painting of the mural. While it might not initially look perfect, there's no clear reason to eliminate it, so keep (C). Choice (D) focuses on the volcano and does not connect the eruption to the mural, so (D) can be eliminated. Choice (C) is the correct answer.

30. **B** On the table, two eruptions are marked: A and B. Notice the eruptions are labeled with the *ka* unit, which is defined as *age in thousands of years*. Therefore, the two eruptions are 8.97 ka, or 8970 years old, and 28.9 ka, or 28,900 years old. The question asks about the *youngest* eruption. Choice (B) is the correct answer.

31. **B** The passage states *we would predict a time period for the eruption between 7400 and 6600 B.C.E.* and the table indicates the eruption is roughly 8,970 years old. Going back in time just under 9,000 years would put the eruption roughly around 6,900 B.C. Choice (B) is the correct answer.

32. **D** This question asks about which statement would be supported by the data, so use the data to go through each of the four statements. Choice (A) is the opposite of what is in the table. The xenocrysts were older than the other particles. Eliminate (A). Choice (B) can be eliminated because there is nothing about the oral tradition in the graphic. Choice (C) does reference the dating method used for the crystals, but this answer can be eliminated because there is no indication that it's the *best* way to determine the age of an artifact. Choice (D) matches the data, indicating that the particles from HDA (the flank of the volcano) are older than the particles taken from the rim. Choice (D) is the correct answer.

33. **A** This question asks about Burke's opinion of the argument of those who support electing officials. In the text, Burke says that they use *paltry artifices* and *substitute a fictitious cause, and*

feigned personages, thereby using weak or untrue arguments. Choice (A) matches that prediction, so don't eliminate it. Choice (B) can be eliminated because even though Burke mentions *fanatics*, he isn't referring to the *sophisters*, and though *universality* might be understood, there's no support for it in the text. Choice (C) doesn't work because the argument, though weak, is current, not antiquated. Eliminate (C). Choice (D) can be eliminated because there is no mention anywhere of *innovation*. Choice (A) is the correct answer.

34.   **A**   This is a Vocab-in-Context question, so go back to the text, find the word *overload* in line 1, and cross it out. Replace it with another word that makes sense in the sentence based on the context of the passage. There is a time contrast in the sentence between *a few years ago* and *now* that can be used for context. Burke says *a few years ago* he would have been *ashamed to overload a matter…*with *unnecessary support* but now the doctrine is *publicly taught, avowed, and printed. Overload* must be referring to something that means *unnecessary support*. Choice (A) is a clear synonym of that phrase, and none of choices (B), (C), or (D) has anything to do with *unnecessary support*. Choice (A) is the correct answer.

35.   **B**   This is a Vocab-in-Context question, so go back to the text, find the word *employ* in line 20, and cross it out. Replace it with another word that makes sense in the sentence based on the context of the passage. *Employ* could easily be replaced with the word *use*, since the abettors are employing the artifices *in order to render the support…invidious*. POE anything that has nothing to do with *use*, leaving (B) as the correct answer.

36.   **A**   This question asks about Paine's beliefs about *leadership by right of birth*. He clearly has a negative view, as evidenced throughout Passage 2 with phrases such as *the evil of hereditary succession, minds early poisoned by importance,* and *monarchy and succession have laid but the world in blood and ashes*. Eliminate anything positive, including (B) because Paine does not view hereditary succession as useful and (D) because Paine does not see hereditary succession as valuable. Compare (A) and (C). Choice (A) might initially look extreme, but remember that a correct answer can contain extreme wording if the text has equally strong wording. Choice (C) can be eliminated because Paine doesn't believe leadership is about *expressing opinions*. Choice (A) is the correct answer.

37.   **C**   This is the first in a paired set of questions, so Parallel POE is a useful strategy here. Begin with the answers for Q38. Check and see if the indicated lines support any of the answers for Q37. Choice (38A) talks about men who consider themselves *born to reign* who *soon grow insolent*. While this might be an excellent argument against the crown, these lines don't support any of the answers to Q37. Eliminate (38A). Choice (38B) is another specific example of problems with the hereditary crown, but none of the answers for Q37 deal with specific examples. Choice (37A) is the closest thing, but that answer says *address all possible reasons* and that answer is just one reason. Eliminate (38B). Choice (38C) is an argument for the hereditary crown, which is the opposite of Paine's point. Eliminate it. Choice (38D) refers to an entire country denying a fact and believing something false. This supports (37C), so connect those

two answers. Without any support from Q38, (37A), (37B), and (37D) can all be eliminated. This leaves the pair of (37C) and (38D) as the correct answers.

38.   **D**   (See explanation above.)

39.   **A**   This question asks about Burke's likely response to Paine's statements in the final paragraph of Passage 2. Paine is clear that he believes the hereditary monarchy, instead of preserving *a nation from civil war*, actually causes wars and rebellions. Burke, on the other hand, says that the people of England *conceive the undisturbed succession of the crown to be a pledge of the stability and perpetuity…of our Constitution.* The two men clearly do not agree, so (B) and (C) can be eliminated. Compare (A) and (D). Whether or not Paine provides specifics about wars and rebellions is irrelevant to Burke's point, so (D) can be eliminated. This leaves (A), which matches the prediction and is the correct answer.

40.   **B**   These were the lines used for the prediction in the previous question. Choice (B) is the correct answer.

41.   **B**   The two passages do not agree, so (A) and (D) can be eliminated. Neither passage presents a method for *resolving the issues*, so (C) can be eliminated. Passage 2 discusses the specifics of England's violent history in relation to hereditary monarchy, a topic never discussed by Burke in Passage 1. Choice (B) is the correct answer.

42.   **C**   Both of these passages deal with hereditary succession and views about the validity of a crown passed down through families. However, this is not all they do. Burke argues for a hybrid of monarchy and elected officials (which is what Payne wants). As a result, their disagreement isn't really so extreme. Burke concedes, especially in the last paragraph, that pure hereditary monarchy is not all it's cracked up to be, while Paine addresses those who support the idea and explains why they are wrong. Choice (C) correctly identifies this purpose and is the correct answer.

43.   **D**   This question asks about the main idea of the passage. It is a general question, so save it for later until after the specific questions are answered. The passage is primarily about new possibilities of human genome editing, weighing the positives and potential dangers of this developing field in science. This supports (D). There is no one long-term study in the passage, making (A) incorrect. Choice (B) is also incorrect because, while there is some background information included in the passage, it is not the primary purpose. Choice (C) is incorrect as well because there are not any competing theories juxtaposed in the passage. Therefore, (D) is correct.

44.   **B**   This question asks about the author's attitude toward CRISPR/Cas9 technology. Attitude questions are general questions, and therefore should be saved until after the specific questions are answered. For tone/attitude questions, first decide whether the attitude is positive, negative, or neutral. Eliminate what doesn't match that general category, and then make a more specific decision from the remaining answers. The author of this passage is generally optimistic, noting CRISPR's potential for disease prevention while understanding the risks involved

at this current state of research. Eliminate any answer choices that are negative or neutral. Choice (A) can be eliminated because the author is concerned. Choice (B) is positive, so keep it. Choice (C) can be eliminated because it's negative. Choice (D) is also positive, so keep that. Compare (B) and (D) using the text. Choice (B) contains the *understanding of risks* while (D) takes the positivity to an extreme not matched in the passage. Therefore, (B) is correct.

45. **B** This is a Vocab-in-Context question, so go back to the text, find the word *editing* in line 13, and cross it out. Replace it with another word that makes sense in the sentence based on the context of the passage. In this case, *editing* refers to *changing* the human genetic material. Choices (A) and (C), *abridging* and *revising* respectively, are both possible definitions of *editing*, but neither matches the context of the passage. No one is trying to shorten or improve the genetic material. Choice (D), *polishing*, does not make sense in context, leaving (B), *altering*, which most means *changing*. Therefore, (B) is correct.

46. **C** This is a paired question, so start with the best evidence question below to match evidence with the answer choices in this question. Choice (47A) does not support any of the choices in Q46, so eliminate it. Choice (47B) supports (46C), so connect both of these and check the other two choices in Q47. Choice (47C) does not pair with any of the choices in Q46, making it incorrect as well. Choice (47D) on first glance pairs with (46A) because both talk about monkey testing, but it does not provide evidence that monkey testing is expensive. Therefore, eliminate (47D). Eliminate (46A), (46B), and (46D) because they are unsupported by evidence in Q47. Since there is only one true pairing between (46C) and (47B), these are the correct answers.

47. **B** (See explanation above.)

48. **D** This is a paired question, so start with the best evidence question below to match evidence with the answer choices in this question. Choice (49A) pairs with (48C), so draw a line connecting these two answer choices. Choice (49B) does not pair with any of the choices in Q48, so it may be eliminated. Choice (49C) supports (48D) because these tests were done in Atlanta, Georgia in the United States, so draw a line connecting those two choices. Choice (49D) does not support any of the choices in Q48. Eliminate (48A) and (48B) because they are unsupported by evidence in Q49. Now, look back at Q48. Choice (48C) cannot be proven by the passage, eliminating this choice along with (49A). Therefore, (48D) and (49C) are correct.

49. **C** (See explanation above.)

50. **C** Use the key word and line reference to find the window for this question. The text states that countries with *high rates of in vitro* fertilization will be the first to attempt clinical applications, supporting (C). Choice (A) is incorrect because it is outside the window and is not related to *in vitro* fertilization. Choices (B) and (D) are incorrect as well because both predict the future, making them impossible to prove. Therefore, choice (C) is correct.

51. **A** Since this question contains a specific phrase and line references, it is easy to find in the text, and therefore a good question to answer before more general questions. *Much too soon* refers to clinical trials of human genome editing, according to Guoping Feng at MIT. He says that it isn't *time to do human-embryo manipulation* and that doing the wrong thing could *send the wrong message to the public—and then the public will not support scientific research anymore.* The correct answer must have something to do with that statement. Choice (A) supports this prediction. Choice (B) might be tempting, but it does not answer the question. Choice (C) is not mentioned by the passage, making it incorrect, and (D) is too strong, stating that genome editing will be an *inevitable failure*. Therefore, (A) is correct.

52. **A** Find the window for this question using the line references and quotations. This quote supports the previous statement that CRISPR technology is not ready for human testing yet. Therefore, it is not *defining* or *refuting* anything, eliminating (C) and (D). While the quote does clarify and go further into detail, Feng is not talking about an *abstract concept*, eliminating (B). Therefore, (A) is correct.

Section 2: Writing and Language

1. **A** In this sentence, the verb *watch* needs to be consistent with the other verbs in the list: *read* and *look*. Therefore, the single word *watch* is the most effective choice. Choices (B) and (C) add unnecessary words, and (D) removes a crucial component of the answer. Therefore, the correct answer is (A).

2. **D** The phrase *the group of accepted "classic" works* should be offset as parenthetical in this sentence. In the absence of parentheses, use punctuation that will be consistent with the non-underlined parts of the sentence. In this case, there is a comma after the word *canon*, so the punctuation that concludes the parenthetical remark should also be a comma. Choices (A) and (B) mix the punctuation unnecessarily, and (C) discards it altogether. Choice (D) is correct.

3. **C** The sentence that follows this idea is as follows: *There is no better example of such a marginalization than that of Native Americans.* The phrase *such a marginalization* suggests that some type of *marginalization* must be mentioned in the previous sentence. Choices (A), (B), and (D) mention other unrelated things, whereas (C) explicitly mentions the *periphery*.

4. **D** Make the verbs within the sentence consistent. The nearest verb, and one that is used as part of this idea, is *identifies*. Therefore, the most consistent form of this present-tense verb is *outlines*, as (D) contains.

5. **B** The underlined word must be something that could contain *military campaigns*. Choices (A), (C), and (D) all refer to types of pleasant conversation, so they are not likely to encompass military campaigns. Choice (B), *contact*, is neutral enough to encompass military campaigns, so even in the instance in which one or more of the other answers were unfamiliar words, (B) makes a good answer.

6. **D**   There is a comma after the word *assimilation*. If the sentence were written as in choice (A), it would contain a comma splice. The two ideas surrounding the comma—*When the wars subsided, the American government started a similarly cruel program of assimilation* and *often this involved the movement of Native American children from their homes to "Indian schools" that sought to remove any trace of tribal inheritance*—are complete, so they cannot be separated by the comma. Choices (B) and (C) would create run-on sentences. Therefore, only (D) fixes that error by giving an incomplete idea after the comma.

7. **C**   The previous paragraph describes the injustices suffered by Native Americans in the early twentieth century. There is no mention of *anti-war demonstrations*, eliminating (A), or *Kenneth Lincoln*'s youth, eliminating (B). Between the remaining two choices, (C) is more effective because it connects to the idea of *assimilation*, whereas (D) is not sufficiently specific.

8. **D**   While the proposed sentence is true, it does not contribute in a substantive way to the information given in this paragraph. With questions like these, make sure that the proposed sentence is crucial to the meaning of the paragraph or passage before adding it. This sentence is not crucial, so it shouldn't be added, for the reason that (D) states.

9. **D**   The last two sentences of this paragraph further describe the positive changes that helped to create the conditions for the Native American Renaissance. These sentences agree with one another and point together toward positive change. The word *Nevertheless* suggests a contrast where none exists in the sentence, so (A) can be eliminated. Choices (B) and (C) point in the right direction rhetorically, but these conjunctions create sentence fragments made all the worse by the commas. Choice (D) is the only word that can work in the context with this particular punctuation.

10. **B**   When answer choices consist of three pronouns (*them*, *these*, and *it*, in this case) and one specific noun (*Native American writers*), the specific noun is almost always correct. The specific noun, given in (B), is correct in this case because it is the only choice that removes all ambiguity from the sentence.

11. **D**   When combining sentences, be sure to look for the shortest option that contains all the necessary information. Choices (B) and (C) are particularly long, and each contains some other issue. Choice (B) changes the punctuation to another form of Stop punctuation, but it does not combine the sentences in any other way. Choice (C) has an ambiguous meaning because of the many modifiers (*in this period*, *of the 1970s and 1980s*, *amid the resulting efflorescence*, and *of Native American writers*) that are strung together. Choice (A) creates ambiguity with the odd combination of words *a resultant efflorescence*. Choice (D) is the only choice that effectively combines and shortens the ideas without introducing new errors.

12. **A**   Choose the word that best fits the context. While the changing leaves may *bode*, *indicate*, or *foretell* the coming of winter, the verb in this sentence will describe the action of the subject, *Anyone who lives in the Mid-Atlantic or New England*. Therefore, the only verb that can apply in this context is the one given in (A), *knows*.

13. **D**   When given the option to DELETE an underlined portion, give it serious consideration: DELETE is often correct. In this case, deleting the underlined portion eliminates extraneous and awkward wording from the sentence, without introducing new errors. Therefore, (D), which says to delete the underlined portion, is the most effective choice.

14. **B**   All of the choices contain the same information; therefore, the most effective route is to choose the most concise of these answers. In this case, the most concise option is (B), which communicates in three words what the other choices communicate in seven or eight.

15. **B**   The phrase *including restaurant owners, hoteliers, and farmers* is a clarifying phrase, giving more detail to the words *business owners*. It should therefore be offset as parenthetical without adding any new commas. Choice (B) accomplishes this goal. Choice (D) cannot be used because the idea that precedes a colon must be complete, and *Many business owners including* is not complete.

16. **A**   The previous sentence states, *Foliage season, however, is a bit more difficult to predict*. This sentence expands on the previous sentence, providing an example or an instance of this difficulty. Therefore, (A), *for instance*, contains an effective transition in linking this idea to the previous one.

17. **C**   The previous idea states *Of course, many people would certainly like to know the cause* of how and why leaves change color in the fall. This sentence continues that idea, but since all the transitions signal continuation, use POE. Choice (A) can be eliminated because it introduces an ambiguous pronoun. Choice (B) can be eliminated because there is no indication that the ideas are happening in any kind of sequence. Choice (D) can be eliminated because it does not sufficiently address the connectedness of the ideas. Only (C) remains as the transition that best connects the two ideas.

18. **A**   This sentence indicates that *scientists* have always had some knowledge of how fall foliage works, so the verb must indicate a past knowledge that has continued into the future. Choices (B), (C), and (D) are all purely in the present, so they can be eliminated. Only (A), *have long known*, effectively communicates that the scientists' knowledge began in the past and continues into the present.

19. **D**   When asked to add an idea to a paragraph, make sure that there is a very good reason to do so. In general, it is best NOT to add new information to the passage. That is true here as well—the proposed sentence may be true, but it does not contribute in a substantive way to the larger purpose of the paragraph. Therefore, the sentence should not be added because it is irrelevant to the paragraph's focus, as stated in (D).

20. **D**   The subject of this verb is *factors*, thereby eliminating the singular verbs contained in (A) and (B). Choice (C) can also be eliminated because it contains the possessive pronoun *their* in a part of the sentence that does not indicate possession. Only (D) remains in giving the correct form of *there* and the appropriately plural verb.

21. **A** The previous sentence states *They found that both reacted to frosts in the fall, but only the highlands reacted to frosts in the spring.* The added detail should continue in this vein, as in (A). Choice (B) does not address climate, (C) does not address the leaves, and (D) is more focused on the spring than the fall.

22. **D** Because the first idea of the sentence—*Combining these findings with climate-change predictions for the next century*—is an introductory idea, the second part of the sentence must contain a complete idea with a subject and a verb. Choices (A), (B), and (C) contain only verbs, so they can be eliminated. This leaves (D), which contains both a subject and a verb.

23. **C** The previous sentence refers to *contemporary U.S. holdings*, so the best available contrast comes from (C), in which *quite an old idea* provides a contrast with *contemporary*. Choices (A), (B), and (D) are free of grammatical errors, but they are not adequately linked to the previous sentence or the next, which cites *One early case.*

24. **A** Read the passage carefully. The regions are listed in this order: *west and south*, *north*, and *southeast*. The states shown in the map must be listed in that order as well: Tennessee is to the *west and south*, Virginia is to the *north*, and North Carolina is to the *southeast*. Choice (A) effectively matches the states to their appropriate regions.

25. **B** The idea after the word *debts*, the idea from *those* to *the Revolutionary War* is not complete, so it cannot be preceded by a semicolon as in (A). Choice (C) can be eliminated because this sentence should have some pause to break up the two parts of the sentence, and (D) can be eliminated because it contains too much punctuation, creating confusion with the other long dashes in this sentence. The best answer therefore is (B), which contains an appropriate colon and no extra punctuation.

26. **D** Both uses of the word *its* refer back to *the state* of North Carolina, and both of the nouns in this part of the sentence—*offer* and *western counties*—belong to North Carolina, so both should take the possessive form of *its*. Choice (D) is therefore the best of the available answers. Remember, *it's* is a contraction of the words *it is.*

27. **C** In keeping with the historical tone of the essay, the verb should be in the past tense, eliminating (D). Choice (A) creates an awkward sentence fragment, so it too can be eliminated. Then, the subject of this verb is *counties*, which is plural, meaning that between (B) and (C), the only possible verb is the plural *were* in (C).

28. **B** Each answer contains essentially the same information, except for (A), which suggests a contrast that is not present in the sentence. When each answer contains the same information, choose the shortest. In this case, the shortest possible answer comes from (B), which fixes the sentence by removing the repetitive use of the word *independence.*

29. **C** A *boarder* is someone who lives at a boarding house. This word has no logical place in this sentence, so (A) and (B) should be eliminated. The same could be said for the word *broader,*

which is an adjective meaning "more broad," eliminating (D). Only (C) remains in its use of the word *border*, which is the part or edge that forms the outer boundary of an area.

30. **A** Sentence 2 begins with the phrase *This time*, but that phrase does not clearly refer to anything in sentence 1. Therefore, the proposed sentence, with its mention of *1789*, should be placed before sentence 2, after sentence 1, because it will clarify the referent of *this time*. Therefore, (A) is correct.

31. **A** When the words *just as* are used to make a comparison within a sentence, they must be followed at some point by the words *so too*. This is an English idiom, a convention of usage that is particular to the language. The SAT tests these idioms but does not do so frequently. The best answer is therefore (A).

32. **A** Read the question carefully. It asks for a word that will *convey an attitude of genuine interest* and *avoid the appearance of mockery*. Choices (B) and (D) appear to be mocking, (B) because it is so informal and (D) because it is overstated. Choice (C) is not specific enough to convey an attitude of genuine interest. Choice (A) effectively meets the goal—when used in this way, *curiosity* conveys the sense of something meriting further inquiry.

33. **C** The final paragraph is a discussion of how the state of Franklin provides the reminder that the borders of and within the United States have often changed and that the shape and make-up of our current fifty states is not necessarily a permanent configuration. Choice (A) refers to only a minor aspect of this and implies a generalization to federally oriented states that may or may not be true. Choices (B) and (D) are not specific. Only (C) effectively fulfills the goal outlined in the question.

34. **A** The first two sentences are characterized by simple present-tense verbs: *live, see, cross, drive*. Therefore, the most logical verb in the underlined portion is *see*, as in (A), which has the same tense and format as the other verbs.

35. **C** The previous sentence states, *Civil engineering as a profession is centuries old and has long been necessary for the functioning of modern government*. The new proposed sentence, *Few governments in the modern world could function without the work of civil engineers*, is worded in a slightly different way, but it mainly restates the information contained in the previous sentence. The proposed sentence should therefore not be added because it does not give any new information, as stated in (C).

36. **B** Civil engineers are portrayed in a positive light, so the word *manipulators* in (D) would not have a place in this sentence. *Foundations* and *pillars*, particularly when referring to something about *society*, are typically used to describe principles (in abstract terms) or architectural structures (in more concrete terms). This eliminates (A) and (C). The best answer, therefore, is (B), *cornerstones*, which has a literal meaning as the stone at the corner of a foundation but also has a figurative meaning that describes any person or thing that is important to a structure.

37. **A**   The information in this sentence restates the information from the quote. That is to say that it puts the quoted information *in other words*, making (A) the best possible answer. Choices (B) and (C) suggest a contrast, but there is no contrast between these two sentences. Choice (D) suggests a move to a different type of description, but this sentence is merely restating or rephrasing the information given in the quote. Therefore, (A) is correct.

38. **A**   Use the context of the sentence. The information that expands upon the idea of *small* projects, *like local roads and power stations*, which is offset by a dash. Therefore, the information that is used the same way to describe *large* projects should also be offset with dashes, two in this case because it appears in the middle of the sentence. Choice (A) gives this punctuation most consistently.

39. **D**   As written, the word *however* appears between two ideas that do not contrast. *Their backgrounds tend to vary* and *specialties can range from architecture to environmental engineering, from ecology to urban planning* are related sentences that move in the same direction. Therefore, the word *however* must be restricted to the first sentence, implying a contrast with some earlier idea. Choice (A) places the *however* in the second sentence, and (B) and (C) use the *however* explicitly to link the two sentences. Choice (D) is the only choice that provides another alternative by separating the ideas into two sentences and putting the word *however* in the first.

40. **B**   When all four answers contain essentially the same meaning, choose the shortest that is free of grammatical errors. In this case, that answer is (B), *creating delivery mechanisms*, which communicates the same information as the other choices in the fewest words.

41. **B**   Pay particular attention to the first few words of sentence 3: *Those who want a greener country.* These must come before the similarly worded beginning of sentence 5: *Those who are less concerned with long-term energy sources.* Both ideas must come after sentence 4, which is the first to discuss *environmental* concerns in a specific way. The best of the available answers, therefore, is (B).

42. **C**   The following sentence states that *The Bureau of Labor Statistics predicts that the field will grow by nearly 20% between 2012 and 2022.* This sentence is concerned exclusively with the growth of the career, so the preceding sentence must signal some kind of preview of this *growth*. Choice (C) does so clearly with the words *constantly growing*. The other choices might sound fine in the context, but they do not fulfill the purpose outlined in the question.

43. **D**   If the underlined portion contains a pronoun, that pronoun must be consistent with the noun to which it refers, *a civil engineer*. Choices (A), (B), and (C) all contain plural pronouns, which would not be consistent. Only (D) contains a singular pronoun.

44. **C**   All four choices are concerned with *civil engineering*, but (A), (B), and (D) add a number of unnecessary words in referring to the profession. Therefore, the best of the available answers is (C), which states the information clearly and concisely.

Section 3: Math (No Calculator)

1. **B** Start by plugging in 9 for x into the function to get $\frac{5}{3}(9) + k = 12$. Solve for k to get $15 + k = 12$ and $k = -3$. Therefore, $g(x) = \frac{5}{3}x - 3$, and $g(-3) = \frac{5}{3}(-3) + (-3) = -5 - 3 = -8$, so the answer is (B).

2. **B** Get rid of the fraction in the second equation by multiplying both sides of the equation by k to get $h = 5k$. Substitute $5k$ for h in the first equation to get $3(k + 2) = 5k$. Distribute the 3 to get $3k + 6 = 5k$. Solve for k to get $6 = 2k$, and $3 = k$, which is (B).

3. **D** Set the expressions in each of the answer choices equal to 1 and solve for y. Choice (A) becomes $\left|2 - y\right| + 2 = 1$ or $\left|2 - y\right| = -1$. The result of an absolute value is always greater than or equal to 0, so this doesn't work. Eliminate (A). The same thing happens with (B) and (C). Only (D) works: $\left|2 - y\right| - 2 = 1$ or $\left|2 - y\right| = 3$, which happens when $y = -1$ or 5. Therefore, (D) is the correct answer.

4. **A** According to the question, $\frac{x + y}{x} = \frac{6}{5}$. Plug in an easy value for x, such as $x = 5$, and solve for y. The equation becomes $\frac{5 + y}{5} = \frac{6}{5}$, so $5 + y = 6$, and $y = 1$. Try these values in the answer choices to see which one works. Choice (A) becomes $\frac{1}{5} = \frac{1}{5}$. This is true, so keep (A), but check the rest of the answers to be sure. Choice (B) becomes $\frac{1}{5} = \frac{11}{5}$, (C) becomes $\frac{5 + 1}{5} = \frac{1}{5}$, and (D) becomes $\frac{5 - 2(1)}{5} = -\frac{1}{5}$. None of these are true, so eliminate (B), (C), and (D), and choose (A).

5. **A** Plug $-2x$ in for x in the function to get $g(-2x) = -4(-2x) - 7 = 8x - 7$, which is (A).

6. **D** Use FOIL to expand the quadratic to get $4(15x^2 - 6x - 10x + 4)$. Use Bite-Sized pieces to see that the first term is $4(15x^2) = 60x^2$. Eliminate (A) and (B). Likewise, the last term must be $4(4) = 16$. Therefore, eliminate (C). Choice (D) is correct.

7. **C** Plug 1 in for k to get $x - 7 = \sqrt{x - 1}$. Plug in the answers to solve. Start with $x = 5$ since 5 appears in two of the answers. If $x = 5$, the equation becomes $5 - 7 = \sqrt{5 - 1}$. Solve both sides of the equation to get $-2 = \sqrt{4}$. The square root of a number is always its positive value. Therefore, this expression is untrue. Eliminate (B) and (D). Next, try $x = 1$. If $x = 1$, the equation becomes $1 - 7 = \sqrt{1 - 1}$. Solve both sides of the equation to get $-6 = \sqrt{0}$. This is also untrue, so eliminate (A). The correct answer must therefore be (C).

8. **C** According to the question, Alexi increased the amount he lifted by 225 − 180 = 45 pounds over 24 − 6 = 18 days. Calculate his daily increase to get 45 ÷ 18 = 2.5 pounds per day, which is (C).

9. **D** In the slope-intercept from of an equation, $y = mx + b$, m represents the slope. Therefore, the slope of the given line is −4. In the standard form of the equation $Ax + By = C$, the slope equals $-\dfrac{A}{B}$. For (A), the slope is $\dfrac{-4}{-1} = 4$. Eliminate (A). In (B), the slope is $-\dfrac{4}{2} = -2$. Eliminate (B). In (C), the slope is $-\dfrac{6}{3} = -2$. Eliminate (C). Therefore, the correct answer must be (D).

10. **B** The first equation is a parabola, because if FOILed out, it would contain an x^2 term, and the second equation is a line, because there is no exponent attached to x. The two can at most have two points of intersection, so eliminate (A). Next, draw a rough sketch of the parabola. Start by finding the roots of the equation by setting each of the binomials in the parentheses equal to 0. If $x − 7 = 0$, then $x = 7$. Therefore, one point on the parabola is (7, 0). If $3x + 4 = 0$, then $3x = −4$, and $x = -\dfrac{4}{3}$. Therefore, a second point on the parabola is $\left(-\dfrac{4}{3}, 0 \right)$. Lastly, plug in 0 for x to get $y = (0 − 7)[3(0) + 4] = (−7)(4) = −28$. Therefore, a third point on the graph is (0, −28). Connecting the three points will result in a sketch that looks roughly like this:

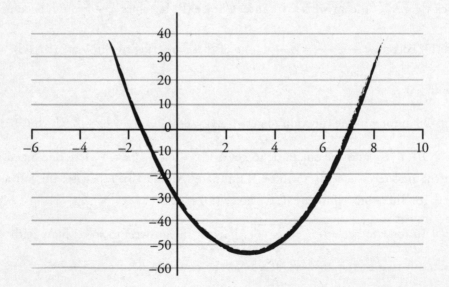

Next, draw the line. Rearrange the equation into slope-intercept form, $y = mx + b$, where m stands for the slope and b stands for the y-intercept. This is $y = \dfrac{1}{3}x + \dfrac{1}{3}$. So, the line has a slope of $\dfrac{1}{3}$, and a y-intercept of $\dfrac{1}{3}$. A rough sketch of the line would look like this:

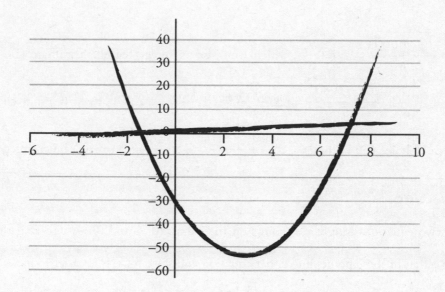

It is clear from a rough drawing of the two equations that the line must cross the parabola twice, and the answer is (B).

11. **A**   There are variables in the answer choices, so plug in. If $d = 10$, then Joan's bouquet costs $10 - 4 = \$6$. The combined cost of both bouquets is $10 + 6 = \$16$, which means that each of them paid $\$16 \div 2 = \$8$ for the bouquets before the tax was added. The tax on each share is $\$8 \times 0.15 = \$1.20$, which means that each of them paid a total of $\$8 + \$1.20 = \$9.20$. Plug 10 in for d in each of the answers to see which answer equals the target of $\$9.20$. Choice (A) becomes $1.15(10) - 2.3 = 11.50 - 2.3 = 9.2$. This matches the target, but check the remaining answers just in case. Choice (B) becomes $2(10) - 1.15 = 20 - 1.15 = 18.85$. Eliminate (B). Choice (C) becomes $2.15(10) - 2 = 21.5 - 2 = 19.5$. Eliminate (C). Choice (D) becomes $2.3(10) - 4.6 = 23 - 4.6 = 18.4$. Eliminate (D). Therefore, the answer is (A).

12. **A**   Multiply both sides of the equation by $(z + 3)$ to get $z - 3 = 8(z + 3)$. Distribute the 8 to get $z - 3 = 8z + 24$. Solve for z to get $z = 8z + 27$, $-7z = 27$, and $z = -\dfrac{27}{7}$. Choice (A) is correct.

13. **C**   Plug in, picking easy numbers. Let $x = 3$, and $v = 6$. The equation becomes $(3)^2 - 3t = \dfrac{6}{3}(3)$.

Solve for t to get $9 - 3t = 6$, and $t = 1$. In the answers, plug in 6 for v and 1 for t to see which answer could return a value of 3 for x. Choice (A) becomes $\dfrac{6}{3} \pm \dfrac{\sqrt{6^2 + 4(1)}}{3} = 2 \pm \dfrac{\sqrt{40}}{3}$, which will not come out to an integer like 3. Eliminate (A). Choice (B) becomes

$$\frac{6}{3} \pm \frac{\sqrt{6^2 + 36(1)}}{6} = 2 \pm \frac{\sqrt{72}}{6}$$, which won't be an integer either. Eliminate (B). Choice (C)

becomes $\frac{6}{6} \pm \frac{\sqrt{6^2 + 108(1)}}{6} = 1 \pm \frac{\sqrt{144}}{6} = 1 \pm \frac{12}{6} = 1 \pm 2 = 3$. Keep (C), but check (D) just

in case. Choice (D) becomes $\frac{6}{6} \pm \frac{\sqrt{6^2 + 4(1)}}{6} = 1 \pm \frac{\sqrt{40}}{6}$. This won't be an integer, either, so

(C) is correct.

14.   **C**   The two equations intersect at points on the y-axis, $(0, s)$ and $(0, -s)$. To find the value of s,

plug either of these points into either equation and solve for s. It is easier to use the first point

in equation A to avoid having to deal with negative signs. Plugging $(0, s)$ into $x = 18y^2 - 2$

results in $0 = 18s^2 - 2$. Add 2 to both sides to get $2 = 18s^2$, then divide both sides by 18 to get

$\frac{2}{18} = s^2$ or $\frac{1}{9} = s^2$. Take the square root of both sides to find that $s = \frac{1}{3}$, which is (C).

15.   **B**   To get i out of the denominator of a fraction, multiply by the complex conjugate

of the denominator. Multiply the top and bottom of the fraction by $(4 - 3i)$ to get

$\frac{(18 + i)(4 - 3i)}{(4 + 3i)(4 - 3i)} = \frac{72 - 54i + 4i - 3i^2}{16 - 9i^2}$. Because $i = \sqrt{-1}$, $i^2 = -1$. Substitute -1 for i^2 to

get $\frac{72 - 54i + 4i - 3(-1)}{16 - 9(-1)} = \frac{72 - 50i + 3}{16 + 9} = \frac{75 - 50i}{25}$. The full equation becomes $3 - 2i =$

$a + bi$. Therefore, $a = 3$, and the answer is (B).

16. $\frac{5}{8}$ or **0.625**

In a right triangle with angles $a°$ and $b°$, $\cos a = \sin b$. Knowing this fact about the complemen-

tary angles of a right triangle makes questions like this easier. Without that knowledge, plug-

ging in can help. Convert 0.625 to a fraction, which is $\frac{5}{8}$. Cosine is defined as $\frac{adj}{hyp}$, so label

the side next to a as 5 and the hypotenuse as 8. Sine is defined as $\frac{opp}{hyp}$, and the side opposite b

is the side that is 5. Therefore, $\sin a° = \frac{5}{8}$ or 0.625 as well.

17. **3** Imagine the triangle as a right triangle with a height of 24 feet and a hypotenuse of $l + \dfrac{1}{4}l + \dfrac{3}{4}l = 2l$. The proportions that hold for the hypotenuse also hold for the height. To solve for the width, set $2l = 24$, which means that $l = 12$, and $\dfrac{1}{4}l = \left(\dfrac{1}{4}\right)(12) = 3$.

18. **1** Multiply the first equation by 2 to get $16x - 10y = 54$. Stack the two equations on top of each other and add them together to get:

$$16x - 10y = 54$$
$$+\ \underline{5x + 10y = 30}$$
$$21x \qquad\quad = 84$$

Solve for x to get $x = 4$. Plug 4 in for x into the second equation to get $5(4) + 10y = 30$. Solve for y to get $20 + 10y = 30$, $10y = 10$, and $y = 1$.

19. $\dfrac{20}{9}$ or **2.22**

The difference in the known p values is $110 - 90 = 20$. The difference in the depths for which the p values are known is $215 - 170 = 45$ feet. Therefore, the pressure increase for every one foot of depth is $\dfrac{20}{45}$, which reduces to $\dfrac{4}{9}$. The question asks for the increase every 5 feet, though, so multiply this value by 5 to get $\dfrac{20}{9}$ or 2.22.

20. **4** Factor x^2 out of the first two terms to get $x^2(x - 4) + 3x - 12 = 0$. Factor a 3 out of the last two terms to get $x^2(x - 4) + 3(x - 4) = 0$. Rewrite the equation to get $(x^2 + 3)(x - 4) = 0$. Therefore, one of the solutions to the equation is $x - 4 = 0$. Solve for x to get $x = 4$. The other solutions come from $x^2 + 3 = 0$, so $x^2 = -3$. This will yield imaginary solutions, so the only real solution is 4.

Section 4: Math (Calculator)

1. **D** There are variables in the answer choices, so plug in. Let $w = 2$. In two weeks, his training time will be $7.2 - (0.2)(2) = 7.2 - 0.4 = 6.8$ seconds. Plug 2 in for w in each of the answers to see which answer equals the target answer of 6.8. Choice (A) becomes $0.2 - 7.2(2) = 0.2 - 14.4 = -14.2$. Eliminate (A). Choice (B) becomes $6.0 - 0.2(2) = 6.0 - 0.4 = 5.6$. Eliminate (B). Choice (C) becomes $7.2 + 0.2(2) = 7.2 + 0.4 = 7.6$. Eliminate (C). Check (D) just to be sure: $7.2 - 0.2(2) = 7.2 - 0.4 = 6.8$. Therefore, the correct answer is (D).

2. **B** Start by converting the yards to inches by setting up the following proportion: $\dfrac{1 \text{ yard}}{36 \text{ inches}} = \dfrac{4 \text{ yards}}{x \text{ inches}}$. Cross-multiply to get $x = (36)(4) = 144$ inches. After the first cut, the yarn's length is $144 \div 2 = 72$. After the second cut, the yarn's length is $72 \div 4 = 18$, which is (B).

3. **C**   Start by subtracting the base fee to get 3.60 – 2.40 = 1.20. Divide this amount by the cost per mile to get 1.20 ÷ 0.30 = 4 miles, so the correct answer is (C).

4. **B**   Let T represent the number of miles Tiki cycled and I represent the number of miles Irina cycled. According to the question, $T + I = 51$, and $T = I - 13$. Substitute the second equation into the first to get $(I - 13) + I = 51$. Solve for I to get $2I - 13 = 51$, $2I = 64$, and $I = 32$. Another approach is to plug in the answers. Either way, the correct answer is (B).

5. **C**   According to the question, resistance = voltage applied ÷ number of amps. Plug the numbers given into the equation to get $9 = 54 ÷ x$. Solve for x to get $x = 6$, which is (C).

6. **C**   According to the sample, 38.7% of the class would be expected to have O-positive blood. $265 × 0.387 ≈ 103$. Therefore, the closest answer is (C).

7. **A**   The total number of 35- to 64-year-old viewers is 63,574 + 20,482 = 84,056. The total number of viewers in that age range who preferred network D is 12,084 + 3,676 = 15,760. Therefore, the probability that a viewer in this age group preferred Network D is $\dfrac{15,760}{84,056} ≈ 0.2$, which is (A).

8. **B**   According to the table, there were 75 total pieces of furniture made, of which 9 were desks made of maple. Therefore, the proportion of maple desks is $\dfrac{9}{75} = \dfrac{3}{25}$. The answer is (B).

9. **A**   Eliminate (C) because a line that is undefined is parallel to the y-axis. Such a line would pass through exactly 2 quadrants. Likewise eliminate (D) because a line with a slope equal to 0 is parallel to the x–axis. Such a line would pass through exactly 2 quadrants. Make a quick sketch of a line that goes through Quadrants I, II, III, such as:

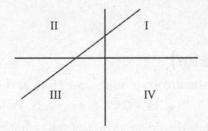

From the drawing, it is clear that the line has a positive slope, so the answer is (A).

10. **D**   For the graph to have x-intercepts at –2, 2, and 5, the expression must equal 0 when $x = -2$, $x = 2$, and $x = 5$. For each answer choice, set each binomial equal to 0 to see if it results in these values for x. For (A) and (C), there is a squared binomial times another binomial. For (A), if $(x - 2) = 0$, $x = 2$, but that root will appear twice, leading to only 2 distinct roots. For this reason, eliminate (A) and (C). For (B), the first root is 2, then $(x + 2) = 0$ gives a root of $x = -2$,

and $(x + 5) = 0$ gives a root of -5. Eliminate (B). The roots for (D) will be 5, 2, and -2, respectively, so (D) is the answer.

11. **C** The animal with the greatest body weight is the one furthest along the x-axis. That animal weighs approximately 125 kilograms. Look to the y-axis to see that the same animal has a brain weight of 140 grams. Therefore, (C) is the correct answer.

12. **D** Remember that the brain weight is given in grams but the body weight is given in kilograms.

    1 kilogram = 1,000 grams. Calculate the ratio of each of the points given in the answers in grams.

    The ratio in (A) is $\dfrac{70}{10(1,000)} = \dfrac{7}{1,000} = 0.007$. The ratio in (B) is $\dfrac{50}{30(1,000)} = \dfrac{5}{3,000} = 0.001\overline{6}$.

    Since this is less than the ratio in (A), eliminate (A). The ratio in (C) is $\dfrac{110}{65,000} = 0.00169$.

    Since this is bigger than (B), eliminate (C). The ratio in (D) is $\dfrac{130}{105,000} = 0.00124$. Since this

    is smaller than (B), eliminate (B) and choose (D).

13. **A** First, because an exponent other than 1 is applied to the fraction, the function is not a linear

    function. Because the scatterplots in (B) and (D) suggest a linear relationship between x and y,

    eliminate (B) and (D). Next, plug in some numbers to see what happens when x gets larger. If

    $x = 1, j = 4$, and $k = -2$, the function becomes $f(1) = \left(\dfrac{4}{1}\right)^{-2} = 4^{-2} = \dfrac{1}{4^2} = \dfrac{1}{16}$. If $x = 100, j - 4$,

    and $k = -2$, the function becomes $f(100) = \left(\dfrac{4}{100}\right)^{-2} = \left(\dfrac{1}{25}\right)^{-2} = 625$. Therefore, according to

    the function, as x increases, y also increases. Of the remaining answer choices, this is not true

    for (C). Eliminate (C). The correct answer is (A). Another option would be to plug in some

    values for the variables j and k and then graph the function on a graphing calculator.

14. **D** Over time, the estimated number of bacteria is clearly decreasing. Therefore, eliminate (A) and
    (C). If the number of bacteria were decreasing linearly, then it would be decreasing by the same
    amount every hour. However, between hours and 0 and 2 the number of bacteria decreased
    by 900,000, whereas between hours 2 and 4 the number of bacteria decreased by only 90,000.
    Since the rate of decrease is not the same every hour, eliminate (B) and choose (D).

15. **C** The value of Pete's bond after one year would be $20{,}000\left(1 + \dfrac{6}{400}\right)^4$, and the value of Roger's

savings bond after one year would be $20{,}000\left(1 + \dfrac{4}{400}\right)^4$. The difference in the value of their

two bonds would be $20{,}000\left(1 + \dfrac{6}{400}\right)^4 - 20{,}000\left(1 + \dfrac{4}{400}\right)^4$. Since both of them started

with savings bonds in the same amount and held them over the same time period, the differ-

ence in the value of the bonds is equal to the difference in their earnings, so the answer is (C).

16. **A** To calculate the slope, plug in two values for x, for example, $x = 2$ and $x = 3$, and find the cor-

responding y-values. When $x = 2$, then $f(x) = 500 + 80(2 - 1) + 70(2) = 720$. When $x = 3$, then

$f(x) = 500 + 80(3 - 1) + 70(3) = 870$. Two points on the graph would then be (2, 720) and

(3, 870). Next, calculate the slope: $\dfrac{y_2 - y_1}{x_2 - x_1} = \dfrac{870 - 720}{3 - 2} = 150$. Now check the answer

choices: For (A), the combined daily cost of the hotel and car rental is $70 + 80 = 150$, so the

correct answer is (A).

17. **B** According to the equation given, the total cost of package P is $400 + 85(x - 1) + 60x$, and the
total cost of package Q is $550 + 75(x - 1) + 50x$, where x is the number of days travelled.
Plug in the answers, starting with a value for a number of days that appears in (B). The cost
of package $P = 400 + 85(8 - 1) + 60(8) = 400 + 595 + 480 = 1{,}475$, and the cost of package
$Q = 550 + 75(8 - 1) + 50(8) = 550 + 525 + 400 = 1{,}475$. The cost of the two packages is the
same at 8 days, which fits the requirements of the question. Eliminate (D), since that range
does not include 8. Now test (A) by trying $x = 7$. Package P would cost $400 + 85(6) + 60(7)$
$= 1{,}330$, and package Q would cost $550 + 75(6) + 50(7) = 1{,}350$. Travel package Q is not less
than or equal to the total cost of travel package P, so eliminate ranges that include 7. This
eliminates (A) and (C). Only (B) is left.

18. **D** Use Process of Elimination. According to Moore's law, the maximum number of transistors
that can be placed on a circuit each year doubles. If there was 1 transistor to start, the next
year there would be 2, then 4, then 8, then 16. The number of transistors would increase more
and more rapidly over the years, which indicates exponential growth. Choice (A) is a flat, horizontal line, showing no growth at all, and (B) has flat sections, showing periods of no growth.
Eliminate (A) and (B). Choice (C) shows growth, but it is a line, which indicates growth at a
constant rate. Eliminate (C). Only (D) shows growth that increases exponentially.

19. **A** The volume of a cylinder can be calculated as $V = \pi r^2 h$. According to the information given,

the radius of each bucket is 0.5 feet and the height of the oil in each bucket is 1.5 feet.

Therefore, the volume of the oil in each bucket is $\pi(0.25)(1.5) \approx 1.1781$ cubic feet. Set up the following proportion: $\dfrac{1 \text{ gallon}}{0.133 \text{ feet}^3} = \dfrac{x \text{ gallons}}{1.1781 \text{ feet}^3}$. Cross-multiply to get $0.133x = 1.1781$. Solve

for x to get $x = 8.858$ gallons per bucket. $55 \div 8.858 \approx 6.2$ buckets. Only round at the last step to

ensure a correct answer when the choices are close together. The question asks for the number of

full buckets, so round this down to 6, which is (A).

20. **B** There is no need to solve all the way for x. Just make the first inequality look like the second one. Solve for $2x$ to get $2x \le 4$. Subtract 5 from each side to get $2x - 5 \le 4 - 5$ or $2x - 5 \le -1$. Therefore, the greatest possible value is -1, and the answer is (B).

21. **D** The question says that the length of arc $\overparen{PQR}$ is 18π. An arc formed by the diameter is a semicircle. The length of a semicircle is equal to half the circumference of the circle, so the circumference of the circle is $18\pi \times 2 = 36\pi$. The formula for the circumference of a circle is $C = \pi d$, so $36\pi = \pi d$. Divide both sides by π to get $36 = d$. The question asks for the length of $\overline{PR}$, which is a diameter, so the length is 36. The answer is (D).

22. **A** The question asks which data points on a scatterplot are below the line $y = x$. To see what happens when a point is below a line, sketch a line on the coordinate plane and a point below it. Notice that the y-coordinate of the point is lower that the y-coordinate of the line at that same value of x. In case of the line $y = x$, a point is below the line if its y-value is less than its x-value. According to the question, the y-value is equal to a city's average temperature in 2010 and the x-value is equal to the city's average temperature in 2000, so find cities in which the average temperature in 2010 is less than its average temperature in 2000. The only city on the chart for which this is true is Miami. Since there is one such city, the answer is (A).

23. **C** The question asks for the approximate percent increase, so an estimate of the temperature will be enough. The top of the 2000 bar is between the 50 and 55 line, closer to 55, so call the average temperature 53. The top of the 2010 bar is between the 55 and 60 line, closer to 55, so call the average temperature 57. To calculate percent change, use the formula $\dfrac{difference}{original} \times 100$. The difference is $57 - 53 = 4$. Since the question asks for a percent *increase*, the original is the smaller value, which is 53. Therefore, the percent increase is about $\dfrac{4}{53} \times 100 \approx 7.55\%$. Since the closest choice is 6%, the answer is (C).

24. **A** The answer choices refer to standard deviation. All that is needed to compute standard deviation is the individual scores. Since this is provided by the table, eliminate (D). The formula to calculate standard deviation is very long and complicated. However, it is not necessary to use the formula here. Just understand that the standard deviation is a measure of how far apart the values are spread out. Notice that a strong majority of students received a 4 on the Physics quiz. Since most of

the students got the same score, the scores are not very spread out. Since the distribution of scores on the English quiz is more even, these scores are more spread out. Therefore, the standard deviation is higher for the English quiz. The answer is (A).

25. **D** The question asks what *must be true*, so expect to plug in more than once. Plug in a value for b such that $b < -b$. Let $b = -3$. If $b = -3$, then $-3 < a < 3$. Let $a = 2$. Go through each statement. Statement (I) says $a < 0$. Since $a = 2 > 0$, cross out (I) and eliminate the choices that include (I): (A) and (C). Since both remaining choices include (III), (III) must be true, so only worry about (II). Since $b = -3$, (II) is true, so keep (II) at least for now. Try to come up with a number a value of b that will satisfy the inequality but make (II) false. Try a positive number. If $b = 4$, then $4 < a < -4$. Since 4 is not less than -4, do not use $b = 4$. Notice that any positive number leads to the same problem. Try $b = 0$. If $b = 0$, then $0 < a < 0$. Again, 0 is not less than 0, so do not use $b = 0$. Since positive numbers and 0 do not satisfy the inequality, only negative numbers do. Therefore, (II) must be true. Eliminate the remaining answer that does not include (II), which is (B). The answer is (D).

26. **A** The question asks for how the number 31 relates to the scatterplot. The number 31 is the y-intercept of the line, or the point at which $x = 0$. The x-axis refers to the number of hours spent on the Internet, and the y-axis refers to the score on the quiz. Therefore, a student who spends no time on the Internet would be expected to score around a 31. Go through the answer choices. Choice (A) says that even students who spend very little time on the Internet are unlikely to score above a 31. This matches the prediction. Also, only one of the data points is above 31. Keep (A). Choice (B) says that even students who spend very little time on the Internet will never score above 31. This is more extreme than the prediction. Also, there is a data point above 31. Eliminate (B). Choice (C) says the lowest score was about 31% of the highest score. This doesn't match the prediction. Also, the highest score is about 34 and the lowest score is about 6, so the lowest score is $\frac{6}{34} \times 100 \approx 18\%$ of the highest score. Eliminate (C). Choice (D) says the highest score on the test was 31. Similar to (B), this is more extreme than the prediction. Also, there is a data point above 31. Eliminate (D). The answer is (A).

27. **C** To determine which polynomial is divisible, plug in a value for x. Let $x = 2$. If $x = 2$, then $r(x) = r(2) = 3(2)^3 + 24(2)^2 + 21(2) = 162$, $s(x) = s(2) = 2^2 + 8(2) + 7 = 27$, and $3x + 4 = 3(2) + 4 = 10$. The question asks which choice is divisible by $3x + 4$, plug in $x = 2$ to each choice and eliminate any choice that isn't divisible by 10. Choice (A) is $r(2) + s(2) = 162 + 27 = 189$. This is not divisible by 10, so eliminate (A). Choice (B) is $r(2) + 2s(2) = 162 + 2(27) = 216$. This is not divisible by 10, so eliminate (B). Choice (C) is $r(2) + 4s(2) = 162 + 4(27) = 270$. This is divisible by 10, so keep (C).

Choice (D) is $2r(2) + 4s(2) = 2(162) + 4(27) = 432$. This is not divisible by 10, so eliminate (D). The only remaining choice is (C).

28. **A** The question asks for what value of c does $g(x) = c$ have one real solution. Since c is on the other side of the equal sign, it is the y-value. Therefore, if $g(x) = c$ has one real solution, it will intersect the line $y = c$ exactly once. Let each answer choice equal c and draw the line $y = c$. Draw $y = 3, y = 1, y = 0$, and $y = -1$. Each line should be a horizontal line crossing the y-axis at 3, 1, 0, and -1, respectively. The lines $y = 1, y = 0$, and $y = -1$ cross the graph of g at three points each. Therefore, if c is any of these values, $g(x) = c$ has three real solutions. The line $y = 3$ crosses g exactly once, so $g(x) = 3$ has exactly one real solution. Therefore, the answer is (A).

29. **B** The question asks for the form of a quadratic in which the minimum value appears. A parabola reaches its minimum (or maximum) value at its vertex, so get the equation into vertex form, which is $y = a(x - h)^2 + k$, where (h, k) is the vertex. Choice (C) is not in this form, so eliminate it. To get g into vertex form, expand using FOIL: $(x - 10)(x + 4) = x^2 + 4x - 10x - 40 = x^2 - 6x - 40$. Eliminate (D), which is not equivalent to this. Get the quadratic into vertex form by completing the square. The coefficient on the x term is -6. Cut this value in half to get -3, and square the result to get 9. Add 9 to both sides (without combining like terms) to get $y + 9 = x^2 - 6x + 9 - 40$. Factor $(x^2 - 6x + 9)$ to get $y + 9 = (x - 3)^2 - 40$. Subtract 9 from both sides to get $y = (x - 3)^2 - 49$. Thus, the vertex is $(3, -49)$ and the minimum value is -49. Choice (B) is correct.

30. **C** There are variables in the answer choices, so plug in. Let $x = 2$. The question states that a is the average of $4x$ and 7. The sum of $4x$ and 7 is $4(2) + 7 = 15$, so the average is $\frac{15}{2} = 7.5$. The question also states that b is the average of $5x$ and 6. The sum of $5x$ and 6 is $5(2) + 6 = 16$, so the average is $\frac{16}{2} = 8$. Finally, the question states that c is the average of $3x$ and 11. The sum of $3x$ and 11 is $3(2) + 11 = 17$, so the average is $\frac{17}{2} = 8.5$. The question asks for the average of a, b, and c. The sum of a, b, and c is $7.5 + 8 + 8.5 = 24$, so the average is $\frac{24}{3} = 8$. Circle 8; this is the target number. Go through the answer choices and eliminate any choice that is not equal to 8. Choice (A) is $x + 4 = 2 + 4 = 6$, so eliminate (A). Choice (B) is $x + 8 = 2 + 8 = 10$, so eliminate (B). Choice (C) is $2x + 4 = 2(2) + 4 = 8$, so keep (C). Choice (D) is $4x + 8 = 4(2) + 8 = 16$, so eliminate (D). The answer is (C).

31. **1.2** The question asks how much of a decrease in target heart rate will occur if the person's age increases by 2 years. Plug in two values of y that are 2 years apart. Start with $y = 20$. If $y = 20$, then $R = \frac{3(220 - 20)}{5} = 120$. Now try $y = 22$. If $y = 22$, then $R = \frac{3(220 - 22)}{5} = 118.8$. To determine the decrease, subtract the two values of R to get $120 - 118.8 = 1.2$. The answer is 1.2.

32. **620** The question asks how many miles into the journey the driver will be at 8:00 P.M. From 1 P.M. to 8 P.M., the driver travels for 7 hours. To determine the distance traveled, use *distance = rate × time* to get $d = rt = (60 \text{ miles per hour})(7 \text{ hours}) = 420$ miles. This is not the answer. Note that at 1:00 P.M. the driver is already 200 miles into his journey. Therefore, the driver has traveled a total of 200 miles + 420 miles = 620 miles. The answer is 620.

33. $\dfrac{25}{4}$, $\dfrac{50}{8}$, or **6.25**

The variables in the question are given in terms of each other, so plug in. Let the first object travel at an acceleration of $a = 4$ for a time of $t = 10$. The displacement is $d = \dfrac{1}{2}(4)(10)^2 = 200$. The second object also has an acceleration of $a = 4$ but for a time of $2.5t = 2.5(10) = 25$. This displacement is $d = \dfrac{1}{2}(4)(25)^2 = 1{,}250$. The question asks for the ratio of velocity of the object that traveled for more time to the velocity of the object that traveled for less time. This is $\dfrac{1{,}250}{200}$. This requires more than four spaces on the answer sheet, so reduce the fraction to get $\dfrac{25}{4}$. (Note that $\dfrac{50}{8}$ is also an acceptable answer, as is 6.25.)

34. **8.16** The question asks for how many pounds are equivalent to 488 shematies. The question states that 12 shematies is equivalent to 1 deben, so set up the proportion $\dfrac{12 \text{ shematies}}{1 \text{ deben}} = \dfrac{488 \text{ shematies}}{x \text{ debens}}$. Cross-multiply to get $12x = 488$. Divide by 12 to get $x = 40.\overline{66}$, so 488 shematies is equivalent to $40.\overline{66}$ debens. The question also says that a deben is approximately equal to 3.21 ounces, so set up the proportion $\dfrac{3.21 \text{ ounces}}{1 \text{ deben}} = \dfrac{y \text{ ounces}}{40.66 \text{ debens}}$. Cross-multiply to get $y = 130.54$, so 488 shematies is equivalent to 130.54 ounces. Finally, the question states that 16 ounces is equivalent to one pound, so set up the proportion $\dfrac{16 \text{ ounces}}{1 \text{ pound}} = \dfrac{130.54 \text{ ounces}}{z \text{ pounds}}$. Cross-multiply to get $16z = 130.54$. Divide both sides by 16 to get $z = 8.15875$. The question asks for the answer to the nearest hundredth, so the answer is 8.16.

35. **43, 44,** or **45**

The question asks about arc, so use the arc formula, $\dfrac{arc}{circumference} = \dfrac{angle}{360}$. The radius is 20, so use the circumference formula to get that the circumference is $C = 2\pi r = 2\pi(20) = 40\pi$. The arc is between 15 and 16, so start with an arc of 15 to get $\dfrac{15}{40\pi} = \dfrac{y}{360}$. Cross-multiply to get $5{,}400 = 40\pi y$. Divide both sides by 40π to get $y = \dfrac{5{,}400}{40\pi} = \dfrac{135}{\pi} = 42.9718$. Now try an arc of 16 to get $\dfrac{16}{40\pi} = \dfrac{y}{360}$. Cross-multiply to get $5,760 = 40\pi y$. Divide both sides by 40π to get

$y = \dfrac{5,760}{40\pi} = \dfrac{144}{\pi} \approx 45.8366$. The angle is, therefore, in between these two values of y. The

question specifies that the answer must be an integer. Therefore, to get credit, grid in one of the

following answers: 43, 44, or 45.

36. **90** The question says that $\dfrac{2}{5}$ of the marbles in the closet must be blue. At the beginning, there are 230

blue marbles and 370 red marbles, so there are a total of 230 + 370 = 600 marbles. 110 red marbles

are added, so there is now a total of 370 + 110 = 480 red marbles and 600 + 110 = 710 total mar-

bles. The question asks how many blue marbles must be added so that $\dfrac{2}{5}$ of the marbles are blue. If

b blue marbles are added, there will be 230 + b blue marbles and 710 + b total marbles. Set up the

equation $\dfrac{230 + b}{710 + b} = \dfrac{2}{5}$. Cross-multiply to get $5(230 + b) = 2(710 + b)$. Distribute to get $1,150 + 5b$

$= 1,420 + 2b$. Subtract $2b$ from both sides to get $1,150 + 3b = 1,420$. Subtract 1,150 from both sides

to get $3b = 270$. Divide both sides by 3 to get $b = 90$. The answer is 90.

37. **1.07** The question asks for the value of r in the bank's interest formula. Interest is a type of exponential

growth. The formula for this is *final amount = original amount*$(1 + rate)^{number\ of\ changes}$. The original

amount is \$5,400 and the rate of interest is 7%. In the formula, rate is in decimal form rather than

percent form, so the rate is 0.07. The bank pays annual interest, so the number of changes is the

number of years, which is y. The final amount is the amount in the bank after y years, which is

A. Plug these into the exponential growth formula to get $A = 5,400(1 + 0.07)^y$ or $A = 5,400(1.07)^y$.

This is now in the same form as the equation provided by the question, $A = 5,400(r)^y$. Since the

question asks for the value of r in the question's formula, which is in the same position as 1.07 in

the standard interest formula, the answer is 1.07.

38. **7,078** As discussed in the explanation for Question 38, $r = 1.07$, so $A = 5,400(1.07)^y$. The question asks for

the value after four years, so $A = 5,400(1.07)^4$. Enter this into a calculator to get about \$7,078.29.

The question asks for the value to the nearest dollar (disregarding the dollar sign), so the answer is

7,078. Without the formula, it is still possible to get the answer. Just add 7% of 5,400 to get the

value after one year, 7% of that new value to get the value after two years, and do that 2 more

times to get the value after four years.

Chapter 11
Practice Test 5

Reading Test

65 MINUTES, 52 QUESTIONS

Turn to Section 1 of your answer sheet to answer the questions in this section.

DIRECTIONS

Each passage or pair of passages below is followed by a number of questions. After reading each passage or pair, choose the best answer to each question based on what is stated or implied in the passage or passages and in any accompanying graphics (such as a table or graph).

Questions 1–10 are based on the following passage.

This passage is excerpted from Robert Louis Stevenson, *Treasure Island,* originally published in 1883. The narrator and his parents own an inn on the English coast.

The stranger kept hanging about just inside the inn door, peering round the corner like a cat waiting for a mouse. Once I stepped out myself into the road, but
Line he immediately called me back, and as I did not obey
5 quick enough for his fancy, a most horrible change came over his tallowy face, and he ordered me in with an oath that made me jump. As soon as I was back again he returned to his former manner, half fawning, half sneering, patted me on the shoulder, told me I
10 was a good boy and he had taken quite a fancy to me. "I have a son of my own," said he, "as like you as two blocks, and he's all the pride of my 'art. But the great thing for boys is discipline, sonny—discipline. Now, if you had sailed along of Bill, you wouldn't have stood
15 there to be spoke to twice—not you. That was never Bill's way, nor the way of sich as sailed with him. And here, sure enough, is my mate Bill, with a spy-glass under his arm, bless his old 'art, to be sure. You and me'll just go back into the parlour, sonny, and get
20 behind the door, and we'll give Bill a little surprise— bless his 'art, I say again."

So saying, the stranger backed along with me into the parlour and put me behind him in the corner so that we were both hidden by the open door. I was very
25 uneasy and alarmed, as you may fancy, and it rather added to my fears to observe that the stranger was certainly frightened himself. He cleared the hilt of his

cutlass and loosened the blade in the sheath; and all the time we were waiting there he kept swallowing as if
30 he felt what we used to call a lump in the throat.

At last in strode the captain, slammed the door behind him, without looking to the right or left, and marched straight across the room to where his breakfast awaited him.
35 "Bill," said the stranger in a voice that I thought he had tried to make bold and big.

The captain spun round on his heel and fronted us; all the brown had gone out of his face, and even his nose was blue; he had the look of a man who sees a
40 ghost, or the evil one, or something worse, if anything can be; and upon my word, I felt sorry to see him all in a moment turn so old and sick.

"Come, Bill, you know me; you know an old shipmate, Bill, surely," said the stranger.
45 The captain made a sort of gasp.

"Black Dog!" said he.

"And who else?" returned the other, getting more at his ease. "Black Dog as ever was, come for to see his old shipmate Billy, at the Admiral Benbow Inn. Ah,
50 Bill, Bill, we have seen a sight of times, us two, since I lost them two talons," holding up his mutilated hand.

"Now, look here," said the captain; "you've run me down; here I am; well, then, speak up; what is it?"

"That's you, Bill," returned Black Dog, "you're
55 in the right of it, Billy. I'll have a glass of rum from this dear child here, as I've took such a liking to; and we'll sit down, if you please, and talk square, like old shipmates."

CONTINUE ➔

When I returned with the rum, they were already
60 seated on either side of the captain's breakfast-table—
Black Dog next to the door and sitting sideways so
as to have one eye on his old shipmate and one, as I
thought, on his retreat.

He bade me go and leave the door wide open.
65 "None of your keyholes for me, sonny," he said; and I
left them together and retired into the bar.

For a long time, though I certainly did my best to
listen, I could hear nothing but a low gattling; but at
last the voices began to grow higher, and I could pick
70 up a word or two, mostly oaths, from the captain.

"No, no, no, no; and an end of it!" he cried once.
And again, "If it comes to swinging, swing all, say I."

1

Which choice is the best synopsis of what happens in
the passage?

A) Two characters make a plan to surprise a third
   character.

B) One character shows another character how to
   properly behave in a parlour.

C) One character unpleasantly surprises another
   character with an unexpected reunion.

D) Two characters reminisce about their time
   together on a ship.

2

Which choice best describes the developmental
pattern of the passage?

A) A detailed analysis of an enthusiastic encounter

B) An inaccurate dictation of a notable conference

C) An apprehensive account of a contentious meeting

D) A dismissive description of an important
   homecoming

3

As it is used in line 5 and line 10, "fancy" most nearly
means

A) elaboration.

B) impatience.

C) imagination.

D) preference.

4

Which emotion does the narrator most sense from
the stranger regarding his imminent meeting with the
captain?

A) The stranger is fearful about the captain's reaction
   to seeing him.

B) The stranger is overjoyed to reunite with the
   captain.

C) The stranger is worried the captain won't
   remember him.

D) The stranger is concerned the captain will be more
   interested in his breakfast than in conversation.

5

Which choice provides the best evidence for the
answer to the previous questions?

A) Lines 24–27 ("I was . . . himself")

B) Lines 31–34 ("At last . . . him")

C) Lines 43–44 ("Come, Bill . . . stranger")

D) Line 71 ("No, no, . . . once")

6

In the passage, the stranger addresses the narrator
with

A) respect but not friendliness.

B) violence but not anger.

C) disgust but not hatred.

D) affection but not trust.

CONTINUE ➡

7

The main purpose of the first paragraph is to

A) introduce a character.

B) criticize a belief.

C) describe a relationship.

D) investigate a discrepancy.

8

As it is used in line 51, "talons" most nearly means

A) weapons.

B) claws.

C) fingers.

D) hooks.

9

Why does the narrator describe the captain's face as something from which "all the brown had gone out of" (line 38)?

A) The captain has grown pale after being on land so long.

B) The captain has washed his face before the meal.

C) The captain has become ill during his walk.

D) The captain has gone pale with fright.

10

Which choice provides the best evidence for the answer to the previous question?

A) Lines 22–24 ("So saying . . . door")

B) Lines 39–42 ("he had . . . sick")

C) Lines 52–53 ("Now, look . . . is it")

D) Lines 59–63 ("When I . . . retreat")

CONTINUE

Questions 11–21 are based on the following passage and supplementary material.

This passage is adapted from Russell W. Belk, "It's the Thought that Counts." © 1976 by University of Illinois at Urbana Champaign.

The phenomenon of selecting an object or service "X" to present as a gift to person "Y" on occasion "Z" is a unique and important act of consumer behavior.
Line Not only must the gift giver attempt to infer the
5 recipient's tastes, needs, desires, and reactions, the gift selection may also be affected by the information which it would appear to convey about the giver and the giver-recipient relationship. The ancient practice of gift-giving is still pervasive and significant in modern
10 cultures. For instance, Lowes, Turner, and Willis (1971) cite a series of British Gallup Polls from 1963-1967, in which it was found that over 90 percent of the adult population did some Christmas gift-giving each year. Another limited sample of middle and upper
15 income families in Montreal, Caron and Ward (1975) found that third- and fifth-grade children received an average of between five and six gifts for Christmas. Both because of its prevalence and because of its strong interpersonal meanings, gift-giving offers a potentially
20 rich area for consumer behavioral explanation.

Gift-giving has been treated from a variety of related theoretical perspectives, focusing primarily on the functions and effects of giving. The preeminent theoretical analysis of the gift-giving process is an essay
25 by French anthropologist-sociologist Marcell Mauss (1923). Based on his examination of gift-giving among numerous primitive, remote, or ancient societies, Mauss concluded that gift-giving is a self-perpetuating system of reciprocity. More specifically, Mauss outlined
30 three types of obligations, which perpetuate gift-giving:
    1. The obligation to give,
    2. The obligation to receive,
    3. The obligation to repay.
The obligation to give may be based on moral
35 or religious imperatives, the need to recognize and maintain a status hierarchy, the need to establish or maintain peaceful relations, or simply the expectation of reciprocal giving. These motives, which do not admit purely selfless giving, become institutionalized
40 in a society so that under appropriate conditions an individual is socially obligated to give. Receiving is seen as similarly obligatory, and avoiding or refusing gifts is construed as an unfriendly or even hostile act. Mauss noted however that there is a certain tension
45 created in receiving a gift since acceptance is an implicit recognition of dependence on the giver. This tension may then be reduced by fulfilling the third obligation, the obligation to repay. Failure to repay or failure to repay adequately results in a loss of status
50 and self-esteem. Adequate or overly adequate repayment, on the other hand, creates an obligation to repay on the part of the original giver, and the cycle is reinitiated.

Schwartz (1967) noted that beyond the functions
55 served by the general process of gift exchange, the characteristics of the gift itself also act as a powerful statement of the giver's perception of the recipient. He also suggested that acceptance of a particular gift constitutes an acknowledgment and acceptance of the
60 identity that the gift is seen to imply. Among children this may lead to lasting changes in self-perceptions, but presumably gifts have less influence on the self-concept of an adult.

Nevertheless, the importance of this symbolic
65 function of gift selection appears clear enough in a gift shop's recent advertisement, which asks, "Do you want your gifts to tell someone how creative you are, how thoughtful you are, or just how big your Christmas bonus was? Do you buy with a specific
70 price or a specific personality in mind?" While the answers to such basic questions about gift selection may be personally evident, the underlying behavioral questions have not been addressed by empirical research.
75 There can be little doubt that gift-giving is a pervasive experience in human life and consumer behavior. Despite the additional variables which gift-giving introduces to conceptions of consumer behavior (e.g. characteristics of the recipient, gifter-
80 receiver similarity, nature of the occasion), the present findings suggest that preference for cognitive balance is a concept which can go far toward explaining gift selection and evaluation.

CONTINUE

GIFT-GIVING AS COMMUNICATION

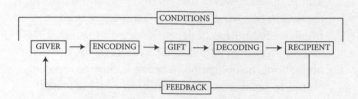

11

The author most likely uses the examples in lines 4–17 of the passage ("Not only . . . Christmas") to highlight the

A) recent increase in consumerism around Christmas time.

B) discrepancies in gift-giving between ancient and modern times.

C) apprehension between gift-givers and receivers.

D) pervasiveness of gift-giving on special occasions.

12

In line 20, the word "rich" most nearly means

A) opulent.

B) embellished.

C) fertile.

D) saccharine.

13

The author indicates that the self-perpetuating system of reciprocity

A) is a form of communication between gift-giver and recipient.

B) functions as a form of status hierarchy.

C) can wreak havoc on a child's concept of him- or herself.

D) requires equal participation in a relationship.

14

Which choice provides the best evidence for the answer to the previous question?

A) Lines 5–8 ("the gift . . . relationship")

B) Lines 34–38 ("The obligation . . . giving")

C) Lines 50–53 ("Adequate or . . . reinitiated")

D) Lines 60–63 ("Among children . . . adult")

15

Schwartz, mentioned in paragraph 4 (lines 54–63), would likely describe the process of gift exchange as

A) stressful.

B) unnerving.

C) intentional.

D) symbolic.

16

The fourth paragraph (lines 54–63) indicates that the acceptance of a gift may be

A) considerate.

B) influential.

C) authoritative.

D) immutable.

17

Which choice provides the best evidence for the answer to the previous question?

A) Lines 58–60 ("He also . . . imply")

B) Lines 60–63 ("Among children . . . adult")

C) Lines 66–69 ("Do you . . . was")

D) Lines 75–77 ("There can . . . behavior")

CONTINUE →

18

As it is used in line 65, "function" most nearly means

A) purpose.

B) tradition.

C) occasion.

D) occupation.

19

The author refers to a gift shop's recent advertisement (lines 65–66) in order to

A) question a former claim.

B) offer a motive.

C) introduce a counter explanation.

D) support an argument.

20

The graph and the passage offer evidence that the communication process of gift-giving predicts that a gift will demonstrate

A) the receiver's self-concept.

B) the amount the gift-giver spent.

C) encoded meaning.

D) the thoughtfulness of the gift-giver.

21

The author would likely attribute the encoding and decoding phases of communication as represented in the graph to

A) an emerging form of conditional approval.

B) an inability to communicate effectively.

C) an increasing amount of pressure on gift-giving.

D) a component of implicit evaluation.

CONTINUE

Questions 22–31 are based on the following passage and supplementary material.

This passage is adapted from Nils Ekholm, "On the Variations of the Climate of the Geological and Historical Past and Their Causes." © 1901 by *Quarterly Journal of the Royal Meteorological Society.* Ekholm's studies are based on new mathematical calculations that show discrepancies among earlier scientists' findings in the study of historical changes in climate.

The atmosphere plays a very important part of a double character as to the temperature at the earth's surface. Firstly, the atmosphere may act like the glass of a green-house, letting through the light rays of the sun
5 relatively easily, and absorbing a great part of the dark rays emitted from the ground, and it thereby may raise the mean temperature of the earth's surface. Secondly, the atmosphere acts as a heat store placed between the relatively warm ground and the cold space, and thereby
10 lessens in a high degree the annual, diurnal, and local variations of the temperature.

There are two qualities of the atmosphere that produce these effects. The one is that the temperature of the atmosphere generally decreases with the height
15 above the ground or the sea-level, owing partly to the dynamical heating of descending air currents and the dynamical cooling of ascending ones, as is explained in the mechanical theory of heat. The other is that the atmosphere, absorbing but little of the
20 insolation and most of the radiation from the ground, receives a considerable part of its heat store from the ground by means of radiation, contact, convection, and conduction, whereas the earth's surface is heated principally by direct radiation from the sun through
25 the transparent air.

It follows from this that the radiation from the earth into space does not go on directly from the ground, but on average from a layer of the atmosphere having a considerable height above sea-level. The
30 height of that layer depends on the thermal quality of the atmosphere, and will vary with that quality. The greater is the absorbing power of the air for heat rays emitted from the ground, the higher will that layer be. But the higher the layer, the lower is its temperature
35 relatively to that of the ground; and as the radiation from the layer into space is the less the lower its temperature is, it follows that the ground will be hotter the higher the radiating layer is.

Now if we are able to calculate or estimate how
40 much the mean temperature that layer is lower than the mean temperature of the ground, we may apply Table I for calculating the mean temperature of the ground, as soon as we know by direct measurements the quantity of solar heat absorbed by the ground.
45 Owing to the clouds and dust floating in the atmosphere, this heat is probably only about a third of that derived by using Langley's solar constant; and is thus about 360 calories per square centimeter during twenty-four hours. This gives, by means of Table I,
50 a temperature of –31°C to the radiating layer. But, according to Arrhenius's estimate, this is at a height of about 7600 meters; and assuming a corresponding decrease of 0.6°C per 100 meters, we find its temperature to be 46°C lower than that of the ground,
55 and thus the mean temperature of the ground equal to 15°C, as it is according to observations.

The table shows the loss of heat by radiation into space from a perfectly black body of the temperature $t°$ centigrade. In gram-calories per square centimeter per
60 24 hours at 7600 meters.

t	Loss of Heat	t	Loss of Heat	t	Loss of Heat
100	2023	20	770	–60	215
80	1624	0	581	–80	145
60	1285	–20	428	–100	94
40	1003	–40	308	–120	57

22

A student claims that over half of solar radiation influences the ground temperature on the earth's surface. Which of the following statements in the passage contradicts the student's claim?

A) Lines 3–7 ("Firstly, the . . . surface")

B) Lines 13–18 ("The one . . . heat")

C) Lines 45–49 ("Owing to . . . hours")

D) Lines 49–50 ("This gives . . . layer")

CONTINUE

23

In the first paragraph (lines 1–11), what does the author claim is the atmosphere's importance to the temperature of the earth's surface?

A) The trapping of all hot air and energy from the sun

B) Controlling the heat energy that is admitted and released

C) The enclosure of all the earth's heat-producing mechanisms

D) The free passage of heat energy to and from the surface

24

The author uses the word "green-house" in line 4 to indicate that

A) the heat on the ground and in the atmosphere of the earth is provided exclusively by solar radiation.

B) most of the heat in the atmosphere comes from radiation from the ground.

C) the agricultural and botanical sectors of the economy are those most affected by climate fluctuations.

D) solar heat enters the atmosphere relatively unobstructed but the same does not apply as it leaves.

25

Based on the passage, the author's statement "the earth's surface is heated principally by direct radiation from the sun through the transparent air" (lines 23–25) implies that

A) when the sun is obscured by clouds the ground is heated principally by other sources of energy.

B) heat generated independently by the ground and by the sun is held in the atmosphere and released as cool air.

C) the heat from the sun that warms the ground must be partially absorbed by the earth's atmosphere.

D) the solar heat reflected back from the earth does not account for all the heat in the atmosphere.

26

The author's use of the words "if," "may," and "as soon as" in lines 39–43 functions mainly to

A) provide definitive evidence that the author's mathematical calculations predict the span of global warming with accuracy.

B) demonstrate that many of the author's conclusions rely on both observable and non-observable factors.

C) support the hypothesis that ground temperatures are warmer than higher temperatures.

D) warn against the indiscretion of earlier scientists who made incorrect claims with insufficient evidence.

27

The author's main purpose in noting the observations of ground temperature is to

A) indicate that the mathematical calculations given in this paragraph correspond to data recorded by others.

B) show the limitations of mathematical formulas in providing precise measurements of observable phenomena.

C) provide an example of one place in which the global temperature has risen because of human activity.

D) underline the importance of mathematical calculations in determining the influence of solar radiation.

28

Based on the table and passage, which choice gives the correct temperature on the ground when the loss of heat is approximately 300 gram-calories per square centimeter for 24 hours?

A) 40°C

B) 6°C

C) −6°C

D) −40°C

CONTINUE

29

Do the data in the table support the author's claim regarding the atmosphere as a heat store?

A) Yes, because at each given temperature, as the temperature decreases, the heat loss decreases as well but by larger and larger intervals.

B) Yes, because at each given temperature, as the temperature decreases, the heat loss decreases as well but by smaller and smaller intervals.

C) No, because at each given temperature, as the temperature decreases, the heat loss fluctuates according to an irregular pattern and series of intervals.

D) No, because at each given temperature, as the temperature decreases, the heat loss increases by larger and larger intervals.

30

According to the table, which of the following pairs of heat-loss values at different temperatures provide evidence in support of the answer to the previous question?

A) 2023 to 1624 and 2023 to 57

B) 1003 to 581 and 581 to 94

C) 1003 to 770 and 770 to 581

D) 308 to 94 and 581 to 57

31

Based on the passage and the table, does the temperature of the atmosphere of the earth stay the same or does it vary with distance from the earth, and which statement made by the authors is most consistent with this data?

A) It varies; "Now if . . . ground" (lines 39–44)

B) It varies; "But, according . . . observations" (lines 50–56)

C) The same; "Firstly, the . . . surface" (lines 3–7)

D) The same; "It follows . . . sea-level" (lines 26–29)

CONTINUE

Questions 32–41 are based on the following passage.

This passage is adapted from Frederick Douglass's speech "On Women's Suffrage" delivered in 1888 to a gathering of women's suffrage activists.

Mrs. President, Ladies and Gentlemen:— I come
to this platform with unusual diffidence. Although I
have long been identified with the Woman's Suffrage
movement, and have often spoken in its favor, I am
5 somewhat at a loss to know what to say on this really
great and uncommon occasion, where so much has
been said.

When I look around on this assembly, and see the
many able and eloquent women, full of the subject,
10 ready to speak, and who only need the opportunity
to impress this audience with their views and thrill
them with "thoughts that breathe and words that
burn," I do not feel like taking up more than a very
small space of your time and attention, and shall not.
15 I would not, even now, presume to speak, but for
the circumstance of my early connection with the
cause, and of having been called upon to do so by one
whose voice in this Council we all gladly obey. Men
have very little business here as speakers, anyhow;
20 and if they come here at all they should take back
benches and wrap themselves in silence. For this is an
International Council, not of men, but of women, and
woman should have all the say in it. This is her day in
court. I do not mean to exalt the intellect of woman
25 above man's; but I have heard many men speak on
this subject, some of them the most eloquent to be
found anywhere in the country; and I believe no man,
however gifted with thought and speech, can voice
the wrongs and present the demands of women with
30 the skill and effect, with the power and authority of
woman herself. The man struck is the man to cry out.
Woman knows and feels her wrongs as man cannot
know and feel them, and she also knows as well as he
can know, what measures are needed to redress them.
35 I grant all the claims at this point. She is her own best
representative. We can neither speak for her, nor vote
for her, nor act for her, nor be responsible for her; and
the thing for men to do in the premises is just to get
out of her way and give her the fullest opportunity
40 to exercise all the powers inherent in her individual

personality, and allow her to do it as she herself shall
elect to exercise them. Her right to be and to do is as
full, complete and perfect as the right of any man on
earth. I say of her, as I say of the colored people, "Give
45 her fair play, and hands off." There was a time when,
perhaps, we men could help a little. It was when this
woman suffrage cause was in its cradle, when it was
not big enough to go alone, when it had to be taken
in the arms of its mother from Seneca Falls, N.Y., to
50 Rochester, N.Y., for baptism. I then went along with it
and offered my services to help it, for then it needed
help; but now it can afford to dispense with me and all
of my sex. Then its friends were few—now its friends
are many. Then it was wrapped in obscurity—now it is
55 lifted in sight of the whole civilized world, and people
of all lands and languages give it their hearty support.
Truly the change is vast and wonderful.

There may be some well-meaning people in this
audience who have never attended a woman suffrage
60 convention, never heard a woman suffrage speech,
never read a woman suffrage newspaper, and they may
be surprised that those who speak here do not argue
the question. It may be kind to tell them that our cause
has passed beyond the period of arguing. The demand
65 of the hour is not argument, but assertion, firm and
inflexible assertion, assertion which has more than
the force of an argument. If there is any argument
to be made, it must be made by opponents, not by
the friends of woman suffrage. Let those who want
70 argument examine the ground upon which they base
their claim to the right to vote. They will find that there
is not one reason, not one consideration, which they
can urge in support of man's claim to vote, which does
not equally support the right of woman to vote.

32

The main purpose of the passage is to

A) qualify the credentials of a speaker.

B) provide support for the suffrage movement.

C) argue for the equal rights of women.

D) compare the sufferings of women to those of
African-Americans.

33

The central claim of the passage is that

A) women should have the floor at this assembly.

B) men should act for women in this movement.

C) women and men have the same justification for voting.

D) the suffrage movement should be less obscure.

34

Douglass uses the word "cause" throughout the passage mainly to

A) clarify his early connection to the suffrage movement.

B) explain why the suffrage movement deserves support.

C) compare the suffrage movement to a baby in a cradle.

D) describe the suffrage movement.

35

According to the passage, Douglass

A) wants to give a great speech, because he has been identified with the suffrage movement.

B) is hesitant to speak, even though he has been identified with the suffrage movement.

C) does not want to speak, though he has been identified with the suffrage movement.

D) is hesitant to give a lengthy speech, since he has been identified with the suffrage movement.

36

Douglass indicates that men

A) should not be speakers in such a movement.

B) should not take too much time and attention.

C) should primarily listen at such a gathering.

D) should voice the wrongs of women publicly.

37

Which choice provides the best evidence for the answer to the previous question?

A) Lines 8–14 ("When I . . . not")

B) Lines 15–18 ("I would . . . obey")

C) Lines 18–21 ("Men have . . . silence")

D) Lines 24–31 ("I do . . . herself")

38

Douglass characterizes the "demands of women" in line 29 as related to injuries that

A) women can best describe and suggest solutions for.

B) men should speak about more eloquently.

C) the civilized world should support heartily.

D) men and women should both be responsible for.

39

Which choice provides the best evidence for the answer to the previous question?

A) Lines 25–27 ("but I . . . country")

B) Lines 32–34 ("Woman knows . . . them")

C) Lines 42–44 ("Her right . . . earth")

D) Lines 45–46 ("There was . . . little")

CONTINUE

40

Which choice most closely captures the meaning of the figurative "cradle" referred to in line 47?

A) Nest

B) Rock

C) Hold

D) Beginnings

41

The surprise referred to in lines 58–74 mainly serves to emphasize how

A) some attendees may have expected different sorts of speeches.

B) male attendees may have expected more arguments than assertions.

C) audience members may not have expected speeches on women's suffrage.

D) speakers may have presented unexpected arguments for the right to vote.

CONTINUE

Questions 42–52 are based on the following passages.

Passage 1 is adapted from Michael B. McElroy and Xi Li, "Fracking's Future." © 2013 by *Harvard Monthly*. Passage 2 is adapted from Natural Resources Defense Council, "Unchecked Fracking Threatens Health, Water Supplies." © 2015.

Passage 1

Supplies of natural gas now economically recoverable from shale in the United States could accommodate the country's domestic demand for natural gas at current levels of consumption for more
5 than a hundred years: an economic and strategic boon, and, at least in the near term, an important stepping-stone toward lower-carbon, greener energy.

The first step in extracting gas from shale involves drilling vertically to reach the shale layer, typically a
10 kilometer or more below the surface. Drilling then continues horizontally, extending a kilometer or more from the vertical shaft, and the vertical and horizontal components of the well are lined with steel casing, cemented in place. The horizontal extension of the
15 casing is then perforated, using explosives; thereafter, water, carrying sand and proprietary chemicals, is injected into the well at high pressure. The water encounters the shale through the perforations, generating a series of small fractures in the rock (hence
20 the nickname, "fracking"); the sand in the water keeps the cracks open, while the chemicals enhance release of gas from the shale. The injected water flows back up to the surface when the pressure in the well is released following completion of the fracking procedure. Then
25 the well starts to produce natural gas.

As many as 25 fracture stages (per horizontal leg) may be involved in preparing a single site for production, each requiring injection of more than 400,000 gallons of water—a possible total of more than
30 10 million gallons before the well is fully operational. A portion of the injected water flows back to the surface, heavily contaminated with the fracking chemicals and others it has absorbed from the shale. Depending on the local geology, this "return water" may also include
35 radioactive elements.

Drillers developing a well must take exceptional care to minimize contact between the wellbore and the surrounding aquifer—often the source of nearby residents' fresh water. Serious problems have arisen
40 in the past from failures to isolate the drilling liquids,

including cases where well water used for drinking became so contaminated that human and animal health was threatened. It is essential that monitoring be in place to ensure the continuing integrity of the seal
45 isolating the well from the aquifer even *after* the well has been fully exploited and abandoned.

Passage 2

The oil and gas industry is rapidly expanding production across the nation, as new technology makes it easier to extract oil or gas from previously
50 inaccessible sites. Over the last decade, the industry has drilled hundreds of thousands of new wells all across the country. These wells are accompanied by massive new infrastructure to move, process, and deliver oil and gas, together bringing full-scale
55 industrialization to often previously rural landscapes.

The sector's growth is spurred by the use of hydraulic fracturing, or fracking, in which often-dangerous chemicals are mixed with large quantities of water (or other base fluid) and sand and injected
60 into wells at extremely high pressure. Unconventional development using advanced fracking methods poses threats to water, air, land, and the health of communities. Studies have shown dangerous levels of toxic air pollution near fracking sites; and oil and
65 gas extraction have caused smog in rural areas at levels worse than downtown Los Angeles. Oil and gas production have been linked to increased risk of cancer and birth defects in neighboring areas; as well as to a risk of increased seismic activity.
70 Constant massive truck traffic associated with large-scale development disrupts communities and creates significant hazards. The millions of gallons of water used in fracking operations not only strain water resources, but end up as vast amounts of contaminated
75 wastewater. Fracking has been reported as a suspect in polluted drinking water around the country. And methane—a potent climate change pollutant—leaks rampantly throughout the extraction, processing, and distribution of oil and gas.
80 Weak safeguards and inadequate oversight have allowed oil and gas producers to run roughshod over communities across the country with their extraction and production activities for too long, resulting in

CONTINUE ▶

contaminated water supplies, dangerous air pollution,
85 destroyed streams, and devastated landscapes. Our
state and federal leaders have failed to hold them to
account, leaving the American people unprotected.
Many companies don't play by the few rules that do
exist; and industry has used its political power at every
90 turn to gain exemptions from environmental laws
designed to protect our air and water.

42

In lines 26–30, the author of Passage 1 mentions the
number of gallons of water primarily to

A) warn of the inevitable dangers of industrial
fracking in small communities.

B) show the variety of ways that natural gas and oil
can be extracted from shale.

C) expand upon the idea that fracking uses only a few
basic elements.

D) establish the size and scope of the industrial
equipment required for fracking.

43

The author of Passage 1 indicates that fracking could
have which positive effect?

A) It could support small, local economies that do
not have other sources of income.

B) It could alter the way scientists understand the
shale layer of the Earth.

C) It could provide resources that meet the needs of
contemporary consumers.

D) It could lower the price that large-scale industrial
firms pay for natural gas.

44

Which choice provides the best evidence for the
answer to the previous question?

A) Lines 1–5 ("Supplies of . . . years")

B) Lines 17–22 ("The water . . . shale")

C) Lines 22–25 ("The injected . . . gas")

D) Lines 30–35 ("A portion . . . elements")

45

What function does the discussion of the aquifer in
lines 36–46 serve in Passage 1?

A) It outlines one significant risk involved in the
process described in earlier paragraphs.

B) It addresses and disputes the concerns of those
whose attitude toward fracking is cautious.

C) It extends a discussion of a significant term that
begins in the previous paragraph.

D) It presents an unexpected new finding that
undermines industry arguments for a certain
practice.

46

As used in line 44, "integrity" most nearly means

A) morality.

B) impermeability.

C) moisture.

D) confidence.

47

The central claim of Passage 2 is that fracking mines
useful resources but

A) the wells that have been built are not sufficiently
productive to justify all the cost.

B) some experts believe that natural gas can be
acquired just as easily from other sources.

C) it may lead some industry executives to believe
that they can mine resources from any place they
choose.

D) it is currently not sufficiently regulated in a way
that is safe for local populations.

CONTINUE ▶

48

As used in line 81, "roughshod" most nearly means

A) productive.

B) rapid.

C) unregulated.

D) industrial.

49

Which statement best describes the relationship between the passages?

A) Passage 2 undermines the optimistic confidence of the author of Passage 1.

B) Passage 2 expands upon some of the concerns expressed less explicitly in Passage 1.

C) Passage 2 argues for certain regulations of which the author of Passage 1 does not approve.

D) Passage 2 describes the process discussed in Passage 1 but does so with more detail and statistics.

50

The author of Passage 2 would most likely respond to the discussion of drillers in lines 36–46, Passage 1, by claiming that these drillers

A) cite their successes in having grown the mining industry throughout the country.

B) often come from small towns themselves and are not likely to abuse the land.

C) have already caused irreparable harm to the American landscape.

D) can be difficult to contact when their work is conducted so far underground.

51

Which choice provides the best evidence for the answer to the previous question?

A) Lines 47–52 ("The oil . . . country")

B) Lines 56–60 ("The sector's . . . pressure")

C) Lines 66–72 ("Oil and . . . hazards")

D) Lines 80–85 ("Weak safeguards . . . landscapes")

52

Which point about the potential effects of fracking is implicit in Passage 2 and explicit in Passage 1?

A) The pollution caused by fracking can affect both the water and the air.

B) The process of fracking requires the use of many billions of gallons of water.

C) The process can contaminate drinking water and thus harm both animals and humans.

D) The economic costs of preparing wells can often cost more than the profits gained from mining.

STOP
**If you finish before time is called, you may check your work on this section only.
Do not turn to any other section in the test.**

No Test Material On This Page

Writing and Language Test

35 MINUTES, 44 QUESTIONS

Turn to Section 2 of your answer sheet to answer the questions in this section.

DIRECTIONS

Each passage below is accompanied by a number of questions. For some questions, you will consider how the passage might be revised to improve the expression of ideas. For other questions, you will consider how the passage might be edited to correct errors in sentence structure, usage, or punctuation. A passage or a question may be accompanied by one or more graphics (such as a table or graph) that you will consider as you make revising and editing decisions.

Some questions will direct you to an underlined portion of a passage. Other questions will direct you to a location in a passage or ask you to think about the passage as a whole.

After reading each passage, choose the answer to each question that most effectively improves the quality of writing in the passage or that makes the passage conform to the conventions of standard written English. Many questions include a "NO CHANGE" option. Choose that option if you think the best choice is to leave the relevant portion of the passage as it is.

Questions 1–11 are based on the following passage.

A Horse of a Different Doctor

Although medical science has made huge bounds in understanding many parts of the body, the brain remains a kind of mystery. A heart attack, for instance, is much easier to identify and prevent than a brain stroke. And mental illness aside, **1** the variety of neurological disorders can make specific brain diagnoses complicated and often unreliable. As a result, the therapeutic resources available to neurologists and those with neurological disorders must necessarily be as vast and diverse as the patient base itself. Disciplines like art therapy, aromatherapy, and horticultural therapy have begun to gain some traction in the popular imagination. Some fields, however, are still awaiting **2** the okay from the people, although their achievements and successes are just as significant. One such field is that of hippotherapy.

1
A) NO CHANGE
B) the variety of different kinds of neurological disorders
C) the differing variety of disorders in neurology
D) disorders that show a variety of differences

2
A) NO CHANGE
B) broader public acceptance
C) something elusive from the public
D) a public to give the thumbs up

CONTINUE ➔

Hippotherapy positions itself at the intersection of physical, occupational, and speech therapy. In this discipline, the characteristic movements of a horse (*hippo-* in Greek) [3] is used to build a foundation for improvements in human neurological functions and sensory processing. Its main difference from therapeutic horseback riding is that hippotherapy uses the movement of the horse as a way to treat a specific ailment. [4] Thus, it is more concerned with learning a skill set and establishing a bond between rider and horse.

[3]

A) NO CHANGE

B) has been used

C) are used

D) used

[4]

At this point, the writer is considering adding the following sentence.

> Therapeutic horseback riding teaches riding skills and is more concerned with emotional and behavioral disabilities.

Should the writer make this addition here?

A) Yes, because it makes the argument that hippotherapy is the more effective of the two disciplines.

B) Yes, because it further clarifies the difference between the two disciplines discussed in this paragraph.

C) No, because it undermines the point the author is trying to make about the validity of hippotherapy.

D) No, because a discussion of therapeutic horseback riding has no place in this particular paragraph.

CONTINUE

[1] Many fields use the basic tenets of hippotherapy, but they each provide a unique spin on the practice. [2] Physical therapists may incorporate hippotherapy to manage a variety of disabilities and, hopefully, cure diseases. [3] Occupational therapists use many of the same features of the horse's movement, but they **5** are similarly plagued by the lack of laboratory support. [4] The research on the effectiveness of hippotherapy is still in the early stages of development, but therapists in a variety of fields, even including speech and language pathology, regularly achieve success with this technique and **6** eagerly to recommended it to their patients. [5] As the name suggests, these therapists are concerned mainly with the movement of the horse as it relates to physical aspects such as balance, posture, and strengthening the core. **7**

The American Hippotherapy Association can provide certification for those wishing to work in the discipline. Physical therapists, occupational therapists, and speech-language pathologists must have practiced for at least three years and had 100 hours of hippotherapy practice before they can sit for the Hippotherapy Clinical Specialty Certification Exam, and the certification lasts for five years. Because the discipline is relatively **8** new, certified, hippotherapists have stringent requirements for staying current on the research within the field.

5

Which choice provides a supporting example that reinforces the main point of the sentence?

A) NO CHANGE

B) use the therapy to develop the cognitive and fine motor skills.

C) work on different maladies and different parts of the body.

D) have a whole different set of requirements and backgrounds.

6

A) NO CHANGE

B) eager recommending of

C) eagerly recommending

D) eagerly recommend

7

To make this paragraph most logical, sentence 5 should be placed

A) where it is now.

B) before sentence 3.

C) before sentence 4.

D) at the beginning of the paragraph.

8

A) NO CHANGE

B) new, certified

C) new, and certified

D) new; certified

CONTINUE ➔

Just as medical science is constantly evolving, **9** so are its alternatives. Hippotherapy may seem a bit out of the ordinary, but if it provides effective relief or treatment for people in pain, the skeptics **10** between doctors and researchers will not hesitate to embrace it. **11** Becoming a hippotherapist is pretty hard, as evidenced by all those hours one has to spend keeping up with the literature.

9

A) NO CHANGE

B) so too are its alternatives.

C) its alternatives also are.

D) its alternatives are, too.

10

A) NO CHANGE

B) above

C) within

D) among

11

The writer wants a concluding sentence that restates the main argument of the passage. Which choice best accomplishes that goal?

A) NO CHANGE

B) Hippotherapy has positioned itself at the crossroads of many disciplines, and it may just be the practice to provide relief in ways the other therapies have not done yet.

C) Many people used bloodletting and radiation regularly before the medical establishment showed how unsafe these practices were.

D) It makes you wonder whether the medical profession is ready for such a crazy discovery.

CONTINUE

Questions 12–22 are based on the following passage and supplementary material.

The Call of the Wilderness

The way science textbooks teach about different ecosystems [12] elicit responses primarily from our visual and tactile senses. We have all seen pictures of the silent sands of the desert and can almost feel the heat radiating from the sands. We all know the ballet of fish and marine life coursing through the vast ocean. Some recent studies, however, have expanded our ideas about these ecosystems by incorporating another one of our senses: sound.

[13] It was Marco Polo who crossed the desert on his way to China, he described the sound he heard as "a variety of musical instruments." Researchers now understand that the curious sound that Polo heard, that odd confluence of pipe organ and [14] cello, probably resulted from the wind blowing across the sand dunes. In a study conducted in the deserts of California, scientists found that the "singing" dunes had dry, tightly-packed layers of sand, with dry sand on top of layers of damp sand. This variation creates an effect similar to that of a musical [15] instrument, a tonal quality coming from the trapping and release of certain frequencies.

12

A) NO CHANGE
B) elicits responses
C) illicit responses
D) illicits responses

13

A) NO CHANGE
B) Marco Polo crossed the desert
C) They called him Marco Polo, he who crossed the desert
D) As Marco Polo crossed the desert

14

A) NO CHANGE
B) cello;
C) cello—
D) cello: it has

15

A) NO CHANGE
B) instrument; a tonal quality coming from the trapping and release of certain frequencies.
C) instrument, a tonal quality that is said to be coming from the trapping and release of certain frequencies.
D) instrument, this quality comes from the trapping and release of certain frequencies.

CONTINUE

16 From among the world's countless ecosystems and throughout that world, the ocean, too, has recently been given a kind of "voice." Although Jacques Cousteau referred to this body of water as *le monde du silence*—"the silent world"—recent research has shown the ocean to be anything but silent. University of Washington biologist Kate Stafford has, for the past five years, recorded sounds in the deep waters of the Bering Strait. **17** For Stafford, sound provides advantage that sight cannot: one can continue to record sound at night or underneath ice cover, and the challenges of deep-sea sound-recording are not nearly as problematic as those of deep-sea diving.

Which choice most smoothly and effectively introduces the writer's discussion of the sounds of the ocean in this paragraph?

A) NO CHANGE

B) Ecosystems are filled with sound, and one such sound in one such ecosystem is the "voice" of the ocean.

C) Another place that has recently been given a kind of "voice" is the ocean.

D) DELETE the underlined sentence.

At this point, the writer is considering adding the following sentence.

> If you go far enough from the coast, the only sounds you will hear are those of distant ships passing in the night.

Should the writer make this addition here?

A) Yes, because it creates a poetic image that complements the main idea of the paragraph.

B) Yes, because it supports the main idea of the passage as a whole.

C) No, because it undermines the argument made by the scientist described in this paragraph.

D) No, because it would be more appropriately placed at the beginning of the paragraph.

CONTINUE

According to Stafford's research, one of the most interesting aspects of the sound of the ocean is **18** its unwillingness to **19** not act so weird. Stafford's team found incredible inconsistencies among the sounds at any particular time of year. This may help to explain the **20** clear direct relationship in whale migrations between 2012-2013 and previous seasons. Recent data shows that it is not at all abnormal for nearly 40 whales to migrate on a single day when, on average, **21** only 14 whales would migrate on that same day. This gives some hint to how marine animals are and will be adapting to climate change in the future. It seems that those with the most flexibility will be those who are least affected.

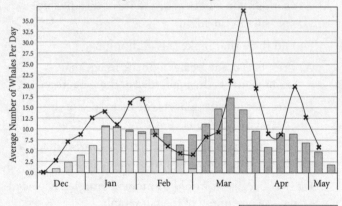

This Season, Compared to the Averages of the Last Ten Seasons

Key
☐ Southbound Whales
☐ Northbound Whales

18

A) NO CHANGE
B) it's
C) their
D) they're

19

A) NO CHANGE
B) follow any discernible patterns.
C) chill out and be normal for a second.
D) play nice with others.

20

Which choice offers the most accurate interpretation of the data in the chart?
A) NO CHANGE
B) definable inverse relationship
C) absolute confluence
D) notable inconsistency

21

Which choice offers an accurate interpretation of the data in the chart?
A) NO CHANGE
B) most whales would typically migrate in the summer months.
C) many more whales migrate southward every single day.
D) over half that number migrate every day in the coldest winter months.

CONTINUE

The work that Stafford and others are doing adds another dimension to how we understand different ecosystems. Sound may clarify the processes of these ecosystems in ways that were not available to researchers before. [22]

The writer wants a conclusion that points toward the role that sound might play in future research into different ecosystems. Which choice results in the passage having the most appropriate concluding sentence?

A) NO CHANGE

B) This is not, of course, to say that no research has ever been done on sound before; that would be an overstatement.

C) Researchers may have missed this sound component, but you have to hand it to them for covering the other parts as thoroughly as they have.

D) The vividness of soundscapes is nowhere more evident than in the experiences of the blind, who can use sound in much the way that sighted people use sight.

CONTINUE

Questions 23–33 are based on the following passage.

Roosevelt's 100 Days

In the 1932 presidential election, up-and-comer Franklin D. Roosevelt [23] won— in a landslide over the incumbent Herbert Hoover, who had done little to avert the crisis that would become known as the Great Depression. [24] And Hoover took office in 1929, the unemployment rate was a mere 3.2%. By 1932, that rate had skyrocketed to 25%.

[25] Roosevelt took office with a clear mandate for action. Even so, no one was quite ready for the legislative whirlwind that would follow. This period became known as Roosevelt's "100 Days." Roosevelt's first action came on March 5, 1933, when an executive order shut down all the nation's banks. At that time, he sent government workers to inspect each bank, [26] although determining which banks would be safe and sustainable to reopen. Four days later, the banks reopened and started business anew.

[23]
A) NO CHANGE
B) won;
C) won,
D) won

[24]
A) NO CHANGE
B) Because
C) When
D) DELETE the underlined portion and begin the sentence with a capital letter.

[25]
Which choice most effectively sets up the paragraph?
A) NO CHANGE
B) Politics could move a bit more quickly in those days.
C) That unemployment rate is remarkably low.
D) Hoover had given up all hope of ending the Depression.

[26]
A) NO CHANGE
B) for
C) thereby
D) whereupon

Roosevelt's main goal was to lift the country from depression and to get the [27] economy operating again. In the 100 days, Roosevelt established programs to aid the poor, such as the $500 million Federal Emergency Relief Association. The Civilian Conservation Corps was established to give unemployed men six-month job assignments on environmental projects, such as national parks. In agricultural regions, Roosevelt sought to control supply as a way to level [28] with demand, and certain projects were geared toward electrifying until-then remote regions. The Tennessee Valley Authority brought dams to the non-coastal southern states, [29] including Tennessee itself, of course, but also the northern parts of Alabama and Mississippi.

27

Which choice provides the most specific information on the areas that Roosevelt hoped to stimulate?

A) NO CHANGE

B) industrial and agricultural sectors

C) whole thing

D) money flowing and the economy

28

A) NO CHANGE

B) on

C) off

D) to

29

Which choice gives an additional supporting detail that emphasizes the importance of the TVA in Roosevelt's larger economic project?

A) NO CHANGE

B) taking account of the fact that farming is difficult without a reliable large body of water.

C) establishing not only more reliable sources of water and work but electricity for millions of Americans.

D) one of many impressive public-works projects completed throughout Roosevelt's tenure.

CONTINUE

Many of the programs, including the Tennessee Valley Authority, continue to exist to this day. Roosevelt's 100 Days were unique in that they not only jumpstarted the American economy at a time when a stimulus was most needed but also laid the groundwork for programs that could persist into the **30** future, past their own moment. Indeed, Roosevelt's "New Deal" remains new even though, at this point, **31** it's nearly eighty years old.

Still, Roosevelt's 100 Days remain the subject of controversy. In Roosevelt's day, there was widespread criticism from those who thought government should play a smaller rather than a larger role in **32** people's day-to-day lives. For many others, Roosevelt's government interventions are a model for how governments should aid citizens in times of need. **33** Clearly, Roosevelt's unadulterated successes would seem odd in an era of political wrangling characterized by gridlock rather than swift action.

30

A) NO CHANGE

B) future.

C) future, which is to say after the present.

D) future, many years beyond when they were created.

31

A) NO CHANGE

B) its

C) they're

D) there

32

A) NO CHANGE

B) peoples'

C) peoples

D) peoples's

33

The writer wants to conclude the paragraph effectively without dismissing the debate described in this paragraph. Which choice best accomplishes this goal?

A) NO CHANGE

B) Unfortunately, even Roosevelt's obvious failures can

C) In either case, Roosevelt's achievements in the first 100 Days of his presidency

D) All of the things described above could accomplish this goal.

CONTINUE

Questions 34–44 are based on the following passage.

Setsuko Hara: In and Out of the Tokyo Spotlight

One of the [34] hammiest board-treaders in the history of Japanese cinema was also one of the most mysterious. Setsuko Hara died in September 2015 at the age of 95, and while she is remembered as perhaps the most formidable actress in Japan's long cinematic tradition, no one had seen her in anything since the 1960s. The actress went into seclusion after the death of her longtime collaborator, the director Yasujiro Ozu.

Hara's first acting role came when she was only 15. The Japanese film industry had divided loyalties at the time, [35] despite its obvious debt to American cinema amid the increasing international tensions with the United States and others that would lead to World War II. Hara's first film, a German-Japanese production called *The Daughter of the Samurai* (1937), emerged among these tensions [36] using as it did the conventions of the American melodrama to promote an early version of what would become Axis propaganda. After her success in this film, Hara became one of the faces of the Japanese propaganda effort during the Second World War.

[34]

A) NO CHANGE
B) most exquisite thespians
C) most emotive of histrionists
D) greatest actresses

[35]

A) NO CHANGE
B) as evidenced by
C) contrasting with
D) enabled by

[36]

The writer is considering the deleting the underlined portion (ending the sentence with a period). Should the writer make this deletion?

A) Yes, because the information is provided in the previous sentence.
B) Yes, because the underlined portion undermines the paragraph's description of the Axis propaganda effort.
C) No, because the underlined portion gives a specific example of how the Axis powers conducted their propaganda campaign.
D) No, because the underlined portion provides information that clarifies an idea central to this paragraph.

CONTINUE

After Japan's defeat in the war, however, Hara's career changed significantly. Directors and audiences discovered her incredible talent acting in quieter dramas. The masterpieces in this mode were Ozu's *Late Spring* (1949) and *Tokyo Story* (1953), in which Hara plays a woman who is torn between the demands of various family members, who in turn **37** represented different generational expectations. Hara could reveal incredible emotion through subtle, almost imperceptible facial expressions and voice modulations. **38** Moreover, her compelling and unique beauty kept screen audiences eagerly engaged.

The subtle conflicts in *Late Spring* capture Hara's particular **39** style of acting in films. Even in the 1940s, Hollywood films were characterized by grand conflicts and even grander emotions. The films of Ozu's late period, especially his collaborations with Hara, however, worked with a much smaller canvas, usually with very few sets, limiting the scenes to a character's **40** office kitchen, living room, or garden. In *Late Spring*, Hara's character Noriko is twenty-seven years old and has not married. Against the **41** council of her friends and family, she has instead chosen to care for her aging widowed father. The conflict and plot are that simple, **42** and Ozu's cinematography and Hara's expressive face show that sometimes the simplest and smallest domestic conflicts can have profound implications.

37
A) NO CHANGE
B) would represent
C) had represented
D) represent

38
A) NO CHANGE
B) In sum,
C) Nevertheless,
D) Meanwhile,

39
A) NO CHANGE
B) acting style.
C) acting methods that were unique to her.
D) acting style in film and presumably in the theater.

40
A) NO CHANGE
B) office, kitchen, living,
C) office, kitchen, living
D) office, kitchen living,

41
A) NO CHANGE
B) council from
C) counsel with
D) counsel of

42
A) NO CHANGE
B) for
C) so
D) yet

CONTINUE →

[1] Hara never formally announced her retirement, though she made her last film in 1963. [2] Rumors have always circulated about Hara's mysterious disappearance from the screen, and viewers' many theories show **43** their grief at having lost such a bright star. [3] Some believe that she had been going blind and did not want to do so in the public eye. [4] In either case, Hara left an indelible mark on the shape of world cinema. [5] Especially in a moment when all cinematic achievement seems to point toward bigger and louder, Setsuko Hara provides the important reminder that smaller and quieter can be just as powerful. **44**

43

A) NO CHANGE

B) one's

C) his

D) your

44

The writer plans to add the following sentence to this paragraph.

> Others believe that her grief over Ozu's death in 1963 kept her from returning to the cinema.

To make this paragraph most logical, the sentence should be placed

A) after sentence 2.

B) after sentence 3.

C) after sentence 4.

D) after sentence 5.

STOP

**If you finish before time is called, you may check your work on this section only.
Do not turn to any other section in the test.**

Math Test – No Calculator

25 MINUTES, 20 QUESTIONS

Turn to Section 3 of your answer sheet to answer the questions in this section.

DIRECTIONS

For questions **1-15**, solve each problem, choose the best answer from the choices provided, and fill in the corresponding circle on your answer sheet. For questions **16-20**, solve the problem and enter your answer in the grid on the answer sheet. Please refer to the directions before question 16 on how to enter your answers in the grid. You may use any available space in your test booklet for scratch work.

NOTES

1. The use of a calculator **is not permitted**.
2. All variables and expressions used represent real numbers unless otherwise indicated.
3. Figures provided in this test are drawn to scale unless otherwise indicated.
4. All figures lie in a plane unless otherwise indicated.
5. Unless otherwise indicated, the domain of a given function f is the set of all real numbers x for which $f(x)$ is a real number.

REFERENCE

The number of degrees of arc in a circle is 360.
The number of radians of arc in a circle is 2π.
The sum of the measures in degrees of the angles of a triangle is 180.

CONTINUE

1

An editor is paid $25 an hour to edit 3 essays and an additional $50 bonus when the edits on all three essays are completed. If the edits on the essays are completed, what expression could be used to determine how much the editor earned?

A) $50y + 25$, where y is the number of hours

B) $25y + 50$, where y is the number of hours

C) $y(25 + 2) + 3$, where y is the number of essays

D) $50y + (25 + 2)$, where y is the number of essays

2

$$(-mn^2 + 2n^2 - 6m^2n) + (2mn^2 - 2n^2 + 3m^2n)$$

The expression above is equivalent to which of the following?

A) $mn^2 + 4n^2 - 9m^2n$

B) $mn^2 - 3m^2n$

C) $3mn^2 - 4n^2$

D) $3m^2n - mn^2$

3

$$\frac{1}{12}x - \frac{1}{12}y = 13$$
$$\frac{1}{3}x - \frac{1}{6}y = 20$$

Which ordered pair (x, y) satisfies the equations above?

A) $(-35, 190)$

B) $(-36, -192)$

C) $(168, 25)$

D) $\left(\dfrac{752}{5}, \dfrac{304}{5} \right)$

4

Kelly is a salesperson at a shoe store, where she must sell a pre-set number of pairs of shoes each month. At the end of each workday, the number of pairs of shoes that she has left to sell that month is given by the equation $S = 300 - 15x$, where S is the number of pairs of shoes Kelly still needs to sell and x is the number of days she has worked that month. What is the meaning of the number 300 in this equation?

A) Kelly must sell 300 pairs of shoes per week.

B) Kelly must sell 300 pairs of shoes per day.

C) Kelly will sell the pairs of shoes in 300 days.

D) Kelly must sell 300 pairs of shoes each month.

CONTINUE

5

A certain amusement park sells half-day passes and all-day passes. The amusement park charges $40 for a half-day pass and $80 for an all-day pass. The amusement park sold a total of 70 passes one day for $4,600. How many all-day passes did the amusement park sell?

A) 25

B) 35

C) 45

D) 60

6

$$5x^2 + 7x - 6 = 0$$

If a and b are two solutions to the equation above and $a < b$, which of the following is the value of $b - a$?

A) $\dfrac{3}{5}$

B) $\dfrac{6}{5}$

C) $\dfrac{8}{5}$

D) $\dfrac{13}{5}$

7

Which of the following must be true if $\dfrac{t + u}{t} = \dfrac{12}{11}$?

A) $\dfrac{u}{t} = \dfrac{1}{11}$

B) $\dfrac{u}{t} = \dfrac{23}{11}$

C) $\dfrac{t - u}{t} = \dfrac{1}{11}$

D) $\dfrac{t + 2u}{t} = -\dfrac{8}{11}$

8

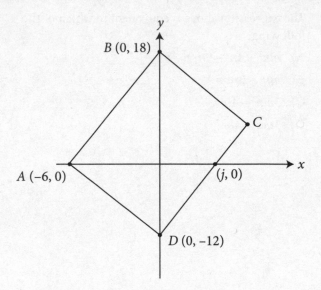

Parallelogram $ABCD$ is shown in the xy-plane above. What is the value of j ?

A) 15

B) 12

C) 4

D) 3

CONTINUE

9

$$x = \frac{y(y-3)}{2}$$

The number of diagonals, x, that can be drawn within a polygon depends on the number of sides, y, of the polygon according to the formula above. If a polygon has at least 7 diagonals, what is the least number of sides it can have?

A) 7

B) 6

C) 5

D) 4

10

The value of a car decreases $500 for every 1,000 miles it is driven. The current value of the car is $23,000, and the car is driven an average of 10,000 miles per year. What will be the value of the car, in dollars, at a point in time y years from now?

A) $23,000 – $5,000$y$

B) $23,000 – 500y$

C) $23,000 – 0.02y$

D) $23,000 – 0.0002y$

11

$$7x - cy = 10$$
$$5x + 2y = 8$$

In the system of equations above, x and y are variables and c is a constant. What must the value of c be if the system of equations has no solution?

A) $\dfrac{14}{5}$

B) $\dfrac{27}{25}$

C) $-\dfrac{27}{25}$

D) $-\dfrac{14}{5}$

12

Which of the following complex numbers is equal to $\dfrac{4 - 7i}{6 + 3i}$? (Note: $i = \sqrt{-1}$)

A) $\dfrac{1}{15} + \dfrac{6i}{5}$

B) $\dfrac{1}{15} - \dfrac{6i}{5}$

C) $\dfrac{2}{3} - \dfrac{7i}{3}$

D) $\dfrac{2}{3} + \dfrac{7i}{3}$

CONTINUE

13

$$g(x) = 2(x^2 + 14x + 7) - 7(x + c)$$

In the polynomial $g(x)$ defined above, c is a constant. If $g(x)$ is divisible by x, what is the value of c ?

A) –2

B) 0

C) 2

D) 5

14

If $3r - s = 10$, then which of the following is equivalent to $\dfrac{27^r}{3^s}$?

A) 27^2

B) 9^4

C) 3^{10}

D) The value cannot be determined from the information given.

15

Which of the following is equivalent to $\dfrac{4n + 9}{n - 5}$?

A) $4 + \dfrac{29}{n - 5}$

B) $4 + \dfrac{9}{n - 5}$

C) $4 - \dfrac{9}{5}$

D) $-\dfrac{4 + 9}{5}$

CONTINUE

DIRECTIONS

For questions 16-20, solve the problem and enter your answer in the grid, as described below, on the answer sheet.

1. Although not required, it is suggested that you write your answer in the boxes at the top of the columns to help you fill in the circles accurately. You will receive credit only if the circles are filled in correctly.

2. Mark no more than one circle in any column.

3. No question has a negative answer.

4. Some problems may have more than one correct answer. In such cases, grid only one answer.

5. **Mixed numbers** such as $3\frac{1}{2}$ must be gridded as 3.5 or 7/2. (If [3 1 / 2] is entered into the grid, it will be interpreted as $\frac{31}{2}$, not as $3\frac{1}{2}$.)

6. **Decimal Answers:** If you obtain a decimal answer with more digits than the grid can accommodate, it may be either rounded or truncated, but it must fill the entire grid.

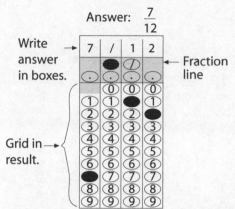

Answer: $\frac{7}{12}$

Answer: 2.5

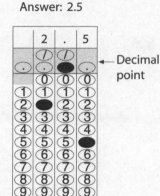

Acceptable ways to grid $\frac{2}{3}$ are:

Answer: 201 – either position is correct

NOTE: You may start your answers in any column, space permitting. Columns you don't need to use should be left blank.

CONTINUE →

16

For what value of x is $37 = \dfrac{x}{20} - 3$?

17

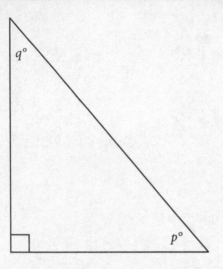

In the triangle above, the cosine of $p°$ is 0.8. What is the sine of $q°$?

18

If $a \neq 0$, what is the value of $\dfrac{9(5a)^2}{(3a)^2}$?

CONTINUE ➡

19

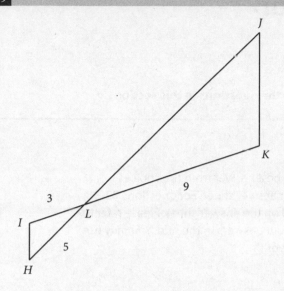

Segment HJ intersects segment IK at L in the figure above. If $\overline{HI} \parallel \overline{JK}$, what is the length of segment HJ?

20

What is the value of y if $z = 5\sqrt{3}$ and $3z = \sqrt{3y}$?

STOP

If you finish before time is called, you may check your work on this section only.
Do not turn to any other section in the test.

Math Test – Calculator

55 MINUTES, 38 QUESTIONS

Turn to Section 4 of your answer sheet to answer the questions in this section.

DIRECTIONS

For questions **1-30**, solve each problem, choose the best answer from the choices provided, and fill in the corresponding circle on your answer sheet. For questions **31-38**, solve the problem and enter your answer in the grid on the answer sheet. Please refer to the directions before question 31 on how to enter your answers in the grid. You may use any available space in your test booklet for scratch work.

NOTES

1. The use of a calculator **is permitted**.
2. All variables and expressions used represent real numbers unless otherwise indicated.
3. Figures provided in this test are drawn to scale unless otherwise indicated.
4. All figures lie in a plane unless otherwise indicated.
5. Unless otherwise indicated, the domain of a given function f is the set of all real numbers x for which $f(x)$ is a real number.

REFERENCE

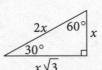

$A = \pi r^2$
$C = 2\pi r$

$A = \ell w$

$A = \frac{1}{2}bh$

$c^2 = a^2 + b^2$

Special Right Triangles

$V = \ell w h$

$V = \pi r^2 h$

$V = \frac{4}{3}\pi r^3$

$V = \frac{1}{3}\pi r^2 h$

$V = \frac{1}{3}\ell w h$

The number of degrees of arc in a circle is 360.
The number of radians of arc in a circle is 2π.
The sum of the measures in degrees of the angles of a triangle is 180.

CONTINUE

1

David has a mobile data plan for which the monthly fee is $20.00 and the data usage fee is $2.50 per gigabyte. Which of the following functions expresses David's cost, in dollars, for a month in which he uses g gigabytes of data?

A) $f(g) = 22.50g$

B) $f(g) = 20g + 2.50$

C) $f(g) = 20 + 250g$

D) $f(g) = 20 + 2.50g$

2

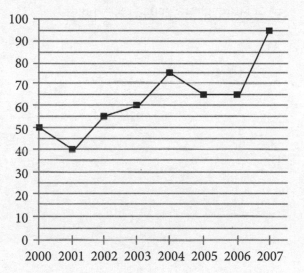

Annual Profits

The line graph above shows the annual profit of a particular clothing store from 2000 to 2007. According to the graph, what was the greatest change (in absolute value) in the annual profit between two consecutive years?

A) $25,000

B) $30,000

C) $35,000

D) $40,000

3

In order to qualify for a fitness competition, a person must be able to complete 30 pull-ups in one minute. Jim can currently do 14 pull-ups in one minute and believes that he can increase that amount by 7 pull-ups each year. Which of the following represents the number of pull-ups that Jim believes he will be able to complete in one minute y years from now?

A) $7y + 14$

B) $7y + 30$

C) $14y + 7$

D) $14 - 7y$

4

$$v = 17 + 2.5t$$

A constantly-accelerating particle is moving in a straight line. After t seconds, the particle is moving at a velocity of v, in meters per second, as shown in the equation above. What is t when v is 67 ?

A) 184.5

B) 67

C) 33.6

D) 20

CONTINUE

5

When function h is graphed in the xy-plane, it has x-intercepts at -4, 2, and 4. Which of the following could define h ?

A) $h(x) = (x - 4)(x - 2)(x + 4)$

B) $h(x) = (x - 4)(x + 2)(x + 4)$

C) $h(x) = (x - 4)^2(x + 2)$

D) $h(x) = (x + 2)(x + 4)^2$

6

When three times a number n is added to 9, the result is 3. What is the result when 4 times n is added to 14 ?

A) -2

B) 3

C) 6

D) 22

7

A coffee shop is filling coffee cups from an industrial urn that contains 64 gallons of coffee. At most, how many 16-ounce cups of coffee can be filled from the urn? (1 gallon = 128 ounces)

A) 4

B) 512

C) 1,024

D) 2,048

8

What is the slope of the line in the xy-plane that passes through the points $\left(5, \dfrac{8}{3}\right)$ and $\left(1, -\dfrac{1}{3}\right)$?

A) -2

B) $-\dfrac{4}{3}$

C) $\dfrac{3}{4}$

D) 2

CONTINUE

9

Number of Fish in Each of 18 Tanks

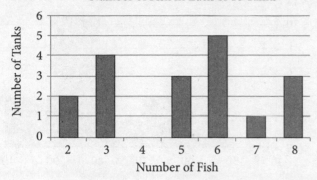

Based on the histogram above, which of the following is closest to the average (arithmetic mean) number of fish per tank?

A) 5

B) 6

C) 7

D) 8

10

A telephone survey was conducted in order to determine if people in City C are more likely to work 9-to-5 office jobs than other jobs. The research team called 5,000 random people between 12 p.m. to 4 p.m. on a Thursday. Of the 5,000 people called, 3,000 did not answer, and 250 refused to participate. Which of the following was the biggest flaw in the design of the survey?

A) The time the survey was taken

B) Population size

C) Sample size

D) The fact that the survey was done by telephone

11

If the function p has exactly four distinct roots, which of the following could represent the complete graph of $y - p(x)$ in the xy plane?

A)

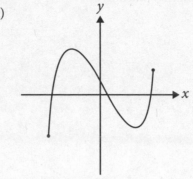

B)

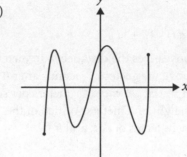

C)

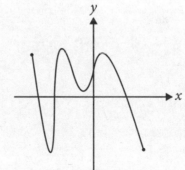

D)

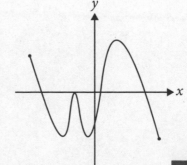

CONTINUE

12

One morning in a particular restaurant, 85 percent of the customers ordered the brunch special. Which of the following could be the total number of customers in the restaurant that morning?

A) 40

B) 42

C) 44

D) 48

13

$$d = -8t^2 + vt + h$$

The equation above gives the distance d, in meters, a projectile is above the ground t seconds after it is released with an initial velocity of v meters per second from an initial height of h meters. Which of the following gives v in terms of d, t, and h?

A) $v = \dfrac{d - h}{t} + 8t$

B) $v = \dfrac{d + h}{t} - 8t$

C) $v = \dfrac{d - h + 8}{t}$

D) $v = d + h - 8t$

14

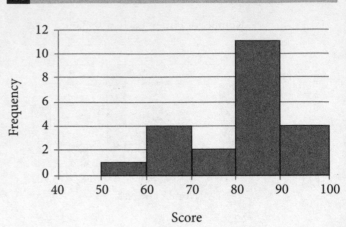

The histogram above shows the distribution of the scores of 22 students on a recent biology test. Which of the following could be the median score of the 22 students represented in the histogram?

A) 68

B) 71

C) 77

D) 84

CONTINUE

Questions 15-17 refer to the following information.

A survey of 130 randomly selected workers in a particular metropolitan area was conducted to gather information about average daily commute times. The data are shown in the table below.

	Commutes by Public Transit	Does not commute by Public Transit	Total
Less than 1 hour	22	46	68
At least 1 hour	29	33	62
Total	51	79	130

15

Which of the following is closest to the percent of those surveyed who commute using public transit?

A) 65%

B) 46%

C) 39%

D) 32%

16

In 2014, the population of the metropolitan area from the survey was about 13 million. If the survey results were used to estimate information about commute times throughout the metropolitan area, which of the following is the best estimate for the number of individuals who used public transit and had an average daily commute of at least one hour?

A) 290,000

B) 2,200,000

C) 2,900,000

D) 6,200,000

17

Based on the data, how many times more likely is it for a person with a commute of less than 1 hour NOT to commute by public transit that it is for a person with a commute of at least one hour NOT to commute by public transit? (Round the answer to the nearest hundredth.)

A) 1.39 times as likely

B) 1.27 times as likely

C) 0.78 times as likely

D) 0.72 times as likely

CONTINUE

18

In order to determine the effect that caffeinated beverage *C* would have on sleep, researchers conducted a study. From a large population of people without sleep disorders, 500 subjects were randomly selected. Half the subjects were randomly selected to consume beverage *C* and the rest did not consume beverage *C*. The results of the study showed that the subjects who consumed beverage *C* slept less than those who did not consume beverage *C*. Based on the design and results of the study, which of the following statements is the best conclusion?

A) Beverage *C* will cause more loss in sleep than all other caffeinated beverages.

B) Beverage *C* will cause a substantial loss in sleep.

C) Beverage *C* is likely to reduce the amount of sleep of people without sleep disorders.

D) Beverage *C* will reduce sleep of anyone who consumes it.

19

The sum of four numbers is 1,764. One of the numbers, *n*, is 40% more than the sum of the other three numbers. What is the value of *n* ?

A) 287

B) 735

C) 1,029

D) 1,260

20

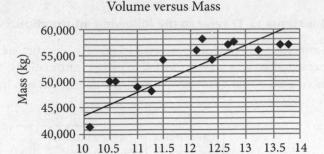

Volume versus Mass

Selin weighs 14 different objects of similar density. The scatterplot shown above shows the volume of each object and the corresponding weight of each object. The line of best fit for the data is shown. For the object that had a volume of 11.5 m³, the actual mass was about how many kilograms more than the mass predicted by the line of best fit?

A) 1,000

B) 2,000

C) 3,000

D) 4,000

CONTINUE

21

Jessica owns a store that sells only laptops and tablets. Last week, her store sold 90 laptops and 210 tablets. This week, the sales, in number of units, of laptops increased by 50 percent, and the sales, in number of units, of tablets increased by 30 percent. By what percentage did total sales, in units, in Jessica's store increase?

A) 20 percent

B) 25 percent

C) 36 percent

D) 80 percent

22

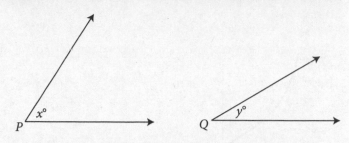

Note: Figures not drawn to scale

For acute angles P and Q shown above, $\cos(x°) = \sin(y°)$. If $x = 3c - 23$ and $y = 7c - 42$, what is the value of c ?

A) 24.5

B) 15.5

C) 9.0

D) 6.0

CONTINUE

23

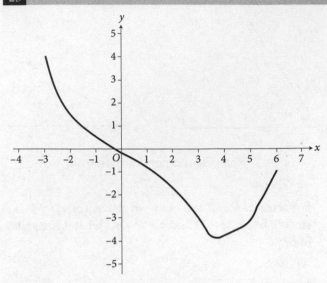

What is the maximum value of the function graphed in the *xy*-plane above, for $-3 \leq x \leq 6$?

A) 4

B) 5

C) 6

D) ∞

24

Matthew constructs a fence around a patch of grass in his backyard. The patch has a width that is 8 feet more than 4 times the length. What is the perimeter of the fence if Matthew's patch of grass has an area of 5,472 square feet?

A) 364 feet

B) 376 feet

C) 396 feet

D) 400 feet

25

In the *xy*-plane, the line determined by the points $(c, 3)$ and $(27, c)$ intersects the origin. Which of the following could be the value of *c* ?

A) 0

B) 3

C) 6

D) 9

26

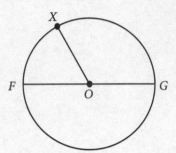

In the circle above, the length of arc $\overset{\frown}{FXG}$ is 14π. If $\overline{FOG}$ is a chord and *O* is the center, what is the length of the segment $\overline{XO}$?

A) 7

B) 14

C) 28

D) 56

CONTINUE ➤

27

Let p and q be numbers such that $-|p| < q < |p|$. Which of the following must be true?

 I. $p > 0$

 II. $|p| > -q$

 III. $p > |q|$

A) I only

B) II only

C) II and III only

D) I, II, and III only

28

A rectangular container with a base that measures 10 feet by 10 feet is filled with jelly beans. The container is divided into regions each with the same height as the container and a square base with sides that measure 1 foot each. Sherman randomly selects ten of these regions and counts the number of blue jelly beans in each region. The results are shown in the table below.

Region	Blue Jelly Beans	Region	Blue Jelly Beans
I	20	VI	22
II	21	VII	25
III	27	VIII	24
IV	31	IX	28
V	19	X	23

Which of the following is a reasonable approximation of the number of blue jelly beans in the entire container?

A) 25,000

B) 2,500

C) 250

D) 25

CONTINUE

29

	Flavor	
Product Type	Frozen Yogurt	Ice Cream
Vanilla		
Chocolate		
Total	32	152

The incomplete table above shows the sales for a particular sweet shop by product and flavor. There were 4 times as many vanilla ice creams sold as vanilla frozen yogurts, and there were 6 times as many chocolate ice creams sold as chocolate frozen yogurts. If there were a total of 32 frozen yogurts and 152 ice creams sold, and no flavors other than vanilla and chocolate were available, which of the following is closest to the probability that a randomly selected ice cream sold was vanilla?

A) 0.250

B) 0.435

C) 0.526

D) 0.667

30

$$\begin{cases} y \geq x \\ 3y < 2x - 3 \end{cases}$$

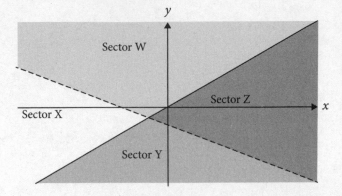

A system of inequalities is graphed above. Which sector or sectors on the graph could represent all of the solutions to the system shown?

A) Sectors Y and Z

B) Sectors W and Y

C) Sector W

D) Sector X

CONTINUE

DIRECTIONS

For questions 31-38, solve the problem and enter your answer in the grid, as described below, on the answer sheet.

1. Although not required, it is suggested that you write your answer in the boxes at the top of the columns to help you fill in the circles accurately. You will receive credit only if the circles are filled in correctly.

2. Mark no more than one circle in any column.

3. No question has a negative answer.

4. Some problems may have more than one correct answer. In such cases, grid only one answer.

5. **Mixed numbers** such as $3\frac{1}{2}$ must be gridded as 3.5 or 7/2. (If  is entered into the grid, it will be interpreted as $\frac{31}{2}$, not as $3\frac{1}{2}$.)

6. **Decimal Answers:** If you obtain a decimal answer with more digits than the grid can accommodate, it may be either rounded or truncated, but it must fill the entire grid.

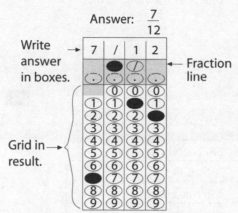

Answer: $\frac{7}{12}$

Write answer in boxes. → Fraction line

Grid in result.

Answer: 2.5

Decimal point

Acceptable ways to grid $\frac{2}{3}$ are:

Answer: 201 – either position is correct

NOTE: You may start your answers in any column, space permitting. Columns you don't need to use should be left blank.

31

At a certain food truck, hamburgers are sold for $5 each and hot dogs are $3 each. If Martina buys one hamburger and h hot dogs and spends at least $20 and no more than $25, what is one possible value of h ?

32

Number of States in 14 Federal Nations			
Nation	States	Nation	States
Australia	6	Micronesia	4
Austria	9	Nigeria	36
Brazil	26	Saint Kitts and Nevis	2
Germany	16	South Sudan	10
India	29	Sudan	17
Malaysia	13	United States	50
Mexico	31	Venezuela	23

The table above lists the number of states in each of the 14 federal nations that have subdivisions called states. According to the table, what is the mean number of states of these nations? (Round your answer to the nearest tenth.)

33

In the xy-plane, the point $(-2, 6)$ lies on the graph of the function $g(x) = 2x^2 + kx + 18$. What is the value of k ?

34

In a certain college dormitory, 108 students are assigned dorm rooms. The dormitory has 26 dorm rooms, each of which is assigned 3 or 5 students. How many of the dorm rooms will be assigned 3 students?

CONTINUE

35

Population of Town A
Each Decade from 1910 to 2000

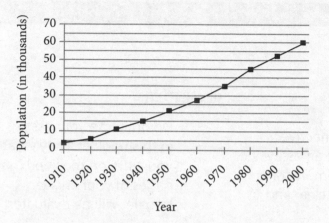

According to the figure shown above, the population of Town A in 1970 was what fraction of the population of Town A in 2000?

36

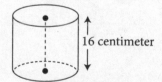

16 centimeter

A wooden block is in the shape of the right circular cylinder shown above. If the volume of the wooden block is 64π cubic centimeters, what is the <u>diameter</u> of the base of the cylinder, in centimeters?

Questions 37 and 38 refer to the following information.

$\omega^2 = \omega_0^2 + 2\alpha\theta$ (angular position – angular velocity)

$\omega = \omega_0 + \alpha t$ (time – angular velocity)

$\theta = \omega_0 t + \dfrac{1}{2}\alpha t^2$ (time – angular position)

A carousel is rotating at an angular velocity of 90 degrees per second. The instant a particular point on the carousel reaches angular position $\theta = 0°$, the carousel operator flips a switch, causing the carousel at a constant angular acceleration to slow down and eventually change direction. The equations above describe the constant-acceleration motion of the carousel, where ω_0 represents the initial angular velocity, ω is the angular velocity as it travels, θ is the angular position of the particular point on the carousel, t is the time since the switch was flipped, and α is the constant angular acceleration ($-12.6°/s^2$).

37

To the nearest degree, at what angular position will the carousel change direction?

38

To the nearest second, how long will it take the carousel to come to a complete stop before it changes direction?

STOP
If you finish before time is called, you may check your work on this section only.
Do not turn to any other section in the test.

SAT Essay

DIRECTIONS

The essay gives you an opportunity to show how effectively you can read and comprehend a passage and write an essay analyzing the passage. In your essay you should demonstrate that you have read the passage carefully, present a clear and logical analysis, and use language precisely.

Your essay must be written on the lines provided in your answer sheet booklet; except for the planning page of the answer booklet, you will receive no other paper on which to write. You will have enough space if you write on every line, avoid wide margins, and keep your handwriting to a reasonable size. Remember that people who are not familiar with your handwriting will read what you write. Try to write or print so that what you are writing is legible to those readers.

You have 50 minutes to read the passage and write an essay in response to the prompt provided inside this booklet.

REMINDER

— Do not write your essay in this booklet. Only what you write on the lined pages of your answer booklet will be evaluated.

— An off-topic essay will not be evaluated.

CONTINUE ➡

As you read the passage below, consider how Jimmy Carter uses

- evidence, such as facts or examples, to support claims.
- reasoning to develop ideas and to connect claims and evidence.
- stylistic or persuasive elements, such as word choice or appeals to emotion, to add power to the ideas expressed.

Adapted from Jimmy Carter, "The President's Proposed Energy Policy." The speech was televised and was delivered on April 18, 1977.

1   Tonight I want to have an unpleasant talk with you about a problem unprecedented in our history. With the exception of preventing war, this is the greatest challenge our country will face during our lifetimes. The energy crisis has not yet overwhelmed us, but it will if we do not act quickly. It is a problem we will not solve in the next few years, and it is likely to get progressively worse through the rest of this century. We must not be selfish or timid if we hope to have a decent world for our children and grandchildren.

2   We simply must balance our demand for energy with our rapidly shrinking resources. By acting now, we can control our future instead of letting the future control us.

3   Two days from now, I will present my energy proposals to the Congress. Its members will be my partners and they have already given me a great deal of valuable advice. Many of these proposals will be unpopular. Some will cause you to put up with inconveniences and to make sacrifices. The most important thing about these proposals is that the alternative may be a national catastrophe. Further delay can affect our strength and our power as a nation.

4   Our decision about energy will test the character of the American people and the ability of the President and the Congress to govern. This difficult effort will be the "moral equivalent of war"—except that we will be uniting our efforts to build and not destroy. I know that some of you may doubt that we face real energy shortages. The 1973 gasoline lines are gone, and our homes are warm again. But our energy problem is worse tonight than it was in 1973 or a few weeks ago in the dead of winter. It is worse because more waste has occurred, and more time has passed by without our planning for the future. And it will get worse every day until we act.

5   The oil and natural gas we rely on for 75 percent of our energy are running out. In spite of increased effort, domestic production has been dropping steadily at about six percent a year. Imports have doubled in the last five years. Our nation's independence of economic and political action is becoming increasingly constrained. Unless profound changes are made to lower oil consumption, we now believe that early in the 1980s the world will be demanding more oil that it can produce.

CONTINUE

6   The world now uses about 60 million barrels of oil a day and demand increases each year about five percent. This means that, just to stay even, we need the production of a new Texas every year, an Alaskan North Slope every nine months, or a new Saudi Arabia every three years. Obviously, this cannot continue.

7   We must look back in history to understand our energy problem. Twice in the last several hundred years there has been a transition in the way people use energy. The first was about 200 years ago, away from wood—which had provided about 90 percent of all fuel—to coal, which was more efficient. This change became the basis of the Industrial Revolution. The second change took place in this century, with the growing use of oil and natural gas. They were more convenient and cheaper than coal, and the supply seemed to be almost without limit. They made possible the age of automobile and airplane travel. Nearly everyone who is alive today grew up during this age and we have never known anything different.

8   Because we are now running out of gas and oil, we must prepare quickly for a third change, to strict conservation and to the use of coal and permanent renewable energy sources, like solar power.

9   …Other generations of Americans have faced and mastered great challenges. I have faith that meeting this challenge will make our own lives even richer. If you will join me so that we can work together with patriotism and courage, we will again prove that our great nation can lead the world into an age of peace, independence, and freedom.

Write an essay in which you explain how Jimmy Carter builds an argument to convince his audience to support his proposed energy policy. In your essay, analyze how Carter uses one or more of the features listed in the box above (or features of your own choice) to strengthen the logic and persuasiveness of his argument. Be sure that your analysis focuses on the most relevant features of the passage.

Your essay should not explain whether you agree with Carter's claims, but rather explain how Carter builds an argument to persuade his audience.

END OF TEST

DO NOT RETURN TO A PREVIOUS SECTION.

1.

YOUR NAME: _____
(Print)
  Last   First   M.I.

SIGNATURE: _____   DATE: __ / __ / __

HOME ADDRESS: _____
(Print)
  Number and Street

_____
  City   State   Zip Code

PHONE NO.: _____
(Print)

IMPORTANT: Please fill in these boxes exactly as shown on the back cover of your test book.

2. TEST FORM

6. DATE OF BIRTH

Month	Day	Year
JAN		
FEB	0 0	0 0
MAR	1 1	1 1
APR	2 2	2 2
MAY	3 3	3 3
JUN	4	4 4
JUL	5	5 5
AUG	6	6 6
SEP	7	7 7
OCT	8	8 8
NOV	9	9 9
DEC		

3. TEST CODE   **4. REGISTRATION NUMBER**

7. SEX
MALE
FEMALE

5. YOUR NAME

First 4 letters of last name | FIRST INIT | MID INIT

The Princeton Review

Test ⑤   Start with number 1 for each new section.
If a section has fewer questions than answer spaces, leave the extra answer spaces blank.

Section 1—Reading

1. A B C D
2. A B C D
3. A B C D
4. A B C D
5. A B C D
6. A B C D
7. A B C D
8. A B C D
9. A B C D
10. A B C D
11. A B C D
12. A B C D
13. A B C D
14. A B C D
15. A B C D
16. A B C D
17. A B C D
18. A B C D
19. A B C D
20. A B C D
21. A B C D
22. A B C D
23. A B C D
24. A B C D
25. A B C D
26. A B C D

27. A B C D
28. A B C D
29. A B C D
30. A B C D
31. A B C D
32. A B C D
33. A B C D
34. A B C D
35. A B C D
36. A B C D
37. A B C D
38. A B C D
39. A B C D
40. A B C D
41. A B C D
42. A B C D
43. A B C D
44. A B C D
45. A B C D
46. A B C D
47. A B C D
48. A B C D
49. A B C D
50. A B C D
51. A B C D
52. A B C D

Section 2—Writing and Language Skills

1. A B C D
2. A B C D
3. A B C D
4. A B C D
5. A B C D
6. A B C D
7. A B C D
8. A B C D
9. A B C D
10. A B C D
11. A B C D
12. A B C D
13. A B C D
14. A B C D
15. A B C D
16. A B C D
17. A B C D
18. A B C D
19. A B C D
20. A B C D
21. A B C D
22. A B C D

23. A B C D
24. A B C D
25. A B C D
26. A B C D
27. A B C D
28. A B C D
29. A B C D
30. A B C D
31. A B C D
32. A B C D
33. A B C D
34. A B C D
35. A B C D
36. A B C D
37. A B C D
38. A B C D
39. A B C D
40. A B C D
41. A B C D
42. A B C D
43. A B C D
44. A B C D

Completely darken bubbles with a No. 2 pencil. If you make a mistake, be sure to erase mark completely. Erase all stray marks.

Test 5 — Start with number 1 for each new section.
If a section has fewer questions than answer spaces, leave the extra answer spaces blank.

Section 3—Mathematics: No Calculator

1. (A) (B) (C) (D)
2. (A) (B) (C) (D)
3. (A) (B) (C) (D)
4. (A) (B) (C) (D)
5. (A) (B) (C) (D)
6. (A) (B) (C) (D)
7. (A) (B) (C) (D)
8. (A) (B) (C) (D)
9. (A) (B) (C) (D)
10. (A) (B) (C) (D)
11. (A) (B) (C) (D)
12. (A) (B) (C) (D)
13. (A) (B) (C) (D)
14. (A) (B) (C) (D)
15. (A) (B) (C) (D)

16. 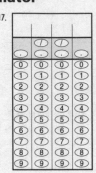 17. 18. 19. 20.

Section 4—Mathematics: Calculator

1. (A) (B) (C) (D)
2. (A) (B) (C) (D)
3. (A) (B) (C) (D)
4. (A) (B) (C) (D)
5. (A) (B) (C) (D)
6. (A) (B) (C) (D)
7. (A) (B) (C) (D)
8. (A) (B) (C) (D)
9. (A) (B) (C) (D)
10. (A) (B) (C) (D)
11. (A) (B) (C) (D)
12. (A) (B) (C) (D)
13. (A) (B) (C) (D)
14. (A) (B) (C) (D)
15. (A) (B) (C) (D)
16. (A) (B) (C) (D)
17. (A) (B) (C) (D)
18. (A) (B) (C) (D)
19. (A) (B) (C) (D)
20. (A) (B) (C) (D)
21. (A) (B) (C) (D)
22. (A) (B) (C) (D)
23. (A) (B) (C) (D)
24. (A) (B) (C) (D)
25. (A) (B) (C) (D)
26. (A) (B) (C) (D)
27. (A) (B) (C) (D)
28. (A) (B) (C) (D)
29. (A) (B) (C) (D)
30. (A) (B) (C) (D)

31. 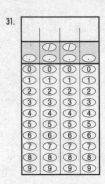 32.  33. 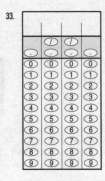 34. 35.

36. 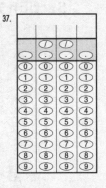 37. 38.

Chapter 12
Practice Test 5:
Answers and
Explanations

PRACTICE TEST 5 ANSWER KEY

Section 1: Reading		Section 2: Writing & Language		Section 3: Math (No Calculator)		Section 4: Math (Calculator)	
1. C	27. A	1. A	23. D	1. B	11. D	1. D	20. D
2. C	28. B	2. B	24. C	2. B	12. B	2. B	21. C
3. D	29. B	3. C	25. A	3. B	13. C	3. A	22. B
4. A	30. C	4. B	26. C	4. D	14. C	4. D	23. A
5. A	31. B	5. B	27. B	5. C	15. A	5. A	24. B
6. D	32. B	6. D	28. C	6. D	16. 800	6. C	25. D
7. A	33. A	7. B	29. C	7. A	17. $\frac{8}{10}$,	7. B	26. B
8. C	34. D	8. B	30. B	8. C	$\frac{4}{5}$,	8. C	27. B
9. D	35. B	9. B	31. A	9. B	or	9. A	28. B
10. B	36. C	10. D	32. A	10. A	0.8	10. A	29. C
11. D	37. C	11. B	33. C		18. 25	11. D	30. D
12. C	38. A	12. B	34. D		19. 20	12. A	31. 5
13. A	39. B	13. D	35. B		20. 225	13. A	or 6
14. A	40. D	14. A	36. D			14. D	32. 19.4
15. D	41. A	15. A	37. D			15. C	33. 10
16. B	42. D	16. C	38. A			16. C	34. 11
17. A	43. C	17. C	39. B			17. B	35. $\frac{7}{12}$
18. A	44. A	18. A	40. C			18. C	
19. D	45. A	19. B	41. D			19. C	36. 4
20. C	46. B	20. D	42. D				37. 321
21. D	47. D	21. A	43. A				38. 7
22. C	48. C	22. A	44. B				
23. B	49. B						
24. D	50. C						
25. D	51. D						
26. B	52. C						

For self-scoring assessment tables, please turn to page 565.

PRACTICE TEST 5 EXPLANATIONS

Section 1: Reading

1. **C** This is a general question about what happens in the passage as a whole. Leave it until the end of the questions because it will be easier to answer once all the specific questions for this passage have been answered. This passage is about a stranger showing up unexpectedly for an unhappy reunion with a former shipmate. Choice (A) might initially look attractive because the narrator and the stranger do hide and then surprise the captain, but there is no *plan* to surprise the captain. Eliminate (A). Choice (B) has nothing to do with the passage and can be eliminated. Choice (C) is a solid paraphrase of the prediction, so keep it. Choice (D) does mention two characters sharing time on a ship, but the passage does not indicate that the two men were *reminiscing* at all. Choice (C) is the correct answer.

2. **C** This is a general question that will be best answered after all of the more detail-oriented questions. Look at the second part of each answer choice. The *encounter* in the passage is not *enthusiastic*, so (A) can be eliminated. There is no *conference*, so (B) can also be eliminated. Choice (C) looks good because the narrator was worried, and the stranger and the captain fought, so keep (C). There is no *homecoming*, so eliminate (D). Choice (C) is the correct answer.

3. **D** This is a Vocab-in-Context question, so go back to the text, find the word *fancy* in lines 5 and 10, and cross it out. Replace it with another word that makes sense in the sentence based on the context of the passage. In the first case, the narrator says that he didn't step back inside *quick enough for his fancy. Fancy* could be replaced with *liking.* See if that also makes sense in the second occurrence. The stranger tells the narrator that he's *taken quite a fancy* to him because the narrator reminds him of his own son, or *the pride of [his] 'art. Liking* definitely fits in that context as well. Choices (A) and (C) can be eliminated immediately. Choice (B) might appear to match the context of the first occurrence of *fancy*, but *impatience* has nothing to do with the prediction of *liking*, so (B) can be eliminated. *Preference* means *liking*. Choice (D) is the correct answer.

4. **A** This question asks about the narrator's sense of the stranger's emotions regarding the coming meeting between him and the captain. Find evidence in the text to predict how the stranger feels about seeing the captain. In the second paragraph, there is plenty of evidence to predict that the stranger feels very bad about the upcoming meeting. The narrator is *uneasy and alarmed*, and he notices that the stranger is *certainly frightened himself.* The narrator goes on to say that the stranger readies his weapon and keeps *swallowing as if he felt...a lump in the throat.* The stranger is definitely not *overjoyed*, so eliminate (B). Choice (D) has nothing to do with the passage, so eliminate it. Choices (A) and (C) both have negative emotions, but the evidence in the text shows the stranger is clearly fearful, not just worried the captain won't recognize him. Choice (A) is the correct answer.

5. **A**   This is a best evidence question, so simply refer to the lines used to predict the answer to the previous question. Choice (A) is the correct answer.

6. **D**   This question asks about how the narrator is addressed by the stranger, so look for evidence in the text to predict what the answer might be. In the text used to answer previous questions, the stranger tells the narrator he has *taken a fancy* to him, but in that same paragraph the stranger swears at the boy *with an oath that made [him] jump.* Eliminate (A) because, while the stranger does address the narrator with friendliness at one point, he never addresses him with respect. Choice (B) is reversed—the stranger does address the boy with anger but he's never violent to him. Choice (C) does not match the prediction. *Affection* in (D) looks good, and later the stranger shows that he does not trust the narrator when he sends him for rum but tells him to leave the door open. Choice (D) is the correct answer.

7. **A**   In order to determine the purpose of the first paragraph, simply look to see what's happening in that paragraph. Throughout the paragraph, the narrator creates a picture of the stranger, from how he looks to how he acts. Choice (A) is the correct answer.

8. **C**   This is a Vocab-in-Context question, so go back to the text, find the word *talons* in line 51, and cross it out. Replace it with another word that makes sense in the sentence based on the context of the passage. Black Dog says he's lost two talons, and then he holds up *his mutilated hand. Talons* must mean *fingers*. Choice (C) is the correct answer.

9. **D**   This question asks why the narrator uses a particular phrase (*all the brown had gone out of his face*), so go back to the text to see what's happening around that phrase. The narrator uses the phrase to describe the captain's reaction to seeing the stranger. Black Dog surprises the captain, who *spun round on his heel…he had the look of a man who sees a ghost, or the evil one, or something worse, if anything can be; and upon my word, I felt sorry to see him all in a moment turn so old and sick.* The narrator uses the phrase to show that the captain is reacting badly to the surprise of seeing Black Dog. Choice (A) does not match that prediction, so it can be eliminated. Choice (B) might be true, but isn't supported by the text. Choice (C) doesn't have any support in the text, either, so it can be eliminated. Choice (D) is a clear paraphrase of the prediction and is the correct answer.

10. **B**   This is a best evidence question, so simply refer to the lines used to predict the answer to the previous question. Choice (B) is the correct answer.

11. **D**   This question asks why the author mentions certain examples. Use the line reference to find the correct window and look for the claim the examples are meant to illustrate. The examples of gift giving are both recent and about Christmas, but they are offered to show that *the ancient practice of gift-giving is still pervasive and significant in modern cultures.* Eliminate (A), as there's no mention of a *recent increase.* Eliminate (B) and (C), since neither *discrepancies* nor *apprehension* is mentioned. Choice (D) matches the prediction and is the correct answer.

12. **C** This is a Vocab-in-Context question, so go back to the text, find the word *rich* in line 20, and cross it out. Replace it with another word that makes sense in the sentence based on the context of the passage. In this case, *rich* refers to the plethora of information that might help to explain consumer behavior. Choices (A) and (B) are actual definitions of the word *rich*, but they don't make sense based on the context. Both of these answers can be eliminated. Choice (C) could work, because when something is *fertile* it is *abundantly productive*, which fits the context of the passage. Choice (D) might connect with the idea of foods that are rich, but that doesn't make sense in this context. Eliminate (D), leaving (C) as the correct answer.

13. **A** This question asks about the *self-perpetuating system of reciprocity*. Notice that the following question is a best evidence question, so Q13 and Q14 can be answered in tandem. Look at the answers choices for Q14 first. Choice (14A) suggests that gift-giving conveys information, which supports (13A). Draw a line connecting those two answers. Choice (14B) deals specifically with the *obligation to give,* and (14C) deals with *repayment*—both refer only to part of the system of reciprocity, and neither supports an answer choice in Q13, so both can be eliminated. Choice (14D) might appear to support (13C), but the lines do not support the idea of wreaking *havoc,* so the relationship is weak. Eliminate (14D). Without any support from Q14, (13B), (13C), and (13D) can be eliminated. That leaves (13A) and (14A) as the correct answers.

14. **A** (See explanation above.)

15. **D** This question asks how Schwartz would view the gift-exchange process. The fourth paragraph presents Schwartz's insights about a gift's ability to reflect *the giver's perception of the recipient* and the implicit acceptance of that perception when a receiver accepts a gift. This point about the process matches well with (D), *symbolic.* Though it may be true that such a process could be *stressful* or *unnerving,* no evidence is given that Schwartz considers it to be so. Thus (A) and (B) can be eliminated. While some givers and receivers may act *intentionally,* there's no evidence that the process always operates that way, so (C) can be eliminated. The best answer is (D).

16. **B** This question asks what the passage says about *the acceptance of a gift.* The fourth paragraph states that accepting a gift constitutes acceptance of the implied identity the gift conveys and that *this may lead to changes in self-perceptions.* The correct answer must have something to do with *a lot of power.* This prediction matches well with (B), *influential.* Eliminate (A), as there's no discussion of the idea that accepting a gift is *considerate.* Eliminate (C) because there is no indication that accepting a gift is *authoritative.* Choice (D) can be eliminated as well because, while accepting a gift may have influence on the recipient, there no evidence that it's *immutable.* Choice (B) is the best answer.

17. **A** This is a specific paired set with Q16, so simply look at the lines used to predict the answer to the previous question. Choice (A) is the correct answer.

18.   **A**   This is a Vocab-in-Context question, so go back to the text, find the word *function* in line 65, and cross it out. Replace it with another word that makes sense in the sentence based on the context of the passage. In this case, *function* refers to the purpose of gift selection, which supports (A). The *nevertheless* at the beginning of the sentence shows a continuation from the previous paragraph. The focus of the previous paragraph was how gift-giving *does* something, not *when* the gifts are given. Therefore, *function* in this context does not have to do with an event. Choices (B) and (C) can be eliminated. Choice (D), *occupation*, does not fit the context of the sentence. Choice (A) is the correct response.

19.   **D**   This question asks why the author mentions *a gift shop's recent advertisement.* Use the line reference to find the window and read for context. Here, the line reference points to the fourth paragraph and to the quoted advertisement. The ad does not question any prior claims or counter any explanations, eliminating (A) and (C). Choice (B) can be eliminated because the advertisement does not *offer a motive* for a certain behavior. The ad supports what was said in paragraph 3, making (D) the correct choice.

20.   **C**   The question asks about information in both the passage and the graph. Use the passage and the graph to answer it. The recipient's self-concept is not included in the graph, nor is the amount of money the giver spent, eliminating (A) and (B). Choice (D) does not work because the thoughtfulness is not measured by the graph. Rather, the graph shows the implicit communication between the gift-giver and recipient, and the passage supports this information in the last paragraph. Therefore, (C) is correct.

21.   **D**   This question asks about the author's thoughts on the graph. For graph-related questions, look at the graph and see what is also supported by the passage. The graph shows the various steps of communication and evaluation in the gift-giving process, as mentioned in the last lines of the passage. *Conditional approval* is not mentioned, making (A) incorrect. While (B) mentions communication, it does not state that parties cannot *communicate effectively*. Similarly, while (C) might be true, it is not supported by the passage, and therefore is incorrect. Choice (D) is supported by the graph and the last lines of the passage and therefore is the correct choice.

22.   **C**   This question asks for a piece of information that *contradicts* the student's claim that *over half of solar radiation influences the ground temperature.* Use the line references given in each of the answer choices to check. Choice (A) refers to a situation in which the atmosphere is *letting through the light rays of the sun relatively easily,* which would confirm rather than contradict the student's claim and should therefore be eliminated. Choice (B) mentions *the temperature of the atmosphere* but does not address solar radiation or ground temperature, so this answer can be eliminated. Choice (C) should be kept because it specifically contradicts the student's claim with these lines: *Owing to the clouds and dust floating in the atmosphere, this heat is probably only about a third of that derived by using Langley's solar constant.* In other words, the *clouds and dust floating in the atmosphere* block the sun's full energy. Choice (D) refers only to the table, not to

the conceptual information regarding the sun's radiation, so it too can be eliminated. Choice (C) is the correct answer.

23. **B** This question asks about the importance of the atmosphere as it influences the temperature of the earth. Use the given line reference to find the window. The relevant information is here: *the atmosphere may act like the glass of a green-house, letting through the light rays of the sun relatively easily, and absorbing a great part of the dark rays emitted from the ground, and it thereby may raise the mean temperature of the earth's surface.* A second purpose is cited here: *the atmosphere acts as a heat store placed between the relatively warm ground and the cold space, and thereby lessens in a high degree the annual, diurnal, and local variations of the temperature.* In other words, the atmosphere plays a crucial role in allowing certain heat in and trapping that heat so it influences ground temperature. Choice (A) is extreme in its use of the word *all*, particularly given that the text indicates that much of the heat is transferred back out of the atmosphere. Eliminate (A). Choice (B) should be kept because it captures the ideas from both quotations without overstating. Choice (C) can be eliminated because it neglects the role of solar radiation. Choice (D) can be eliminated because the words *free passage* are extreme—the passage indicates that the atmosphere absorbs *a great part of the dark rays emitted from the ground*. Choice (B) is the correct answer.

24. **D** This question asks why the author uses the word *green-house* to describe the effects in this passage. Use the given line reference to find the window. The relevant information is here: *like the glass of a green-house, letting through the light rays of the sun relatively easily, and absorbing a great part of the dark rays emitted from the ground.* In other words, the atmosphere is like a greenhouse in that it lets in more heat than it lets out. Choice (A) may be partially true (though it is extreme in its use of the word *only*), but it does not match the prediction because it does not answer the question as to why the word *green-house* is used. Eliminate (A). Choice (B) can also be eliminated because it neglects the role of solar radiation entirely. Choice (C) is deceptive in that it applies the term *green-house* literally rather than figuratively. Eliminate (C). Choice (D) matches well with the prediction and captures both the idea of solar radiation and the atmosphere's role in absorbing it. Choice (D) is the correct answer.

25. **D** This question asks which of the answers can be supported by the quoted statement and its surrounding context. Read the quotation carefully—the word *principally* indicates that most but not all of this energy comes from solar radiation. Choice (A) states a version of this, but there is no indication in the quotation or the passage that clouds block out solar radiation entirely, nor that ground heat does whatever heating solar energy cannot. Eliminate (A). Choice (B) correctly implies that heat can be generated by the sun and other sources, but this choice then goes on to state that the heat is held in the atmosphere and released as cool air, which is untrue. Eliminate (B). Choice (C) may seem plausible, but it overlooks the green-house effect described throughout this passage, which states that solar energy passes relatively unobstructed into the earth's atmosphere. Eliminate (C). Choice (D) takes proper account of the word *principally* by

stating that the heat in the atmosphere comes from the sun and other sources and that heat may be generated from non-solar sources. Choice (D) is thus the correct answer.

26. **B** This question asks why the author uses a few particular words in this context. The window is given by the line numbers in the passage. The cited lines read: *Now if we are able to calculate or estimate how much the mean temperature that layer is lower than the mean temperature of the ground, we may apply Table I for calculating the mean temperature of the ground, as soon as we know by direct measurements the quantity of solar heat absorbed by the ground.* The conditional language here implies that many factors must be considered as one calculates these values. Choice (A) overstates the confidence this language implies in the calculations, so this choice should be eliminated. Choice (B) is true, given the author's indication that the calculations will depend on mathematical formulas and constants in combination with some experimental observations. Choice (C) cannot be supported in the passage because it presumes the knowledge that the described calculations are setting out to find. Choice (D) identifies a harsh critique of earlier scientists where none is present in any part of the passage. Choice (D) can thus be eliminated. Choice (B) is the correct answer.

27. **A** This question asks why the author notes the observations of ground temperature. Using the chronology of previous questions, look for the lead words *observations* and *ground temperature* in the last paragraph. They appear in the last part of the last sentence: *assuming a corresponding decrease of 0.6°C per 100 meters, we find its temperature to be 46°C lower than that of the ground, and thus the mean temperature of the ground equal to 15°C, as it is according to observations.* Taken as a whole, the phrase *as it is according to observations* implies an agreement between the calculated data and the data observed by measurement. In this sense, the author cites the observations as a way to show the correctness of his calculations. Choice (A) captures the importance of the *observations*, so this answer should be kept. Choice (B) would undermine the importance of the mathematical calculations, when in fact the mention of *observations* is used to show the value of mathematical calculations. Eliminate (B). Choice (C) cites a contemporary theory of climate change, one that is not identified in the passage itself, so (C) should be eliminated. Choice (D) can be eliminated because it does not address the importance of the *observations* cited in the question. Choice (A) is the correct answer.

28. **B** This question asks for a combination of information from the table and passage. The relevant information in the passage is indicated by the data *1000 gram-calories per square centimeter for 24 hours.* This refers to the *Loss of Heat* columns in the chart, which are given in this unit. A *Loss of Heat* of 300 corresponds to a temperature of approximately −40°C. However, as the passage indicates, the figures given in the chart indicate the temperature at an elevation of *7600 meters.* Therefore, for the numbers given in the chart, *we find its temperature to be 46°C lower than that of the ground.* In other words, when the temperature on the chart is −40°C, the temperature on the ground must be approximately 6°C, or 46°C warmer, which corresponds with (B). Choices (A) and (D) pull the number directly from the chart but do not account for the information in the passage. Choice (C) confuses the negative signs. Choice (B) is the correct answer.

29. **B** This question asks whether the data from the chart support the author's claim regarding the atmosphere's *heat store*: *the atmosphere acts as a heat store placed between the relatively warm ground and the cold space.* This information is then expanded upon with the detail that *the higher the [atmospheric] layer, the lower is its temperature relatively to that of the ground.* Since this layer of atmosphere is located between the hot earth and cold space and the earth temperature gets colder with higher elevation, the loss of heat will be less as colder earth temperatures come nearer to space temperatures. Despite this technical explanation, this question can be answered with aggressive POE, particularly by looking at the given reasons rather than the "Yes" and "No" components of each answer. Choice (A) can be eliminated because it states that heat loss decreases at larger intervals at lower temperatures, which is not true. For each twenty-degree temperature interval, the heat-loss intervals shrink. In other words, whereas the heat loss at temperatures 100°C and 80°C goes down approximately 400, the heat loss at temperatures −100°C and −120°C goes down only 37. Choice (B) should be kept because it correctly establishes this relationship. Choices (C) and (D) can be eliminated because they cite incorrect relationships between temperature and loss of heat. Choice (B) is the correct answer.

30. **C** This question asks for a piece of information that will support the conclusion in the previous question. The correct answer to the previous question stated that *as the temperature decreases, the heat loss decreases as well but by smaller and smaller intervals.* This agrees with the information given in the chart. Choice (A) shows a widening gap between two heat-loss values, but it does not show the shrinking intervals mentioned in Q29. Eliminate (A). Choice (B) shows large intervals in heat-loss values, which make it difficult to form any conclusion. Eliminate (B). Choice (C) shows adjacent heat-loss values that decrease at smaller and smaller intervals, so keep this choice. Choice (D) shows decreasing values, but these are random and cannot be used to support a conclusion. Eliminate (D). The correct answer is (C).

31. **B** This question asks whether the temperature of the atmosphere varies relative to the distance from the ground. The chart does show variations in temperature, but it does not show variations in height. Therefore, the answer cannot be gleaned from the table alone and must be more explicitly stated within the passage. Choice (A) does hypothesize that temperatures may be different at the ground and at certain heights, but it does not offer conclusive proof and thus should be eliminated. Choice (B) offers conclusive proof of the relationship in the lines, *we find its temperature to be 46°C lower than that of the ground.* Choice (C) can be eliminated because it does not discuss different distances from the earth. Choice (D) can be eliminated for the same reason. Choice (B) is the correct answer.

32. **B** This question asks about the main purpose of the passage, or why this passage was composed. To answer it, ask why Douglass is speaking at this convention. He refers to his *early connection with the cause* as well as *having been called upon to do so by one whose voice in this Council we all gladly obey.* Now look for an answer choice that best fits these reasons. Choice (A) reflects a statement in paragraph 2 (*Men have very little business here as speakers, anyhow*), but does not fit this prediction. Choice (B) is consistent with the prediction. Choice (C) does not have

support in the passage, which explicitly states that *our cause has passed beyond the period of arguing*. Choice (D) reflects a statement in paragraph 2 (*I say of her, as I say of the colored people, "Give her fair play, and hands off"*), but does not fit this prediction. Choice (B) is the correct answer.

33.   **A**   This question asks for the central claim of the passage. To answer it, look for an answer choice that fits the most parts of the text, and eliminate answer choices that are true, but fit only part of the text. Choice (A) has support in paragraph 1 and several points of paragraph 2. Choice (B) contradicts the passage, which says that men *can neither speak for her, nor vote for her, nor act for her*. Choice (C) has support in the end of paragraph 3. Choice (D) slightly contradicts the passage, which indicates that the suffrage movement has become less obscure. It could be true that it should become less obscure still, but the passage doesn't say this, and so this cannot be the passage's central claim. Having eliminated (B) and (D), compare (A) and (C). Since (C) has less support, it is less likely to be the central claim; eliminate (C). Choice (A) is the correct answer.

34.   **D**   This question asks why Douglass uses the word *cause* throughout the passage. To answer it, find each time the word *cause* appears and take note of what Douglass is doing in each case. The first time, in paragraph 2, Douglass explains why he is speaking at this convention, and refers to his early connection to the cause. The second time, also in paragraph 2, he refers to the history of *this woman suffrage cause*. The third time, in paragraph 3, he refers to the convention of women and uses the phrase *our cause*. Putting these ideas together, it is clear that Douglass uses the word *cause* to refer to the women's suffrage movement. Now look for an answer choice that best fits this prediction, and eliminate answer choices that are either false, or true for only one instance of *cause*. (Remember, the question asks how Douglass uses the word *throughout* the passage.) Choice (A) could be true, since it refers to his early connection, but this better fits the first two uses of the word *cause*. Choice (B) goes beyond the scope of the passage: Douglass is not explaining why the movement deserves support; he assumes that it does, and that it is already clear to most people in attendance that it does. Eliminate (B). Choice (C) does not fit any of the uses of the word *cause*. Eliminate (C). Choice (D) could be true, since in each of the three uses of the word *cause* Douglass is referring to the suffrage movement. Now compare (A) and (D), and see that (A) kind of fits two out of three uses of the word, and that (D) completely fits three out of three uses of the word. Choice (D) is the correct answer.

35.   **B**   This question asks for something true about the passage. Notice that the first half of each answer choice addresses Douglass's speaking, and that the last half of each answer choice addresses his identification with the movement. Start by choosing the easier half and using POE. If that is the first half, begin by finding what the passage says about Douglass speaking. In paragraphs 1 and 2, Douglass indicates that he feels diffidence, that he is at a loss for words, and that men really have no business speaking here. Thus, (A) can be eliminated right away:

Douglass is not saying that he wants to give a great speech. Choice (C) also seems extreme, since he is in fact speaking. Eliminate (C). The first half of choices (B) and (D) are similar, and fit the text. Now look at the second half of (B) and (D). According to (B), he is hesitant to speak *even though* he is connected to the movement. That fits. According to (D), he is hesitant to speak *since* he is connected to the movement. This makes no sense. Eliminate (D). Choice (B) is the correct answer.

36. **C**   This question is a excellent question for the Parallel POE strategy because it contains no line reference and no useful lead word. Douglass mentions *men* throughout the passage, so use the line references provided in the next question to help eliminate answer choices. Begin with (37A). Douglass says that he doesn't want to take *more than a very small space of... time and attention*. This could support (36B), so draw a line connecting those two answers. Choice (37B) talks about how he ended up speaking at the gathering, which doesn't support any of the answers from Q36. Eliminate (37B). Choice (37C) says that *men have very little business here as speakers* and that they should *take back benches and wrap themselves in silence*. This supports men *primarily listening*, so draw a line connecting this to (36C). Choice (37D) does not support any of the answers for Q36, so eliminate it. Without support from Q37, (36A) and (36D) can both be eliminated. Now compare the remaining pairs of (36B)/(37A) and (36C)/(37C). The question asks what Douglass indicates *about men*. While he does say that he doesn't want to take up much time, he's speaking specifically about himself and not men in general. The (36B)/(37A) pair can be eliminated. This leaves (36C)/(37C), which is consistent with the text and the question. The correct answers are (36C) and (37C).

37. **C**   (See explanation above.)

38. **A**   This question asks how the *demands of women* in line 29 are related to some kind of injuries. To answer it, find the phrase, and read a bit before and after to understand the context. Douglass says: *I believe no man, however gifted with thought and speech, can voice the wrongs and present the demands of women with the skill and effect, with the power and authority of woman herself.* He goes on to say that woman *knows and feels her wrongs as man cannot...* and *she is her own best representative.* Therefore, the demands of women are something that women can better speak about than men can. Look for an answer choice that fits this prediction. Choice (A) fits this prediction; keep it. Choice (B) can be eliminated because Douglass does not argue that the injuries are for men to speak about. Choice (C) can be eliminated because there is no evidence anywhere that the *world should support* injuries to women. Choice (D) may be true, but it doesn't fit the prediction. Choice (A) is the correct answer.

39. **B**   This question asks for the best evidence to answer question 38. Look back at the lines used to predict the answer to the previous question. Lines 27–31 and 31–36 were used. Choice (B) is the correct answer.

40. **D**   This question asks for the meaning of the word *cradle*, which the passage uses figuratively. Find the word in the passage, and read it in context: *It was when this woman suffrage cause*

was in its cradle, when it was not big enough to go alone, when it had to be taken in the arms of its mother from Seneca Falls, N.Y., to Rochester, N.Y., for baptism. Douglass is referring to the history of the movement, so the word *cradle* here means something like its early years. Choices (A), (B), and (C) have nothing to do with this prediction; eliminate them. Choice (D) fits this prediction exactly. Choice (D) is the correct answer.

41.　**A**　This question asks what the surprise referred to in lines 58–74 serves to emphasize. To do this, first find the word *surprise*, read it in context, and then determine what the author is trying to emphasize. Read the window: *There may be some...period of arguing.* Douglass says that some people attending were expecting arguments about women's suffrage, but were surprised to find no arguments. Look for an answer choice that fits this prediction. Choice (A) refers to *different sorts of speeches,* which could refer to *arguments vs no arguments.* Keep (A). Choice (B) may be attractive because of the reference to *more arguments than assertions,* but the text does not explicitly say what the gender of *some well-meaning people* is. Eliminate (B). Choice (C) can be eliminated. Although the phrase *may not have expected* might look good on its own, the answer as a whole clearly does not match the prediction. Choice (D) can be eliminated, because the arguments weren't *unexpected.* It was the lack of arguments that was surprising. Choice (A) is the correct answer.

42.　**D**　This question asks why the author mentions the number of gallons in discussing fracking. Use the given line reference to check: *As many as 25 fracture stages (per horizontal leg) may be involved in preparing a single site for production, each requiring injection of more than 400,000 gallons of water—a possible total of more than 10 million gallons before the well is fully operational.* Phrases like *as many as* and *more than* are there to draw attention to the size and scale of these numbers. Choice (A) can be eliminated because of the extreme language of the word *inevitable* and because it does not address the size of the fracking operation. Choice (B) can be eliminated because this passage discusses a single method, fracking, for extracting natural gas from shale. Choice (C) can be eliminated because while water might be described as a *basic element,* there is no indication that *only a few* of these basic elements are at play in fracking. Choice (D) should be kept because it reflects the passage's language of size and scale. Choice (D) is the correct answer.

43.　**C**　This question asks for some positive aspect of fracking in Passage 1. Notice that the following question is a best evidence question, so this question and Q44 can be answered in tandem. Look at the answers for Q44 first. The lines in (44A) mention that the natural gas from fracking can *accommodate the country's domestic demand for natural gas at current levels of consumption for more than a hundred years.* These lines match with (43C), which paraphrases that information. Connect these two answers. Next, consider the lines for (44B). These lines describe the way that high-pressure water is used to perforate the shale layer. The shale layer is mentioned in (43B), so those answers can be connected, though the connection is tentative. Next, consider the lines for (44C). These lines complete the description of how fracking extracts natural gas from the shale layer, but the lines have no match in Q43, so (44C) can be eliminated. Next, consider the lines for (44D). These lines set up the discussion of water contamination and pollution in the next paragraph, but the lines have no match in Q43, so (44D) can be eliminated. Without any support from Q44, (43A) and (43D) can be eliminated. Consider the remaining pairs of answer choices in the context of the passage. The positive aspect of fracking is that it produces a lot of natural gas. Choices (43B) and (44B) can be eliminated because they do not contain this positive aspect. Choices (43C) and (44A) are the correct answers.

44.   **A**   (See explanation above.)

45.   **A**   This question asks why the author discusses the *aquifer* in the given lines. Use the line reference to find the window in which the *aquifer* is discussed. In the final paragraph of Passage 1, the aquifer is mentioned twice: *Drillers developing a well must take exceptional care to minimize contact between the wellbore and the surrounding aquifer—often the source of nearby residents' drinking water* and *It is essential that monitoring be in place to ensure the continuing integrity of the seal isolating the well from the aquifer even* after *the well has been fully exploited and abandoned*. In both sentences, the *aquifer* is mentioned as something that must be isolated and protected from the outflowing water used to frack. Choice (A) should be kept because it points to the *significant risk* that the aquifer could be contaminated. Choice (B) may address the concerns of those who worry about fracking, but it does not *dispute* those concerns, so (B) can be eliminated. Choice (C) can also be eliminated because the word *aquifer* does not appear before the final paragraph of Passage 1. Choice (D) can be eliminated because there is no indication that water contamination is a *new finding*. Choice (A) is the correct answer.

46.   **B**   This question asks for the meaning of the word *integrity* in this context. Remember the Vocab-in-Context strategy. Cross out the word, and use the surrounding context to fill in another word that makes sense based on the passage. Earlier sentences refer to the need to *minimize contact between the wellbore and the surrounding aquifer* and to *failures to isolate the drilling liquids*. The word in the blank should therefore mean something like "solidness," or any of a number of words that mean the opposite of "leakiness." Choice (A) does provide one definition of the word *integrity*, but that definition does not agree with the prediction based on the context above, so (A) can be eliminated. Choice (B) matches the prediction, so it should be kept. Choice (C) may be deceptive because this paragraph discusses water at such length, but the word *moisture* does not match the prediction and should be eliminated. Choice (D) provides another possible definition of the word *integrity*, but that definition does not match the context, so (D) can be eliminated. Choice (B) is the correct answer.

47.   **D**   This question asks for some aspect of Passage 2's main idea—something negative, as evidenced by the word *but* in the question. Because this question deals with Passage 2 as a whole, it is best to save it for later, after the more detail-oriented questions. The evidence appears throughout the passage—the first paragraph describes fracking's usefulness, but the remaining two paragraphs discuss its risks. The last paragraph is vicious in its criticism of *Weak safeguards*

and inadequate oversight. In short, the author of Passage 2 sees the potential value of fracking, but he does not consider it to be regulated in a way that protects local populations. Choice (A) does not address safety, only cost, so this answer can be eliminated. Choice (B) might be true, but it is not addressed in the passage, so it can be eliminated. Choice (C) is deceptive because while the author of Passage 2 does believe that industry executives flout the rules, there is no indication that these executives believe *they can mine resources from any place they choose.* This is extreme language that is not supported by the passage. Eliminate (C). Choice (D) effectively paraphrases the evidence presented in the passage, so it should be kept. Choice (D) is the correct answer.

48.   **C**   This question asks for the meaning of the word *roughshod* in this context. Remember the Vocab-in-Context strategy. Cross out the word, and use the surrounding context to fill in another word that makes sense based on the passage. These lines continue the author's critique of industry leaders and overseers, who have created insufficient regulations and have been lax in enforcing the regulations that do exist. Therefore, the word in the blank should mean something like "without restriction" or "without care." Choice (A) could certainly describe the industries that have used fracking to generate a good deal of natural gas, but this does not match the prediction, so (A) can be eliminated. Choice (B) could also describe the industries that have quickly transformed certain rural landscapes, but this does not match with the prediction, so (B) can be eliminated. Choice (C) matches nicely with "without restriction" and "without care," so it should be kept. Choice (D) is deceptive because the sentence describes industrial processes, but the word in the blank should mean "without restriction," and (D) does not match. Choice (C) is the correct answer.

49.   **B**   This questions asks about the relationship between the two passages. This question should be done last because it asks about the main ideas of both passages. Passage 1 gives an overview of the process of fracking and hints at some of its dangers. Passage 2 is primarily concerned with these dangers and is less admiring of fracking's ability to extract natural resources. Choice (A) can be eliminated because Passage 1's author is not blind to the dangers of fracking and his attitude could not be described as *optimistic confidence.* Choice (B) should be kept because it offers a reasonable paraphrase of the relationship between the two passages. Choice (C) can be eliminated because there is no indication that the author of Passage 1 would disapprove of any particular regulations. Choice (D) can also be eliminated because Passage 2 is less concerned with the process of fracking than is Passage 1. Choice (B) is the correct answer.

50.   **C**   This question asks how the author of Passage 2 might respond to the referenced lines in Passage 1. The lines in Passage 1 discuss both the care that drillers must take to ensure that pollution does not occur and the risks associated with such pollution. Notice that the following question is a best evidence question, so this question and Q51 can be answered in tandem. Look at the answers in Q51 first. The lines in (51A) discuss the expansion of the mining industry. There is no match for this answer choice in Q50, so (51A) can be eliminated. Next, consider the lines for (51B), which continue the discussion of the proliferation of the practice of

fracking. These lines match with (50A), which cites the mining industry's success and growth. Connect these two answers. The lines for (51C) refer in a general way to increased industrial production, but they do not address the risks of drilling in particular. Choice (51C) can be eliminated because it does not match with any of the answers in Q50. Next, consider the lines for (51D). These lines match almost exactly with (50C), so these two answers should be connected. Without any support from Q51, (50B) and (50D) can be eliminated. Consider the remaining pairs of answer choices in the context of the passage. Passage 2's tone is overwhelmingly critical, so the author of Passage 2 is not likely to cite the successes of the mining industry in response to a claim about drillers' risks. Choices (50A) and (51B) can be eliminated because they are not sufficiently critical. Choices (50C) and (51D) are the correct answers.

51. **D** (See explanation above.)

52. **C** This question asks for something that is *implicit* (or implied) in Passage 2 and *explicit* (or stated outright) in Passage 1. Consider each answer separately and use POE. Choice (A) can be eliminated because Passage 2 explicitly states that fracking causes air and water pollution, and Passage 1 is concerned only with water pollution. Choice (B) can be eliminated because Passage 2 mentions the *millions of gallons of water used in fracking operations* but doesn't give any indication that it could also be *billions*. Passage 2 also focuses on the effects of fracking rather than the process. Choice (C) should be kept because Passage 2 addresses the effects of fracking on drinking water but does not specifically mention animals, whereas Passage 1 states explicitly, *Serious problems have arisen ... including cases where well water used for drinking became so contaminated that human and animal health was threatened.* Choice (D) can be eliminated because neither passage addresses the costs in setting up wells for drilling. Choice (C) is the correct answer.

Section 2: Writing and Language

1. **A** The words *variety* and *difference* mean roughly the same thing in this context, so having versions of both words in the same answer would be redundant. The best choice is therefore (A), which contains only the word *variety*.

2. **B** All choices express essentially the same idea, so choose the one that expresses that idea in a way that is consistent with the tone of the passage. Choices (A) and (D) are too informal and can be eliminated. Choice (C) is too vague in its mention of *something elusive*. This leaves (B), which expresses a definitive idea and does so in a way that is in keeping with the tone of the passage.

3. **C** The subject of the underlined verb is *movements*, which is plural and therefore requires a plural verb, thus eliminating (A) and (B). Choice (D) would not make sense in the context, because it changes the meaning, saying that the movements *used* to do something. Instead, they are being used to do something. Only (C) remains, which matches the rest of the paragraph with its tense and the subject of the sentence with the plural verb *are*.

4. **B** As the paragraph now stands, its last sentence contains an ambiguous pronoun. It is unclear whether the *it* at the beginning of the last sentence refers to *difference, therapeutic horseback riding, hippotherapy, way,* or *ailment.* The addition of the new sentence would clarify that pronoun, so the sentence should be inserted, thus eliminating (C) and (D). In addition, the sentence helps to further clarify the differences between *therapeutic horseback riding* and *hippotherapy,* making (B) the correct answer.

5. **B** The first and second sentences of this paragraph describe the different applications of hippotherapy within different disciplines, stating that many fields *use the basic tenets of hippotherapy, but they each provide a unique spin on the practice.* Choice (A) would not contribute a useful detail in this regard, and (C) and (D) do not actually offer any specific examples. Choice (B) is therefore the best of the available answer choices in that it describes the work of occupational therapists by providing a specific example.

6. **D** The underlined verb should be consistent with the other verb in this part of the sentence, *achieve.* This eliminates all choices except for (D), which contains the verb *recommend,* which is in the simple present and matches *achieve.*

7. **B** The clues in this sentence are the references to *therapists* who are concerned with *physical aspects.* The only other sentence that discusses physical therapists is sentence 2. Sentence 4 should therefore go after sentence 1 because it refers *back* to the physical therapists mentioned earlier in the paragraph. Therefore, the best answer is (B).

8. **B** Although the underlined portion makes it seem that *new* and *certified* are both adjectives modifying a single noun, in fact, *new* is the end of the previous idea and *certified* is the beginning of the next one. The first idea, *Because the discipline is relatively new,* is incomplete and introduces the second idea, so there should be a comma after the word *new,* eliminating (D). There is no reason to insert a pause in the phrase *certified hippotherapists,* so the best available answer is (B).

9. **B** The words *Just as* at the beginning of the sentence require the words *so too* to complete the idiom, in the same way that *neither* requires *nor* or *not only* requires *but also.* Given the necessity of the words *so* and *too,* (A), (C), and (D) can all be eliminated, leaving only (B).

10. **D** In this sentence, choose a word that establishes the relationship between the *skeptics* and the *doctors and researchers.* Choices (B) and (C) can be eliminated because the relationship they create is illogical. Choice (A) can also be eliminated because it implies a division between doctors and researchers, where none is stated in the passage. Only (D) remains, suggesting that the *skeptics* are those *among* the medical community at large.

11. **B** Read the question carefully. It asks for a choice that *restates the main argument of the passage.* The passage as a whole is about hippotherapy, so this should be in the answer, eliminating (C). Choice (D) undermines the passage's claim that hippotherapy is gaining in popularity. Choice (A) mentions hippotherapy, but it can be eliminated because it is too informal and cites only

a minor detail rather than the passage's central argument. Only (B) remains, as it fulfills the goal outlined in the question.

12. **B** The word *elicit* is a verb meaning "to evoke or draw out." The word *illicit* is an adjective meaning "illegal." In this case, nothing illegal is being described, and the underlined part of speech is a verb, so (C) and (D) can be eliminated. Then, the subject of the underlined verb is *way*, which is singular, and thus requires the singular verb *elicits*, as in (B).

13. **D** Choice (A) creates a comma splice because it separates two complete ideas—*It was Marco Polo who crossed the desert on his way to China* and *he described the sound he heard as "a variety of musical instruments*—with only a comma. Choices (B) and (C) create the same mistake. Only (D) fixes the mistake by making the first part of the sentence incomplete.

14. **A** The word *cello* is the last word in the phrase *that odd confluence of pipe organ and cello*. As the comma before the word *that* indicates, this phrase is meant to be set off as unnecessary information. Therefore, in order to remain consistent with the non-underlined part of the sentence, the entire phrase should be set off with commas, as in (A).

15. **A** Choice (B) can be eliminated because it uses a semicolon to set off a complete idea from an incomplete idea, when a semicolon should be used to separate only complete ideas. Choice (D) can be eliminated because it contains two complete ideas but insufficient punctuation—only a comma, not a semicolon or a period. Choices (A) and (C) state the same idea, but (A) does so more concisely, so (A) is the better of the two answers.

16. **C** This paragraph shifts the focus from the desert to the ocean, so there must be a phrase or sentence at the beginning to signal that shift, thus eliminating (D). Choices (A) and (B) provide this transition, but they do so in wordy, awkward ways. Choice (C) is relatively simple, but it does not contain any less information that (A) and (B), and it fulfills the purpose outlined in the question.

17. **C** The passage as a whole is all about sound—the sound of the seemingly silent desert sands or the seemingly silent ocean. The passage is mainly concerned with showing that these, especially the ocean, are actually noisy places. The proposed sentence goes against that general argument, so the sentence should not be added to the passage at all, thus making (C) the most appropriate answer.

18. **A** The underlined pronoun refers back to the word *ocean*, which is singular. The plural pronouns given in (C) and (D) can therefore be eliminated. Then, the sentence is referring to the *ocean's unwillingness*, so the possessive form *its* should be used, not the contraction *it's*. The best answer is thus (A).

19. **B** All four answers express essentially the same idea, but (A), (C), and (D) do so in oddly informal language. Only (B) is in keeping with the general tone of the passage and is therefore the best answer.

20. **D** The line graph and the bar graph on the chart show almost no consistency with one another, so the choices that describe a consistent relationship—(A), (B), and (C)—can be eliminated. Only (D) accurately describes the chart.

21. **A** Because the trends in this chart are so erratic, it is crucial to work with only single data points. At the point in March described earlier in the sentence, when there were 40 whale sightings, the average was approximately 14. Choice (A) captures this relationship. Choice (B) is not supported in the chart because summer months are not shown. Choice (C) is false by any measure. Choice (D) suggests that over 20 whales migrate every day in some other months (whatever those coldest winter months are), a claim which is not substantiated by information in the chart.

22. **A** Read the question carefully. It asks for *a conclusion that points toward the role that sound might play in future research into different ecosystems.* In fact, the paragraph already contains this information, so there is no reason to add a new sentence. In order words, that goal can be fulfilled most directly and concisely with NO CHANGE to the passage.

23. **D** Punctuation should only be used when it has a clear and definite purpose. In this case, there is no need for any punctuation, so the best available option is to eliminate punctuation entirely, as (D) does.

24. **C** When given the option to DELETE the underlined portion, give it serious consideration. It is often correct. In this case, however, the underlined portion must be kept—without it, there is only a comma separating two complete ideas. This eliminates (D). This sentence and the next one create a sequence—from 1929 to 1932. Therefore, the best of the available answers will be a word that indicates time, as only (C), *When*, does.

25. **A** This and all subsequent paragraphs are about Roosevelt and his legislative action when he took office in 1933. Of the four answers, the only one that mentions Roosevelt is (A), and this answer effectively sets up the information that is to follow.

26. **C** This sentence describes Roosevelt's action to send *government workers to inspect each bank.* The reports from these inspectors would allow government officials to determine *which banks would be safe and sustainable to reopen.* There is a cause-and-effect relationship established between these ideas, which (A) and (B) disrupt. Choice (D) provides the appropriate relationship, but this word cannot be used idiomatically with the non-underlined word, *determining,* that follows. Only (C) remains—it establishes the correct relationship and can be used in the context.

27. **B** Read the question carefully. It asks for the choice that *provides the most specific information on the areas that Roosevelt hoped to stimulate.* Choices (A), (C), and (D) may each be true, but none fulfills the question's demand for *specific information.* Only (B) does so in listing two specific sectors of the economy.

28. **C** This sentence refers to an action that would control *demand*. The best combination of words that refers to this action is *level off*, as in (C). Choice (A), *level with*, means "to be honest with." Choices (B) and (D) do not create idiomatically logical phrases.

29. **C** Read the question carefully. It asks for a detail that *emphasizes the importance of the TVA in Roosevelt's larger economic project*, a project, as the passage indicates, of stimulating the economy and reducing unemployment. Choices (A) and (D) do not fulfill any part of this purpose, and (B) gives a detail about the TVA but does not connect it to Roosevelt's larger project. Therefore, (C) most effectively fulfills the goal outlined in the question.

30. **B** All four answers express essentially the same idea, so the most effective answer will be the most concise. In this case, that answer is (B), which expresses in a single word what the other answers express in more.

31. **A** The underlined pronoun refers back to *Roosevelt's "New Deal,"* which is singular, thus eliminating (C), which is plural, and (D), which is not a pronoun. Then, the underlined pronoun should be the contraction *it is*, as in (A). The possessive pronoun given in (B) would create a sentence fragment, in addition to the fact that the *it* is not in possession of anything.

32. **A** This sentence refers to the *day-to-day lives* belonging to *people*. Therefore, the best answer is (A), which gives the possessive form *people's*. Choice (C) is not possessive. With (B) and (D), remember that everything that comes before the apostrophe must be a word—*peoples* (when used in this way) is not a word.

33. **C** This paragraph describes a debate about the legacy of Roosevelt's legislative activity, citing arguments from those on either side of the issue. Only (C) remains neutral in this debate with the words *In either case*.

34. **D** All four choices express a similar idea, that of an actress who excels in some way. Choice (A) is informal and potentially sarcastic, so it can be eliminated. Choices (B) and (C) are unnecessarily elevated as they are written in a tone that is not in keeping with that of the rest of the passage. Choice (D) is the most direct and keeps with the tone of the passage, in that it is sufficiently formal but not overblown in its use of language.

35. **B** This sentence states that *the Japanese film industry had divided loyalties at the time*, and it cites a *debt to American cinema* and *tensions with the United States and others* which led to war. There is no contrast established in the sentence, eliminating (A) and (C). Nor was it the Japanese film industry's loyalties that *enabled* the tensions between nations that led to war, eliminating (D). Only (B) works effectively in this contrast by establishing the correct relationship between the ideas in the sentence.

36. **D** This paragraph mentions the Japanese film industry's divided loyalties and tensions between nations, and the underlined portion explains how these tensions played out in the particular

film. The underlined portion should be kept because this information is not given anywhere else in the passage, thus eliminating (A) and (B). The information in the underlined portion refers to something that *would become Axis propaganda* and is more general than specific, eliminating (C). Choice (D) is the correct answer in that it correctly states that the underlined portion should be kept because it clarifies the idea about divided loyalties that comes before it and connects to the sentence that follows it.

37. **D** This part of the sentence describes the film *Late Spring* in the present tense, as evidenced by the verbs *plays* and *is*. The underlined verb should therefore be in the present tense as well, eliminating (A), (B), and (C), leaving only (D) as the correct answer.

38. **A** This paragraph as a whole celebrates Hara's performance in *Late Spring*. The last sentence of the paragraph contributes to that celebration, so it should be introduced with a word that indicates a continuation, as only (A) does. Choice (B) can be eliminated because this sentence contains a detail, not a summation. Choice (C) can be eliminated because there is nothing in this sentence that contrasts with previous information. Choice (D) can be eliminated because it suggests a concurrent event, when in fact this sentence gives an additional detail about an event already being described.

39. **B** All four answers express essentially the same idea, so the most effective answer will be the most concise. In this case, that answer is (B), which expresses in a two words what the other answers express in more.

40. **C** This sentence refers to *very few sets*, suggesting that the terms in this list must each represent one of those sets. Choice (A) suggests that one of those sets is an *office kitchen*, which does not make sense. Choices (B) and (D) create similar errors in suggesting *living* and *kitchen living*, respectively, as possible sets. Only (C) creates a logical list by separating as possible sets an *office*, a *kitchen*, and a *living room*.

41. **D** The word *council* is used only as a noun and typically refers to a group of people brought together to deliberate a significant issue. The word *counsel* can be used as either a noun or a verb, and the word refers to either giving advice (in the verb form) or the advice itself (in the noun form). In this sentence, the word refers to the advice of *her friends and family*, so *counsel* must be used, eliminating (A) and (B). Then, the character is receiving the advice *of* this group, making (D) the better of the remaining answers.

42. **D** The first part of the sentence characterizes the plot and conflicts as *simple*, while the second part suggests that the plots are also very *profound*. As a result, the conjunction that links the ideas must indicate a contrast, eliminating (A), (B), and (C) and leaving only (D).

43. **A** The underlined pronoun refers back to the noun *viewers*, meaning that the pronoun must be plural. Of the available choices, only (A), *their*, provides such a pronoun. Though *your* can be plural, the viewers would not be referred to as "you."

44. **B** Note the first word of the proposed sentence: *Others*. This word must link with some first group. That group is indicated in sentence 3 by the word *Some*. Therefore, the most effective placement of the proposed sentence would be between sentences 3 and 4, or after sentence 3, as (B) states.

Section 3: Math (No Calculator)

1. **B** Come up with the expression in bite-sized pieces. Notice that all of the choices use the variable y, which represents the number of hours for (A) and (B) but the number of essays for (C) and (D). The number of essays is given but the number of hours is not. Therefore, the variable has to represent the unknown value, the number of hours. Eliminate (C) and (D). The editor is paid $25 per hour. The total amount that the editor is paid for his or her time can be found by multiplying 25 by the number of hours. The remaining choices use y to represent the number of hours, so the product is $25y$. Eliminate the remaining choice that doesn't include $25y$, which is (A). Only one choice remains. To see why (B) is correct, note that the $50 bonus must be added to the editor's earnings for time spent. Also, the bonus is for *all three* essays rather than *each* essay, so it should only be added once. The answer is (B).

2. **B** Use bite-sized pieces and eliminate answer choices after each step. Start by combining $-mn^2 + 2mn^2$ to get mn^2, and use this to eliminate (C) and (D). Now combine the $2n^2$ terms, which cancel and should not appear in the correct answer. Use this to eliminate (A). The answer is (B).

3. **B** The question is made more complicated by fractions, so get rid of the fractions. Multiply both sides of the first equation by 12 to get $x - y = 156$. Multiply both sides of the second equation by 6 to get $2x - y = 120$. Subtract the first equation from the second equation.

$$\begin{array}{rcr} 2x - y = & 120 \\ -\underline{(x - y = } & \underline{156)} \\ x \quad\quad = & -36 \end{array}$$

Eliminate any choice that doesn't include $x = -36$. Eliminate (A), (C), and (D). Only one choice remains. To see why $y = -192$, plug $x = -36$ into the non-fraction version of the first equation to get $-36 - y = 156$, and solve for y. The answer is (B).

4. **D** The problem discusses how many shoes Kelly must sell in a month. Eliminate (C) because 300 days does not fit the problem. Since x is the number of days she works each month, plug in $x = 0$ to see how many shoes she starts with at the beginning of the month. The value for S would be 300 at day 0. Therefore, (D) is the answer.

5. **C** Since there are actual numbers in the answer choices, plug in the answers, starting with one of the middle two choices. Start with (B), which is 35. The question asks for the number of all-day passes sold, so assume that there were 35 all-day passes sold. Since there were a total of 70

passes sold, there must have been a total of 70 − 35 = 35 half-day passes sold. The park sells all-day passes for $80 and half-day passes for $40. Since there were 35 of each sold, the park took in a total of $80 × 35 = $2,800 for all-day passes and $40 × 35 = $1,400 for half-day passes. Therefore, the park took in a total of $2,800 + $1,400 = $4,200. However, the question states that the park took in $4,600, so eliminate (B). Since the total should be greater, the park needs to sell more of the $80 tickets. Therefore, the number of all-day passes sold has to increase. Eliminate (A) as well. Only (C) and (D) remain. Since 60 is easier to work with than 45, try (D). If 60 all-day passes are sold, then 70 − 60 = 10 half-day passes are sold. The park takes in $60 × 80 = $4,800 from all-day passes. Since this is already too high, eliminate (D). Only one choice remains. The answer is (C).

6. **D** To find the solutions to a quadratic equation, either factor or use the quadratic formula. When the coefficient on the x^2 term is not 1, factoring is more difficult than usual but not impossible. Since 5 is prime, one factor will have $5x$ and the other will have x, so write $(5x\ \ )(x\ \ ) = 0$. Now find two factors of 6 that fit the equation. Since the sign on 6 is negative, one factor is negative and one is positive. To fit the equation, one of the factors must be multiplied by 5 and added to the other to get 7. The only pairs of factors of 6 are 1 and 6 and 2 and 3. Since $5 \times 2 + (-3) = 7$, the equation can be factored as $(5x - 3)(x + 2) = 0$. Set each factor to 0 to get $(5x - 3) = 0$ and $x + 2 = 0$. Solve each factor to get $x = \dfrac{3}{5}$ and $x = -2$. Another way to find the values for x of a quadratic in the form $ax^2 + bx + c$ is to use the quadratic formula, $x = \dfrac{-b \pm \sqrt{b^2 - 4ac}}{2a}$. In this case, $a = 5$, $b = 7$, and $c = -6$. Either way of solving yields the solutions $\dfrac{3}{5}$ and -2. Since the question specifies that $a < b$, $a = -2$ and $b = \dfrac{3}{5}$. The question asks for $b - a$, which is $\dfrac{3}{5} - (-2) = \dfrac{3}{5} + 2 = \dfrac{3}{5} + \dfrac{10}{5} = \dfrac{13}{5}$. The answer is (D).

7. **A** Look at the denominators of the fractions to find easy numbers to plug in. Try $t = 11$. Now look at the numerator to see that $t + u = 12$, so u would then equal 1. Plug these values into the answers to see which is true. Only (A) works, so it must be the answer.

8. **C** Opposite sides of a parallelogram are parallel, and parallel lines have the same slope. Use the slope formula: $\dfrac{y_1 - y_2}{x_1 - x_2}$. Segment AB has a slope of $\dfrac{18 - 0}{0 - (-6)} = \dfrac{18}{6} = 3$. Segment DC is paral-

lel to AB and must have the same slope, so $3 = \dfrac{0 - (-12)}{j - 0}$. Then $3 = \dfrac{12}{j}$, so $3j = 12$, and $j = 4$. The answer is (C).

9. **B** Since the problem involves algebra and asks for the least possible value of y, plug in the answers starting with the smallest number. Try (D). If $y = 4$, then $x = \dfrac{4(4-3)}{2} = \dfrac{4(1)}{2} = \dfrac{4}{2} = 2$, so a polygon with 4 sides only has 2 diagonals. This is not at least 7, so eliminate (D) and try (C). If $y = 5$, then $x = \dfrac{5(5-3)}{2} = \dfrac{5(2)}{2} = \dfrac{10}{2} = 5$. This is not at least 7, so eliminate (C) and try (B). If $y = 6$, then $x = \dfrac{6(6-3)}{2} = \dfrac{6(3)}{2} = \dfrac{18}{2} = 9$. This is greater than 7, so choose (B).

10. **A** The question asks for the value of the car y years from now. Determine the value of the car each year. The car is driven 10,000 miles each year. Set up a proportion to determine the decrease in the value each year. Since the car's value decreases $500 for every 1,000 miles driven, set up a proportion: $\dfrac{\$500}{1{,}000 \text{ miles}} = \dfrac{x}{10{,}000 \text{ miles}}$. Cross-multiply to get $1{,}000x = 5{,}000{,}000$. Divide both sides by 1,000 to get $x = 5{,}000$. Therefore, the car's value decreases by $5,000 each year. Plug in a value for y, such as $y = 2$, and calculate the value of the car. After 2 years, the car's value decreases by $10,000, so the value then would be $13,000. Go through each answer, plug in $y = 2$, and eliminate each choice that is not equal to $13,000. Choice (A) is $23,000 − $5,000(2) = $23,000 − $10,000 = $13,000. Keep (A). Choice (B) is $23,000 − $500(2) = $23,000 − $1,000 = $22,000. Eliminate (B). Choice (C) is $23,000 − $0.02(2) = $23,000 − $0.04 = $22,999.96. Eliminate (C). Choice (D) is $23,000 − $0.0002(2) = $23,000 − $0.0004 = $22,999.9996. Eliminate (D). The answer is (A).

11. **D** The problem states that the system of equations has no solution, which means that the lines are parallel and the slopes are equal. The slope of a line in standard form $Ax + By = C$ is given by $-\dfrac{A}{B}$, so the slope of the first line is $-\dfrac{7}{-c} = \dfrac{7}{c}$. The slope of the second line is $-\dfrac{5}{2}$. Set the

slopes equal to each other to solve for c: $\dfrac{7}{c} = -\dfrac{5}{2}$. Now cross-multiply to get $-5c = 14$, and

divide both sides by -5 to find that $c = -\dfrac{14}{5}$. Alternatively, convert each line into the form

$y = mx + b$ to find the slopes and set them equal. In either case, the answer is (D).

12. **B** Start by multiplying both the numerator and denominator of the given expression by the com-

plex conjugate of the denominator: $\dfrac{4 - 7i}{6 + 3i} \times \dfrac{6 - 3i}{6 - 3i}$. Use FOIL to get $\dfrac{24 - 12i - 42i + 21i^2}{36 - 18i + 18i - 9i^2}$.

Combine like terms to get $\dfrac{24 - 54i + 21i^2}{36 - 9i^2}$. Plug in $i^2 = -1$, since the problem says that

$i = \sqrt{-1}$. This gives $\dfrac{24 - 54i + 21(-1)}{36 - 9(-1)} = \dfrac{24 - 54i - 21}{36 + 9} = \dfrac{3 - 54i}{45}$. To make this look like

the answer choices, turn the expression into two fractions and reduce: $\dfrac{3}{45} - \dfrac{54i}{45} = \dfrac{1}{15} - \dfrac{6i}{5}$,

which is (B).

13. **C** If a polynomial is divisible by x, each term in the simplified form of the polynomial must have x as a factor. Write $g(x)$ in simplified form. If $g(x) = 2(x^2 + 14x + 7) - 7(x + c)$, distribute to get $g(x) = 2x^2 + 28x + 14 - 7x - 7c$. Combine like terms to get $g(x) = 2x^2 + 21x + 14 - 7c$. The two terms without x as a factor are 14 and $-7c$. In order for the polynomial to be divisible by x, $14 - 7c$ must equal 0, so that only the terms with x as a factor remain. If $14 - 7c = 0$, add $7c$ to both sides to get $14 = 7c$. Divide both sides by 7 to get $c = 2$. The answer is (C).

14. **C** Plugging in would normally be a good idea for a question like this, but this is the no-calculator section. Exponent questions are always easier to handle when the bases are the same, so

rewrite 27 as 3^3. Use the rules of exponents to work out the expression as $\dfrac{27^r}{3^s} = \dfrac{(3^3)^r}{3^s} = \dfrac{3^{3r}}{3^s}$.

Now that the terms have the same base, remember the MADSPM rule that division means

subtraction of the exponents, so $\dfrac{3^{3r}}{3^s} = 3^{3r-s}$. The problem states that $3r - s = 10$, so $3^{3r-s} = 3^{10}$

and (C) is the answer.

15. **A** This question contains variables in the question and in the answer choices, so plug in. Use

$n = 10$ so the calculations are straightforward. Then, $\dfrac{4n + 9}{n - 5} = \dfrac{4(10) + 9}{10 - 5} = \dfrac{40 + 9}{5} = \dfrac{49}{5}$.

This is the target value, so plug 10 in for n in the choices to find the one that matches the target. Start with (A): $4 + \dfrac{29}{n-5} = 4 + \dfrac{29}{10-5} = 4 + \dfrac{29}{5} = \dfrac{20}{5} + \dfrac{29}{5} = \dfrac{49}{5}$. This matches the

target, so keep (A) but remember to check all four choices when plugging in. Move to (B):

$4 + \dfrac{9}{n-5} = 4 + \dfrac{9}{10-5} = 4 + \dfrac{9}{5} = \dfrac{20}{5} + \dfrac{9}{5} = \dfrac{29}{5}$. This doesn't match the target, so eliminate

(B). Try (C): $4 - \dfrac{9}{5} = \dfrac{20}{5} - \dfrac{9}{5} = \dfrac{11}{5}$. This doesn't match the target, so eliminate (C). Try (D):

$\dfrac{4+9}{-5} = \dfrac{13}{-5}$, which will be a negative number and won't match the target, so eliminate (D).

Choice (A) is the answer.

16. **800** To solve for x, isolate the variable. First add 3 to both sides to get $40 = \dfrac{x}{20}$. Then, multiply both sides by 20 to get $x = 40 \times 20 = 800$. The answer is 800.

17. $\dfrac{8}{10}, \dfrac{4}{5}$, or **0.8**

In any triangle with angles of 90°, $x°$, and $y°$, cos x = sin y. Therefore, if cos p = 0.8, then

sin q = 0.8 as well. Alternatively, remember from SOHCAHTOA that the cosine of an angle

is the ratio of the adjacent side to the hypotenuse. The value 0.8 can also be written as $\dfrac{8}{10}$.

Plug in 8 as the base of the triangle (adjacent to $p°$) and 10 as the hypotenuse. Sine is opposite

over hypotenuse. To find the sine of $q°$, find the opposite side, which is 8, and the hypotenuse,

which is 10. The sine of $q°$ is therefore $\dfrac{8}{10}$, which can also be written as $\dfrac{4}{5}$ or 0.8. Any of these

are acceptable answers.

18. **25** Plug in a value for a that will be easy to use without a calculator. If $a = 2$, then

$\dfrac{9(5a)^2}{(3a)^2} = \dfrac{9(5 \times 2)^2}{(3 \times 2)^2} = \dfrac{9(10)^2}{(6)^2} = \dfrac{9(100)}{36}$. Reduce this fraction now, rather than multiplying it

out, since 36 is divisible by 9. The fraction becomes $\dfrac{100}{4}$, which is 25. The answer is 25.

19. **20** Vertical angles are congruent, so $\angle HLI = \angle JLK$. Also, $\angle IHL = \angle KJL$ because $\overline{HI} \parallel \overline{JK}$. Like-

wise, $\angle HIL = \angle JKL$. These triangles are similar, and similar triangles have proportional side

lengths, so set up a proportion, which will help find $\overline{HJ}$: $\dfrac{3}{9} = \dfrac{5}{JL}$. Cross-multiply to find that

$45 = 3(\overline{JL})$, and divide both sides by 3 to find that $\overline{JL} = 15$. The question asks for the length of

$\overline{HJ}$, which is 5 (from $\overline{HL}$) plus 15 (from $\overline{JL}$) for a total length of 20, which is the answer.

20. **225** Start by plugging $z = 5\sqrt{3}$ into the second equation to get $3(5\sqrt{3}) = \sqrt{3y}$. Distribute the 3 on the left side to get $15\sqrt{3} = \sqrt{3y}$. Square both sides to get rid of the square root signs: $225 \times 3 = 3y$. Divide both sides by 3 to get $225 = y$.

Section 4: Math (Calculator)

1. **D** Translate the information in the question into an expression in bite-sized pieces. The monthly fee is $20.00 and the data usage fee is $2.50 per gigabyte. Start with the fee for data usage. The usage is $2.50 per gigabyte used, so to get the fee in a month in which David used g gigabytes, multiply g by 2.50 to get 2.50g. Eliminate any answer choice that doesn't include 2.50g: (A), (B), and (C). Thus, only (D) remains. To determine why (D) is correct, note that the word *and* translates to +, so add 20 to 2.50g to get 20 + 2.50g. The answer is (D).

2. **B** The question asks for the greatest change between consecutive years. Go through each year and determine the change in each. From 2000 to 2001, there is a decrease of $50,000 – $40,000 = $10,000. From 2001 to 2002, there is an increase of $55,000 – $40,000 = $15,000. From 2002 to 2003, there is an increase of $60,000 – $55,000 = $5,000. From 2003 to 2004, there is an increase of $75,000 – $60,000 = $15,000. From 2004 to 2005, there is a decrease of $75,000 – $65,000 = $10,000. From 2005 to 2006, there is no change. From 2006 to 2007, there is an increase of $95,000 – $65,000 = $30,000. The greatest is $30,000, which is (B). Alternatively, ballpark. Look at the graph and notice that the change from 2006 to 2007 appears to be the steepest, so this difference would have to be the answer. The answer is (B).

3. **A** There are variables in the answers, so plug in. Currently Jim can do 14 pull-ups in a minute. He believes that he can increase this amount by 7 each year. Therefore, he believes that in 1 year he can do 14 + 7 = 21 pull-ups, and in 2 years he can do 21 + 7 = 28 pull-ups. Now plug $y = 2$ into each of the choices and eliminate any that isn't equal to 28. Choice (A) is 7(2) + 14 = 28, so keep (A). Choice (B) is 7(2) + 30 = 44, so eliminate (B). Choice (C) is 14(2) + 7 = 35, so eliminate (C). Choice (D) is 14 – 7(2) = 0, so eliminate (D). The answer is (A).

4. **D** The question gives an equation and a value for one of the variables in the equation. Plug in the given value to solve for the value of the other variable. If $v = 67$, the equation becomes $67 = 17 + 2.5t$. Subtract 17 from both sides to get $50 = 2.5t$. Divide both sides by 2.5 to get $t = 20$, so the answer is (D).

5. **A** The question asks for the equation of a function that could possibly define h. Each of the equations in the choices is in factored form. If a factor of the equation of a function is in the form $(x - r)$, r is one of the roots, or one of the x-intercepts. Since the roots of this function are −4, 2, and 4, the roots are $(x - (-4))$ or $(x + 4)$, $(x - 2)$, and $(x - 4)$. The only equation with all of these factors is (A), so the answer is (A).

6. **C** Translate the first statement into an equation. The phrase *three times a number n* translates to $3n$. The phrase *is added to* translates to +. The word *is* translates to =. Therefore, the sentence translates to $3n + 9 = 3$. Solve this for *n*: subtract 9 from both sides to get $3n = -6$, then divide both sides by 3 to get $n = -2$. This is (A). However, the question does not ask for the value of *n*, so (A) is a trap answer. The question asks for *the result when 4 times n is added to 14*. The phrase *4 times n* translates to $4n$. The phrase *is added to 14* translates to + 14. Therefore, *4 times n is added to 14* translates to $4n + 14$. Since $n = -2$, $4n + 14 = 4(-2) + 14 = -8 + 14 = 6$. The answer is (C).

7. **B** The question asks for how many 16-ounce cups can be filled from a 64-gallon urn. First, convert the 64 gallons into ounces. Use a proportion: $\dfrac{1 \text{ gallon}}{128 \text{ ounces}} = \dfrac{64 \text{ gallons}}{x \text{ ounces}}$. Cross-multiply to get $x = (128)(64) = 8{,}192$. Now determine the number of 16-ounce cups that can be filled from an 8,192-ounce urn. Use another proportion: $\dfrac{1 \text{ cup}}{16 \text{ ounces}} = \dfrac{y \text{ cups}}{8{,}192 \text{ ounces}}$. Cross-multiply to get $16y = 8{,}192$. Divide both sides by 16 to get $y = 512$. The answer is (B).

8. **C** To determine the slope of a line, use the slope formula, $slope = \dfrac{y_2 - y_1}{x_2 - x_1}$. Let $\left(1, -\dfrac{1}{3}\right)$ be (x_1, y_1) and $\left(5, \dfrac{8}{3}\right)$ be (x_2, y_2). The slope is $\dfrac{\dfrac{8}{3} - \left(-\dfrac{1}{3}\right)}{5 - 1} = \dfrac{\dfrac{8}{3} + \dfrac{1}{3}}{4} = \dfrac{\dfrac{9}{3}}{4} = \dfrac{3}{4}$. The answer is (C).

9. **A** The question asks for the average number of fish per tank. The average is $\dfrac{total}{number \ of \ things}$. The *things* in this case are the tanks. Since the title of the graph says that there are 18, the average is $\dfrac{total}{18}$. The *total* is the number of fish. To determine this, use the histogram. There are 2 tanks with 2 fish each, so these 2 tanks have a total of $2 \times 2 = 4$ fish. There are 4 tanks with 3 fish, so these 4 tanks have a total of $4 \times 3 = 12$ fish. There are no tanks with 4 fish, so ignore that column. There are 3 tanks with 5 fish, so these 3 tanks have a total of $3 \times 5 = 15$ fish. There are 5 tanks with 6 fish, so these 5 tanks have a total of $5 \times 6 = 30$ fish. There is 1 tank with 7 fish, so this 1 tank has a total of $1 \times 7 = 7$ fish. There are 3 tanks with 8 fish, so these 3 tanks have a total of $3 \times 8 = 24$ fish. Therefore, all the tanks have a total of $4 + 12 + 15 + 30 + 7 + 24 = 92$ fish, and the average number of fish per tank is $\dfrac{92}{18} = 5.\overline{1}$. The question asks for the *closest* choice, which is (A).

10. **A** The question asks for the design flaw in the survey. The survey was conducted to determine whether people in City C are more likely to work 9-to-5 office jobs than other jobs. The survey was conducted exclusively during the time in which people would be working at 9-to-5 office jobs.

Therefore, people at this type of job would be less likely to answer the call. Choice (A) matches the prediction, so keep (A). Choice (B) is population size. Population size is not necessarily a design flaw, since the population size is not given. Eliminate (B). Choice (C) is sample size. If the sample size were significantly less than the population size, this fact could lead to unreliable results. However, since population size is not known, sample size cannot be determined to be a design flaw. Eliminate (C). Choice (D) refers to the fact that the telephone was used. Since the problem does not mention telephone use by people with different types of jobs, there's no reason to believe that using a telephone to conduct the survey would make the results less reliable. Eliminate (D). The correct answer is (A).

11. **D** The question asks which graph could represent $y = p(x)$ and says that function p has exactly four roots. A *root* of a function is an x-value for which the y-value is 0. The y-value is 0 for all points on the x-axis, so p has to have exactly four x-intercepts (points where the graph intersects the x-axis). Go through each choice and determine the number of x-intercepts. Choices (A) and (C) have three x-intercepts, so eliminate these. Choice (B) has five intercepts. Since the question states that p has *exactly* four roots rather than *at least* four, eliminate (B) as well. Only (D) has exactly four x-intercepts, so the answer is (D).

12. **A** The question states that 85% of the customers ordered the brunch special. Since the question asks for which choice could be the number of customers, plug in the answers by taking 85% of each choice. Eliminate any choice that doesn't result in a whole number of customers. Start with (A): 85% of 40 is $(0.85)(40) = 34$. Since this is a whole number, this could be the number of customers, so the answer is (A).

13. **A** The question includes variables and uses the phrase *in terms of*, so plug in. Since an equation is given with d isolated, plug in for the other variables, t, v, and h, and calculate d. Let $t = 2$, $v = 10$, and $h = 20$. In this case, $d = -8t^2 + vt + h = -8(2)^2 + (10)(2) + 20 = 8$. The question asks for the value of v, so the target answer is 10. Go through the choices and eliminate any answer that is not 10. Choice (A) is $v = \dfrac{8 - 20}{2} + 8(2) = 10$, so keep (A). Choice (B) is $v = \dfrac{8 + 20}{2} - 8(2) = -2$, so eliminate (B). Choice (C) is $v = \dfrac{8 - 20 + 8}{2} = -2$, so eliminate (C). Choice (D) is $v = 8 + 20 - 8(2) = 12$, so eliminate (D). Only (A) matches, so the answer is (A).

14. **D** The question asks for what could be the median of 22 scores. The median of an even number of numbers is the average of the middle two when the numbers are listed in order. In this case, it is the average of the 11th and 12th score. Find the location of the 11th and 12th scores on the histogram. There is 1 score from 50 to 60. There are 4 scores from 60 to 70, so there are 5 scores from 50 to 70. There are 2 scores from 70 to 80, so there are 7 scores from 50 to 80. There are 11 scores from 80 to 90, so there are 18 scores from 50 to 90. Since the 11th and 12th scores were passed at the 80 to 90 interval, they must be in this interval. Therefore, the median must be within this interval, as well. The only choice within this interval is 84, so the answer is (D).

15. **C** The question asks for a percent, which is $\dfrac{part}{whole} \times 100$. The *part* is the total number of those surveyed who use public transit, which is 51, and the *whole* is the total number of those surveyed, which is 130. Therefore, the percent is $\dfrac{51}{130} \times 100 \approx 39$. The answer is (C).

16. **C** The proportion of people who fit the requirements in the survey can be expected to be the same proportion of people who will fit the requirements in the general population. First, find the number of commuters surveyed who used public transit and had an average daily commute of at least 1 hour. Find the column for *Commutes by Public Transit* and the row for *At least 1 hour*. At the intersection is 29, so this is the number of those surveyed who used public transit and had an average daily commute of at least 1 hour. Since the total number of those surveyed is 130 and the total population of the population is 13,000,000, set up the proportion $\dfrac{29}{130} = \dfrac{x}{13,000,000}$. Cross-multiply to get $130x = 377,000,000$. Divide both sides by 130 to get $x = 2,900,000$. The answer is (C).

17. **B** The question asks how many times more likely it is for a commuter whose average daily commute is less than 1 hour not to take public transit than it is for a commuter whose average daily commute is at least 1 hour not to take public transit. The term *more likely* refers to probability, so determine the probability of each. Go to the table and find the number of commuters who commute less than 1 hour and do NOT commute using public transit. Find the *Does Not Commute by Public Transit* column and the *Less than 1 hour* row. At the intersection is 46, so this is the number of commuters who commute less than 1 hour and do NOT commute using public transit. Now look in the same row under the *Total* column to find that the total number of commuters who commute less than 1 hour is 68. Therefore, the probability is $\dfrac{46}{68}$. Now do the same for the probability that someone who commutes at least one hour does not take public transit. Find the row for those who commute *At least 1 hour* and the columns for *Does Not Commute Using Public Transit* and *Total*. In this row, the number under *Does Not Commute by Public Transit* is 33 and the number under *Total* is 62, so the probability is $\dfrac{33}{62}$. The question asks *how many times more likely* is the first probability than the second. Set up the equation $\dfrac{46}{68} = \dfrac{33}{62}x$. Divide both sides by $\dfrac{33}{62}$ to get $x \approx 1.27$. The answer is (B).

18. **C** The question asks for the best conclusion from the study. The study takes a random sample of subjects without sleep disorders and gives half of them beverage *C*. The subjects who consume beverage *C* sleep less than the subjects who don't consume it. This would seem to indicate that beverage *C* caused people without sleep disorders to sleep less. Go through each of the choices. Choice (A) is incorrect because the study doesn't compare different caffeinated beverages. It only compares consuming beverage *C* to not consuming it. Choice (B) is incorrect, because the study does not indicate *substantial* loss is sleep. Furthermore, the sample only includes people without sleep disorders, so any conclusion must be restricted to this population. Choice (C) is similar to the prediction, so keep this choice. Choice (D), like (B), does not restrict the conclusion to people without sleep disorders. The answer is (C).

19. **C** The question involves algebra, asks for a value, and includes numbers in the answers, so plug in the answers. First, eliminate any answers that don't make sense: since *n* is 40% larger than the sum of the other three numbers, *n* will have to be greater than half of 1,764. Eliminate (A) and (B). Try one of the remaining answers, such as (D). If *n* = 1,260, then the remaining three numbers would add up to 1,764 − 1,260 = 504. Since 1,260 is not 40% more than 504, eliminate (D) and choose (C). If desired, check (C): if *n* = 1,029, then the other three numbers add up to 735. Since 735 + 40% (735) = 735 + 294 = 1,029, (C) is the correct answer.

20. **D** The question asks how much more the 11.5 m³ object weighed than was predicted by the line of best fit. This question can be solved by determining the actual weight of the object and the weight predicted by the line of best fit. However, finding the actual amounts is not necessary. Instead, simply find the difference between the two. Volume is represented by the horizontal axis, so find 11.5 on the horizontal axis. Trace straight up to the data point. From that point, trace the line downward, counting the number of intervals to the line of best fit. There are four intervals. Go to the vertical axis to determine the number of kilograms per interval. The labels are 5,000 kilograms apart, and there are 5 intervals between each label. Therefore, each interval is $\frac{5,000}{5} = 1,000$, so 4 intervals are 4,000 kg. The answer is (D).

21. **C** The question asks the percent increase in total sales. Since the number of laptops and the number of tablets are different, don't just add the two percent increases. Thus, (D) is a trap answer. A percent change is always equal to the expression $\frac{difference}{original} \times 100$. The *original* is the total number of units sold last week, which is 90 + 210 = 300. To get the difference, get the increase in laptops and the increase in tablets separately and then add. There is a fifty percent increase in laptop sales,

so the increase is $\frac{50}{100} \times 90 = 45$. There is a thirty percent increase in tablet sales, so the increase

is $\frac{30}{100} \times 210 = 63$. Therefore, the total *difference* is $45 + 63 = 108$, and the percent increase is

$\frac{108}{300} \times 100 = 36\%$. The answer is (C).

22. **B** According to the question, $\cos(x°) = \sin(y°)$. This can only be the case if the two angles are complementary, meaning the measures of the two angles have a sum of 90°. The question asks for the value of c, and there are numbers in the answer choices, so plug in the answers. Start with (B). If $c = 15.5$, then $x = 3(15.5) - 23 = 23.5$ and $y = 66.5$, so $x + y = 23.5 + 66.5 = 90$. Thus, the two angles are complementary, and the answer is (B).

23. **A** The question asks for the maximum value for $-3 \leq x \leq 6$. This is the domain sketched in the graph, so only worry about the points on the sketch. The value of the function is equal to each y-value. Although the values of the function appear to be increasing toward ∞, they do not actually go to ∞ within the points sketched, so eliminate (D). Since the question asks for the maximum value of the function, which is the maximum y-value, find the highest point on the graph. This appears on the far left. Draw a horizontal line to the y-axis to see that this line crosses the y-axis at 4. Therefore, the y-value at this point, or the maximum value of the function, is 4. The answer is (A).

24. **B** The question says that the width is 8 feet more than 4 times the length. Take this statement and

translate it into an equation. Translate *the width* to w. Translate *is* to =. Translate *8 feet more than*

to _____ + 8, leaving room on the left for what follows. Translate *4 times the length* to $4l$. There-

fore, the statement translates to $w = 4l + 8$. The question also says that the area is 5,472. The area

of a rectangle can be found using the formula $A = lw$. Substitute $A = 5{,}472$ and $w = 4l + 8$ to get

$5{,}472 = l(4l + 8)$. Distribute the l on the left side to get $5{,}472 = 4l^2 + 8l$. Since this is qua-

dratic equation, get one side equal to 0 by subtracting 5,472 from both sides to get

$0 = 4l^2 + 8l - 5{,}472$. This is a difficult quadratic to factor, so use the quadratic formula,

$l = \dfrac{-b \pm \sqrt{b^2 - 4ac}}{2a}$, where $a = 4$, $b = 8$, and $c = -5{,}472$. Substitute these values to get

$l = \dfrac{-8 \pm \sqrt{8^2 - 4(4)(-5{,}472)}}{2(4)}$. Use a calculator to get that $8^2 - 4(4)(-5{,}472) = 87{,}616$ and that

$l = \dfrac{-8 \pm \sqrt{87{,}616}}{2(4)}$. Take the square root of 87,616 to get $l = \dfrac{-8 \pm 296}{2(4)} = \dfrac{-8 \pm 296}{8}$. Since

length can only be positive, don't take the negative into account and $l = \dfrac{-8 \pm 296}{8}$ becomes

$l = \dfrac{-8 + 296}{8} = \dfrac{288}{8} = 36$. If $l = 36$, then $w = 4l + 8 = 4(36) + 8 = 152$. To find the perimeter, use

$P = 2l + 2w = 2(36) + 2(152) = 376$. The answer is (B).

25. **D**   The line intersects the origin as well as the points $(c, 3)$ and $(27, c)$. Questions about lines in the

xy-plane often involve slope, so determine the slope of this line. Any two points can be used to find

the equation of a line (including the slope). Note that since the line intersects the origin, it inter-

sects point $(0, 0)$ as well as the other two points. Use points $(0, 0)$ and $(c, 3)$ to calculate the slope:

$slope = \dfrac{y_2 - y_1}{x_2 - x_1} = \dfrac{3 - 0}{c - 0} = \dfrac{3}{c}$. The slope can also be determined using points $(0, 0)$ and $(27, c)$:

$\dfrac{c - 0}{27 - 0} = \dfrac{c}{27}$. Since these two slopes must be equal, $\dfrac{3}{c} = \dfrac{c}{27}$. Cross-multiply to get $c^2 = 81$. Take

the square root of both sides to get $c = \pm 9$. Since only 9 is a choice, the answer is (D).

26. **B**   Since $\overline{FG}$ is a chord that includes the center, it is a diameter. Therefore, arc $\overset{\frown}{FXG}$ is a semicircle.
Since the length of the semicircular arc is 14π, the circumference of the circle is $14\pi \times 2 = 28\pi$. The
formula for circumference is $C = 2\pi r$, so $28\pi = 2\pi r$. Divide both sides by 2π to get $r = 14$. The question asks for the length of the segment $\overline{XO}$. Since $\overline{XO}$ is a radius, the length is 14. The answer is (B).

27. **B**   Since the question says *must be*, plug in multiple values of p and q. Make sure that all values of p
and q satisfy the inequality $-|p| < q < |p|$. Let $p = 4$ and $q = 2$. Go through each statement and
eliminate any statement that is false. Statement (I) is $4 > 0$, which is true, so keep Statement (I).
Statement (II) is $|4| > -2$, which is true, so keep Statement (II). Statement (III) is $4 > |2|$, which is
true, so keep Statement (III). Try other values that might change the results. Since the question
involves absolute values, try negative numbers. Let $p = -4$ and $q = -2$. In this case, Statement (I)
is $-4 > 0$, which is false, so cross out (I). Eliminate (A) and (D), since they include Statement (I).
Since both remaining choices include Statement (II), Statement (II) must be true, and no more
testing of Statement (II) is necessary. Test Statement (III) using the same values of $p = -4$ and
$q = -2$: $-4 > |-2|$. This is false, so cross out Statement (III), and eliminate (C). The answer is (B).

28. **B**   The question asks for a reasonable estimate for the number of blue jelly beans in the entire container.

The number of blue jelly beans is given for each of ten regions. Determine the total number of regions in the container. The container has a base of 10 feet by 10 feet, so the area of the base of the entire container is $A = s^2 = (10)^2 = 100$. Each region has a base of 1 foot by 1 foot, so the area of the base of each region is $A = s^2 = (1)^2 = 1$. To get the number of regions, divide the area of the base of the container by the area of the base of each region to get $\frac{100}{1} = 100$. One way to get an estimate of the number of blue jelly beans in the entire container would be to find the average number of blue jelly beans in the counted regions and multiply that number by 100. The question asks for an approximation, though, and the answer choices are spread apart, so ballpark. All of the numbers in the table are around 25. Therefore, 25 is a reasonable estimate for the average number of blue jelly beans, and the total number of jelly beans should be about $25 \times 100 = 2{,}500$. The answer is (B).

29. **C** The question states that there are four times as many vanilla ice creams sold as vanilla frozen yogurts. Let x be the number of vanilla frozen yogurts sold; therefore, $4x$ is the number of vanilla ice creams sold. The question also says that there are six times as many chocolate ice creams sold as chocolate frozen yogurts, so let y be the number of chocolate frozen yogurts sold and $6y$ be the number of chocolate ice creams sold. Since there are a total of 32 frozen yogurts sold, $x + y = 32$. Since there are a total of 152 ice creams sold, $4x + 6y = 152$. Since there are two equations with two variables, it is possible to solve for the variables. Stack and add the two equations, trying to eliminate the chocolates to solve for the vanillas: multiply both sides of the first equation by -6 to get $-6x - 6y = -192$, then stack and add the equations like this:

$$
\begin{aligned}
4x + 6y &= 152 \\
\underline{-6x - 6y} &= \underline{-192} \\
-2x &= -40
\end{aligned}
$$

Divide both sides by -2 to get $x = 20$. The question asks for the probability that a randomly selected ice cream sold is vanilla, which will be calculated by dividing the number of vanilla ice creams sold ($4x$) by the total number of ice creams sold (152). Since $x = 20$, the number of vanilla ice creams sold is $4x = 4(20) = 80$. The probability that one ice cream is vanilla is $\frac{80}{152} \approx 0.526$. The answer is (C).

30. **D** To graph an inequality, start by graphing the equation. If the inequality sign is $\geq$, draw the equation as a solid line and shade above. If the inequality sign is $\leq$, draw the equation as a solid line and shade below. If the sign is $>$ or $<$, use the same rule as $\geq$ or $\leq$, respectively, but use a dashed line instead of a solid line. Use the inequalities given. Start with $y \geq x$. Since the inequality sign

is ≥ rather than >, the graph is the one with the solid line. Since the inequality sign is ≥, shade the solution above the line. Therefore, since only Sectors W and X are above the solid line, eliminate any choice that includes Y and Z. Eliminate (A) and (B). Now look at the inequality $3y < 2x - 3$. Divide both sides by 3 to get $y < \frac{2}{3}x - 1$. Since the inequality sign is <, the solution is below the dashed line. Since Sector W is above the dashed line, eliminate (C). The answer is (D).

31. **5 or 6** Martina spends between \$20 and \$25, inclusive, and she buys one hamburger at a cost of \$5. This would leave her at least \$20 – \$5 = \$15 and at most \$25 – \$5 = \$20 for hot dogs. In the first case, \$15 total divided by \$3 per hot dog would get her 5 hot dogs, so 5 is one possible value for h. If she spent up to \$20 on hot dogs, she could get \$20 divided by \$3 per hot dog for 6.67 hot dogs. She can only buy whole hot dogs, so 6 is another possible value of h. Therefore, the two possible correct answers are 5 and 6.

32. **19.4** The question asks for the average, so get the total and divide by the number of things. To get the total, add the number of states for each nation. The total is 6 + 9 + 26 + 16 + 29 + 13 + 31 + 4 + 36 + 2 + 10 + 17 + 50 + 23 = 272. Divide 272 by the 14 nations to get $\frac{272}{14} \approx 19.4285714$. Rounded to the nearest tenth, the answer is 19.4.

33. **10** The question gives the equation of a function and a point on the graph of the function. Plug the point into the equation. Substitute $x = -2$ and $y = g(x) = 6$ to get $6 = 2(-2)^2 + k(-2) + 18$. Simplify the right side to get $6 = 26 - 2k$. Subtract 26 from both sides to get $-20 = -2k$. Divide both sides by -2 to get $10 = k$. The answer is 10.

34. **11** The question asks how many rooms will be assigned three students. Consider the possibility that all rooms have three students. How many left over students would there be? If 26 rooms are assigned three students, then there are 26 × 3 = 78 students. However, the question says that there are 108 students, so there are 108 – 78 = 30 left over. These left over students have to be assigned to 5 student rooms. Since each room already has three students, to make five student rooms, pair the remaining students and add each pair to one of the three student rooms. Since there are 30 left over students, they make 15 pairs, so 15 rooms of three students become five-student rooms. Since there are a total of 26 rooms, there are 26 – 15 = 11 three-person rooms. The answer is 11.

35. $\frac{7}{12}$ The question asks for what fraction Town A's 1970 population was of Town A's 2000 population. To determine the population in 1970, find 1970 on the horizontal axis, trace straight up to the curve, then straight across to the vertical axis. It hits the vertical axis on the only line between 30 and 40, so the population in 1970 was 35,000. (Note that the vertical axis label indicates that the population is in thousands.) To determine the population in 2000, find 2000 on the horizontal

axis, trace straight up to the curve, then straight across to the vertical axis. It hits the vertical axis at 60, so the population in 2000 was 60,000. Therefore, the fraction is $\frac{35,000}{60,000} = \frac{35}{60} = \frac{7}{12}$. The answer is $\frac{7}{12}$.

36. **4** The question states that the volume of the cylinder is 64π cubic centimeters. The formula for volume of a cylinder is $V = \pi r^2 h$. Plug in $V = 64\pi$ and $h = 16$, as indicated by the figure, to get $64\pi = \pi r^2 (16)$. Divide both sides by 16π to get $4 = r^2$. Take the square root of both sides to get $2 = r$. Note, however, that the question asks for the *diameter* and not the radius. Since the diameter is twice the radius, $d = 2r = 2(2) = 4$. The answer is 4.

37. **321** This question asks for angular position, which is in equation 1 and represented by θ. Write down known variables and solve. When the carousel changes direction, the angular velocity is 0. Use the first equation, $\omega^2 = \omega_0^2 + 2\alpha\theta$. Plug in $\omega = 0$, $\omega_0 = 90$, and $\alpha = -12.6$ to get $0 = 90^2 + 2(-12.6)\theta$. Simplify the right side to get $0 = 8,100 - 25.2\theta$. Add 25.2θ to both sides to get $25.2\theta = 8,100$. Divide both sides to get $\theta = 321.4286$. Rounded to the nearest degree, the answer is 321.

38. **7** The question asks for time. Write down known variables, then choose the equation that gives only time as the unknown. This is equation 2. When the carousel changes direction, the angular velocity is 0. Use the second equation, $\omega = \omega_0 + \alpha t$. Plug in $\omega = 0$, $\omega_0 = 90$, and $\alpha = -12.6$ to get $0 = 90 + (-12.6)t$. Simplify the right side to get $0 = 90 - 12.6t$. Add $12.6t$ to both sides to get $12.6t = 90$. Divide both sides by 12.6 to get $t = 7.1429$. Rounded to the nearest second, the answer is 7.

Chapter 13
Practice Test 6

Reading Test

65 MINUTES, 52 QUESTIONS

Turn to Section 1 of your answer sheet to answer the questions in this section.

DIRECTIONS

Each passage or pair of passages below is followed by a number of questions. After reading each passage or pair, choose the best answer to each question based on what is stated or implied in the passage or passages and in any accompanying graphics (such as a table or graph).

Questions 1-10 are based on the following passage.

The following passage is from Charlotte Brontë, *Shirley*, originally published in 1849. Robert Moore is a mill owner and Reverend Helstone is the local parson.

Cheerfulness, it would appear, is a matter which depends fully as much on the state of things within as on the state of things without and around us. I
Line make this trite remark, because I happen to know
5 that Messrs. Helstone and Moore trotted forth from the mill-yard gates, at the head of their very small company, in the best possible spirits. When a ray from a lantern (the three pedestrians of the party carried each one) fell on Mr. Moore's face, you could
10 see an unusual, because a lively, spark dancing in his eyes, and a new-found vivacity mantling on his dark physiognomy; and when the rector's visage was illuminated, his hard features were revealed all agrin and ashine with glee. Yet a drizzling night, a somewhat
15 perilous expedition, you would think were not circumstances calculated to enliven those exposed to the wet and engaged in the adventure. If any member or members of the crew who had been at work on Stilbro' Moor had caught a view of this party, they
20 would have had great pleasure in shooting either of the leaders from behind a wall: and the leaders knew this; and the fact is, being both men of steely nerves and steady-beating hearts, were elate with the knowledge.

I am aware, reader, and you need not remind me,
25 that it is a dreadful thing for a parson to be warlike; I am aware that he should be a man of peace. I have

some faint outline of an idea of what a clergyman's mission is amongst mankind, and I remember distinctly whose servant he is, whose message he
30 delivers, whose example he should follow; yet, with all this, if you are a parson-hater, you need not expect me to go along with you every step of your dismal, downward-tending, unchristian road; you need not expect me to join in your deep anathemas, at once so
35 narrow and so sweeping, in your poisonous rancour, so intense and so absurd, against "the cloth;" to lift up my eyes and hands with a Supplehough, or to inflate my lungs with a Barraclough, in horror and denunciation of the diabolical rector of Briarfield.
40   He was not diabolical at all. The evil simply was— he had missed his vocation. He should have been a soldier, and circumstances had made him a priest. For the rest, he was a conscientious, hard-headed, hard-handed, brave, stern, implacable, faithful little man; a
45 man almost without sympathy, ungentle, prejudiced, and rigid, but a man true to principle, honourable, sagacious, and sincere. It seems to me, reader, that you cannot always cut out men to fit their profession, and that you ought not to curse them because their
50 profession sometimes hangs on them ungracefully. Nor will I curse Helstone, clerical Cossack as he was. Yet he was cursed, and by many of his own parishioners, as by others he was adored—which is the frequent fate of men who show partiality in friendship and bitterness
55 in enmity, who are equally attached to principles and adherent to prejudices.

CONTINUE ➤

Helstone and Moore being both in excellent spirits, and united for the present in one cause, you would expect that, as they rode side by side, they would
60 converse amicably. Oh no! These two men, of hard, bilious natures both, rarely came into contact but they chafed each other's moods. Their frequent bone of contention was the war. Helstone was a high Tory (there were Tories in those days), and Moore was a
65 bitter Whig—a Whig, at least, as far as opposition to the war-party was concerned, that being the question which affected his own interest; and only on that question did he profess any British politics at all. He liked to infuriate Helstone by declaring his belief in the
70 invincibility of Bonaparte, by taunting England and Europe with the impotence of their efforts to withstand him, and by coolly advancing the opinion that it was as well to yield to him soon as late, since he must in the end crush every antagonist, and reign supreme.

1

Which choice best summarizes the passage?

A) A character becomes increasingly hostile as he travels with his fellow associate.

B) A character describes his reasons for disliking for another character.

C) Two characters in the same profession become increasingly competitive.

D) Two characters traveling together eagerly await confrontation.

2

The main purpose of the opening sentence of the passage is to

A) show the contrast between the clergymen's cheerfulness and the narrator's gloom.

B) provide an allegorical representation of the clergymen's journey.

C) issue a general statement that helps to clarify the characters' emotional states.

D) characterize the narrator's perspective on the characters' violent intentions.

3

During the course of the second paragraph, the narrator's focus shifts from

A) assessment of the reader's sentiment to the desire to chastise the clergymen.

B) acknowledgment that clergymen should be peaceful to admonition for anti-clergy prejudices.

C) reflection on the clergymen's behaviors to identification of their manners and appearance.

D) generalization about peaceful men to the details of two particular clergymen.

4

The references to "rancour" and "denunciation" at the end of the second paragraph mainly have which effect?

A) They reflect the narrator's fear of clergymen.

B) They reveal the reader's empathetic understanding of clergymen.

C) They illustrate the narrator's sense of dismay at clergymen.

D) They capture the reader's potential sense of disapproval of clergymen.

5

The passage indicates that Moore's behavior is mainly characterized by

A) attitudes that do not align with his profession.

B) indignation at his travel partner's political views.

C) a willingness to engage in confrontation.

D) impatience with his travel partner's apparent superiority.

CONTINUE

6

The passage indicates that while the narrator acknowledges a certain evil in the third paragraph, Helstone is actually a

A) sympathetic clergyman.

B) harmless soldier.

C) righteous citizen.

D) ruthless warmonger.

7

Which choice provides the best evidence for the answer to the previous question?

A) Lines 7–14 ("When a . . . glee")

B) Lines 24–26 ("I am . . . peace")

C) Lines 42–47 ("For the . . . sincere")

D) Lines 51–56 ("Yet he . . . prejudices")

8

At the end of the third paragraph, the comparison of Helstone to a Cossack mainly has the effect of

A) illustrating his nature as soldier-like.

B) suggesting the likelihood of an altercation.

C) contrasting the natures of the two men.

D) conveying the belligerence of a course of action.

9

The passage indicates that, despite their excellent spirits, the men sometimes found each other's company to be

A) intolerable.

B) mundane.

C) vexing.

D) comforting.

10

Which choice provides the best evidence for the answer to the previous question?

A) Lines 24–26 ("I am . . . peace")

B) Lines 42–47 ("For the . . . sincere")

C) Lines 60–62 ("These two . . . moods")

D) Lines 63–65 ("Helstone . . . bitter Whig")

CONTINUE

Questions 11–21 are based on the following passage and supplementary material.

This passage is excerpted from John W. Murphy and John T Pardeck, "The Current Political World-View, Education and Alienation." Originally published 1991.

In American society everything is a commodity and education is no exception. Of course, this means that every aspect of life is assumed to have a cash value
Line and can be purchased for the right price. Also, every
5 person is a consumer, who enters the marketplace searching for a bargain. Although this scenario may be appropriate for describing the sale of shoes, when education is approached as a commodity the learning process may be seriously compromised.
10 　　Nonetheless, most students view education to be a product they are buying. Like good customers, students expect their education to meet their needs and assume a form they find palatable. Accordingly, students demand to have a significant amount of
15 control over their education, so as to guarantee the most favorable outcome possible. On the other hand, administrators must offer a competitive product, or revenues will decrease. Yet is the image of a buyer confronting a seller appropriate to describe how
20 students should relate to their school? The claim at this juncture is that education should not be exchanged in a manner similar to other products. Indeed, the worth of education is depreciated by this demarche.
　　In what ways do students participate in their
25 education? Usually their desires are voiced in the form of teacher evaluations. What is mostly revealed by this process is that students want, and demand, to be entertained. Like a competent sales representative, a teacher must be attractive, witty and capable of gaining
30 and retaining the attention of students. Additionally, material must not be dull or require much effort, or students will quickly become aggravated. For as every astute businessman knows, customers do not want to be hassled. Securing a favorable evaluation, therefore,
35 requires that a teacher adopt the demeanor of the television personalities who are invoked constantly to sell products to students.
　　Also similar to wise consumers, students strive to make the best deal possible. Translated into economic
40 terms, this means that the greatest rewards should be gained through the least amount of effort. Hence preparing students to take exams, organizing both their work and leisure time and summarizing their

reading assignments have become very profitable
45 businesses. Entrepreneurs who provide these and other services are well known to students. On the other hand, cheating has become rampant. Consistent with the ethos of consumerism, achieving some sort of advantage is considered to be essential to
50 beating the competition. Unfortunately the view has been conveyed that only through a series of dubious maneuvers can success be attained. In this climate, why should the message that becoming educated is hard work find a receptive audience?
55 　　From an administrative perspective, the curriculum offered by a school must be competitive. Creating an enticing array of courses is considered to be indispensable to attracting students and keeping enrollment figures high. Hence capitalizing on fads
60 has become normative, as witnessed by the recent proliferation of degrees and courses with captivating titles. In fact, many schools hire high paid advertising consultants to develop promotional material and discover untapped markets.
65 　　But education is trivialized when it is treated as a commodity. Content, in short, is replaced by form, for flash and glitter sell products. Difficult subjects are avoided, while the term relevant is reserved to describe the trendy courses that administrators have
70 begun to promote. Clearly the integrity of education is jeopardized when educational policies are dictated by the vagaries of the marketplace and ephemeral imagery is used to describe profound ideas that can be understood only through dedicated study.

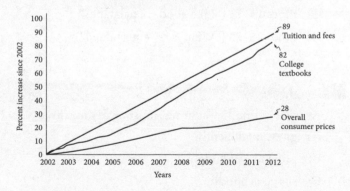

Estimated increases in New College Textbook Prices, College Tuition and Fees, and Overall Consumer Price Inflation, 2002–2012

Excerpted from the Government Accountability Office report to Congressional Committees from June 2013.

CONTINUE ▶

11

The main purpose of the passage is to

A) advocate for the marketing of education to students.

B) argue a position on a decidedly complex topic.

C) weigh the merits of educational products in the marketplace.

D) evaluate statistics about treating education as a commodity.

12

In the passage, the author makes which concession to the view that every person is a consumer in the marketplace of life?

A) The implied contract which exists between buyer and seller has educational value.

B) It may be valid when one is discussing the sale of some types of goods.

C) Students and administrators benefit from negotiating over the price of higher education.

D) A person engages with all aspects of a product when he or she assigns it monetary value.

13

Which choice provides the best evidence for the answer to the previous question?

A) Lines 2–4 ("Of course . . . price")

B) Lines 6–9 ("Although this . . . compromised")

C) Lines 11–13 ("Like good . . . palatable")

D) Lines 26–28 ("What is . . . entertained")

14

As used in line 13, "assume" most nearly means

A) guess intelligently.

B) pretend grudgingly.

C) suppose blindly.

D) take on readily.

15

The main purpose of the 4th paragraph (lines 38-54) is to

A) concede the logic of an attitude with which the author disagrees.

B) demonstrate that cheating results in serious consequences later in life.

C) provide a contrast to the view of teachers as salesmen.

D) argue against cheating or the use of educational preparation businesses.

16

As used in line 57, "enticing" most nearly means

A) pulling.

B) deceptive.

C) appealing.

D) suggestive.

17

Which choice best supports the authors' claim that schools have already begun to incorporate some facets of the popular marketplace into their educational materials?

A) Lines 16–18 ("On the...decrease")

B) Lines 59–62 ("Hence capitalizing...titles")

C) Lines 65–66 ("But education...commodity")

D) Lines 67–70 ("Difficult subjects...promote")

CONTINUE ▶

18

The main idea of the final paragraph is that

A) focus on profit can undermine the effectiveness of true education.

B) ephemeral imagery cannot lead to an understanding of complex ideas.

C) education seems unimportant when it is present in the economic marketplace.

D) modern educators ignore difficult subjects in favor of trendy topics.

19

Data in the graph about estimated increases in prices from 2002 to 2012 most strongly support which of the following statements?

A) Overall consumer prices increased the same amount each year.

B) Overall consumer prices have not increased in the period since 2002.

C) Increases in college tuitions and fees exceed those of consumer prices.

D) Prices of college textbooks decreased from 2005 to 2006.

20

Data in the graph indicate that the greatest difference between the percent increase since 2002 of college tuition and fees and that of overall consumer prices occurred during which period?

A) 2004 to 2005

B) 2008 to 2009

C) 2010 to 2011

D) 2011 to 2012

21

Data in the graph provide most direct support for what idea in the passage?

A) Schools are interested in revenue.

B) Students have an expectation that school should be entertaining.

C) Teacher evaluations reflect the students' perceptions.

D) Content is replaced by flashy slogans.

CONTINUE

Questions 22–32 are based on the following passages.

Passage 1 is adapted from Connie Weaver, et al., "Contributions to Nutrition." ©2014 by the American Society for Nutrition. Passage 2 is from David Stuckler and Marion Nestle, "Big Food, Food Systems, and Global Health." © 2012 by PLOS Medicine.

Passage 1

Both fresh and processed foods make up vital parts of the food supply. Processed food contributes to both food security (ensuring that sufficient food is available) and nutrition security (ensuring that food quality meets human nutrient needs).

Line
5

Nutrition scientists, public health professionals, agricultural economists, food scientists, and other professionals dedicated to meeting the food and nutritional needs of people around the globe recognize
10 that fresh, local foods cannot meet all nutritional requirements. Food processing is necessary.

Although nutritional security (quality) and food security (quantity) both depend on food processing, in recent years there has been considerable public
15 controversy over the nutritional contribution that processed foods make to the American diet.

If enrichment and fortification were not present, large percentages of the population would have had inadequate intakes of vitamins A, C, D, and E, thiamin,
20 folate, calcium, magnesium, and iron. When nutrients from enrichment and fortification were included, the percentages of the population with inadequate intakes decreased substantially for vitamin A, vitamin D, folate, and iron.
25 Clearly, this type of food processing, of adding nutrients to foods, has greatly benefitted nutrient intakes in the United States.

Thus, processed foods are nutritionally important to American diets. How, then, do we enhance the
30 contribution of processed food to nutritional security and food security?

Rather than limiting processed foods in the diet, it may be more productive to encourage the best available food options, namely, those that provide
35 fewer constituents to limit and more nutrients to encourage for the calories consumed.

One disadvantage of commercial food processing techniques is that they are poorly understood. Commercial food processing involves techniques that
40 are difficult for the general public to grasp and that

are out of their control, thus introducing a lack of transparency and generating suspicion and concerns about safety in some individuals.

In addition, concerns about the nutritional content
45 and other aspects of the production of processed foods, such as sustainability and cost, have led to criticisms of processed foods as "ultra-processed" and not compatible with good nutrition. However, the type and extent of processing do not necessarily correlate
50 with the nutritional content of the product.

Passage 2

Global food systems are not meeting the world's dietary needs. About one billion people are hungry, while two billion people are overweight. Underlying both is a common factor: food systems are not driven
55 to deliver optimal human diets but to maximize profits.

To understand who is responsible for these nutritional failures, it is first necessary to ask: *Who rules global food systems?* By and large it's "Big Food," by which we refer to multinational food and beverage
60 companies with huge and concentrated market power. Three-fourths of world food sales involve processed foods, for which the largest manufacturers hold over a third of the global market.

We see three possible ways to view this debate. The
65 first favors voluntary self-regulation, and requires no further engagement by the public health community. The second view favors partnerships with industry.

The third approach is critical of both. It recognizes the inherent conflicts of interest between corporations
70 that profit from unhealthy food and public health collaborations. Because growth in profit is the primary goal of corporations, self-regulation and working from within are doomed to fail.

We support the critical view, for several reasons.
75 Any partnership *must* create profit for the industry, which has a legal mandate to maximize wealth for shareholders. We also see no obvious, established, or legitimate mechanism through which public health professionals might increase Big Food's profits.
80 Big Food attains profit by expanding markets to reach more people, increasing people's sense of hunger so that they buy more food, and increasing profit margins through encouraging consumption of

CONTINUE ➡

products with higher price/cost surpluses. Although
85 in theory minimal processing of foods can improve
nutritional content, in practice most processing
is done so to increase palatability, shelf-life, and
transportability, processes that reduce nutritional
quality.
90   To promote health, industry would need to make
and market healthier foods so as to shift consumption
away from highly processed, unhealthy foods. Yet,
such healthier foods are inherently less profitable.
The only ways the industry could preserve profit is
95 either to undermine public health attempts to tax and
regulate or to get people to eat more healthy food while
continuing to eat profitable unhealthy foods. Neither is
desirable from a nutritional standpoint.

22

The authors of Passage 1 indicate which of the
following about the addition of nutrients to foods?

A) It has a helpful impact.

B) It should be increased significantly.

C) It may require further investigation.

D) It gives people unnecessary extra vitamins.

23

Which choice provides the best evidence for the
answer to the previous question?

A) Lines 2–5 ("Processed food . . . needs")

B) Lines 29–31 ("How then . . . security")

C) Lines 32–34 ("Rather than . . . options")

D) Lines 37–38 ("One disadvantage . . . understood")

24

The authors of Passage 1 indicate that food
enrichment methods

A) often involve industrial machinery.

B) lead to employment opportunities.

C) are the leading source of thiamin.

D) are not comprehended by all people.

25

As used in line 40, "grasp" most nearly means

A) comprehend.

B) clutch.

C) squeeze.

D) reach.

26

The authors of Passage 2 refers to "Big Food"
primarily to suggest that global food systems

A) result from a varied, competitive marketplace.

B) involve regions served by single companies.

C) should be simplified through local markets.

D) are largely dominated by a few extremely
influential companies.

27

According to the authors of Passage 2, what do profit
margins and price/cost surpluses have in common?

A) They typically coincide with ethical practices.

B) They are more important than other concerns
held by companies.

C) They are key elements of economic theory.

D) They are best increased through expanding
markets.

28

The possibilities offered in the final paragraph
(lines 94–97) of Passage 2 have primarily which
effect?

A) They show the only ways that industry could
promote health.

B) They demonstrate the unlikelihood of industry
marketing healthier foods.

C) They refer to government controls to illustrate
excessive regulation.

D) They supply positive steps to emphasize the
impossibility of corporate charity.

CONTINUE ➡

29

The main purpose of each passage is to

A) support a side in an argument about whether to promote vitamin intake through food.

B) discuss the nature of large-scale food production as it relates to nutrition.

C) compare the need for food security with the desire for nutrition security in the American diet.

D) emphasize the importance of sustainable processing in certain foods of the American diet.

30

Which choice best describes the relationship between the two passages?

A) Passage 2 discusses the underlying processes of a solution that Passage 1 describes in specific detail.

B) Passage 2 presents a plan to clarify the several misunderstood processes presented by Passage 1.

C) Passage 2 outlines an objective perspective that clashes with the opinions discussed in Passage 1.

D) Passage 2 explores the problematic nature of a system embraced by Passage 1.

31

On which of the following points would the authors of both passages most likely agree?

A) A thorough discussion of global food systems and content should address adequate nutrition.

B) Well-prepared, non-processed meals are generally more appealing than most processed foods.

C) Previous discussions of nutrition contained less suspicion of processed foods than those discussions do today.

D) People who avoid processed foods due to nutrient concerns are unlikely to be overweight.

32

Which choice provides the best evidence that the authors of Passage 2 would acknowledge some aspect of the statement made in lines 48–50 of Passage 1?

A) Lines 61–63 ("Three-fourths . . . market")

B) Lines 80–84 ("Big Food . . . surpluses")

C) Lines 84–89 ("Although in . . . quality")

D) Lines 90–92 ("To promote . . . foods")

CONTINUE

Questions 33–42 are based on the following passage.

The following passage is adapted from Bruce Ackerman and Jennifer Nou, "Hey, what about the 24th? The constitutional amendment about voting rights that the Supreme Court forgot." © 2008 in *Slate* online magazine.

Americans have long fought hard to protect the right to vote and a generation ago emphatically rejected the idea of paying for the ballot. As the civil
Line rights revolution reached its peak, Congress and
5 the states in 1964 enacted the 24th Amendment, forbidding any "poll-tax or other tax" in federal elections. Yet, remarkably enough, this basic text went unmentioned by the Supreme Court when it upheld Indiana's photo-ID law this week.
10 Indiana's law insists on a photo ID to vote, which in turn requires documents, like a birth certificate or passport, that verify identity. Getting these papers costs voters money as well as time and effort. This leads to the question the court failed to ask: Does the extra
15 expense violate the absolute ban on all "taxes" imposed by the 24th Amendment?

The leading Supreme Court decision about this amendment provides a starting point. In *Harman v. Forssenius*, Virginia responded to the new
20 constitutional prohibition by allowing citizens to escape its poll tax if they filed a formal certificate establishing their place of residence. Otherwise, they would be obliged to continue paying a state tax of $1.50 if they wanted to cast a ballot. Lars Forssenius
25 refused to pay the tax or file the residency certificate and brought a class action suit attacking the statute as unconstitutional.

The Supreme Court agreed with Forssenius in 1965, only a year after the amendment came into force. Chief
30 Justice Earl Warren emphasized that Virginia's escape clause for avoiding the $1.50 was unconstitutionally burdensome: "For federal elections," he explained, "the poll tax is abolished absolutely as a prerequisite to voting, and no equivalent or milder substitute may be
35 imposed." Although the Roberts Court divided sharply this week over Indiana's voter ID law, Warren's opinion gained the support of all the sitting justices except the conservative Justice John Marshall Harlan—and even he concurred in the result.
40 *Harman* casts a shadow over Indiana's photo-ID law. On the face of things, Indiana provides identification free of charge, but so did Virginia when it required proof of residence. Like Virginians trying

to avoid the tax, Indianans must file paperwork to get
45 their IDs. And their burden is often heavier. It was enough for a Virginian to swear that he or she was a resident in front of witnesses or a notary public. Indianans must also travel to the Bureau of Motor Vehicles to get a photo ID as well as pay for supporting
50 documents like a birth certificate or passport. They can escape the requisite fees only by casting a provisional ballot and then taking another trip to a local official to swear that they are too poor to comply. And they must repeat this humiliating procedure every time they cast
55 a ballot.

Like Indiana, Virginia told the court that a certificate of residency was necessary to preserve the integrity of its elections. But in 1965, the justices would have none of it. According to *Harman*, the 24th
60 Amendment could not be satisfied by a showing of "remote administrative benefits"—especially when other less burdensome devices were available for proving residency. In particular, the court pointed out that Virginia could ask voters to take an oath and rely
65 on the threat of punishment to deter lying. The same is true today in Indiana.

We don't suggest that the Roberts Court isn't clever enough to find a way around *Harman*. Our point is that the justices didn't even try. They ignored the 24th
70 Amendment and restricted themselves to the equal-protection clause of the 14th in deciding the Indiana case. Narrowing their vision didn't help them reach a consensus. The nine justices produced four very different opinions, none of which gained more than
75 three votes.

This sort of thing doesn't happen every day in the life of the court—indeed, we can't think of another case in which the justices utterly failed to address the most obviously relevant provision of the constitutional text.
80 If they had squarely confronted the law and language of the 24th Amendment, there is a fair chance that Justices Stevens and Anthony Kennedy would have switched sides, creating a new majority for striking down the Indiana law.
85 Perhaps the majority will choose to turn its back on *Harman* and uphold the state's exclusionary law. But at the very least, the justices should provide Indianans, and the rest of us, with an explanation for their decision to trivialize a solemn constitutional
90 amendment enacted only 44 years ago.

CONTINUE ➡

33

The central problem that the authors describe in the passage is that Indiana's photo ID law

A) may run counter to a constitutional amendment, despite a Supreme Court ruling.

B) forces voters to spend time and money acquiring background checks.

C) divided the Roberts Court sharply on a matter of federal and state importance.

D) led the Supreme Court to take an overly wide view in ignoring the 24th amendment.

34

The authors use the phrase "remarkably enough" (line 7) mainly to emphasize the Supreme Court's

A) complete disregard for the U. S. Constitution.

B) partial ignorance of the Bill of Rights.

C) notable divergence from established law.

D) qualified reliance upon political polls.

35

The passage claims that which of the following casts doubt on the recent Supreme Court decision?

A) The civil rights movement

B) A later decision by the same Court

C) The views of Anthony Kennedy

D) The Department of Motor Vehicles

36

Which choice provides the best evidence for the answer to the previous question?

A) Lines 10–12 ("Indiana's law . . . identity")

B) Lines 24–27 ("Lars Forssenius . . . unconstitutional")

C) Lines 28–29 ("The Supreme . . . force")

D) Lines 48–50 ("Indianans must . . . passport")

37

As used in line 29, "force" most nearly means

A) violence.

B) power.

C) field.

D) effect.

38

As used in line 59, "have" most nearly means to

A) accept as legally reasonable.

B) obtain appropriate documents.

C) issue a ruling upon.

D) reread the relevant parts of the Constitution.

39

It can be reasonably inferred that "exclusionary" (line 86) is a term generally intended to

A) emphasize the difference between state and federal rights.

B) criticize a state law that may in fact be unconstitutional.

C) emphasize the solemnity of a trivialized amendment.

D) criticize the prejudiced actions of elected officials.

40

The authors contend that on the subject of voter-ID laws the present-day Supreme Court has

A) ruled in favor of Forssenius.

B) insisted on a heavier burden.

C) favored one amendment over another.

D) refused to explain its decision.

CONTINUE ➡

41

Which choice provides the best evidence for the answer to the previous question?

A) Lines 28–29 ("The Supreme . . . force")

B) Line 45 ("And their . . . heavier")

C) Lines 69–72 ("They ignored . . . case")

D) Lines 87–90 ("But at . . . ago")

42

The eighth paragraph (lines 76–84) is primarily concerned with establishing a contrast between

A) the positions of Stevens and Kennedy.

B) a historical rule and a present anomaly.

C) a law in Virginia and a law in Indiana.

D) the decisions of Roberts and Warren.

CONTINUE

Questions 43–52 are based on the following passage and supplementary material.

The following excerpt is adapted from Ramez Naam, "Arctic Sea Ice: What, Why, and What Next." © 2012 by *Scientific American*.

On September 19th, NSIDC, the National Snow and Ice Data Center, announced that Arctic sea ice has shrunk as far as it will shrink this summer, and
Line that the ice is beginning to reform, expanding the
5 floating ice cap that covers the North Pole and the seas around it. The Arctic Sea Ice extent this September was far smaller than the previous record set in 2007. At 3.4 million square kilometers of ice coverage, this year's Arctic minimum was 800,000 square kilometers
10 smaller than the 2007 record. That difference between the previous record and this year's is larger than the entire state of Texas. An ice-free summer in the Arctic, once projected to be more than a century away, now looks possible decades from now. Some say that it
15 looks likely in just the next few years.

Conditions in the Arctic change dramatically through the seasons. In the depths of winter, the Earth's tilt puts the Arctic in 24 hour-a-day darkness. Temperatures, cold year round, plunge even lower. The
20 sea surface freezes over. At the height of summer, the opposite tilt puts the Arctic in 24 hour-a-day sunlight. While it's a cold, cold place even at these times, the constant sunshine, warmer air, and influx of warm waters from further south serve to melt the ice. The ice
25 cap usually starts shrinking in March, and then reaches its smallest area in mid-September, before cooling temperatures and shorter days start the water freezing and the ice cap growing once again.

When scientists and reporters talk about an ice-
30 free Arctic, they're usually speaking of the Arctic in *summer*, and especially in September, when ice coverage reaches its minimum. The amount of ice left at that minimum has indeed been plunging. In 1980, the ice shrank down to just under 8 million square
35 kilometers before rebounding in the fall. This year's minimum extent of 3.4 million kilometers is less than half of what we saw in 1980. Strikingly, two thirds of the loss of ice has happened in the 12 years since 2000. The ice is receding, and the process, if anything,
40 appears to be accelerating.

Artic Sea Ice Minimum Area

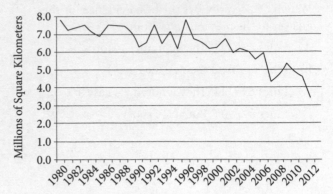

Data: NSIDC. Graphic: Ramez Naam

Arctic sea ice coverage in September has dropped in half since 1980, and the drop appears to be accelerating.

As recently as a few years ago, most models of the Arctic ice anticipated that summers would remain icy until the end of the 21st century, and well into the 22nd century. But the trend line above makes that look
45 unlikely. The amount of ice remaining, this year, is about the same as the ice *lost* between the mid-1990s and today. If ice loss continued at that pace, we'd see an ice-free summer sometime around 2030, give or take several years.
50 Is that plausible? Opinions differ substantially, even among climate scientists. At one end of the spectrum are those who see the ice lasting in summer for another 20 or 30 years, or perhaps even a bit longer. For example, Lars-Otto Reierson, who leads the Arctic
55 Monitoring and Assessment Programme told Reuters that most models predict the summer ice disappearing by 2030 or 2040. Similarly, a paper published this year in *Geophysical Research Letters* by multiple scientists, including several from the National Snow and Ice Data
60 Center, found that an ice-free summer in the Arctic in the "next few decades" was a "distinct possibility." A recent assessment from Muyin Wang at the University of Washington and James Overland at the National Oceanographic and Atmospheric Administration,
65 using the most up to date Arctic ice models and data, projected a nearly ice-free Arctic around 2030. And Cecilia Bitz, a professor of Atmospheric Sciences at the University of Washington at part of the Polar Science Center sees a 50/50 chance that the Arctic will be ice-
70 free in summer in the next few decades.

CONTINUE →

On the other end of the spectrum are those who think the melt could happen much sooner. Peter Wadhams, who leads the Polar Ocean Physics Group at the University of Cambridge, has predicted since 2008
75 that the Arctic ice could be gone in summer by 2015. He now believes there's a chance that it could happen even sooner. Similarly, Mark Drinkwater, the European Space Agency's senior advisor on polar regions and a mission scientist for the CryoStat satellite that
80 measures arctic ice, believes that the Arctic could be ice-free in September by the end of this decade.

When will the ice melt? While the range of possibilities is wide today, it's shrunk dramatically from just a few years ago, when most climate scientists
85 expected the ice to survive through the 21st century. Now the question is whether it will be gone in decades —or in mere years.

43

The first paragraph serves mainly to

A) inform the reader that Arctic ice is starting to return.

B) compare the size of an Arctic area to a U. S. state.

C) illustrate dramatic changes in polar weather conditions over the last century.

D) present a trend that is occurring differently than expected.

44

As used in line 13, "projected" is closest in meaning to

A) hurled.

B) seen.

C) hypothesized.

D) illuminated.

45

According to Naam, the Earth's tilt is significant primarily because it

A) causes the sea surface to freeze and the ice cap to grow further.

B) accounts for seasonal differences in the Arctic.

C) explains why the ice-free summer is accelerating in recent years.

D) exposes the Arctic to constant daylight and melts portions of ice.

46

Which choice provides the best evidence for the answer to the previous question?

A) Lines 12–15 ("An ice-free . . . years")

B) Lines 16–21 ("Conditions in . . . sunlight")

C) Lines 29–32 ("When scientists . . . minimum")

D) Lines 37–40 ("Strikingly, two . . . accelerating")

47

As used in line 47, "pace" most nearly means

A) walk.

B) loss.

C) rate.

D) measure.

CONTINUE

48

Based on information in the passage, it can reasonably be inferred that climate scientists

A) agree that the polar ice is receding, but disagree about the rate of acceleration.

B) disagree that the polar ice is receding, but agree about the rate of deceleration.

C) are uncertain about whether the polar ice is receding, but agree that it should be studied.

D) are certain that the polar ice is receding, but cannot say whether it will rebound.

49

Which choice provides the best evidence for the answer to the previous question?

A) Lines 50–51 ("Is that . . . scientists")

B) Lines 57–61 ("Similarly, a . . . possibility'")

C) Lines 66–70 ("And Cecilia . . . decades")

D) Lines 77–81 ("Similarly, Mark . . . decade")

50

In the graph, what general trend in the area of Arctic sea ice is depicted?

A) An overall decline

B) A geometric series of rises and falls

C) An arithmetic series of dramatic changes

D) A temporary shrinkage

51

Which concept is supported by the passage and by the information in the graph?

A) The Arctic ice-free summer will be upon us within decades.

B) The Arctic ice-free summer may not be a scientific fact.

C) The Arctic ice-free summer may come sooner than the 22nd century.

D) The Arctic ice-free summer will not come as swiftly as some have predicted.

52

How does the graph support the author's point that Arctic ice is receding?

A) It shows that the change in ice from 2007 to 2012 is similar in size to the state of Texas.

B) It suggests that the amount of ice could drop to zero within a few years.

C) It indicates a loss of 3 million square kilometers of ice from 1980 to 1990.

D) It presents a trend of sharp and noticeable decline since 2000.

STOP
If you finish before time is called, you may check your work on this section only.
Do not turn to any other section in the test.

No Test Material On This Page

Writing and Language Test

35 MINUTES, 44 QUESTIONS

Turn to Section 2 of your answer sheet to answer the questions in this section.

DIRECTIONS

Each passage below is accompanied by a number of questions. For some questions, you will consider how the passage might be revised to improve the expression of ideas. For other questions, you will consider how the passage might be edited to correct errors in sentence structure, usage, or punctuation. A passage or a question may be accompanied by one or more graphics (such as a table or graph) that you will consider as you make revising and editing decisions.

Some questions will direct you to an underlined portion of a passage. Other questions will direct you to a location in a passage or ask you to think about the passage as a whole.

After reading each passage, choose the answer to each question that most effectively improves the quality of writing in the passage or that makes the passage conform to the conventions of standard written English. Many questions include a "NO CHANGE" option. Choose that option if you think the best choice is to leave the relevant portion of the passage as it is.

Questions 1–11 are based on the following passage.

A Dirty Job Worth Having

As people become more sensitive to the idea of preserving certain ecosystems, **1** yet more attention must be paid to the land. The central challenge of maintaining an ecosystem, especially by artificial means, is that ecosystems have a tendency to change, particularly with the dual influence of human **2** reacting and a

1

A) NO CHANGE
B) and
C) for
D) DELETE the underlined portion.

2

A) NO CHANGE
B) reacts
C) interacting
D) interaction

CONTINUE ➡

rapidly altering climate. **3** <u>Still,</u> one career that has grown by leaps and bounds in the last fifty years is that of the soil conservationist, whose land-use surveys guide both public and private entities as to how to work within sustainable ecosystems.

Take, for example, the factors that must be considered **4** <u>when building a beach house.</u> Coastal areas are particularly susceptible to the influence of **5** <u>things eroding because of the water from the ocean and in the air.</u> In this context, a soil conservationist might be asked to conduct a survey of the region in order to determine where it would be safest to build. After all, one's dream house would not be quite so ideal if it were at constant risk of collapsing, shifting, or **6** <u>to deteriorate</u> with the ground beneath it.

3

A) NO CHANGE
B) Nonetheless,
C) Finally,
D) Therefore,

4

Which choice most effectively sets up the subject discussed in this paragraph?

A) NO CHANGE
B) in performing these tasks.
C) with the changes in the seasons.
D) if you are doing soil conservation.

5

A) NO CHANGE
B) erosion
C) what erodes
D) the process of erosion

6

A) NO CHANGE
B) deteriorating
C) deteriorate
D) structures deteriorating

CONTINUE

In more agricultural communities, the work of a soil conservationist might take a different form. Farmers, after all, are not necessarily concerned with building structures on the land—instead, they are concerned with land that will yield reliable crops. [7] In these cases, soil conservationists employ a variety of techniques. Of these techniques each in its way is geared toward preserving or reviving land where crops are grown. The goal in these situations is to mimic the biology of "virgin land," or land that has never been farmed. Soil conservationists might advise on farming techniques [8] or chemical supplements that can help the land produce to its full potential. With the efforts of soil conservationists, no-till farmlands, lands that are not farmed with traditional plowing implements, [9] which has grown dramatically, nearly doubling in the fifteen years since 2000.

[7]

Which choice most effectively combines the underlined sentences?

A) Soil conservationists, in these cases, are ways of preserving or reviving land where cops are grown, and they will use a variety of techniques to do it.

B) In these cases, each one of them is geared toward the idea of preservation or revival as to crops, and the soil conservationists employ a variety of techniques to that end.

C) Geared toward preserving or reviving land where crops are grown, soil conservationists in these cases employ a variety of different techniques.

D) In these cases, soil conservationists employ a variety of techniques, each in its way geared toward preserving or reviving land where crops are grown.

[8]

At this point, the writer is considering adding the following information.

—such as no-till or terrace methods—

Should the writer make this addition here?

A) Yes, because it demonstrates the advantages of the methods described later in the sentence.

B) Yes, because it gives specific instances of the techniques discussed in this sentence.

C) No, because it distracts from the sentence's main focus on soil conservationists.

D) No, because it provides an unnecessary detail that interrupts the sentence's flow.

[9]

A) NO CHANGE
B) which have
C) have
D) has

CONTINUE

Soil conservation can be applied to any ecosystem, but its details tend to be rather technical. As a result, most people who work as soil conservationists tend to study agricultural science or environmental studies in college. From there, however, the paths diverge. Clearly, someone working on the eastern seaboard would need a different knowledge base from that of someone working in the deserts of the Southwest, the **10** plains of the Midwest, or the forests of the Northwest. **11** In all cases, however, soil conservationists do truly fascinating work, seeking as they do to continue to strike the balance between natural spaces and the people who live in them.

10

A) NO CHANGE

B) areas without trees

C) plains-like ecosystems

D) barren wasteland

11

Which choice most clearly ends the passage with a restatement of the writer's claim?

A) NO CHANGE

B) In all of these places, soil conservationists do essential work, but just as much is required of the builders and contractors who accompany them.

C) Soil conservationists work in both the public and the private sectors, but the public is better because it can be enjoyed by all.

D) Because the desert is unique, the skills that soil conservationists learn in places like Arizona are valuable but difficult to transfer between regions.

CONTINUE

Questions 12–22 are based on the following passage.

A Bigger Piece of the Peace

—1—

Nobel Prizes have been given since 1901 as a way to honor outstanding achievements in Physics, Chemistry, Literature, Medicine, and Economics. There may be some controversy as to who earns these awards in many cases; **12** therefore, there can be no doubt that the winners are always accomplished in their fields and have contributed something significant to their **13** disciplines and the world at large.

12

A) NO CHANGE

B) for example,

C) however,

D) fightingly,

13

A) NO CHANGE

B) disciplines,

C) disciplines, it's

D) disciplines, for example

CONTINUE

—2—

The Nobel Peace Prize may be a good deal more controversial, but it is by no means any less significant. **14** The prize is given each year "to the person who shall have done the most or the best work for fraternity between nations, for the abolition or reduction of standing armies and for the holding and promotion of peace congresses." Time and again we see the **15** committee rewarded bravery in the face of adversity. This is a difficult thing to quantify, but the Peace Prize is as important as the other prizes and contributes to **16** their common goal: to make the world a better place.

14

At this point, the writer is considering adding the following sentence.

> One of the most important prizes of all time, the 1962 prize in Physiology, was given to Francis Crick, James Watson, and Hugh Wilkins, for their discovery of the structure of DNA.

Should the writer make this addition here?

A) Yes, because it cites an important moment in Nobel Prize-giving history.

B) Yes, because it explains the typical genetic makeup of a Nobel Prize winner.

C) No, because it implies that all Peace Prize winners must also be scientists.

D) No, because it distracts from the paragraph's main focus on another prize.

15

A) NO CHANGE

B) committee reward

C) committee's rewarding

D) committees' reward

16

A) NO CHANGE

B) they're common goal,

C) they're common goal;

D) their common goal;

CONTINUE

—3—

It is probably no surprise that Martin Luther King, Jr., won the award in 1964 amid his non-violent campaign for civil rights in the United States. By 1964, and certainly by the time of his death in 1968, Baptist **17** minister King's, influence spanned the globe, not only for people of color seeking civil rights, but also for all **18** those people's friends, family, and loved ones. King was also the first African-American man to gain this particular kind of stature in the United States and on the world stage.

—4—

19 When given to first-year President Barack Obama, there was a good deal more controversy surrounding the award in 2009. In this case as in the others, however, the Nobel Peace Prize seeks to award the intangible, the unquantifiable, and the hopeful. Whether Burche, King, Obama, or the hundreds of other recipients, all winners provide the important reminder that people work every day to make the world a better place.

17

A) NO CHANGE
B) minister King's
C) minister, King's,
D) minister, King's

18

Which choice gives a specific supporting detail that is most similar to the details already in the paragraph?

A) NO CHANGE
B) the people throughout the world.
C) who thought the Nobel Prize should be awarded to someone who deserved it.
D) those who championed a cause in non-violent ways.

19

A) NO CHANGE
B) There was a good deal more controversy surrounding the award in 2009, when it was given to first-year President Barack Obama.
C) In 2009, when it was awarded, first-year President Barack Obama received the Prize with a good deal more controversy.
D) When it was awarded to first-year President Barack Obama in 2009, a good deal more controversy surrounded the award.

CONTINUE

—5—

King may be the most famous African-American recipient of the Nobel Peace [20] Prize. The honor was first given to a lesser known but no less illustrious figure, Ralph Bunche, in 1950. After a difficult childhood punctuated by an illustrious educational and political career, Bunche was one of the many tasked with trying to resolve the Arab-Israeli conflict that had erupted after World War II. The work began with a scare, as the UN's appointee, the Swedish Count Folke Bernadotte, was assassinated by members of the underground Lehi group. After this tragic event, Bunche, Bernadotte's chief aide, became the UN's chief mediator, and his long negotiations began with the Israeli representative Moshe Dayan. These negotiations, many of which were done while the two men shot pool, became the 1949 Armistice Agreements, concluding the 1948 Arab-Israeli Conflict and earning Ralph Bunche [21] the Nobel Peace Prize from the year 1950.

Question [22] **asks about the previous passage as a whole.**

20

Which choice most effectively combines the sentences at the underlined portion?

A) Prize: the

B) Prize, while the

C) Prize for the

D) Prize, yet the

21

Which choice most closely matches the stylistic pattern established earlier in the sentence?

A) NO CHANGE

B) 1950's Nobel Prize for Peace.

C) the 1950 Nobel Peace Prize.

D) the Nobel Prize for 1950's Peace.

Think about the previous passage as a whole as you answer question 22.

22

To make the passage most logical, paragraph 5 should be placed

A) where it is now.

B) after paragraph 1.

C) after paragraph 2.

D) after paragraph 3.

CONTINUE

Questions 23–33 are based on the following passage and supplementary material.

Conserving the Trees that Conserve the Earth

The most obvious facet of global warming is the rise in global temperatures. What many do not understand quite as well, **23** however, are the factors that contribute to that rise in global temperatures. The rise in carbon dioxide (CO_2) levels, for instance, is commonly cited as a reason, but what exactly does this chemical compound do?

For instance, every time you breathe, you inhale oxygen and a number of other compounds, and you exhale CO_2. Factories, cars, and other heavy machinery perform **24** functions that could be called analogous on a much larger scale. Because of the heavy output from this wide variety of industrial sources, the earth's atmosphere is bombarded **25** . This excess carbon dioxide creates what is known as a greenhouse effect, wherein heat enters the atmosphere but not all of it leaves. CO_2 does not absorb

---

23

A) NO CHANGE

B) thereby,

C) correspondingly,

D) thus,

24

A) NO CHANGE

B) the functions of an analogy

C) functions that are like analogies

D) analogous functions

25

At this point, the writer is considering adding the following information

> with more CO_2 than it can process or release naturally back into the area outside the earth's atmosphere

Should the writer make this addition here?

A) Yes, because it defines the role that the trees in the Amazonian rainforest play in modulating the earth's CO_2 levels.

B) Yes, because it states why high levels of CO_2 can be a problem in the earth's atmosphere.

C) No, because it mentions the process of absorbing CO_2, which blurs the essay's focus on the Amazonian rainforest.

D) No, because it undermines the passage's central claim that the earth can absorb CO_2 naturally.

CONTINUE

heat energy from the sun, but where the compound is concerned, **26** it's always absorbing heat energy released from the earth. Here's the problem: while the carbon dioxide can release some of that heat into space, it also releases some back to the earth, creating a kind of self-perpetuating cycle of rising temperatures. Since 1960, carbon dioxide has increased at a steady rate, **27** as temperatures have increased along exactly the same curve.

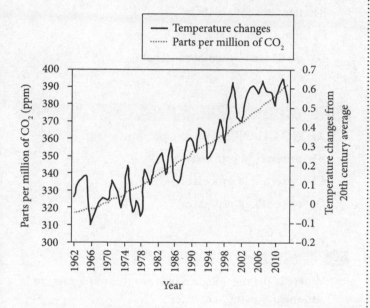

There are some earthly mechanisms to absorb and **28** chill out the levels of carbon dioxide in the atmosphere, but many of these industrial processes have depleted or overwhelmed these mechanisms. For instance, trees need carbon dioxide to perform their basic functions, but the number of trees required to offset carbon emissions is staggering. An independent analysis found that the number of trees required to offset the emissions of one modest coal plant **29** operating in a small city in Connecticut and would then require 52 million trees!

CONTINUE

26

A) NO CHANGE

B) its

C) they're

D) there

27

Which choice offers an accurate interpretation of the data in the chart?

A) NO CHANGE

B) but the temperatures have shown no general increase despite the rising CO_2 levels.

C) whereas the temperature changes peaked in 1989 for no apparent reason.

D) and although temperatures have fluctuated, those have generally increased as well.

28

A) NO CHANGE

B) kill

C) reduce

D) mellow

29

A) NO CHANGE

B) operating in a small city in Connecticut, where it would

C) operating in a small city in Connecticut would

D) operating in a small city in Connecticut, it would

Still, there are lots of trees on the earth, and alongside many of the carbon caps that many countries and industries have begun to impose, people are starting to take the ideas of *re*forestation and conservation more seriously. A team of over 150 researchers produced the first comprehensive map of the Amazon rainforest's ecosystem and **30** said, "that half of the Amazon could be deforested by 2050.

[1] But there is a silver lining to the findings in this research. [2] Because of the team's efforts, as many as 57% of Amazon tree species could be eligible for the International Union for the Conservation of Nature's red list of threatened species. [3] Other polluting behaviors would need to change as well for significant emission reversals, but protecting the Amazon's trees could **31** temper some of those polluting behaviors in the meantime and into the future. [4] This could be a first major step in part of the much longer process, **32** or series, of processes, to get the earth's carbon levels back to appropriate ranges. **33**

30

A) NO CHANGE
B) said that
C) said, that
D) said—that

31

A) NO CHANGE
B) temper some of them
C) temper some of it
D) do its part by tempering them

32

A) NO CHANGE
B) or series of processes,
C) or series; of processes
D) or series, of processes

33

Where is the most logical place in this paragraph to add the following sentence?

This could go a long way toward reforesting the Amazon rainforest, adding a significant boost to the 390 billion individual trees that currently grow there.

A) Before sentence 1
B) Before sentence 2
C) Before sentence 3
D) Before sentence 4

CONTINUE

Questions 34–44 are based on the following passage.

Original Adaptations and Rewrites

Literary influence can take many forms. Therefore, the results of this influence can take many forms—novels, poems, critiques, and countless others. Every great writer works within a literary tradition established by the great writers who came before. Sometimes that influence is [34] formal, in any case—as in the case of a writer who uses the forms created by an earlier writer to discuss new topics. Sometimes that influence is more literal—as in the case of those writers who take marginal characters from earlier works [35] and sometimes poems or movies are included.

[1] Perhaps the most famous instance of such a work is the epic blank-verse poem *Paradise Lost*, written by John Milton and first published in 1667. [2] It was by this alternate route, Milton claimed, that he could help to "justify the ways of God to men." [3] This work retells the biblical story of Adam and Eve and their exile from the Garden of Eden. [4] With the framework set by the biblical story, *Paradise Lost* offers a unique interpretation, [36] just as the story focuses on the fallen angel Satan rather than on the human characters. [5] As such, *Paradise Lost* is considered essential reading for those interested in matters both aesthetic and theological. [37]

34

A) NO CHANGE
B) formal—
C) formal, nevertheless—
D) formal, therefore—

35

Which choice provides information that best supports the claim made by this sentence?

A) NO CHANGE
B) but don't cite the author's name at all.
C) and build new literary worlds around them.
D) yet still consider it entirely their own.

36

A) NO CHANGE
B) wherein
C) from which
D) into it

37

To make this paragraph most logical, sentence 2 should be placed

A) before sentence 2.
B) before sentence 3.
C) before sentence 4.
D) before sentence 5.

CONTINUE

The practice of adapting literary works, particularly the great classics of a 38 language; to unique ends has continued. The 1966 novel *Wide Sargasso Sea* was British author Jean Rhys's prequel to the 1847 novel *Jane Eyre*. Toward the end of *Jane Eyre*, it is revealed that one of the novel's central characters, Mr. Rochester, has a wife locked away in one of the rooms of his castle. Rhys's novel tells this wife's story, foregrounding the cruelty of British imperialism and the oppressive society that awaited women in England. As Milton had before, Rhys uses a well-known work to 39 overtake an alternate story.

More recently, Algerian writer Kamel Daoud 40 he adapted Albert Camus's novel *The Stranger* into his own unique work, *The Meursault Investigation*, first published in Algeria in 2013. Camus's novel centers on the protagonist Meursault, 41 who kills an anonymous Arab man for vague reasons. Daoud's novel starts with Camus's

38

A) NO CHANGE
B) language
C) language,
D) language—

39

A) NO CHANGE
B) tell
C) manifest
D) ideate

40

A) NO CHANGE
B) adapted
C) he adopted
D) adopted

41

A) NO CHANGE
B) he kills
C) whom killed
D) killing

CONTINUE

basic outline, but *The Meursault Investigation* is
[42] deferent from *The Stranger* in that it writes the
backstory of that man and gives him a name, Musa. [43]
Daoud's narrative follows the observations of Musa's
brother Harun and offers a critique of European views that
refuse to acknowledge the existence of non-Europeans.
"By claiming your own name," Daoud said in an interview,
"you are also making a claim of your humanity and thus
the right to justice."

Although some of these works may not seem quite
as "original" as the original texts, they in fact make literal
what all other texts merely imply [44] and do not state.
Daoud refers to his novel as part of a "dialogue with
Camus," but we should not forget that even the greatest
works of literature are speaking to someone.

42

A) NO CHANGE
B) different, than
C) different than
D) different from

43

At this point, the writer is considering adding the
following sentence

> The history of Franco-Algerian relations goes
> back centuries as France was the occupying
> colonial power in Algeria from 1830 to 1962.

Should the writer make this addition here?

A) Yes, because it situates Daoud's novel in an
   essential historical context.

B) Yes, because it gives an example of a global
   conflict that one writer might have drawn upon.

C) No, because it contradicts the passage's larger
   claim that literature cannot be defined by
   historical events.

D) No, because it strays from the paragraph's main
   focus with an idea that is not elaborated upon.

44

A) NO CHANGE
B) as well.
C) similarly.
D) DELETE the underlined portion, and end the
   sentence with a period.

STOP
If you finish before time is called, you may check your work on this section only.
Do not turn to any other section in the test.

Math Test – No Calculator

25 MINUTES, 20 QUESTIONS

Turn to Section 3 of your answer sheet to answer the questions in this section.

For questions **1-15**, solve each problem, choose the best answer from the choices provided, and fill in the corresponding circle on your answer sheet. For questions **16-20**, solve the problem and enter your answer in the grid on the answer sheet. Please refer to the directions before question 16 on how to enter your answers in the grid. You may use any available space in your test booklet for scratch work.

NOTES

1. The use of a calculator **is not permitted**.
2. All variables and expressions used represent real numbers unless otherwise indicated.
3. Figures provided in this test are drawn to scale unless otherwise indicated.
4. All figures lie in a plane unless otherwise indicated.
5. Unless otherwise indicated, the domain of a given function f is the set of all real numbers x for which $f(x)$ is a real number.

REFERENCE

$A = \pi r^2$
$C = 2\pi r$

$A = \ell w$

$A = \frac{1}{2} bh$

$c^2 = a^2 + b^2$

Special Right Triangles

$V = \ell w h$

$V = \pi r^2 h$

$V = \frac{4}{3}\pi r^3$

$V = \frac{1}{3}\pi r^2 h$

$V = \frac{1}{3}\ell w h$

The number of degrees of arc in a circle is 360.
The number of radians of arc in a circle is 2π.
The sum of the measures in degrees of the angles of a triangle is 180.

CONTINUE

1

$$2x + 3y = -9$$
$$x - y = -2$$

Which of the following ordered pairs (x, y) satisfies the system of equations above?

A) $(-3, -1)$

B) $(-1, -3)$

C) $(1, 3)$

D) $(3, 1)$

2

$$x = 4(x + y)$$

If (x, y) is a solution to the equation above and $x \neq 0$, what is the value of $\dfrac{y}{x}$?

A) $\dfrac{3}{4}$

B) $\dfrac{1}{4}$

C) $-\dfrac{3}{4}$

D) $-\dfrac{5}{4}$

3

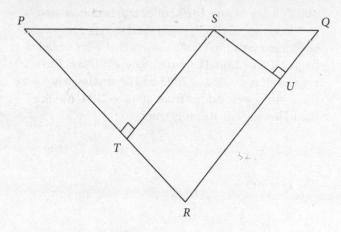

Note: Figure not drawn to scale.

Triangle PQR is isosceles with $PR = QR$ and $PQ = 64$. If the ratio of ST to $SU = 5{:}3$, what is the length of $\overline{SQ}$?

A) 8

B) 24

C) 32

D) 40

4

Buster estimates the expected profit, in dollars, from one week's operation of his family's chocolate-covered banana stand using the expression $4cd - 200$, where c is the number of expected customers of the banana stand each day, and d is the number of days the banana stand will be open during that week. Which of the following is the best interpretation of the number 4 in the expression?

A) Each customer is expected to buy 4 chocolate-covered bananas.

B) The price of a banana increases by $4 every day.

C) The number of customers will increase by a factor of 4 every day.

D) The banana stand charges $4 for each chocolate-covered banana.

CONTINUE

5

The number of Java Jim's coffee stores that existed in 2003 is approximately one-half the number of additional Java Jim's coffee stores that were added from 2004 to 2014. If approximately 700 Java Jim's coffee stores existed in 2003 and approximately y Java Jim's stores were added from 2004 to 2014, which of the following equations is true?

A) $\dfrac{1}{2}y = 700$

B) $2y = 700$

C) $700y = \dfrac{1}{2}$

D) $700y = 2$

6

Stream Supreme, a streaming movie service, charges a monthly fee of $7 for membership and $1.75 per movie streamed. Another streaming movie service, Download Empire, charges a monthly fee of $4 for membership and $2.25 per movie streamed. If m represents the number of movies streamed in a particular month, what are all the values of m for which Stream Supreme's total monthly charge is less than that of Download Empire?

A) $m < 4$

B) $5 \le m \le 6$

C) $6 \le m \le 7$

D) $m > 6$

7

$$q = \frac{\left(p_e - p_{wf}\right)k}{\mu d}h$$

The formula above models the productivity index, q, in barrels per day, of an oil well with a pressure differential of $(p_e - p_{wf})$, a permeability of k, a pay zone thickness of h, a viscosity of μ, and a drainage factor of d. Which of the following gives h in terms of q, p_e, p_{wf}, k, μ, and d ?

A) $h = \dfrac{\mu q d}{k}$

B) $h = \dfrac{k}{\mu q d}$

C) $h = \dfrac{\mu q d}{\left(p_e - p_{wf}\right)k}$

D) $h = \dfrac{\left(p_e - p_{wf}\right)k}{\mu q d}$

8

$$s = 110 + 4C$$

The equation above is used to model the relationship between the number of scoops, s, of ice cream sold per day at a particular ice cream shop, and the temperature, C, in degrees Celsius. According to the model, what is the meaning of the 4 in the equation?

A) For every increase of 1°C, four more scoops of ice cream will be sold.

B) For every decrease of 1°C, four more scoops of ice cream will be sold.

C) For every increase of 4°C, one more scoop of ice cream will be sold.

D) For every decrease of 4°C, one more scoop of ice cream will be sold.

CONTINUE

9

While saving money to pay for graduate school, Stephan created a plan in which the amount of money he saves each month is increased by a constant amount. If Stephan's savings plan requires that he save $145 during month 3 and that he save $280 during month 12, which of the following describes how the money Stephan saves changes between month 3 and month 12 of his savings plan?

A) Stephan increases the amount he saves by $5 each month.

B) Stephan increases the amount he saves by $15 each month.

C) Stephan increases the amount he saves by $60 every 6 months.

D) Stephan increases the amount he saves by $45 every month.

10

Which of the following equations, when graphed in the xy-plane, will include only values of y that are less than 2 ?

A) $y = -x^2 + 3$

B) $y = |-x| - 1$

C) $y = x^3 - 4$

D) $y = -(x - 1)^2 + 1$

11

If $f(x + 1) = 3x - 4$ for all values of x, what is the value of $f(-4)$?

A) -19

B) -16

C) -13

D) -10

12

$$\frac{5 - i}{2 - 3i}$$

If the expression above is rewritten in the form $a + bi$, where a and b are real numbers, what is the value of a ? (Note: $i = \sqrt{-1}$)

A) -2

B) -1

C) 1

D) $\dfrac{17}{13}$

CONTINUE

13

What is the sum of all values of p that satisfy the equation $3p^2 + 24p - 6 = 0$?

A) $-6\sqrt{2}$

B) -8

C) 8

D) $6\sqrt{2}$

14

The parabola with the equation $y = ax^2 + bx + c$, where a, b, and c are constants, is graphed on the xy-plane. If the parabola passes through the point $(-1, -1)$, which of the following must be true?

A) $a - b + c = -1$

B) $a - b - c = -1$

C) $a + b = 1$

D) $b - c = -1$

15

If $(px + 5)(qx + 3) = 8x^2 + rx + 15$ for all values of x, and $p + q = 6$, what are the two possible values for r ?

A) 2 and 4

B) 7 and 12

C) 22 and 26

D) 29 and 39

CONTINUE

DIRECTIONS

For questions 16-20, solve the problem and enter your answer in the grid, as described below, on the answer sheet.

1. Although not required, it is suggested that you write your answer in the boxes at the top of the columns to help you fill in the circles accurately. You will receive credit only if the circles are filled in correctly.

2. Mark no more than one circle in any column.

3. No question has a negative answer.

4. Some problems may have more than one correct answer. In such cases, grid only one answer.

5. **Mixed numbers** such as $3\frac{1}{2}$ must be gridded as 3.5 or 7/2. (If $\boxed{3\ 1\ /\ 2}$ is entered into the grid, it will be interpreted as $\frac{31}{2}$, not as $3\frac{1}{2}$.)

6. **Decimal Answers:** If you obtain a decimal answer with more digits than the grid can accommodate, it may be either rounded or truncated, but it must fill the entire grid.

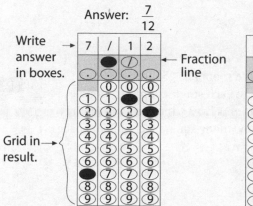

Answer: $\frac{7}{12}$ Answer: 2.5

Write answer in boxes. →   ← Fraction line

Grid in result. →   ← Decimal point

Acceptable ways to grid $\frac{2}{3}$ are:

Answer: 201 – either position is correct

NOTE: You may start your answers in any column, space permitting. Columns you don't need to use should be left blank.

CONTINUE ➡

16

What is the value of y if $(4y + 8) - (7y - 12) = 11$?

17

At a hotel, each double room has 25 more square feet of floor space than each single room. If 2 double rooms and 4 single rooms have a total of 1400 square feet of floor space, how many square feet of floor space does a double room have?

18

One angle of a right triangle measures $a°$, where $\cos a° = \dfrac{3}{5}$. What is $\sin(90° - a°)$?

19

If $x + 3$ is a factor $x^2 + kx + 2k$, where k is a constant, what is the value of k ?

CONTINUE

20

$$x^3 - 3x^2 + 5x - 15 = 0$$

What real value of x is a solution to the above equation?

STOP

If you finish before time is called, you may check your work on this section only.
Do not turn to any other section in the test.

Math Test – Calculator

55 MINUTES, 38 QUESTIONS

Turn to Section 4 of your answer sheet to answer the questions in this section.

DIRECTIONS

For questions **1-30**, solve each problem, choose the best answer from the choices provided, and fill in the corresponding circle on your answer sheet. For questions **31-38**, solve the problem and enter your answer in the grid on the answer sheet. Please refer to the directions before question 31 on how to enter your answers in the grid. You may use any available space in your test booklet for scratch work.

NOTES

1. The use of a calculator **is permitted**.
2. All variables and expressions used represent real numbers unless otherwise indicated.
3. Figures provided in this test are drawn to scale unless otherwise indicated.
4. All figures lie in a plane unless otherwise indicated.
5. Unless otherwise indicated, the domain of a given function f is the set of all real numbers x for which $f(x)$ is a real number.

REFERENCE

The number of degrees of arc in a circle is 360.
The number of radians of arc in a circle is 2π.
The sum of the measures in degrees of the angles of a triangle is 180.

CONTINUE

1

A pizzeria sells pizzas in individual slices or in pies of 8 slices. On a certain day, the pizzeria sold a total of 364 slices, 84 of which were sold as individual slices. Which of the following shows the number of pies, n, sold on that day?

A) $n = \dfrac{364 + 84}{8}$

B) $n = \dfrac{364}{8} + 84$

C) $n = \dfrac{364}{8} - 84$

D) $n = \dfrac{364 - 84}{8}$

2

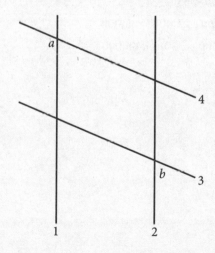

In the figure above, lines 1 and 2 are parallel, and lines 3 and 4 are parallel. If the measure of $\angle a$ is 125°, what is the measure of $\angle b$?

A) 40

B) 55

C) 110

D) 125

3

	Cream filling	No filling	Total
White chocolate	5	15	20
Dark chocolate	7	3	10
Total	12	18	30

A box contains 30 pieces of chocolate, distributed as shown in the table above. Each piece is made of either white chocolate or dark chocolate, and each piece contains either cream filling or no filling. If one piece is selected at random, what is the probability that the piece is either white chocolate with cream filling or dark chocolate with no filling?

A) $\dfrac{8}{30}$

B) $\dfrac{12}{30}$

C) $\dfrac{20}{30}$

D) $\dfrac{22}{30}$

CONTINUE

4

An isosceles triangle has perimeter T and sides of length x, x, and y. Which of the following represents x in terms of T and y ?

A) $x = T - y$

B) $x = T - 2y$

C) $x = \dfrac{T - 2y}{2}$

D) $x = \dfrac{T - y}{2}$

5

$$2x + 3y = -6$$
$$x - 4y = 19$$

Which ordered pair satisfies the system of equations shown above?

A) $(-9, 4)$

B) $(-3, 4)$

C) $(-1, -5)$

D) $(3, -4)$

6

When 6 times the number n is subtracted from 8, the result is 20. What is the result when 3 times the number n is subtracted from 5 ?

A) -2

B) 8

C) 11

D) 20

7

At 12 P.M. on Sunday, there are 25,000 people in a football stadium that holds 65,000. Every minute after 12 P.M., the number of people in the stadium increases by 550. If m represents the time, in minutes, after 12 P.M., which of the inequalities below gives the set of minutes in which the football stadium is below capacity?

A) $550m < 25{,}000$

B) $550m < 65{,}000$

C) $550m + 25{,}000 < 65{,}000$

D) $25{,}000 - 550m < 65{,}000$

CONTINUE

Number of United States Residents With Health Insurance in 2015, in Thousands

Income in dollars	Age in years						Total
	Under 19	19-25	26-34	35-44	45-64	65 and older	
Under 25,000	12,499	4,881	6,146	6,387	13,314	7,359	50,586
25,000-49,999	15,624	6,102	7,683	7,984	16,643	9,200	63,236
50,000-74,999	14,061	5,491	6,915	7,185	14,978	8,278	56,908
75,000-99,999	10,936	4,271	5,378	5,589	11,650	6,439	44,263
100,000 and above	24,998	9,762	12,293	12,774	26,628	14,718	101,173
Total	78,118	30,507	38,415	39,919	83,213	45,994	316,166

The table above shows the number of U.S. residents with health insurance in 2015, in thousands, categorized by age group and annual income. According to these results, if a U.S. resident with health insurance who was 35-64 in 2015 is selected at random, what is the approximate probability that this resident had an income between $50,000 and $74,999 ?

A) 0.20

B) 0.25

C) 0.40

D) 0.80

CONTINUE

9

A truck traveled at an average speed of 70 miles per hour for 4 hours and had a fuel efficiency of 18 miles per gallon. Approximately how many gallons of fuel did the truck use for the entire 4-hour drive?

A)   4

B) 10

C) 16

D) 20

10

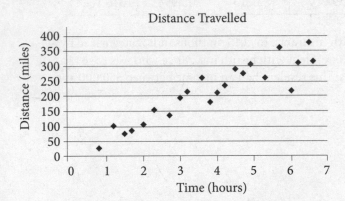

Distance Travelled

The scatterplot above shows the distances and times spent traveling for 22 trips by a driver. What is the time, in hours, of the trip represented by the data point farthest from the line of best fit (not shown)?

A)   4

B)   6

C)   8

D) 10

11

$$t_b = 212 - 0.0018a$$

The temperature at which water boils varies with altitude. The formula above models the relationship between t_b, the temperature at which water boils, in degrees Fahrenheit, and a, the altitude, in feet. Which of the following equations expresses altitude in terms of the temperature at which water boils?

A) $a = \dfrac{0.0018}{t_b - 212}$

B) $a = \dfrac{t_b + 212}{0.0018}$

C) $a = \dfrac{t_b - 212}{0.0018}$

D) $a = \dfrac{212 - t_b}{0.0018}$

CONTINUE

12

Which scatterplot below expresses a positive association that is not linear? (Note: A positive association between two variables is one in which higher values in one variable correspond to higher values in the other variable, and vice versa.)

A)
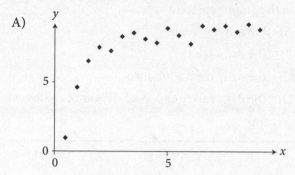

B)
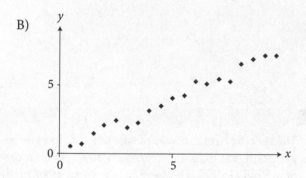

C)
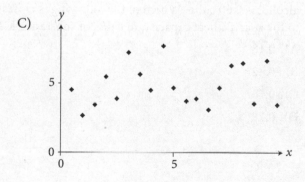

D)
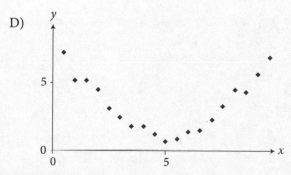

13

$$v = \frac{h - m}{t} + 4.9t$$

For an object thrown straight upward, the formula above gives the relationship between v, the initial speed in meters per second, t, the time in seconds after the object was thrown, h, the height after t seconds, and m, the initial height from which the object was thrown. Which of the following expresses h in terms of v, t, and m ?

A) $h = -4.9t^2 + vt - m$

B) $h = -4.9t^2 + vt + m$

C) $h = -4.9t^2 - vt + m$

D) $h = 4.9t^2 - vt - m$

14

$$65x + y = 455$$

A grocery store receives a shipment of oranges and consistently sells the same number of oranges each day. The equation above models the number of oranges, y, that remain x days after the shipment is received. What does it mean that (7, 0) is a solution to the equation?

A) It takes 7 days after the shipment until none of the oranges are remaining.

B) There are 7 oranges in the shipment.

C) It takes 7 days for oranges to be sold to 455 customers.

D) After the shipment, 7 oranges are sold each day.

CONTINUE

Questions 15 and 16 refer to the following information.

A minor-league baseball player is offered a short-term contract by three teams: the Eagles, the Hawks, and the Jays. Each contract consists of a signing bonus, a daily salary, and a daily meal allowance, as shown in the table below.

Team	Signing bonus, b (in dollars)	Salary, s (in dollars per day)	Meal allowance, m (in dollars per day)
Eagles	1400	140	40
Hawks	1200	160	50
Jays	1500	130	30

The player's total compensation, C, for each contract in terms of the number of days, d, is given by the formula $C = b + (s + m)d$.

15

For what number of days, d, would the player's total compensation including signing bonus, salary, and meal allowance with the Eagles be greater than the total compensation with the Jays?

A) $d < 5$

B) $d > 5$

C) $d < 6$

D) $d > 6$

16

The relationship between the player's total compensation, C, for a contract with the Hawks as a function of the number of days, d, for which the contract lasts is graphed in the xy-plane, with d on the x-axis and C on the y-axis. What does the y-intercept of the graph represent?

A) The signing bonus

B) The daily salary

C) The daily meal allowance

D) The daily salary and meal allowance combined

17

The specific heat capacity of substance K, in calories per gram (cal/g), is approximately 30% less than that of methyl alcohol. The specific heat capacity of methyl alcohol is 0.60 cal/g. Which of the following is closest to the specific heat capacity, in cal/g, of substance K?

A) 0.18

B) 0.42

C) 0.56

D) 0.78

CONTINUE

18

In the xy-plane, if $(-1, 0)$ is a solution to the system of inequalities $y < x + c$ and $y < -x - d$, which of the following must be true about c and d ?

A) $c = d$

B) $c = -d$

C) $c < d$

D) $d < c$

20

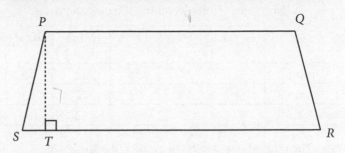

In quadrilateral $PQRS$ above, $PS = QR$, and $\overline{PQ}$ is parallel to $\overline{SR}$. If PQ and SR were both decreased by 75% and PT were quadrupled, how would the area of $PQRS$ change?

A) The area of $PQRS$ would be quadrupled.

B) The area of $PQRS$ would be increased by 75%.

C) The area of $PQRS$ would be decreased by 75%.

D) The area of $PQRS$ would be unaffected.

19

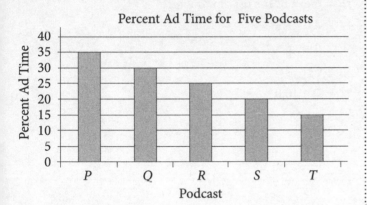

Percent Ad Time for Five Podcasts

A company advertises on five different podcasts: P, Q, R, S, and T. The graph above shows the amount of time used for the ad on the five different podcasts as a percentage of total run time. Each podcast runs for the same length of time, and the costs to advertise on podcasts P, Q, R, S and T are \$400, \$350, \$200, \$180, and \$150, respectively. Which of the following podcasts provides the most ad time per dollar?

A) Q

B) R

C) S

D) T

CONTINUE

21

Number of times watching the news per week

	Never	1-2	3-4	More than 4	Total
Group A	7	14	18	11	50
Group B	4	13	21	12	50
Total	11	27	39	23	100

The table above shows the results of a survey in which 100 people were asked how often they watched the news. Group A consisted of people who were registered voters, and Group B consisted of people who were not registered to vote. If one person is randomly chosen from among those who watch the news fewer than three times a week, what is the probability that the person was a member of Group A ?

A) $\dfrac{21}{38}$

B) $\dfrac{4}{50}$

C) $\dfrac{21}{50}$

D) $\dfrac{38}{100}$

22

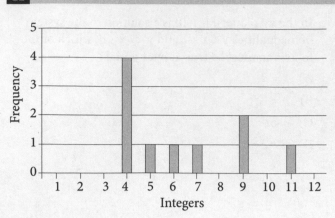

The bar graph above shows the distribution of randomly selected integers from 1 to 12. What is the mean of the list of numbers?

A) 5.5

B) 6.3

C) 7.0

D) 10.0

CONTINUE

Questions 23-25 refer to the following information.

A team of scientists measures the volume of various samples of different gases with a constant pressure of 0.1 atm and a constant temperature of 610 K. The graph below plots the volume of each sample against the amount of the gas.

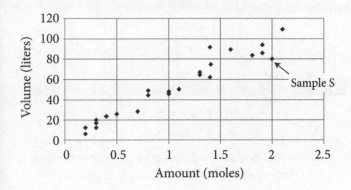

Volume-Amount Relationship among Samples of Gases

The ideal gas law predicts that at this pressure and temperature, the volume of an ideal gas can be modeled by the equation $V = 50n$, where V is the volume in liters and n is the amount of the substance, measured in moles. Assume that the relationship is valid for greater amounts of the substance than are shown in the graph. (A mole is approximately 6.022×10^{23} molecules.)

23

According to the data provided, what is the volume, in <u>milliliters</u>, of Sample S ?

A) 8×10^4

B) 2×10^3

C) 8×10^1

D) 4×10^1

24

There are three samples shown of approximately 1.4 moles. Which of the following is closest to the range of volumes of these four samples, in liters?

A) 30

B) 20

C) 9

D) 3

25

Based on the ideal gas law, what is the volume, in liters, of a sample that contains 1,200 moles?

A) 6,000

B) 24,000

C) 36,000

D) 60,000

CONTINUE

26

Let the polynomials f and g be defined by $f(x) = 3x^3 + 6x^2 + 11x$ and $g(x) = 8x^2 + 15x + 7$. Which of the following polynomials is divisible by $3x + 7$?

A) $j(x) = 2f(x) + g(x)$

B) $k(x) = f(x) + g(x)$

C) $m(x) = f(x) + 2g(x)$

D) $n(x) = f(x) + 3g(x)$

27

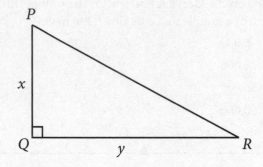

Given the right triangle PQR above, which of the following is equal to $\dfrac{y}{x}$?

A) $\cos P$

B) $\cos Q$

C) $\tan P$

D) $\tan Q$

28

Let the function f be defined by $f(x) = (x - 1)(x + 7)$. Which of the following is an equivalent form of f in which the minimum value of f appears as either a coefficient or a constant?

A) $f(x) = x^2 - 7$

B) $f(x) = x^2 + 6x - 7$

C) $f(x) = (x + 3)^2 - 16$

D) $f(x) = (x - 3)^2 - 20$

29

$$4a - j = 7a + 3$$
$$4b - k = 7b + 3$$

In the equations shown above, j and k are constants. If j is k plus 1, which of the following is true?

A) a is b plus $\dfrac{1}{3}$.

B) a is b minus $\dfrac{1}{3}$.

C) a is b minus 1.

D) a is b minus 3.

CONTINUE

30

If the average (arithmetic mean) of $3x$ and 11 is a, the average of $4x$ and 6 is b, and the average of $5x$ and 7 is c, what is the average of a, b, and c, in terms of x?

A) $x + 2$

B) $x + 3$

C) $2x + 4$

D) $4x + 8$

CONTINUE

DIRECTIONS

For questions 31-38, solve the problem and enter your answer in the grid, as described below, on the answer sheet.

1. Although not required, it is suggested that you write your answer in the boxes at the top of the columns to help you fill in the circles accurately. You will receive credit only if the circles are filled in correctly.

2. Mark no more than one circle in any column.

3. No question has a negative answer.

4. Some problems may have more than one correct answer. In such cases, grid only one answer.

5. **Mixed numbers** such as $3\frac{1}{2}$ must be gridded as 3.5 or 7/2. (If  is entered into

    the grid, it will be interpreted as $\frac{31}{2}$, not as

    $3\frac{1}{2}$.)

6. **Decimal Answers:** If you obtain a decimal answer with more digits than the grid can accommodate, it may be either rounded or truncated, but it must fill the entire grid.

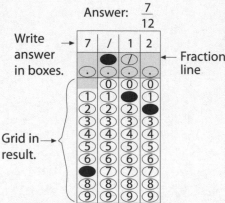

NOTE: You may start your answers in any column, space permitting. Columns you don't need to use should be left blank.

CONTINUE →

31

A scientist estimates that the water level of a lake is dropping by 2.25 inches per year. If this trend continues, how many years will it take for the water level in the lake to drop by 27 inches?

32

A car factory that operates 24 hours a day and 7 days a week produces one car every 20 minutes. How many cars does the factory produce in 3 days?

33

Scores in the game of bowling range from 0 to 300 per game, inclusive. Vito's average score in the first 6 games of a bowling tournament was 200. What is the lowest score he can receive in his 7th game and still have an average score of at least 240 for the entire 12-game tournament?

34

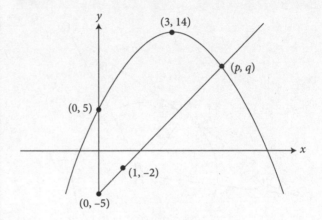

The *xy*-plane shows a point of intersection between a line and a parabola. The point of intersection has coordinates (p, q). If the vertex of the parabola is at $(3, 14)$, what is the value of p ?

CONTINUE ➤

35

To purchase a car, Harry makes a down payment, and every month thereafter, he pays a fixed amount to the car dealer. The total amount, *T*, in dollars, that Harry has paid after *m* months can be represented by the equation $T = 175m + 350$. According to this equation, how much, in dollars, was Harry's down payment? (Disregard the $ sign when gridding your answer.)

36

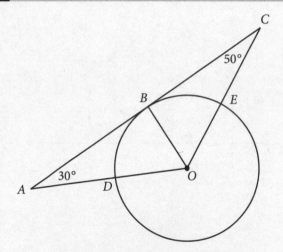

In the figure above, line segment *AC* is tangent to the circle with center *O* at point *B*. Line segments *AO* and *CO* intersect the circle at points *D* and *E*, respectively. If the circumference of circle *O* is 72, what is the length of minor arc $\overset{\frown}{DE}$?

Questions 37 and 38 refer to the following information.

The population of a small town is currently 800. A statistician estimates that the population of the town will decline by 14 percent per year for the next five years. The statistician models the population, *P*, of the town after *x* years using the equation $P = 800(k)^x$.

37

In the equation above, what value should be used for *k* ?

38

According to the statistician's model, what will the population of the town be, to the nearest whole number, after five years?

STOP
If you finish before time is called, you may check your work on this section only.
Do not turn to any other section in the test.

No Test Material On This Page

SAT Essay

DIRECTIONS

The essay gives you an opportunity to show how effectively you can read and comprehend a passage and write an essay analyzing the passage. In your essay you should demonstrate that you have read the passage carefully, present a clear and logical analysis, and use language precisely.

Your essay must be written on the lines provided in your answer sheet booklet; except for the planning page of the answer booklet, you will receive no other paper on which to write. You will have enough space if you write on every line, avoid wide margins, and keep your handwriting to a reasonable size. Remember that people who are not familiar with your handwriting will read what you write. Try to write or print so that what you are writing is legible to those readers.

You have <u>50 minutes</u> to read the passage and write an essay in response to the prompt provided inside this booklet.

REMINDER

— Do not write your essay in this booklet. Only what you write on the lined pages of your answer booklet will be evaluated.

— An off-topic essay will not be evaluated.

CONTINUE ➔

As you read the passage below, consider how John Kerry uses

- evidence, such as facts or examples, to support claims.
- reasoning to develop ideas and to connect claims and evidence.
- stylistic or persuasive elements, such as word choice or appeals to emotion, to add power to the ideas expressed.

**The following is adapted from the article "Saving Our Future By Saving Our Oceans,"
written by John Kerry for National Geographic in June 2014.**

1   The ocean covers almost three-quarters of our planet and sustains life on Earth as we know it. But our ocean is at grave risk today—and we know the reason why.

2   Human activity threatens the world's ocean. Often illegal international fishing practices are decimating fisheries. A garbage patch twice the size of Texas floats in the Pacific Ocean, evidence of the trash we cast into our waterways. Rising carbon dioxide levels from emissions increase ocean acidity, endangering coral reefs and other marine life.

3   The warning could not be starker: Unless these trends are reversed, the effects across the planet will be profound. The damage will be felt whether you live on a coastline or hundreds of miles from the nearest ocean's edge. The ocean produces half the world's oxygen, creates the clouds that bring fresh water, and regulates our climate. More than a billion people eat fish as their primary source of protein. Fishing is a $500-billion global industry, and one in six jobs in the United States is marine related.

4   The good news is that we know what is behind the degradation of the ocean. We know the steps required to counter the dangers and restore the health of our ocean for this generation and those to come. We know the science to change the future for the ocean.

5   What we also know is that the global political will to address this urgent peril has yet to be summoned. We must change the equation. The plight of the ocean compels us to fight complacency and build consensus for action.

6   The United States has demonstrated that we can make progress. We have begun to restore fish stocks and sustain the livelihoods of our fishermen. We have reduced the flow of waste into the marine environment and launched intensive studies of the effects of rising acidity levels on sea life. Some other nations are also addressing the challenges in innovative ways.

7   But governments will not undertake this enormous campaign without prodding from the private sector—from businesses that depend on a healthy ocean, from nongovernmental organizations committed to saving the ocean, and from all of us who recognize that the ocean is a defining feature of life on our planet.

CONTINUE

8   That's why we will hold the State Department's first ocean conference on June 16 and 17. Government leaders from around the world—heads of state and foreign ministers—will join scientists, environmentalists, and business leaders to discuss the threat to our ocean and the steps that should be taken to reverse the damage and restore the balance.

9   We intend to create a global movement to protect the ocean and its resources. We will debate real solutions and come up with concrete plans for implementing them. We also have sent out a call to action that lays out the crucial steps all of us can take to ensure that a healthy ocean allows us to continue to enjoy its bounty.

10 Because I come from Massachusetts, the sea has been a constant in my life. But stewardship of the ocean is more than just a personal passion for those of us who hail from coastal communities. Just as this issue was a priority for me as a senator, it is a priority for me now as Secretary of State, because it means jobs, health, industry, and the safety of our planet.

11 I've been around enough to know that governments can't solve all of these problems alone. Just as we share a common dependence on the ocean, we must join together in a common endeavor to save the ocean from the damage caused by humans.

12 In a few days, I will ask leaders from around the world to take action to save our ocean. I'm convinced the ocean conference will be an important catalyst, that governments and experts can lead the way. But I know it will take more to win this crucial struggle

13 What we do as individuals will ultimately make the difference. Some acts are simple. Don't throw trash into waterways. Buy sustainable seafood. Volunteer at least one day a year to clean beaches or waterways in your community. Other acts require a sustained commitment by people everywhere to make certain saving the ocean is a priority for their governments.

14 In observing World Oceans Day yesterday, we recognized that protecting our ocean is not a luxury. It is a necessity that contributes to our economy, our climate, and our way of life. Working together, we can change the current course and chart a sustainable future.

Write an essay in which you explain how John Kerry builds an argument to persuade his audience that there are benefits to saving the oceans. In your essay, analyze how Kerry uses one or more of the features listed in the box above (or features of your own choice) to strengthen the logic and persuasiveness of his argument. Be sure that your analysis focuses on the most relevant features of the passage.

Your essay should not explain whether you agree with Kerry's claims, but rather explain how Kerry builds an argument to persuade his audience.

END OF TEST

DO NOT RETURN TO A PREVIOUS SECTION.

The Princeton Review®

Completely darken bubbles with a No. 2 pencil. If you make a mistake, be sure to erase mark completely. Erase all stray marks.

1.

YOUR NAME: _____
(Print)   Last   First   M.I.

SIGNATURE: _____ DATE: ___ / ___ / ___

HOME ADDRESS: _____
(Print)   Number and Street

_____
City   State   Zip Code

PHONE NO.: _____
(Print)

5. YOUR NAME

First 4 letters of last name | FIRST INIT | MID INIT

(bubbles A–Z for each column)

IMPORTANT: Please fill in these boxes exactly as shown on the back cover of your test book.

2. TEST FORM

3. TEST CODE

4. REGISTRATION NUMBER

6. DATE OF BIRTH

Month	Day	Year
JAN		
FEB	0 0	0 0
MAR	1 1	1 1
APR	2 2	2 2
MAY	3 3	3 3
JUN	4 4	4
JUL	5 5	5
AUG	6 6	6
SEP	7 7	7
OCT	8 8	8
NOV	9 9	9
DEC		

7. SEX
- MALE
- FEMALE

The Princeton Review®

Test 6
Start with number 1 for each new section.
If a section has fewer questions than answer spaces, leave the extra answer spaces blank.

Section 1—Reading

1. A B C D
2. A B C D
3. A B C D
4. A B C D
5. A B C D
6. A B C D
7. A B C D
8. A B C D
9. A B C D
10. A B C D
11. A B C D
12. A B C D
13. A B C D
14. A B C D
15. A B C D
16. A B C D
17. A B C D
18. A B C D
19. A B C D
20. A B C D
21. A B C D
22. A B C D
23. A B C D
24. A B C D
25. A B C D
26. A B C D
27. A B C D
28. A B C D
29. A B C D
30. A B C D
31. A B C D
32. A B C D
33. A B C D
34. A B C D
35. A B C D
36. A B C D
37. A B C D
38. A B C D
39. A B C D
40. A B C D
41. A B C D
42. A B C D
43. A B C D
44. A B C D
45. A B C D
46. A B C D
47. A B C D
48. A B C D
49. A B C D
50. A B C D
51. A B C D
52. A B C D

Section 2—Writing and Language Skills

1. A B C D
2. A B C D
3. A B C D
4. A B C D
5. A B C D
6. A B C D
7. A B C D
8. A B C D
9. A B C D
10. A B C D
11. A B C D
12. A B C D
13. A B C D
14. A B C D
15. A B C D
16. A B C D
17. A B C D
18. A B C D
19. A B C D
20. A B C D
21. A B C D
22. A B C D
23. A B C D
24. A B C D
25. A B C D
26. A B C D
27. A B C D
28. A B C D
29. A B C D
30. A B C D
31. A B C D
32. A B C D
33. A B C D
34. A B C D
35. A B C D
36. A B C D
37. A B C D
38. A B C D
39. A B C D
40. A B C D
41. A B C D
42. A B C D
43. A B C D
44. A B C D

Test 6   Start with number 1 for each new section.
If a section has fewer questions than answer spaces, leave the extra answer spaces blank.

Section 3—Mathematics: No Calculator

1. Ⓐ Ⓑ Ⓒ Ⓓ
2. Ⓐ Ⓑ Ⓒ Ⓓ
3. Ⓐ Ⓑ Ⓒ Ⓓ
4. Ⓐ Ⓑ Ⓒ Ⓓ
5. Ⓐ Ⓑ Ⓒ Ⓓ
6. Ⓐ Ⓑ Ⓒ Ⓓ
7. Ⓐ Ⓑ Ⓒ Ⓓ
8. Ⓐ Ⓑ Ⓒ Ⓓ
9. Ⓐ Ⓑ Ⓒ Ⓓ
10. Ⓐ Ⓑ Ⓒ Ⓓ
11. Ⓐ Ⓑ Ⓒ Ⓓ
12. Ⓐ Ⓑ Ⓒ Ⓓ
13. Ⓐ Ⓑ Ⓒ Ⓓ
14. Ⓐ Ⓑ Ⓒ Ⓓ
15. Ⓐ Ⓑ Ⓒ Ⓓ

16.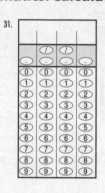
17.
18.
19.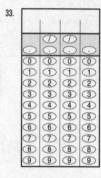
20.

Section 4—Mathematics: Calculator

1. Ⓐ Ⓑ Ⓒ Ⓓ
2. Ⓐ Ⓑ Ⓒ Ⓓ
3. Ⓐ Ⓑ Ⓒ Ⓓ
4. Ⓐ Ⓑ Ⓒ Ⓓ
5. Ⓐ Ⓑ Ⓒ Ⓓ
6. Ⓐ Ⓑ Ⓒ Ⓓ
7. Ⓐ Ⓑ Ⓒ Ⓓ
8. Ⓐ Ⓑ Ⓒ Ⓓ
9. Ⓐ Ⓑ Ⓒ Ⓓ
10. Ⓐ Ⓑ Ⓒ Ⓓ
11. Ⓐ Ⓑ Ⓒ Ⓓ
12. Ⓐ Ⓑ Ⓒ Ⓓ
13. Ⓐ Ⓑ Ⓒ Ⓓ
14. Ⓐ Ⓑ Ⓒ Ⓓ
15. Ⓐ Ⓑ Ⓒ Ⓓ
16. Ⓐ Ⓑ Ⓒ Ⓓ
17. Ⓐ Ⓑ Ⓒ Ⓓ
18. Ⓐ Ⓑ Ⓒ Ⓓ
19. Ⓐ Ⓑ Ⓒ Ⓓ
20. Ⓐ Ⓑ Ⓒ Ⓓ
21. Ⓐ Ⓑ Ⓒ Ⓓ
22. Ⓐ Ⓑ Ⓒ Ⓓ
23. Ⓐ Ⓑ Ⓒ Ⓓ
24. Ⓐ Ⓑ Ⓒ Ⓓ
25. Ⓐ Ⓑ Ⓒ Ⓓ
26. Ⓐ Ⓑ Ⓒ Ⓓ
27. Ⓐ Ⓑ Ⓒ Ⓓ
28. Ⓐ Ⓑ Ⓒ Ⓓ
29. Ⓐ Ⓑ Ⓒ Ⓓ
30. Ⓐ Ⓑ Ⓒ Ⓓ

31.
32.
33.
34.
35.

36.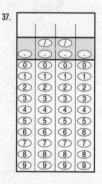
37.
38.

Chapter 14
Practice Test 6:
Answers and
Explanations

PRACTICE TEST 6 ANSWER KEY

Section 1: Reading		Section 2: Writing & Language		Section 3: Math (No Calculator)		Section 4: Math (Calculator)	
1. D	27. B	1. D	23. A	1. A	11. A	1. D	20. D
2. C	28. B	2. D	24. D	2. C	12. C	2. B	21. A
3. B	29. B	3. D	25. B	3. B	13. B	3. A	22. B
4. D	30. D	4. A	26. A	4. D	14. A	4. D	23. A
5. C	31. A	5. B	27. D	5. A	15. C	5. D	24. A
6. C	32. C	6. B	28. C	6. D	16. 3	6. C	25. D
7. C	33. A	7. D	29. C	7. C	17. 250	7. C	26. C
8. A	34. C	8. B	30. B	8. A	18. $\frac{3}{5}$ or 0.6	8. A	27. C
9. C	35. B	9. C	31. A	9. B		9. C	28. C
10. C	36. C	10. A	32. B	10. D	19. 9	10. B	29. B
11. B	37. D	11. A	33. C		20. 3	11. D	30. C
12. B	38. A	12. C	34. B			12. A	31. 12
13. B	39. B	13. A	35. C			13. B	32. 216
14. D	40. C	14. D	36. B			14. A	33. 180
15. A	41. C	15. B	37. D			15. B	34. 5
16. C	42. B	16. A	38. C			16. A	35. 350
17. B	43. D	17. B	39. B			17. B	36. 20
18. A	44. C	18. D	40. B			18. D	37. 0.86
19. C	45. B	19. B	41. A			19. B	38. 376
20. D	46. B	20. D	42. D				
21. A	47. C	21. C	43. D				
22. A	48. A	22. D	44. D				
23. A	49. A						
24. D	50. A						
25. A	51. C						
26. D	52. D						

For self-scoring assessment tables, please turn to page 565.

PRACTICE TEST 6 EXPLANATIONS

Section 1: Reading

1. **D** This question asks for the best summary of the passage, so save it until the end of the question set. To answer this question, look for an answer that fits the majority of the text and rely on POE. Choice (A) incorrectly states that a character *becomes increasingly hostile*; eliminate it. Choice (B) incorrectly states that a *character describes* something; the narrator does so. Eliminate (B). Choice (C) states that two characters are *in the same profession*, which is not true, and that they *become increasingly competitive*, which is not true; eliminate it. Choice (D) states that two characters are *traveling together*, which is true, and that they *eagerly await confrontation*, which may sound extreme, but which does fit the mention of a *frequent bone of contention* and that one character *liked to infuriate* the other. Choice (D) is the correct answer.

2. **C** This question asks for the main purpose of the opening sentence. To answer this question, go back to the first paragraph and carefully read the sentence to determine its purpose. The first sentence describes *cheerfulness* in general before the paragraph moves forward with specific descriptions of the cheerfulness of the characters. Eliminate any answers that have nothing to do with this prediction. Choice (A) incorrectly mentions a *contrast* and *the narrator's gloom*; eliminate it. Choice (B) refers to an *allegorical representation,* which is not present in the text. Eliminate this answer. Choice (C) matches the prediction, so keep it for now. Choice (D) incorrectly refers to *violent intentions*; eliminate it. Choice (C) is the correct answer.

3. **B** This question asks how the narrator's focus shifts in the second paragraph. To answer this question, carefully read the second paragraph to determine what's happening. At the beginning of the paragraph, the narrator says that it is *dreadful* for a parson to be *warlike* and that he remembers *distinctly whose servant he is,* so the narrator is referencing a parson being a *man of peace.* In the second half of the paragraph, the narrator continues by saying to the *parson-haters* that he will not go along *every step* of their *dismal, downward-tending, unchristian road.* The correct answer must have something to do with the shift from acknowledging the parson as a man of peace to disagreeing with those who are anti-parson. Choice (A) can be eliminated because the narrator does not want to chastise the clergy. Choice (B) matches the prediction, so keep it for now. Choice (C) can be eliminated because the second part of the paragraph has mention of the clergy's *manners and appearance*; eliminate it. Choice (D) is too general in its discussion of *peaceful men*; eliminate it. Choice (B) is the correct answer.

4. **D** Go back to the second paragraph to see how the words are used. The narrator says *if you are a parson-hater* he's not going to *go along* with the *poisonous rancor* and *horror and denunciation* toward a rector. The correct answer should have something to do with *showing strong anti-clergy sentiments.* Choice (A) can be eliminated because the narrator has no *fear* of clergymen. Choice (B) can be eliminated because it has nothing to do with the prediction. Choice (C) doesn't match the

prediction because the narrator is speaking to those who are anti-clergy, not illustrating his own *sense of dismay*. Eliminate this answer. Choice (D) mentions the *disapproval of clergymen* in the prediction, and the *reader* in the answer choice is supported by the narrator's use of *you*. Choice (D) is best supported by the text and is the correct answer.

5. **C** This question asks about *Moore's behavior*. The passage talks more about Helstone, but there is evidence in the passage to predict the answer for this question. In the first paragraph, the narrator says that both of the men knew that there were those who would have had *great pleasure in shooting either of [them]* and that the two men were *elate* with this knowledge. The final paragraph says *you would expect... they would converse amicably. Oh no!* and then goes on to say that Moore *liked to infuriate Helstone*. It's clear from the text that Moore likes to fight and pick fights, so the correct answer should reflect this. Choice (A) is deceptive: It contains words seen in the text but describes Helstone rather than Moore. Eliminate it. Choice (B) also describes Helstone rather than Moore, so it can be eliminated. Choice (C) is a solid paraphrase of the prediction, so keep it. Choice (D) is deceptive because the word *superiority* seems to match *reign supreme*, but that answer choice does not match the prediction. Eliminate it. This leaves (C) as the correct answer.

6. **C** The question asks how Helstone might be described and refers to the narrator's acknowledgement of *a certain evil* in the third paragraph. Look in the third paragraph to see that the narrator's larger point about Helstone is that he is not temperamentally suited to being a priest and *should have been a soldier*. On the whole, he is described positively, though some of his limitations are noted. Eliminate (A), as in the text he is described as *a man almost without sympathy*. Eliminate (B) because Helstone is not a soldier. Keep (C), as Helstone is described as *conscientious, true to principle* and *honourable*. Eliminate (D) because its tone is negative and there's no evidence to support such an extreme characterization. The correct answer is (C).

7. **C** The question asks for the best evidence to support the correct answer to the previous question. Look for the answer choice that refers to lines used for the prediction for Q6. Choices (A) and (B) can be eliminated, as those lines come from the first and second paragraphs, respectively. Choices (C) and (D) are both from the third paragraph and both describe Helstone, but (C) contains the list of characteristics that best supports that Helstone is a righteous citizen. Since the lines in (C) were useful in making the prediction in question 6, eliminate (D). Choice (C) is the best answer.

8. **A** This question asks the effect of comparing Helstone to a Cossack. To answer this question, look at the comparison in context. The narrator says, "*Nor will I curse Helstone, clerical Cossack as he was. Yet he was cursed....*" Thus, being a Cossack is something bad. Choice (A) could be true, so keep it for now. Choice (B) refers to an event, rather than a person; eliminate it. Choice (C) refers to two men, rather than only Helstone; eliminate it. Choice (D) refers to an action, rather than a person; eliminate it. The only remaining answer is (A), so select it. Choice (A) is the correct answer.

9. **C** This question asks how the men found each other's company sometimes. To answer this question, read paragraph 4 and find that they *chafed each other's moods*, had a *frequent bone of contention*, and that one *liked to infuriate* the other. There is no evidence that they found each other *intolerable*, only that they annoyed each other. Eliminate (A). Choice (B) is irrelevant to the text, so it can be eliminated. Choice (C) matches the idea that they annoyed each other, so don't eliminate it. Choice (D) can be eliminated because it's a positive word, and the two men were not *comforting* each other. Choice (C) is appropriately negative for the passage. Choice (C) is the correct answer.

10. **C** This question asks for the best evidence for the answer to Q9. To answer this question, start by eliminating choices that refer to the wrong paragraph: (A) refers to paragraph 2 and (B) refers to paragraph 3; eliminate both. Choices (C) and (D) refer to paragraph 4; compare them. Since (C) contains the phrase *chafed each other's moods*, keep it. While (D) does mention a difference between the two men that could potentially cause trouble, the lines themselves don't show that trouble. Eliminate (D). Choice (C) is the correct answer.

11. **B** This question asks about the main purpose of the passage. Because this is a general question, save it until the end of the question set. Choice (A) is the opposite of the text, so it can be eliminated. Choice (B) is possible, so keep it for now. Choice (C) is neutral, but the author of the passage definitely has a negative opinion about marketing education, so eliminate it. Choice (D) incorrectly states that the passage's focus is on *evaluating statistics,* so eliminate it. Choice (B) is the correct answer.

12. **B** The question asks about the *concession* the author makes to the view that people are *consumers in the marketplace of life.* That means the author disagrees with the view, but the correct answer will agree with it. Because this question is the first in a paired set, the answers to Q13 can be used to help with POE. Begin with Q13 and see if any connections can be made to answers in Q12. Choice (13A) says that every aspect of life has *cash value* and *can be purchased.* While this does agree with the view presented in the question, these lines do not support any of the answers for Q12, so (13A) can be eliminated. Choice (13B) says *this scenario may be appropriate for the sale of shoes....* This agrees with the idea that people are consumers, and these lines support (12B). Connect these two answers. Choice (13C) might initally seem to support (12C) because of the mention of *students*, *price*, and *customers*, but a careful reading shows these two answers don't actually support each other. Eliminate (13C). Choice (13D) talks about the students wanting *to be entertained*, which isn't mentioned in any of the choices for Q12. Eliminate (13D). Without support from Q13, (12A), (12C), and (12D) can be eliminated. Choices (12B) and (13B) are the correct answers.

13. **B** (See explanation above.)

14. **D** This question asks what *assume* means in context. To answer this question, find the word and read a few lines above and below. Substitute an alternate word or phrase that makes sense in the context, then compare that word to the answer choices. A phrase like "take on" could work well.

Choices (A), (B), and (C) all refer possible definitions of assume, but none of them fit the context of the passage, so eliminate them. Choice (D) fits the prediction and is the correct answer.

15. **A** This question asks about the main purpose of the fourth paragraph. To answer it, carefully read the fourth paragraph and determine why the author included it in the passage. In the paragraph, the author translates the educational experience into economic terms, presenting the idea that *achieving some sort of advantage is considered…essential to beating the competition.* He goes on to explain how cheating and *dubious maneuvers*, though *unfortunate*, have become rampant because that is an easier way to achieve success. Choice (A) matches the text because the author does explain the *logic of an attitude* (cheating) and he does disagree with that attitude. Choice (B) is something the author may agree with outside of the text, but that's not what the fourth paragraph is about. Eliminate it. Choice (C) has nothing to do with the paragraph and can be eliminated. Although he doesn't agree with cheating, the fourth paragraph does not argue against cheating, so (D) can be eliminated. Choice (A) is the correct answer.

16. **C** This question asks what *enticing* means in context. To answer this question, find the word and read a few lines above and below. Substitute a word or phrase that makes sense in the context, then compare that word or phrase to the answer choices. A word like "attractive" could work well. Choices (A), (B), and (D) do not fit this prediction; eliminate them. Choice (C) matches this prediction; select it. Choice (C) is the correct answer.

17. **B** This question asks for the best support for a particular claim (that schools have already begun to incorporate some facets of the popular marketplace into their educational materials). To answer this question, consider whether and how each answer choice would affect that claim. Choice (A) describes what administrators *must* do, rather than what they have already begun to do, so eliminate it. Choice (B) describes something that *has become normative*, so this could fit; keep it. Choice (C) is in the present tense and has the wrong tone, so eliminate it. Choice (D) refers to courses that administrators *have begun to promote*, so keep it. Now compare (B) and (D) to each other: (B) mentions a *proliferation of degrees and courses*, while (D) mentions *courses*. Choice (B) connects more specifically to the *advertising consultants* mentioned in paragraph 5. Choice (B) is the correct answer.

18. **A** This question asks what the main idea of the last paragraph is. To answer this question, read the paragraph and make a prediction of what that summary will be, such as the following: education is hurt when it is treated like a commodity. Look for answers that match this prediction, and eliminate answers that express the main idea of some other paragraph, the main idea of the entire passage, or a secondary idea of the last paragraph. Choice (A) contains both ideas from the prediction (education hurt, treated like a commodity), so keep it. Choice (B) is true, but is a secondary point in the last paragraph. This answer is too narrow, so it can be eliminated. Choice (C) is tempting, as it has the correct tone, but *unimportant* is not the same as *hurt*; eliminate it. Choice (D) is deceptive, using concepts from the last paragraph to say something that the paragraph itself does not say; eliminate it. Choice (A) is the correct answer.

19. **C** This question asks what statement is supported by the data in the graph. To answer this question, look at the graph and notice any obvious trends, such as the following: all three lines show a positive increase, a small one with overall consumer prices and a big one with college textbooks and tuition and fees. Choice (A) mentions an increase, so keep it. Choice (B) says there is no increase, so eliminate it. Choice (C) mentions an increase, so keep it. Choice (D) says there is a decrease, so eliminate it. Now compare (A) and (C). Choice (A) does not match the graph because the line does not rise consistently, and (C) matches the information in the graph. Choice (C) is the correct answer.

20. **D** This question asks during which period the difference was largest between college tuition and fees and overall consumer prices. To answer this question, look at the graph and see that this was in 2012. Choice (D) is the correct answer.

21. **A** This question asks what idea in the passage is most directly supported by the graph. To answer this question, note that the graph is measuring prices. Now eliminate answers that do not concern prices, which are (B), (C), and (D). Choice (A) is the correct answer.

22. **A** This question asks about what the authors of the passage indicate about the addition of nutrients to food. This topic is covered throughout the whole passage, so there's no specific window to look for the answer. Notice that it's the first in a paired set, though, so this question can be done in tandem with Q23. Look at the lines given in the answers to Q23 first and see if they support any answer choices in Q22. Any answer choices that neither support nor have support can be eliminated. Start with (23A). The lines say that processed food contributes to *both food security... and nutrition security*. This could support (22A) because contributing to food and nutrition security is a helpful impact. Connect those two answers. Choice (23B) says that processed foods *are nutritionally important* and then goes on to ask how we can *enhance the contribution to...nutritional...and food security*. This refers to the securities mentioned in (23A), so connect this to (22A) as well. Choice (23C) presents a contrast between *limiting processed foods* and *encouraging best available food options*. These lines don't support any of the answers for Q22, so (23C) can be eliminated. Choice (23D) mentions a *disadvantage* in that the techniques *are poorly understood*. These lines may initially seem to support (22C), but there's no indication from the text that they *may require further investigation*. Even though it might make sense that something poorly understood would need further investigation, that's not in the text. Eliminate (23D). Without any support from Q23, (22B), (22C), and (22D) can be eliminated. There are two answer choices connected to (22A), so now go back and carefully reread each of the support lines. Choice (23A) is a statement of fact, clearly showing the *helpful impact*. Although (23B) also mentions the same ideas, those lines ask about how to enhance the contributions, rather than stating them as fact. Eliminate (23B). Choices (22A) and (23A) are the best answers.

23. **A** (See explanation above.)

24. **D** This question asks about food enrichment methods, which are mentioned throughout the passage. Save this question until the others have been answered. Choice (A) can be eliminated because there is no information about how the food enrichment is done. Choice (B) can be eliminated because there is no mention of *employment opportunities*. *Thiamin* is mentioned in the fourth paragraph, so don't eliminate (C). Choice (D) can be supported by lines 37–38, which say that a disadvantage of the processing techniques is that they *are poorly understood*. Compare (C) and (D). Although thiamin is mentioned, there is no indication that processed foods are the *leading source* of thiamin. Choice (D) is directly supported by the text and is the correct answer.

25. **A** This question asks what *grasp* means in context. To answer this question, find the word and read a few lines above and below. Substitute a word or phrase that makes sense in the context, then compare that word or phrase to the answer choices. A word like "understand" could work well. Choice (A) matches that prediction; keep it. Choices (B) and (C) are definitions for *grasp*, but they don't fit the context of the passage. They can be eliminated. Choice (D) refers to physical grasping; eliminate it. Choice (A) is the correct answer.

26. **D** This question asks what Passage 2's reference to "Big Food" suggests about global food systems. To answer this question, see what the passage explicitly says: that a few companies rule global food systems. Choices (A) and (C) do not mention companies; eliminate them. Choice (B) refers to single companies that serve individual regions, and (D) refers to a few companies that dominate. Choice (D) most clearly matches what the text actually says; (D) is the correct answer.

27. **B** This question asks what profit margins and price/cost surpluses have in common in Passage 2. To answer this question, read paragraph 6, which mentions both things in a sentence that states that the main goals of these companies is to increase profits. So the profit margins and price/cost surpluses must have this in common: the goal of increasing profits. Choice (A) is not supported by this prediction; eliminate it. Choice (B) could be true; keep it. Choice (C) could be true; keep it. Choice (D) goes beyond what the passage says; the passage does not indicate that they are BEST increased by expanding markets; eliminate it. Compare (B) and (C). Choice (B) refers to the concerns of companies, and (C) refers to economic theory in general. The passage never treated economic theory in general, so (C) is too broad to answer the question. Choice (B) is the correct answer.

28. **B** This question asks what effect the possibilities mentioned in Passage 2 have. To answer this question, read the relevant selection in the context of the paragraph. The passage states that industry can only make profits by doing things that are not good nutritionally. Choice (A) uses words from the paragraph, but suggests the opposite of what the text says; eliminate it. Choice (B) supports the meaning of the last paragraph; keep it. Choices (C) and (D) do not fit the text; eliminate them. Choice (B) is the correct answer.

29. **B** This question asks about the main purpose of both passages. To answer this question, start by eliminating choices that are true for one passage only, or are not true for either passage.

Choice (A) is too specific and fits Passage 1 only; eliminate it. Choice (B) could be true; keep it. Choice (C) is too specific and fits some of Passage 1 only; eliminate it. Choice (D) is also too specific to be a main idea; eliminate it. Choice (B) is the correct answer.

30. **D**   This question asks how Passages 1 and 2 are related to each other. To answer this question, consider the overall impression of both passages: Passage 1 says that American food processing is great, and Passage 2 says that global food systems are problematic. This does not involve *underlying processes* and there is no *solution* in Passage 1, so eliminate (A). Passage 2 does not present a *plan* relating to *processes* presented in Passage 1, so eliminate (B). Each passage seems to have an opinion, rather than *an objective perspective*, so eliminate (C). Choice (D) says that Passage 1 embraces a system, which matches the prediction, and that Passage 2 explores the problematic nature of a system, which also matches the prediction. Choice (D) is the correct answer.

31. **A**   This question asks what the authors of both passages would most likely agree on. To answer this question, eliminate choices that fit only one passage (or neither). Choice (A) mentions adequate nutrition, which both passages examined, so this is possible, even though only Passage 2 concerned global food systems; keep it for now. Nothing matching (B) is mentioned in either passage; eliminate it. Almost nothing matching (C) is mentioned in either passage, although Passage 1 discusses *suspicion*; eliminate (C). Choice (D) is absent from Passage 2, and Passage 1 indicates the opposite to be true. Choice (A) is the correct answer.

32. **C**   This question asks what in Passage 2 matches what is said in a specific part of Passage 1. To answer this question, first review the specific part of Passage 1, and note that it concerns *processing* and *nutritional content*. Choice (A) has processing, but no nutrition; eliminate it. Choice (B) has no processing and no nutrition; eliminate it. Choice (C) has processing and nutrition; keep it for now. Choice (D) has processing and mention of *healthier foods*; keep it for now. To decide between (C) and (D), review the specific part of Passage 1, and note that it focuses on processing and nutrition not necessarily correlating, which means that they might be independent of each other. Choice (C) states that processing *can improve nutritional content*, but that most processing actually serves to *reduce nutritional quality*. Choice (D) states that industry could make healthier foods. Choice (D) seems to point in one direction, whereas (C) points in two directions, which better fits the prediction. Choice (C) is the correct answer.

33. **A**   This question asks what the central problem is regarding Indiana's photo law. To answer this question, select an answer choice that fits several paragraphs and eliminate answer choices that fit only one paragraph (or none of them). Choice (A) fits the last sentence of paragraph 1, as well as several parts of the passage afterwards; keep it for now. Choice (B) is true, but it is only mentioned in paragraphs 2 and 5. Choice (C) is true, but it is only mentioned in paragraph 4; eliminate (C). Choice (D) is only mentioned in paragraph 7, so can be eliminated for that reason; it is also inaccurate, since the Supreme Court took a *restricted* view, not a wide one. Between (A) and (B), (A) is closer to the main idea of the entire passage. Choice (A) is the correct answer.

34. **C** This question asks what the phrase *remarkably enough* emphasizes about the Supreme Court. To answer this question, find the phrase in the first paragraph and read carefully for context. The author uses the phrase to indicate something notable or out-of-the-ordinary. Choice (A) can be eliminated because there is no evidence of *complete disregard* for the Constitution. The passage doesn't suggest *ignorance* of the Bill of Rights, just that it was surprising that the Supreme Court didn't use language that was previously very important. Eliminate (B). Choice (C) matches the prediction, so keep it. Choice (D) is irrelevant to the prediction, so eliminate it. Choice (C) is the correct answer.

35. **B** This question asks about a claim that casts doubt on the recent Supreme Court decision. Because this is the first in a paired set, use the answers from Q36 to work through answers for Q35. Eliminate any answer choices that don't provide support for other answers. Choice (36A) gives a specific details about Indiana's law, which aligns with the Supreme Court decision to uphold voter ID law. Eliminate (36A). Choice (36B) is an example of a specific individual who disagrees with the law, which could cast a small amount of doubt on the decision. There is no corresponding answer in Q35, though, so (36B) can be eliminated. Choice (36C) mentions that the Supreme Court agreed with the man who challenged the law. That would cast doubt on the decision, and supports (35B). Connect those two answers. Choice (36D) is specific details about the process of getting an ID, which has nothing to do with whether or not the Supreme Court decision is a good one. Eliminate (36D). Without support, (35A), (35C), and (35D) can all be eliminated. This leaves (35B) and (36C) as the correct answers.

36. **C** (See explanation above.)

37. **D** This question asks what *force* means in context. To answer this question, find the word *force*, read a few lines above and below, and insert another word that would fit based on the context. Something like "effect" could work. Choices (A) and (B) refer to other meanings of force that don't match the context of the passage, and (C) is part of the term "force field." Choice (D) matches the prediction exactly, so pick it. Choice (D) is the correct answer.

38. **A** This question asks what *have* means in context. To answer this question, find the word *have*, read a few lines above and below, and insert another word that would fit based on the context. Something like "believe" could work. Choice (A) could fit; keep it for now. Choices (B), (C), and (D) do not fit this prediction, so eliminate them. Choice (A) is the correct answer.

39. **B** This question asks what the word *exclusionary* is used for. To answer this question, read in context to see that it refers to a state law. Choice (A) refers to a difference that is not the issue here. Choice (B) fits the prediction. Choice (C) could be true, but is not what the word in question is used for. Choice (D) does not fit anything in the passage. Choice (B) is the correct answer.

40. **C** This question asks what the authors claim (*contend*) the present-day Supreme Court has done regarding voter-ID laws. To answer this question, go back to the passage and see what is said about the present-day Supreme Court. Choice (A) refers to the past Supreme Court, so

eliminate it. Choice (B) is deceptive. Although the phrase *heavier burden* is in the text, it does not refer to the Supreme Court. That phrase refers to the burden on Indianans to get paperwork completed. Choice (C) is supported by paragraph 7, which states that the Supreme Court ignored the 24th Amendment and relied on the 14th. Choice (D) recalls paragraph 9 but is extreme: The passage does not say that the Supreme Court has *refused* to explain its decision. Choice (C) is the correct answer.

41. **C** This question asks for the best evidence for the answer to Q40. To answer this question, simply refer back to the lines used to answer Q40. Choice (C) is from paragraph 7, is relevant, and it is the correct answer.

42. **B** This question asks what contrast the eighth paragraph primarily makes. To answer this question, read the eighth paragraph and note the contrast, rewording if necessary. Something like "considering the Constitution vs. not considering it" would work. Choices (A), (C), and (D) are not mentioned in paragraph 8; eliminate them. Choice (B) could fit as a summary of the prediction: The Constitution is the historical rule, and the anomaly is the current Court's not considering it. Choice (B) is the correct answer.

43. **D** This question asks for the main purpose of the first paragraph. To answer this question, read the first paragraph, then summarize what the author uses this first paragraph to do. Several sentences indicate that the amount of ice is shrinking at a rate much faster than what was initially predicted. Look for an answer that matches this idea. Only one sentence talks about the ice reforming, so (A) is too specific; eliminate (A). Although the size is compared to a U.S. state in this paragraph, that's not the paragraph's main purpose; eliminate (B). Choice (C) may be tempting due to the first half, but it is flawed due to the second half; eliminate (C). Choice (D) fits, since the trend of the ice melting is occurring much faster than scientists originally predicted. Choice (D) is the correct answer.

44. **C** This question asks for the meaning of *projected* in context. To answer this question, find the word and read a few lines above and below. Substitute a word or phrase that makes sense in the context, then compare that word or phrase to the answer choices. A word like "thought" could work well. Compare this prediction to the answer choices. Choice (A) is a different meaning of *projected*, and (B) and (D) do not fit the prediction. Choice (C) fits the prediction and is the correct answer.

45. **B** This question asks why Naam says the Earth's tilt is significant. To answer this question, read paragraph 2, which says that the tilt puts the Arctic in complete darkness or complete sunlight in different seasons. The correct answer will have something to do with the tilt affecting sunlight and darkness in different seasons. Choices (A) and (D) are each only true for one season; eliminate them. Choice (C) is inaccurate, and (B) fits the prediction. Choice (B) is the correct answer.

46. **B** This question asks for the best evidence for the answer to Q45. Since the evidence came from paragraph two, look at where the answer choices come from. Choices (A), (C), and (D) are

from the wrong paragraph, so eliminate them. Choice (B) is from paragraph two, and matches the prediction for Q45, so (B) is the correct answer.

47. **C** This question asks for the meaning of *pace* in context. To answer this question, find the word and read a few lines above and below. Substitute a word or phrase that makes sense in the context, then compare that word or phrase to the answer choices. A word like "rate" could work well. Compare this prediction to the answer choices. Choice (A) refers to a different meaning of *pace*; eliminate it. Choices (B) and (D) do not fit the prediction; (C) does. Choice (C) is the correct answer.

48. **A** This question asks about a reasonable inference that can be made about *climate scientists* based on the passage. There is no line reference, and climate scientists appear throughout the passage. Notice that this is the first question in a paired set, so use the best evidence answers in the next question to help with POE. Start with the answers to Q49 and eliminate any that don't support answers in Q48. Choice (49A) states that *opinions differ substantially... among climate scientists.* It's not clear from the line what those opinions are, but the answers in Q48 do have *agree* and *disagree* options, so these lines could work. Don't eliminate (49A). Choice (49B) mentions a paper in which *multiple scientists* agree about the possibility of *an ice-free summer.* No disagreement or uncertainty is mentioned, so these lines can't support any answer choices for Q48. Eliminate (49B). Both (49C) and (49D) mention specific scientists by name. Neither of those choices is broad enough to support any answers for Q48, so they can both be eliminated. This leaves (49A), but there's no clear connection to any of the answers in Q48. Go back to the text and read the window for this line to determine what the scientists' differing opinions are. Just before that line reference, the text discusses the amount of ice and what would happen if it continued to melt at its current pace. Therefore, the differing opinions must have something to do with the rate of ice melt. Eliminate (48C) and (48D). Compare the remaining two choices. Choice (48A) correctly matches the information in the text. Choices (48A) and (49A) are the correct answers.

49. **A** (See explanation above.)

50. **A** This question asks how the graph depicts the general trend in the area of Arctic sea ice. To answer this question, look at the graph and draw a line that best fits the overall trend. The amount of sea ice overall goes down over time, with some fluctuations up and down. Choice (A) could fit; keep it. Choice (B) could be tempting, but it is not a geometric series; eliminate it. Choice (C) exaggerates the changes, which are not dramatic; eliminate it. Choice (D) is not supported, since the graph does not show that the shrinkage is temporary. Choice (A) is the correct answer.

51. **C** This question asks which concept is supported by the passage and by the information in the graph. To answer this question, consider both the passage, which indicates that the ice is shrinking and will be gone at some point in the future, and the graph, which shows the amount of ice dropping over a 30-year period. Choices (B) and (D) are contradicted by both the passage and the graph; eliminate them. Choice (A) is possible, but is not necessarily true

based on information in the passage or the graph. Choice (C) has the best support from both the passage and the graph. Choice (C) is the correct answer.

52. **D** This question asks how the graph supports the author's point that Arctic ice is receding. To answer this question, go back to the text to see the specific points made by the author, then see how the graph relates to those points. Although (A) fits the text, it does not fit the graph; eliminate it. Choice (B) is mentioned in the passage as a possibility, but this is not a point the author makes; thus, eliminate it. Choice (C) does not accurately depict the graph; eliminate it. Choice (D) fits both the author's point and the graph. Choice (D) is the correct answer.

Section 2: Writing and Language

1. **D** Choose DELETE unless there is some very good reason not to. In this case, (A), (B), and (C) add unnecessary transitions to a sentence that already contains a transition in the word *As*. Additionally, *yet*, *and*, and *for* are all FANBOYS, and when used with a comma, these words operate as Stop punctuation, which links only complete ideas. The phrase *As people become more sensitive to the idea of preserving certain ecosystems* is incomplete, so it cannot be followed by Stop punctuation. The best option is therefore to DELETE the underlined portion, as (D) suggests.

2. **D** The odd pairs of *human reacting* and *human reacts*, as in (A) and (B), can be eliminated because they do not make sense in this or any other context. The same can be said for (C), *human interacting*. Choice (D) presents the most viable option, *human interaction*, and is therefore the best answer.

3. **D** In order to choose an appropriate transition word, consider the ideas that must be linked. The idea that precedes the transition word reads as follows: *The central challenge of maintaining an ecosystem, especially by artificial means, is that ecosystems have a tendency to change, particularly with the dual influence of human interaction and a rapidly altering climate.* The idea that comes after the transition word reads as follows: *one career that has grown by leaps and bounds in the last fifty years is that of the soil conservationist.* These ideas agree with one another, especially given the first sentence's claim that people have *become more sensitive to the idea of preserving certain ecosystems.* Of the available transition words, the only one that signals agreement in this way is (D), *Therefore.*

4. **A** The question asks which answer most effectively sets up the subject of the paragraph, so start by figuring out the subject of the paragraph. This paragraph is primarily concerned with the role a soil conservationist might play in helping to *determine where it would be safest to build a dream house* in a *coastal area.* Choices (B) and (D) are not specific, so they can be eliminated. Choice (C) does not address the coastal region, so it too can be eliminated. Choice (A) mentions *building a beach house*, so it is the only choice that is adequately specific and germane to the topic of the paragraph.

5. **B** All four choices refer to the same idea, that of erosion, so the best answer will be the most concise. Choice (B), *erosion*, provides that conciseness because it expresses the idea in a single word.

6. **B** The items in a list must be consistent with one another. In this case, the first two items in the list are *collapsing* and *shifting*, so the only consistent option is (B), *deteriorating*. Choice (D) also contains this word, but this choice adds the unnecessary word *structures*. Choice (B) is therefore the correct answer.

7. **D** For long combination questions like this one, use POE on answers that do not make sense. Choice (A) can be eliminated because it says that soil conservationists *are ways of preserving land*, when in fact the soil conservationists *provide* these ways. Choice (B) can be eliminated because the phrase *each one of them* is ambiguous. Choice (C) is awkwardly phrased because of the excessive phrases *in these cases* and *a variety of different*. Choice (D) is therefore the best of the available answers because it states the idea directly and without excess or ambiguity.

8. **B** The phrase *farming techniques* could be clarified by the proposed information, so that information should be added. The mention of *no-till farming* does not demonstrate the advantages of the method, however, so (A) can be eliminated. Choice (B) is more effective: *no-till farming* and *terrace methods* provide specific examples of the *farming methods* mentioned in the sentence.

9. **C** The subject of the underlined verb is *farmlands*, which is plural. Choices (A) and (D) contain singular verbs, so these choices can be eliminated. The word *which* in (B) creates a sentence fragment, so this too can be eliminated. Choice (C) is the correct answer: It contains a verb that agrees with the non-underlined subject and does not add unnecessary words.

10. **A** Choice (A) seems good, but check the other answer choices to see if one is better. Choice (D) is offensive to people living in the Midwest, so it should be eliminated. Choices (A), (B), and (C) each express similar ideas, so the best answer will be the most concise and the most consistent with the phrasing of the other items in the list, *deserts of the Southwest* and *forests of the Northwest*. In this case, the most concise of the answers is (A), *plains*.

11. **A** The passage as a whole is concerned with describing the work of soil conservationists and the importance of the work these conservationists do. Choice (A) encapsulates that idea effectively. Choice (B) undermines the importance of soil conservationists, and (C) gives a value judgment that the passage has not discussed and that is unfair to one group of soil conservationists. Choice (D) is too concerned with a particular ecosystem. Choice (A) is therefore the best answer.

12. **C** In order to choose an appropriate transition word, consider the ideas that must be linked. The idea that precedes the transition word reads as follows: *There may be some controversy as to who earns these awards in many cases*. The idea that comes after the transition word reads as follows: *there can be no doubt that the winners are always accomplished in their fields and have contributed something to their disciplines and the world at large*. These ideas contrast, especially given the words *controversy* and *no doubt*, and the only word that effectively signals this contrast is (C), *however*.

13. **A** Use POE to eliminate words that don't belong in the context. Choice (C) creates an ambiguous pronoun in its use of the word *it*. Choice (D) anticipates an example, but no example is forthcoming. Choice (B) cuts out these words, but it creates a new problem—the phrase *the world at large* now has no clear place within the sentence. The best answer is therefore (A), which establishes that the work of Nobel recipients is significant to their disciplines *and* to the world at large.

14. **D** If there is no good reason to add new information, don't add it. This new information about Watson and Crick is interesting, but it does not belong in this paragraph, which focuses on the Nobel Peace Prize. Choices (A) and (B) can be eliminated, then, because they suggest that the sentence should be added. Choice (C) correctly states that the sentence should not be added, but its reason is untrue. Choice (D) better captures the reason the sentence should not be added: The sentence does not contribute in a significant way to the main idea of the paragraph.

15. **B** As the verb *see* indicates, this sentence should be in the present tense, eliminating (A). Choice (D) can be eliminated because there is no indication that multiple committees give the award. Choices (B) and (C) express essentially the same idea, but (B) does so in a more direct way that avoids the awkward *-ing* construction in (C). Choice (B) is therefore the best of the available answers.

16. **A** This sentence refers to a *common goal* belonging to some group—in other words, *their common goal*. The form given in (B) and (C), *they're*, is the contraction *they are*, which has no place in this sentence. Choices (B) and (C) can be eliminated. Choice (D) can also be eliminated because it contains a semicolon, which cannot be used with anything other than complete ideas. The idea *to make the world a better place* is not a complete idea, so the semicolon cannot punctuate this sentence. Only (A) can work, as it uses the correct form of the pronoun and punctuation that is appropriate to the context. A colon must come after a complete idea, but what comes after it can be either complete or incomplete.

17. **B** Unless there is a reason to use a comma, don't use one. In this case, the word *King's* is needed to make the sentence complete. Because it is essential to the completeness of the sentence, it should not be offset with any commas. Choice (B) is therefore the best of the answers.

18. **D** The question asks for a supporting detail that is most similar to the detail already in the paragraph. This sentence mentions *people of color seeking civil rights*, but it also mentions that King's influence *spanned the globe*. Choice (A) does not fit with these large ideas, (B) is not adequately specific, and (C) undermines King's importance. Only (D) adequately fulfills the question's requirement of a *specific supporting detail* and ties this sentence to the *non-violent campaign* mentioned in the previous sentence.

19. **B** When faced with long, confusing sentences, use POE aggressively. In this case, the incorrect answers—(A), (C), and (D)—all create misplaced or dangling modifiers. Choice (C), for example, contains the modifier *when it was awarded*, but that modifier seems to be describing *first-year President Barack Obama*, which does not make sense. Choice (B) is the only choice that is free of any such incoherence and is therefore the best answer.

20. **D**   Choice (A) changes the punctuation but does not combine the sentences in a meaningful way. Choice (B) introduces the transition word *while*, which does not create the desired contrast between the two sentences. Choice (C) introduces the transition *for*, which makes it seem that King is famous *because* Bunche was the first. Only (D) is truly effective at combining the ideas, stating that King was the most famous *yet* Bunche was the first African-American to win the prize.

21. **C**   Use the other similarly phrased items in the sentence to determine the best form of the underlined portion. These other items are *the 1949 Armistice Agreements* and *the 1948 Arab-Israeli conflict*. The choice that best preserves this format is (C).

22. **D**   Martin Luther King, Jr., is discussed in paragraph 3. Paragraph 5 begins with the idea that *King may be the most famous African-American recipient of the Nobel Peace Prize*, thus suggesting that paragraph 5 must come after paragraph 3. This eliminates (B) and (C). Choice (A) can also be eliminated because paragraph 4 must come at the end—it describes a recent recipient of the Nobel Peace Prize and offers some concluding remarks. The best placement for paragraph 5, therefore, would be directly after paragraph 3, as (D) suggests.

23. **A**   The first two sentences of this paragraph establish a contrast between the *most obvious facet* and *What many do not understand quite as well*. These two phrases require a contrasting transition, so *however* in (A) is the best response.

24. **D**   Since all four answer choices express the same idea, choose the shortest that does not introduce any grammatical errors. In this case, the shortest answer is (D), *analogous functions*, which accomplishes what the other answers do in the fewest words.

25. **B**   The idea given in the passage, *Because of the heavy output from this wide variety of industrial sources, the earth's atmosphere is bombarded*, is complete grammatically. However, the meaning of the word *bombarded* is not entirely clear. The proposed insertion could clarify the word *bombarded*, so it should be added. The insertion is not helpful in defining anything about the *Amazonian rainforest*, which is not mentioned in the passage, so (A) can be eliminated. Choice (B), however, states the value of the inserted idea and correctly states that the idea should be inserted. Choice (B) is therefore the correct answer.

26. **A**   The underlined pronoun refers back to CO_2, which is singular. The pronoun should be consistent with this singular noun, thus eliminating (C) and (D). (In fact, *there* is not a pronoun at all.) Of the remaining two pronouns, *it's* is the contraction *it is*, and *its* provides a possessive pronoun. This phrase should read *it is always absorbing heat energy*, indicating the need for the contraction given in (A).

27. **D**   According to the graph, carbon-dioxide parts per million have increased with almost linear consistency. Temperature changes have also increased, though in an irregular pattern. Choice (A) can be eliminated for stating that the two curves are *exactly the same*. Choice (B) states that

temperatures have not increased at all, when the graph shows that they have. Choice (C) is untrue. Only (D) is consistent with the information in the graph and is therefore the correct answer.

28. **C** Choose the word that best fits the style and tone of the passage. Choices (A) and (D) are too informal for the tone of the passage. Choice (B) is also a bit informal and overstates the idea of the sentence. Only (C) works in the context in a way that is consistent with the passage's style and tone.

29. **C** This long sentence may seem to require additional punctuation or linking words, but pay attention to the verb *would*, which the answer choices do not change. The subject of this verb is the word *number*, from *the number of trees required to offset the emissions of one modest coal plant operating in a small city in Connecticut*. Quite a long phrase! Even so, that phrase should not be broken up by any punctuation, nor should the subject and verb be split by transition words such as those found in (A) and (B). Choice (D) adds the word *it*, which stands in for the subject *number* again, but has no transition. Only (C) appropriately leaves out extra words and punctuation.

30. **B** Use the context. If this is an actual quotation, a second set of punctuation marks should appear at the end of the quote. No second set appears, thus eliminating (A). In fact, this sentence does not need any punctuation at all—the comma in (C) and the long dash in (D) break up the flow of the sentence unnecessarily. When there is no need for punctuation, don't add it! Choice (B) is the best of the available answers.

31. **A** The main differences among the answer choices have to do with the pronouns. The word *temper* remains essentially the same. The choice is instead between *those polluting behaviors* in (A); *them* in (B) and (D); and *it* in (C). Pronouns are concise substitutes, but they are never as precise as specific nouns. Therefore, when, as in this question, the answers list three pronouns and one specific noun, choose the specific noun. Choice (A) contains that specific noun, and this answer provides the best option because there is no room for ambiguity.

32. **B** The underlined portion is offset as unnecessary information, which is included to clarify the statement made in this passage about the *longer process* of getting the earth's carbon levels *back to appropriate ranges*. As such, the whole phrase, *or series of processes*, should be offset by commas (as it is in this sentence), thus eliminating (C) and (D). Choice (A) has too many commas, splitting up the phrase unnecessarily. Choice (B) is therefore the best of the available answers.

33. **C** Use the language of the sentence. The first word is *This*, which refers to something that could *go a long way toward reforesting the Amazon rainforest*. As such, the previous sentence must contain some plan or course or action. Sentence 2 provides exactly that in its mention of the trees that could be placed on the *list of threatened species*. The proposed sentence should therefore be placed after sentence 2 and before sentence 3, as (C) indicates.

34. **B** Look at the changes among the answer choices. There are three choices with transition words and one without. For the sake of conciseness, if the sentence can stand without the transition

words, don't include them! In this case, the sentence is complete without the transition words, so the best answer is (B).

35. **C** Read the question carefully. It asks for a sentence that best supports this sentence's claim. There's not a tremendous amount of context in this sentence, *Sometimes that influence is more literal—as in the case of those writers who take marginal characters from earlier works.* Use POE. Choices (A) and (B) are irrelevant, so they can be eliminated. Choice (D) can also be eliminated because the word *it* creates ambiguity within the sentence. As a result, the best of the available answers is (C), which continues the thought established in the beginning of the sentence without creating new grammatical errors.

36. **B** On questions that test idioms and odd transitions words, use POE. Choice (A) can be eliminated because the phrase *just as* means "at that exact moment," which would not apply here. Choice (C) can be eliminated because this construction would imply that the story focuses *from* the interpretation, which does not make sense. Choice (D) can be eliminated because the word *it* in this context would be awkward and ambiguous. Only (B) remains, suggesting that *in* the story's interpretation, the characters act in a certain way.

37. **D** The key words in sentence 2 are *this alternate route*. Sentences 1 and 2 do not contain any mention of alternatives, but sentence 4 does with the words *rather than*. Sentence 4 describes how Milton's *Paradise Lost* was an alternate take on a biblical story, so the words *this alternate route* in sentence 2 must refer directly back to sentence 4, as (D) does.

38. **C** The words *particularly the great classics of the language* are offset in this sentence as unnecessary or parenthetical information. There are three ways to offset this information—with commas, dashes, or parentheses—so the underlined portion should have punctuation that is consistent with the rest of the sentence. The phrase *particularly the great classics of the language* is initially offset with a comma, so it should be concluded with a comma as well, as in (C).

39. **B** Choose a word that is consistent in style and tone with the rest of the passage. Use POE to eliminate words that don't make sense in the context, such as *overtake*, in (A). Choice (C) can also be eliminated because the word *manifest* means "to show or demonstrate," and one cannot *manifest a story*. Choice (D) may be unfamiliar (*ideate* means "to form an idea of"), but (B) works appropriately in the context and does not elevate the level of vocabulary in the context. Choice (B) is therefore the better answer, whatever the definition of *ideate* may be.

40. **B** To *adopt* is "to take on or assume," as an idea or a name. The word can also refer to taking on the legal guardianship of children. To *adapt* is "to suit to a new purpose" or "to modify." In this sentence, the latter definition applies, eliminating (C) and (D). Choice (A) can also be eliminated because the word *he* repeats the subject of the sentence unnecessarily. Choice (B) is therefore the best of the available answer choices.

41. **A** Although the answer choices are relatively short, this problem is testing a wide variety of concepts, so the most effective option is to use POE. Choice (B) creates a comma splice because

it makes the sentence's second idea, *he kills an anonymous Arab man for vague reasons*, into a complete idea. The sentence is written in the present tense, so (C) is incorrect as well. Choice (D) creates an ambiguous modifier, making the sentence sound as if *Camus's novel* is doing the *killing*. Only (A) remains as a viable answer, as it gives the correct tense and the pronoun *who* refers clearly back to *Meursault*.

42. **D** The word *deferent* means "respectful," and it takes the preposition *to*, so (A) can be eliminated. Choices (B) and (C) can also be eliminated because the word *different* always takes the preposition *from*. The word *than* is used for comparisons—for example, this apple is bigger *than* that apple. Because the word *different* is not used in this kind of comparison (can one thing be *differenter* than another?), it does not take the preposition *than* but rather *from*. Choice (D) is the only one of the answers that uses the correct preposition.

43. **D** If there is no good reason to add new information, don't add it. This new information about Franco-Algerian relations is interesting, but it does not *have* to be in this paragraph. Choices (A) and (B) can be eliminated because they say the sentence should be added. Choice (C) can also be eliminated because there is nothing in the passage to suggest that it is making a larger claim about the separation of literature and historical events. Choice (D) is therefore the best answer, correctly giving a viable reason for why the sentence should not be added.

44. **D** Choose DELETE unless there is a very good reason not to. In this case, (A) can be eliminated because *do not state* is redundant with the word *imply*. Choices (B) and (C) give information that is already implied in the phrase *all other texts*. The best option, therefore, is to DELETE the underlined portion, as (D) states.

Section 3: Math (No Calculator)

1. **A** The question involves Algebra and has numbers in the answers, so plug in the answers. Start with (B). Using the values given in (B), the first equation becomes $2(-1) + 3(-3) = -9$. Solve the left side of the equation to get $-2 - 9 = -9$ or $-11 = -9$. This isn't true, so eliminate (B). Whether to go up or down may not be clear, so just choose a direction. Using the values given in (A), the first equation becomes $2(-3) + 3(-1) = -9$. Solve the left side of the equation to get $-6 - 3 = -9$, or $-9 = -9$. That works, so plug the values into the second equation to get $-3 - (-1) = -2$. Solve the left side of the equation to get $-3 + 1 = -2$, and $-2 = -2$. Since the values given in (A) work in both equations, the correct answer is (A).

2. **C** The question gives an equation in terms of x and y and asks for an expression involving both. To solve this, plug in for one variable and solve for the other. Since there are two instances of the variable x in the equation, plug in for x. Let $x = 4$. Plug this into the equation to get $4 = 4(4 + y)$. Distribute the 4 to get $4 = 16 + 4y$. Subtract 16 from both sides to get $-12 = 4y$. Divide both sides by 4 to get $y = -3$. The question asks for $\frac{y}{x}$, which is $-\frac{3}{4}$. The answer is (C).

3. **B** The question involves multiple triangles and ratios. This is often an indication that the question involves similar triangles. The question gives the ratio of the lengths of $\overline{ST}$ and $\overline{SU}$. Since these two segments are sides of triangles PST and QSU, respectively, determine whether these two triangles are similar. All that is needed to prove that two triangles are similar is to find two pairs of congruent corresponding angles. Since both triangles have a right angle, there is one pair. Also, the question states that triangle PQR is isosceles with $PR = QR$. In an isosceles triangle, equal angles are opposite equal sides, so $\angle P \cong \angle Q$. Thus, triangles PST and QSU have a second pair of congruent corresponding angles and are similar. Therefore, all corresponding sides have the same ratio. The question asks for the length of $\overline{SQ}$, which is opposite the right angle. Since $\overline{PS}$ is also opposite a right angle, $\overline{PS}$ and $\overline{SQ}$ are corresponding. Therefore, their lengths are in a ratio of 5:3. On any ratio question, use the ratio box to keep track of the parts of a total and the actual numbers. Draw a 3 × 3 table, and label the columns $\overline{PS}$, $\overline{SQ}$, and $\overline{PQ}$, respectively. The top row of a ratio box is the ratio, so fill in the ratio with 5 under $\overline{PS}$ and 3 under $\overline{SQ}$. The bottom row is for actual numbers. Since the actual length of $\overline{PQ}$ is 64, fill in 64 in the third row under $\overline{PQ}$. The result is below.

$\overline{PS}$	$\overline{SQ}$	$\overline{PQ}$
5	3	
		64

The numbers in the top row form an addition equation, so add 3 and 5 to get 3 + 5 = 8 and fill in 8 in the top row under $\overline{QR}$. Each column in the ratio box forms a multiplication equation. Since 8 × 8 = 64, fill in the middle row under $\overline{PQ}$ with 8. This is the multiplier for all parts of the ratio, so fill in 8's across the middle row.

$\overline{PS}$	$\overline{SQ}$	$\overline{PQ}$
5	3	8
8	8	8
		64

The question asks for the length of $\overline{SQ}$. Multiply the ratio number for $\overline{SQ}$, which is 3, by the multiplier of 8 to get an actual length of 24. The answer is (B).

4. **D** Use Process of Elimination. Profit = Revenue − Expenses. According to the question, profit = $4cd - 200$. Therefore, the expression $4cd$ must be related to the revenue the chocolate-covered banana stand brings in. Since c represents the number of expected customers, and d is the number of days, the 4 must be related to revenue dollars. Eliminate (A) and (C) since neither of these answers is related to dollars. The question does not say that the price of bananas increases on any given day, so it's safe to assume that the price of a chocolate-covered banana remains the same irrespective of the day it is bought. Therefore, eliminate (B). The correct answer is (D).

5. **A** According to the question, 700 coffee stores existed in 2003, which is one-half of the number of coffee stores that were added from 2004 to 2014. Therefore, $2 \times 700 = 1{,}400$ stores were added from 2004 to 2014. Plug $y = 1{,}400$ into each of the answer choices to see which one works. Choice (A) becomes $\frac{1}{2}(1{,}400) = 700$, or $700 = 700$. Since this equation works, keep it, but check the other answers. You'll see that only (A) works, so (A) is the correct answer.

6. **D** Plugging in could work on this question, but it may take a few tries to get down to one answer choice. A faster way to the answer is to translate the information in the question into an inequality and solve it. The question asks for values of m for which Stream Supreme's monthly cost is less than Download Empire's. *Less than* translates into <, not ≤, so eliminate (B) and (C). To watch m movies, the cost with Stream Supreme would be \$7 for the monthly fee plus \$1.75 for each movie, or $\$7 + \$1.75m$. The cost with Download Empire would be $\$4 + \$2.25m$. Therefore, the inequality is $\$7 + \$1.75m < \$4 + \$2.25m$. Subtract \$4 from both sides to get $\$3 + \$1.75m < \$2.25m$, then subtract \$1.75m from both sides to get $\$3 < \$0.50m$. Divide both sides by \$0.50 to get $6 < m$, so the answer is (D).

7. **C** Solve the equation for h. Start by multiplying both sides of the equation by μd to get $q\mu d = (p_e - p_{wf})kh$. Next, divide both sides by $(p_e - p_{wf})k$ to get $\dfrac{q\mu d}{(p_e - p_{wf})k} = h$. The correct answer, (C), simply reorders the variables in the numerator, which is permissible since numbers can be multiplied in any order.

8. **A** The question asks for the relationship between s and C. Plug in values for C to determine the effect on s. To start, plug in $C = 4$ and $C = 0$ to determine what happens where there is an increase or decrease of 4°C. If $C = 0$, then $s = 110 + 4(0) = 110$. If $C = 4$, then $s = 110 + 4(4) = 126$. As the temperature, C, increases by 4 degrees from 0 to 4 there is an increase in s of $126 - 110 = 16$, so eliminate (C). Also, as C decreases by 4 degrees from 4 to 0 there is a decrease in s of 16, so eliminate (D). Now, test a temperature change of 1°C. Plug in $C = 1$ to compare the results to those from $C = 0$. If $C = 1$, then $s = 110 + 4(1) = 114$. Therefore, as the temperature decreases from $C = 1$ to $C = 0$, there is a decrease in the number of scoops sold of $114 - 110$. Choice (B) says there would be an increase, so eliminate (B). On an increase from $C = 0$ to $C = 1$, there is an increase of 4. This is what is described in (A), so the answer is (A).

9. **B** Information is given about Stephan's plan over a period of 9 months. Find the increase in savings over that time: $\$280 - \$145 = \$135$ increase in savings over the 9-month period. Find the increase each month: $\$135 \div 9 = \$15$ additional savings per month, which best matches (B).

10. **D** Since graphing on a calculator is not an option, try plugging in some numbers. Let $x = 10$. Choice (A) becomes $y = -(10^2) + 3 = -100 + 3 = -97$. Since y is less than 2, leave (A), but check

the remaining answers just in case. Choice (B) becomes $y = |-10| - 1 = 10 - 1 = 9$. Since y is greater than 2, eliminate (B). Choice (C) becomes $y = 10^3 - 4 = 1000 - 4 = 996$. Eliminate (C). Choice (D) becomes $y = -(10 - 1)^2 + 1 = -81 + 1 = -80$. Since this value for y is less than 2, keep (D). When plugging in more than once, try some weird numbers too. Next, try $x = 0$ in the remaining answer choices. Choice (A) becomes $y = -(0^2) + 3 = 0 + 3 = 3$. Since this is a value greater than 2, eliminate (A). Therefore, the correct answer is (D).

11. **A** The question asks for the value of $f(-4)$. If the function equation were given in $f(x)$ form, -4 would replace x. However, the function is written in $f(x + 1)$ form, so -4 replaces $x + 1$. Since $-4 = x + 1$, subtract 1 from both sides to get $x = -5$. Therefore, $f(-4) = 3(-5) - 4 = -15 - 4 = -19$. The answer is (A).

12. **C** To get rid of the fractions, get the i out of the denominator by multiplying the expression by the conjugate of the denominator. Multiplying the expression by $\dfrac{2 + 3i}{2 + 3i}$ is the same as multiplying by 1, so it won't change the value. This becomes $\dfrac{(5 - i)(2 + 3i)}{(2 - 3i)(2 + 3i)} = \dfrac{10 + 15i - 2i - 3i^2}{4 + 6i - 6i - 9i^2} = \dfrac{10 + 13i - 3i^2}{4 - 9i^2}$. Since $i = \sqrt{-1}$, $i^2 = -1$. Substitute -1 for i^2 to get $\dfrac{10 + 13i - 3(-1)}{4 - 9(-1)} = \dfrac{10 + 13i + 3}{4 + 9} = \dfrac{13 + 13i}{13}$. Divide by 13 to get $1 + i$. Therefore, if $a + bi = 1 + i$, then $a = 1$, and the answer is (C).

13. **B** For all quadratic equations in the form $y = ax^2 + bx + c$, the sum of the roots equals $-\dfrac{b}{a}$. In the equation given, $-\dfrac{b}{a} = -\left(\dfrac{24}{3}\right) = -8$. Without that handy trick, it is still possible to answer the question using the quadratic formula to find the roots. Then add them together to get -8. Either way, the answer is (B).

14. **A** The parabola passes through the point $(-1, -1)$, so plug $x = -1$ and $y = -1$ into the equation of the parabola. The equation of the parabola is $y = ax^2 + bx + c$, so $-1 = a(-1)^2 + b(-1) + c$. Simplify this equation to get $-1 = a(1) + b(-1) + c$ and $-1 = a - b + c$. The correct answer is (A).

15. **C** Start by expanding the left side of the equation to get $pqx^2 + 3px + 5qx + 15 = 8x^2 + rx + 15$. Subtract 15 from both sides of the equation to get $pqx^2 + 3px + 5qx = 8x^2 + rx$. The two x terms on the left can be combined as $(3p + 5q)x$. When two quadratics are equal to each other, the coefficients on the x^2 terms on both sides are equal, and the coefficients on the x terms on both sides are equal. From this, it can be determined that $pq = 8$ and $3px + 5qx = rx$. Simplify the second equation by dividing by x to get $3p + 5q = r$. Given that $2 \times 4 = 8$ and that the problem states that $p + q = 6$, one of the values for either p or q could be 2 and the other could be 4. If $p = 2$ and $q = 4$, then $3(2) + 5(4) = r$.

Solve the right side of the equation to get $6 + 20 = r$, and $26 = r$. The only choice with 26 as one of its answer is (C).

16. **3** To solve for y, isolate the variable. First distribute the negative sign to get $4y + 8 - 7y + 12 = 11$. Combine like terms to get $-3y + 20 = 11$. Subtract 20 from both sides to get $-3y = -9$. Divide both sides by -3 to get $y = 3$. The answer is 3.

17. **250** Let d represent the square footage of a double room, and s represent the square footage of a single room. According to the question, $d = s + 25$. Solve the equation for s to get $s = d - 25$. According to the question, $2d + 4s = 1,400$. Substitute $d - 25$ in for s to get $2d + 4(d - 25) = 1,400$. Distribute the 4 to get $2d + 4d - 100 = 1,400$. Combine like terms to get $6d - 100 = 1,400$. Solve for d to get $6d = 1,500$, so $d = 250$.

18. $\dfrac{3}{5}$ or **0.6**

There is a useful trigonometry rule that states $\cos \theta = \sin(90 - \theta)$. Therefore, $\sin(90 - a°) = \cos a° = \dfrac{3}{5}$. Without knowing that rule, it is still possible to answer this question. Draw a right triangle and label one of the acute angles as $a°$ and the other as $(90 - a°)$. If $\cos a° = \dfrac{3}{5}$, the side adjacent to the angle with $a°$ is 3 and the hypotenuse is 5. Now find $\sin(90 - a°)$: it is the value of the side opposite $(90 - a°)$ over the hypotenuse, or $\dfrac{3}{5}$. This can also be entered as 0.6 in the grid-in box.

19. **9** The question says that $x + 3$ is a factor of $x^2 + kx + 2k$. By definition, this means that $x^2 + kx + 2k = 0$ if $x + 3 = 0$. If $x + 3 = 0$, subtract 3 from both sides to get $x = -3$. Plug this value in for x into the equation $x^2 + kx + 2k = 0$ to get $(-3)^2 + (-3)k + 2k = 0$. Simplify the equation to get $9 - 3k + 2k = 0$. Combine like terms to get $9 - k = 0$. Add k to both sides to get $9 = k$. The answer is 9.

20. **3** Factor x^2 out of the first two terms to get $x^2(x - 3) + 5x - 15 = 0$. Factor 5 out of the last two terms to get $x^2(x - 3) + 5(x - 3) = 0$. Factor out the $(x - 3)$ from both parts of the left side and rewrite the equation as $(x^2 + 5)(x - 3) = 0$. If $x^2 + 5 = 0$, then $x^2 = -5$, which results in 2 imaginary values for x: $\sqrt{-5}$ and $-\sqrt{-5}$. Therefore, the real value of x is when $x - 3 = 0$, and $x = 3$.

Section 4: Math (Calculator)

1. **D** Translate the information in the question into an equation. The question asks for the number of pies sold. The store sold a total of 364 slices, 84 of which were individual slices. Since individual slices sold do not affect the number of pies sold, these 84 slices should not be counted. In order not to count them, subtract them from the total to get the total number of slices sold as parts of pies. Therefore, eliminate any choice that does not include $364 - 84$. This

eliminates (A), (B), and (C). Only (D) remains. To determine why (D) is correct, note that 364 – 84 represents the number of slices sold in pies. To get the number of pies, divide this total by the number of slices in each pie, which is 8. Therefore, the number of pies sold is $\frac{364 - 84}{8}$. The answer is (D).

2. **B** In this scenario, parallel lines are cut by another set of parallel lines, and two kinds of angles are created—big and small. All the small angles are equal to each other, all the large angles are equal to each other, and any large angle plus any small angle equals 180°. The given angle, $\angle a$, is a big angle, and $\angle b$ is a small angle. So $125 + \angle b = 180$, and angle $\angle b = 55°$, which is (B).

3. **A** According to the table, there are 5 white chocolate pieces with cream filling, 3 dark chocolate pieces with no filling, and 30 total pieces in the box. Therefore, the probability of selecting a piece that is either white chocolate with cream filling or dark chocolate with no filling is $\frac{5 + 3}{30} = \frac{8}{30}$, which is (A).

4. **D** The perimeter of a triangle is the sum of the individual sides. Plug in for the sides. The question says that the sides have length x, x, and y, so let $x = 3$ and $y = 4$. Thus, the perimeter is $T = 3 + 3 + 4 = 10$. The question asks for the value of x, which is 3, so this is the target number. Plug $T = 10$ and $y = 4$ into each choice and eliminate any that are not equal to 3. Choice (A) is $3 = 10 - 4$. Since this is false, eliminate (A). Choice (B) is $3 = 10 - 2(4)$. Since this is false, eliminate (B). Choice (C) is $3 = \frac{10 - 2(4)}{2}$. Since this is false, eliminate (C). Choice (D) is $3 = \frac{10 - 4}{2}$. Since this is true, the answer is (D).

5. **D** To solve a system of equations, stack and then add them to try to make a variable disappear. To do this, it may be necessary to manipulate the equations first. In this case, multiply the second equation by –2 to get $-2x + 8y = -38$. Stack and add the equations.

$$\begin{array}{r} 2x + 3y = -6 \\ \underline{-2x + 8y = -38} \\ 0x + 11y = -44 \end{array}$$

Therefore, the result is $11y = -44$. Divide both sides by 11 to get $y = -4$. Eliminate any answer choice for which the y-coordinate is not -4: (A), (B), and (C). Only (D) remains. To determine why the x-coordinate is 3, plug $y = -4$ into one of the equations. Try the original form of the second equation. If $x - 4y = 19$, then $x - 4(-4) = 19$, and $x + 16 = 19$. Subtract 16 from both sides to get $x = 3$. The answer is (D).

6. **C**   Translate the question. The first part of the question indicates that $8 - 6n = 20$. Solve for n to get $-6n = 12$, and $n = -2$. The question is asking for the value of $5 - 3n$. Substitute -2 for n to get $5 - 3(-2) = 5 + 6 = 11$. Choice (C) is correct.

7. **C**   Translate the question. Given that there are 25,000 attendees at 12 P.M. and the number of attendees increases by 550 every minute, the number of attendees m minutes after 12 P.M. can be expressed as $25,000 + 550m$. The full capacity of the stadium is 65,000. To calculate the time prior to the stadium reaching full capacity, the equation would read $25,000 + 550m < 65,000$. Choice (C) is correct.

8. **A**   According to the table, the total number of residents between the ages of 35 and 64 who have an income between $50,000 and $74,999 is $7,185 + 14,978 = 22,163$. These numbers are all in the thousands, but the total will be as well. Those extra zeros cancel out when making the probability, so don't worry about them. The total number of residents between the ages of 35 and 64 is $39,919 + 83,213 = 123,132$. Therefore, the approximate probability that a resident randomly selected in this age range has an income between $50,000 and $74,999 is $\frac{22,163}{123,132} \approx 0.18$. The closest answer is 20%, which is (A).

9. **C**   The question says the truck traveled at an average speed of 70 miles per hour for 4 hours. If the speed and time are given, multiply them to get the distance, so $d = (70 \text{ mph})(4 \text{ hours}) = 280$ miles. The truck has a fuel efficiency of 18 miles per gallon. Set up a proportion: $\frac{1 \text{ gallon}}{18 \text{ miles}} = \frac{g \text{ gallons}}{280 \text{ miles}}$. Cross-multiply to get $280 = 18g$. Divide both sides by 18 to get $g \approx 15.56$. The question says *approximately*, so select the closest choice, which is (C).

10. **B**   The question asks about the data point farthest from the best fit line, so draw an estimate of the best fit line onto the graph itself. It should look something like this.

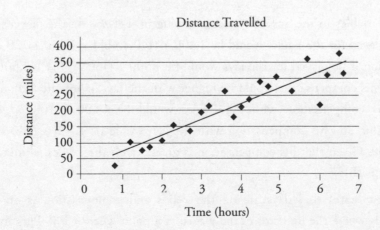

Notice that one point is far away from the line, the point at about (6, 220). The question asks for the time of the trip represented by this data point. Since time is represented by the x-axis, the time is 6 hours. The answer is (B).

11. **D** Start by subtracting 212 from both sides of the equation to get $t_b - 212 = -0.0018a$. Multiply both sides of the equation by -1 to get $-t_b + 212 = 0.0018a$. Divide both sides by 0.0018 to get $\dfrac{-t_b + 212}{0.0018} = a$. Reorder the terms in the numerator to get $\dfrac{212 - t_b}{0.0018} = a$. This matches (D).

12. **A** The question asks for the scatterplot with a positive association that is not linear. First eliminate any answer that does not have a positive association. In a positive association, y increases as x increases, so eliminate any choice for which this is not true. Eliminate (C), since it doesn't appear to have a clear positive or negative association. Eliminate (D), since it decreases then increases, so it's not consistently increasing. The question asks for the one that is not linear, so eliminate the answer that is linear. A linear association is one in which a line rather than a curve best fits the data points. In (B), the data points roughly form a linear pattern, so eliminate this choice. The answer is (A).

13. **B** Start by multiplying the entire equation by t to get $vt = h - m + 4.9t^2$. Isolate the h by adding m and subtracting $4.9t^2$ on both sides to get $vt + m - 4.9t^2 = h$. Reorder the terms to get $-4.9t^2 + vt + m = h$, which is (B).

14. **A** The question says that x refers to the number of days after the shipment is received and y refers to the number of oranges that remain. Therefore, since (7, 0) is a solution, there are 0 oranges remaining 7 days after the shipment. Go through each choice and determine whether it reflects this information. Choice (A) seems to be consistent with this, so keep (A). Choice (B) says that there are 7 oranges, but 7 refers to days rather than oranges, so eliminate (B). Choice (C) refers to 455 customers, but since there is no information about how many oranges are sold to each customer, the number of customers cannot be determined. Eliminate (C). Similar to (B), (D) refers to 7 oranges rather than 7 days, so eliminate (D). The answer is (A).

15. **B** There are variables in the answer choices, so plug in. Let $d = 4$. The player's total compensation if he played for the Eagles would be $1,400 + (140 + 40)4 = 1,400 + 720 = 2,120$, and his compensation if he played for the Jays would be $1,500 + (130 + 30)4 = 1,500 + 640 = 2,140$. Given that his compensation would be higher with the Jays, eliminate (A) and (C). Next, try $d = 6$. His compensation with the Eagles would be $1,400 + (140 + 40)6 = 1,400 + 1,080 = 2,480$, and his compensation with the Jays would be $1,500 + (130 + 30)6 = 1,500 + 960 = 2,460$. Given that his compensation is greater with the Eagles, eliminate (D). The correct answer is (B).

16. **A** The question states that days are on the x-axis and compensation is on the y-axis. The y-intercept is where the line crosses the y-axis, at a point where $x = 0$. Plug in 0 for days, and the function becomes $y = b + (s + m)0$. Simplify the function to get $y = b$. Therefore, when $x = 0$, y is equal to b, which is the signing bonus. Choice (A) is correct.

17. **B** Start by using Process of Elimination. The question states that substance K has a heat capacity that is lower than that of methyl alcohol. Eliminate (D) since it is greater than 0.6. To calculate the heat capacity of substance K, find 30% of 0.6, which is $0.3 \times 0.6 = 0.18$. Therefore, the heat capacity of substance K is $0.6 - 0.18 = 0.42$, so (B) is correct.

18. **D** If a point is a solution to two inequalities, it means that point is on the graphs of both. Plug $x = -1$ and $y = 0$ into both inequalities and solve them for c and d, respectively. The first inequality becomes $0 < -1 + c$. Add 1 to both sides to get $1 < c$. The second inequality becomes $0 < -(-1) - d$ or $0 < 1 - d$. Add d to both sides to get $d < 1$. If $d < 1$ and $c > 1$, then $d < c$, and the correct answer is (D).

19. **B** The question asks for which podcast had the most ad time per dollar. To get this for each podcast that is a choice, divide the amount of ad time by the cost of the ad. To get the amount of ad time, take the percent of ad time multiplied by the length of each podcast. However, since the length of each podcast is the same, the percent can be used rather than the amount itself. The ad times per dollar for Q, R, S, and T, respectively are $\frac{30}{\$350} \approx 0.086$ per dollar, $\frac{25}{\$200} = 0.125$ per dollar, $\frac{20}{\$180} = 0.111$ per dollar, and $\frac{15}{\$150} = 0.1$ per dollar. Since R has the greatest result, the answer is (B).

20. **D** The formula for the area of a trapezoid is $A = \frac{1}{2}(b_1 + b_2)h$, where b_1 and b_2 represent the two bases, or the two parallel sides on the trapezoid, and h represents the height, or the perpendicular distance between the two bases. Plug in for the bases and height. Let $b_1 = 4$, $b_2 = 8$, and $h = 3$. The area is $A = \frac{1}{2}(4 + 8)(3) = 18$. The question says that PQ and SR are decreased by 75% and PT is quadrupled. Since PQ and SR are parallel, they are b_1 and b_2. Decrease each of these by 75%. 75% of 4 is $\frac{75}{100}(4) = 3$, so decrease by 3 to get $b_1 = 4 - 3 = 1$. 75% of 8 is $\frac{75}{100}(8) = 6$, so decrease by 6 to get $b_2 = 8 - 6 = 2$. Since PT is perpendicular to the two bases, it is the height. Since the height is quadrupled, the new height is $4 \times 3 = 12$. Therefore, the new area is $A = \frac{1}{2}(1 + 2)(12) = 18$. Since the area is unchanged, the answer is (D).

21. **A** According to the table, 11 people never watch the news, and 27 people watch between 1 and 2 times a week, which makes $11 + 27 = 38$ people who watch the news fewer than 3 times a week. Of those viewers, there are $7 + 14 = 21$ people who belong to Group A. Therefore, the probability that a person randomly chosen from among those who watch fewer than 3 times a week is a member of Group A is $\frac{21}{38}$. Choice (A) is correct.

22.   **B**   Use the graph to determine the frequency of each integer. There are four 4's, one 5, one 6, one 7, two 9's, and one 11. To get the mean, take the sum of these numbers and divide by the number of terms. The sum is $4 + 4 + 4 + 4 + 5 + 6 + 7 + 9 + 9 + 11 = 63$. Count the numbers to get that there are 10 numbers. Therefore, the average is $\frac{63}{10} = 6.3$. The answer is (B).

23.   **A**   Find the point representing Sample S on the graph. The volume of the sample is represented by the vertical axis, so trace the horizontal line from Sample S to the vertical axis at 80. However, this is 80 liters and the question asks for milliliters. The answer should begin with an 8, so eliminate (B) and (D). There are 1,000 milliliters in a liter, so set up the proportion $\frac{1,000 \text{ mL}}{1 \text{ L}} = \frac{x \text{ mL}}{80 \text{ L}}$. Cross-multiply to get $x = 80,000$. The choices are in scientific notation. Since 80,000 is an 8 followed by four 0's, it is equal to 8×10^4. The answer is (A).

24.   **A**   The question asks for the range, or the difference between the greatest and least values, of the volume of the three samples of approximately 1.4 moles. The horizontal axis represents amount. Go just to the left of the line representing 1.5 moles, trace a line straight upward and cross three points. To determine the volume of the sample represented by each point, trace a line directly to the left of each point and see where it crosses the vertical axis, which represents volume. The highest point is between 80 and 100 liters, closer to 100, so it between 90 and 100. The lowest is between 60 and 80 liters, closer to 60, so it is between 60 and 70. Therefore, the range must be greater than $90 - 70 = 20$ and less than $100 - 60 = 40$. The only choice in this range is 30, so the answer is (A).

25.   **D**   According to the ideal gas law prediction given, $V = 50n$, where V is the volume and n is the number of moles. The question asks about a sample with 1,200 moles, so the volume is $V = 50(1,200) = 60,000$. The answer is (D).

26.   **C**   There is a variable in the question, so plug in. If $x = 2$, $f(x) = 3(2^3) + 6(2^2) + 11(2) = 24 + 24 + 22 = 70$, $g(x) = 8(2^2) + 15(2) + 7 = 32 + 30 + 7 = 69$, and $3x + 7 = 3(2) + 7 = 13$. In the answers, plug in 70 for $f(x)$ and 69 for $g(x)$ to see which answer is divisible by 13. Choice (A) becomes $j(x) = 2(70) + 69 = 140 + 69 = 209$, which is not divisible by 13. Eliminate (A). Choice (B) becomes $k(x) = 70 + 69 = 139$, which is not divisible by 13. Eliminate (B). Choice (C) becomes $m(x) = 70 + 2(69) = 70 + 138 = 208$. $208 \div 13 = 16$. Keep (C), but check (D) just in case. Choice (D) becomes $n(x) = 70 + 3(69) = 70 + 207 = 277$, which is not divisible by 13. Eliminate (D); the answer is (C).

27.   **C**   The question asks for which of the trigonometric function in the choices is equal to $\frac{y}{x}$. The answer choices include two different functions and two different angles, so use POE (Process of Elimination) in bite-sized pieces. The function cosine is equal to $\frac{opp}{hyp}$. Since neither x nor y is the hypotenuse, eliminate the choices that use cosine, (A) and (B). The only two remaining choices use tangent, which is $\frac{opp}{adj}$. Therefore, $\frac{opp}{adj} = \frac{y}{x}$. Since P is opposite side y, $\frac{y}{x} = \tan P$. The answer is (C).

28. **C** The given equation of $f(x)$ is a quadratic equation which when graphed will be a parabola. The minimum value of a parabola is the vertex. The vertex form of a quadratic equation is $y = a(x - h)^2 + k$, where (h, k) is the vertex. Eliminate (B), since it is not in the vertex form of the equation. Expand the function to get $f(x) = x^2 + 7x - x - 7 = x^2 + 6x - 7$. Eliminate (A), since it is not an equivalent form of this quadratic. Set the quadratic to 0 to get $x^2 + 6x - 7 = 0$. Complete the square to get $(x^2 + 6x + 9) - 7 = 0 + 9$. Factor the equation to get $(x + 3)^2 - 7 = 9$. Subtract 9 from both sides to get $f(x) = (x + 3)^2 - 16$. The correct answer is (C).

29. **B** Simplify the top equation to get $-j = 3a + 3$. Multiply both sides of the equation by -1 to get $j = -3a - 3$. Substitute $k + 1$ for j to get $k + 1 = -3a - 3$. Solve for k to get $k = -3a - 4$. Simplify the bottom equation to get $-k = 3b + 3$. Multiply both sides of the equation by -1 to get $k = -3b - 3$. Therefore, $-3a - 4 = -3b - 3$. Solve for a to get $-3a = -3b + 1$, and $a = b - \dfrac{1}{3}$. Choice (B) is correct.

30. **C** There are variables in the question and answer choices, so plug in. If $x = 3$, $3x = 9$, $4x = 12$, and $5x = 15$. Use these values to find the values of a, b, and c. *Average = total ÷ number of things*, so $a = \dfrac{9 + 11}{2} = \dfrac{20}{2} = 10$, $b = \dfrac{12 + 6}{2} = \dfrac{18}{2} = 9$, and $c = \dfrac{15 + 7}{2} = \dfrac{22}{2} = 11$. Now take the average of a, b, and c: $\dfrac{10 + 9 + 11}{3} = \dfrac{30}{3} = 10$. Plug $x = 3$ into the answers to see which one matches this target number. Choice (A) becomes $3 + 2 = 5$, (B) becomes $3 + 3 = 6$, (C) becomes $2(3) + 4 = 10$, and (D) becomes $4(3) + 8 = 20$. Choice (C) is correct.

31. **12** Let y represent number of years. Set up the following equation: $2.25y = 27$. Divide both sides by 2.25 to get $y = 12$.

32. **216** Given that the car factory produces one car every 20 minutes, it produces 3 cars in 1 hour. Since the car factory operates 24 hours a day, the factory produces $3 \times 24 = 72$ cars per day. Therefore, in 3 days the factory produces $72 \times 3 = 216$ cars.

33. **180** To average 240 over all 12 games, Vito must score a total of $240 \times 12 = 2{,}880$ points. In his first 6 games, Vito scored a total of $6 \times 200 = 1{,}200$ points. To find the least number of points he would need to earn on his 7th game, calculate the maximum number of points Vito could get on his last 5 games. If he bowled a perfect game for the last 5 games, he would receive a total of $5 \times 300 = 1{,}500$ additional points. Add this to the total of his first 6 games to get $1{,}200 + 1{,}500 = 2{,}700$ points scored. Therefore, the minimum number of points Vito must score on his 7th game is $2{,}880 - 2{,}700 = 180$ points.

34. **5** Only two points on the parabola are given. However, one of the points is the vertex, so use the vertex form of the equation of a parabola: $y = a(x - h)^2 + k$, where (h, k) is the vertex. Plug the point

(3, 14) in as the vertex to get $y = a(x - 3)^2 + 14$. To determine the value of a, plug in the other point (0, 5) to get $5 = a(0 - 3)^2 + 14$. Simplify the parentheses to get $5 = a(-3)^2 + 14$, and square -3 to get $5 = 9a + 14$. Subtract 14 from both sides to get $-9 = 9a$. Divide by 9 to get $a = -1$. Therefore, the equation of the parabola is $y = -(x - 3)^2 + 14$. To determine the point of intersection, find the equation of the line, which contains the points (0, −5) and (1, −2). The equation of a line can be put into the form $y = mx + b$, where m is the slope and b is the y-intercept. The y-intercept is the point at which $x = 0$. Since (0, −5) is on the line, the y-intercept is −5. Now get the slope by using the formula $m = \dfrac{y_2 - y_1}{x_2 - x_1}$. Let $(x_1, y_1) = (0, -5)$ and $(x_2, y_2) = (1, -2)$, so $m = \dfrac{-2 - (-5)}{1 - 0} = \dfrac{-2 + 5}{1} = -2 + 5 = 3$. Therefore, the equation of the line is $y = 3x - 5$. Now set the two equations equal to each other to get $-(x - 3)^2 + 14 = 3x - 5$. FOIL $(x - 3)^2$ to get $-(x^2 - 6x + 9) + 14 = 3x - 5$. Distribute the negative to get $-x^2 + 6x - 9 + 14 = 3x - 5$. Combine like terms to get $-x^2 + 6x + 5 = 3x - 5$. To solve a quadratic, get one side equal to 0. Subtract $3x$ from and add 5 to both sides to get $-x^2 + 3x + 10 = 0$. Divide both sides by −1 to get $x^2 - 3x - 10 = 0$. Factor to get $(x - 5)(x + 2) = 0$. Set both factors equal to 0 to get $(x - 5) = 0$ and $(x + 2) = 0$. Solve the two equations to get $x = 5$ and $x = -2$. Since the point (p, q) is in Quadrant I, the x-coordinate is positive, so use $x = 5$. Since p is the x-coordinate, the answer is 5.

35. **350** The total amount paid = monthly payments + his down payment. In the function given, the $175m$ represents the monthly payments, which means his down payment must have been the 350 dollars.

36. **20** A line of tangency is always perpendicular to the radius of the circle. Therefore, $\angle ABO = 90°$ and $\angle CBO = 90°$. Given that the interior angles of a triangle add up to 180°, $\angle AOB = 60°$, and $\angle BOC = 40°$. The interior angle $\angle AOC = 60° + 40° = 100°$. To determine the circumference of minor arc $\overarc{DE}$ set up the following proportion: $\dfrac{\text{angle}}{360°} = \dfrac{\text{minor arc}}{\text{circumference}}$. In this case, $\dfrac{100°}{360°} = \dfrac{x}{72}$. Cross-multiply to get $360x = 7{,}200$. Divide both sides by 360 to get $x = 20$.

37. **0.86** The decay formula states that *final amount = original amount* × $(1 - rate)^n$. The rate is 14% per year, which is written as a decimal in the decay formula. Therefore, $k = 1 - 0.14 = 0.86$.

38. **376** Use the decay formula, *final amount = original amount* × $(1 - rate)^n$, and the value for k found in the last question to find the population in 5 years. Plug 800 in for the original amount, 0.86 in for k, and 5 in for x to get $P = 800(0.86)^5 \approx 376$. Without the formula, it is still possible to get this question right. Just use a calculator to find the population after 1 year, which would be $800 - 0.14(800) = 688$. Then do it again for the population after 2 years: $688 - 0.14(688) = 591.68$. Continue the process 3 more times to find the population after five years, which will round to 376.

RAW SCORE CONVERSION TABLE — SECTION AND TEST SCORES

Raw Score (# of correct answers)	Math Section Score	Reading Test Score	Writing and Language Test Score	Raw Score (# of correct answers)	Math Section Score	Reading Test Score	Writing and Language Test Score
0	200	10	10	30	530	28	29
1	200	10	10	31	540	28	30
2	210	10	10	32	550	29	30
3	230	11	10	33	560	29	31
4	240	12	11	34	560	30	32
5	260	13	12	35	570	30	32
6	280	14	13	36	580	31	33
7	290	15	13	37	590	31	34
8	310	15	14	38	600	32	34
9	320	16	15	39	600	32	35
10	330	17	16	40	610	33	36
11	340	17	16	41	620	33	37
12	360	18	17	42	630	34	38
13	370	19	18	43	640	35	39
14	380	19	19	44	650	35	40
15	390	20	19	45	660	36	
16	410	20	20	46	670	37	
17	420	21	21	47	670	37	
18	430	21	21	48	680	38	
19	440	22	22	49	690	38	
20	450	22	23	50	700	39	
21	460	23	23	51	710	40	
22	470	23	24	52	730	40	
23	480	24	25	53	740		
24	480	24	25	54	750		
25	490	25	26	55	760		
26	500	25	26	56	780		
27	510	26	27	57	790		
28	520	26	28	58	800		
29	520	27	28				

*Please note that these scores are best approximations and that actual scores on the SAT may slightly vary, depending on individual adaptations made by the College Board.

CONVERSION EQUATION 1 — SECTION AND TEST SCORES

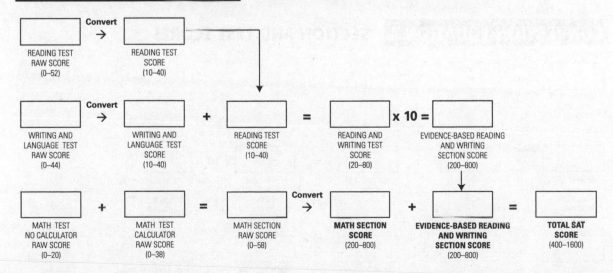

CONVERSION EQUATION 2 SECTION AND TEST SCORES

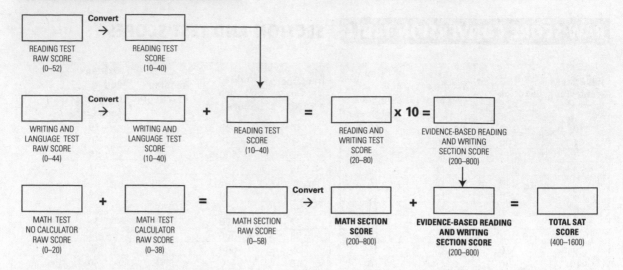

READING TEST RAW SCORE (0–52)
Convert →
READING TEST SCORE (10–40)

WRITING AND LANGUAGE TEST RAW SCORE (0–44)
Convert →
WRITING AND LANGUAGE TEST SCORE (10–40)
+
READING TEST SCORE (10–40)
=
READING AND WRITING TEST SCORE (20–80)
x 10 =
EVIDENCE-BASED READING AND WRITING SECTION SCORE (200–800)

MATH TEST NO CALCULATOR RAW SCORE (0–20)
+
MATH TEST CALCULATOR RAW SCORE (0–38)
=
MATH SECTION RAW SCORE (0–58)
Convert →
MATH SECTION SCORE (200–800)
+
EVIDENCE-BASED READING AND WRITING SECTION SCORE (200–800)
=
TOTAL SAT SCORE (400–1600)

CONVERSION EQUATION 3 SECTION AND TEST SCORES

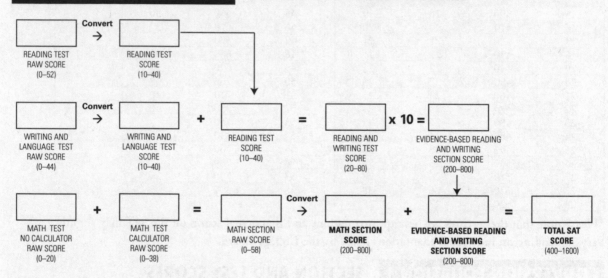

READING TEST RAW SCORE (0–52)
Convert →
READING TEST SCORE (10–40)

WRITING AND LANGUAGE TEST RAW SCORE (0–44)
Convert →
WRITING AND LANGUAGE TEST SCORE (10–40)
+
READING TEST SCORE (10–40)
=
READING AND WRITING TEST SCORE (20–80)
x 10 =
EVIDENCE-BASED READING AND WRITING SECTION SCORE (200–800)

MATH TEST NO CALCULATOR RAW SCORE (0–20)
+
MATH TEST CALCULATOR RAW SCORE (0–38)
=
MATH SECTION RAW SCORE (0–58)
Convert →
MATH SECTION SCORE (200–800)
+
EVIDENCE-BASED READING AND WRITING SECTION SCORE (200–800)
=
TOTAL SAT SCORE (400–1600)

CONVERSION EQUATION 4 SECTION AND TEST SCORES

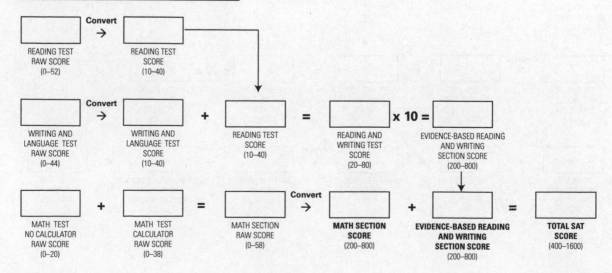

READING TEST RAW SCORE (0–52)
Convert →
READING TEST SCORE (10–40)

WRITING AND LANGUAGE TEST RAW SCORE (0–44)
Convert →
WRITING AND LANGUAGE TEST SCORE (10–40)
+
READING TEST SCORE (10–40)
=
READING AND WRITING TEST SCORE (20–80)
x 10 =
EVIDENCE-BASED READING AND WRITING SECTION SCORE (200–800)

MATH TEST NO CALCULATOR RAW SCORE (0–20)
+
MATH TEST CALCULATOR RAW SCORE (0–38)
=
MATH SECTION RAW SCORE (0–58)
Convert →
MATH SECTION SCORE (200–800)
+
EVIDENCE-BASED READING AND WRITING SECTION SCORE (200–800)
=
TOTAL SAT SCORE (400–1600)

CONVERSION EQUATION 5   SECTION AND TEST SCORES

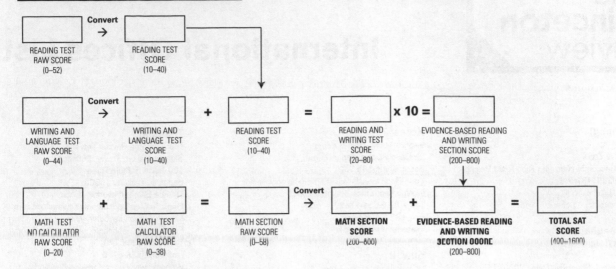

CONVERSION EQUATION 6   SECTION AND TEST SCORES

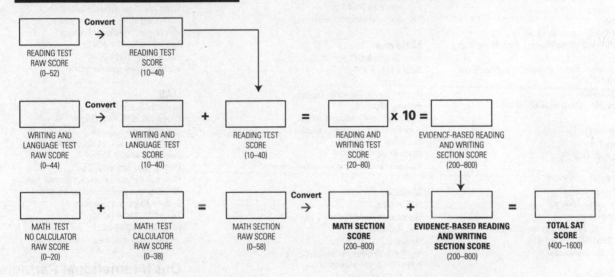

International Offices Listing

China (Beijing)
1501 Building A,
Disanji Creative Zone,
No.66 West Section of North 4th Ring Road Beijing
Tel: +86-10-62684481/2/3
Email: tprkor01@chol.com
Website: www.tprbeijing.com

China (Shanghai)
1010 Kaixuan Road
Building B, 5/F
Changning District, Shanghai, China 200052
Sara Beattie, Owner: Email: sbeattie@sarabeattie.com
Tel: +86-21-5108-2798
Fax: +86-21-6386-1039
Website: www.princetonreviewshanghai.com

Hong Kong
5th Floor, Yardley Commercial Building
1-6 Connaught Road West, Sheung Wan, Hong Kong
(MTR Exit C)
Sara Beattie, Owner: Email: sbeattie@sarabeattie.com
Tel: +852-2507-9380
Fax: +852-2827-4630
Website: www.princetonreviewhk.com

India (Mumbai)
Score Plus Academy
Office No.15, Fifth Floor
Manek Mahal 90
Veer Nariman Road
Next to Hotel Ambassador
Churchgate, Mumbai 400020
Maharashtra, India
Ritu Kalwani: Email: director@score-plus.com
Tel: + 91 22 22846801 / 39 / 41
Website: www.score-plus.com

India (New Delhi)
South Extension
K-16, Upper Ground Floor
South Extension Part–1,
New Delhi-110049
Aradhana Mahna: aradhana@manyagroup.com
Monisha Banerjee: monisha@manyagroup.com
Ruchi Tomar: ruchi.tomar@manyagroup.com
Rishi Josan: Rishi.josan@manyagroup.com
Vishal Goswamy: vishal.goswamy@manyagroup.com
Tel: +91-11-64501603/ 4, +91-11-65028379
Website: www.manyagroup.com

Lebanon
463 Bliss Street
AlFarra Building - 2nd floor
Ras Beirut
Beirut, Lebanon
Hassan Coudsi: Email: hassan.coudsi@review.com
Tel: +961-1-367-688
Website: www.princetonreviewlebanon.com

Korea
945-25 Young Shin Building
25 Daechi-Dong, Kangnam-gu
Seoul, Korea 135-280
Yong-Hoon Lee: Email: TPRKor01@chollian.net
In-Woo Kim: Email: iwkim@tpr.co.kr
Tel: + 82-2-554-7762
Fax: +82-2-453-9466
Website: www.tpr.co.kr

Kuwait
ScorePlus Learning Center
Salmiyah Block 3, Street 2 Building 14
Post Box: 559, Zip 1306, Safat, Kuwait
Email: infokuwait@score-plus.com
Tel: +965-25-75-48-02 / 8
Fax: +965-25-75-46-02
Website: www.scorepluseducation.com

Malaysia
Sara Beattie MDC Sdn Bhd
Suites 18E & 18F
18th Floor
Gurney Tower, Persiaran Gurney
Penang, Malaysia
Email: tprkl.my@sarabeattie.com
Sara Beattie, Owner: Email: sbeattie@sarabeattie.com
Tel: +604-2104 333
Fax: +604-2104 330
Website: www.princetonreviewKL.com

Mexico
TPR México
Guanajuato No. 242 Piso 1 Interior 1
Col. Roma Norte
México D.F., C.P.06700
registro@princetonreviewmexico.com
Tel: +52-55-5255-4495
+52-55-5255-4440
+52-55-5255-4442
Website: www.princetonreviewmexico.com

Qatar
Score Plus
Office No: 1A, Al Kuwari (Damas)
Building near Merweb Hotel, Al Saad
Post Box: 2408, Doha, Qatar
Email: infoqatar@score-plus.com
Tel: +974 44 36 8580, +974 526 5032
Fax: +974 44 13 1995
Website: www.scorepluseducation.com

Taiwan
The Princeton Review Taiwan
2F, 169 Zhong Xiao East Road, Section 4
Taipei, Taiwan 10690
Lisa Bartle (Owner): lbartle@princetonreview.com.tw
Tel: +886-2-2751-1293
Fax: +886-2-2776-3201
Website: www.PrincetonReview.com.tw

Thailand
The Princeton Review Thailand
Sathorn Nakorn Tower, 28th floor
100 North Sathorn Road
Bangkok, Thailand 10500
Thavida Bijayendrayodhin (Chairman)
Email: thavida@princetonreviewthailand.com
Mitsara Bijayendrayodhin (Managing Director)
Email: mitsara@princetonreviewthailand.com
Tel: +662-636-6770
Fax: +662-636-6776
Website: www.princetonreviewthailand.com

Turkey
Yeni Sülün Sokak No. 28
Levent, Istanbul, 34330, Turkey
Nuri Ozgur: nuri@tprturkey.com
Rona Ozgur: rona@tprturkey.com
Iren Ozgur: iren@tprturkey.com
Tel: +90-212-324-4747
Fax: +90-212-324-3347
Website: www.tprturkey.com

UAE
Emirates Score Plus
Office No: 506, Fifth Floor
Sultan Business Center
Near Lamcy Plaza, 21 Oud Metha Road
Post Box: 44098, Dubai
United Arab Emirates
Hukumat Kalwani: skoreplus@gmail.com
Ritu Kalwani: director@score-plus.com
Email: info@score-plus.com
Tel: +971-4-334-0004
Fax: +971-4-334-0222
Website: www.princetonreviewuae.com

Our International Partners

The Princeton Review also runs courses with a variety of
partners in Africa, Asia, Europe, and South America.

Georgia
LEAF American-Georgian Education Center
www.leaf.ge

Mongolia
English Academy of Mongolia
www.nyescm.org

Nigeria
The Know Place
www.knowplace.com.ng

Panama
Academia Interamericana de Panama
http://aip.edu.pa/

Switzerland
Institut Le Rosey
http://www.rosey.ch/

All other inquiries, please email us at
internationalsupport@review.com